THE MUSIC
OF
ANTHONY BRAXTON

Anthony Braxton — Photo: Bill Burkhart

THE MUSIC OF ANTHONY BRAXTON

Mike Heffley

Excelsior Music Publishing Company • New York

AN EXCELSIOR MUSIC TRADE PAPERBACK

Published by:
Excelsior Music Publishing Company
a division of the
ZINN PUBLISHING GROUP:
Zinn Communications, Inc. / New York

Hardcover Edition: Greenwood Publishing Group, Inc.

Copyright © 1996 by Excelsior Music Publishing Co.

All rights reserved. No part of this book may be reproduced or transmitted in any form or by any means, electronic or mechanical, including photocopying, recording, or by any information storage and retrieval system, without the written permission of the Publisher, except where permitted by law.

ISBN: 0–935016–18–X

Printed in the United States of America

Library of Congress Cataloging-in-Publication Data

Heffley, Mike.
    The music of Anthony Braxton / by Mike Heffley.
       p.   cm. — (The Excelsior profile series of American composers)
    Includes index.
    ISBN 0–935016–18–X
    1. Braxton, Anthony—Criticism and interpretation. I. Series.
ML410.B834H44   1996
781.65′092—dc20   95–7385
                                                                        CIP
                                                                         MN

Dedicated to my nephew Jason Becker,
who rushed to his own glory serving the Muse
before his family knew what hit them.

I don't see my creativity as being separate from my life, so I'd like as a person to grow and develop and deal with the planet that's on its way up, then my music will continue to mirror that same relationship. It's just a question of gravitational intrigue.

Anthony Braxton

Contents

Figures 5
Acknowledgments 8
Introduction: Millennial/Gravitational Intrigue 10

first arrow . . . from the bow of the past
    Evocation 23
    Chapter One: The Music's Grandparents 27
    Chapter Two: The Music's Parents 52

second arrow . . . on the string of the present
    Invocation 143
    Chapter Three: The Musician's Words 146
    Chapter Four: The Musician Speaks 183

third arrow . . . in the five fingers of the archer
    Provocation 207
    Chapter Five: The Solo Music's Axis (Tradition/Innovation) 212

fourth arrow . . . whistling through the air of the future
    Convocation 259
    Chapter Six: Duo Music 262
    Chapter Seven: Trio Music 303
    Chapter Eight: Quartet Music 336
    Chapter Nine: Large Ensemble Music 417

fifth arrow . . . in the eye of the bull
    Chapter Ten: The Music's Muse 445
    Appendix: Anthony Braxton's
        Introduction to "Catalogue of Works" 463
    Sources 468
    Index 481

Figures

Fig. I:	A Braxtonian schematic of this book	14
Fig. 1.1:	Braxton's 141(+20+96+120D) expressed graphically	31
Fig. 2.1a:	Typical rhythm from the Jalisco region of Mexico	54
Fig. 2.1b:	*Habanera* rhythm from Cuba	55
Fig. 2.1c:	From Braxton's *23G* (alto sax)	55
Fig. 2.1d:	From Braxton's *23G* (bass)	55
Fig. 2.2a:	From Hildegard of Bingen's *Symphonia*	61
Fig. 2.2b:	Schema of the modal system	61
Fig. 2.2c:	From Braxton's *40N*	61
Fig. 2.3a:	Bars 16–19 of William Billings' *Dunstable*	63
Fig. 2.3b:	Opening of Charles Ives' *Symphony No. Four*, third ("fugue") movement	63-64
Fig. 2.3c:	Braxton's *105A* (D section)	64
Fig. 2.4a:	From *The Cry of My Beloved* by Timothy Swan	66-67
Fig. 2.4b:	From Braxton's *6J*	67
Fig. 2.4c:	From Braxton's *37*	67
Fig. 2.5a:	From 10th-century chant *Beata Gens*	69-70
Fig. 2.5b:	The hexachord system of solmization	71
Fig. 2.5c:	From Braxton's *76* and *136*	72
Fig. 2.5d:	From *Beata Gens*	72-73
Fig. 2.6a:	Opening of Ives' *Symphony No. Four*	76–77
Fig. 2.6b:	From Braxton's *147*	78
Fig. 2.6c:	Breakdown of a few lines from Obrecht's *Missa si dedero*	78-79
Fig. 2.6d:	From Billings' anthem *Blessed is He that Considereth the Poor*	79
Fig. 2.7:	Score page from Braxton's *58*	81
Fig. 2.8:	From Braxton's *40P*	87
Fig. 2.9:	From flute part to Braxton's *96*	89
Fig. 2.10:	From Braxton's *55*	94
Fig. 2.11a:	Opening bars of *Donna Lee*	98
Fig. 2.11b:	From Braxton's *23B*	99
Fig. 2.12a:	From Charles Mingus' *What Love*	111
Fig. 2.12b:	From Ornette Coleman's *Una Muy Bonita*	111
Fig. 2.12c:	From Braxton's *23M*	111-12
Fig. 2.13:	From Braxton's *23E*	114
Fig. 2.14a:	From Webern's *Six Pieces*	125
Fig. 2.14b:	From Stockhausen's *Kontra-Punkte*	126
Fig. 2.15:	From Braxton's opera *Trillium M*	133-34
Fig. 5.1:	A "biogram"	215

Fig. 5.2:	From Braxton's classroom materials about his musical paradigm, an outline called *Tri-Metric Modeling*	217-18
Fig. 5.3:	Paradigma of recording of *Goodbye, Pork-Pie Hat*	221
Fig. 5.4:	Paradigma of *Victory Ball*	224
Fig. 5.5:	Solo alto "language" music paradigma	233
Fig. 5.6:	Paradigma of *Donna Lee*	235
Fig. 5.7:	Paradigma of *8F*	238
Fig. 5.8:	Composition notes for *99G*	251
Fig. 5.9:	Paradigma of *106C*	252
Fig. 6.1a:	From *85*	267
Fig. 6.1b:	From *86*	268
Fig. 6.1c:	Paradigma of *Embraceable You*, *85*, *86*, and *87*	269
Fig. 6.2:	From bass part to *40A*	270-71
Fig. 6.3:	Paradigma of *6A* and *69P* (with John Lindberg)	272
Fig. 6.4:	From *101* (with Giorgio Gaslini)	279
Fig. 6.5:	Paradigma of *136* (with Marilyn Crispell)	284
Fig. 6.6:	Paradigma of *140* (with Marilyn Crispell)	285
Fig. 6.7:	Paradigma of *95* (with Ursula Oppens and Frederick Rzewski)	287
Fig. 6.8:	Paradigma of free improv (with Max Roach) and *86* (with Gino Robair)	289
Fig. 6.9:	Paradigma of free improvs (with Derek Bailey, Evan Parker, and Richard Teitelbaum)	295
Fig. 6.10:	Paradigma of *74A* (with Roscoe Mitchell) and *64* (with George Lewis)	296
Fig. 6.11:	From *74A*	298
Fig. 7.1:	Graphic representation of *6D*	308
Fig. 7.2:	From composition notes to *6E*	309-10
Fig. 7.3:	From score of *76*.	320
Fig. 7.4a:	Example of "clouds" of improvised sound from *94*	324
Fig. 7.4b:	A square-note line from Obrecht's mass	325
Fig. 7.5:	From the composition notes to *94*.	325
Fig. 7.6:	Two systems from *107*	327
Fig. 7.7:	Graphic titles of *110A(+108B+69J)*	332
Fig. 8.1:	From Braxton's *82* (for four orchestras)	354
Fig. 8.2:	Quartet instrumentation/personnel since late '60s	356
Fig. 8.3:	Graphic representation of quartet music through the *6*, *23*, *40*, *69*, "Golden Peak," and Coordinate System periods	359
Fig. 8.4:	From composition notes to *6A*	366
Fig. 8.5:	From *23M*	372
Fig. 8.6:	From *23G*	376
Fig. 8.7:	From *40(O)*	384
Fig. 8.8:	From *50*	385-86
Fig. 8.9a:	From *69C* and *32* (played simultaneously).	388

Fig. 8.9b, c:	From composition notes to *69C*	389
Fig. 8.10:	From *69E*	390
Fig. 8.11:	From composition notes to *84*	394
Fig. 8.12:	The twelve religious symbols that formed the visual component of *96*	400
Fig. 8.13:	From *105A*	404
Fig. 8.14:	From liner notes to *Performance 9/1/79*	405-06
Fig. 8.15:	From *110A*	406
Fig. 8.16:	From composition notes to *114*	407
Fig. 8.17	Graphic title of *131*	408
Fig. 8.18:	Graphic title to *161*	413
Fig. 9.1:	From score to *171*	421-22
Fig. 9.2:	From trombone part to *112*	425-26
Fig. 9.3:	From score to *100*	428
Fig. 9.4:	From score to *102*	430
Fig. 9.5:	From score to *42*	433
Fig. 9.6:	Prototype of Braxton's new representation of his paradigm	441
Fig. 10.1:	The author's picture of Braxton's place on (what he calls) the Universal Axis	449
Fig. 10.2:	Titian's *The Allegory of Prudence*	450

Acknowledgments

First and primary thanks go to Dr. Bernard Dobroski, dean of the School of Music at Northwestern University, and to Professor Anthony Braxton, chair (at this writing) of the Wesleyan University Department of Music. Without their help in my initial professional projects with Professor Braxton and my Northwest Creative Orchestra, I would never have had the opportunity to conceive and develop this book and the papers and thesis preceding it.

Next in line are the friends and colleagues whose input on my research was generous and welcome: Dr. Douglas Blandy, of the University of Oregon (UO) Arts Education department; Neill Archer Roan, in his former capacity as Director of Marketing and Programming at the Hult Center for the Performing Arts in Eugene; Dr. Edwin Coleman II, of the UO Department of Ethnic Studies; and Professor Steve Owen, head of the UO Jazz Studies Program. Special thanks to my Antioch University faculty advisor Jon Saari, for editorial suggestions informed by his literary expertise; and to Graham Lock, and Art Lange for their input and friendly support and encouragement. Also to my editors and readers: Stuart Saunders Smith, Rebecca Miller, and Chris Bakriges; to informal consultants among my teachers and colleagues at Wesleyan and Yale Universities: Jon Barlow, Alvin Lucier, Neely Bruce, and John Szwed; to my publishers, William and David Zinn, for the humanity and sensitivity accompanying the professionalism of their production and distribution of my manuscript; and to those with whom I worked (by phone and mail) at the offices of their co-publishers, Greenwood Press: Jim Sabin, Andrea Mastors, and Jeanne Lesinski (particularly the latter, for the care with which she scrutinized my manuscript on its last go-around).

A very special mention is due the late Edward Kammerer, former Associate Dean and Horn Professor of the UO School of Music. His unexpected illness and death caused grief in many quarters, and took from me a treasured friend and ally who was the first of my many colleagues to help me open the door to the musical work in Oregon that led to this book.

I would also like to acknowledge my debt to Carl (Arzinia) Richardson and Malinké Robert Elliot. My longstanding friendships with both have helped raise the issues discussed in these pages from the academic and aesthetic to the viscerally human level (art is an angel, but most so when it serves as well as guides human souls). Also, my friend and fellow musicophile Dale McBride, who not only availed me of his comprehensive collection of Braxton recordings and liner notes, but helped me order them.

Special thanks to Steve Norton for his chronological cross-referenced list of Anthony Braxton's compositions and recordings. The patterns it revealed provided the underpinning and suggested the arc of the book's musical analyses. Professor Robert Dickow, at the University of Idaho, also has my heartfelt gratitude (and relief) for the *gratis* and crucial gift of his computer expertise and resources.

Finally, on the most personal levels, thanks go to Richard Greene and Sandra Boynton for their respective roles in my physical support and survival; and to Geneva Heffley and Karin Thompson for their crucial emotional moorings. Those roles were definitely not bit parts among the others, even though—perhaps because—they weren't played for the sake of the book.

One more word of appreciation about Professor Braxton's help: I've known not a few people who have had talents and journeys similar to his who have encountered not half the frustrations and dilemmas, yet have developed twice the bitterness and anger. If he had been one of them, I doubt I would have gotten close enough to recognize everything I've tried to present in this book, nor would I have cared to.

For material deemed in excess of "fair use" standards, I gratefully acknowledge permission to use excerpts of the following previously published material: Anthony Braxton's self-published writings and musical scores, by permission of the author; Art Lange's writings, by permission of the author; Graham Lock's writings, by permission of the author; a photograph of Titian's "Allegory of Prudence," by permission of The National Gallery of London; Francis Davis' *In the Moment: Jazz in the 1980s* and *Outcats*, and Robin Maconie's *The Works of Karlheinz Stockhausen*, by permission of Oxford University Press; R.P. Morgan's *20th Century Music* (Copyright © 1991 by W.W. Norton & Co. All rights reserved. Reprinted by permission of W. W. Norton & Co.); Charles Ives' *Symphony No. 4* (copyright © 1969 by Associated Music Publishers, Inc. (BMI) International Copyright Secured. All Rights Reserved. Reprinted by permission); Ad de Vries' *Dictionary of Symbols and Imagery*, by permission of North Holland Publishing (NY); John Blacking's *A Commonsense View of All Music*, by permission of Cambridge University Press; Wilfrid Mellers' *Music in a New Found Land*, by permission of Georges Borchardt Inc.; assorted excerpts from *The Woman's Encyclopedia of Myths and Secrets*, by Barbara G. Walker, reprinted by permission of HarperCollins Publishers, Inc.; and Karlheinz Stockhausen's *Kontra-Punkte No. 1* and Anton von Webern's *Six Pieces for Orchestra, Op. 6*, used by permission of European American Music Distributors Corporation, sole U.S. and Canadian agent for Universal Edition (London) Ltd., London.

Introduction

Millennial/Gravitational Intrigue

Flesh knows what spirit knows, but spirit knows it knows.

Charles Williams

My editor, the composer Stuart Saunders Smith, started me on my way through this book with the concept of "a biography of a music." As he explained it, this would be distinct from a biography of the musician, in its relative unconcern with details of Anthony Braxton's personal and professional history. It would rather lie somewhere between a musicological treatise on and a journalistic portrait of the music. "Think of the music as a living entity," he said, "with its own messages and role to play in the history of ideas and culture."

Players and aficionados intimate with the jazz tradition (or, as Braxton prefers, "trans-African tradition of creative music") will attest to the music's very personal identity. We often speak of it in such a way that those words "the music" are charged with nuances that whisper something more like "the spirit," "the friendly and terrible god," "the mystery," "the force," or "the plan." This one transcendent identity is infused with the more immanent and many personalities of its servants, the players, and part of their service is precisely to define just what "The Music" is up to in a given time and place.

The Music's "biography" in Braxton, then, also serves the concept the publishers had for this book as a portrait of a contemporary American composer in the Western art music tradition. Braxton's music has been a distinct and irrepressible voice in its Africanized Western-gone-global musiculture,[1] that forged by both the jazz and art music traditions in both Europe and America. It has proven a seminal synthesis of the two, joining and furthering the soul and scope of both.

As such, it has attracted much attention. The early jazz press coverage, in the late 1960s-early 1970s, was both hostile and laudatory—primarily the latter, but both in the extreme. Braxton's staying power, underscored by a stream of recordings kaleidoscopic in their conceptual and sonic variety, has won him both a passionate following and mainstream acknowledgment from such snapshooters of culture as *The Village Voice*, *The New Yorker*, *Stereo Review*, *Time*, and *Newsweek*.[2] Good reviews of his recordings far outnumber bad, and those on terms he himself has managed to define over the years. He has become a respected academic who keeps busy with teaching, live performances, recordings, and commissions. With the 1994 MacArthur "genius" award, he has finally received the best acknowledgment and support his culture can offer.

Yet his music has not become the same sort of musical coin of the realm as that of comparably innovative artists whose work was generally absorbed after two or three decades: Charlie Parker, Thelonious Monk, John Coltrane, or even Charles Ives, John Cage, or Karlheinz Stockhausen. Composers such as Cage, Philip Glass, John Adams, and Steve Reich (three of whom Braxton has worked with) claimed or are claiming their niches beyond the margins. Artists closer to Braxton's sound and approach (e.g., Steve Lacy, Cecil Taylor, Anthony Davis, and Leroy Jenkins) are doing so, with prestigious awards and grants and healthy media attention. Still more familiar names—such as Keith Jarrett or the Marsalis brothers—have, like the others, built bridges between the improviser's and the composer's traditional and/or creative worlds. Most make music with more commercial appeal.

To those familiar with and responsive to Braxton's work, this seems unfortunate. In many crucial ways, he was "there" first, fastest, and most surely and comprehensively. At the same time, the reasons for such obscurity are also easy to discern. Braxton has never been a concert artist dabbling with jazz or improvisation (as, for example, Aaron Copland or Stravinsky; or, more recently, André Previn, Stockhausen, or Günther Schuller), nor a jazz artist dabbling in concert music (as were Benny Goodman, Woody Herman, or "Third Streamers" such as the Modern Jazz Quartet). He hasn't had both feet, alternately, in each tradition in a more direct way, as Jarrett or the Marsalises with their recordings of the classical repertoire. From the first he has rather envisioned and expanded a common ground between the improviser's, composer's, conductor's and interpreter's respective approaches to music. He has, in fact, gone so far down this road, in the company of such select and specialized performers, that it can no longer be called the footpath of a scout. By now, it is a well-nigh paved and delineated multi-lane highway, leading from the most familiar music to some of its farthest reaches, half-staked out for settlement. Indeed, much of the ground Braxton has broken is settled, but more by a new generation of scouts[3] than by the general public most in need of new ground. Moreover, part of Braxton's absorption in his new "road" work has been to develop an idiosyncratic use of language that suits its referents but means little to those not yet traveling his route. The need, therefore (motivating this book), is to present and clarify the musical ground that's been broken.

I have the advantage of having two other recent close looks at Braxton's work as part of my source material. Graham Lock's *Forces in Motion: Anthony Braxton and the Meta-Reality of Creative Music* and Ronald Radano's *New Musical Figurations: Anthony Braxton's Cultural Critique*,[4] and the several shorter writings of each (especially Lock's superb liner notes and Radano's academic work),[5] provide much information and insight that has informed my study (though I have tried to avoid reinventing any of their wheels). I could scarcely improve on Lock's literate, lively journalism or Radano's comprehensive scholarly assessment. While my approach and material overlaps with both of theirs, mine is the account of musician first, journalist and scholar second. It is the musician's experience of learning and playing Braxton's music, specifically, as well as the African American, Western European, and American experimental idioms he draws on that motivates what I deem most important to say, and how to say it.

It is significant to me that Lock is European; his book lies in the tradition of Europe explaining the import of the African American culture to America's (ironically) Eurocentered readers. It is also significant that the American Radano is an academic; his book too is part of a tradition, of an American intelligentsia explaining America's emerging culture to itself, again, in the face of bias—that of a disdain for the world of Western arts and letters that springs from an historical Euro-American *hostility* to Europe.

I believe this two-edged cultural sword offers some clues about the reasons for Braxton's struggle (and that of similar artists—e.g., Ornette Coleman) for recognition. It is a sword that has historically blocked widespread understanding of and respect for American (especially African American) artists and thinkers. However, it may well be a barrier fast becoming history indeed. This book will hopefully offer a look at this artist and thinker that will clearly position him beyond that wall, and bring many more of us into our own motion with him on his road.

I would, then, recommend that the most serious readers read Lock and Radano first, as I have before writing. When at sea in the bark of my book—focused on the music as a transcendent, sentient being—attention will be continually drawn through, rather than to, Braxton. His aspiration to universalism[6] will be put to the test, as we consider his work not as a dwelling for him and a spectacle for us, but rather as a (literally) engaging variation on the processes of life and creativity in which we all share. To bring Braxton's own writings into the metaphor mix, access to them and those of Lock, Radano, and my own will provide an all-terrain, four-wheel drive vehicle perfect for the new highway and surrounding territories running through Braxton's recordings.

My approach here has several distinguishing traits and intents, stemming from my relationship to this subject. I have worked both as a musician and a journalist of Braxton's genre—that place in the jazz tradition where it breaks out of its Western song-form structures and forges new platforms, from anywhere, everywhere, and (the) "nowhere" (of creative free play) for its improvisational statements. I have grown up on Braxton's music, hearing it as an aspiring trombonist just three years his junior in the late 1960s, when it made its first public debut. I have always been aware of his work as solidly rooted in convention and tradition—and in their timeless bio-mythological roots—and as equally dogged in its pursuit to further same. I hope to convey this grounded balance of new and familiar to the reader, to end with an impression of a music that is relevant and exciting for what it brings forth as much as for what it artfully veils. Braxton and his body of work have become for me a garden of earthly delights with an open door and divinable lore; if this book succeeds, no reader will feel it a glimpse into a narrowly esoteric or eccentric realm.

Part of my strategy for achieving this success was made possible by Braxton's own written aids to his music, from his early liner notes to his self-published books. After examining the voluminous literature about him and his work by others, I have foregone a survey of them here in favor of his own words as the discourse to which I wish to offer my own musical analyses and assessments in the latter chapters. (The serious researcher can access the literature I originally selected to review in the Bibliography. For the most complete list of

introduction 13

works on Braxton, see Gray and Radano.) I did bring in some of that literature when I felt it made a point needed for my research.

Readers even passingly aware of Braxton's music, the literature on it, and his own writings may well wonder at the possibility—even the desirability—of broadening its mass appeal. This artist has generated for some three decades now a music and a use of language that seem to many the very embodiment of convolution and complexity, solipsistic obfuscation and even pretentiousness, all threatening more often than enhancing the undeniable musicianship and creativity behind them. The trap waiting for any writer seeking to unravel and explain it is that his or her book will be the same compendium of arcane and subjective abstraction as (or, conversely, will dilute and distort) its subject. The avoidance of that trap lies in finding the ways Braxton's work succeeds, by his lights and those of his fans, and reflecting those ways and that success in one's writing.

I have designed my chapters as different windows progressively revealing increasingly sophisticated aspects of the one open system his music is. They might be schematized (after Braxton's own fashion of visualizing invisible structures and components of music and sound) as done in Figure I.

Figure I (a Braxtonian schematic of this book, next page) is offered as a demonstration of Braxton's process of visualizing the invisible—both music and concept—with symbols, their shorthand legends, and stylized drawings of real-world scenes. It may seem unnecessarily arcane (as does Braxton's work to many) at first glance, but as I walk you through it, notice how much less tediously than words it conveys concepts and facts.

First, both shapes—the concentric circles and the tipped hourglass—are ancient and universal. The circles are images from some of the very earliest known drawings by anyone anywhere. They traditionally signify, among other things, the female in nature, and they do so here.[7] As signaled by the male symbol at the lower left, the circles represent a view of the book seen from the "male" experience of reading right through it in a linear fashion. In other words, while the mode of perception is most linear/male, the thing perceived is most global/female. Thus the book/subject is experienced holistically with every step through it, drawing the reader to the central point of gravity forward from the first four and backward through the last five chapters (the point where Braxton picks up his horn, learns the music of his world and begins to add his own to it).

Fig. I.b "turns the circles around" to reveal their extension through a third dimension. The tipped hourglass shape, an ancient symbol for time, is made by the five arrows of time running from left to right (your reading experience, my writing experience, Braxton's music's evolution, the Muse's music's evolution, and . . . all four together as an entity). (The arrow, by the way, is also among those earliest primal drawings, as a symbol for the male genitalia. The semi-circular bow is also both an ancient musical instrument and, with the arrow, a weapon.) I conceive of this as the archetypally female perceptual experience of the manifold male trajectories through "her" body in search of conception. As the archetypal male "sees" her circles all at once, globally, so she "sees" his lines in their entirety.

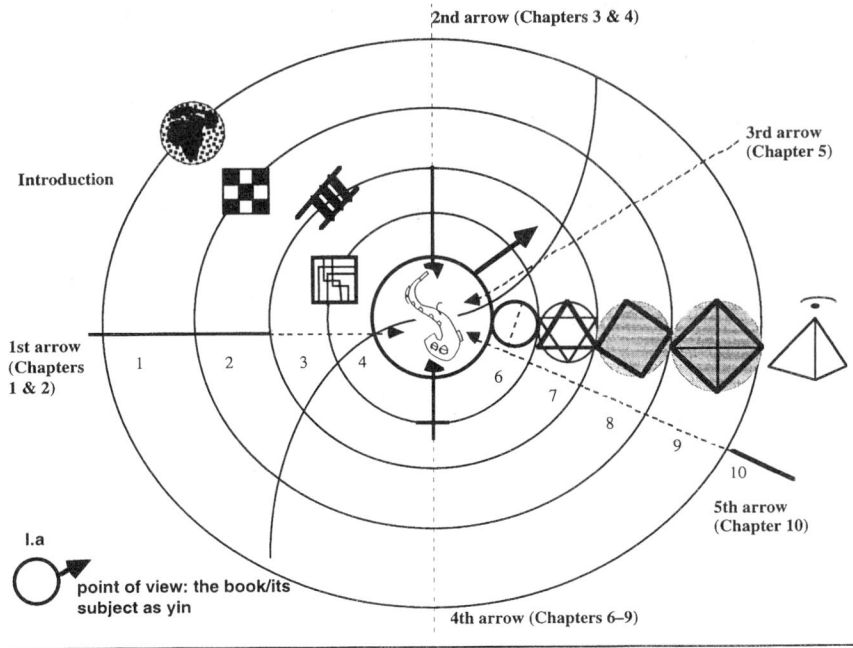

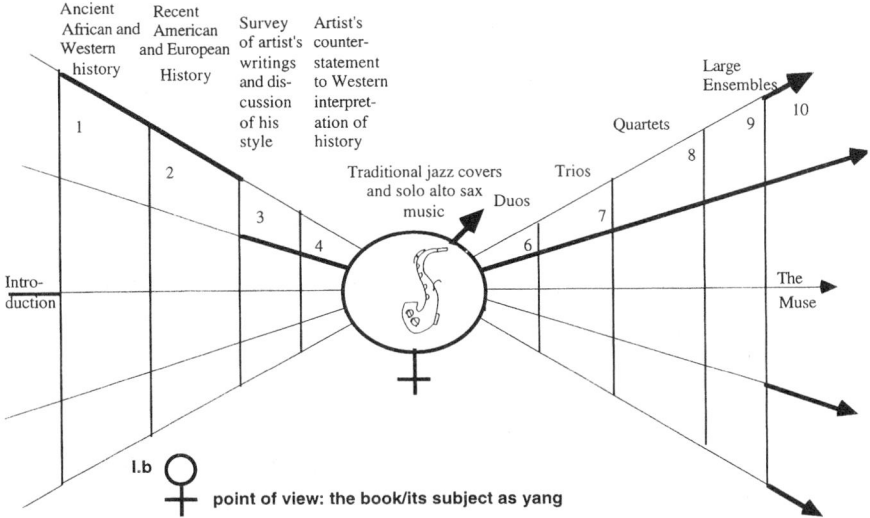

(It will become clear why I chose to represent the plan of the book as one thing perceived from two complementary points of view, and those points of view as archetypally male and female, as you read. For now, simply enjoy the elegance of the conceit.)

Notice how some sections of line are broken or light and others solid. This represents here and in illustrations to follow the distinction between potential and its actualization. This is an important distinction in a book about the

introduction

creation of something concrete from something abstract, and is especially useful in discussing Braxton, who experiments with the ordering and re-ordering of the abstract as much as the concrete realm.

In Fig. I.a, the five arrows are solid in the sections they are intended to denote; the fact that they're broken in the other sections denotes the continuum of the reading experience, of the book, of its subject's many aspects. The S-curved line snaking through the circle to make it a yin-yang symbol denotes the dimensionality revealed in I.b. Imagine it as the abstract truth of what you experience as a straight line, since the circles are actually parts of a continually moving vortex through which you must spiral continuously, even though you feel yourself to be going straight through a series of discrete zones. Imagine the circles moving counter to each other, to indicate the constant friction and tension of paradox that never resolves but always generates and motivates: part of its "gravitational intrigue."

In Fig. I.b, the horizontal line drawn for "all five arrows" is broken until Chapter Five and solid through and after it. This denotes the potential from which the music was/is conceived—its material (matter, mater, mother)—and the actual music. Chapters Five through Nine grant the arrow its solidity because they are about the music; Chapter Ten does so because it is about the Muse, the music's source outside of spacetime (thus the arrows pointing up and down become broken and open, by infinity, around Ten). The up and down directions denote the dual sensation of ascent—sometimes a struggle to climb, sometimes a heavenly float—and descent—sometimes a terrifying plunge, sometimes a blissful sink—one is subject to when one simply tries to proceed with equilibrium: "one" being me trying to write, you trying to read, Braxton trying to create, the Muse trying to manifest, or all trying at once.

The icons of globe, chess board, railroad tracks, electronic schema, and saxophone (drawn by Braxton for this figure) denote various literary devices extracted from Braxton's world to organize the first half of the book's information most aesthetically. The geometric figures in circles 6–9, and the pyramid at 10, signal the essence of the music unfolding in different contexts. As Figure I covers the whole book, these similar figures will signal the essence of the music of their particular chapter.

Finally, the numbers 0 through 9 themselves, and their interrelationships, are as charged with primal symbolism as are the circles and arrows. That symbolism is beyond the scope of this caption, but some of it is included elsewhere (mostly the excerpts from de Vries leading the latter chapters). Suffice it to say that the numbers were used and ordered in this figure and throughout the book with respect to such symbolism and inter-dynamics.

As Braxton himself seeks for his work to be a true slice of cosmic life, so do I for my book about it.

The Introduction and Conclusion should be seen as subscendent and transcendent, respectively, to the body of the book: an "outside" to the "inside" of the structure organizing the material, a space where we can anticipate and reflect on it. I think of the "sub" and "trans" aspects of these sections as relative—not hierarchically fixed—as suggested by the open space around the circles. The Conclusion is also as immanent as it is transcendent; thus the section/chapter umbrella it shares with the book's main content.

"Chapter One: The Music's Grandparents" and "Chapter Ten: The Music's Muse" comprise a temporal pair of binoculars that reach past the limits of historical (Chapter One) and futuristic (Chapter Ten) mythmaking for their outer edges, and also encompass the more known and knowable about world musiculture in their magnifying glass. Braxton's music goes far and consciously into humanity's primal mammalian roots; it also includes works that could only be performed if humans had spread throughout the galaxies and learned to communicate therein instantaneously (despite the speed of light). There exist data and informed speculation from the fields of biology, sociology, archaeology, anthropology, and physics that frame those far reaches in a sympathy with, if not corroboration of, the artist's conceits.

Braxton's music also incorporates, again consciously and deeply, the esoteric principles handed down from ancient and occult history through African and Western (mostly—more generally and peripherally from shamanic tribal and Asian) cultures, to America. The historical narrative delineating those "forces in motion" through spacetime is synopsized mostly from the most time-nonspecific, uncontroversial data of standard references,[8] departing from that base to draw on sources more specifically relevant to Braxton's role.

Chapter Ten sees the biography of a music metamorphose to that of a Muse: a living metamusical, metaphysical entity—a god, a *loa*, an archetype, a "force in motion"—with its own discernible persona and purpose through spacetime. The artist, we'll see, is not so hard to understand; he's simply a man who's been doing a do-able, divinable craft. The resulting music, and the writing about it, are discernible enough; both are there to be traced and grasped by normally functional minds led by the heart to do so.

The Muse, on the other hand, is both the mystery and self-awareness of transcendent human being itself and will always be as inscrutable and familiar, as glorious and mundane, as complex and simple as a sunset or a planet. Literature from the latest physics and psychology will be invoked, again, as corroborations of the ancient and perennial wisdom summarized in Chapters One and Two and of Braxton's work.

The first section—Chapter One with "Chapter Two: The Music's Parents"—and part of the fourth ("Chapter Nine: The Large-Ensemble Music") present, respectively, the musical traditions and voices with which Braxton aligns himself, and his own musical vision in full "symphonic" bloom. The large-ensemble work subsumes his axial role as performer, brings out that of the composer, activating and maximizing the creative potential in the world of other musicians, the music world at large. The author speaks from personal experience as such an "other" musician in such an ensemble.

Chapter Two also narrows the binocular focus of One and Ten to American and post-Columbian European history. Braxton claims direct descendance from black and white American gospel/folk/blues, Euro-American Independent experimental art music, march music, post-tonal European, and, of course, jazz traditions; he names specific artists for special influence. At first glance, many of these claimed affinities may seem wholly unlikely. Chapter Two highlights their links to and common historical and aesthetic ground with Braxton's music. "Chapter Eight: Quartet Music" ties up the threads of Chapters Four through Seven, which strive to present the music from its maker's point of view, and on his terms. If the picture emerging from those chapters can be likened to a

introduction 17

creative storm, Chapter Eight clears their clouds away, lets both rainbow and sunshine make harmony out of the watery work of the music. An overview of the *ouevre* is offered, and an exploration of its synchronicities and other "metameaningful" features indulged.

"Chapter Three: The Musician's Words" considers briefly the way the general and music media have defined and presented Braxton's music to the public over the years, observes both the opportunities and constraints of such attention, and the premises underlying it. It then examines difficulties a typical reader will have with Braxton's writings and suggest ways (and reasons) to overcome them. "Chapter Seven: Trio Music" continues the musical analysis, through trio recordings and unrecorded trio works. A transcendent arc spanning Braxton's entire body of work—that rainbow over the storm—begins to appear.

"Chapter Four: The Musician Speaks" lets the artist speak for himself, in contradistinction to much of the media. It establishes the author's response to and acknowledgment of the primary authority of the artist's words, and their status of primary source informing the musical analysis and assessment in the remaining chapters. "Chapter Six: Duo Music" traces duo recordings, continuing to construct from them the process and portrait of Braxton the composer begun in Chapter Five, a role inseparable from that of performer/improviser. Attention is drawn to the special significance of the duo dynamic as it reflects its extramusical manifestations in the artist and the larger culture (the corresponding associations of trio, quartet, and large-ensemble dynamics are similarly noted).

"Chapter Five: The Music's Axis (Tradition/Innovation)" looks at Braxton's technical and conceptual foundation in the mainstream jazz and concert music of his time (his whole time: recordings from this and all other categories span the three decades of his recording career) and at his solo excursions into innovative restructuring (his word) of same.

Note the shared categories encircled in Fig. I.a, with the accompanying logos: the first and tenth chapters, with the globe; the second and ninth, with the chess board; the third and eighth, with the railroad track; the fourth, sixth, and seventh, with the electronic schematic; and the fifth, alone with the saxophone. The images and the shared, embedded, and linked circles denote literary strategies—metaphors of globalism, chess, trains, and electronic engineering borrowed from Braxton's youth (all 50 years of it), to conceptualize his original music and its external influences and impact. The sheerly visual and numerical aspects of the figures—the circles, the logos, the tipped hourglass shape; and the sets, symmetries, and relationships of the 10 digits used from zero through ten (sections *one* and *two* of *two* chapters each, sections *three* and *five* of *one* chapter, section *four* of *four* chapters; *ten* chapters; *one* introduction; and the various instrumental combinations)—signal something key about the body of the book, and about Braxton's music.

Visuals—diagrams, drawings, schemata—and numbers (and alphanumeric and geometric visuals of numbers and their relationships) figure large in both Braxton's music and his explanations of it. My use of both here is offered as a conceptual touchstone through the potentially overwhelming convolutions of them to come. My circles convey the way I've tried to spiral through my material and tie the end of the book up with its beginning, just as Braxton's latest fruits are the issue of the same kind of seeds they contain. My *logi* mirror some of the visualization premises and techniques the artist has developed for his music, and the numbers and their orderings and relationships mirror those generated in the music. If the visuals and numerical patterns begin to lose meaning in density as we explore the music, try to look beyond them and any thought of "meaning" as you think of this: nature is full of repetition and complexity; of singularity, duality, trinity, quaternity, and (arguably) infinity; of sights and sounds all running on together at once, intermingling and manifesting and mutating constantly; the human nervous system is processing *all* sensory/rational data in the same neural network, to form its *one* manifold reality; and music generally, not just Braxton's, is an art form made from sound in time; that time is defined by periodicity, and that periodicity is measured by numbers, especially one, two, three and their multiples. Since Descartes, numbers may have become intangibly abstract, but in hearkening back to Pythagoras and his Western torchbearers in the mystical and occult traditions, we feel the life of numbers in the mind indeed, but in a mind not detached from the body nor the rest of the universe, from its most mundane to its most mysterious phenomena. "Zero" is self-swallowing nature (the snake with its tail in its mouth) in the void of space; "one," with "turn," is in the very word "universe;" "two" is yin and yang, symmetry and conflict, in their myriad flesh and form; "three" has its flesh in the male/female/offspring engine of life; "four" bears the structure of spacetime in seasons, the elements, the encompassed directions, to name a few clear examples. Pictograms and ideograms evoke, invoke, and conceptualize human psychic connections to such realities; alphabets and words, and mathematical systems, are simply those pictures shorthanded up a notch and sequenced together; sights sing and sounds are seen in the keenest states of mind where the oneness of the all and the interreflection of the many are apparent, for which artists/mystics invent their language, movements, images, and sounds.[9] Braxton simply musicalizes all this more explicitly and urgently than many in his genre. The best way to "understand" his terms and systems, and the schemata and structure of his pieces, is to let them sate the insatiable mind right off; then let their contents touch the heart, soul, and spirit.

As for calling the chapter sections "arrows," the explanation is begun in the caption to *Figure I*, but not completed until the book's final pages. I'll allow you the pleasure of its unfolding aesthetic revelation.

Finally, a word about supplementary sections. In keeping with the emphasis on Braxton as a self-defining composer, I've included his "Introduction" to his "Catalogue of Works," as printed in his *Composition Notes A–E*. Early and partial versions of the catalogue itself can be seen in Lock and Radano; Braxton's own complete and current catalogue is too long to include here. However, I do paraphrase the bulk of its brief blurbs on each piece in my Chapter Eight; and information about how to order both catalogue and specific scores and parts (and Braxton's books) directly from Braxton's publishing company is included with his "Introduction," in the Appendix. Since my book is a close look at his performance practices, theoretical constructs, and views on music and culture as though they were generally relevant and accessible to typical musicians and educators, I felt this particular excerpt to be the best use of this space, and the best complement to the supplementary sections of the other two (English-language) books on the artist.

Sources include some unpublished works, videos, and lectures not cited in footnotes that contributed to the book's conceptual ambiance; Ad de Vries'

introduction

Dictionary of Symbols and Imagery,[10] listed there, is the source of several of my chapters' display quotes beginning "From the occult definition of"; and the "Recordings Cited" includes private tapes. My few unnotated references to statements attributed to Braxton are drawn from numerous private conversations that have taken place over the course of the seven years I've known him; two long formal phone interviews were conducted and transcribed expressly for this book.

Some personal background seems more appropriate before than after the body of the book, to ground the reader in its approach and conception. I will be looking at several elements—Braxton's music, media perceptions of it, Braxton's perceptions of the media, and, self-consciously, my own processes of representing all that (so as best to speak to the *issue* of representation central to much of it)—from the viewpoint of a creative person, specifically a musician in Braxton's genre. My conclusions about his and others' writings and music are shaped by and grounded in my own experience as both a writer and a musician.

Those two experiences have for twenty years intertwined and fed each other. When I first started writing, it was more as a poet and literary storyteller than as a journalist or academic. The experience of writing in the creative mode—that mode's relationship between the mechanics and spirit of language—was much closer than this "nonfiction" one (although those last quotes are used here ironically) to the experience of making music by wrestling sounds from instruments into musical statements spun out of notes, scales, song forms, and more experimental elements. The same holistic intensity, focus, and rapture prevailed; the cerebration, however keen, did not, as it traditionally does in this mode.

My decision to become a journalist, some ten years after I had been actively playing and writing music (and writing poetry and fiction), was a conscious attempt to cover a subject I felt I knew firsthand, and to improve upon the journalism I was reading. As a player, I consistently resented and disdained most of that, especially reviews of the music I considered most interesting and adventurous. I developed an abiding passion to set the record straight. I didn't couch the problem in racial/cultural terms so much as creative/noncreative: "These people aren't artists," I can still hear my younger self declaim with passion, "aren't even trying to be. How dare they set themselves up as experts and judges?" (The same feeling was often roused by academics.) That gut indignation provided much of the motivation for me to rein in my own initial creative flights of literary fancy to harness language to the twin oxen of journalism and scholarship—which did not come easily, naturally, or quickly (I'm 47 now, and while I have been selling music journalism regularly on and off for over 20 years it is only for the last ten that I have begun to develop my own voice and messages, and only in the last five have I extended those to regional and national mainstream music magazines and scholarly journals).

I view my youthful disdain for journalists and scholars of this music as an immature passion, one turning increasingly to respect as I myself struggle to enter their respective discourses. However, this book, though I hope it contributes to both of those discourses, is not consistently crafted nor entirely evaluable by their criteria. It seeks to speak in the same voice that speaks the music itself—the voice of the Muse—to fellow musicians and music lovers.

That voice either speaks or it doesn't, and must shape and follow its own criteria and judgments on the fly. If it speaks, it is for us journalists and scholars to listen, and let it inform — not necessarily affirm — our positions.[11]

---

1. Following the example of my subject, I've coined a couple of words (only two; his own will be quite enough to deal with) to aid my discussion. *Musicultural* draws on the ethnomusicological inclusion of music with its cultural context; its distinguishing connotations are (1) its emphasis on the discipline and field of music as primary and the culture contextualizing it as secondary, rather than the other way around (thus I'll more commonly speak of the African American musiculture as the set from which the subset of the culture as a whole derives than I will the reverse, sheerly for the sake of the musician's focus and perspective); and (2) its presumption of a transcultural, panhistorical, global "family" of music makers engaging in a similarly universal and timeless discourse, rather than of a particular tribe, nation, people, period or paradigm (thus I'll speak of the American musiculture, or the Western musiculture, as members along with the African or African American musicultures of the one world musiculture).

The other word is *paradigma*. Combining "paradigm" and "schema," it tags my variations (mostly in Chapters Five and Six) on Braxton's own diagram of his general paradigm/system for composing and improvising. Since he conceives his many creations as coming from this one paradigm/system, I found it useful to seek the relationship of my selections from that many to that one.

2. Chip Stern ("Kelvin *7666* = Blip-Bleep," *Village Voice* June 11, 1979) called him "the Buckminster Fuller of music;" Whitney Balliett (*New Yorker*, April 4, 1977: 84): "Grass will never grow on Anthony Braxton"; Herbert Saal ("Two Free Spirits," *Newsweek* Aug. 8, 1977: 52–53) called him "...the most innovative force in jazz"; and Chris Albertson ("Braxton's Basics," *Stereo Review* Aug. 1985: 71) "the most important jazz composer/player since John Coltrane." See Ronald M. Radano ("Braxton's Reputation," *Musical Quarterly* LXXII (1986 #4): 503–22 for a good survey of coverage by jazz-specific media and general publications with jazz coverage; and Gray, next note.

3. See John Gray, *Fire Music: A Bibliography of the New Jazz, 1959–1990* (New York/Westport, CT/London: Greenwood Press, 1991) for a comprehensive source guide through the subject; and 120–26, for sources on Braxton.

4. Lock: London: Quartet Books, 1985; Radano: Chicago/London: University of Chicago Press, 1993. For convenience, I've used the paperback reprint of Lock's book (*Forces in Motion: The Music and Thoughts of Anthony Braxton*, New York: Da Capo Press, 1988) for research; footnotes on Lock refer to that edition.

5. See Lock's liner notes to *Solo (London) 1988*, the three quartet CD sets *Quartet (London/Birmingham/Coventry) 1985*, and the CD reissue of *Composition 96* (see Recordings Cited for catalogue data) and Radano's Ph.D. dissertation *Anthony Braxton and his Two Musical Traditions: The Meeting of Concert Music and Jazz* (University of Michigan, 1985).

6. "I never intentionally made a separation between the folk and pop musics and Western art and classical music traditions as a young guy, in terms of my listening. I grew up with Chicago urban blues—Curtis Mayfield, Bobby Blue Bland—that tradition was always in my house. Playing in [a commercial band called] the Melody Makers and in the army band exposed me to the dance band repertoire, American show tunes, marches, and so on. I was always attracted to the American song form tradition. After experiencing the music of Ruth Crawford and Charles Seeger, I became interested in American country music, and the field recordings of Alan Lomax. What

we did in the AACM [Association for the Advancement of Creative Musicians] was a response to Coltrane and Ornette Coleman, a clarification of what history was, especially for African Americans—but even then, in that context, I had defined my aesthetic as not accepting artificial separation from musics I liked. Now, at 45, looking back, I see the American song form, [John Philip] Sousa, Coltrane, Ornette, [Paul] Desmond, Warne Marsh and Lennie Tristano, [John] Cage, and [Karlheinz] Stockhausen as my influences. I had not planned to become a universalist, but when I look back I see I was interested in the universal musics before I even knew I was.

"We act in our country as though African American musicians were never influenced by European Americans and vice versa, but the real history of our country is just the opposite. The universalist axis has been happening all along. I have tried to build my model based on a tenet structure that respects what I learn about life as it relates to the Asian, African, European and feminist viewpoint—all my influences—so I try to cover individual, group, synthesis, and architectural (form) postulations in terms of both my own and universal goals and targets" (Anthony Braxton, telephone interview (February 25, 1993)).

7. See Robert Farris Thompson, *Flash of the Spirit: African and Afro-American Art and Philosophy* (New York: Random House, 1983: 7) for a picture of three concentric circles within a square as the sign of the Goddess Earth generated by the Yoruba people, who, along with peoples from The Congo (now Zaire), constituted much of the population of American slaves.

8. Mostly the *New Grove* dictionaries of *Jazz*, *American Music*, and *Music and Musicians* (London: Macmillan; New York, Groves Dictionaries of Music, 1988 and 1986, respectively; and London: Macmillan; Washington, DC: Groves Dictionaries of Music, 1980). Even the more specific sources cited throughout the first two chapters are not always picked for their latest words in scholarly discourse so much as their pointed resonance with my subject and approach and their accessibility to the general reader.

9. *Synesthesia* is the word for this scrambling of sensory data and receptors, and is commonly reported by artists and mystics intensely engaged with a medium or discipline.

10. Amsterdam/Holland: North Holland Publishing Co., 1974.

11. Since I finished this work much scholarship on representing and contextualizing the music has come out that would have certainly influenced in its own right my own Muse's voice, had the timing been right. Most notably so, editor Krin Gabbard's companion anthologies *Representing Jazz* and *Jazz Among the Discourses* (Durham and London: Duke University Press, 1995), especially the contributions of Jed Rasula, Robert Walser, and John Corbett to the latter.

first arrow . . .

from the bow of the past

Evocation

Good biographies often start with a long look at their subjects' parentage and world. This biography—of a music's Muse—will do that. Unlike a person, however, a Muse lives outside of time; its music exists in all time. The godfather and godmother of both Muse and music might best be imaged as, respectively, Mystery and History.

Mystery is the *potentia* we call (in its subscendence) the subconscious, both collective and personal, and (in its transcendence) the vision, also collective—cultural, or universal—and personal, that compels us to learn and create. History is the *actu* continuum of knowledge and events generated by those who attempt not only to know but to express the Mystery.

As godparents to Braxton's music (think of him as the delivering doctor, or midwife), these are the best guides through the vast range of the first two chapters. Those are a synopsis of, in Chapter One, human myth, imagination, and thought as it has run from prehistory through the Western and African streams—the "grandparents"—that converged in the Americas; and, in Chapter Two, through the "trans-African" and "trans-European" musicultural lineages Braxton claims (and so names) and aligns himself with (the "parents"). Such "godparents," with such "grand/parents," are helpful, because although both are beyond the individual human scale, they are not beyond the collective human—archetypal—scale of the Muse. They are thus still within the purview of the human experience, the part Braxton himself claims for and through his work (we are about to assess a composer who has written music to be performed simultaneously in different star systems, and who claims access to the last "2000 to 5000 years of our legacy as a species.")[1]

The range of Braxton's influences and musical ambitions is enormous. What is compelling about the vast range of musical traditions and musicians this music maker claims, and why? That is the question driving this section.

In tracing the lineages with which Braxton expresses affinity and seeks to extend, we establish context. The need for context is great because Braxton's music, more than that of many of his peers, takes on so many disparate musical legacies with such disarming (detractors would say disingenuous) aplomb that his syntheses have easily (and often) been mistaken for absurd pastiche, or clinical attempts to create life in the test tubes of a laboratory, as opposed to the more organic, less presumptuous gestures we call good art.

The American musical community has mostly seen Braxton as what critic Francis Davis has called an "outcat,"[2] a (specifically jazz-traditional) figure marching to some different drummer. That Braxton has busied himself throughout this isolating experience—spelled by a brief period of mainstream jazz media attention in the mid- to late-1970s—at finding an anchor within tradition's premises and principles, while mining it for new possibilities, has been noticed only by some, heralded by fewer.

The first step toward grasping its substance is to notice the specific threads of Braxton's own African American tradition, then those of traditions he chose, when old enough to choose, to feed and inform his own music. America's potentially greatest gift to the world is a culture born of that world's most extremely opposite (thus most mutually hostile) groups; they are here. Braxton has chosen to embrace them—or take them all on—rather than seek refuge in and/or from any of them.

While this section will bring out Braxton's influences, then, to counter the image of the outcat who is too *far* out, we should yet clarify the nature of influences on an artist who seeks to be, and is widely accepted as, definitive as well as derivative. William Cole's words about John Coltrane fit Braxton:

> I don't think that a man of Trane's potential would listen to what another person is playing and directly imitate him. I think he would listen to find out what the other player is playing that he cannot play, and then he would try to work that expansion of capacity into his own playing . . . So, in an individual like Trane, an influence would be an unconscious departure from what was continuously evolving in his music.[3]

Braxton expresses this for himself when discussing his own way of analyzing and assimilating the work of various saxophonists and then consciously responding to it with his own approach.[4] Similarly, in conversation, he has pointed out that even those of his compositions directly inspired by someone else's work don't therefore necessarily sound like that work.

Again, what, if not sound and style, bespeaks the nature of Braxton's relationship to his influences? What about them is he most interested and invested in? Braxton's three decades of music are the unfolding of a potential first tapped in the two to three years of musical experiments and experiences during his time in the Association for the Advancement of Creative Musicians (AACM), in the late 1960s—but it is important to take seriously the fact that the AACM members studied and discussed mystical and religious writings from throughout the world and history as much as music, in their quest to contextualize and feed *their* music.

For this section, then, I go back through the AACM as Mystery School to Braxton the student at Roosevelt College, who rejected there the formal study of music in favor of philosophy and Oriental thought, beginning a lifelong interest in comparative studies of philosophical, religious, occult, and mystical traditions. I go back even further, to his personally primal Afrocentric encounters with the West, in his childhood encounters with the Baptist and Catholic churches.

Braxton's formal college study was brief, and he has never devoted himself as an "organization man" to a particular dogma or creed,[5] but a foundation of philosophy and musicultural history pervades his music from its beginnings. Indeed, the "Philosophical" is one of three parts (the other two are "Architectural" and "Ritual and Ceremonial;" see Fig. 5.5) of what he calls his "tripartite" musical system. Through his three-volume *Tri-Axium Writings*,[6] Braxton articulates this philosophical aspect, and generalizes and signifies much of the history and thought specified in this section as the context in which to understand the music itself. (Braxton's spelling of "axium" signals—as distinct from the more passive conventional definition of "axiom"—his notion of the present as an *axis* upon which he/humanity is positioned to draw from the past to determine the future.) Accordingly, I mix history, Braxton's work as a whole, and pertinent thought and research from various fields to create a real-world scenario of that notion.

The reader may well question whether an historical synopsis of such sweep and detail is not too extensive to remain relevant to the work of a single artist. The answer is that we live in a time of unprecedented access to historical information, world travel and communication, interdisciplinary dialogue and collaboration, and therefore equally broad personal assimilations of same. This material will not seem so far flung once we get into the more microscopic and direct looks at Braxton's music. The latter is much like the concentric circles in Fig. I, or perhaps a series of locked Chinese boxes that contain each other; the human history of evolution, ideas, and events is a ring of keys that will allow us to sort and open those boxes before examining their contents and putting them back together.

The first locked box, to be opened by the very scope and detail of this section, is Braxton's well-nigh absurd artistic ambition. He *claims* this reach, and his music reflects that detail (the distillation of both into a book's worth of reading itself says something about the feasibility of such a claim, and about its possible mode of operation). What's more, he has a sense of his place in the vast chronology—thus my choice of "Millennial" in the Introduction. This information is Braxton's *mythos*, in the same way the Lutheran's Bible was Bach's, or the mix of German music pedagogy and *vodou* rites in New Orleans' Congo Square was Louis Armstrong's. It also resonates with the *mythos* of his Muse—in Western mythological terms, Hermes (Thoth, Mercury, Gabriel) Lord of the Roads, Lord of Thieves, who travels everywhere throughout spacetime, defining the routes and boundaries separating everything, able by virtue of the definer's role (that of *logos*) to *re*define, *re*route, and *re*direct the flow and balance of the *kosmos* so ordered.

The historical continuum and issues considered in these two chapters are alluded to, if not detailed so, in Braxton's *Tri-Axium Writings*. Many of the sources I cite, or similar ones—from the sciences, history, mythology, psychology, and philosophy—can be found stocked and well worn on the shelves of his office walls (likewise most of the recordings). His readings in Western arts and letters have fed the same quest for the soul and taproot of the music as the parallel backtracks down Afrocentric lines he also took with so many of his peers, especially in the AACM, in the 1960s. They led to a sense of the Greco-Roman/Judeo-Christian West as a civilization built from the cultural remnants of ancient Egypt. Like the work of many important composers—certainly the Westerners who most influenced him, from Ives to Schoënberg to Cage to Stockhausen—Braxton's includes dimensions directly issuing as much from the thought and events of history as of his own time and place. African American music has evolved as a gradual recasting of ever more of the Western world into an ever-deeper, broader, subtler African context. Braxton's role in that process has a distinct and unique resonance with much of the West's historical and timeless themes and motifs.

In this section we'll begin unlocking the Chinese boxes of Braxton's music and put their contents on display next to similar yet more familiar gems: selections from Braxton's scores, recordings, and *Composition Notes* that parallel selections from the work of the influences he claims. This will provide the ground for the overwhelmingly *Braxtonian* world we'll enter and explore in the other sections. The delight and surprise in these comparisons of an individual with his world lie in the discovery of concrete musical statements in a voice whose consistency might have kept their diversity hidden to any but such a methodical treasure hunt—statements that, when recast from the fragmented context of that diversity into the integrated one of that voice, stand as that voice's single statement. It is there we hear the Muse singing, and speaking.

Chapter One

The Music's Grandparents

> *I see and claim all the devices of the last 2000–5000 years as part of our legacy as a species.*
>
> Anthony Braxton, on the scope of his influences

Primate Music

One scholar's quest for the primal tongue of both music and language has led him to observe the behaviors of our nearest primate cousins, African chimps, in response to regular celestial events such as nightfall and thunderstorms.[7] Dudley Young sees clues there of how early hominids might have started a tradition of nocturnal prayers/songs still alive in rituals such as military Taps, Bantu night drumming, Protestant Evensong, and bedtime prayers.

Chimps, as night comes on, take to their arboreal nests and drum and hoot together in an "evening chorus" that "arises soothingly, a kind of mellow hum on which they float happily into sleep." The purpose, writes Young, seems to be to warn off predators and reassure each other—but it is the darkness that triggers it. This signal from their environment provokes a response that makes their unity as a group both palpable and explicit. If palpable then manipulable, magnifiable; if explicit, then the unity is that of a united front, a group consciousness, facing the fearful mystery of night and its dangers.

The chimps address the sky more violently when it produces thunderstorms, but in the same concerted way. What starts as disparate, defiant and terror-tinged shrieks and motions becomes, literally, a group song and dance that ends more as a collectively patterned (into chorus and principal solo "dancer-singers") statement of ecstatic identification—a duet—with the storm.

Anthony Braxton's music is one whose phylogeny *consciously* recapitulates the ontogeny of the music of the world. Its relevance to Young's ideas lies in those aspects of it that sound like animals sound;[8] these aspects comprise our second locked box, and Young's and other such research the key that opens it. From the cathartic primal screams in the upper registers of the highest reeds, to the lumbering growls of the lowest, to the more pensive whimpers and whines and snuffles and snorts he has worked out all along his various horns, Braxton's audial palette has painted uncanny pictures of barking dogs, pan-mammalian terror and rage, bears coming out of hibernation, whales and birds and dolphins croaking and squeaking and chirping, bovines lowing a human lament.

African American music, of course, has distinguished itself by such sounds. Eurocentric purists have historically disdained the growls and whinnies of jazz horn players as vulgar; others have taken obvious delight and pleasure, even power, from them. In the larger picture, shamans everywhere everywhen have gone to great lengths to take on the ways of various animals to attain particular attributes of consciousness and life energy. The Western mainstream itself is coming back to such an approach, through its environmental movement (with musical expressions such as those of Paul Winter) and its New Age mental health and self-realization techniques (from Arthur Janov's primal screamers in the early 1970s to the back-to-the-Goddess wing of the Women's Movement and the painted drummers of the Men's Movement).

The fact is, of course, humans are animals, and need to remember it and feel it to be fully human, both individually and collectively. We need to make the sounds and gestures, develop the vocal (not just verbal) and body language that leads to successful mating, protection of self and others, survival strategies and enhancers of every sort. This aspect of Braxton's music is perhaps the best place to start. Its logic rests in the pre-rational heart, the visceral emotions of the limbic brain, the autonomic rhythms and cycles of blood and breath, and the fight-or-flight surges of adrenalin that mark our trek through life. It also grounds the highest spiritual impulses in their deepest biological roots. Braxton's motto since childhood ("Play or die!")[9] may best be understood as such a bio-spiritual imperative impervious to less compelling conventional ideas of what sounds "right" (and makes money) and what doesn't.

I love the old horror movies. To be inches away from some 20-foot slobbering monster, just about to gobble you up. How real can you get?

Anthony Braxton

Hunter/Shaman Music

Our experience as human animals has not been so simple as that group awe and coziness with the elements and their cycles. We have been both hunters and hunted, as much of our own as of other species. Again, the prehistoric tradition of taking on the identity of the bear, the hoofed beast, the eagle or the hawk, of painting and contemplating their images in the firelit caves, of making their sounds and motions, of observing and marking the biorhythms and habits both of our prey and our enemies—all this, the roots of magic, religion, and art, sprung from and grew in the soil of the survival instinct and its strategies. (This is a very different picture than that of Maslow's "hierarchy of needs,"[10] in which creative and spiritual fulfillment are achieved in the most rarefied garden at the peak of a life that has covered its basic needs and is leisurely and safely pursuing its fulfillment.) The bodies of our first instruments came from those of the plant and animal life around us, at a time, and for a long time, when we were keenly aware of the spirits therein.

Botanist/author Terrence McKenna spells out the nature of that shamanic tradition's magic and power, and the influence of it on what he sees as the decline in the West of the literate tradition.[11] He speaks of language and music as stemming from the same process in the brain and nervous system that literally creates reality (in a sense mystics have always meant and even physicists are starting to mean now).[12] His field studies of an Amazon Indian tribe's use of psychotropes go far toward explaining the psychic connections between visual images, language, and music so highly developed in Braxton's work.

The Amazon tribe known as the *Ayahuasqueros* ritualizes chanting while on tryptamine hallucinogens as a means of directing a visual hallucination shared by the group. McKenna, who participated in the ritual, describes it as a way of making an animant, shared pictorial art form, using the colors, shapes, and images commonly experienced on psychotropes.

McKenna theoretically projects this phenomenon onto prehistoric evolution. Small amounts of psilocybin, he writes, improve visual acuity, which increases hunting success, which increases reproductive success; slightly higher doses stimulate sexual arousal, and the effects that has on the nervous system (heightened focus and concentration, a nervous energy level). Still higher doses stimulate the language-forming function of the brain, which gives rise to the use of sound (song) and its visual correspondents as symbolic of emotional and conceptual abstraction.

Whether or not psilocybin functioned, as McKenna suggests, as an "evolutionary catalyst"[13] leading proto-human primates to their eventual human potential, we know that the African American oral tradition of both music and language has been feared and scorned (and matched) by white America for its associations with marijuana, alcohol, cocaine, opium, heroin, and other mind-altering substances. This history resonates with similarly used (let's leave "abused" out of this particular discussion) substances in shamanic ritual everywhere and everywhen. The African American tradition is similarly famous for its creativity with language, as displayed in the so-called "jive" talk generated by artists from Louis Armstrong through Lester Young to Dizzy Gillespie, chronicled and discussed by authors such as Mezzrow and Sidran.[14] Finally, to finish what admittedly has suffered the fate of stereotype, black music in America has presented sexuality in a context that white America, not without mixed feelings and trauma, can be said to have accepted as more healthy and realistic than the one it inherited from its own Judeo-Christian tradition of flesh-renunciation.

All of this contextualizes richly the times in which Braxton came of age and formed his artistic voice and vision. It serves as a key to his third locked box, the one that contains his general compulsion to visualize his music; to infuse it with nervous, mercurial energy; and to develop new visual and verbal languages to image and explain it. A child of the 1960s, Braxton escaped the alcohol and heroin culture of his immediate musical predecessors. However (without getting into his personal habits), he and his peers and their music were certainly exposed to the effects of psychotropes. Certainly many who have experienced this syncretic stimulation of, most commonly, marijuana on music, language, and the generation of internal and receptivity to external visual experiences would describe it in terms that corroborate McKenna's.

McKenna's theories are extrapolations on prehistory from a present culture. Anthropologists have made similar extrapolations from similar evidence onto prehistoric cultures in a more direct line to those of present-day Africa and Europe. Ethnographies of modern day Stone Age peoples (most notably the San tribe of Africa) suggest that the geometric patterns such as concentric circles and squares, triangles, spirals, grids, patterns of dots, crosses, and various combinations of same that abound throughout the rock art of the Paleolithic and Neolithic worlds were likely representations of "entoptic" images—those generated within the optic nerves themselves—experienced in altered states brought on by stimuli as varied as "psychoactive drugs, fatigue, sensory deprivation, intense concentration, auditory driving, migraine, schizophrenia, hyperventilation, and rhythmic movement."[15] (Four of those, of course, come with a serious wind player's occupation; the rest are at least occupational hazards, if not inevitable to the human condition to some degree.)

The relevance to Braxton of this primal connection between visuals and music, and the role of same in culture, should by now be clear. That they have been an enigma to so many for so long may be because Braxton has developed them intuitively, independently, without himself fully understanding their nature (indeed, that may explain many other such enigmas more accurately and charitably than to ascribe them to pretentiousness and bluff).

Braxton colleague trumpeter/composer Leo Smith's mention (see last footnote) of letters and numbers as the "outside meaning" of mystical pictographs brings to mind the nature of the origin of the alphanumeric system used today for language, music notation, and mathematics. Its letters and numbers have their roots in such pictures and have served both alphabetical and numerical functions (as Roman numerals still do). The pictures came first and were associated with the *sounds* of the words for their referents (thus the letter A was originally a picture of a bull, for which the Hebrew word was "aleph;" the Greek letter/numeral "iota" has a phallic origin, in the depiction of a seed (sperm) being spouted, to denote the tiny unit of origin, numbered "1," of the many and vast; the letter M was originally a picture of a water-wave, and so on). The initial visual meaning was eventually lost in the forging of such a phonetic code, and the symbols could be strung together in enough combinations to be functionally infinite, to abstract new mental images.

This historical progression from visual images and sounded word to an alphanumeric code of fixed components that can be mutably combined to form the multileveled logic of language and mathematics (including the formulaic-visual narratives of algebra and geometry) is perhaps the key to the fourth locked

the music's grandparents

Braxton box: the one that contains the *specific* visual and numerical images with which he orders, notates, and titles his music. Those titles convey the abstract meaning of his music, including its syntax and grammar, just as letters and numbers do—*arbitrarily*—the abstract meaning of language.

For example: *141(+20+96+120D)* denotes a primary piece nesting part or all of three other pieces, one of which (120D) is part (D) of a lettered series in a number (120) set. Each of these four pieces may also fall into a broad category of pieces—such as Kelvin, Cobalt, or some other designation chosen not as a direct musical referent but as a simple, often poetic, code he assigns to a given musical concept he wants to develop. Each may also have a graphic and/or formulaic title, both of which may or may not reflect something about Braxton's private, subjective conception of the music. What all this *means* transcends the meanings of its components as the "order" scientists now find transcending "chaos"[16]—as, for that matter, the meaning of language transcends the jumble of sounds and images alphanumerics started out to be. Both meanings are as mysterious, epiphenomenal—and known—as consciousness itself. The global commonalty of all peoples in this process resonates with Braxton's universalist, rather than racially, historically or culturally specific, declarations for his music.

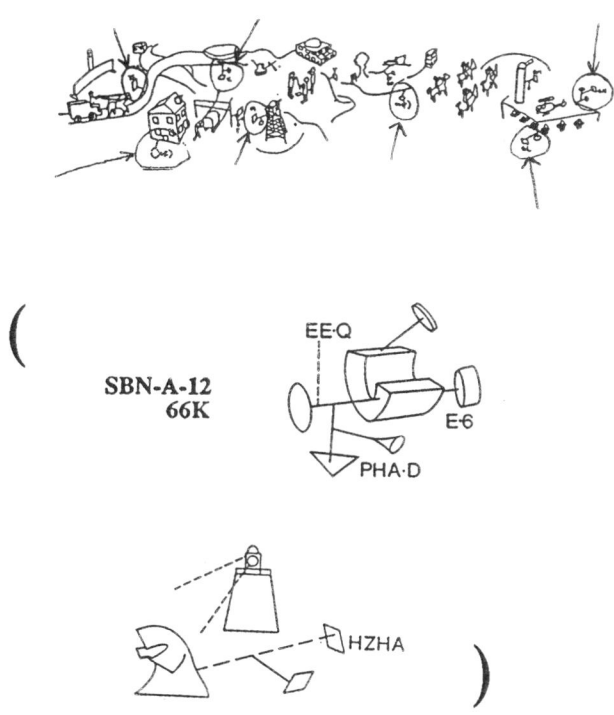

Fig. 1.1: 141(+20+96+120D) *expressed graphically. The top graphic title, of* 141, *is what Braxton calls the primary identity of* 141 (+20+96+120D). *Within its execution, material from the other three is included to aid new*

improvisations; this material Braxton calls sub-identity formings. A consideration of this visual representation yields insight into its musical referent. Notice the small geometric "tags," with letters and numbers (too tiny at this scale, so circled), positioned at various points within the top picture. Think of the three subidentity titles as magnified details of the top picture; notice that as the titles evolved from earliest to latest (20–96–120D), they started as alphanumerics, added geometric shapes, then added real-world pictures to both of those. This reflects the way (universal) entoptic images are generated first, then (culturally specific) hallucinations later on, in the kind of trance state brought on by music (it also images Plato's vision of the absolute ideal realm from which material variations emanate, and the general development of art from symbol to realistic representation).

The musical experience might be thought of as the internal "videos" the artist's creativity has generated to go with his musical statements; the geometrics and alphanumerics are as spontaneous and evanescent as the music, as fixed and fluid at once. That is, they mean something as they're born and evoke that something when recalled, but that something is itself mutable, like a dream, a river, or a living thing.

Racial Memories

The last in a series of migrations from Eurasia across the Bering Strait to North America took place some 15,000 years ago.[17] To this primary population we can add the likelihood of early Polynesian, African, Middle Eastern and even European explorations across both Pacific and Atlantic oceans, some of which may have been seminal influences on the great South American civilizations discovered by 16th-century Europeans. By that time, the native Americans, like the Africans, had developed magical cultures with a mythos of immanence (unlike the Christianist emphasis on the transcendent); they also featured, across their highly heterogeneous spectrum, a balance between male and female in both mythology and social structure that contrasted starkly with the patriarchy of the Catholic church. They were also, of course, dark-skinned.

About the time of that last Eurasian migration, Mesolithic and Neolithic groups now known as the battle-axe cultures lived in the forest and coastal areas of Northern Europe, especially Denmark. They seem to be the most likely forerunners of the patriarchal nomadic tribes which, from about 2400 B.C., began to sweep in periodic waves of conquest, on horses, down from the Caucasus region of Russia onto the matriarchal cultures in the Middle and Near Eastern lands of Anatolia, Persia, Mesopotamia, India, Egypt, Sumer, Canaan, and India. These peoples are now referred to as Caucasians, Indo-Europeans, Indo-Iranians, Indo-Aryans, and Aryans.

These Aryans:

• worshipped a male storm god who was pictured on a mountain, having descended from the sky, brandishing lightning or (volcanic?) fire;

• equated their own light skin with that god's light, thus equating both skin and light with "good"; equated the darker-skinned (and more civilized) peoples and the deities (mostly female, often depicted with a serpent) with "bad"; and institutionalized this white racism and male sexism into every dark-skinned, matriarchal culture they conquered, from Persia to India to Egypt;

• seem to have had close ties with the Abrahamic clans of the early (light-skinned) *h'brus* (the Egyptian word for "slaves"), who borrowed from their patriarchal social structure and their god's persona and power;

• had a tendency, once they conquered a people and their deity and had established their rulership, to accommodate themselves to the conquered culture. Thus do we find their priest-caste elite hierarchically dominating among the Celts as Druids, the Indians as Brahmins, the Persians as Zoroastrians, the Sumerians and Assyrians through Hurrian and Kassite underlords, the Egyptians through the followers of Hor, and even, possibly, the Hebrews, through the priest-caste tribe known as the Levites.

What would start out as a mythological imposition of the male sky/storm/mountain/fire god over all other gods and goddesses, and a political imposition of an Aryan warrior/priest elite caste over a subjugated people relatively quickly became a more tangled hierarchy, as Aryan nobles intermarried with their non-Aryan underlings and as myths subsequently merged in reflection of such social mixing.

This pattern of conquest and assimilation took place between the different groups of Aryans as well as between each group and its non-Aryan victims. As more intercourse occurred, more racial, religious, and sexual hierarchization became the legacy of dark-skinned peoples previously free of it. The idea of the white male standing as the good and powerful god's governor on earth was thus implanted in those cultures' mass consciousness from within, from their "father's" side, as it were; the image of the white as an uncivilized but powerful barbarian was inherited from the more cultured position held by the "mother" in ancient times.

This syndrome surged throughout the ancient world, nomadic Aryans taking and ruling already established cultures; adopting the ways therein, yet for their own god; doing much of this by forced slave labor, causing the society to fall in on itself out of the sheer human inability of both oppressor and oppressed to sustain such terms; then falling into the hands of a temporarily stronger Aryan or Aryan-molded rival, and so on.

In the European discovery of America, then, we see two worlds which, though they had lost widespread knowledge of each other, began from a common Eurasian land base. The dark-skinned Far Eastern groups migrated overland around the Pacific to the Americas, north and east, with the planet's spin; and the light-skinned passed their culture southward through Semitic and then Greco-Roman-European peoples westward, against the spin, across the water. We see then a single landmass of peoples splitting into opposite directions to meet each other again in the Americas.

Their meeting was intuited and defined in the myths of both races. The natives had their stories of white gods coming from the East, and the Europeans romanticized the noble savage still living in his Edenic golden age (some Medieval maps even labeled the Eastern lands "Paradise"). Their first big clash took place first in South America, where the native civilization was greatest both in terms of its plunder potential and of its potential to be defined as the enemy. That is, its spirit was a "city-sized" elaboration on magic, myth, and immanence, its rituals including the human sacrifice Christianity had mythologized. The *conquistadors* were Spanish Catholics at the time of the Inquisition, one of the most intolerant, militant, imperialistic, and dogmatic expressions of Christendom's history.

These first conquests of a whole civilization by a handful of whites can be understood in terms of both biology and mythology. Both sides felt the whites had the power of God/gods on their side because of mythological expectations of white gods coming from the East; and both felt the natives were being punished for some fundamental flaw when strange new diseases wiped out millions of natives yet none of the immune white carriers.

The motion of this historical force is at the heart of African American music generally, and Braxton's specifically. It is the motion of the warrior spirit in both sides of the battle, in an eternal fluctuation that makes conquest and defeat eternally transient situations, each experienced alternately by both sides, put to rest finally only by the peace and satisfaction of both together. In Braxton's music, its aspect is that intensity that screams, roars, and signifies beyond the viscerally animal and with the unmistakably human intelligence—that aspect which the music's *cognoscenti* describe as "bad," "dangerous," the music of a "monster," "burning," "smoking." It is the force that will always be in motion to one degree or another until the ancient racial enmity—or, for that matter, violence and war themselves—and their lingering legacies are somehow transformed (as they are in music, or Braxton's beloved games, chess and football).

After that historical shift from a feminine to a masculine cosmology, the accumulated knowledge and its symbolic media continued to shape both African and Western cultures. Its unbroken historical line can be found not only throughout occult, religious, and secular streams of Western society today, but in African peoples from the Ethiopians to the Pygmies.[18] We'll come back to Africa; for now, let us trace literacy and the development of the transcendent cosmology in the West.

History

For me, having the opportunity to begin studying information related to the Nile Valley Mysteries Complex, as well as the writings of the ancient Europeans, has made all the difference in the world in the emergence of my own aesthetic and what it would open up for me in terms of form building, vibrational dynamics or philosophical dynamics, and synthesis dynamics.

Anthony Braxton

As the Fig. I caption relates, the earliest known symbols drawn by anyone are representations of male and female genitalia. These (nudged by the entoptic process?) developed over time into stylizations—circles, triangles with the peak pointing both up and down—that became the building blocks of pictography, thence hieroglyphy, thence alphanumerics and literacy. As ancient and primal are the examples of counting dots, thought to be women's early measurements of the lunar and their own menstrual cycles.[19]

We move from speculation on mystery to that on history with writing. The abstract and realistic symbols used for ritual magic by countless human bands developed into the mythologies, emblems, organizational and structural media of communication both of tribes and of whole civilizations. Those of Africa and what we now call the West, along with the Middle Eastern and Slavic world, developed much more interactively than either did with, of course, ancient American, Asian, and Indian cultures (although what is of passing interest to our global-Millennial approach is the synchronistic way cultures and their consciousness have mirrored and paralleled each other in mutual—but perhaps not absolute—isolation).[20]

The first exactly dated year in (Western) world history is (the equivalent of) 4241 B.C., from the Egyptian calendar of 360-day years and twelve months of 30 days each. The earliest cities of Mesopotamia were established then, so it stands well as an arbitrary kickoff time for the civilization we call Western. More than that, it truly is the beginning of that civilization's mass consciousness codified through the literate media in which we still swim, with our act of writing and reading (musical scores, as well as books), through written history, literature, myth, science, and philosophy, before all those fields stood up so firmly against each other in specialization.

Goddess

Feminist scholar Barbara Walker speaks of the rise of arts and sciences in ancient Egypt in the context of the Goddess mythos:

> Besides creating the world and everything in it, the Goddess created the civilized arts: agriculture, building, weaving, potting, writing, poetry, music, the graphic arts, calendars, and mathematics. These seem to have developed mostly in the hands of women as outgrowths of the maternal nest-building, communication, and play behavior.[21]

Speaking of the Hindu scriptures, she notes they attribute to the Goddess

> alphabets, pictographs, mandalas and other magical signs, hence her title of Samjna (sign, name, image). The Brahmavaivarta Purana says . . . the Goddess gave birth to the Vedas, the rhythms of the Ragas, day and night, the year, the month, the seasons, the inch, the second, and all other units of measurement; also logic, grammar, the days of the week, Time, Death, Nourishment, Memory, Victory, religious rituals, the trinity of eons, and all the gods.

Walker further depicts the Goddess as the "Great Mother Kali Ma," to be the source of the Sanskrit language and, in her hands, its power to generate creation—a concept picked up later by the Neoplatonic Christian concept of the *logos*.

> Sanskrit matra, like the Greek meter, meant both "mother" and "measurement." Mathematics is, by derivation, "mother-wisdom." Root words for motherhood produced many words for calculation: metric, mensuration, mete, mens, mark, mentality; geo-metry, trigono-metry, hydro-metry, etc. Women did temporal and spatial calculations for so long that, according to the Vayu Purana, men once thought women were able to give birth because they had superior skill in measuring and figuring. Men imagined that if they could master these feminine skills, they could give birth, too . . . In pre-Hellenic Greece the alphabet was attributed to the original three Muses, who were identical with the Fates or Gaeae, eponymous mothers of Greek tribes.

These passages are offered as a fifth master key to what might, locked, seem a rather incidental but is in fact a fundamentally important box: Braxton's feminism. Walker isn't saying so much about the individual men and women at the dawn of civilization as she is about the metaphysic that inspired them. As the next chapter will bring out, women—the feminine force in motion—have played a relatively undersung but crucial role in the history of what at first glance seems a predominantly male (jazz, and, in some aspects, African American cultural) tradition. Further, many of the key figures—Lester Young, Miles Davis, Ornette Coleman, Cecil Taylor, and Braxton himself—exude in their different ways that fertile androgyny artists of genius often exhibit in their equally potent measures of strength and gentleness, savvy and innocence, vulnerability and force. This is male feminism at its most self-invested—the feminism, if you will, of the sperm whose male force is such that it actually gets "him" through to the egg, thus to the union that leads to the death/transformation/new life of separate male and female. As we'll see, it figures subtly but significantly in Braxton's music both personally and on the transpersonal levels of Muse and Millennium.

In this time period when I talk of my music I talk not so much of a composition or instrumental performance as I do of the system of my music: a tripartial model that seeks to cast perceptual and vibrational and ritual dynamics in a context that will establish fresh possibilities for fusing as we begin to move into the post-Aristotelian Aquarian era.

Anthony Braxton

As the cultural power shifted to patriarchy, science also began to advance. Egypt, Babylonia, India and China were all making systematic astronomical observations and constructing calendars accordingly. Sumeria developed a

the music's grandparents

numerical system around multiples of six and twelve; iron, papyrus, potters' wheels and kilns, and bows and arrows all started to come into use.

The next thousand years bring in the beginning of the Semitic alphabet and the Ten Commandments, the Israeli age of the Judges, and the first Israeli king, Saul, in conquered Canaan; the beginning of a true Iron Age in Palestine and Syria; the movement of the Greeks from the shores of the Caspian Sea toward the Eastern Mediterranean, the rise of the Cretan-Mycenean culture, the Trojan War, the abolition of the monarchy in Athens, and a primitive Greek alphabet.

The 300 years before the sixth century B.C. were even more action-packed (at least in the written record), too much so to describe in detail. Suffice it to say that they ushered in the fall of Israel to the first of a long line of conquerors, Sheshonk I of Egypt; the foundation of Rome and the expansion of the Phoenicians and Greeks; a continuing civilization in China with highly advanced mathematics and astronomy; and the Celtic presence in England.

In Greece, classic paganism based on the Gaea-Uranus-Titans-Olympians mythology was in full bloom, later giving way to the worship of Apollo and Bacchus-Dionysus, and later still to the mysticism of the Orphic cult. Sappho of Lesbos was writing, the Indian Vedas were completed, the Hebrew prophets had had their say, and Lao-Tze had had his.

And so we come to the sixth century B.C., time of Confucius, Zoroaster, the Ionian philosophers (the "Seven Wise Men of Greece"), of the first written collection of the Hebrew prophets—and of Pythagoras. The prophets' writings represent the anti-Egyptian generative impulse of the Judeo-Christian mythos, and Pythagoras represents the beginning of the Greco-Romanization of the Egyptian knowledge systems underpinning Western theology, philosophy, science, and aesthetics to come.

Pythagoras

Arthur Koestler[22] wrote about the Ionian philosophy and the popularity of the Orphic cult as a background to the genius of Pythagoras. The Ionians included Thales of Miletos, Anaximander, and Anaximenes who collectively developed abstract geometry (literally "earth measurement") and began to ask what we know as scientific questions (what is the universe made of? how does it work?). The Ionians were materialists, atheists in the sense that they saw the gods of their spacetime as human projections onto the natural processes they wanted to divine.

However, another sort of reaction against the gods occurred in the Orphic cult. Orpheus, you'll recall, was the singer/musician so skillful and enchanting that he charmed Pluto into letting him lead his wife Eurydice back out of the underworld, on the condition that he not look back to see if she was following him out. He couldn't help himself and so lost her to Hades.

Orpheus was so heartbroken that he turned his back on all other women, which eventually enraged those of Thrace who lusted for him. In one of their roaring rites of wine and flesh around the goat-god of fertility, Bacchus-Dionysus, they tore his body to pieces, which the sympathetic Muses buried at the foot of Mt. Olympus. The head, however, had been thrown into the river

Hebrus, down which it floated, still singing, into the sea and thence to Sappho's isle of Lesbos for a separate internment.

Recall the fifth locked box, the feminism of the male force imbued by female energy by virtue of that one-in-a-million successful union (between sperm and egg), the fertile androgyny that permeates mythology. The singing head received by Sappho resonates fiercely with our times, and, as coming pages will show, our subject, especially when harmonized with another Orphic myth.

> Dionysus . . . is the beautiful son of Zeus and Persephone; the evil Titans tear him to pieces and eat him, all but his heart, which is given to Zeus, and he is born a second time. By devouring the god's flesh, the Titans have acquired a spark of divinity which is transmitted to man; and so is the desperate evil that resided in the Titans. But it is in the power of man to redeem this original sin, to purge himself of the evil portion of his heritage by leading an otherworldly life and performing certain ascetic rites. In this manner he can obtain liberation from the "wheel of rebirth"—*his imprisonment in successive animal and even vegetable bodies, which are like carnal tombs to his immortal soul*—and regain his lost divine status[23] (emphases mine, to hearken back to the animism of shamanism, and the role therein of psychotropes).

The Orphic cult therefore evolved into a reaction against the Bacchanalian-Dionysian emotional release of the here and now, an afterlife-eyeing asceticism, with a mythology, ritual, and spirit that prefigured those of Christianity. It was also the first proto-Western religious practice that opened itself up to other tribes and nations.

Pythagoras, says Koestler,[24] united both Orphic and Ionian reactions, one a renunciation and the other a redemption of the world from false, enslaving gods, into a religious philosophy that was also a science.

Like the legendary Orpheus, Pythagoras is best known for his connection with music. He is attributed with the discovery of the overtone series produced by dividing a vibrating string, and their numerical relationships. From music, numbers were seen throughout the rest of nature, from the planets to the body to the psyche. To Pythagoras, musical ecstasy—*ekstasis*, from *ek* (out), plus *histanai* (to place) equals a being put out of its place, distraction, astonishment—found its very self-consciousness in the understanding of numbers. Unlike the associations of dry, cold, passionless abstraction numbers hold for many today, Pythagoras saw them as a sparkling, pure link for the human mind to the workings of *logos* in nature. Music was the song of numbers, stars were their plotted points, all mystery was divinable by the yet greater mystery of numbers. Harmony (*armonia*, a fitting) was the tuning of the strings to the Music of the Spheres (the Pythagorean scale built on the numerical intervals between the observed bodies of the solar system), and catharsis (*katharsis*, purification) the ministration of music as medicine to "tune" the sick body. Numbers were behind it all, behind rocks and planets, and the philosopher had only to learn their rules. Theories (from *thea*, spectacle, and *theoris*, spectator) were to the Pythagoreans' immediate predecessors (Orphic cultists) originally "'a state of fervent religious contemplation, in which the spectator is identified with the suffering god, dies in his death, and rises again in his new birth.'"[25]

Pythagoras formed a brotherhood around his system, an elitist group only for the initiated, since this new knowledge was seen as a possible Pandora's Box for the universe (as, indeed, it has proven to be).

The most important thing is to keep doing the music, so all your intellectual constructs keep referring to something real and alive.

Anthony Braxton

Plato

The following quote from *The Republic* Koestler sees as anti-Pythagorean, which of course it is, on the surface. However, it might just as well be a symptom of a zeal to refine, enrich Pythagoras' *ekstasis*. In "Book VII" Plato says that the actual physical stars are only dim shadows of the real world of ideas: ". . . let us concentrate on (abstract) problems, said I, in astronomy as in geometry, and dismiss the heavenly bodies, if we intend truly to apprehend astronomy."[26]

This position led to two logical—and disastrous—conclusions: (1) that pure abstract reasoning was the best way to figure out how the physical world worked, and (2) that there was a qualitative difference between stations of a hierarchical "Chain of Being."

From the first premise we got Plato's *a priori* reasoning that the universe must be a sphere, since that was the most perfect form, and that the motion of the heavenly bodies was in perfect circles at uniform speed: philosophy as science. From the second we got the gnostic idea of the evil nature of all matter, of our own bodies, of the opposingly good nature of our minds, our links to the realm of Pure Idea (*nous*).

Aristotle

Aristotle, then, applied these positions to the physical world. Physics, through him, became a study of this mutable, base world we inhabit; astronomy became a kind of sky-geometry of a supramundane, immutable celestial, semi-divine region—the last step out of the finite spherical universe into the immaterial region of *nous*, then to the absolutely infinite cause, the "unmoved Mover" of even the Ideal Forms of *nous*. (More directly relevant to the course of Western medieval and Renaissance music, Aristotle's pupil Aristoxenus wrote two treatises, one "Harmonics" and the other "Rhythmics." The former dealt with the mathematics of intervals and their arrangements into modes and scales; the latter similarly applied mathematics to the durations of the pitches of those arrangements, overlapping with the study of "metrics" (poetic meter). Significantly, much more of his writings on harmonic than those on rhythmic theory survived.)

Later on, in the Egyptian Claudius Ptolemy, Aristotle's theory of crystalline spheres within spheres upon which the stars, sun, moon, and planets revolved around the circular disc of the earth was refined into a complex theory of epicycles to try and explain various transgressions of the "true" circular motions ascribed to them by Plato. The only partial success of this attempt didn't bother him because, being a good Platonist, he ascribed those transgressions to other laws, divine/celestial ones which rational mortals could never divine (Ptolemy's *Harmonics* was a more successful application—to music theory—of his vast, labrynthian intellect). The Egypto-Roman Plotinus, in the Greek tradition as it continued after the advent of Christianity, is often considered an early Western mystic because of his teaching of "the One," the ineffable causal ultimate which emanates the lesser orders of *nous*, the World Soul (sort of a combination of the Greek *logos* and the Indian *prajna*, or life-energy; or the Chinese *wu li*, patterned organic energy) and, last and also least, pure matter. It was Plotinus who said "he blushed because he had a body."[27]

Jesus

If all the above represents the *mind* of the Muse's Western face, the figure of Jesus brings us to the *heart*. Western European music stems from Greco-Roman and Judeo-Christian learning and mythology, through the plainchant; African American music stems from the fervent expressions of the black church.

The New Testament accounts represent a crossroads of Greco-Roman and Jewish history with the world of ideas that can hardly be summed up in a paragraph or two. What might best be drawn from them into this survey is a picture of a bridge. From the pre-Christian to the post-Christian life of the collective Western psyche, the events revolving around the figure of Jesus served as food for that life's millennia-long global musings. A glance at the four broad cultural forces interacting at this point, and at Jesus' relationship to them, reflects Braxton's own cultural-historical stage and role in this music born of the Judeo-Christian West and Africa.

The mainstream of Jesus' culture was that of the Pharisees, who embodied the forces of reaction and conservatism. Traditionalists hostile to innovative change, obsessed with the letter and afraid of the spirit that created it, they came to personify oppression and hypocrisy. The dynamic between Jesus and the Pharisees makes for a sound metaphor of that between what Braxton calls "restructuralists"—musicultural innovators who develop the tradition, saving it from stagnation, usually in the face of resistance and ignorance—and the status quo. It's a dynamic he sees as universal, one he applies to aspects of figures as diverse (yet similar) as the medieval woman composer Hildegard of Bingen, the Connecticut Yankee Charles Ives, and Arnold Schönberg, as well as more jazz-specific figures such as Charlie Parker, Charles Mingus, John Coltrane, and Ornette Coleman.

The Sadducees were the Hellenized Jews determined to relativize their magical Hebrew tradition to merge it with the prevailing Greco-Roman world view. They image liberal secularists of every sort, those who are out of touch with their own spiritual roots through seeking to assimilate for the sake of consensus without real substance (such as musicians driven by the marketplace). The Zealots image all oppressed who would call for separatism, revolution,

the music's grandparents   **41**

justice, even vengeance. And the Essenes can stand for those who would beat the destructive dilemma of the world with a monastic retreat and isolated pursuit of otherworldly wisdom.

Jesus had elements of all four. He thoroughly honored the Pharasaic scriptural tradition, the Sadducee impulse to relativize and synthesize that tradition with others, the Zealot passion for justice, and the equal passion for holiness of the Essenes. But what he added to those was the authority of his own personality, and his sense of that—along with everything else—as the full expression of a *universal* personality. The resulting scandal and his mythological survival and transcendence of it offer us another key to yet another box: that containing the nature of Braxton's problems with the American music community and its larger sociocultural context—his music's associations with both the black militancy of the 1960s and with European classical influences—and of that world's problems with him, and of the solutions the problems themselves continue to generate. What greater scandal—and promise—than that figure who affirms your greatest potential while at the same time affirming that of your most threatening enemy?

The Birth of the Modern West: Augustine's Neoplatonism

Modern secular Western philosophy and science continued to grow through the Greco-Roman theology of the early-to-medieval Christian church and its parent Jewish tradition. A quick survey of that will bring us up to the European discovery of America, and the next chapter.

Through the Catholic church, the Greek *logos* principle took on the person of Jesus; the occult wisdom that had developed through and for ancient civilizations was claimed by and for the early church, in Rome's attempt to preserve its crumbling empire in sanctification.

Hans Küng[28] points out the initial Greek tendency to over-spiritualize Jesus, devaluing his (and by implication all) humanity, and the Roman impulse to explain his significance in terms of a contractual agreement between humanity and God. Ironically, the two impulses found their joint stability (in musical as well as philosophical terms) in the figure of an African—Augustine of Hippo.

In 313 A.D., with the Edict of Milan, the Roman Emperor Constantine officially sanctioned Christianity as the religion of the Empire. A century or so later, just after Alaric the Visigoth sacked Rome, Augustine—intellectual humanist, sensualist, worldly lover of Rome turned ascetic lover of God—reconfirmed Plato over and above Pythagoras and all other Greeks ("prostituted with the influence of obscene and filthy devils")[29] in his vision of a holy City of God.

The ancient Greeks who wrote about music, for all their intellectualism, were still closely rooted in actual music making.[30] By the time of Augustine, it was more purely an academic study, but not in the narrowly specialist sense of modern times; philosophers and scholars treated it as part of the core of arts and letters, something of general and universal relevance. Augustine's *De musica* comprised six books on "rhythmics," the first five written well before his conversion. McKinnon's words strike a loud chord in the context of Braxton's music and its role in his time and place (specifically, his unflagging efforts to convey the metamusical "forces in motion" of which his music is only the expression):

> There is a different mood about the sixth book . . . it is more deeply and fervently neo-Platonic, and even neo-Pythagorean with its numerical view of reality. In the first book, the basic theme of the superiority of the spiritual over the material—or at least of the intellectual over the practical—is already announced; thus the typical aulos player is no more a musician in the true sense than a nightingale because he too is ignorant of the science underlying the sounds he produces . . . This way of thinking is deepened and enriched in book 6 where Augustine describes a series of hierarchically ordered musical "numbers." At the lower end are sensible or corporeal numbers, that is, the musical sounds produced by the player and felt by the auditor. At the upper end are "judicial numbers" whereby the soul evaluates the equality and harmony of the lesser numbers. These judicial numbers in turn reflect a "numberliness" (*numerositas*) that pervades creation and which ultimately reflects the eternity and immutability of God.[31]

Koestler, on the other hand, calls "the destruction of the Pythagorean union of natural and religious philosophy, the denial of science as a way of worship, the splitting up of the very texture of the universe into a vile lowland and ethereal highlands, made of different materials, governed by different laws" a "dualism of despair," a "legacy of one bankrupt civilization: Greece at the age of the Macedonian conquest, to another bankrupt civilization: the Latin world at the age of its conquest by the Germanic tribes."[32] Augustine was horrified at the sight of his beloved civilization falling to the unlearned European barbarians. Whereas in retrospect his idealism may be seen as excessive and negatively portentous, at the time it may have been the visceral passion of survival. With the infusion of a new spiritual power into the best (most transcendent) of its wisdom and peace-preserving order, he may have seen hope of saving the thread of civilization and culture (dating back to Egypt) he loved as much before as after his conversion. The Empire did indeed rise as a City of God—the church—after falling as a state.

Augustine went on to write six more books—*de melo* (on harmonics)—comprising with the first six a total treatise. *De musica* was to be the first of a series of books on liberal arts, but his north African contemporary, Martianus Capella, proved to be his torchbearer for that. Capella's *De nuptiis Philologiae et Mercurii* is an allegory spanning nine books that depicts the marriage of Philology (learning) and Mercury (eloquence); seven of the books are treatises (spoken by the wedding's bridesmaids): *Grammatica, Rhetorica, Dialectica, Arithmetica, Musica, Geometrica,* and *Astronomia*. The first three would reemerge after the "Dark Ages" (from which plainchant was born after a long gestation) with the revival of classical learning as the *Trivium* of language arts, and the rest as the *Quadrivium* of mathematical arts.

The rise of the church marked the West's affair with what Arthur Lovejoy called the "otherworldly God." The "word" of the Platonic hierarchy between the ethereal highlands of *nous* and the vile lowlands of *phenomena* became the "flesh" of the Church Universal and Triumphant on earth. This hierarchical dualism of spirit and flesh, abstract and concrete, mind and body was never absolute or consistent, but it was the fundamental principle underlying that medieval world of celibate saints, profligate popes, flagellants, mystics, and marauders that gave birth to Western music.

(As mentioned above, I've made this reach back [some will see it as an overreach, no doubt] to lay the foundation Braxton himself sketched in his *Tri-Axium Writings*—one of musical mythos more than history. The history informs the mythos, of course, but ancient history—especially that of Egypt and its relevance to African America[33]—is too distant to be invoked as any kind of authority for an aesthetic. That same distance, however, magnifies its power as myth, and for an artist that power is often more compelling than that of history anyway. I've chosen here to make known my awareness of the critiques of both black and white intellectuals leveled against the afrocentric egyptologists, then to proceed to give the latter the benefit of the doubt throughout the book, in deference, first, to Braxton's Muse and, second, to my own. The appeal of afrocentric egyptology for me has always resonated with that old saw of my Western education: Egypt is the cradle of civilization. Further, the problem I have with African-American critics of afrocentrism is their parochial and (understandable, but globally untenable) bourgeois "Americentrism.")

It is curious—but also in keeping with his reputation for otherworldliness—that Braxton's musical philosophy (and music) syncs up more with the Medieval than the Renaissance-through-Romantic periods of Western civilization, picking it up again in the 20th century. Curious, because despite said reputation, Braxton's relationship to his music is nothing if not concrete; the god he meets there (as in the work of one of his favorite composers, Hildegard of Bingen) may indeed be otherworldly to many, but not to him. In fact, Braxton's kinship with Augustine's Neoplatonism is perhaps best understood as an African version of a Pythagorean embrace: immanence empowered by its very surrender to transcendence. With that, his understandably African view of the West makes sense of this kinship: the time he pinpoints as the beginning of the West's departure from its own proper place in the world, from its spiritual parameters, is concordant with its geographical expansion, the Age of Exploration and subsequent colonialism, the rise of the slave trade, and of the Enlightenment humanism that made man the measure of all things, and God his conceit.

As it happened, the Europeans transplanted to the Americas were more concurrent with the beginnings than with the farthest removes of that departure. For all its kinship with and wielding of the European force, white America was in large part a spore population from a pre-Enlightenment Renaissance peasantry with one foot still in the Middle Ages . . . and with the other, scarcely noticed, tapping time to the dances of a people with much more of themselves rooted in a much earlier age.

Africa in the West

> *Though quintessence of negritude from across the seas, Queequeg is also an Indian when he smokes his tomahawk peace pipe; and though Ishmael fares better with the cannibal biscuit than Queequeg does in the Presbyterian chapel (where people tend to sit by themselves), together they dream the dream of an ampler form of worship in which animal power and angelic aspiration may be gathered in a single party.*
>
> Dudley Young

The *New Grove Dictionary of Jazz* makes a point in its "Jazz" entry that is worth building on here:

> It has been said that jazz, in a half-century, recapitulated the history of four centuries of European music, moving from the *heterophonic polyphony* of the early New Orleans style, through the big-band *romanticism* of the 1930s, to the *chromaticism* of bop and the *free-form experiments* after 1960.[34] (emphases mine)

The analogy between the first New Orleans jazz bands and medieval European polyphony begs expansion in our millennial context. The musical connection suggested is the phenomenon of multiple melodic lines interweaving simultaneously over a *cantus firmus*. We can follow that connection back even further, to establish the deepest kinship between African and European cultural legacies.

Moving back by parallel steps from turn-of-the-century New Orleans and from medieval Europe, we can say that the apocryphal first *single* line sung over a blues bass figure mirrored early European ornamentations on a monophonic liturgical chant. Both expressions are of a beginning mastery over the seed material—blues and plainsong—bearing the respective musical traditions to come. Improvisation is beginning to happen as form has been mastered, context established.

We can say, too, that the first transformations of a European American hymn, or folk ballad, into an African American spiritual, or blues, mirror the first plainchants, in that each is an expression couched in media imposed from without. The Africanization of Christianity—in music, by the development of gospel—is not unlike the European Christianization of the Greco-Roman civilization—in music, by the use of Greek modes to construct the sacred chants—that was in decline throughout the early medieval period (and about to be reborn, in the Renaissance). Both gospel and plainchant were the incredibly vulnerable breakthroughs of a new soul's voice speaking through media transmitted by a hostile or dying culture from which the new soul had to distinguish and protect itself.

Going back further, we can see the enslaved field hand's first attempts to preserve (and preserve himself on) his native West African rhythms in the chop

the music's grandparents

of the hoe, and in his improvised syncopating cries above it, as a reflection of Pythagoras' discovery and systematization of the overtone series. If this begins to seem forced, consider: for the West, Pythagoras served up the first major paradigm shift from the ancient to the modern secular rationalistic world view; his contributions stand right on the border between music as esoteric magic and music as scientifically perceived and mathematically conceived art.

For the African, the paradigm shift was as momentous, if more violent. He had to learn to restate the complex magical data that had been transmitted and memorized in media he no longer had—in the drum, by a culture no longer there for him—in his new situation of forced labor, on the decidedly unmagical terms of the culture that had misperceived and destroyed his. He had to conceive as a fiercely thinking individual what had formerly been transmitted and received in a nonrational and collective mode, in order to recreate it in his new situation.

Finally, we get back all the way to the newly arrived African slave moaning her first laments in her native language on a strange soil and the Hebrew psalmist in captivity crying out to God, "How shall we sing the lord's song in a strange land?"[35] The music at this point is still in embryo, the cry before the song, conceived in trauma to develop in the fire.

African America and (Judeo-Christian) European America thus meet as two cultures with similar mythologies and histories of slavery, oppression, exodus, diaspora, lost kingdoms and glories, falls from grace, wandering, vulnerability, strength forged in weakness, crucifixion, resurrection, and love and faith through it all. This kinship is the crucial root to tap in coming to see Braxton's as the American music it is for Americans from every background. It is a kinship African Americans have been forced to appeal to for sheer survival; but it is also one that white America has felt the need to enjoy, however much it has also needed to deny and resist it. This black-white love-hate dynamic is another key to yet another box, in which Braxton's international following and relative lack of it in the American cultural arena have both been locked. A quick selective look at European, African, and American musicultural history will bring us into that arena and Braxton's work there.

The rhythmic sophistication of pre-American African music[36] was comparable to the harmonic and melodic sophistication of medieval Europe, and both cultures seem to have improvised/composed in much the same way: by varying slightly and methodically many well-known patterns, a sort of orderly creative process anchored by the pleroma of traditional material. In European music, moreover, improvisation is documented as early as the fourth century, in a reference Augustine made to the *jubilus*. This was a melodic outburst widely thought to be triggered by the last syllable of certain alleluias in the spoken liturgy: " . . . the expression of a mind poured forth in joy."[37] To put it in Greco-Roman terms of the time that are still usable currency, thanks to the Jungians,[38] such improvisations were instances of *Dionysian* music: spontaneous improvised expressions of ecstasy, or of *any* madness, whether divine or infernal—very like possession by a *loa*, or spirit, in Haitian and New Orleans *vodou*. They contrasted with the calmer, more predetermined and orderly *Apollonian* music of the composition that inspired the improvisation, as the various ceremonial structures in *vodou* determine which of many *loas* is to be invoked, and as the European American song forms would come to inform the nature of African American jazz improvisations.

When polyphony started in the West, improvisation went on to become as Apollonian—as methodical and codified—as composition had always been. Medieval texts instructed singers how to improvise a melody to fit with a given chant. The skill flourished in the Baroque era, with the *basso continuo* and *basso ostinato* systems of improvisational bases, and the latitude given performers who knew how to improvise on them within the more fixed forms. By classical times, improvised sections were segregated from fixed in *cadenzas*, until even these eventually came to be written out. It is interesting to note that it was around the time of the last great improvisers, Beethoven and Liszt, that music programs began to be offered as commercial ventures by entrepreneurs to paying audiences, and that performers and composers began to develop their respective specialized "star" personae.[39] Perhaps the economic incentives toward control, spectacle, and predictability played the main part in this move away from spontaneity.

In any case, as improvisation waned, it was Dionysus, not Apollo, who suffered. Jazz addressed that problem for many Westerners, especially in its early years—but it has always been a healthy balance of intellectual as well as emotional prowess and exercise for those who played it.

European secular and liturgical music had evolved to a point by the Renaissance that was arguably its closest historical convergence with the African tradition, through the Arab-Moorish connection, as evidenced by certain musical elements: the creation of pulse for dancing; the creation of polyrhythmic layers by numerous simultaneous variations on a melodic (rhythmic, in Africa) line; the creation of harmonic textures by the same process; a shifting tonal center defined by independent modes, or scales, similar in North Africa and Europe; and a functionalism that tied the aesthetics of music to the whole range of human activity from work to wooing to worship. This connection has survived and thrived in much of the rural strain of American music, much of which has inherited vestiges of the "pagan" Europe Michael Ventura mentions (below).

Tonal improvisation over steady rhythm are the main musical elements that distinguish jazz from the European music of the last few centuries—yet, in fact, it was initially the rhythm that was improvised. The West African rhythms that gave jazz its initial heartbeat were not primarily improvised in their native culture.[40] They were part of a vast inherited musical tradition passed down and circulated by ear and memory, much like the classical Indian musical tradition's stock of melodic and rhythmic patterns.[41]

The West African civilizations current with the time of the slave trade were as sophisticated as African American music would fast become. Ventura writes:

> As late as the mid-nineteenth century the Yoruba city of Abeokuta ran six miles along the bank of the Ogun River and had a population estimated at 200,000. Its craft industries thrived—ironwork, carpentry, tailoring, farming, tool-making, textiles. And this [at once tribal and urban] culture had been thriving for centuries, a city probably older than, say, New York is now.[42]

Ventura describes the sophistication of their culture's metaphysical underpinnings, the profundity and complexity of which was actually created and conveyed—"expressed" is too weak a word—by the drums. The metaphysics were similar to those of India, China, Native America, and pre-Christian Europe. They envoiced the pagan religions, the conviction, writes Ventura, that "religious worship is *bodily* celebration, a dance of the entire community; or, as it would have been called in Europe when such belief had been driven underground, a 'sabbat.' The mind-body split that governs European thought seems never to have entered African religion, African consciousness—at least not until imported there by missionaries."

When the Africans in North American slavery lost their culture and its voice in the drums, they essentially started its music from scratch, as much as possible. They improvised patterns against a basic beat in any way they could (with a hoe, or a shout) that had the *feel* of those remembered, to invoke— without drums, or common language, or freedom—their now much-needed spirits.

As their exposure to and mastery over the European musical materials grew, the Africans continued to infuse those materials with that improvised rhythmic base. Improvisation became the primary rather than secondary process, and it was a process that had the corner on the rhythm market. By that time, except in the country and folk traditions, improvisation and counterrhythms had almost entirely disappeared from European American concert and popular music.

In the *vodou* culture of Haiti (and, to a more limited degree, New Orleans), the West African drums were never lost. *Vodou* is the transplanted West African metaphysic that triggered and celebrated the interaction of (as opposed to the European distinction between) the spiritual and material realms. The different rhythms played on the drums corresponded to different "gods," or *loa*, and the goal of playing them was to open the worshipers to possession by the *loa*. We should perhaps bring up to date the synopsis of European thought, to get a sense of the development of the spirit-flesh split that was behind the white fear and loathing of—and raving lust for—such possession.

Arthur Lovejoy's classic book *The Great Chain of Being*[43] traces the Platonic conception of a hierarchical continuum between the material universe and its spiritual source as it developed through two millennia of Western thought. Early Christian theologians and mystics lived with the concept comfortably enough, but medieval scholars started fretting over its intrinsic dilemma: how could there be an unbroken continuum between Very God, ineffable infinite, and gross matter? Yet if the Great Chain was broken, how could it be perfect? Why did, how could, an essentially self-sufficient Creator need to burden Himself with something as essentially flawed as matter?[44]

By medieval times, writes Lovejoy, the strain between the Neoplatonic notion of the Creator as Pure Idea infinitely detached from the *phenomena* He creates—the "otherworldly God"—and that of a self-transcending, generative Absolute Good from which everything emanates—the "thisworldly God"—was too great to tolerate. The otherworldly (Neoplatonic) prevailed, but had the thisworldly one caught on, we might have seen, with the beginning of the Christian church, a reinstatement of the creative artist/philosopher/natural scientist to the old Pythagorean status as a wise and holy man. Instead, we got the monastic ideal of celibacy, asceticism, and contemplation, a monotheism much like the Eastern monism that also scorned the material realm, though more as illusion than as evil.

But the thisworldly strain didn't die out completely. Thomas Aquinas, in reinstating Aristotle (thus a respect for nature), helped usher in the humanism of the Renaissance. Descartes, says Küng, was an admirer of the naturalists Aristotle and Galileo, though his famous "I think, therefore I am" would seem to place him in the Platonic tradition, with its emphasis on mentation. Shift the emphasis to being ("I am"), however, and you get "I am, therefore God is, since I, finite, conceive (think) Him, infinite. Therefore the material world is, and is what it seems, and can be divined."

Descartes' *a priori* assumptions and faith in reason would be challenged over time by Immanuel Kant, Henri Poincarré, Kurt Gödel, and Karl Popper, but "with him begins priority of . . . consciousness over being, of personal freedom over cosmic order, of questioning in *immanent rather than transcendent terms*"[45] (emphasis mine). Blaise Pascal was a Platonic swing of the pendulum back from Descartes' updated Aristotelianism: feeling, intuition, faith are as important as reason.

We begin to notice a Western dynamic: Plato/Aristotle, Augustine/Aquinas, Pascal/Descartes—the Janus-like double Western face of faith and sight. But one's sight always focused most clearly in proportion to one's faith in one's eyes, and one's faith always soared in direct proportion to one's sense of a clear perception of its object. Lovejoy continues to trace the seesawing of the two impulses through thinkers such as Leibniz, Berkeley, Robinet, Voltaire, Rousseau, Samuel Johnson, and Hegel. He spends most of his book on the debate between two 17th-century Germans, F.W.J. Schelling and F.H. Jacobi, in whom he sees its resolution. The conflict between the otherworldly and the thisworldly God had to be resolved, as it was in the beginning of the church, in Neoplatonism. But this time it was the otherworldly that went under.

Schelling, says Lovejoy, won the debate. Unfortunately, European thought—through Hegel and his 18th- and 19th-century heirs espousing the scientific age's progressive perfectibility (Comte, Strauss, Feuerbach, Schleiermacher, Marx) and their 20th-century heirs (Freud, Skinner, the existentialists, the God-is-Dead theologians)—went as excessively far into thisworldliness as they previously had into otherworldliness. Schopenhauer was the first philosopher to turn this around, with his look to Eastern thought, and others have followed that path (a path leading directly, in music, to John Cage, one of Braxton's main influences).

When Europeans first clashed with Native Americans, the otherworldly God was still in full force in Europe, and remained so in the first European American societies (see next chapter). Throughout the time of the slave trade and the displacement and genocide of Native Americans the pendulum was swinging to a thisworldly God with whom the spirit of social Darwinism was compatible. By the time of the full 20th-century flower of that spirit—in the two world wars, the Holocaust, Hiroshima and Nagasaki, the cold war—the gravity, if you will, of the situation pulled the pendulum back again. It is now swinging through the end of colonialism, a promising struggle against racist and sexist oppression, peace between the superpowers, peace (albeit uneasy) in the Middle East, and a global reclamation of traditional cultural roots (albeit nasty in the Balkans).

Concurrent with this 20th-century pull on the pendulum is the end of tonality in Western European music; the rise of improvisation through jazz to a global art music; and, starting with Charles Ives, the flowering of a non-

the music's grandparents

Eurocentric European American experimental tradition of concert music. Those are the forces in motion, and those are some of their musical expressions. It is on that global-historical stage set that we approach the Millennium, a time charged with mythological associations with both apocalypse and paradise.

But before we get there we need to focus here more closely on the place where the actors on this stage came together and merged their various lines, in the Americas.

---

1. Anthony Braxton, telephone interview (February 25, 1993).

2. Francis Davis, *Outcats: Jazz Composers, Instrumentalists, and Singers* (New York: Oxford University Press, 1990).

3. William Cole, *John Coltrane* (New York: Schirmer, 1976: 32).

4. Lock, Graham. *Forces in Motion: The Music and Thoughts of Anthony Braxton* (New York: Da Capo Press, 1988: 101).

5. An exception to this occurred briefly in the early 1970s when he, along with Chick Corea, investigated Scientology. Elitist attitudes encountered there quickly turned him off to it.

6. Anthony Braxton, *Tri-Axium Writings 1, 2, & 3* (Oakland, CA: Frog Peak Music, 1985, available through Braxton; see back page).

7. Dudley Young, *Origins of the Sacred: The Ecstasies of Love and War* (New York: St. Martin's Press, 1991: 97–98). For even more pointed reading along these lines, see Robert Jay Russell's *The Lemur's Legacy: The Evolution of Power, Sex, and Love* (New York: Jeremy P. Tarcher/Putnam, 1993). Russell's discussion of language and human gender dynamics parallels the way they figure in Braxton's music. Finally, for an excellent complement to this book's approach to pan-species, pan-temporal, pan-personal—essentialist, if I may use that term non-pejoratively—aspects of Braxton's music, see John Bleibtreu's *The Parable of the Beast* (Toronto: Macmillan/Collier, 1968), especially his rigorous discussion of "The Molecular Memory" (85–116).

8. See Saal, above, and Lock, 111, for a typical example. Lock also excerpts Braxton's own notes to *99G* ("you must become the dog") on *Solo (London) 1988*.

9. Peter Rothbart, "Play or Die," (*Down Beat*, February, 1982: 20–23).

10. Abraham Maslow, *Toward a Psychology of Being* (Princeton: New Jersey: Van Nostrand, 1962).

11. Terrence McKenna, *The Archaic Revival* (San Francisco: Harper, 1991).

12. Amit Goswami, with Richard Reed and Maggie Goswami, *The Self-Aware Universe: How Consciousness Creates the Material World* (New York: G.P. Putnam's Sons, 1993).

13. McKenna, 207. Re: the connection between music and language, Ben Sidran's superb *Black Talk* (New York: Da Capo Press, 1981) discusses African American musiculture (including its use of language) as part of that ancient shamanic-oral tradition, and has inspired much of the thrust of this book.

14. See Mezz Mezzrow and Bernard Wolfe, *Really the Blues* (New York: Random House, 1946), Sidran and others on jazz *patois*. While Braxton's use of language is certainly not the stereotypical "jive," I would submit that it is in the tradition of such verbal invention. Once understood so, even the most difficult and obscure of his writings come to the life of an ancient and still-living oral tradition moving into literate media to reassert itself as the root of such media.

15. J. D. Lewis-Williams and T. A. Dawson, "The Signs of All Times: Entoptic Phenomena in Upper Paleolithic Art" (*Current Anthropology*, Vol. 29, no. 2, Apr. 1988: 201–17). See also the videotape *Images of Another World* (BBC/Arts &

Entertainment) for an engaging look at the phenomenon of entoptic images and their universal role in the evolution of disparate visual art and symbol systems. See Lock, *Forces in Motion*, 1988: 10 for one of Braxton's longtime friends' and collaborators' (Leo Smith) comments on the composer's connection to this primeval symbol generation.

16. James Gleick, *Chaos: Making a New Science* (New York: Viking, 1987).

17. See the works of Georges Dumézil, J. P. Mallory, Ram Chandra Jain, and Robert Drews for information and theories about the Indo European invasions dating from around 5000 B.C. Also, some of this and following information about ancient Goddess-worshiping cultures in Barbara Walker's (headings) "Agni," "Lightning," "Mountain," and "Caste" (*The Woman's Encyclopedia of Myths and Secrets*, San Francisco: Harper & Row, 1983).

18. W. Kirk MacNulty, *Freemasonry: A Journey through Ritual and Symbol* (London/New York: Thames & Hudson, 1991); Albert Churchward, *Signs and Symbols of Primordial Man: The Evolution of Religious Doctrine from the Eschatology of the Ancient Egyptians* (London/New York: E.P. Dutton & Co., 1910); and National Public Radio music critic Tom Manoff's research for a book in progress on ancient roots of current myths and symbols, delivered in lecture at the University of Oregon, August 16, 1993.

19. Manoff lecture, above.

20. Biologist Rupert Sheldrake suggests a sort of collective sub/superconscious informing such global synchronicities in his *The Presence of the Past: Morphic Resonance and the Habits of Nature* (New York: Times Books, 1988). Musically, common ground can be found between these isolated cultures in (roughly) the pentatonic scale, and the (mostly minor) modes and preponderance of the octave, fifth and fourth derived therefrom.

21. Walker ("Motherhood"), for this and next two citations. See also Robert Graves, *The White Goddess: A Historical Grammar of Poetic Myth* (London: Faber & Faber, 1952).

22. Arthur Koestler, *The Slepwalkers: A History of Man's Changing View of the Universe* (New York: Grosset & Dunlap, 1963).

23. Ibid., 34.

24. Ibid., 28.

25. Ibid., 37.

26. Quoted in Koestler, 52.

27. Quoted in Koestler, 86.

28. Hans Küng, *On Being a Christian* (New York: Doubleday, 1976).

29. Ibid., 88.

30. See Barker ("Archaic Greece") and McKinnon ("Christian Antiquity") in James McKinnon, *Antiquity and the Middle Ages From Ancient Greece to the 15th Century* (Englewood Cliffs, NJ: Prentice Hall, 1991).

31. McKinnon, 82–3.

32. Koestler, 85.

33. See Tom Carson's "Greece is the Word: Afrocentrism and Its Discontents" (*Village Voice*, April 16,1996: 20-21) for a glimpse at the criticisms of the scholarship pioneered by Diop, Ben-Jochannon, and Bernal. Crouch (*The All-American Skin Game*, New York: Pantheon Books) is an example of one of several African-American such critics.

34. *New Grove/Jazz*, "Jazz," 580.

35. Psalm 137.

36. See Samuel Charters, *The Roots of the Blues: An African Search* (Boston/London: Marion Boyars, 1981) for a sense of how this might have been.

E.g., from p. 16, about a *jali* (storysinger): "The accompaniment he played on the kora was a repetitive, highly rhythmic figure that was light in texture and contrasted brilliantly with the dark tone of his voice. The structure of the song seemed to be built more on extended melodic phrases than it did on recurring verse patterns and I could hear sudden changes of mood in the tone and timbre of the voice. It was a technically exciting, and at the same time complex and demanding musical style.

"At first I was surprised at how little the music sounded like the blues. The busy, running accompaniment figure in the kora had no definite points of stress accent. I couldn't tap my foot to the rhythm the way I could with a blues. There were no harmonies, none of the melodic figures that set the blues apart. I couldn't follow the verses; since he was singing in Mandingo, I couldn't even follow the words. But at the same time so much of the mood and style had overtones of something I had heard before. I had the uncanny feeling that I was hearing one of the early blues men, only now he was singing a different style of song. The vocal timbres, the shaping of the melody, the rhythmic openness of the singing all seemed to be directly related to the blues."

37. *New Grove/Music & Musicians*, "Improvisation" (Vol. 9, pp. 31-52). McKinnon points out that this connection of the *jubilus* with the *alleluia* is speculation, and that it is more "explicitly defined as a type of work song, sung 'either in the harvest, in the vineyard, or in some other arduous occupation,' not a liturgical chant of any sort" (78-79)—an interesting resonance with the early African-American work song.

38. See Robert Moore and Douglas Gillette, *King, Warrior, Magician, Lover: Rediscovering the Archetypes of the Mature Masculine* (San Francisco: Harper, 1990); and Jean Shinoda Bolen, *Goddesses in Everywoman: A New Psychology of Women* (San Francisco: Harper & Row, 1984).

39. See Jacques Chailley, *40,000 Years of Music: Man in Search of Music* (New York: Farrar, Straus & Giroux, 1964: 29). Also the video series *The Music of Man*, hosted by Yehudi Menuhin (Chicago: Public Media, 1987) on the first Venetian opera houses.

40. In fact, they weren't even "syncopated," a term that implies a dichotomy between a "regular" and an "irregular" rhythm; see Burton W. Peretti, *The Creation of Jazz: Music, Race, and Culture in Urban America* (Urbana and Chicago: University of Illinois Press, 1992: 12).

41. See Charters, and *New Grove/Music & Musicians* ("African Music"), Vol. 1, pp. 144-52.

42. Michael Ventura, "Hear That Long Snake Moan" (*Whole Earth Review* no. 54, Spring 1987: 28), for this and next citation.

43. Arthur Lovejoy, *The Great Chain of Being: A Study of the History of an Idea* (New York: Harper & Row, 1960: 97-98). Key to the thrust of my study: "through the Middle Ages there were at least kept alive, in an age of which the official doctrine was predominantly otherworldly, certain roots of an essentially 'this-worldly' philosophy: the assumption that there is a true and intrinsic multiplicity in the divine nature, that is to say, in the world of Ideas; that, further, 'existence is a good,' i.e., that the addition of a concrete actuality to universals, the translation of supersensible possibilities into sensible realities, means an increase, not a loss, of value; that, indeed, the very essence of good consists in the maximum actualization of variety; and that the world of temporal and sensible experience is thus good, and the supreme manifestation of the divine."

44. Küng, 420-23.

45. Lovejoy, 158.

Chapter Two

The Music's Parents

We have also sound-houses, where we practise and demonstrate all sounds, and their generation. We have harmonies which you have not, of quarter-sounds, and lesser slides of sounds. Divers instruments of music likewise to you unknown, some sweeter than any you have, together with bells and rings that are dainty and sweet. We represent small sounds as great and deep; likewise great sounds extenuate and sharp; we make diverse tremblings and warblings of sounds, which in their original are entire. We represent and imitate all articulate sounds and letters, and the voices and notes of beasts and birds. We have certain helps which set to the ear do further the hearing greatly. We have also divers strange and artificial echoes, reflecting the voice many times, and as it were tossing it: and some that give back the voice louder than it came, some shriller, and some deeper; yea, some rendering the voice differing in the letters or articulate sound from that they receive. We have also means to convey sounds in trunks and pipes, in strange lines and distances.

Francis Bacon (1624)

Chess, which exists predominantly in two dimensions, is one of the world's most difficult games. Three-dimensional chess is an invitation to insanity. But human relationships, even of the simplest order, are like a kind of four-dimensional chess, a game whose pieces and positions change subtly and inexorably between *moves, whose players stare dumbly while their powerful positions deteriorate into hopeless predicaments and while improbable combinations suddenly become inevitable. To make matters worse, some games*

the music's parents

are open to any number of players, and all sides are expected to win.

Robert Grudin

From occult definition of **chess***: 1. the entertainment, where the two sexes could meet on equal terms: playing chess was even recommended by the laws of courtly love . . .*

Both African and European streams of American music can be seen as having developed along three demographic lines: the rural, the urban, and the cultural elite. Both the streams and the lines, of course, interpenetrate and cohere, but they are also broad and distinct enough to use as frameworks for the macro-sweep desired here.

Imagine (in deference to Braxton the chess buff) American music's history taking place on a chess board. Imagine the black and white pieces and squares as the disparate cultures and individuals interacting to make the music. Call the board the spacetime window of the Americas from the first arrival of Europeans. Since so much in this music is happening at any given time from so many directions, we'll trace the moves of a given piece back and forth in time, rather than try to keep track of all simultaneously. And since Braxton realizes his music as a microcosm of that particular chess game, we'll see what aspects of his music, if any, its various moves evoke.

Latin Music: The Rook

The rook—the castle-like piece that moves straight across the chess board—might best image the Latin influence in the jazz tradition. It was one of the first, straight from (more) medieval (than Renaissance, in spirit) Spain through the Arab slave-holding castles of Ghana to the present time and place, yet in North America it has always been a flavor that's sneaked in from the side, as a rook in chess castles with a king.

Latin American rhythms are rooted in the mix of 16th-century Spanish, Portuguese, and North African Moorish cultures of the first European invaders; in the West African tribal rituals of their few slaves; and in indigenous American tribal musics. Despite the cruelty of the *conquistadors*, the Catholic culture that came to dominate the Caribbean and Central and South America has had from the first a somewhat healthier relationship with the native and African cultures around it. It played out the ancient pattern of Aryan conquest followed by assimilation, in the widespread intermarriage of both people and their gods (i.e., the adaptation of Catholicism and African and native mythologies with each other). This in contrast to the arguably more psychotic edge of the later, whiter Protestant North American brands (heirs to the legacies of Luther and Calvin) of racism. Perhaps the African Moorish conquest and occupation of Spain and Portugal in their then-recent history gave these *conquistadors* the human and cultural contact necessary to temper the racism. Whatever the reason, the Latin American model, however flawed, suggests to its northern cousins something of the potential and payoffs of synthesis in this racial-cultural mix.

Musically, the synthesis has expressed itself in a certain tidiness and control absent in North American jazz. Afro-Hispanic rhythms, while complex and exciting, are also more measured and measurable, less ambiguous than their African American counterparts in jazz. On the European side, Latin music has been shorter on harmonic, melodic, and extended improvisational complexities than those in jazz.

Latin rhythms always had a strong presence in New Orleans, with its early history of Spanish governance. They've figured prominently since then throughout the music, from the big bands of Don Azpiazu and Xavier Cugat to the Afro-Cuban beboppers to the more recent Afro-Cuban, Argentinean, and Brazilian voices.

On the surface, Braxton's music seems to have borrowed little from this part of the tradition. Throughout all of this consciously synthesizing composer's 300-plus works, only a handful are direct allusions to either Latin or Native American music. A few more allude to Asian traditions;[1] most are described as "trans-African" or "trans-European" expressions. However, a major aspect of Braxton's musical synthesis—his "pulse tracks"—mirrors something about the Latin model.

Braxton has developed what he calls "pulse tracks" from his own rhythmic creativity. These are essentially transcriptions of rhythmic patterns he generates by composing or improvising a sequence of syncopated accents against a basic pulse, to then serve as the foundation on which to build melodic, harmonic, timbral, and contrapuntal musical expressions. Like the Afro-Cuban *clavé*—the (typically) two-measure "building block" pattern (see Fig. 2.1b)—they fix in Western notation African patterns that originated as extensions or improvisations on the pulse. In Latin music these patterns have functioned as entry points into more sophisticated polyrhythmic improvisation; in their notated form they provide a common ground between African rhythmic and the European elements of harmony and melody, themselves framed in simpler and more symmetrical meters than their original oral-traditional versions.[2] (A similar compromise in North American jazz is the jazz pedagogy that has codified the subtle syncopations and "swings" we've come to associate with 4/4, 3/4, 12/8 and 6/8 in *those* Western metric terms).

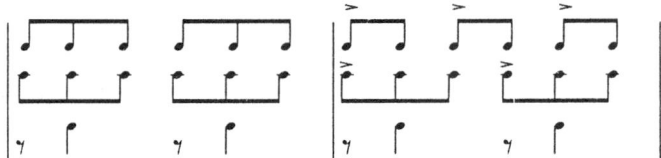

Fig. 2.1a: Typical rhythm from the Jalisco region of Mexico[3]

the music's parents 55

Fig. 2.1b: *Habanera* rhythm from Cuba[4]

Fig. 2.1c: From Braxton's *23G* (alto sax)

Fig. 2.1d: From Braxton's *23G* (bass)

Fig. 2.1a is a basic and typical Afro-Hispanic polyrhythm (made famous in Leonard Bernstein's West Side Story*). The addition of accents in the second bar and the staggering of the bottom line an eighth-beat ahead of the top two present the non-Western pulses as asymmetrical impositions over a symmetrical Western meter.*

Fig. 2.1b shows the Afro-Cuban habanera *rhythm, a force in jazz since the music's beginning. As notated here, the representation combines even and odd accents in one voice, again set within the symmetry of the 2/4 field.*

Fig. 2.1c shows the accented notes in bars 12–15 of the alto sax part to Braxton's 23G,[5] indicates to the drummer and bassist where to play his "sound attacks," thus foregoing the timekeeping functions that would commonly go with such regular (post-bop) eighth-note lines as well as *"free" departures from them that make for a feel of no pulse. Fig. 2.1d shows such accents in sync with the bass line.*

The brief cycle of simple syncopations over an even pulse, or the clavé *(e.g. 2.1b), is repeated as a support for dancing and for the harmonic-melodic elements. The sound attacks in 23G are also simple syncopations on an even pulse that are cycled repeatedly, here as a basis for improvisation. Their cycle, however, runs the first 18.5 of the piece's 59 bars. Braxton staggered those two lengths so as to create both asymmetry and isorhythmic regularity within the piece. As these "pulse tracks" developed into complete pieces in their own right—as opposed to one of several aspects of a complete piece—Braxton began layering several together, for the sort of polyrhythmic texturing common to both non-Western music and Western music in the 20th and before the 16th centuries.*

This device of Braxton's put in literate terms the theretofore (and still) mostly oral tradition in improvisation of creatively dividing and accenting the conventionally notated meter. He usually leaves the articulation of that regular pulse behind entirely, in favor of those accents, a move that has distinguished the heart of his music and provoked charges of his inability to swing, and his artificial and clinical approach to the "natural" phenomenon of swing.

In fact, outsiders to the African cultures cannot truly be possessed *by* the rhythm and its *loa* (to jump from Cuba to Haiti) until they learn *to* possess— i.e., generate—it. Braxton developed his pulse tracks well after the rhythmic nuances of swing and of bop and post-bop artists such as Charlie Parker, Thelonious Monk, Miles Davis, and John Coltrane and even Ornette Coleman were assimilated by the musiculture. The pulse tracks were conceived as "next steps" into the rhythmic field defined by the common musical discourse of such artists. As we'll see in Chapter Eight, they were combined to form the same sort of multilayered rhythmic "floor" as the polyrhythmic juxtapositions shown in Fig. 2.1a, common to African-based music throughout the Americas.

The Bishops: Black Church, White Church

The Age of Exploration and the rise of nationalism were Renaissance phenomena, but it was the Reformation that made the New World the arena for the religious struggles of an emergent Protestantism against its own parent Roman Catholicism, as well as those of its own seemingly inevitable factionalism (if Luther could say I AM in defiance of the Catholic ("universal") Church, why not everyone else in defiance of him, each other, or, ultimately, even themselves? Braxton alludes to this throughout *Tri-Axium* with his words on the rise of individualism at the expense of responsibility to the collective). African Americans were pulled into these struggles, which also forged the Western metamusical context—the black church—for their own emerging musiculture.

Again, perhaps a reminder of the immediate currency of historical context is in order before we continue. Braxton told Lock—whose book continually tried to crack the artist's metaphysical underpinnings, with little success—

> I believe very much in God; and in the last ten years, which have brought me and my family to our knees because of the intensity of our struggle and the poverty that we've been dealing with, this has only increased my convictions about the oneness of . . . wonder, and how fortunate it is to exist. And when I say I believe in God, by that I'm only saying that I believe in God.[6]

Lock's frustration at such generality was due not so much to a willful reserve on Braxton's part as to the difficulty one who is actively engaged in something has in being detached and analytical about that engagement in any fixed sense. It might be more fruitful to examine the milieu itself in which Braxton clearly meets his Maker. It is the same milieu, of the music, that produced Duke Ellington, who said of his later concerts of sacred music that in them he was finally expressing what had been in his heart about the music all his life; Thelonious Monk, whom Miles Davis summed up as from the "sanctified" church tradition; Charles Mingus, whose *Wednesday Night Prayer Meeting* explicated the revivalist energy permeating all of his music; Rashaan Roland Kirk's version of *The Old Rugged Cross*, and fascination with glossolalia (speaking in tongues); and John Coltrane's entire body of explicitly devotional music, both fervent and serene.[7] (With all of them, we might associate the New Testament writings about the beginning of a "Spirit-filled" church; when we add Braxton to their company, we must bring in the Book of Revelations.) What is the nature of the shared mythology (and its music) surrounding belief in God in black and white America *circa* 1994, with the new Millennium just around the corner? What are its roots and most current fruits?

The thread of the Western thought examined in the last chapter continued in the first American religion-based social experiments and took a turn early on that would distinguish America from Europe. The Congregationalists were led by the Mather family and Jonathan Edwards, a philosopher-theologian with a strong neoplatonic base. Their communities were theocracies, and for some time it seemed as though they might be the model for American government. Arrests, exiles, public whippings and hangings of "witches" in Salem and dissenters, papists, and other "heretics" were common in late 1600s Boston. To their credit—or perhaps inevitably, in the face of the overwhelming pluralism that followed—the Congregationalists changed their direction toward liberalism and tolerance.

But these are the people who founded the great universities and, later, industries: the American cultural elite, whose role in American music has come to be, over time, that of patron-philanthropists and scholars. The more grassroots religious traditions were the ones that most gave rise and shape to that music, and they sprang from another reform movement within the Anglican Church: Methodism, the movement that suited best the rough-and-ready Westward expansion, as well as the contact with the magical ecstasies of African and Native American spirits.

It was the Methodists, through the First and Second Great Awakenings of American religion in the first half of the 19th century, who led directly to the white American churches that fostered spiritual experiences of ecstasy and the paranormal such as speaking in tongues, prophesying, and the clairvoyance and telepathy claimed by Pentecostal and Charismatic groups. This distinctly American brand of Christianity was opposed to mere intellectual submission and life devotion to a doctrine of faith (or, alternately, the scientific "sight" of materialism). It was this same European American tradition that would give form to the early black church, to which African Americans brought their own Ring Shout call-and-response and other traditions. (Poetically just, it was the Wesley brothers John and Charles, namesakes of the academic home base of both John Cage and Braxton—Wesleyan University—who started Methodism.) The name alludes to the new *methods* the passionate youth brought to their religious practice: observation of the Lord's Supper every Sunday, a fast every Wednesday, and a constant review of their personal lives in the light of Scripture.

The Wesleys founded a Methodist society of 30 to 40 members in Georgia in 1736. Working themselves mostly in England, Scotland, and Ireland, John was the movement's central organizing force and Charles its Orpheus (he wrote 6,500 hymns!). Their American connection was George Whitfield. His solution to the early American hodgepodge of European sects was what academics might call a *structuralist* approach—an ecumenical, highly emotional, intellectually simple *revival* of the broad *universals* all the *denominations* shared (emphases denote the first widespread usage of now-standard words; the singularly American spin on "universals" pertains particularly to Braxton's musical vision, as does the very practice of recruiting old words for new, homespun concepts. Braxton might call the Wesleys *restructuralists*).

The Second Great Awakening, begun in the early 1800s, furthered this impulse with social as well as theological activism, an important part of which was abolitionism. Lyman Beecher was a seminal initiator of what was called voluntarism: the formation of "societies," "associations," and "unions" of concerned individuals against social ills (the American social template underpinning the structure of the Association for the Advancement of Creative Musicians). Another prime mover, Charles Grandison Finney, made Oberlin College (over which he presided) a major stop on the underground railroad that carried escaped slaves to points north.

Among blacks, this period saw the beginnings of their American church tradition. Dr. Thomas Coke, an English colleague of John Wesley, officiated at the birth of the Methodist Episcopal Church, in Baltimore in 1784. When he went back to England, the American Francis Asbury took over, eventually putting the circuit preacher into American folklore. In 1816, ex-slave Richard Allen started the first denomination exclusively for blacks, the African Methodist Episcopal Church.

The circuit preachers in both black and white communities instigated what were essentially *ad hoc* churches built on emotional and highly charged "revivals," not unlike Haitian *vodou* ceremonies in their religious fervor. A "second blessing," not unlike visitations and possessions by *loa*, rewarded the truly holy, those who made it a point not just to know about but to know God. These revivals, or camp meetings, became the primary social as well as religious functions of the 19th-century frontier expansion. Baptists did particularly well in this frontier settlement of soul turf. (To touch base with the music for a moment, this history is the direct forbear of the kinds of experiences rock- and jazz-oriented players started seeking and finding, eschewing urban secularism, through their music in the 1960s. Recorded examples include many from

Coltrane and Ayler, Pharoah Sanders, Rashaan Roland Kirk, Mingus, and Coleman. The Pentecostalist/Millennialist/Fundamentalist strains of American frontier Christianity generally resonated most closely with the more rural urban centers of the Kansas, Texas, and California traditions—those of the West Coast (mostly white) "cool" players, of Count Basie, Lester Young, Charlie Parker (all Kansas), Mingus (California), and Coleman (Texas, and California)—that spawned those key figures in the music generally and in Braxton's lineage specifically.)

Beecher's famous daughter, *Uncle Tom's Cabin* author Harriet Beecher-Stowe, carried his abolitionist torch. Her words, written shortly before the Civil War, express a social conscience that balanced the Methodist revival's emotional swells, in a tone that suggests something Malcolm X might have said to Martin Luther King, Jr.:

> We believe in no raptures, in no ecstasies, in no experiences that do not bring the soul into communion with Him who declared He came to set at liberty them that are bound and bruised . . . It is quite necessary that those who profess to be the exponents of religion before the community, should have some deeper and higher idea of what religion is. So that when they go forth with the Apostolic message, "Repent and be converted every one of you," they need not be met with the scornful reply, "Converted, sir, converted to what? Converted into a man who defends slavery—converted into one who dares not testify against a profitable wickedness—converted into a man whose religion never goes into his counting house—converted into a man who has no conscience in his politics, and who scoffs at the higher law of God?"[8]

Following the Civil War, the Holiness Sects, which eventually led to black and white Pentecostals (a.k.a "Sanctified," and "Holy Rollers") emerged as Methodism's cutting edge. As Darwinism came across the Atlantic, churches that had previously differed only slightly in doctrine began to polarize into "modernists," who tried to accommodate the new scientific theories, and "fundamentalists," who resisted their theological implications with a call to rally around the "fundamentals" of the faith. The first fundamentalists were not benighted fanatics so much as intellectually conservative theologians trying to reconcile the integrity of their religious *experience*, as well as faith, with the troubling suggestion of our Darwinian "ascent" from the animal world. (This goes to the discussion above about the links with and distinction from other animals humans have pursued in, respectively, the African and Western traditions.)

One such theologian was Charles Parham, who founded Bethel Bible College in Topeka in 1900. Parham, inspired by his reading of the biblical account of glossolalia (speaking in tongues) as a sign of the Holy Spirit, established the Pentecostal church. Pentecostalism spread, through Parham and his students, throughout Kansas, Missouri, and Texas. In 1905, at one of his bible schools in Houston, Parham enrolled as a student a black preacher named

William J. Seymour, who took the movement to Los Angeles. From there it spread to Europe and to the rest of the United States.

It may be no accident that it was an African American man who got this movement off the ground for both black and white churches (ironically, one leading, through the music, directly back *to* our links with the animal world). The seminal role of black gospel music on the American music scene is widely acknowledged,[9] and perhaps affirmed by this popular worship style, with its improvisatory, participatory, emotional practice of glossolalia, of prophesying as the Spirit led in a service, of being "slain in the Spirit." Originating mostly among the poorest and least educated blacks and whites, Pentecostalism initially was an integrated group at a time when segregation was the norm.

The 19th century set the stage, then, for a national emergence of an African-European musicultural synthesis. Blacks succeeded in establishing a Western social and religious context that would allow their African impulses to thrive; whites established a parallel context that would take their European heritage in a direction more in line with such impulses and away from the intolerant, oppressive line they themselves left Europe to escape and eschewed in themselves once here.

The Rural Roots: Black and White Pawns

Braxton claims the field recordings made by Alan Lomax[10] as a major influence on his own music. The deepest rural roots of the black folk traditions of blues and gospel lead directly to jazz; the European side came more from "civilized" (urban) pedagogy. In Braxton's music, the rural white folk tradition that has led to American experimental concert music also looms large.

Best seen as the pawns (the first grassroots movers) in our chess game, many of the earliest poor North American blacks and whites had their first meetings as fellow slaves.[11] The country music tradition is rooted in the tune and lyric stock of Renaissance England, Scotland, and Ireland (that stock also contributed the Western harmonies and forms used in the blues). Its premier instrument was the fiddle; white country musicians took up the African-derived banjo with as much relish as the African Americans would later take up the European saxophone. The European ancestors of white Americans predated the widespread imperialism and colonialism, predated the slave trade as a major socioeconomic institution and the corresponding social institutionalization of white racism, predated the Enlightenment and the Industrial Revolution in Europe. The various ethnic and rural music traditions, both secular and religious, have survived as oral more than literate traditions, and the history of poor whites struggling against exploitation and oppression by the rich and powerful runs parallel to that of blacks.

Braxton has an avowed affinity for the Western music of the late medieval period and matches some of its melodic, harmonic, and rhythmic approaches and effects in his own work.[12] This medieval and Renaissance tradition continued unbroken throughout early American hymnody.

the music's parents

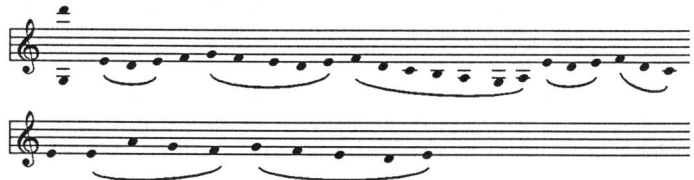

Fig. 2.2a: From Hildegard of Bingen's *Symphonia*.[13]

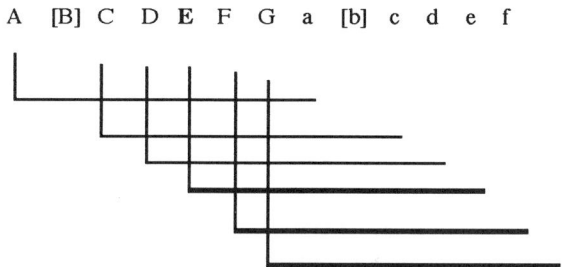

2.2b: Schema of the modal system. The various classical Greek names of the modes would distract from the point here: tonal centers variously defined by the scales built on them (the bold **E** indicates the phrygian mode of the above example). The addition of equal temperament and then chromaticism to the diatonic platform of this principle brings us to the way it's used by Braxton and others in these times.

2.2c: From Braxton's *40N*. Much of Braxton's music, both improvised and composed, is modal in nature, often patterned over a drone. The brackets around the notes are mine, to show the way Braxton shifted the modes of this piece.

Fig 2.2: Hildegard of Bingen (1098–1179) is one of Braxton's favorite medieval composers. Her music (not to mention her gender) set her apart from her contemporaries in much the same way as Carlo Gesualdo 500 years later, or Braxton in his time.

Fig. 2.2a shows the extraordinary range (after the clef sign) of one of her pieces (like Braxton, she was also given to sudden intervallic leaps). Unusually for her time, she used more than one mode in one piece. Like Braxton, she developed her own distinct vocabulary and syntax—in her case, of melodic patterns— and organizational principles which she applied creatively to the modes (and mores) behind the generation of her music.[14]

Fig. 2.2b shows the way the modal system worked—templates of interval patterns extracted from what we've come to know as the diatonic C scale (with a variable "b") that place the center of "tonal gravity" on each of six of the scales' seven tones (excluding the variable "b"). Braxton's notes claim 40N "contributed to my awareness of modalism and the power of one note."

Braxton's 40N (2.2c) was inspired by Indian classical (modal) music; even so, it stands well in comparison to early Western modal music, especially this from Hildegard in the more Eastern-sounding phrygian mode.

(No seamless, consistent link, nor unbroken historical continuum between these two or any succeeding such examples is asserted, neither by the author nor his subject. The point is the broad resonances between concepts and techniques. However, the suggestion of a link between early Western and Middle Eastern, African, and Indian music is intended.).[15]

Shape-Note Music

Wilfrid Mellers calls the roots of white America a

> rag-bag of European traditions . . . In this sense America is an extreme evolution from the European consciousness; we see in America what happened to "the mind of Europe" when, separated from the traditions of a civilized past, it was faced with nothing but land—not a country at all, but the material out of which countries are made. One might almost say that America begins with the disintegration of the Middle Ages and the triumph of humanism. In Europe's High Renaissance flesh and spirit were one; *but belief in man's individual will in the long run led to spiritual impoverishment* . . . (emphasis mine; Braxton makes much of this point; see Chapter Four)[16]

The 18th-century New England hymnodists, not yet so impoverished, composed hymns, psalms, anthems, and "fuging tunes" based on English and German Reformation music.

> The half-intuitive composers, thinking modally, like folk-singers, did not know how to achieve the highly civilized equilibrium between horizontal polyphony and vertical homophony that characterized their European forebears. Yet their rawness was also their authenticity. Their "mistakes" in harmony and part-writing could be at times inspired; indeed, they were not mistakes at all, since they were a creative manifestation of their identities.[17]

As Mellers points out, it was a later critical view of the hymnodists that labeled them crude and primitive, a perspective formed by 19th-century Americans affecting European *personae*. Their criticisms could have as easily applied to the medieval composer Machaut and to such 20th-century composers as Ives, Stravinsky, Schönberg and, for that matter, Braxton. They all comprise

Fig. 2.3a: Bars 16–19 of William Billings' *Dunstable*.[18]

2.3b: Opening of Charles Ives' *Symphony No. Four*, third ("fugue") movement.[19]

2.3c: Braxton's *105A* (D section) shows *his* use of the fugal approach. The notated and improvised sections (the shapes, with beats for duration designated above them) are staggered; this way of composing has developed from this point in Braxton's work to the "C[onnector]-class" and "signature logic" pieces, which feature overlapping written and staggered improvised material in increasingly recognizable interactive restatements.

As with other major currents of both Western and African traditions, Braxton's composerly connection to the fugue isn't obvious but is deep. That is, it is also a major current in his work, in his practice of alternating brief written with brief notated phrases in one part's line then staggering that line against another of similar construction (Fig. 2.3c). The mature realization of this device, heard in his most recent quartet music, lies in what he calls "signature logic" pieces and, most recently, "C(onnector)-class prototypes," in which the written material of all parts overlaps, appearing and vanishing successively in each voice of the collective improvisation, like some ball thrown around by swimmers in a water sport. Besides sharing the fugue's staggered juxtapositions of the same material, it also makes its vertical harmonies/textures by the same layering of horizontal constructions.

what Braxton would call an "affinity continuum," despite all their radical differences. The common ground of that continuum lies in their variously "horizontal" approaches: a melody or line with its own integrity serves to suggest rhythmic and pitch contours and relationships; other equally self-integrated lines that may be very close, distant, or opposed in one or more aspect are added, always intentionally—to amplify, challenge, or reconcile with each other in an infinite variety of ways—but not always predictably. In all, in one way or another, the literate conventions of Western scoring and composing are more flexible than rigid in their service to the Muse: in the medieval, Renaissance, and early American composers because they hadn't yet been dominated by vertical considerations (either harmonic or metric); and in the moderns because they consciously broke free of such conventions. New England hymnody was written in simple harmonic configurations and repetitive forms such as the rondo and variation, since its composers had little skill or interest in the modulatory techniques of 18th-century European music. The American Europhiles objected to the hymnodists' prosodic (read "oral") tradition that freed meter from bar lines, left time changes to be inferred from verbal stresses, and gave melody a greater weight than harmony, which in its turn thus flowered in striking (but unsanctioned) ways.

It's interesting to trace these qualities through the African American lineage of Charlie Parker, and Ornette Coleman to Braxton. All alto saxophonists, all seminal figures in the course of the music, together they neatly define an arc removing it from the Western diatonic-metric system that had governed it since Bach. Parker's pitch extensions pushed the envelope into chromaticism; his rhythmic pyrotechnics soared equally free of regular meter.[20] Coleman's free pulse and pan-tonality demonstrated new melodic realities, songs, making homes out of that expanded harmonic and rhythmic field.[21] Braxton's knack for universalizing and combining such infinitely disparate personal expressions into a system that accommodates and unifies them made those homes into a community. The arc described is an African way out of the most Eurocentric urban America (through Parker) through the rural America whose European culture is rooted in a closer connection to the rest of the world (through Coleman) to a reconnection with the West as a whole (through Braxton), which is itself turning back to that closer connection. The spirit of this trans-European musiculture right up through Charles Ives and the musico-dramas of the churches, well into the 20th century, has been characterized by the disdain for European cosmopolitan humanism and the mix of stoicism and rapture, rugged self-sufficiency and community spirit, rustic physicality and piety that seems to go with the life of the land more than that of the city.

The most famous New England hymnodist was and is William Billings. He said something about art and artists that set the tone for the next two centuries of American experimental musicians, something especially applicable to Braxton: "Every composer should be his own Carver."[22] He set another precedent, built upon by the American composers who write about their art—from Harry Partch to John Cage to Braxton—when he wrote that he would acknowledge no rules based on precedent or authority that seemed irrelevant to an aboriginal New Englander. (One such rule was the use of parallel fifths, which he ignored with delight, describing their "noise" as "luscious and fulsome." Two hundred years later, Braxton also found himself rebelling against the same rule, taught in an American college, when he first took up music as a young man.) Billings always gave melody primacy over harmonic considerations, and he always indulged rules of any sort only until "Fancy . . . gets upon the wings, seems to despise all form, and scorns to be confined or limited by any formal prescriptions whatever."[23]

Moving from this American branch of early Western music back to its roots there, Guillaume Dufay's *Missa L'Homme Armé* is a striking example of the harmonic effect of modalism in polyphonic music. Tonal centers and syllabically altered vocal timbres shift in a non-modulatory, rhythmical way under parallel melodic statements; each shift creates the musical excitement of a mobile tonality that we also hear in Miles Davis' *So What*, or Coltrane's *Impressions* (a Braxton solo-sax staple). Medieval music derived its system from recast Greek modes, themselves perhaps linked through the Pythagoreans with Egyptian concepts of tonal arrangements and systems. These in turn share the approach of the ancient Chinese and Indian systems, which posit the successions of tones (which the West would later hierarchize into scales) in a non-hierarchical pattern of equally "valid" vibrations, each with its particular impact on the individual nervous system and collective ritual function and meaning. In the hymnodists and their counterparts in the American folk and gospel traditions, directly aligned as they are with medieval Europe, the modal approach forms the very root of the American art music that would take shape through Charles Ives and others in the 20th century.

the music's parents

Fig. 2.4a: From *The Cry of My Beloved*, by Timothy Swan.[24]

2.4b: (Barless) segment of Braxton's *6J* with parallel fifths.

2.4c: These four pitches variously voiced comprise the harmonic field of *the* precursor (Braxton's *37*) to the spate of saxophone quartets that came on the scene in the 1980s. Braxton used these chords as source material for much of his later large-ensemble work.

Fig. 2.4: Parallel harmony as used in early Western and non-Western music essentially conceives of harmony as texture, or of intervals as part of one sound (an articulation of overtones?), rather than two with a relationship begging definition. Early American hymnodists used it so (2.4a), as does Braxton (2.4b), for effect among the more (recently) conventional harmonic movement in the rest of each example. In Braxton's mature ensembles, especially his quartet, duets often feature either unison or parallel lines, the next most common being random chromatic harmonies. The latter are the staple of both large-ensemble music, where pitch is often undetermined but intuited interactively according to the group's listening and playing skill level, and of Braxton's notated music, which he often writes spontaneously (not formulaically) but with a desire to hear and work specific clusters of pitch. Parallel harmonies (2nds and 6ths more than 4ths, 5ths, and octaves) also result from using one unspecified clef for all the instruments. Fig. 2.4c is an example of some of his most static harmonic writing, for saxophone quartet. The notes change octave and order, but never pitch; the effect is of an Indian harmonium droning to field improvisation.

Philosophically, this way of making music complements the American dream of freedom from the social hierarchy and imbalance between master and slave (if we think of melody and its mode as primary and its relationship to other melodies within that mode as secondary); of diversity in unity (if those priorities yield both individual and collective contentment); of music as a joiner rather than a separator of flesh and spirit (if we think of the individual part magnified rather than exploited by the whole); and thus as a physical force that heals, provides balance in, makes whole, reconciles the individual and the collective. Braxton has indicated his sensitivity to this understanding numerous times in interviews, such as in the following:

> I have tried to build my model based on a structure that respects what I learn about life as it relates to the Asian, the African, the European, and the feminist viewpoints—all my influences—and reflects them in its architectural, its individual, its collective, and its synthesis postulations . . . a musical performance or composition can give insights into sociopolitical processes in its soundspace microcosm, in the way the musicians interact with each other.[25]

Mellers discusses the presence of chance that increasingly became an element in this early European American music as it spread from colonial enclaves to an expanding rural culture throughout the 19th century. This element, like modalism, would flower in both American experimental music and the jazz tradition. Discussing a "shape-note" score, Mellers writes:

> If, on paper, the music looks crude and gauche, we must remember that it is not paper-music. It came empirically from the sound made by massed voices: as, indeed, the technique of medieval organum [instrumental music] had originally done. The sonority the music produces in performance is extraordinarily impressive and resonant, the more so because the New Englanders' habit of allowing men or women to sing any part—'up' or 'down' according to sex—was, in the remoter rural areas, adopted with complete spontaneity. The consequent octave doublings give the sound its awe-inspiring reverberation: nor is it ever certain which part will receive the main emphasis, since that depends on the proportionate number of people who decide to sing each part. The shape-note tunes proliferated with remarkable rapidity, and the revivalist sects that flourished in every state took them up the more readily because they could appeal

the music's parents

> immediately to the illiterate. Shape note method encouraged the singers to make up their own versions of the tunes on the spur of the moment, so that a wild heterophony must often have resulted. This would have accorded, musically, with the physical excesses of revivalist fervour; and contemporary descriptions make clear that this was not far removed from the ritual exercise of voodoo-worship. In the South the shape-note tunes were the main 'white' source for the Negro's spirituals; together, white and black Christian sought a refuge from Calvinistic fire and brimstone.[26]

This could almost be a description of a performance of one of Braxton's works for large ensemble. They are typically written to accommodate any number and kind of instruments, and a wide skill range of players.

> By this time the shape-note tunes had ceased to be a part of American 'art' music and had become part of the origins of the American folk-art that is jazz: not until the twentieth century did they play a part in the evolution of art music, as we can see in the setting of the 67th Psalm by Charles Ives. It says much for the vitality of this indigenous American music that...it should still be performed, in much the same manner, in the remoter regions of the Southern states. *Meanwhile, however, the development of art-music in the American cities was associated with the assimilation, and then perhaps with the imposition, of European models*[27] (emphasis mine).

Be – a – ta _____ *gens*

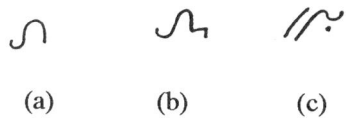

(a) (b) (c)

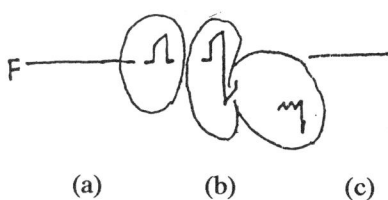

(a) (b) (c)

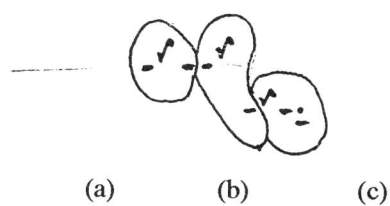

(a) (b) (c)

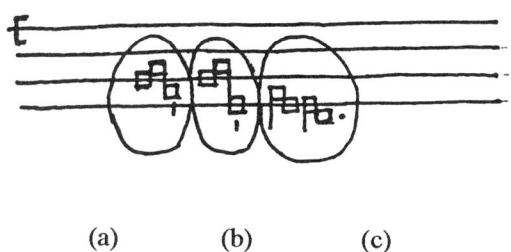

(a) (b) (c)

the music's parents

Fig. 2.5a: The top line suggests the development of neumes from the motion of a hand in air; the next four lines show their evolution through some 500 years (and the same pitches for the same chanted three syllables "dom-i-nus" into the square-note notation of the 14th and 15th centuries.[28]

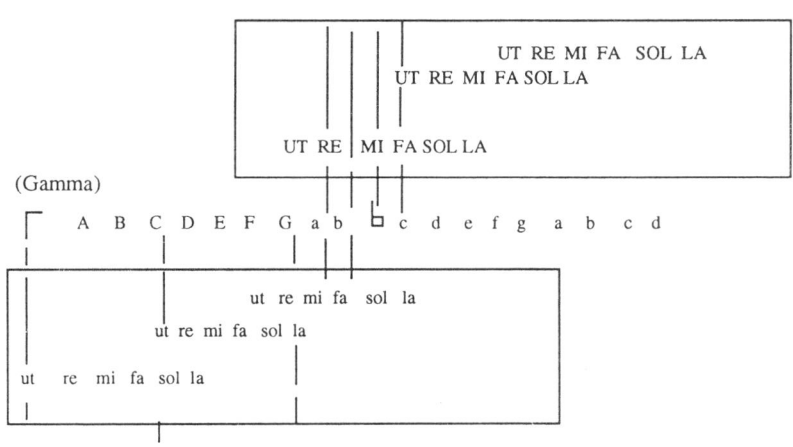

2.5b: The hexachord system of solmization dating roughly to the time of Hildegard. This became known as the musical "gamut" (from the Greek "gamma" and "ut," is indeed the source of the word), and is still found in shapenote hymn books such as the one containing the hymn selection above. Although conceived as an anti-oral, pro-literacy movement, this system's way of signalling the rhythmic and intervallic intricacies of Western polyphony to musically nonliterate singers has in effect kept Western musiculture's *oral* traditional aspect and its mythology alive in North America. Moreover, the practice of "lining out," a call-and-response style of singing memorized tunes to text alone, dates from the Reformation and is practiced by many African- and European American Baptist groups today.

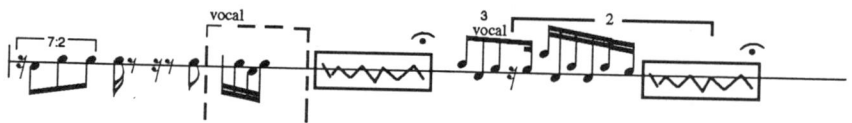

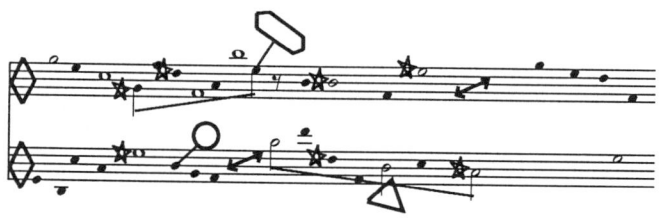

2.5c: Braxton's *76* and *136* reflect several traits of the examples above it. *76*'s (first line) parts for unschooled vocalists go back to the device of pitch designations woven around and relative to a single tonal line. Its second line uses the triangle (and even a long square note, such as in medieval notation) to denote duration and pitch alterations. *136* has developed this use of shapes in an interesting reversal of their medieval origins. Here, musical literacy is presumed, while the shapes suggest improvisational elements and approaches to apply to the notes as written. Whereas the neumes and early shape notes sought to codify and eventually standardize the oral tradition of the chant, Braxton's shapes are intended to reintegrate the static literate tradition with its dynamic oral roots.

2.5d: Facsimile of material from *Beata Gens*. The horizontal line through these early "notes" (discrete points extracted from the neumes) was originally scratched by scribes onto the manuscript as an informal pitch orientation. They later evolved into our staves.

Braxton's use of triangles, circles, and squares in his music has been ongoing, changing slightly over time or from piece to piece, from the beginning. Used as supplements to regular notation rather than the hybrids of traditional shape notes, Braxton has consistently put them to the same general use: as indicators of pitch attributes (duration, attack, inflection) and context (relationship to other pitches, exactitude of interpretation) that especially target musically nonliterate readers.

Fig. 2.5c shows music written for unschooled vocalists; though standard notation is used, obviously pitch is undetermined. A gesture like this finds its match, again, in the neumes and in Western music's very earliest notation (Fig. 2.5d). They obviously didn't specify pitch, but just as obviously specified the details of a fluctuation and flow of it—its "gravitational intrigue," in tandem with the mystery of the words—to people who already had much knowledge about what they meant. In other words, they were literate devices put to the service of, rather than putting to death, an oral tradition.

Charles Ives

Ives is generally acknowledged to be the first singularly American composer, the one who defined the Europhiles as a dead end and the one who made "experimental" and "American" virtually synonymous in the world of art music. His was the first music from European America to successfully synthesize, in the Renaissance/Reformation tradition as Americanized through the hymnodists and the folk tradition, popular and high culture. If for "popular" you read "flesh," and for "high," "spirit," you begin to see Ives' resonance with the African *vodou* (not to mention his direct exposure to Harlem's ragtime). Ives was motivated by creative freedom and passion more than what he considered the effete and confining European conventions. We might say that he was the first to codify and personify as high culture, American-style, ideas and practices that had been evolving all along anyway—polyrhythms, polymeters, chance/improvisation, microtonalism. It also might be more accurate to say about this and his other essential traits that he stands more as a kindred spirit to than a mentoring influence on Braxton, whose music has also served to systematize theoretically and in literate terms qualities from the oral/aural African American tradition which have their European and European American counterparts in American music.

Indeed, most of Ives' most distinguishing features resonate that way with Braxton. To name some of the most key, they are:

• his dogged amateurism, in the sense that he didn't expect to make money from his art, and so permitted himself freedom from commercial considerations;

• his largely self-imposed creative isolation. Braxton has always collaborated with a wide range of musicians, but his admonition to "stay away from the musicians"—an exact echo of Ives—is, as with Ives, also a

prescription for creative integrity and liberation, from artistically impure peer pressure and distraction;
- a musical humor and whimsy that lighten the potentially oppressive weightiness of his cosmic aspirations;
- his claim to absolute creative freedom in self-sufficiency. Braxton has said he believes people should "be born and be creative," without taking on a lot of conditioning; Ives spoke of his music as a search for "the inner invisible activity of truth," the end that justified even the most unconventional means.

This spirit, as American as the Revolution and the Emancipation, is described well by Moore, and might well describe Braxton:

> The Yankee composers rationalized their musical calling on the basis of redemptive culture: the doctrine that musical culture could redeem the American spirit . . . As Yankees, they considered themselves leaders of a progressive movement *peculiarly American and, therefore, universal.* By directly experiencing the ordering principles of redemptive culture, audiences could understand the meaning of their identity as Americans . . . The keystone of redemptive culture, musical art connected and completed two sides of an arching spiritual structure. *Music both sustained and was supported by tradition, on the one hand, and by the prophetic future, on the other. While the composer, as artist, represents creative freedom, his freedom is contingent, responsible to an ideal past and an ideal future.* However much the Yankee composer feared the power of critics, implicitly he recognized that the success of redemptive culture hinged on critical mediation. *As essayist or educator, the composer himself often explained music, tradition, and the prophetic future in terms of each other.* He believed an ideal criticism would help the artist court the public[29] (emphases mine, for their resonance with the "Philosophical" aspect of Braxton's music system; see Chapter Three, on *Tri-Axium Writings*).

Ives' most obvious musical influence on Braxton was his way of writing music that incorporated two or more clashing pieces. The inspiration for this was the experience of hearing two different bands within earshot but at a distance from each other. Braxton:

> I can still recall the excitement I felt when my family would tell me stories about famous 'big band' battles (some of which took place in my own neighborhood) where two or more ensembles would participate in making the music at the same time . . . There has always been something special about the reality of different ensembles making music in the same physical universe space that has excited my imagination. It is as if the whole of the universe were swallowed up—leaving us in a sea of music and color . . . One of the first compositions that would affect me was the fourth symphony of

Charles Ives which, although involving only one orchestra, achieved a multi-orchestral breakthrough anyway . . . [30]

. . . an interesting fascination, in the common light of two artists who revel in integrating and synthesizing from what so many others preferred to segregate ("high" and "low" culture, black and white traditions) and keep polarized.

Like Braxton, Ives was not without his critics, and even those speak similarly. Ives' contemporary and fellow composer Virgil Thomson saw Ives' work, however ingenious, as suffering from a lack of full commitment (since Ives was an amateur composer, in between a fulltime work and family schedule), and therefore often facile but not as profound as the thought behind it.[31] This emotional glibness and superficial eclecticism born of an eccentric intellect is the very thing Braxton has been charged with.

What is interesting in the light of Thomson's critique is to continue scanning this American Independent tradition—from Ives through Thomson through, say, Adams, Glass, and Reich, on the minimalist path; and through Partch and Varèse to Cage, on what we might call the maximalist path (definition of that forthcoming)—and to observe what Thomson's criticism says about his own (pro-development) criteria, and what Ives' place in that history says about the potential place of Braxton therein, with whom Ives shares so many personal and artistic traits.

I would argue, in defense of Ives' and Braxton's penchant for pastiche, that its greatness lies in the very thing Thomson dislikes. It is an expression of a transcendence of, rather than lack of grounded connection to, phenomena; however deeply the stuff of the music might be felt (and who can deny the passion and poignancy in Ives?), it comes and it goes; those of us who make it have to take care that we don't come and go with it—just as with history, or with life, seen spiritually.

Ives' *Symphony No. Four* and, say, Braxton's *Composition Nos. 147* and *151*, share this quality (see Fig. 2.6): they roil and meander through spacetime like a rich but aimless garden of sound, except for occasional fleeting epiphanous moments in which a heartbreakingly poignant statement emerges just long enough to be glimpsed, then dissolves again. The effect is much more striking than if that motif had been stripped of its oceanic chaos, dried off and stuck in a fenced yard for all the developed world to memorize then forget, and neglect to its ruin.

Ives' music wasn't even considered playable until the 1950s, and since then has universally been declared timeless. Its innovations paralleled those of Stravinsky and Schönberg, in synchronistic isolation. The music of Virgil Thomson—as that of Henry Cowell, Carl Ruggles, Aaron Copland, and Glass, to suggest the lineage—succeeded quite well in distilling various American essences, but they are only distillations of elements that were much more interesting, and connected to the larger world, when mixed together in the briny soup of Ives' music.

the music's parents

Fig. 2.6a: Opening of Ives' *Symphony No. Four*[32]

2.6b: Parallel articulations of a familiar movie theme charged with mythological associations from Braxton's *147*. Such discernible statements floating on a sea of sound constitute the "signature logics"—sonic lighthouse beams on seas of half-improvised sound—of Braxton's later music.

the music's parents

[musical notation: four lines of rhythmic patterns with ties and brackets]

2.6c: Breakdown of a few lines from Obrecht's *Missa si dedero*, an early mass. The ties indicate suspensions across the beat; bracketed figures show patterns of two and four within the one-within-the-three of the *perfectum* (triple) cycle of mensuration.

2.6d: From Billings' anthem *Blessed is He that Considereth the Poor*[33]

Snippets such as these—the hymn opening Ives' masterpiece and the much shorter echo of the theme from Close Encounters of the Third Kind *acting as a "signature logic"—set as they are like cool islands of order on an ocean of warm chaos—bring to the order that is life a context missing in music that weeds out the chaos and makes of the order an inexorable center.*

Notice that "chaos'" currents of quintuple and quadruple phrases against triple (6/8) meter floating around Ives' metrically even hymn. This kind of complex subdivision of the meter, considered so wildly avant-garde in his (and Stravinsky's, Schönberg's, and Stockhausen's and Braxton's) work, is in fact another ancient musical convention that connects the West, through its medieval legacy, to the rest of the world. Medieval music's cycles of mensuration (or, roughly, measures; more accurately, phrases) were mazes of this sort of suspension and staggered layering of the pulse (Fig. 2.6c); even Billings (2.6d), the most conventionally constrained between medieval and modern, and European and American worlds, exhibits elements of the layerings of three against two and four (the short vertical lines above the staves), and of clumps of 5/8 breaking up the 4 meter.

John Phillip Sousa, Ruth Crawford Seeger

Another American composer whose work is dear to Braxton—and is the sort of material Ives used in the way jazz musicians use that of the American songbook—is John Philip Sousa. While this may seem the most unlikely of a host of unlikely allegiances, the following quote by Sousa sheds light on it (remember Braxton's concept of music as viscerally functional, and of composing as an exacting and rewarding discipline):

> A march speaks to a fundamental rhythm in the human organization and is answered. A march stimulates every center of vitality, wakens the imagination . . . But a march must be good. It must be as free from padding as a marble statue. Every line must be carved with unerring skill. Once padded, it ceases to be a march. There is no form of composition wherein the harmonic structure must be more clearcut. The whole process is an exacting one. There must be a melody which appeals to the musical and the unmusical alike. There must be no confusion in counterpoints.[34]

Sousa's music hit Braxton in his formative years, when he played in an army band (he can still be seen, sopranino in hand, stepping across the Wesleyan football field during home-game halftimes). The economic and focused craftsmanship Sousa expresses is the very thing Braxton sees in the very different so-called "cool" white jazz influences (more on which ahead).[35]

Braxton seems to have passed over the music of 20th-century American composers such as Wallingford Riegger, Roger Sessions, and Elliott Carter, who *were* in touch with Europe, in his reach back to their sources in Schönberg and Webern. A notable exception from this conceptual circle is Ruth Crawford Seeger, who, though influenced by European serialism, was as original in the use she put it to as is Braxton, and in many of the same ways. Even though Seeger's impact on Braxton was not as extensive as that of other male composers, it has a special significance that justifies attention,[36] in the context of Braxton's feminism, about which also more ahead.

the music's parents 81

Fig 2.7: Score page from Braxton's Composition 58 *(composer's score). Most of this march is conventional, including its 6/8 meter. This page shows where he starts to have fun with it, redistributing the eighth note accents so that the steady "boom-chk-chk boom-chk-chk" goes off (in the reeds, trumpets, and trombones) into "chk-chk-boom (rest) chk chk-chk-boom (rest) chk chk-chk boom (re-e-st...) Boom!" and so on, splaying off so like a part out of the Obrecht mass we've been looking at, and that against counter parts (tuba, bells, percussion).*

John Cage, Harry Partch

The other Americans in this lineage Braxton names as influences—Harry Partch and John Cage, most notably—we might call maximalists (like Braxton) not because their music was busy and dense but because they didn't derive it from some portion of Ives' or the Europeans' work, but rather (like Braxton) furthered the *approach* of their European and American influences, by getting their music in a wide-open embrace of their own world and time.

Cage and Partch can be seen as the (musicultural) end of the Western odyssey that began with Columbus. Columbus sought the East, not a New World; Cage, like the twentieth-century philosophers who took Schopenhauer's cue, finally got there, along with millions of Americans—especially on the Pacific Rim—of his and then Braxton's generation, in the popular surge of

Eastern religions-philosophies, American-style. These appealed to a diversity of Americans for the light they shone at the end of our Western, and Western-oppressed, tunnels (Braxton, recall, was and is perennially a student of such things).

Musically, Cage built a platform with its foundation in Schönberg's (as, philosophically, in Schopenhauer's) breakthrough, but its main planks came from the East, in a sheer gasp for freedom from abstractions and rules: chance, *I Ching*-style synchronicity, as determinant elements in musical syntax and structure; an Eastern relationship with numbers and their magic that recalled the West's own Pythagorean beginnings; an acceptance of both sounds and silences in their infinite variety of possible expressions and durations as part of the composer's palette; and a concern for the inadequacy of language as developed in the literate tradition to keep up with the music, and an attempt to re-tool it to do so.

Cage's Zen Buddhist point of view informed his music and his words about both it and music generally. Some of those speak particularly to Braxton's own role:

> ... more and more a concern with personal feelings of individuals, even the enlightenment of individuals, will be seen in the larger context of society. We know how to suffer or control our emotions. If not, advice is available. There is a cure for tragedy. The path to self-knowledge has been mapped out by psychiatry, by oriental philosophy, mythology, occult thought, anthroposophy, and astrology. We know all we need to know about Oedipus, Prometheus, and Hamlet. What we are learning is how to be convivial. "Here Comes Everybody."[37]

Cage's "reasons for open-mindedness about the future of music"[38] include electronic and computer technology and the "interpenetration of cultures formerly separated," both of which have excited Braxton from his beginnings, and increasingly do so. Cage's words about the religious spirit becoming social, Mankind as Family, Earth as Home, Music's ancient purpose ("to sober and quiet the mind, thus making it susceptible to divine influences"), all echo the way Braxton talks to his student ensembles, exhorting them to learn how to be a part of the musical family, to find the balance between personal and collective fulfillment therein.

Cage espoused an American form of benign and pragmatic anarchy, voiced by Thoreau:

> "That government is best which governs not at all"...Less anarchic kinds of music give examples of less anarchic states of society. The masterpieces of Western music exemplify monarchies and dictatorships. Composer and conductor: king and prime minister. By making musical situations which are analogies to desirable social circumstances which we do not yet have, we make music suggestive and relevant to the serious questions which face Mankind.[39]

His words about words offer a way out of the dilemma Braxton voiced about "words being the most sophisticated weapon"[40] used in the cause of Western oppression (they also take us back to our starting point of music and language as they first evolved in us):

> Since words, when they communicate, have no effect, it dawns on us that we need a society in which communication is not practiced, in which words become nonsense as they do between lovers, in which words become what they originally were: trees and stars and the rest of primeval environment. The demilitarization of language: a serious musical concern.[41]

Braxton's distinctions from Cage are as well defined as their common ground. He decided the "self" Cage tried so diligently to remove from his music was just as much a part of the larger "nature" Cage felt "self" impeded. He also felt Cage went farther into pure abstraction than was musically or otherwise sound.[42] Cage was a modern Western man who embraced the East for its integration of the otherworldly and the thisworldly God, but not particularly Africa for her outright celebration of the thisworldly God. Braxton claimed what he could from Cage and added what he felt was still missing (a conceptual comparison between Cage's *4'33"* —the three sections marked "Tacet"—and Braxton's *9*, in which the musician makes music by shoveling coal, shows well the similarity and difference between the two composers).

If Columbus finally reached the East through Cage, he can be said to have come finally to peaceful, respectful Western terms with Native America in Partch. Partch renounced both chance and electronics—the former as uninteresting, the latter as impersonal and artificial—as he embraced his own relationship with the natural world. He made instruments from natural objects and materials, devised his own scales, systems, and poetics to create a context of ritual magic and spectacle for his music. Reactively, he criticized and mocked conventional culture; proactively, he celebrated the individual's capacity to create original mythology-philosophy and art from a direct personal relationship with nature and nature's soul.

Braxton's links with Partch are thickest in his later music, that beginning with his first Ritual and Ceremonial pieces in the late '70s/early '80s. Human (or at least anthropomorphic) figures began to appear in the drawings— "summation identity figures"—that helped "title" his works. Theatrical elements in performance increased (e.g.: *Composition 95*—see Chapter Six), and a personal mythology came to life in subtitles and texts (such as *When Chancey Speaks, the Number '3' Changes Lights*, subtitle to Braxton's *151*, which compares with Partch titles such as *And on the Seventh Day Petals Fell on Petaluma*).

Partch *maximized* microtonal and timbral possibilities, as Cage did chance and the synchronistic events and numerical patterns to which it gave rise, as Ives did the combinations inherent in both European and American traditions, and as Braxton would form, timbral/tonal vocabulary, and improvisational techniques from the jazz tradition. Again, all share primarily an approach and spirit, only secondarily a musical vocabulary.

The Blues

Of the three broad traditions Braxton draws from—African American, European American, and European—the first is the most extensive and primal, of course, because it is his own. It is the *urgrund* from which the others grew, both in his personal and in the larger transpersonal musicultural history (in that it is also the most generally primal source feeding both global and American music). It spans a range from ancient (in its African and first American expressions) to the most multifaceted, futuristically visionary (in innovators from Charlie Parker to John Coltrane to Albert Ayler, from Sun Ra to Cecil Taylor to Ornette Coleman, and a modern host including Braxton and others of like mind) to the most formalized classical (in the unbroken line of black American composers-performers from Newport Gardner *circa* 1746 to Olly Wilson, Talib Rasul Hakim, and, again, Braxton and his peers today).

Braxton grew up in the modern blues bedrock, Chicago. That urban musiculture had direct links to the Southern one a generation or two before it, and that musiculture was still full of Africanisms.[43] There was a figure in the Chicago of Braxton's youth whose *persona* and messages shed a particularly striking light on how this blues tradition could be perceived and understood. But before we talk about Sun Ra, let's glimpse the sort of thinking about the blues and its pre American African roots that he and his generation of African American artists and intellectuals would have had to confront: the blues and African music as "primitive."

Mellers' book, though dated, serves that purpose well, for its look at American music as a whole fabric. It examines *as* American, woven in an American web of interconnections, the music of the pilgrims and slaves through that of the white American composers and jazz artists to that of the blues, ragtime, and jazz artists of both colors. Its musical analyses and musicultural insights are strong, and its sympathy with that which it deems primitive usually keen. Finally—along with that of the first scholarly books on jazz, and of some of the best of the latest, on Braxton's generation—it is the viewpoint of a European, which fact speaks resonantly to Braxton's unique relationship with Europe via his most primal African American base.

For all his sympathy, Mellers' book is built on the assumption that pre-Westernized African peoples were pre-civilized.[44] In the light of Robert Farris Thompson's description (see footnote 41, Chapter One) of a West African urban center with a rural *feel* to it—a legacy which could have informed both the African rural and urban experience in America—we can leave aside the "primitive" slant and extract points for our purposes here: music as a greaser-of-the-wheels-of-mundane-life, as a reconnection to the healthy life of the land as opposed to urban decadence, and the traditional relationship between pitch/inflection and meaning—not vague, inarticulate emotion, nor Morse-code-like rhythmic analogues, but sound-triggered cognition (such as McKenna described in the *Ayahuasqueros* tribal chants). As we'll see, Braxton's work is marked by attempts to develop these qualities.

The African treatment of European materials in America was not only melodic (monodic) as opposed to harmonic, it was textural, in its handling of both melody and harmony; pitch and timbre, whether in solo, unison, or harmonized voices, was of central importance in the arrangement of those

the music's parents

materials. And, again, the net result was something more akin to early-Renaissance than to later European music (elsewhere Mellers, like Groves, describes the evolution of harmony from heterophony in jazz as analogous to that in Western medieval music, with ornamentations on the old gradually forming the heart of the new musics: the "vertical" music of Europe that culminated in Baroque, and of America as voiced in the big-band orchestrations as developed by such as Fletcher Henderson and Duke Ellington). These too are thoughts to carry into our look at Braxton's work.

Let's return for now to his relationship to the blues, and to the information that set them, for him, in an unbroken spectrum including Howlin' Wolf and Stockhausen. Braxton:

> People say I don't play the blues—I've always played the blues, but I never argue about those kinds of things. What we call the blues is not just notes, it's a vibrational understanding that's been transmitted and encoded, and it's manifested in various forms of music in various different ways. Still, there is a science to different periods of blues playing, and that information is important. It just depends on how you want to look at it: there's the blues as manifested in one particular style or projection and then there's what the blues is really affirming, and that's manifested on many different levels.[45]

What is the "vibrational understanding" that is being transmitted and encoded in so many ways? The pithy lyrics for which the blues are famous convey anecdotally what it is, inseparable as they are from their vocal expressions. Sidran cites one of thousands of such lines: "I don't worry 'bout a thing 'cause I know nothing's going to be all right." He notes[46] that jazz is the result of a black voice (blues) in a peculiarly white context (Western harmony); i.e., you can put a blues spin on everything, as Parker was said to do, and as Braxton says above: pop song forms, other cultures' musics, even classical music (e.g., Gershwin's *Rhapsody in Blue*). Sidran observes the blues as the African's American experience.[47] The first African American solo artist was a blues singer, using the guitar as a simulation of the community-chorus as a response to his call. This new isolated individualism was part of the general fall from the grace provided by the displaced African's communal culture. At the same time, it was a preservation of that culture, by restructuring it in the new American context. The first blues singers and players were thus what Braxton calls "restructuralists," artists who redefine the rules of the game of art-making.

But what were they restructuring? African culture, of course, mostly West African culture. But what, in the global and historical arenas, was that culture? Something more primitive than the more evolved West? No one asserts that much these days, even benignly, and with good reason. Still, do we then say that African tribal cultures and civilizations represent a development made parallel to and in relative isolation from that of the West (until the slave trade), resulting in different but equally advanced fruits (for example, the African systems of rhythm as a match to the European systems of harmony)?

Braxton's understanding of the blues—African musiculture's American expression, from the early Ring Shouts to the most current improvisational ensembles—is framed by a different viewpoint, one informed by scholarship and thought as recent as his own time. Before identifying that viewpoint, let's add a bit more to the quote from Cole above about influences. The idea of taking in one's cultural influences in order to add to them by distinguishing oneself from them—carving out a new and unique voice and song—is also an African tradition.[48] If we then take these aspects of the blues tradition and stack them next to Braxton's music, we see some strong connections.

First of all, Braxton made his first big mark on the scene with *For Alto*, a two-record album of solo alto sax improvisations. The groundbreaking concepts then concerned the potential of a single-line instrument to articulate a complete music—a horizontal, or a-harmonic music; and the potential of a music based on rhythm and sound—textures, pitch and timbral variations replete with "vibrato, tremolo, and overtone effects"[49] as well as other sound-rhythm extensions. He did it in a solo voice, after the fashion of the first Africans to leave the insulation of their cultural "ring" and take on the European arena with the African musical metaphysic.[50] He disputed Western musical conventions that had cropped up since medieval and Renaissance times, and, in his middle age no less than in his youth, he generally sees the potential in music to be one of reshaping society at large through the multitude of individual psyches away from the Western (especially American) dilemmas of racism, sexism, materialism, and earth-raping and toward the more balanced orientations of older, wiser cultures. Which brings us back to his viewpoint of the blues, and to Sun Ra.

Lock points out[51] that the acquisition of a personal name to supplant or augment that inherited through slave masters is a time-honored blues tradition (e.g. Leadbelly, Jelly Roll, Muddy, Lightnin', etc.). Herman Blount took on the name Sun Ra because it transported him back past European America, past Western European civilization, past the poetry of his native ghetto culture and into the *persona* of the god-king of what the West itself calls the "cradle of civilization:" Egypt. Ra's readings in African history led him to a picture of ancient Egypt as a quintessentially black African empire, one from which, through Greece and Rome, the Western world got its start. Contemporary African American scholarship around this subject has burgeoned since the 1950s period of Braxton's childhood and Sun Ra's first discovery of George James and other black Egyptologists.[52]

The result of this thinking and knowledge is that the blues tradition, in all its expressions through the black church, through popular music and jazz, and through the black classical tradition, is recast as the vestiges of a musiculture solidified in ancient Egypt. This Egypt had as much concourse with the empires of the African interior as with those off its continent. The "blues people" thus represent not the evolution of a primitive folk catching up with the West, nor even the continuing refinement of a differently developed culture foreign to the West and trying to adapt to it. Rather, they are those whose African American musiculture provides an access to the very source of the Western culture. Perhaps this explains the abovementioned speed and profundity with which the African American musiculture recapitulated the evolution of almost a thousand years of Western music in the two short centuries since African Americans tackled European instruments and concepts: they were *remembering* something they once knew rather than learning something foreign, and they were recollecting its former potency and purity more than learning its present decadence (saxophonist

the music's parents   **87**

Sidney Bechet, for example, called jazz "the remembering song"). In any case, this viewpoint captures our concern—Braxton's *personal* mythology of the blues—better than any based in the reality of a marginalized down-and-outer.

It is the vestigial embodiment of that same mythological Egypt that Braxton also sees in the West, especially in its mystical traditions as handed down through the Rosicrucians, the Freemasons, and hundreds of artists, spiritual mavericks, scientists and philosophers who have managed to have some success in bringing the mainstream literate (post-Enlightenment, rationalistic, scientific) culture back in line with the balance of its own oral spiritual, holistic, magical/mythical roots. This is the legacy Braxton claims when he champions both pre- and post-tonal European music, and when he stakes his own claim on European as much as on African American cultural turf.

Fig. 2.8: 40P *(1976) is a free extended line (much like Eddie Harris'* Freedom Jazz Dance *or Ornette Coleman's* Blues Connotation) *weaving around a minor chord vamping on a repeated rhythm. Abrams varies and shifts the chords on the vamp, while Braxton solos on contrabass clarinet; then Braxton plays (and alters) root notes in the same rhythm while Abrams solos. Braxton wrote this about the piece: "... an atonal line structure whose structural nature is positioned somewhere in between the works of composers like Charles Mingus and Ornette Coleman ... The reality of this music moves to reawaken our memories about the last five hundred years by calling our attention to the primary basis of the 'blues' ... a vibrational blues structure that reestablishes what this continuance can mean in the open space implications of the music.*

The blues will go on forever."[53] *(emphases mine, to link with this chapter's discussions of Coleman).*

This is a simple example of how something perceived as "avant-garde" from the Western perspective is in fact, rather, radical in its return to roots. The modern blues tradition as it has evolved in the music industry dates only to the late 1800s, when musical Africanisms crossed with the couplet-and-refrain (AAB) style of English balladry. To "free" the blues—or whatever words and music are being made—from the Western harmonic and metric structure shaping them to then go where they will—which freedom Mingus indeed started and Coleman furthered—is not to lose boundaries into thin air but rather to dig into their psychic roots (expressed timbrally beautifully here by the choice of low reed). Specific historical roots are evoked too; the "last five hundred years" takes us back to the European discovery of America and subsequent rise of the slave trade. 40P has a form and structure, but they are de-rigidified to better serve the life they contain, much as a Spanish flamenco piece or West African jali's story-song are today and would have been during Europe's Age of Exploration.

Ornette Coleman, with whom Braxton lived for a time and whom he acknowledges as the inspiration for his decision to be a composer, also resonates with this broad-based legacy shared by black and white rural America, including the ecstasies of the church.[54] In the '50s and '60s, Coleman shocked the black more than (arguably) the white elements of the jazz and classical communities when he redirected the improvisational rules of the music away from Western song forms and harmonic system to the more organic ground of melody and counterpoint cycling freely through repetition and variation common to Africa and premodern Europe.[55]

Coleman grew up in Texas, which has both strong fiddle and blues traditions; he brought a distinctly country sound to what people called his "free" jazz. One of its freedoms was from harmonic structure (chords); another was from metrical structure (though not from regular pulse; Braxton, with the AACM, led the way in that). Coleman's approach tapped the root in the music that predated the mergers of the field hollers and work songs with the couplet/refrain (AAB) form of the Anglo American ballads that flourished between 1870 and 1915, mergers that gave birth to the standard blues and jazz structures.

Second-line Pawns: Gentrified Black, Gentrified White

Minstrelsy, Ragtime

Plantation songs, such as those made famous by Stephen Foster, were a minstrel-show staple throughout the last century. Musically, they were European stylizations that *simulated* African syncopation (in other words, didn't "swing"). They suggested African musical colors by overuse of the sixth interval and the

the music's parents

"amen" cadence from the subdominant to the tonic chord. The spiritual, as popularized abroad by Fisk University's Fisk Jubilee Singers, combined with the plantation songs to establish a widely embraced presence of the African American culture, however Europeanized, in white America.

Ragtime developed after Emancipation, when black pianists could travel and work in saloons, dance halls, and brothels (*Groves* says, "it is thought to be a transfer of the music previously done on banjo").[56] The piano is a percussive instrument as much as melodic-harmonic; the syncopation of ragtime (originally "ragged time"; later generations might have called it polyrhythmic) was much more complex than anything any other single instrument could produce, and it caught the ears of the whole American public by the end of the 19th century.

Mellers dismisses ragtime as black music emasculated in its attempt to be white.[57] In this, he is aligned with many European and European American scholars who look to African and African American culture as a sort of noble savagery in which they might find respite from their disenchantment with their own less noble but also less savage civilization. The necessary condition for this respite is that the effete stay the effete and the savage the savage. If the savage dares lay claim to an expression deemed effete, he or she is rebuked and scorned. Braxton, ever the cross-cultural synthesist, has spoken out often against such denigrations.

Fig. 2.9: From flute part to Composition 96. Pianist Cecil Taylor has called the piano "88 tuned drums";[58] Braxton's instructions to ensemble members trying to read his scores depict the pitch range this way, giving rhythm primacy. This example from 96 shows Braxton's rhythmic offsets (and one line of his horizontally layered pitch relationships) at about as high a level of density and complexity as they get. Nevertheless, they aren't any more so than a typical moment of focused improvisational abandon (e.g., Cecil Taylor's, or anyone's, not just Braxton's) might produce. In fact, this is the sort of thing Braxton improvises at the piano, which he uses to compose, and which moved him to create a solo alto sax music through which to develop as a composer. Braxton's way of getting young music students who've never heard of him or his music to play this material is to tell them to target the down beats and hit as many as they can; the rest, he says, will begin to fall in place with repeated attempts. It

does. The lesson: literate media can mystify and complexify what is, in the fact of oral/aural experience, simple and direct.

Because the piano is so like a one-instrument orchestra, it evolved a solo tradition parallel to that of the conventional jazz band (as we'll see when we delve into Braxton's music, his use of the piano reflects this relationship more than the one in which piano serves the more hierarchical end of holding *down* the harmonic matrix for the *upper* voices to solo *over*). In this century's beginning, ragtime led to the stride and blues (a.k.a. barrelhouse or boogie-woogie) styles of playing. Stride was essentially ragtime—single bass notes or octaves alternating with backbeat chords in the left hand and florid figures in the right—with more improvisation, and with the looser rhythmic feel of the new "hot" music of the 1920s (then recently dubbed "jazz"). Blues was more rhythmic, less harmonically ambitious, and consisted of a single-note bass line in the left and single-note melodies in the right, both often repeated. The blues pianists worked mostly in the south and midwest; Fats Waller was among the schooled stride pianists of the northeastern cities.

Braxton names Waller (who was also a formally trained Bach fanatic) as one of the three sources of the solo piano music that inspired him to create his solo saxophone music (the other two were Arnold Schönberg and Karlheinz Stockhausen). Braxton viewed his saxophone as a piano equivalent. It was not an instrument, obviously, that could match the keyboard's polyphonic potential, but one which, through extended and alternate techniques, could be mined for equally valuable musical ore that was equally refinable for ensembles of instruments and for theoretical constructs, and equally presentable on its own in concert and recordings. Additionally, Braxton's first and some of his most significant notated scores are for solo piano; these have continued to figure prominently in his quartet music (see Chapter Eight). In his trio music, the piano has often been called in as a sort of rhythmic and textural reflection of music originally conceived for three single-line instruments (e.g., 6D; see Chapter Seven). One of his most important works, *Composition 95* (we'll see why, in Chapter Six), was scored for two pianos.

In short, Braxton the composer drew much from the African American solo piano tradition impressed upon him from popular ragtimers such as Scott Joplin through the stride style of Fats Waller through Art Tatum (via Muhal Richard Abrams) to Thelonious Monk and Cecil Taylor—and, of course, the various pianists he's collaborated with, whom we'll meet in the third and fourth sections. Braxton's music has served to liberate the solo piano tradition from its timekeeping and chordal functions and bring out its potential for expanded virtuosity. In other words, his use of the piano in ensemble is very much an appropriation of the solo piano for his own brand of "ensembles of soloists."

Albert Murray defines the jazz tradition as part and parcel with the blues tradition; his *Stomping the Blues* ranges from the pre-jazz Mississippi Delta to the beboppers' New York.[59] As jazz became established in major urban centers, its richest soil continued to come from more rural regions, all their roads leading through the cities to New Orleans, then Chicago, then New York.

The cities have functioned as the busiest, most intense crossroads of Euro- and Afrocentric currents. Finite opportunities and resources, paying markets, competition and cooperation were all there in fullest force. In the beginning, the challenge to blacks was to master the Western harmonic system; to whites it was the African rhythmic base and improvisational skills; to both, it was to come to terms with the cultural premises underlying each others' musical spins in order to fulfill the promise and potential of the common American culture and its music. (Perhaps this explains why social struggles and experimentation, such as those concerning sexual and racial mores, often come about in the arts before other parts of the society.) This struggle for such mastery by all the musicians cast them in the role of musical warriors, or knights.

The Knights: Urban Blacks and Whites

New Orleans

The most important of the early urban flowerings of jazz took place in New Orleans. Of all American cities, it really was *the* multicultural gathering ground. First inhabited by Native Americans, it fell to the first Spanish settlers with their African slaves, making it early on a mainland American city with a full measure of the Latin American influence. Later it took in the French presence, and later still the English.

In New Orleans, true to these roots, intermarriage and other cultural intimacies happened more naturally, and kinships were less denied; many pockets of such populations mellowed into models of racial harmony.[60] Most importantly to jazz, the drums were never outlawed, only limited to Congo Square. There they, with dance, evolved over time from a religious ritual into a musical performance.

The earliest "dance" bands, from which "jazz" would start to come, still stuck fairly close to the more brittle rhythms of ragtime. They consisted of violin, cornet, clarinet, trombone, drums, double bass, and banjo or guitar. Gradually, the saxophone family—novelty instruments in both vaudeville and European classical music—replaced the clarinet as the choice jazz woodwind voice. Through such players as Sidney Bechet, Coleman Hawkins, Lester Young, Charlie Parker, John Coltrane, Sonny Rollins, Ornette Coleman, and Braxton, saxophones would take on a preeminent significance among jazz instruments unmatched in any other music.

By the late 1920s and early 1930s, jazz had entered the mainstream of white America as an important popular music, by way of New Orleans, St. Louis, San Francisco, Los Angeles, Chicago, Kansas City, and New York. The time for this was ripe for sociocultural reasons as much as aesthetic ones. The old white American survivor's ethic of hard work, rugged individualism, and emotional taciturnity subsided as the country finally became more or less settled and governed. World War I exposed thousands of Americans to less racist and more sensual white societies, not to mention the stark face of mortality. Pleasure and self-expression became more acceptable, and dance halls, cabarets, Tin Pan Alley, fancy restaurants, and Broadway theaters proliferated. Sound recording technology and cinema spread the new spirit to the masses. The forces behind the 1920 Prohibition law were a backlash to this spirit and provoked an even stronger reaction in the new, mostly young "libertines." The modern entertainment industry was born, and jazz was central to it. The very time was called the Jazz Age.

For their part, African Americans migrated north, especially to Chicago (Braxton's parents among them), in great numbers. It was in the 1920s that the first recordings of black bands—which is to say the first of the jazz recordings that would prove historically important—were made. New Orleans trombonist Kid Ory cut them in Los Angeles, his new home base. King Oliver's Creole Jazz Band cut many more in Chicago, which was fast preempting New Orleans as the center of the music. It was that band's alumni, in the 60-some Hot Five and Hot Seven recordings done by Louis Armstrong from 1925 to 1927, that really brought the music to the rest of the world's attention, and to the American public's total embrace.

The big-band era had its seeds in the larger dance orchestras of the '20s and early '30s. Both white (Paul Whiteman, Ben Pollack, Red Nichols) and black orchestra leaders (Jimmie Lunceford, Fate Marable, Bennie Moten, Duke Ellington, Fletcher Henderson) were competing to entertain, with a variety of trials and errors. Both camps tried to strike the right balance between popular dance music, "symphonic" (sweet) *arrangements* of New Orleans jazz elements, and spirited *presentations* of the New Orleans (hot) players themselves, as featured soloists. The musical dynamic between these smooth society ensembles and the rocking, boisterous New Orleans solo improvisers led to the thing called swing.

In the hands of clarinetist/saxophonist Sidney Bechet, pianist Jelly Roll Morton, and trumpeter Louis Armstrong, a certain lightness and looseness had come into the music. "Swing" has always been one of those words that signifies much to the *cognoscenti* but is hard to define. Some of the palpable musical elements that bore it were

- the use of vibrato only at the end of phrases or long notes that, in contrast to the "legit" style of unflagging vibrato, served to release or introduce tension, rather than sustain it;
- a speech-like spicing of the melodic line with accents and pitch and dynamic nuances;
- a placing of the notes slightly around, before, or behind the beat rather than squarely on it;
- a division of that beat from ragtime's two to early jazz's four to, finally, swing's uneven eighth notes, resulting in a more relaxed yet also busier sound.

Braxton's music has been conspicuously criticized for not "swinging"—but so has that of Lester Young, Miles Davis, John Coltrane, Thelonious Monk, Charlie Parker and Dizzy Gillespie, Charles Mingus, and a host of other such luminaries throughout the music's history—*whenever it departed from the norm, as both/either African and/or European American cultures defined it, in a given time.* "In advance of" might be more accurate than "away from," given that the charges were dropped on all of the above offenders over time, including Braxton,[61] though he has arguably gone so much further "in advance" with his

the music's parents

music that it may take more time for the mainstream to catch up. In any case, these charges suggest one admittedly ambiguous but definable trait of "swing": that which the consensus of informed opinion, sooner or later, more or less universally perceives as such in the music (is it simply the relaxation that comes with mastery of and familiarity with anything?).

Jazz receded somewhat during the years of Prohibition and into the Great Depression. The public was not in its earlier Jazz Age mood nor prosperity, and many saw the music as a fad that had had its day. When it came back, however, it came on strong. White big bands such as those of Benny Goodman, the Dorseys, Glenn Miller, Artie Shaw, Harry James; and the black ensembles led by Lunceford, Chick Webb, Ellington, and Count Basie filled a hunger for dance music, strong in both cultures, that coincided with the 1933 repeal of Prohibition.

These bands were stating the latest words in the jazz lexicon, but improvisation did not play that large a part. Solos were short and simple; the main thrust was rhythmic and compositional. Improvisation was always important to the musicians themselves, however, and most of them developed it in jam sessions "after the gig."

Basie's band was somewhat the exception to this polarization; it was closer in spirit than many to the blues, and the midwestern blues at that. The force of these roots in the big-band format showed through arrangements that were often layers of riffs and textures put together spontaneously, to feature both the ensemble and soloists in a relaxed, fruitful interaction. The rural feel also included a wide-open sense of space in the sound, in which the diversity of the soloists' styles and the ensemble's collective ideas had room to play themselves out. The Basie band's famous relaxed rhythmic feel and minimal use of notes can be understood as the necessary musical environment for open-minded but grounded experimentation. Whether or not it was consciously intended, it did provide that environment, suffused as it was with another one of jazz's many numinously charged qualities: "cool."

Basie tenorist Lester Young is seminal to the modern concept of cool, and of Braxton's major influences, both African- and European American. Lock quotes Braxton as saying, "I was coming from a Lester Young forming affinity continuum: from Lester Young on through Bird to Konitz, to Marsh, then into Jackie McLean."[62] Young's career bridged the Jazz Age of the 1920s and the bop era of the 1940s. It was a bridge built in the swing era of big bands, which led directly from the earlier Fletcher Henderson through the bebop bands to Sun Ra, and, through Count Basie's and Charles Mingus' large ensembles to the flowering of Braxton's music in large ensembles (see Chapter Nine). To really get to the essence of Young, we have to consider another major piece in our chess game.

The Queen

Think back to the ancient matriarchal Old World cultures touched on in the last chapter. Recall especially the presence of the snake as a symbol of worship, as we look at a fascinating figure who virtually established the New Orleans voodoo (from *vodou*) culture that would have been suppressed anywhere else in the country, and maybe there as well without the force of her personality.

Marie Laveau, a racially mixed free woman of color, was known by 1830 as the "queen of the voodoos" in New Orleans, where she reigned until her death in the 1880s. Her embrace of both *vodou* and Catholicism, her connections to several cultures (her father was a rich white landowner), and her politically strong and active presence as a community spiritual leader throughout the Civil War and Reconstruction had the effect of legitimizing a culture with shadowy associations. Ventura writes, "What elsewhere in the South was a people that had to disguise its expression and conceal its spirit became in her reign a true culture, a culture that felt its identity deeply *as a culture*. And only out of such intensely felt culture could a creation like jazz be born."[63]

Laveau's dances in Congo Square, some with serpents and fish, were legendary for their skill and spirit. Her influence is still signaled by women such as blues singer Victoria Spivey, who as late as the 1960s used as a personal logo a picture of a woman "wearing" a snake on her shoulders; and St. Louis author Luisah Teish, a modern *vodou* priestess active with the important players from the Black Artists Group (close Braxton collaborators) of the same decade.[64]

The *New Grove Dictionary of Jazz* has some 30 to 40 entries about male

Fig 2.10: From Braxton's Composition 55 *(composer's score). This sax sectional is one of many such throughout Braxton's works for his extension of the big band ("creative orchestra") inspired by the masters (Ellington and Basie as well as Sun Ra) of that tradition. His are characterized by atonality and intervallic leaping, but they share the tight couplings and doublings common to the straight repertoire, with perhaps more flair toward the "supersax" approach of harmonizing a section presumed to consist of players who are all "first chair."*

artists for every one about a female. Jazz has primarily been the sport of male instrumentalists; even those few males who sing often play an instrument as well, which has rarely been the case with the women. Of the women *Grove* does mention, the names of only a handful approach household-word status—Bessie Smith, Billie Holiday, Sarah Vaughan, Ella Fitzgerald, Dinah Washington—but those few have had an impact, both as musicians and as cultural icons of womanhood, that have proven a subtle but formidable match for the male chauvinism entrenched in both black and white American traditions.

The early blues vocals that set the stage for modern jazz singing had a distinct gender split. Men like Leadbelly and Blind Lemon Jefferson dominated a country, street-singing tradition that has evolved through urban migrations, generations, and technology into modern rock and roll. But it was a group of women who *first* recorded the blues, in the early 1920s. They were closer to vaudeville and thus to the jazz performance style than men like Jefferson and Leadbelly, and they set the emotional, technical, and expressive parameters on which later jazz and non-rock pop singing styles were built. Ma Rainey, Bessie Smith, and Mamie Smith made the first of the highly successful race records of the time, which exposed African Americans (and the white Americans and Europeans who were interested) *en masse* to the best of their music. Many of them even led their own groups in which some important men—including saxophonist Coleman Hawkins, in Mamie Smith's Jazz Hounds—got their starts. Other women, such as Ethel Waters, drew, again, on a vaudeville background to expand from the blues into presentations of Tin Pan Alley songs for musical theater in a jazz style.

Braxton, in his *Tri-Axium Writings 1* ("Trans-African Music"), gives Louis Armstrong his due as the major figure he was (see Chapter Four). In fact, Lil Hardin, Armstrong's first wife, played a major role in furthering Armstrong's career once he arrived in Chicago.[65]

Braxton has also expressed his profound disagreement with the critics who panned Billie Holiday's later work by going so far as to say hearing it changed his life.[66] Holiday got her famous nickname "Lady Day" from Braxton's "affinity continuum" forbear, Lester Young. These two enjoyed a profound rapport that looks, in hindsight, like the delicate balance of the gender forces at the eye of their more volatile hurricane. This dynamic is worth examining for its importance to both Braxton's music and the larger jazz tradition, because both Young and Holiday turned and furthered the tide of the music with their particular magic and power.

Holiday took the blues and the popular song material of vocalists into an emotional depth that never swallowed up her presence of mind. Where Bessie Smith might have exorcised her pain by obliterating it in song, or numerous others from Louis Armstrong to Ella Fitzgerald lightened it by effectively singing it away, Holiday carved melodic lines on lyrics that unflinchingly traced the emotional power and shadings being expressed. She was intrepid in this way, a combination of vulnerability and inspiration that made her a timeless beacon for all musicians.

Part of her strength and stability through her rocky path came from her enduring friendship with Young. That they loved to make music together was simply a manifestation of their bond. They weren't lovers—each had their own mates or affairs—but they were certainly soul mates. Holiday had a lot of trouble with men; Young's nickname for her surrounded her with an aura of gentility and refinement she could grow into and draw on for protection over her difficult life.

For his part, Young was also troubled by men, in a sense. He was widely loved and respected for his talent, but he was also envied and left to flounder for his eccentric, almost feminine manner in a time and culture of macho camaraderie. He had trouble being taken seriously by business and media people because he kept to himself and his music in a world of his own language and mannerisms. He spoke softly in his own private slang, part of which tagged everyone he liked, men and women, with the nickname "Lady," which stood to him for class and elegance.[67] Holiday accepted and cherished what he was, which surely empowered and affirmed him in his upstream swim as much as he did her in hers. His playing style was much lighter and more refined—"whiter"—than that of his peers, and if he hadn't had the confidence to stick to it, they would have blown him away. And if they had, swing would have had a much harder time transforming into bebop, as it did largely through his influence. In the highly competitive jam sessions of his day, Young was perceived as blowing everyone else away, even the paragon of the heavier, less cerebral and more emotional "black" style, Coleman Hawkins. Young's ideas were endless; they floated and soared like light above the heat of the rest of the music, kept coming on after others had spent themselves. Young was in all these ways similar to Braxton in character, genius, and in his ups and downs with his peers.

Amiri Baraka has scoffed, rightly, at the notion that the greatest advances in jazz came when black artists mastered white concepts or styles.[68] Still, Baraka may be missing the point. The best *American* music *does* happen when the most disparate cultures (and, for that matter, genders and generations) succeed in achieving a mutually enhancing synthesis.

Young is not among the category of players Braxton cites as his main models—the restructuralists—but he is the supreme example of a *stylist* who arguably opened up as many doors as such innovators as Parker, Coltrane, or Coleman.

The quality Lester Young embodied—"cool," as it came to be known in jazz—is one that defined some of the most vital streams of the music to come through Parker, Miles Davis, the white players who influenced Braxton, and Braxton himself. When "cool" has been criticized, it's been called "cold." Young took heat for it; the beboppers were considered cold by many; white players like Marsh, Lennie Tristano, Konitz, Stan Getz, and Desmond have all suffered varying degrees of neglect and reverse, "Crow Jim" discrimination over it; and Braxton has certainly carried the burden for it in his own time. Yet all these players have also been acknowledged and proven as more vital, universal, and noteworthy in the history of the music than a host of other, less problematic artists.

What is this quality? What makes it so fertile and problematic at the same time?

Thompson talks about the importance of "cool" among the (matriarchal, goddess-oriented) Yoruba people of Africa, a quality he sees matched in American jazz musicians:

> Like character, coolness ought to be internalized as a governing principle for a person to merit the high praise, "His heart is cool" (*okan e tutu*). In becoming sophisticated, a Yoruba adept learns to differentiate between forms of spiritual coolness . . . So heavily charged is this concept with ideas of beauty and correctness that a fine carnelian bead or a passage of exciting drumming may be praised as "cool.". . . Coolness, then, is a part of character . . . To the degree that we live generously and discreetly, exhibiting grace under pressure, our appearance and our acts gradually assume virtual royal power. As we become noble, fully realizing the spark of creative goodness God endowed us with . . . we find the confidence to cope with all kinds of situations. This is *ashe*. This is character. This is mystic coolness. All one. Paradise is regained, for Yoruba art returns the idea of heaven to mankind wherever the ancient ideal attitudes are genuinely manifested.[69]

The "grace under pressure," the "generosity and discretion" the jazz artists who exhibit cool have manifested, lay in their ability and willingness to leave the safety of their own psychological and emotional moorings, both those of their cultures and their individual egos, in order to build the bridges that can and must be built between their own worlds and those foreign, even hostile, to them. The blacks who have done it are those who are secure enough in their blackness to remove it from its given context and try it out in less amenable and familiar but potentially more rewarding contexts. The whites who have made significant contributions to jazz are not those content to appreciate "black" rhythmic and improvisational grace and intensity from a safe distance but instead claim them as part of a common humanity, even if their own expressions of them will never be from within the same original cultural context. Those compelled by cool are compelled to vulnerability by strength, and compassion, in the promise of greater strength and understanding.

Cool has fortified and inspired those possessed by and possessing it to swim upstream against the currents in which they were spawned, sometimes at great personal cost, often ignored or put down, and to connect on the very highest level of the synthesis' potential. Cool is not cold, even though its warmth doesn't come from the home fire's hearth; its own body heat keeps it warm as it strikes out on its nighttime journey.

The Kings of Bop and Cool—Check!

By the beginning of World War II, big-band swing was in its heyday as America's popular music, but the young musicians coming up saw it in decline. A new generation of African Americans was waking up to the racial and social situation in the culture and getting a sense that they could change it. They had seen their music spread abroad and throughout the country, and they were becoming more aware of it as theirs. They resented what they saw as the commercial appropriation of it and the exploitation of them by whites, and they turned away from trying to please the white culture in favor of pleasing their own, where at least they were understood and welcomed. They turned away from older entertainers such as Louis Armstrong, Fats Waller, Cab Calloway and others, whom they saw as show business Uncle Toms. They struck a very different pose.

Charlie Parker and Dizzy Gillespie were the high priests (or, as per our chess game, the black kings launching an unguarded offensive against the white king) of this exclusively, at first, African American quantum leap. Both were veterans of the swing era, Kansas City-based Parker particularly influenced by Lester Young. Gillespie had pioneered the harmonic underpinnings of bop in his characteristically conscious, probing way as a big-band soloist and arranger. He "altered" chords by shifting their pitches chromatically, which at first sounded very discordant to audiences. Parker had more of an intuitive knack for creating bop's sweeping harmonic extensions and polyrhythmic patterns, by playing his long alto lines of even eighth notes outside the pulse and metric structure in remarkably cohesive ways. Both expanded the improvisational palette to include the notes stacked above the basic triad that had previously been used only for color in passing. Both were also intellectuals with a studied awareness of the arts and letters of Western culture.

The attainment of bop was a musical apotheosis for African Americans. It took shape in small groups more concerned with playing for each other and peers than for the public, much like early European string quartets. It allowed for a technical virtuosity and conceptual sophistication that matched those of the European classical tradition, and that also matched and expanded on the rhythmic base that had *always* surpassed that of European music. It was informed by the global and social awareness that would light the way for the Civil Rights Movement and the predominantly white Beat literary/social and hippie movements of the next two decades that would prove so important to white American culture. Bop validated the music that came before it and opened the way for that to come after as deserving of the culture's highest regard. It was a move that put the white (cultural) king in check, by mastering his own (musical) terms and strategies.

Fig. 2.11a: Opening bars of *Donna Lee*.[70]

the music's parents 99

2.11b: From Braxton's *23B*.

Fig 2.11: Donna Lee *with Braxton's 23B. Braxton calls the latter an "atonal version" of the former. In performance, it often starts on the high concert G above the half-note transitional section, the same note that opens* Donna Lee; *the contour of the line from that point also reflects the original's.*

Covers of traditional jazz material and the music of masters he particularly admires—e.g., Thelonious Monk, Lennie Tristano, and most recently, Parker (at this writing, he has just recorded a tribute to Charlie Parker CD in Europe)— have made up a substantial part of Braxton's recorded and live output from the beginning. In fact, he was the first jazz artist ever to call a jazz recording (of standards) In the Tradition (see Chapter Five). Those who insulate themselves from the implications of his work by dismissing it as outside the "jazz" game are either willfully or ignorantly mistaken.

Charlie Parker

Many writers and fellow musicians have named Young as Charlie Parker's main influence. To a great degree, he obviously was an influence, but Parker— definitely a restructuralist—himself said once, "I was crazy about Lester. He played so clean and beautiful. But I wasn't influenced by Lester. Our ideas ran on differently."[71]

Of Parker, Green asks:

> How can a man complicate an art form technically and at the same time simplify it emotionally? He can only achieve this if his emotional depth is so profound that not only can it cleanse the existing form with its attendant rules and conventions, but can accept further complexities and still manage to retain the effect of simplicity. That is why Charlie Parker might be said to have possessed a melodic gift greater than any other jazz musician before him.[72]

Young is famous for his lyrical sweetness, while Parker is more often thought of as a rhythmic and harmonic genius, but Green's point is well taken. Critics and peers were hostile to bop in many quarters, calling it cold and cerebral—exactly the response Braxton has provoked. But time has proven that Parker's genius lay not in abandoning the melodic heart in favor of the harmonic mind, but of expanding both in a balanced relationship—in other words, breaking the stereotype of African American genius being of heart and blood, but not, like European genius, of mind. Braxton is enjoyed by his audience precisely for bringing as much heart as intellect to the leading edge of exploration of new territory, where *heartless* head is a fearful thing but where heart (consistent with its etymology) means courage. To make the musical connection, Braxton's expansion (following Coleman) of the tonal palette past tonality and the rhythmic divisions bop made on the basic two-, three-, and four-meters into yet more varied divisions on more diverse meters are an obvious step or two down the same lines the bop masters laid down, themselves continuing the tradition of Africanizing Western premises.

Braxton was put off by Parker when he first heard him, in the same way others were, for the same reasons. He was used to a sweeter, more accessible sound, from Young through white players. But Parker was the quintessential blues player, a restructuralist because he could take that same "vibrational information" encoded and transmitted in the blues and extend it into the highest Western and urban complexities of chromaticism and African complexities of rhythm. Braxton didn't fail to unearth this in due course, and his own treatments, however elastic, of *Donna Lee* and other bop standards (see Chapter Five) would become an important part of his mature music.

Perhaps the spirit, however, would again play an even larger role for Braxton than its actual musical expression in his influence, as this quote about the latter from Green might well apply to Braxton:

> He was a lone musical spirit to whom compromise was an alien and uncomprehended thing. The playing speaks without compromise. There is no fooling when Parker plays. He puts into it everything he knows and feels. The best he can hope for is that somehow the emotional force of the performance will convey itself to ears unversed in the laws of harmonic exploration.[73]

Above the Game:
Black Meets White Where Grays Are Cool

Parallel to the bop revolution was a mainly white move toward a new sort of symphonic jazz, this one more musically fertile than that of the 1920s. The big bands of Stan Kenton, Claude Thornhill, Woody Herman, and Boyd Raeburn drew not only on bop but on the then current European art music, especially that of Stravinsky and Debussy, for harmonic, voicing, and tonal texturing devices. Their playbills would include symphony-like tone poems and suites. Small groups featuring Thornhill arranger Gil Evans, Gerry Mulligan, Lennie Tristano, Lee Konitz, and Warne Marsh cropped up and made some even more cerebral music that mystified the listeners but fascinated fellow musicians. Until Miles Davis came in on the band with Evans and Mulligan, this music—now actually called the "cool school"—was as predominantly white as bop was black. But even Davis' band was a flop with the public, although its recording *Birth of the Cool* went on to become a classic.

Braxton's very first sax influence, as mentioned, was Paul Desmond, whose style fell within this area of the music, as well as in Young's shadow. It may be that growing up exposed to white culture through the media but not in person (Braxton didn't have much personal contact with whites until high school), his own personality traits, and the timely occurrence of Brubeck's popular success combined to give this curious and gifted teenager easy access to Desmond's playing. In any case, something gave him early on an openness to the white aesthetic that was unthreatened by the sociopolitical complexities struggled with by his fellow militants/musicians. He certainly claimed his right from the first, even during the peak of the nationalism and militancy with which his own public image was associated, to acknowledge and honor white jazz masters.

What are the musical characteristics of the white "cool" styles that spoke so sympathetically to Braxton? What in his own music did they feed and inform?

Lee, while seeing a polarity between white and black expressions in jazz, also points out the spectrum they define as one that successfully synthesizes "hitherto divorced elements of the human personality."[74] White players had difficulty with the music, he says, because they initially lacked access to it. When they did, their understanding and treatment, especially of rhythmic and expressive techniques, remained much of the time at the level of parody. As jazz evolved, it became a badge of honor among intellectual white critics to champion what was genuine about black jazz and artificial in white. Very few blacks were going to kick about this, in the highly competitive, high-stakes, and usually racially inequitable game of the music business (although, as Braxton points out, musical camaraderie has been an integrated phenomenon from early on too, among a few cursed/blessed with the gift of genius, such as Louis Armstrong and white trombonist Jack Teagarden, to name only one of many such bonds to follow).

Lee's diagnosis of white inadequacy in the beginning revolves around the very things Braxton likes most about his own white musical heroes. Lee says that the white bands of the 1920s didn't have ears "acute enough to make the fine distinctions of accent and weight, and they did not perceive the nature of the balance between rhythmic insistence and rhythmic variety"; and that the black *sound*, even on sentimental ballads, had a roundness to it that came from the blues, whereas whites were hearing jazz as merely hotter versions of Victorian drawing room music, "and thus sought after a cruder version of the violinist's *vibrato* and *portamento* techniques. In the hands of dance musicians the latter became a rather tasteless *glissando* in crude emulation of the alterations of pitch used in the blues."[75]

If white mastery in jazz would thus be defined by the strengthening of these weaknesses, then Braxton, as we see in Lock, responded to just the right things in the music of Paul Desmond and Warne Marsh: their sounds and the "gravallic" (or "gravillic," Braxton neologisms derived from "gravity," a force he ascribes metaphorically to the attraction of a given pulse or tone) *weight* of their musical inventions, established by their ways of relating to rhythm.

Noting the exception of Miles Davis, Lee begins his discussion of the post-bop cool school as a predominantly white movement to embrace the advances bop made on elements held in high regard in the Western European tradition—harmony and composition—while "refining" out the "heldover" Africanisms of hot tone, extreme emotional expression, and driving beat. "These were transmuted into a thinner tone without vibrato, a very restrained use of blues techniques, and a clear, lightly swinging beat."[76]

Of Tristano and company, Braxton's main source of inspiration, Lee writes:

> Other than in smoothness of tone and attack, he differed from his contemporaries in his use of unusual passing notes, and movements into bitonality, together with the construction of asymmetrical phrases and striking cross rhythms. His approach was conscious in the way which that of a conservatory composer is, and his music has much the same virtues and limitations.[77]

While Lee ends up calling the cool school "retrogressive" in the evolution of jazz, he accedes several positive contributions that have clear significance for Braxton and other experimenters of the 1960s: single-line instruments were allowed to stand on their own without a piano (in Gerry Mulligan's groups), and improvisation free of song forms (though not their basic harmonic-melodic logic) took place and succeeded, in Tristano's work with horns and rhythm section, even on record. Marsh is *the* seminal influence on Braxton from this school. Davis' analysis of him bears quoting:

> Laboring in relative obscurity ... Marsh has matured into one of the most stimulating improvisers in jazz. His cool, liquid style is spiked with paradox. Playing a pop standard, he will frequently dissolve its melody completely in an attempt to isolate and purify its harmonic base. Yet the new melodies he stretches over the chords are usually appealing and memorable in their own right, and the *ideal* of melody is something he bears proudly and carefully aloft, as though it were a sacred chalice from which he were (*sic*) determined not to spill one sacred drop. Although he is a melodic player, however, he is not

really a lyrical one in the conventional sense—his tone is one of the palest and brittlest in jazz. He has a knack for rhythmic displacement, and he uses silence and space almost as tellingly, if not as mischievously, as Thelonious Monk did—he speaks of *"the ability to play the rests and give them meaning, too."* But because he is not a virile, breast-beating swinger, many of his rhythmic subtleties are lost on all but his most attentive and sophisticated audiences. Above all else, there is an inner-directed quality to Marsh's best solos, a feeling of rigorous soul-searching as intense as that which one hears in John Coltrane, but more diffident in character. There is nothing purgative, nothing Promethean, or sheerly physical about Marsh's solos. Rather, one hears in them what critic Harvey Pekar has described as *"the kind of intense concentration a scientist must feel when deeply involved in his work."* No doubt it is this quality of passionate intellectual involvement which draws some listeners to Marsh at the same time it keeps larger numbers seeking simpler, more immediate pleasures away. (emphases mine: recall the importance to Cage of silence as a musical concept; and Braxton often describes his composing work as that of a scientist in his laboratory)[78]

About Desmond, Braxton told Lock the sound was the first thing that attracted him; after that, the logic.

It looked like he was a very slow player, but in fact he was making very quick decisions, and because he understood his craft so well his music has this air of easiness about it, as if it's just kind of floating . . . Desmond understood how to get to the point quicker than most players ever learn. This is a lightning-fast improviser, who understood sound logic and how to prepare the event.[79]

When Lock asked Braxton if any of his records showed Desmond's influence, he said:

All of my recordings show the influence of Paul Desmond. But remember, I never wanted to imitate anybody because that would insult the masters [elsewhere, however, Braxton says, "I used to play very much like Paul Desmond and Warne Marsh before I began to digest and learn from Coltrane's music" —M. H.] What I liked about them was that they found their own way . . . It's the ones who've put together their own language, their own syntax, their own way of being—those are the ones I'm interested in. That's why I love Paul. Plus, he understood how not to let even ruffles and flourishes get in the way of singing from the heart.[80]

It was after taking in the Desmond sound and style that Braxton first heard Charlie Parker, with whom at first, he says, he didn't click. Neither did he really understand him. As he grew a taste for Parker, he still never idolized him to the extent that most saxophonists did, calling him one of several "restructuralists on a continuum with Lester Young, Coleman Hawkins, and Wardell Gray."

In trying to describe his concept of "gravallic" visually, Braxton draws lines with peaks and valleys (depicting high and low intervals) that move from left to right like an EKG reading of a heartbeat, with an imaginary transecting flat line broken by the pulse of the beat.[81] The relationship between the pulse and peaks and valleys is where the gravillic profundity or lack of it will manifest. Braxton describes Marsh's gravillic contour thus:

> If we break down one of Marsh's solos with respect to the time, we find all kind of inner gravillic—*pockets*—completely ametrical, completely outside of the time, which rebalance his phraseology, the nature of his construction, in a unique way. He demonstrates this in every period of his music: his vocabulary, the relationship of his forming to gravillic balances, has always been unique.[82]

The control over gravillic contour might be likened to a juggler who can do the basic moves so fast that he creates an optical illusion of stillness in his motion, as though his objects were suspended in midair. The master is one who can manipulate that illusion, in breathtaking ways, as well as create it. Some examples of this sort of mastery that have become familiar to jazz lovers are Count Basie, Thelonious Monk, and Miles Davis. All three developed a concept that made use of the spaces between sounds in unprecedented ways. Monk especially stands out for this—and for the same sort of misunderstanding from his peers Braxton says Marsh and the cool players generally have experienced.

Many jazz critics have dismissed cool players as conservative to the point of sterility. Braxton sees this approach differently. On Marsh:

> It's so inside of the chord changes, he's really somewhere else. It's like you know the context so well that you're free: you're free because you understand the rules to such a level that you can do anything you want. That's what freedom is. You can't be free unless you have a context to be free in.[83]

Marsh's music so moved and informed Braxton that he used it as a jumping-off place from which to construct his own very different gravillic contour, one with what he calls "angle attacks";[84] Marsh's musical "vocabulary" gave Braxton ideas for his own "intervallic languages."

Perhaps as importantly, Marsh became a role model Braxton could turn to to weather his own hard times as an artist. Ironically, the reverse discrimination he perceived in critical reception of the cool players was something he could identify with as one blasted for not being "black" enough. He told Lock that Marsh wasn't accepted because he's from the European mystic lineage. Like Desmond, and Lee Konitz, his music has in it his heritage as a trans-European man: all of his solutions do not come from Africa . . . He was interested only in the music and in developing an evolution . . . so they, the powers-that-be, couldn't use him. They could use someone who, for instance, would take Charlie Parker's language and function under the mentality of the "jazz musician" that has been perpetrated in this time period. Marsh, by contrast, was talked about as being cold and academic, no feeling, not swinging. Fortunately I'd read all those reviews of Warne Marsh, so when I started getting the same reviews that didn't hurt me too much.[85]

Marsh's influence (and that of the whole Tristano circle, of which for Braxton Marsh was the point man) was no youthful flash in the pan. It has instead increased in power over time. This is in keeping with the very thing Braxton says excites him most (and has himself demonstrated by now): the commitment over time a master such as Marsh brings to his music. One of Braxton's most recent recordings is *Eight (+3) TristanoCompositions*, dedicated to Marsh. It may best be described as white hot; it combines the fluidity and inventiveness of the cool players so dear to Braxton with the fiery intensity of tone and rhythm associated with the "energy music" started by Coltrane and carried through Pharoah Sanders and Albert Ayler. Braxton describes, in the liner notes, a reunion with Marsh's music he had in the early 1970s (the beginning of a time when Braxton was most lauded by the jazz press as an important artist):

> I put on the record to the composition "You Stepped Out of a Dream" . . . and Warne started to play . . . Nothing happened for me! But, of course, it couldn't. I had been listening to Coltrane, Ayler, Mitchell, etc.—music that reaches out and shakes you (if you're lucky)—but with Warne . . . well, you had to come to it "somewhat differently." I played the solo again, and, of course, it was special—his work is a unique and profound offering that was always "master's level." It was my listening that had been off. I never made that mistake again. Some music(s) are not on the "surface," but that doesn't mean it's not there.

Critic Art Lange, in the same liner notes, writes thoughtfully of the affinities between Braxton and the cool school.

> In fact, Marsh, Tristano, and Lee Konitz played melodies that sought the sort of freedom that Braxton has subsequently espoused (that is, within a common understanding of structure; a democratic, flexible, cooperative creation of form). Their phrases all but burst through the strictures of the song forms they tried to circumvent with their wily arrangements, reharmonizations, rephrasings. They approached atonality, but never adopted it outright, on its own terms; and their frequent contrapuntal passages equated a collective freedom of choice,

again, within a set context . . . Then too there are those unorthodox intervals, the emphasis on linear improvisations (which become especially elastic in Braxton's solos), and both's ingenuity within "set" forms. Too, the "pretzel logic" of Warne Marsh's unique brand of improvising has inspired Braxton's willingness towards spontaneous complexity, and recognition of the beauty in unusual shapes and eccentric assertions.

But the way Lange captures Braxton's treatment of this uniquely American material (ironically, this most European of American jazz never caught on much in Europe, as African American music always has) is worth quoting at length for the way it redeems, *circa* 1990, the instances of bad press both Braxton and his cool white influences have attracted:

> Most importantly, no matter what you think about the original Tristano performances, this music is *not* "cool"—with feverish intensity, volcanic dynamics, explosive technique, aggressive attitudes . . . there is an enormous amount of drama here, and none of it is sedate, reticent, or bloodless. Note the treacherously difficult heads on tunes like "Two Not One," "Dreams," "Lennie's Pennies," and "April," and the hang-on-to-the-roller-coaster-with-your-fingernails-for-dear-life endings, where the question is not how they can find the notes at all at such breathless tempos, but how are they able to invest them with such meaning, such emotion? Note how Braxton puts his personal stamp on the music, retaining his own stylistic character—and adding an unquenchable sense of emotional urgency—to his solos, stretching the material without distorting its nature, and avoiding mimicking Marsh and Konitz's solutions to these compositional conundrums . . . Note the commitment, note the risks taken, note the rewards. Then give credit where it's due, marvel, and enjoy.[86]

In his obviously heartfelt and profound love affair with the European American music and musicians mentioned here, Braxton personalizes a point of immense significance to American culture: the problem of racism is best understood as a subset of a larger spiritual problem, one that suggests a more profound and potent spiritual *solution* than mere racial tolerance. From the first Irish and English indentured servants; through William Billings and the other hymnodists; through the poor whites of the folk and white gospel traditions;[87] through composers such as Ives, Seeger, Partch, and Cage, and jazz players such as Desmond, Tristano, Konitz, and Marsh, there has been a *white* American culture that has had its own experience of oppression, persecution, malign/benign neglect, ridicule, misunderstanding, and belated (after death, or close to it) accolades from the mainstream *Eurocentric* culture. While it can never be said that such whites have been vulnerable to the degree of economic and strictly racial hostility their black counterparts have suffered, it does remind us that black people—their music, art, culture, humanity—have always been as important to a certain part of white America as they have been to themselves, and for the same visceral, life-or-death reasons. This affinity and love between European- and African American cultures is as real as—and hopefully, in the long run, more potent than—their estrangement and enmity. Anthony Braxton embodies and expresses it as do few of his peers, white or black.

Free Black Pawn to White King—Checkmate!

It was at this point in the history of jazz that its struggle for an audience and a mature identity began in earnest. It was no longer a popular music, however culturally significant. Throughout the 1950s and 1960s it grew through a healthy diversity of styles and voices, but its struggle in the marketplace was dire. The sociopolitical hegemony of Eisenhower/McCarthy/Nixon put a bipolarized shadow spin on it: egghead intellectualism and rampant hedonism, emotional aloofness and manic depression. Such associations would prove transient to the music itself, of course, which would go on to move the culture in its new directions, relegating the more oppressive one to the shadows—but not overnight. We had the cool, then modal, then symphonic statements of Miles Davis; the mainstream and funky grooves of Art Blakey and Horace Silver; the fiery hard-bop then post-bop dervishes of John Coltrane; and a host of other sounds from a handful of originators and a bevy of imitators all over the musical spectrum. But that spectrum remained the one laid down since the turn of the century: improvisations on American song structures that stretched and turned them inside out the way Gustav Mahler, around the time of jazz's birth, milked the last drops of the Western tonal system that had ruled since Bach.

Braxton teaches a course at Wesleyan University on the music of Charles Mingus, John Coltrane, and Ornette Coleman. Those three figures serve well the story of the music's move from the "bebop soundspace" to those opened up in the 1960s, and explored so thoroughly since by Braxton.

Mingus

I believe in God, I just jumped some bars. And that's what my music is about, man.

Charles Mingus

Some of Braxton's echoes of Mingus are obvious, others less so but more profound. Mingus started out as a bassist with bands from jazz's New Orleans beginnings (Louis Armstrong, Kid Ory with Barney Bigard), its swing period (Lionel Hampton, Ellington, Earl Hines), and gained his first real name with the beboppers of his own age group (Gillespie and Parker, Miles Davis, Billy Taylor, Bud Powell, Howard McGhee, Stan Getz, Konitz—the whole spectrum of black and white, young and old, hot and cool, East and West Coast).

As he matured into a full-time leader, he blossomed as a composer, bringing out and developing many of the fundamental principles that distinguish composition for improvisers from classical composing. Of course, the New Orleans and early Chicago groups, and those of Duke Ellington and Count Basie had pioneered these principles, but Mingus furthered them more than anyone then, carrying the whole spirit from the "Dixieland," "Swing," and "Bebop" greats (that he'd actually played with) in his one concept. This embrace of the "oldest" and "newest" as the same "trans-African" song—contrary to distinctions imposed on it by both marketplace and Western cultural arena—prefigured the stance of Braxton and his AACM peers.

Mingus' infamous anger, as fully expressed in his music as in his personal life, made passionately human sense in the context of the times: pre-civil rights movement, bland-to-mean political culture of Eisenhower, McCarthy, and Nixon, a decline in popular support of the music proportionate to its reach for its heights. Mingus was neither cool nor beat, as was the more common response of artists and intellectuals, not in his music itself nor in his attempts to present it on his own terms. Like the innovators of the 1960s, he expressed African American outrage on a transpersonal (through his own personal) level, often working with poetry, theater, and allusions to visual arts and science (Darwin, Freud) to do so. On the pragmatic level, he was one of the first of his time and genre to insist on recording his own compositions and to start his own musician-run label to do it, as artist co-ops of the 1960s (like AACM) would try to do. Every strategy he came up with had the thrust of getting the music away from players who ran on automatic for passive listeners, which was the direction bebop was going in its departure from the dance and social background role (indeed, it had a lock on Braxton and his peers that they had to shatter with force, whatever their love for it). Mingus wanted to bring the life of the *mind* and imagination into the same visceral, sociable, immediate expression as that of the unthinking, conventionally programmed *body*.

Some of those strategies included sections of "planned chaos"—in *Wednesday Night Prayer Meeting*, to image a Sanctified service; unusual pulses and meters, sometimes several at once; hemiola-like suspensions and subdivisions over and within conventional meter; tempos that sped up and slowed down gradually on the run, or entirely melismatic (barless, rubato) pieces (such as *What Love,* in 131.5/4 meter!). They include (what Braxton would call) "combination logics," such as *Self-Portrait in Three Colors*, which weaves together three successively entering independent melodies (Braxton's *6D* would pick this up), a "portrait" that evokes Braxton's own penchant for the number three, and echoes Mingus' "In other words, I am three," from his autobiography.[88] Another such strategy resonant with Braxton lay behind the premise for improvisation he once gave to Yusef Lateef: a picture (of a coffin).[89]

The obvious parallels abound. Mingus' and his players' straight-eight, pre-swing phrasing drew fire for "not swinging"; some found him difficult for being so passionate about blackness, others for his European classical leanings and fondness for Lennie Tristano; musicians respected but also were intimidated by his music, which looked impossible on paper but which he managed to draw out from many. Generally, Mingus extended instrumental techniques and improvisational platforms, all in the service of mastering Western frameworks with African hands.

The subtler parallels are perhaps even deeper, since they come to the fore in the more mature work of both Mingus and Braxton: specifically, the episodic, almost cinematic nature of Mingus'—and, lately, Braxton's—work. It seems no coincidence that Mingus grew up in the movie capital of the world, was passionate about the world of painting, and dabbled in studio and soundtrack projects throughout his life. Webern was the one who brought the concept of the perfectly distilled moment into post-tonal music, but American pop culture itself has a place where the most adventurous and wide-ranging such music might find its niche: the cinema.[90] The visual and dramatic logic of the cinema demands of music that it find and distill its expressive essence, infuse it with the proper emotion, and control the development of both in time windows ranging from very small to extended—and then move suddenly, with little or no transition, to the next (possibly very different) scene and do the same. Much of what Braxton calls Mingus' "descriptive music" does just that, sometimes with verbal narration, sometimes with sufficiently evocative musical effects.

The titles Mingus gave his pieces were as important to their intellectual and emotional energy and effect as anything. They recall Partch: *All the Things You Could Be By Now if Sigmund Freud's Wife Was Your Mother, She's Just Miss Popular Hybrid, Once There Was a Holding Corporation Called Old America, Meditations on a Pair of Wire Cutters,* or *The Shoes of the Fisherman's Wife Are Some Jive-Ass Slippers.* Like Partch's, they also prefigure some of Braxton's recent titles: *What About Moveable Sign Post Strategies?* and *When Chancey Speaks, the Number 3 Changes "Lights."* The titles of both artists suggest a musical mythology of place, passions, and events that come into clear detail in proportion to the music's function as a means rather than an end. Like movie music, these works are mature because the musical craft is no longer the focus; mastered, it is simply the vehicle of transport to and within the mythical realm. Mingus' mythical realm was that of the heroic survivor, keeping heart, mind, and faith for the good fight in a sad, cruel, funny, fallen but ultimately redeemed world. Braxton's, judging from his recent texts, notes, and libretti (see Chapter Nine), is more that of the wide-eyed, intrepid explorer, surveying and charting a raw, fresh wilderness charged and crackling with the clash of elemental forces and a futuristic civilization laced with interstate highways and communications systems, and people going about their happy-to-manic, scary business. As different as the two worlds may be, the shoulders of Mingus were broad, and Braxton's footing on them is sure.

Ornette Coleman

Besides Mingus, there were a few experimental artists in jazz throughout the 1950s, but none as radical as Ornette Coleman. Thelonious Monk's music suggested some new terrain to new players, such as the soprano saxist Steve Lacy; pianist Cecil Taylor started out then but didn't connect with audiences as much as he later would. Coleman's primary significance (cultural as much as musical) lay in two areas: his abandonment of Western harmonic and metrical structures and of equal-temperament tuning standards, and validation by credentialed Western/ized figures such as pianist John Lewis and conductor Günther Schuller. It was this combination of revolution against and connection with the European spirit on the level of cultural elite (the white king in our chess game) that made Coleman's music the one to open the door for jazz onto the entire musical spectrum of the world, from its many primal roots to its most sophisticated fruits.

With Coleman, the music came full circle, in a sense. Jazz *qua* jazz began when the blended rural folk traditions of African and European America hit the cities; it evolved as an increasingly fertile synthesis. By the time of bop, it was an expression worthy of a cultural respect and support it has only recently won. Coleman went back before the synthesis started even in the folk traditions, evoking the field hollers, shouts, and pulse of slaves not yet constrained even by a symmetrical blues structure.[91] His melodies and improvisations had no bar lines, no conventionally even lengths, no harmonic constraints. His instrumentation had no Western-style hierarchy between (low) percussion and bass and (high) horns; those instruments' roles began to bleed into each other.

Like Braxton, Coleman was hailed as "the new Bird" by his advocates, and scorned as a charlatan by many musicians and critics, black as well as white. For many whites, the mystification came in Coleman's abandonment of the common musical ground; for the blacks, it was a matter of having a hard-won mastery of a foreign culture's turf undermined by a shrugging off of the rules.[92] In this, the music was reflecting the larger social tensions between the two communities pulling in the opposite directions of integration/assimilation and a return to cultural autonomy/distinction. Critics compared Coleman with Cage, Boulez, Elliott Carter, and Stockhausen. This is an interesting glimpse of the increasing alignment between the African American and Western vanguards that surged in the 1960s and has continued through Braxton and others.

For Braxton, Coleman's influence took a while to sink in. As did Parker's, when it did, it sank in deep. Coleman's contribution to the music was to free that melodic genius that soared in Young and Parker over the harmonic and metric conventions of the West, with their musical reflections of hierarchy and ultimately arbitrary aesthetic value systems that straitjacketed rhythms, timbres, pitches, melodic statements, and contrapuntal harmonic development, into new forms and sounds of his own personal invention. For the music of Braxton and others, Coleman's gift was to validate and suggest an infinite palette of form, arrangement, and pitch, timbre, and rhythm. Though Braxton and others would develop this gift much further than the man who gave it, any piece of Braxton's music that isn't bound by the American song form, including even the blues structures that were originally European hymns and folk ballads, owes a debt to Coleman.

Again, it is worth noting that Coleman was of particular interest to whites, especially those in high cultural places. Paradoxically, he was more African in his approach than most of his peers. Like Parker, and to a lesser degree Young, he was received with hostility by many purists. The resonance between the Western and African tributary-continua of the mythical Egyptian source was beginning to increase in their convergence.

the music's parents 111

Fig. 2.12a: From Charles Mingus' *What Love*:[93] shades of Hildegard...

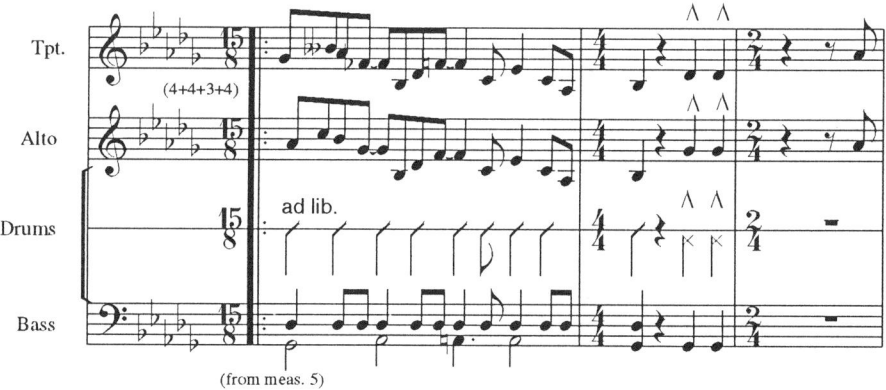

2.12b: From Ornette Coleman's *Una Muy Bonita*:[94] shades of Günther Schuller (the notation; Coleman's is more idiosyncratic)...

2.12c: From Braxton's *23M*: no stems, no shades...

Fig 2.12: In a reversal of his more typical rhythmic generation of pitch, Braxton wanted to see this arrangement of pitches with no stems or metric divisions (23M) find their own rhythmic weight and "gravitational intrigue" in a given performance.

The interesting thing about a comparison of his work to that of his two most significant (compositional) predecessors from the African American tradition is his typical proactive attempt to forge a workable synthesis between Western notation and African oral tradition. The written *forms of the works of both Mingus and Coleman have for the most part gone out to the world in Western terms that inadequately convey the music of the recordings. The collections cited here, while better than average for the practicing and thinking musician's needs, nonetheless feature disclaimers about the efficacy and accuracy of their representations. Coleman's fake-book charts typically indicate things such as "disregard the form" and "chordal instruments not on original recording" after dividing the music into regular bars and supplying chord symbols.*

Braxton's experiments in notation, as complex and/or vague as they often look (this example's a simple one), consistently enhance and inform a listening experience that conventional notation would more likely obscure or obfuscate. They also, like this one, hearken back to the West's oral roots and literate media of same (medieval manuscripts).

John Coltrane

The final major influence from the African American jazz saxophone tradition we'll look at is the continuum formed by John Coltrane and Albert Ayler.

Braxton said of his playing before hearing Coltrane, "I was the only black man in America who would call 'Take Five' at a jam session. You had to play with brushes when playing with Braxton before he heard Mr. Coltrane's music."[95]

Braxton in his youthful debut as a public player of note was associated with the most radical, militant, uncompromising intelligentsia of his time, forged in the fire of Malcolm X and other black nationalists. The music associated with this expression was correspondingly fiery, full of catharsis, purgation, and unrelenting intensity of volume, speed, and hard-edged-to-screaming timbre. Braxton identifies the source of this musical energy as Coltrane and, carrying it further, Ayler.

Kofsky and Wilmer are good sources for the feel of Coltrane's and Ayler's music as a musicultural expression of those times. Cole is an even better source for an understanding of the same energy beyond its function as reflector of a transient historical situation. It is that level—of music as metaphysics in sound, sonic shamanism—that is of most enduring relevance to Braxton, who lived through those volatile times with visible conviction but was not to limit his idealism to the rage of youth.

Braxton's words to Lock about believing in God are worth going back to in full, in the light of Coltrane's influence:

> I believe very much in God; and in the last ten years, which have brought me and my family to our knees because of the intensity of our struggle and the poverty that we've been dealing with, this has only increased my convictions about the oneness of . . . wonder, and how fortunate it is to exist. And when I say I believe in God, by that I'm only saying that I believe in God . . . I'm very interested in trying to understand for myself how to live, how to be the best person that I can possibly be—whatever that means. And I'm trying to understand what it does mean. This kind of information can be obtained in many different directions (though it seems to me that they all go back to the Negative Confessions) . . . [96]

The Negative Confessions were an ancient Egyptian code of ethics thought by Dr. Yosef A. A. Ben-Jochannon to be the source of the Ten Commandments.[97] Braxton goes on to cite Coltrane (along with Schönberg and Stockhausen) as bringing the *musical* inspiration to his spiritual path.

Again, Cole, quoting composer Fela Sowandé to explain Coltrane's music: "By far the most important single factor in African music is the full recognition and practical endorsement and use of the metaphysical powers of Sound."[98] Sowandé explains in other passages how sound is divided into functions ranging from the highest ritual and ceremonial to recreation and entertainment; Cole points out how this is expressed in the African American tradition by the establishment of a personal sound, or voice, as the goal of the mature player.

Ayler would take the frequency level attained by Coltrane at his peak and essentially start there, with little build-up; what build-up there was was in the context not of harmonic complexity but of folk tunes disgorging from the depths of the psyche. The result was to push the music right over the collectively psychic edge into a new world, which Braxton and his peers would explore and map.

The Braxton compositions and improvisations that draw on that high blast of energy and cathartic thrashing, then, represent Braxton's working of the Coltrane-Ayler continuum, which he has done throughout his recordings. Its function has been to give voice to the prophet in the belly of the beast, and, once out of it, to the passion and exuberance of survival and hope for the future.

Fig 2.13: Composition 23E. *Braxton's treatments of the "post-Coltrane/post-Ayler continuum"—his version of what was often called "energy music" in the 1960s and 1970s—are distinguished by what we might call his chromatic modalism. For example, if we recall that modes are arrangements of intervals that can be applied to any pitches, then apply that theoretical freedom to the chromatic scale, we come up with an access to all twelve tones that allows for patches of modal tonality within an atonal field (in figure, those patches are segmented off, and the modes they imply stated). The improviser's oscillation between these patches, when quick, creates an effect that simulates*

the music's parents 115

atonality, melting into a modal tonality when slower. The G# in this piece acts as the tonal center generating and calling back in all such oscillations.

Again, Coltrane's Impressions, *or his* Miles' Mode *(or, to cite one with a more direct line to Western roots,* Greensleeves*) are classic examples of this.*

Despite the importance of this influence, it should be remembered that that importance lies chiefly in its inspiration toward individuation. Coltrane and Ayler found their voices; once Braxton heard them, he had to leave them behind to find his own. That voice would emerge as something different in the Chicago of the AACM period (late-1960s), however informed by all the aforementioned. As Lock writes,

> Braxton's "Tri-Axium Writings," a massive philosophical/historical/spiritual discourse on black creative music and its relation to world culture, seeks to transform our basic understanding of what creativity is. Reading it, the continuity of the African American tradition becomes clear; because if the sound of the new Chicago music was very different from that of the Ayler/Coltrane high-energy axis, its intention, on a fundamental level, was very similar: to affirm and explore the spiritual dimensions of the music.[99]

In his liner notes to *Three Compositions of New Jazz* from that period, Braxton writes:

> We're on the eve of the complete fall of Western ideas and life values. We're in the process of developing more meaningful values, and our music is a direct expression of this . . . You are your music. If you try to vibrate toward the good, that's where your music will come from.

He would probably chuckle at the young man's words now, but his work is still consistent with the critique embedded in them, and that critique with his respect for Western European culture and its American offshoots. He's positioned himself as the loyal opposition, out to restore rather than destroy.

Braxton defined his own special interest in the AACM as one in the relation of form to movement, and of music to visual formations. He would quickly dissociate himself from any narrow cultural chauvinism and display a mind hungry for information from all quarters of the world. He was also to establish his personal inclinations as leaning toward the scholarly, the self-made academic, and the aspirer to a priestly-shamanic role in a culture that he knew might not recognize such a role, or at least not in him. Such a role in Eurocentric American society—which Braxton would leave and transcend, but then return to and participate in again, over time—was filled, officially anyway, by the classical composer. That was the musical figure who got what little cultural acknowledgment and support (public and donated monies) the not-historically-culturally-minded young American society had to give. That (and its academic ancillary office) was the social niche that most fit who Braxton really was and what he was doing, and it did have its African American manifestation.

Before we finish with the African American classical tradition, however, we need to look at the third great 20th-century influence-continuum (the first being trans-African and the second trans-European, both in North America): the European.

Black King Mates White King: The European Connection

The poetic justice in this is blatant. Braxton took his (let's call it) trans American music to Europe in the late 1960s/early 1970s, after making big waves with it on the jazz scene here; he and his peers helped spark European improvisers into their own "free" (spontaneously improvised) music scene; he himself continued to forge a music more concerned with European post-Modern structure, notation, and concept than the Europeans themselves, who reacted as if to centuries of such concern with the sonic abandonment of the roster of the Free Music Production (FMP), Incus and similarly radical labels; that music enjoyed a period of popularity in the American jazz scene in the late 1970s. Finally, when his mature and developed work picked up in the United States again, in the late 1980s, it positioned him to take on the mantle of a modern composer—a role one might expect him, per tradition, to have prepared for formally by some serious work in Europe.

Meanwhile, back in the States, also to be expected (there), the more commercial fusions of jazz with pop and rock music got started. Miles Davis went this way, opening up the extensive use of sequencers, drum machines, and synthesizers to the standard horn-bass-keyboard-percussion mix. Groups such as Weather Report, the Brecker Brothers' Dreams, and Chick Corea's Return to Forever made solid inroads both commercially and technologically. Keyboardist Herbie Hancock, guitarist George Benson, and producer Quincy Jones are still going strong down this road. Ornette Coleman has even tried to travel it, with his Prime Time groups, and his collaborations with guitarist Pat Metheney. Then of course there are the neo-bop and neo-Dixie revivals initiated by Wynton Marsalis, and revivals and resurgences of the music of old lions such as Frank Morgan, Dexter Gordon, Sonny Stitt, Art Pepper, and Johnny Griffin, along with a plethora of reissued, filmed, and printed material on the music.

Many of those who have stayed in touch with only this American fork in the road were not very aware of the new-music scene that concurrently burgeoned in Europe and Canada. It has become a stronger presence over the last ten or so years, leading more to commissions and concert productions for artists such as Braxton, fellow AACM-er Leroy Jenkins, George Lewis, Anthony Davis and others. If the late 1940s/early 1950s music of the post-Parker neo-bop groups are now on the agendas of the Lincoln Center and the Smithsonian, the musical legacies from the 1960s may be positioned to take their place just around the Millennial corner.

In some ways, Braxton's relationship with European musiculture seems even more significant than that with the two—European American and African

the music's parents

American—already covered. He was born an African American, and has lived as one in a Eurocentric America; but he *chose* Europe, was drawn to it, and not just on the intellectual and aesthetic planes. He's said many times that if it weren't for Western Europe, he would not have survived during the 1970s and 1980s; his music has found an audience and support base there that has yet to be matched in his own country, even though he chose to return and work here, and feels most at home here. His first college studies were of Western philosophy, and the concerns he expresses in both his own voluminous writings and in his many interviews show the influence of German philosophical literature (one wag compared his verbal/literate style to a 19th-century German philosopher on acid. His wife Nickie suggested a genealogy likely rooted in German Moors).

Of course, Europe has long been a haven for (especially African-) American, jazz musicians, for its relative lack of racism and other cultural problems peculiar to the United States, but Braxton's connection to European culture is more than that of grateful guest to good host. His personality and art, and history itself, have combined to draw him in that direction.

If we continue looking for common historical and aesthetic links between traditions usually seen as disparate, the Europe of Braxton's century teems with fertility. Braxton has made his main connection with the European art music tradition through the music of Arnold Schönberg and developed through that of Karlheinz Stockhausen. While there are certainly many other European composers he's expressed familiarity with and interest in—notably Wagner, Bach, Mozart, Beethoven, Webern, Berg, and Xenakis—the 20th century as expressed through Schönberg and Stockhausen is what has had the most impact on him and his work. Accordingly, after some background discussion on the history in Western art music of a musical element reintroduced to the world on a highly developed level by jazz—improvisation—we'll limit our focus to these two composers.

Braxton has positioned himself, in the gradual and unpremeditated way of authenticity, as a composer not just in the American tradition but in the Western tradition. His vision of his own work has drawn its power not from opposition to nor avoidance of so much as engulfment of the problems confronting it. We've seen this power at work in his conception of African America as a constructive vestige of the Egyptian cradle of European culture, and of European America as best embodied in a mystical lineage of allies standing with him against the destructive aspects of Western civilization. When we see his interactions with Europe, through Schönberg and Stockhausen, we see the third connection that creates the charged triangle. The Western dragon is mounted by the African knight-king-magus with the American armor, not to slay but to befriend and direct, and ride.

The following Braxton quote from Lock supplies a sense of his general posture toward the Western tradition:

> Bach, Beethoven, Mozart, all of the master Europeans who solidified Western art music were instrumentalists and improvisers as well as composers. Notation wasn't used then as a choking device to stop the blood, the dynamic, of the culture; it was later, when the technocrats made the process more important than the results, that we got the so-

called crisis of Western art music, which is still with us. In fact, we can see the same mind-set entering the bebop continuum: now they're making bebop so "correct," it will be bopbe or something—it won't be the same music that Charlie Parker and John Coltrane played . . . If you look at Bach, Mozart, Harry Partch, Fletcher Henderson, Duke Ellington—all of those people, though on the surface they seem very different, there's an awful lot in common there . . . *There was a law, an order, about the music, and improvisation was used to establish the nature of that law system.* It's the same for Duke Ellington's music, or any restructuralist who's trying to establish a body of work...I'm interested in structure because the concept of structure can be transmitted on several different levels; the understanding being that *there are things to be transmitted, to be forwarded . . . The significance of form is that information can be carried forward; a given form can make given variables come into play.*[100] (emphases mine, to evoke the presence of, and suggest the presence of purpose in, the Muse)

In Europe, parallel with the first rise of jazz in the world, it was the door opened by Arnold Schönberg that led to the resurgence of spontaneity and chance in Western art music.

Arnold Schönberg

It is hardly a coincidence that the mathematical techniques of music originated in Vienna, the home of logical positivism. The inclination towards numerical games is as unique to the Viennese intellect as is the game of chess in the coffee house.

Theodor Adorno

Schönberg's immediate Viennese and larger European society was in a state that makes America in the 1960s, even for blacks, look like a walk in the park. Economies and cultures were unmoored and thrashing, long-held philosophical and sociopolitical premises were crumbling; music was undeniably experienced as an expression and a prophecy of these dire and dangerous times, and violent riots against or chauvinistic displays for a concert's program were common.

As Braxton has done for his time and place, Schönberg took on the part of the theoretical and aesthetic genius driven to help the old ways pass and usher in the new. He also suffered ridicule, hostility, and neglect for his pains; indeed, he invited them, with his personal and artistic integrity and passion for freedom. Born a Jew, he was raised Catholic and converted to Protestantism as a young adult. That in itself, in Catholic Vienna, was asking for trouble. Then, when Hitler rose to power, he re-embraced Judaism.

Schönberg's "affinity continuum" (to borrow from Braxton) was from Wagner through the late German romantics, especially Mahler. He established himself early on as one whose genius lay in compositional thinking and theorizing. It is important to remember, however (and to apply to Braxton, the lover of sweet, lyrical, melodic jazz), that he himself virtually stumbled upon this talent in the service of an abundance of *heart* that needed to be expressed. He was pushing at boundaries of expression in the passionate conviction that, as Braxton said, there was something to express. That something was not an Apollonian logic isolated from Dionysian experience of spiritual transport; the logic was the means, the transport their end, the "variables" Braxton says come into play as a result of form. Schönberg was, as Braxton is, motivated to his mental complexities by a proportionate abundance of feeling and passion; the intellectual processes and fruits in their turn generate more feeling and passion. In such highly integrated and disciplined artists, it doesn't work to separate or hierarchicize intellect and feeling; it is also inaccurate to dismiss their processes as contrived, forced by an imbalance of intellect imposed on the creative impulse. Such critiques say more about the shortcomings, of both mind and heart, in those who make them.

Schönberg spoke of his own breakthrough in the program notes to the first performance of his *Opus 15* songs: "For the first time I have succeeded in coming near an ideal of *expression and form* which I had in mind for years . . . *Now that I have finally embarked on the path* I am conscious that I have broken all barriers of a past esthetic."[101]

Morgan describes Schönberg's innovation as a re-organization of pitch functions initiated by an emphasis on the intervals the diatonic system defines as dissonances, to the point where they cease resolving into their implied consonances. Pitches and intervals were set free to stand on their own, with no reference to the (ultimately arbitrary) rule of the diatonic hierarchy of tonal relationships. "For the first time in Western music since the Renaissance," Morgan writes, "the triad was no longer accepted as the sole harmonic reference from which all other vertical sonorities were derived and to which they owed their meaning."[102]

In the absence of these underlying assumptions—as long held as absolute and empirical in Western music before Schönberg as Newtonian physics were in science before Einstein—it quickly became clear that every new musical expression now had something new to express: the existential freedom and responsibility to define itself.

> What is most revolutionary about this music is precisely that each work establishes its own methods, its own special set of references. There is no "given" language, no grammar of relationships that can be assumed in advance and then relied upon in the process of composition and of listening. Musical structure has become "contextual," defined by the network of referential associations set out within each separate composition.[103]

It is exciting, of course, to see this freedom manifest through other traditions, such as the American, as we've seen it do in both its African and European faces; but it is *dramatically* exciting to see it manifest in the tradition where it had been curtailed the most, and where it had curtailed that of others the most. Braxton's sensitivity to and sympathy with the import of this drama has always been keen and responsive.

Also exciting is the realization of Schönberg's music as a *return* to pre-diatonic principles—such as heterophonic counterpoint rather than homophonic harmony—in Europe (principles that, as we've seen, took root in America and its music) rather than a leap into a sheerly atonal future (Schönberg himself preferred the term "pan-tonal").[104] The following from Adorno might have been said about Braxton:

> At first the complex chords strike the naive ear as "false," as an inability to do things correctly . . . Schönberg's earliest compositions—*particularly the Piano Pieces* . . . shocked the audience much more through primitivism than through their complexity.[105] (emphasis mine: the piano pieces were one of the first main inspirations of Braxton's solo sax music)

Cecil Taylor's vision of the piano (after exposure to classical conservatory training) as "88 tuned drums" and Schönberg's restructuring of Western music into his system of 12 (or, on the piano, 88) pitches floating free of diatonic obligations together define ground Braxton sees as common. One might say that Schönberg composed from his rational system, whereas Taylor improvises freely and intuitively—but Schönberg's rules didn't preclude creative decisions that could vary widely between composers, determined by sheerly personal style; and the decisions Taylor makes in performance are in accordance with aesthetics and concerns, however subjective, *he's* consistently developed and refined throughout his working life. More to the point, Braxton's solo sax music (he names *8C* as a good example) takes its inspiration from Schönberg for its use of atonality as color, and emotional affect. (Interestingly, in light of the above discussion of Mingus' cinematic aspects and Braxton's longstanding engagement with visual/theatrical experience through his music, Schönberg became interested in the potential and challenges of film music—which revolve around tone as color and emotional affect—right around the time of his first piano music, 1931.

Schönberg's conscious and synchronistic connections to the groundbreakers from his culture's other disciplines are obvious. The parallels in science have already been noted; Morgan also mentions Freud as a Viennese contemporary of Schönberg and compares Freud's disturbing and exciting probings into personal and collective psychic substrata to Schönberg's increasingly conscious upheaval of the Western musicultural premises that gave meaning to individual composers' expressions and the masses' experiences of them. He also touches on Schönberg's connection to the visual arts in Kandinsky and the German expressionists (Braxton first discovered Schönberg's piano music through his attraction to a Kandinsky painting on an album cover, and his desire to "hear music that sounded like that painting looked").[106]

Schönberg's crystallization of his innovations into a system happened gradually and as a result of a "crisis of intuition."[107] Like Braxton, Schönberg's deft handling of life on the edge served only to intensify his hunger to be rooted in the tradition behind that edge. He was compelled to take the tonal system and all its historical and philosophical associations and implications even more seriously than one who wasn't so driven to go beyond it. And, like Schönberg's, Braxton's force of passion and expressive skills fast reached their limits in the old, tired, overmined veins and called on him to scout out new ones with his equally prodigious creative intellect.

When Braxton was first doing the solo saxophone concerts he would later be celebrated for initiating in the "new jazz" of the 1960s, he ran up against the dead end of improvising on unstructured "freedom" quite soon. After ten minutes of inspiration, he found he was resorting to forty minutes of repetition of personal clichés, and he found that "horrible." That experience was what pushed him into a proactive construction of forms and other premises for improvisation in his own music.

More than any of Braxton's influences, Schönberg may resonate with his need to create a *system* for his music as much as the music itself, a context as informed by the past as Socratically open to the future; as conservative as liberal, in the radical sense of both words; and as thoughtful and reflective as inspired and cathartic. For a complete picture of both systems, one must read what their creators and others have written about them, study the histories leading up to them, and apply that material to the music each composed.[108] In thumbnail, however, we say it all when we say (1) that Schönberg had the unsentimental, un-nostalgic passion, the genius, the integrity under pressure of neglect and persecution, and the patience and persistence to free notated Western art music from the harmonic straitjacket it had begun weaving for itself after medieval and Renaissance times; and that his work as a composer transcended his medium to join with parallel developments in other Western disciplines, implicating and defining, reshaping, the culture as a whole with them; and (2) that Braxton matches those traits in his own role, which has been to free the art of improvisation from the pre-Schönberg (i.e., tonal) American song form (including the formalization of the blues), and to offer *systematic* and *universal* alternatives to it; and that Braxton's work as a composer and improviser is similarly informed and empowered by the larger philosophical, scientific, aesthetical-theoretical, and sociopolitical thinking of his time and place.

Braxton isn't the only artist making the sort of *musical* contributions he's making; but, like Schönberg, or Freud, or Einstein, he may be the main one to chart and codify hitherto unconscious assumptions and processes so comprehensively and methodically for his own time and place and genre. The value in such work lies in its power to open up areas of untamed psychic wilderness and put them within reach, make them inhabitable. It can mean the difference between life and death to the spirit and vision of both the creative community and the larger culture when the tamed lands they do inhabit have ceased to support them, or become contaminated.

Stockhausen

If Schönberg's/Braxton's system building was motivated in large part by a crisis of intuition, the music of Stockhausen may be broadly characterized as intuition inspired by a crisis of faith in the concept of drawing many cups of water (individual works) from the same well (*any* system, whether diatonic or chromatic). Paradoxically, the close and extremely narrow handling of Schönberg's system by his student Anton Von Webern opened wide the doors to going beyond it into our postmodern world of creating *contexts* as spontaneously and variously as we have always invented *contents* within a given context. By focusing on the 12-tone row as a compositional end rather than a means, Webern essentially demonstrated the option of finding complete creative fulfillment and expression in the making of a form, much like the painter Mondrian took the "cubes" of the first cubist painters out of their role as building blocks and presented them as artistic statements in their own right (and as Mingus did in the jazz arena of his time and place). Schönberg had expanded the tools of his trade to serve more expression; Webern freed them from that personal expression, set them forth as their own expression. In so doing, he begged the questions "What is being expressed? Who is expressing it?" Stockhausen took it on himself to answer those questions, as has Braxton.

Braxton's comments to Lock on Stockhausen are worth quoting at length for what they say about both Stockhausen's music and Braxton's relationship to musical influences so far from, even hostile to, his own soil:

> Stockhausen is awesome. He's such a master visionary that I even buy records of his that I *hate*; that's how much I respect him. In every period of his work he's demonstrated excellence and a unique understanding of form. Experiencing his music and his visions would help me try to function to my complete potential; reading his analysis books would inspire me to systematize and calibrate every aspect of my music. It was Stockhausen who showed me the beauty and excitement of every aspect of music science . . . It's true that both Stockhausen and Cage have exhibited, in my opinion, profound racist tendencies; but as I get older I find myself very much aware that I know a lot of racists, but I know very few racists who have been able to contribute the kind of information to humanity that Cage and Stockhausen have. Experiencing the music of Cage and Stockhausen would be the final part of my own equation, in terms of understanding what I wanted to do with my life.[109]

This ability and willingness to recognize and access information from every quarter is one of Braxton's strong suits, and, to ground it once again in his own roots, he reminds Lock that what he learned from Cage and Stockhausen they learned "from their masters, who learned it from their masters: Europeans are not the only people to establish a forward-information complex; they learned from the Egyptians."[110]

Elsewhere Braxton tells Lock, comparing Stockhausen to Coltrane, how the composer helped him develop his solo alto saxophone approach:

> I wanted to create a particular language for the saxophone . . . Separation was the only thing I could figure out: focusing on particular areas, parameters, I could work within; separating elements as a basis for establishing a sound logic. That seemed a practical way to continue, as opposed to the idea that whatever you play is interesting so you just keep playing . . . it seems to me that structure

gives one the possibility of defining the space in a way where it can be evolutionary. So, I was interested in developing a music and a music system then, from that point, extending it. My last influences, those being Stockhausen and John Coltrane, showed me beyond a doubt how to do it: you establish a point, you work, you try to develop it.[111]

In his writings and interviews (see Bibliography), Stockhausen has made it clear that this "pointillistic" approach is a conscious expression of the ancient mystical tenet that the many comes from the one, and the vast from the infinitesimal, in music as in the cosmos.

After describing Coltrane's approach through bop through modal, and so on, Braxton said:

Stockhausen would demonstrate another evolution by establishing a particular piece with a language, then the next piece would be another language, another syntax . . . without trying to develop any one line, he would demonstrate this extended understanding of form and of putting events together...I decided to take both of these approaches; to start first at several different points and then try to generate from those points.[112]

Stockhausen is slightly older than Braxton, but his music made its greatest impact during the 1960s, when Braxton had just started working. The common ground of the two composers can be mapped partially by looking at their similar responses to the ideas and history of that time, and partially by similar backgrounds and personalities.

Giving his own account of his connection to the European tradition, Stockhausen named Webern as a pioneer of the new spirit of the post-1950 aesthetic in which he began his own work. Succeeding a tradition based on the variation and development of a single idea, Webern suggested—and Stockhausen ran with—the idea that pitch configurations are at the service of givens of tempo, timbre and other musical elements, rather than the other way around. Melody and harmony function as random kaleidoscopes refracting the light of these givens, and the atmospheres and abstractions rooted mainly in them.[113] This turnaround brought the West to an even more rarefied and esoteric site than that scouted out by Schönberg and Berg. The irony in comparing it to the African American ideologies of freedom in the '60s, lies in its stigma as overly cerebral, since they arrived at it through eschewing that spirit of cerebration in favor of a (no less complex) rhythmic and auditory intuition.

Stockhausen came from a poor rural background; he did not inherit the world of international musiculture, rather became one of its shapers by sheer dint of self-developed talent. The spiritual orientation to which his music adheres was stimulated early in his life during World War II, when he worked in a hospital near the front lines. He suggests the motivation to abandon linear development of an idea through time, in favor of a succession of timeless moments, with the following words:

> I was 16... Death was an everyday affair for me...Enemy bombers attacked the hospital, firing like crazy. Almost half the wounded died. We carried the corpses into the chapel and threw them on top of one another...We had no time. We had to take care of the new arrivals...From childhood onwards, I often directly experienced death as a moment of transition, possible at any time...and directly followed by another form of existence. My view of art and all my work as a composer have been shaped by that experience.[114]

What's more, along with all German intellectuals of that time, Stockhausen was denied access to many modern developments in the humanities and sciences, those banned from 1933 to the end of the war. One for whom such currency is food, Stockhausen turned to catching up with his century as fervently as one who had been starved.

Again citing Webern's work (as a musical analogy of the science of the nuclear age, in its microscopic explorations of musical elements and constructs, its reduction of the *motif* to the intervals themselves), he understood his own approach as an even further atomisation of musical sound, down to tones and partials.

> And the laws of relativity and chance criteria of microstructures within the single sounds and spectra . . . I was very much aware in 1951 that I was part of a new epoch; and that an epoch which had started hundreds of years ago, even 200, 500 years ago with the way of thinking of the ancient Greeks, had finished during the last war.[115]

The following Stockhausen remarks, in the light of Braxton's quote about moving from an Aristotelian to an "Aquarian" age, underscores the way these particular artists, and artists generally, fall naturally into the realms of metaphysics and their earthly expressions in Muses and mythologies, swallowing whole epochs and cosmos as if they were themselves works of art:

> I have found that what I am trying to do in music has been better expressed than I could express it myself in the books by the Indian Sri Aurobindo. His work will shape the whole new era of Aquarius.[116]

Touching on another lesson learned during the war, Stockhausen says:

> I learnt during the war and after it that specific ideology would bring trouble and hatred and destruction. And I had no reason to trust any adult, because they would change with the change of the system and compromise with any new situation. I found that ideology was something I couldn't rely on, and that I should attach myself to the divine.[117]

the music's parents   **125**

One aspect of Stockhausen's thought stands in stark contrast to Braxton's love for Sousa, though it resolves itself in the common ground of jazz. Maconie quotes Stockhausen as saying,

> The periodic beat, which makes people march without knowing it . . . . I am very sensitive to this because that was exactly the way the Nazis tuned in the whole population with marching music on the radio, and whether it's marching music, pop or even a rock beat, I don't like it . . . [118]

Words to ponder whenever volatile social conditions bring out the beast, whether on the streets of Oklahoma or Berlin—and especially interesting in the light of the rebukes Braxton has long and publicly suffered for not being willing or able to "swing," and his clear renunciations from the beginning of either the racialistically militant's or supplicant's camps.

2.14a: From Webern's's *Six Pieces for Orchestra, Op. 6*, copyright 1956 by Universal Edition A.G., Wien, Copyright renewed. All Rights Reserved. Used by permission of European American Music. Distributors Corporation, sole U.S. and Canadian agent for Universal Edition A.G., Wien.[119]

2.14b: From Stockhausen's *Kontra-Punkte Nr. 1* copyright 1953 by Universal Edition (London) Ltd., London. Copyright renewed. All Rights Reserved. Used by permission of European American Music. Distributors Corporation, sole U.S. and Canadian agent for Universal Edition (London) Ltd., London.[120]

Fig. 2.14: Braxton claims both the Webern and the Stockhausen excerpted here as having an impact on his own work from the beginning (he gives his 11 *as an example). Webern distilled the essence of Schönberg's serialism into phrases; Stockhausen microscoped it further into single pitches, then, through electronic technology, into the vibrational dynamics within a single pitch. Braxton's fascination with texture and timbre (especially in his language musics) and irregular rhythms can be seen as an acoustic, macroscopic analog of that European zoom from diatonic to chromatic to pointillistic to electronically enhanced sonic field. More: his development of the twelve sonic identities that comprise his music system into mythological characters (see Chapter Nine) brings the fields of sound and music (and by implication, the universe) back to the life they enjoy in ancient and contemporary animistic and Western spiritual contexts. There are* angels *dancing on the head of that pin (sound).*

Maconie then points out that jazz's way of handling surface chaos and freedom with deep structure influenced Stockhausen's own derigidification of rhythmic elements—which, as we'll see, is the same path Braxton has taken and furthered, to the same place.

Morgan says something about Stockhausen that might have been said in relation to some of Braxton's scores.

> Stockhausen . . . takes a relatively large time segment as his basic unit and *divides* it to arrive at individual durations . . . This accounts for the extraordinary (and at times seemingly meaningless) complexity of the notated rhythmic relationships: the individual durations are conceived not so much as absolute values, calculated for their own worth, but as merely approximate subdivisions of larger

values. Only these larger values are really 'fixed,' since—as the composer was certainly aware—no pianist could possibly play the indicated durations accurately.[121]

Even so, Braxton's scores have scared off many players by their complexities; but when he conducts his changing time signatures with their impossibly juxtaposed figures, he sets up a larger time frame within which a player can *try* to do the impossible; he's more interested in the result that sounds from the attempt's inevitable "failure" than in correct execution.

Along with the textures and rhythmic layerings of big-band jazz in Stockhausen's music, his experimental electronic group was part of the same general thrust Braxton contributed to in Europe in the 1970s. Morgan paints a picture of their loose connections and common influences.

> One of the earliest and closest parallels is that between the music of the "free jazz" movement, initiated by the saxophonist Ornette Coleman...in the late 1950s, and such 1960s free-improvisation groups as MEV [Musica Elettronica Vita, with which Braxton performed and recorded] and Stockhausen's "intuitive music" ensemble . . . In subsequent years numerous prominent jazz artists, including Anthony Braxton . . . have continued in this direction, developing complex and extended forms of jazz that draw extensively upon the language of contemporary concert music.[122]

However, as Braxton himself has done with the descriptor "free," Stockhausen decried its problems well in advance of its more general decline in public favor. In acknowledging the valuable potential for musical models of utopian as well as practicable human community, Stockhausen found the actuality grossly wanting.

> Free jazz is relevant in so far as it leads individual players to collaborate in a collective creative process. But what they did this year at . . . with internationally known free jazz players was just chaos. Everyone played as loud and as fast as possible, and everyone at once. There were hardly any solos, and when there were, they were full of unconscious citations of idioms I would rather get rid of. But that's what always happens when people say "Let's be free." It produces chaos and destruction because they have never learnt to use freedom as a means of restricting oneself, so that others can also be free. It was very interesting, for instance, that in this free music there was rarely any silence to enable one musician to play for awahile.[123]

As we'll see in later chapters, these words might have been spoken by Braxton. On the other hand, Braxton has voiced reservations about Stockhausen's work as profound as those he's expressed about Cage's:

> The total body of the music is the most important alternative aesthetic and vibrational reality for America that's happened since black people were brought here as slaves . . . The activity of Louis Armstrong right through Ellington and all the names you know so well, is talking about an alternative reality, and always has been...And I don't mean improvisation *per se*. Cage and Stockhausen call this "intuitive" music when they mean improvised, because they can't deal with the fact. If they would deal with improvised music, they'd have to redocument it; and they don't want to do that because both of them are vying for Beethoven's place. I'm saying that improvisation has nothing to do with new or old music. I disagree with the concept that realigning of structure is sufficient to call something "new" music. The only time you get a new music is when you get a new reality.[124]

The first door Stockhausen would open onto musical elements that weren't notated came in 1954. Stockhausen was influenced by Cage when the latter reintroduced to Western art music the element of chance, one that had vanished with improvisation.[125] Schönberg's American ersatz student Cage—the European American mystic spawned in the American musiculture where African Americans and native Americans and Asian Americans had all done their share to maintain an atmosphere that kept improvisation and music-as-spiritual-ritual alive even in secularized Western contexts—was bringing that fire back to rekindle Europe, through Boulez and Stockhausen (especially, over time, the latter).

Maconie goes on to point out Stockhausen's proclivity for the reconciliation of opposites; the impact of his emotional nature on his outwardly impersonal and "objective" music; and, again, the impact of jazz big bands on his work, evident

> in its opposition of solo and block sonorities, its delineation of structure by changes of timbre and density, and its characteristically "sprung" rhythms. An awareness of jazz timing, and of its intuitive discipline, peculiar instrumental combinations, and exceptional blend of sonorities, all are constant features of Stockhausen's approach to music from the *Sonatine* to *Trans*.[126]

Of Braxton's other main European influence, Stockhausen said:

> During his lifetime Schönberg was generally thought to be of absolutely no significance. Even the most advanced musicians, those the public viewed as such, and the official administrators of musical life thought Schönberg a sick man and an idiot. People are now starting to discover what a great musical prophet he was, mainly as a result of the spiritual content of his work, which will exert an influence long into the future . . . Future generations make a more accurate choice since their perspective is completely different to a

selection made under the impact of shock, surprise, and what is generally termed fashion . . . Contemporary music is always everything that human beings who compose can themselves be and initiate. So that always involves the entire range of music from the most elementary of physical products, animalistic in their links with the human body and aimed at exciting muscles and nerves, to the most spiritual music whose unprecedented aspects proclaim a new being capable of vibrating with it...From time to time there appears a composer who is not just a specialist but completely universal, a composer who deploys all the octaves of expressiveness, inventiveness and discovery. In that very rare instance one can find in a single composer an exceptionally wide range of works, taking in highly subtle compositions in absolute harmony with elemental nature and pieces that are totally spiritual. Such a composer doesn't always exist on the same level of spirituality. He is everything between an animal and the gods.[127]

Like both Schönberg and Stockhausen, Braxton grew up, as a minority, outside of the economic mainstream. He came of age in a volatile place (Chicago) in a volatile time (the 1960s). The parts of African America he was most in touch with were the radical political and cultural intelligentsia, who were feeling both threatened and emboldened by the perceived crumbling of the repressive face of white America around them. Militants were being slain in shootouts with police in Chicago and other big cities, and talk of large-scale revolution accompanied all these incidents and the demonstrations and confrontations that surrounded them. Braxton and the AACM were associated with this foment in the same way, say, Bob Dylan was associated with the first white sociopolitical protests. To hearken back to the primal image of the hunter running and shouting-singing for his life, his music—like that of the supposedly loftiest and most cerebral and esoteric of the Western civilization around him—was not an intellectual-aesthetic leisure pursuit to cap off a hierarchy of fulfilled needs. It was his scream to survive and thrive, as an artist, as a man, as an African American—and, right there with his two German musical heroes trying to restructure their own crumbling worlds, as a Westerner.

Like Stockhausen, only for more American reasons, Braxton would not have access to much of the knowledge about non-Western and contemporary Western, and alternative Western music that he needed to grow until he was old enough to seek it out and incorporate it into his music independently of, usually counter to, his culture's priorities and systems of support and acknowledgment. Much more than Stockhausen, he would have to believe in himself and his path over the long haul in the face of much critical and public hostility and neglect, and even the same from his peers. Like Stockhausen, he would conscientiously eschew "isms"—ideology—even those superficially in sympathy with him, resting instead in the integrity of and faith in his own vision. Like Stockhausen, he would be drawn to the larger cycles of history, and attempt to make a positive contribution of very much the same sort. Like Stockhausen, he seeks to reconcile opposites: "Musical structures can be oppressive and reflect oppression.

I am trying to make flexible, inclusive systems, and a system that respects bridges between polarities."[128]

Stockhausen:

> The serpent always lurks within exotic charms, leading people to lose the protective paradise of self-assurance. The great shock occurs when someone who approached an unfamiliar culture with harmless curiosity is so moved by this experience that he or she falls head over heels in love with it...Once this primal ground has been touched, a yearning to experience the whole, bringing to life the entire range of diversity, can no longer be stilled.[129]

Braxton:

> The musicians are the ones whose heart goes out to the music, and the music takes it wherever it will, and suddenly you find yourself aligned with this guy whose life is very different from yours, but something profoundly links you, and it's the music. It would have been very nice for me to just say fuck Stockhausen and Cage, it would have made my life easier, but that wasn't the relationship I wanted to have with my discipline. Being open to it gives me a chance to reshape it to my own aesthetic based on whatever my needs are at the time. I see all the devices of the last 2000 to 5000 years as part of our legacy as a species.[130]

Black and White Kings and Queens: Beyond the Game

From his beginnings in music, Braxton has approached it as both fun and high art, both carnal and spiritual joy, both emotional and intellectual fulfillment. He has dealt with it as both scholar and creator, and has intuited the common threads connecting all the influences charted above. He has staked his claim as a composer first, instrumentalist close and connected second, and has paid his dues in America and her Western father Europe. When he presents in the studied and practiced terms of a Western composer the music he has worked out, he is claiming a place in another American tradition.

African American Classical

As Lock points out,[131] African American composers in the classical tradition have not been taken seriously, as though they were being uppity for entering this "high-culture zone," even though the first notated music happened in Egypt, and Western art music descended in part from Moorish sources. He also notes that black notated music is not the rigid thing white scores have been,

the music's parents

where the players are slaves to it. He might also have mentioned that this robotic literal interpretation of white classical notated work is only a few centuries old even in the West, that improvisation and much less rigid scores were common up to romantic times.

In America, an African American concert music tradition predates jazz. While this might seem at first glance to have only a tenuous relationship to the jazz tradition, its composers are in fact much more connected to all African American music than classically trained white American musicians have been to European American music.[132] This is still so in these post-tonal times, in the music of Braxton and others of like mind. These classical artists, spanning generations back to the country's beginnings, serve as powerful models for two potent truths: (1) culture and race can be transcended by creativity's passion and discipline, given equal opportunity for education and training and access to forum, and (2) if African Americans are not only capable of but embracing, on the deepest, most personal level, this transcendent affirmation of the spirit and legacy of European culture, then European American artists and audiences are as capable, if willing, of claiming the African legacy as their own human one, not that of some "other."

Newport Gardner, Elizabeth Greenfield, Blind Thomas Bethune, George Bridgetower, and Chevalier de Saint Georges pioneered this tradition from the earliest colonial times—part of a small but unbroken line of free blacks who formed societies to compose and perform notated music. Many performers have embraced the Western art music tradition, from Paul Robeson to Marian Anderson to Jessye Norman, in this century alone. Many composers and performers have straddled both jazz and classical worlds as composers and improvisers.

The classical tradition as developed through American blacks started in the northern colonies, then states, among the "Free African societies" that developed in the 1770s and the also new churches of that time and place, congregations of the African Methodist Episcopal Church. European musical principles and techniques, along with general Anglo-Saxon education, were more accessible to these free people, and the European American hymn stock provided the first composers' initial musical materials. It was reworked to convey the African American style of improvising and altering the music and lyrics of these hymns in worship. By the 1820s there was a whole school of composers (they included James Hemmenway, Aaron J. R. Connor, William Xappo, and Henry F. Williams), spawned by the Philadelphia composer/bandleader Frank Johnson (whom Braxton singles out as a special influence), scattered throughout New York, Boston, Baltimore, and other urban centers. Later in the century, Justin Holland, Joseph Postelwaite, and Blind Thomas Bethune, all bandsmen and concert instrumentalists as well as composers, capitalized on an enormous demand for sheet music and performances, including piano arrangements of operatic arias from the works of Bellini and Donizetti. By and large, their music was indistinguishable from that of their white counterparts, except for occasional racial themes, such as Johnson's *Recognition March of the Independence of Hayti*.

After slavery was ended, as mentioned above, plantation and gospel songs found popularity throughout Europe, Australia, and the Far East through choral groups such as the Fisk Jubilee Singers and the Hampton Institute Singers.

Many minstrel show and New York musical and Tin Pan Alley composers had formal training and made a big mark on the music publishing industry of the time. One of the most notable works of this period was *Treemonisha*, by Scott Joplin, the first folk opera written by an American.[133]

Harry T. Burleigh was a turn-of-the-century composer who pioneered a black musical nationalism similar in intent to what, for example, Béla Bartók did for his native Hungarian folk music. Black folk songs, idioms, issues, and poetry were treated in concert and program works, manifestos were published, "all-Negro composer" concerts staged. The music was neoromantic in style, favored small groups and solos, and fused the black material with European structures and procedures. Antonin Dvořák and Samuel Coleridge-Taylor were European inspirations for this movement, thanks to their unabashed interest in and respect for African American culture. Burleigh, Will Marion Cook, R. Nathaniel Dett, J. Rosamond Johnson, Clarence Cameron White, and Harry Lawrence Freeman were the early nationalistic composers; William Grant Still, William Dawson, Florence Price, Hall Johnson, Edward Boatner, Frederick Hall, and John Wesley Work embodied the movement's apex. These composers made important contributions to the Harlem Renaissance and the African American cultural movements that brought their work closer to that of jazz artists in the times since.

Composers from the 1940s on have had to suffer less racist hindrance, to education and training anyway, than their peers in jazz, and many studied at the best European institutions with the most eminent teachers, going on to create and hear performed symphonic works. Composers such as Howard Swanson, Ulysses Kay, George Walker, and Julia Perry developed a generally neoclassical body of work throughout the 1940s and 1950s. The next generation, represented well by the Society of Black Composers formed in 1968, added avant-garde techniques of the time, including aleatory and electronic. Neoromanticism, neoclassicism, and nationalism in this tradition of African American music were history; Hale Smith, T. J. Anderson, Noel Da Costa, Frederick Tillis, Roger Dickerson, Carman Moore, Olly Wilson, Wendell Logan, and Dorothy Rudd Moore were coming up with titles like Anderson's *Essay* for orchestra, and Logan's *Proportions for Nine Players*. Braxton has come to his musical maturity through the jazz tradition, but from the beginning that path didn't exclude this part of the classical tradition. His own personal classical influences happen to be predominantly European, but he insists on the significance of composers like Joplin and other ragtimers, and on William Grant Still (who studied with Edgard Varése, one of Charlie Parker's mentors), and on the host of others too often seen as fish out of water in this position.

In fact, this tradition is perhaps most important sheerly as a precedent, put in place to expand upon greatly. Perhaps its fulfillment lies in the new *persona* of the African torchbearer of the West's ancient Egyptian paradigm, conceived as a grand restoration of long lost balances between pitch and pulse, pitch and pitch (pitch is just high-frequency pulse), individual and collective, notation and improvisation. Musical balances that, perhaps, reflect metamusical balances that have also been lost. Francis Davis quotes pianist/composer Anthony Davis (no relation), who has been making waves in the world of modern opera lately:

Leo Smith, one of Braxton's AACM colleagues introduced me to a different concept of playing which involved the idea of composition, rather than improvisation, being of central importance in the ongoing development of black music. I think that Leo is one of the most important and underrated composers to emerge since Ornette Coleman. I think that Leo, along with Anthony Braxton, laid the foundation for what's happening in music now. We're in a new period, and some people are confused by what they're hearing, because the music is developing chiefly in the area of composition, not in terms of what people have been taught to listen for—new directions in improvisation...Most of my music is composed—written out. I think that improvisation is just one available option within the larger framework of a given piece. As a composer, the dynamic of a piece is more important to me, in a sense, than the performances of the individuals playing the piece. It's almost closer to the classical tradition of interpretation, of realizing a given work of music, than it is to the jazz-oriented concept of showcasing a soloist or creating a vehicle for a group of different individuals.[134]

The classical musicians in Europe and America both are waking up to this wedding between improvisation and notation. They are as hungry to improvise—to spontaneously compose—as modern Communists have been to democratize.

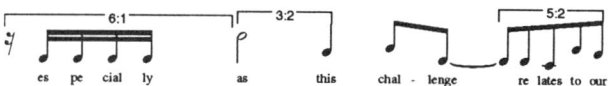

Fig 2.15: From Braxton's opera, Trillium M. *This use of text is typical to his most recent music, in which people speak as well as sing. This coupling of words with notes shows the simplest way into the rhythmic complexities of the latter—we speak them all the time. It also (with Schönberg's sprechstimme) connects full circle with the origin of Western art music, in chanted texts, as well as, possibly (if Young and McKenna are right), the prehistoric urgrund of both music and speech.*

David Balakrishnan, violinist and composer with the Turtle Island String Quartet, a group that writes and improvises in a mainstream jazz style, says

> It's amazing how many string players don't realize how easy it is to open that door and to improvise, in a jazz style especially. There is such a big *angst* put on it, that you have to have some sort of divine inspiration to be an improviser, when actually, although it does take hard work, the rules of the game are very simple [Braxton often says the same thing about composing—M. H.]. The word itself is easily misunderstood. Improvisaton is playing completely from your soul— it gives you the spontaneous feeling, which is the single most important thing about music . . . Classical players seem to have worked themselves into a corner interpreting other people's work. They've gradually lost the improvisational tradition that was so strong even through Beethoven, who was a tremendous improviser.[135]

In addition to the many instrumental ensemble works he has written and recorded that further instrumental art music, Braxton has gotten deeply involved with opera. In this, with Davis, he is aligned with an American tradition dating to the Colored American Opera Company of the 1870s. His other AACM colleague, violinist Leroy Jenkins, is another taking this path, and numerous African American classical performers have taken to opera stages recently.

In fact, this move in the music can also go back past America, through Africa, to Egypt. What are opera and ballet but the high Western expression of the total creative involvement of the human being in a "courtly" ritual ceremony? The mythical, magical power of the written word of the script; the visual art of the sets, masks, and costumes; the choreography, the acting and singing, the rhythm and sound and harmony and melody: put them all together in a new celebration of your own common humanity, world, and dreams and you and all the other black and white pieces have put all the forces in motion and played the game right off the board.

1. *69P* is Latin-inspired, *77E* Asian-influenced.
2. See Vernon W. Boggs, *Salsiology: Afro-Cuban Music and the Evolution of Salsa in New York City*, (New York: Excelsior, 1993: 7–8).
3. From *New Grove/Music & Musicians* ("Latin America . . . Folk Music, Central America and the Carribean," Vol. 10, pp. 521–22).
4. Ibid.
5. See Ronald Radano, *New Musical Figurations: Anthony Braxton's Cultural Critique* (Chicago/London: University of Chicago Press, 1993: 201–3) and *Anthony Braxton and his Two Musical Traditions: The Meeting of Concert Music and Jazz* (University of Michigan, 1985: 194–99) for a good look at this seminal (to Braxton's pulse tracks) piece.
6. Graham Lock, *Forces in Motion: The Music and Thoughts of Anthony Braxton.* (New York: Da Capo Press, 1988: 280).
7. See Duke Ellington's *Sacred Concerts* (Miami Beach, FL: Hansen House, 1979); Mingus' *Wednesday Night Prayer Meeting* (with his comments, in Sue Mingus, ed. *Mingus: Not a Fakebook*), and *The Music of John Coltrane* (both from Milwaukee, WI: Hal Leonard Publishing, 1991). My comment on Kirk is based on a live performance in Berkeley, California, in the late 1960s, in which he talked about glossolalia as practiced in the black church as a setup to his performance of the hymn.
8. Edwin S. Gaustad, ed., *History of Religion in America to the Civil War* (Grand Rapids, MI: William B. Eerdmans, 1982: 406).
9. See Bernice Johnson Reagon, "Nurturing Resistance" (*Reimaging America: The Arts of Social Change*, O'Brien, M. and Little, C., eds., Philadelphia/Santa Cruz: New Society Publishers, 1990: 1–8).
10. Hear Alan Lomax, ed., *Afro-American Spirituals, Work Songs, and Ballads* and *Anglo-American Shanties, Lyric Songs, Dance Tunes, and Spirituals* (Washington, D.C.: Library of Congress, Division of Music, Recording Laboratory, 1942 and 1956 respectively); *Roots of the Blues* and *Sounds of the South* (Atlantic SD 1348 and 1346, respectively); and see *Folk Songs of North America* (New York: Dolphin/Doubleday, 1975).
11. African slaves and Irish and English indentured servants were typically housed together in the 1700s, before the slave trade took off and when race was generally less important than status in people's minds (see Robert Hinton's "The Black Tradition in American Modern Dance," *American Dance Festival Curatorial Guide*, project directors Gerald E. Meyers and Stephanie Reinhart, 1990: 4); the dance and music of both peoples came together intimately then. A similar African/Irish merger occurred in the 1600s, when Oliver Cromwell's brother Henry, occupying governor of a ravaged Ireland, sold thousands of Irish women and children to the West Indies as slaves, where the women were mated with African men; the modern reggae musiculture comes from that merger (see Ventura).
12. This is due less to deliberate study and imitation than to a natural and unstudied historical affinity, through both African and American cultural continua, with that period of the West. Especially striking are the similarities between Braxton's use of the hemiola (regrouping of several small cycles of beats into differently accented cycles of different duration) and similar ways of subdividing regular pulse; his use of drones and modes; his approach to harmony and counterpoint through melody and timbre, rather than the other way around; and even his notation. Early Western neumes are thought to be cursive depictions of a choirmaster's hands leading others in the traditional inflections and phrasings of chants. As the hand described the central tone and intervals above and below it in space, gesturing for accents and inflections, so the neumes suggested the vocalization of the chant. The

neumes essentially described pitch flowing in the air, as sound does. Over time, they were positioned on a reference line (early staves), and broken up into discrete target points of sound (notes). (Wesleyan professor Jon Barlow has developed a system of hand motions to conduct early vocal music that approximates the shapes of the neumes, showing how they might have developed from such gestures.)

Braxton's work mirrors this process. Each phrase in each part of his larger scores has the integrity of a single chanted text (as opposed to a cog in some Cartesian harmonic machine), and is conceived as a soundline flowing in space to land on a target pitch/pulse (thus "gravitational intrigue"; a propos of all this, the lowest of the early medieval clefs was called the *claves graves*). Braxton has a system of hand-signalling and directing elements of his improvisational system to his ensembles, many of which are direct counterparts to the symbols on his scores.

13. See *New Grove/Music & Musicians,* "Hildegard of Bingen," Vol. 8, pp. 553–56.

14. Ibid.; see also Matthew Fox, *Hildegard of Bingen's Book of Divine Works, with Letters and Songs* (Santa Fe, NM: Bear and Company, 1987). From choirmaster Brendan Doyle's "Introduction" (364): "Hildegard . . . once said that *singing* words reveals their true meaning directly to the soul through bodily vibrations. I think we can conclude from this statement that her world view centers around an intimate relationship between body (the mouth, throat, vocal chords, diaphragm, and lungs) and spirit (the breath). The goal of creation for Hildegard is that all creatures sing with one voice the same praises. We wake up to an awareness of eternity, a revelation of the inexhaustibility of feeling, through song.

"Hildegard's compositions are incredibly physical. This makes wonderful sense if we realize that she was a physical scientist as well as a musician. Singing her music comes close to hyperventilation at times. When she writes about the Spirit, you know she understands the Spirit as wind, as breath, because you become the wind. When she writes about Divine Mysteries, you sing out of the deepest space of your physical being from the comfort of normal range to the extremes of your vocal potential. Her music reveals that we, too, are divine mysteries. And living is profoundly erotic."

15. Turn-of-the-century German musicologist Oskar Fleischer's *Neumenstudien: Abhandlugen uber mittealterliche Gesangs–Tonschriften* (Leipzig 1895, Berlin 1897, Berlin 1904) began to make the connections between early Western music with Indian, Middle Eastern and African cultures, but that line has yet to be seriously pursued.

16. Wilfrid Mellers, *Music in a New Found Land* (New York: Hillstone, 1964: 3).

17. Ibid., 7.

18. From "The Singing Master's Assistant (1778)" (*The Complete Works of William Billings,* Nathan, Hans, ed., Vol. II, The American Musicological Society and the Colonial Society of Massachusetts, Boston: University Press of Virginia, 1977: 258).

19. Associated Music Publishers, Inc., New York, 1965.

20. See Michael Levin and John S. Wilson, "No Bop Roots in Jazz," a 1949 interview with Charlie Parker in which he distances his music from "jazz" and suggests its future development into the 12-tone system (reprinted in *Down Beat,* February, 1994: 24).

21. See Howard Mandel's 1987 interview with Ornette Coleman, "The Color of Music" (reprinted in *Down Beat,* February, 1994: 44).

22. *New Grove/American Music,* "Billings, William," Vol. 1, pp. 215–19.

23. Mellers, 13.

24. From *The New England Harmony* (compiled by Timothy Swan; Northampton, MA: Andrew Wright, 1801).
25. Braxton, telephone interview (February 25, 1993).
26. Mellers, 16–17
27. Ibid., 17.
28. The original "neumed" text (*Beata Gens*) and the three subsequent versions of it (309 St. Gall, VII. 34 (Bénévent), and BN 903) are in *Paléographie Musicale: Les principaux manuscrits de chant gregorien, ambrosien, mozarbe, gallican: publiés en facsimilés phototypiques* (Berne: Editions H. Lang, 1969). The fourth version is from the *Liber Usualis* ("authored" and published by the Catholic Church): 1048. Comparison made by Jon Barlow.
29. M. S. Moore, *Yankee Blues: Musical Culture and American Identity* (Bloomington: Indiana University Press, 1983: 63).
30. See liner notes to *For Four Orchestras*. The second and fourth movements of Ives' *Symphony No. Four* are the classic examples of this effect, where dreamy meanderings in the strings and reeds are constantly jolted and swallowed up by boisterous brass marching in through some warped snatch of a march or hymn. Braxton's *Composition 19*, for 100 tubas (four groups of 25 converging at a crossroads on parade), took Ives' conceit out of the concert hall into the streets.
31. Virgil Thomson, *Twentieth-Century Composers: American Music Since 1910*, Vol. I (New York: Holt, Rinehart and Winston, 1971: 25).
32. Ives, Charles, *Symphony No. Four* (Associated Music Publishers, Inc., New York, 1965: 4).
33. From "The New England Psalm-Singer" (1770) (*The Complete Works of William Billings,* Kroeger, Karl , ed., Vol. I, The American Musicological Society and the Colonial Society of Massachusetts, Boston: University Press of Virginia, 1977: 344).
34. Mellers, 257–58.
35. Braxton, telephone interview (October 18, 1993).
36. See M. Gaume's, *Ruth Crawford Seeger: Memoirs, Memories, Music* (New Jersey/London: Scarecrow Press, 1986). Some of the following quotes and points about the work Seeger did with her ethnomusicologist husband Charles, might most effectively show the connections between these two American composers. Seeger
- had a strong sense of music as a sociocultural force;
- shied away from the world of the "professional" musician;
- distinguished herself uncompromisingly even from her influences;
- was strongly influenced by the ethnomusicological research of the Lomaxes;
- endured struggles with poverty because of and for the sake of her work;
- endured the slings and arrows of outrageously unsympathetic and insensitive interviewers/reviewers;
- saw her role as a composer of experimental music, to "work out disciplines which would expand musical technique and give it wider horizons . . . New techniques must be worked out, experimented with, for a long time before the balance can be reached out of which what can be called a true American music can arise" (Gaume, 203);
- was seen by others, and proven by time, as a success in that role.

37. John Cage, *Empty Words: Writings '73–'78* (Middletown, CT: Wesleyan University Press, 1979: 179).
38. Ibid., 180, for this and next citation.
39. Ibid., 183.
40. Joe Carey, "Anthony Braxton Interview," (*Cadence*, March 1984: 5–10).
41. Cage, 184; also resonates with Young (footnote 7, Chapter One).

42. Carey, 8–10.
43. E. Lee, *Jazz: An Introduction* (London: Kahn & Averill, 1972: 13–15) mentions Lomax' documentation of a Ring Shout in Louisiana as late as 1934.
44. Mellers, 263.
45. Lock, 166.
46. Ben Sidran, *Black Talk* (New York: Da Capo Press, 1981: 34).
47. Ibid., 33.
48. Ibid., 25.
49. Ibid., 25.
50. Braxton has a particular love for the solo traditions from around the world. His record collection on reserve for students learning about his solo sax–generated music system ranges from solo classical to experimental to jazz recitals, to bardic storysingers from the spectrum of tribal peoples from Iceland to Africa.
51. Lock, 20.
52. See Basil Davidson, "The Ancient World and Africa: Whose Roots?" (*Race and Class*, Vol. 29, no. 2, 1987).
53. Braxton (*Composition Notes C*), 150–51.
54. See John Litweiler's *Ornette Coleman: A Harmolodic Life* (New York: William Morrow and Co., 1993) for a sense of Coleman's messianic persona during the 1960s.
55. See Charters' (122–23) description of *jali* music as melodic cycle (rather than harmonic field). Re: Braxton's similarity to African and pre-modern blues in his primacy of melody over harmony and his suspended rhythmic texturings: "All of the older singers had a repertoire of faster dance pieces, which seemed to antedate the classic guitar blues . . . The accompaniments were flailing repetitive rhythmic patterns, and the voice was only loosely connected to the pulse of the guitar . . . One piece I'd recorded . . . had almost no harmonic change at all—and in modern blues playing there have been a number of bands who play long improvisatory pieces without harmonic change.

"What I found more interesting than the lack or presence of harmonic changes was the obvious use of rhythmic texturing—the same kind of texturing that was characteristic of the *griot* music and certainly has left its imprint on every other African musical style."
56. *New Grove/Jazz*, "Ragtime" (as a development from African banjo music), Vol. 2, pp. 345–46; see also Eric Lott, *Love and Theft: Blackface Minstrelsy and the American Working Class* (New York: Oxford University Press, 1993); and Braxton's version of Scott Joplin's "Maple Leaf Rag" on *Duets 1976* (with Muhal Richard Abrams, Arista AL 4101, 1976).
57. Mellers, 277.
58. Valerie Wilmer, *As Serious As Your Life: The Story of the New Jazz* (London: Quartet Books, 1977: 45).
59. Albert Murray, *Stomping the Blues* (New York: Da Capo Press/Plenum Publishing, 1976).
60. This gave rise to the Southern saying, "There ain't no white people in New Orleans," and Bessie Smith sang a line about the city being a "right fine place . . . whatever the folks do, the white folk do it too" (in Ventura, Michael, "Hear That Long Snake Moan," *Whole Earth Review*, no. 54, Spring, 1987).
61. See Radano, Ronald, "Braxton's Reputation," (*Musical Quarterly*, vol. 57, 1986, no. 4: 503) for a look at both bad and good press; see also Chapter Three and Bibliography. See Josef Woodard's "Structure, Vocabulary and Tradition: Saxophonist Anthony Braxton" (*Option*, No. 23 (November/December 1988: 1–3) for Braxton's own recollection of writers unsympathetic to him.

the music's parents   **139**

---

62. Lock, 68.

63. Ventura, 39.

64. Braxton's groundbreaking *37* for saxophone quartet was recorded (*New York, Fall 1974*, Arista 4023) by him with Julius Hemphill, Oliver Lake, and Hamiett Bluiett, three Black Artists Group luminaries who later would, with David Murray, form their own highly successful World Saxophone Quartet. I know of Teish through my association with Malinké Robert Elliot, who, with Hemphill in the 1960s, started BAG and, with me, started Pacific Rim Players in the late 1980s.

65. Hardin was a university-trained pianist and composer, as well as a singer. She worked in King Oliver's Creole Jazz Band, which Louis joined when he first left his native New Orleans for Chicago. She and Armstrong married after working together for two years, and shortly thereafter left Oliver for wider opportunities. For Lil, that meant leading her own groups, but it was she who also determined Louis' next move.

She encouraged him to move to New York and work with the leading dance orchestra there, the Fletcher Henderson group. Henderson, with the help of his arranger Don Redman, forged the style of writing and arranging for the big band that would define the swing era to come, a time when white America finally embraced jazz as its favorite music. He hired Armstrong to bring in the fire of jazz to an orchestra in danger of fading into its own polite sweetness, a fate suffered by the leading white orchestra leader Paul Whiteman, who met a dead end when he tried to "symphonize" jazz for white audiences. Armstrong's work with Henderson as a jazz soloist gained him the attention of the most important musicians and journalists on the most important scene, and his influence as the genius of the new "hot" music began to be felt. After a year with Henderson, he returned to Chicago to play in the group Lil was leading.

66. Braxton, lecture, University of Oregon (Eugene), January 30, 1989.

67. M. Green, *The Reluctant Art: The Growth of Jazz* (New York: Horizon Press, 1963: 95–96).

68. Amiri Baraka, in *New Perspectives on Jazz* (Baker, David, ed., Washington, DC and London: Smithsonian Institution Press, 1986: 57–68).

69. Thompson, Robert Farris, *Flash of the Spirit: African and Afro-American Art and Philosophy* (New York: Random House, 1983: 16).

70. Author's transcription (this tune was written by Miles Davis, but is often attributed to Charlie Parker).

71. Green, 100.

72. Ibid., 169.

73. Ibid., 188.

74. Lee, 47.

75. Ibid., 50–51.

76. Ibid., 113.

77. Ibid., 113.

78. Francis Davis, *In the Moment: Jazz in the 1980s* (New York: Oxford University Press, 1986: 157–58).

79. Lock, 62–63, *Coventry* CD.

80. Lock, 64, 106.

81. See Lock (100) for a graphic depiction of this.

82. Ibid., 101.

83. Ibid., 102.

84. For graphic depiction, see Lock, 102.

85. Ibid., 103–04.

86. Braxton, *Eight (+3) Tristano Compositions 1989* (Hat Art CD 6052, 1990).

87. Hear B. F. White, *White Spirituals from the Sacred Harp* (NW 205 New World Records).
88. Charles Mingus, *Beneath the Underdog: His World as Composed by Mingus* (New York: Knopf, 1971: 1).
89. Brian Priestley, *Mingus, a critical biography,* (London/New York : Quartet Books, 1982: 94.
90. Hear *The Carl Stalling Project: Music from Warner Brothers Cartoons, 1936–58* (United States: Warner Bros. Records, 1990).
91. See Mellers, 347 and Litweiler, 100, on Coleman and the blues.
92. Miles Davis in Troupe on free players (indexed), especially Ornette Coleman; also see Joe Goldberg, *Jazz Masters of the 50s* (New York: Macmillan, 1963).
93. Sue Mingus, ed., 152–3. Andrew Homzy, music professor at Concordia University in Montreal, writes there, "Unlike the pieces by his contemporaries, there is no fixed format in a Mingus composition. This lead sheet therefore is a composite rendering, a rebuilding of the basic components to assemble a practical (and simplified) representation of the music. When playing Mingus' music, today's musicians should exercise the same creative and exploratory modes of interpretation as did the composer."
94. Günther Schuller, ed., *A Collection of the Compositions of Ornette Coleman* (New York: MJQ Music, Inc., 1961: 30).
95. Braxton, Lock's *Coventry* CD interview.
96. Lock, 280.
97. Yosef Ben-Jochannon, *Africa, the Mother of Western Civilization* (New York: Alkebu-Lan Associates, 1971).
98. Cole, 68.
99. Lock, 37.
100. Ibid., 232–33.
101. R. P. Morgan, *Twentieth-Century Music* (New York: W.W. Norton & Co., 1991).
102. Ibid., 68.
103. Ibid., 69.
104. See *New Grove/Music & Musicians* ("Schönberg, Arnold"), Vol. 16, p. 708: "The music of the ensuing second period is often called 'atonal.' Schönberg considered this terms nonsensical, preferring 'pantonal.'"
105. Theodor Adorno, *Philosophy of Modern Music* (New York: The Seabury Press, 1973: 41n). Elsewhere he writes, "Counterpoint is unquestionably the actual beneficiary of twelve-tone technique. It has attained primacy in composition. Contrapuntal logic is superior to harmonic-homophonic logic because it has always liberated the vertical from the blind force of harmonic convention . . . *For the first time . . . since the waning of the Middle Ages*—and in an incomparably more rational disposition over the means—twelve-tone technique has crystallized into a genuine polyphonic style . . . Schönberg proved his ability as an exponent of the most mysterious tendencies in music in that he no longer imposed polyphonic organization upon the material but rather derived it from the material itself" (90–1); and "The origins of atonality as the fulfilled purification of music from all conventions contains by its very nature elements of barbarism. In Schönberg's outbursts—often hostile to culture—this purification repeatedly causes the surface to tremble. The dissonant chord, by comparison with consonance, is not only the more differentiated and progressive; but furthermore, it sounds as if it had not been completely subdued by the ordering principle of civilization—in a certain respect, *as if it were older than tonality itself. In the midst of such chaos the style of Florentine Ars Nova—the combining of voices without concern for harmony, accomplished*

merely through the senses of untrained musicians—can easily be confused with many thoughtless products of "linear counterpoint". (40–41; emphases mine)

106. Comments to tutorial student group, Wesleyan University, October 16, 1993.
107. Adorno, 40–41.
108. Interestingly, Braxton's system, like Schönberg's, is built on twelve elements (see Chapter Five).
109. Lock, 150–51.
110. Ibid., 152.
111. Ibid., 51.
112. Ibid., 50–51.
113. Karlheinz Stockhausen, *Towards a Cosmic Music* (England: Element Books, 1989: 8).
114. Ibid., 94.
115. Stockhausen, 10–11. Braxton might have said these words.
116. Ibid., 10–11.
117. Ibid., 11.
118. Robin Maconie, *The Works of Karlheinz Stockhausen* (London: Oxford University Press, 1976: 8–9).
119. Webern (Vienna: Universal Edition, 1956: 22–23).
120. Stockhausen (London: Universal Edition, 1953: 4–5).
121. Morgan, 347.
122. Morgan, 417.
123. Morgan, 373–74.
124. Peter Occhiogrosso, "Anthony Braxton Explains Himself" (*Down Beat*, August 12, 1976: 49).
125. Ibid., 370–73.
126. Ibid., 326. See also Barry Bergstein, "Miles Davis and Karlheinz Stockhausen: A Reciprocal Relationship" (*Musical Quarterly,* Winter, 1992: 502–25) for a good look at Stockhausen's connections with the American muse in another of its major voices.
127. Ibid., 53.
128. Braxton, telephone interview (February 25, 1993). (For the researcher interested in exploring some specific musical connections—or perhaps what the invisibility of them says about the nature of Braxton's relationship to his influences—Braxton credits Stockhausen's *Gruppen* and *Carré* as inspirations for his multi-orchestral works, and *Klavierstucke IV, VI* and *X* for his solo work. *Inori*, he says, informed his *Composition 102.*)
129. Stockhausen, 31.
130. Braxton, telephone interview (February 25, 1993).
131. Lock, 317.
132. *New Grove/American Music*, "Afro-American Music," Vol. 1, pp. 13–21.
133. An interesting side note: modern pianist/composer McCoy Tyner, who was part of the John Coltrane revolution in the 1960s, has dreams of reviving such productions that include music and theater and dance, citing *Treemonisha* as a precedent (in private interview, Medford, Oregon, summer of 1991).
134. Davis, 6.
135. Mike Heffley "Turtle Island String Quartet: America's String Savers?" (*Chamber Music,* Spring 1991: 26–29).

second arrow . . .

**on the string
of the present**

Invocation

The *New Grove Dictionary of Jazz* entry on Braxton gives a brief biographical history and includes the following:

> As a wind player, Braxton stands solidly within jazz traditions. He is among the finest free-jazz alto saxophonists, and his contrabass clarinet playing deserves particular mention . . . He is also a fluent performer on all members of the saxophone and clarinet family and on percussion instruments—reflecting his interest in exploring timbral contrasts. He expanded his repertory in the 1970s to include bop improvisation. As a composer, he is justifiably irritated by the attempts to categorize his music as either free jazz or contemporary art music (surprisingly, it has not been termed "third stream," though it offers perhaps the finest examples of this concept). He makes use of geometrical designs, poetic arrangements of numbers and letters, and human and animal figures as titles of individual pieces on his albums. As well as works for small groups, Braxton has written humorous pieces for parade band and ambitious compositions for large orchestra, some of which have incorporated theatrical elements.[1]

What's interesting about this blurb is its context. Imagine it in a jazz magazine with a mainstream, conservative-commercial focus; it would feel like the argument of a writer voicing a minority opinion. Now imagine it in a publication devoted to new, adventurous music; it would feel like what one would expect there too, an advocacy journalism at odds with the first magazine. The reader of both is exposed to, more than any given *content*, a *context*: American cultural pluralism, in full thousand-flower bloom.

A serious dictionary, however, has an air of cultural consensus and neutral authority that makes one take its words as a judgment open to little dispute; they read like the distillation of long-settled debates. *New Grove*'s words, taken so, are a serviceable bridge from the worlds of Western journalism and scholarship to the alternative world of letters Anthony Braxton felt compelled to create.

Braxton was, in the mid-to-late 1980s, at the age when many people have midlife reflections on what has been and what will be for them. In his case, the process included a voluminous documentation in print: the completion of his own self-published writings (begun in the early 1970s) about his overarching musical philosophy, musical output, and projections on the global music scene couching both. Taken together, the writings from the music journalists *about* Braxton and those *by* Braxton (about his own work as well as those areas that comprise its context: music history, performance philosophies and methodologies, sociocultural contexts and currents) serve as a richly stereoscopic pair of lenses through which to view his music.

This section seeks to grind those lenses to their focal point. Its two chapters are constructed to look at the simple transcendent arcs shaped by volumes of complex, inevitably (because true-to-life) paradoxical, repetitive and exploratively rambling material forged and evolving over some three decades. We'll explore those arcs for their expression of the conceptual platforms—the public's and his own—on which Braxton's music rests.

Chapter Three will briefly summarize and comment on the media coverage of Braxton's music, before surveying his own writings; Chapter Four will select from the latter those parts that speak to the history and perspective surveyed in the first section, commenting on them in passing. We'll look at the peculiar challenges Braxton's writings pose to a sympathetic reader, how best to meet them, and what rewards lie beyond them.

This look at Braxton's writings is meant to complement the comparably voluminous literature by others on him in a particular way. Braxton's own words should be taken as the definitive source and final word on the subject of his music, but they're so idiosyncratic, specialized, and hard to access (since self-published, or limited to liner notes and interviews by others) that their impact on the academic, music, and general cultural communities is, to date, far less than that of the secondary sources. Of those, the *New Grove* blurb (its context more than its words) works, again, as a bridge, to a mainstream acceptance of the artist's own terms. It carries the ambiance of an authoritative, cohesive American cultural reference that sits comfortably on the international shelf next to its European and other counterparts. It is within that ambiance that I would frame this section.

Braxton is an artist with universalist traits and aspirations, but like all such he operates from a solid base in the cultural idioms specifically native to him: African American first, nested in mainstream American second, with the larger Western and global base nesting those. My interest in reviewing the literature was (1) to survey and summarize the most music-specific and widely read, broad and general coverage; (2) to survey and summarize the less widely read, more advocatory coverage, from album liner notes and new-music publications; and (3) to survey and summarize the private interviews published in Braxton's books (which overlap with both of the above).

My reasons for comparing this public press with Braxton's own books went to the ongoing soul-searching in the academic and commercial arts and humanities complex through matters of cultural democracy and multicultural consensus, a search that's been intense in the jazz and American experimental music traditions, with their respective eschewals of Western cultural primacy. Braxton is vitally involved with both traditions. Jazz, of course, has had its hard time (as respected art, not always as popular entertainment) because of its non-Western cultural base; the American experimental tradition, while mostly defined and furthered by whites in European concert tradition, has foundered similarly both because of its non-Western elements and its own American defiances of European musical conventions.

Braxton's version of this two-pronged iconoclasm extends to the written word (as did Cage's, Sun Ra's, and Ornette Coleman's, along with many contemporary librettists and performance artists). His use of language is as original as his music, as profound and purposeful—and as rooted in universal human experience and traditions as it is in his own personality. However, those traditions and that experience are not solely the Western ones underpinning conventional academic and journalistic writing. Chapter Four will explore what they are, and how they relate to those Western premises, both in the specifically Western and international arenas.

Braxton is unique not only for his longtime, evolved work in both jazz and experimental-music traditions, but for that work in the face of a press, however interested and sympathetic, with a different set of aesthetic and philosophical premises than his own. While that difference is still alive and well, he has survived and even thrived long enough to see his premises take root in the emergent (if not yet dominant) music scene, and thus in a fair share of the media.

To discuss Braxton's books (and even his liner notes) in great detail would require one or more books itself; here I would give a faithful rendering of their broad outlines. Lock, again, has already done much of that[2] but my goal is to supplement Lock's outlines with discussions of the difficulties most readers would have with the books, and arguments for why and suggestions for how those difficulties should be overcome (in other words, why they should read Braxton rather than only Lock's, Radano's, or my synopses).

In talking about this body of music that has proven itself on the critical terms of both jazz and Western art music—and in talking so *in* those terms—I hope to ground Braxton's shapes, concepts, and hieroglyphs in the very concrete experience he shares with many. In so doing, I hope to articulate and affirm the vitality and importance of Braxton's ideals and principles, not only as those of a private man's private artistic universe, but as the universals, singularly expressed, that he declares them to be. In doing *that*, I hope to celebrate a part of the American music tradition that has languished in the shadows of too many of its less profound offerings.

Chapter Three

The Musician's Words

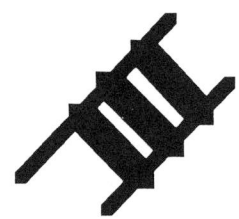

Reporters and reviewers who assume that their role is to determine how well blues music measures up to standards based on principles formulated from the special conceptions and techniques of European concert-hall music are misguided not only as to the most pragmatic function of criticism but as to the fundamental nature of art as well. For art is always a matter of idiomatic stylization, it transcends both time and place. Thus criticism, the most elementary obligation of which is to increase the accessibility of aesthetic presentation, is primarily a matter of coming to terms with such special peculiarities as may be involved in a given process of stylization . . . Such being the nature of the creative process, the most fundamental prerequisite for mediating between the work of art and the audience, spectators, or readers, as the case may be, is not reverence for the so-called classics but rather an understanding of what is being stylized plus an accurate insight into how it is being stylized. Each masterwork of art, it must be remembered, is always first of all a comprehensive synthesis of all the aspects of its idiom.

Albert Murray

The greatest philosophers took pains not to be quotable; they expressed their most serious ideas not through direct statement but rather through implication, allusion, repetition, contrast, symbol, irony, and context; they floated their proofs in time. To them the concise explanation was anathema, the accommodating professor as undesirable as a jeering mob.

Robert Grudin

I think the journalism that surrounds the music has traditionally been very dangerous, because what's happened is that the basic thrust of journalism has always moved to make the music move into the same affinity alignment that we had with language . . . .We need the journalistic community to educate the people about what has really been happening in the music.

Anthony Braxton

The Music's Press

European writing about American jazz has done the music a service that could profitably inform the ethical debates and identity crises of Western ethnomusicologists. The jazz tradition presents a musical microcosm of the African and European cultural conflicts, and it suggests some of their resolutions, in America. Western musical premises, with the Western legacy as a whole, founded and framed America's cultural arena, but African spins on those premises increasingly compel it, Africanizing it as it has Westernized its thralls.

European journalists and scholars have appreciated this dynamic from its turn-of-the-century beginnings. The French Hugues Panassie (in the 1930s) and André Hodeir[3] (in the 1950s) raised the level of discourse on jazz from popular-entertainment journalism to the "serious" criticism and scholarship formerly reserved for Western art music. The results in the music included an expansion from the American commercial entertainment to the broader Western cultural arena, starting in the 1920s, leading to a steady increase in emigration by (mostly) African American "jazz" musicians to Europe, from where they've sensed the most (in Braxton's case, often the only) Western support and understanding. In addition to Lock's studies are Wilmer's and Gray's works, all of which surpass most work by their American counterparts on Braxton's genre as a whole.

The quotations around the words in the last paragraph themselves denote this shift. Artists dating from the earliest days of the music—Duke Ellington is a good example—have defied the authority of such categories as Eurocentrically racist and classist. This defiance surely made its strongest points once it had *sufficiently* mastered Western musical premises, in the dazzling chromaticism of bop, from Charlie Parker to John Coltrane. In Anthony Braxton, seminally, the defiance had new points to make. In the 1960s, he and his peers moved on from the American songbook (including the rigidifying of blues into symmetrical harmonic/metric structures) to claim the texts and scripts of the rest of the world, and to fashion their own spins thereon. They thus moved off of the platform of

Western arts and letters on which the "jazz" and "serious music" press had developed and taken their respective stands.

Radano speculates that

> despite the consistent praise of Braxton, the critics' repeated references to a controversy suggests that a dispute of some dimension must have existed. One suspects that critical reviews rarely appeared in print because many of those who disliked Braxton's music probably preferred not to write about it, and reviewers with more tentative opinions may have curbed their rebuffs in fear of seeming reactionary.[4]

There are some reviews that are less than glowing, which many artists would shrug off or take in stride, especially since they were exceptions to the rule. Braxton—perhaps because of the atmosphere of hostility to his music from some quarters, and the general volatility of the times—was outspoken in his arguments with their premises.

After citing some mention of the reasons for Braxton's lack of favor with a minority of reviewers ("pretentious," "devoid of the element of swing essential to jazz," "clinical and bloodless"), Radano notes the overwhelmingly good press.[5] In chronicling the marketing and media presentation (or failure of it) of Braxton's music, and the rise and fall of its popularity between 1974 and 1977, his point of interest is that Braxton ran into problems not because of critical rejection or dismissal of his music so much as because he scrambled the lines between "jazz" and "concert music" in people's minds. *"Braxton's words about music were the principal source of controversy about him,"* he writes. *"Indeed, this fact is of signal importance when evaluating a musician whose forebears in jazz expressed little interest in and some contempt for verbalizing musical experience"*[6] (emphasis mine. This is a point that frames further discussion of Braxton's synthesis of oral and literate traditions—which, in his music, means improvisation and notation).

Of the major serial coverage (see Bibliography), a bit by Gene Santoro, frequent contributor to *Down Beat*, is pertinent here. Reviewing Lock's book for *The Nation*, he wrote:

> Shaman, seer, mystic: These concepts, devalued by our society, describe almost exactly Braxton's Pythagorean belief (and the belief of almost every culture but the post-Enlightenment West) in the power of art to affect the world . . . the music is what matters, and Braxton's matters a lot. Listening to it in this extended format lets it surround you with its varied preoccupations and goals in a useful and provocative way. The sheer length forces and allows you to react to its kinetic changes of mood, texture, form and concept as musicians onstage have to. Look at it as a chipping away at the barrier between audience and performer, observer and participant, people and culture, that has haunted Western civilization since the Industrial Revolution and its intellectual arm, the Enlightenment.[7]

To summarize the bulk of such coverage, it is safe to say that Braxton enjoyed overwhelmingly positive treatment by the mainstream jazz press and the general media's jazz coverage from the first. The critical assessments have been good; the attention and respect given Braxton's opinions (even negative ones about the music business and media), ideas, and goals have been evident in the regular lengthy coverage; the significance of Braxton's work, established for most existing and new audiences by *Down Beat* and other music magazines, was acknowledged by major mainstream magazines. Yet Braxton sees himself, as others see him, as someone who got short shrift, compared to many of his peers, by that press and business. Why? What exactly has been the problem? We'll come back to that question.

From 1980 to 1985, books on jazz coming out devoted much space to Braxton, sometimes his own chapter; this sort of press has culminated in the three books devoted entirely to him now out. To summarize the composite thrust of the books devoted in part or whole to Braxton, we can say, first, that the sheer amount of print devoted to his work is a statement about his generally accepted importance as an artist in the jazz tradition (Ullman, Berendt, Litweiler, Wilmer, Lock, Heffley); a composer in the American experimentalist tradition (Lock, Radano, Heffley); and a visionary and cultural innovator of broader appeal than both traditions, making music as a means to the larger ends of literally changing the world (Lock, Smith, Heffley).

To summarize coverage by advocacy journalists,[8] we might note that, like Braxton himself, it started out (in the magazines *Coda* and *Cadence*) steeped lovingly in tradition but decidedly positioned on the forward-looking, scouting edges thereof. It is a press that virtually grew up with Braxton and his peers, serving readers as an alternative to a (perceived) complacent, conservative music press. It was obviously an enterprise of love more than money in its early years, one that matured steadily over time not into a big-business operation but certainly a healthy and professional one (the above publications plus *Wire*, the now defunct *Ear*, and *Option*, with a few others). In fact, it often overlaps with the current jazz press in content, now that that press, in publications such as *Down Beat* and *Musician*, has expanded its own scope in pace with the culture, and music/music-journals once considered radical and controversial have established their turfs. Nevertheless, Braxton's role in this press has always been central, compared to the eccentricity still ascribed to him in the other.

Music journalists are assumed to work from a position of, if not absolute and informed neutrality and objectivity, at least viability as a relatively unobtrusive liaison between musicians and the musically curious, and the music lover. Writers of liner notes are granted more bias toward the artist. Often they are also journalists. One reads their good reviews in a magazine and supposes them to express opinions unconflicted by interests other than artistic quality. One reads the same good reviews on artists' albums and knows they've been paid to promote said artist. One nonetheless assumes (properly or not), especially with well-known writers, that they wouldn't hire themselves out to such work if they weren't sincere about their endorsement. Liner notes from a respected journalist are perhaps the next entry point to an artist's work after the media coverage.

Liner notes by a fellow musician, especially a collaborator, can come with different biases, but also different insights (perhaps a reader's relationship with music, passive or active, determines her affinity with a musician's or a non-musician's perspective). A reader has to decide whether the artist's self-interest is clouding his judgment or whether his self-investment is improving it. (A similar decision must be made about notes written by a recording's producer, which occurred as rarely with Braxton's work as notes by a fellow artist. Most were written by journalists or Braxton himself.)

Finally, liner notes written by the artist can either far surpass all the above by giving the readers more of what they are primarily interested in, or fall far short, giving them none of what they are looking for (explanation of a mystery in terms they understand). A record company will, of course, welcome the former, but guard against the latter.

Braxton often wrote his own liner notes, when possible, especially throughout the 1970s, when he felt his own words were most needed and those of others least helpful. Braxton's notes we'll examine shortly; those written by others include all of the above types.

To summarize all of this quarter-century's worth of serious media attention paid to Braxton, it is clear that the international mainstream jazz and general media have acknowledged his importance, but also that he ran into much hostility from some quarters there. The more new-music-friendly media (also international) have likewise recognized him, without the controversy but also without as broad a readership. Commercial endorsements of his recordings have come from respected journalists. In the academic community we see two scholars' published work, both extending through dissertation into published book.

Braxton, for his part, has expressed reservations about the very process of painting such portraits, even when they are flattering. Much of what he says in interviews and writes in his own books about those reservations is aligned with the thrust of a piece by one of those writers—Amiri Baraka—whom, ironically, Braxton has named as a Braxton-disparager.[9]

Baraka's talk at a convention of jazz educators, researchers, artists, and journalists[10] addressed the subject of media coverage of the music. His focus was on the effect of jazz criticism on the art form. He looked at the music critics who write for the sorts of magazines audiences and academics look to for their own information and understanding. In all art forms, he noted, critics and artists often have a natural adversarial relationship; in jazz, this has always been exacerbated by the cultural and racial disparities between the predominantly black artists and the overwhelmingly white critics.

Baraka maintained that good criticism must stem from an understanding of what the artist and art form are intending and meaning; one would be foolish to criticize a Picasso for not painting realistically enough. In the case of black music, he said, the ignorance of and bias against the real nature of the music is tinged with the same sort of repression the Nazis exercised against the modern and "non-Aryan" arts of their time and place. The widespread banning of the drum was an indication of its political threat. He said that the "rhythmic sophistication of the African was forced into vocal expression that was highly sophisticated from its beginnings" and a "percussive style was brought to any instruments blacks played—fiddle, jawbone, broom, body, feet, sticks, and later horns and piano." This rhythmic expression was the very heart of a culture that was systematically and systemically inferiorized for the gain of slavery.

Baraka sees this history as still very much alive in jazz criticism. The music's great artists have been panned and/or trivialized while alive, and redefined, enshrined—and capitalized upon—when dead.

> The main institutions of jazz criticism are like any of the more basic American institutions in relationship to the African American people: they are white supremacist, fundamentally exploitative, and self-serving. Earlier, these critical institutions simply dismissed African cultures as savage, or later as nonexistent, as the alien African became the more familiar Negro slave. The only "culture" and art a slave had were, at most, imitative and witless.

Any other way of seeing it would call into question the premises upon which white prestige and power were based. Those premises, in a nutshell, were based on an aesthetic that distinguished spiritual from material reality, as opposed to joining the two.

One quote from Baraka resonates keenly with Braxton:

> The formalism of the jazz critical establishment celebrates form as content and as formal "invention." Craft and structure are exalted, but "objectionable" content is denigrated as having flaws in technique.

Applied to Braxton, this says that his highly idiomatic playing, speaking, writing, and notating styles are both his desired goals as well as the very things his critics have considered anathema. But then he made his debut in the 1960s, when, as Baraka says, the "upsurge of black writers on jazz . . . was a reflection of the black masses' simultaneous cry for self-determination (at its most practical, beginning with self-definition)." He argues that this self-determination had to swim upstream against the white (racist) critical, academic, and corporate networks that bestowed significance and economic clout on its favorites. "The older, more outrightly racist denunciation of the music has been succeeded by an equally racist attempt to pirate it. Every major writing job on African American music is held by whites. Most institutions that deal with it are white-dominated." He goes on to cite common effects of this domination: starvation wages for performance and recording, even by those declared "legends" and "geniuses"; selective critical attention favoring the most conservative use of the tradition, at the expense of more important innovative artists emerging; and exaltation of white derivative artists at the expense of black definitive ones. Braxton, of course, has not been so favored, has been an important and definitive innovator, and has consciously taken on that upstream swim.

Writer Roberta Penn sees a current expression of the phenomenon Baraka describes in the shadow side of the high cultural status jazz (*qua* jazz) has attained through neoconservative stylists led by Wynton Marsalis, in mainstream venues such as Lincoln Center.[11] Penn writes of artists who are instead following Braxton's upstream swim, and who look to him as a model:

> The importance of this new generation of improvisers is, for the most part, being overlooked or ignored by the jazz community, which seems to treat it as either a media darling to be patronized or an aberration to be kept hidden in the closet. And the players have not exactly tried to bust down the old bastions of jazz, perhaps because they fear being sucked into it . . . But these artists are taking on a new audience, though it is not yet large enough to put them on the cover of *Time* magazine or among the commercial heroes on the *Billboard* charts. "The innovative people aren't getting in the news," vibist Gary Burton explains. "I know who's good and who isn't by listening to the 3,000 kids at Berklee. I don't hear them talking about the young guys in the suits, they're talking about players like guitarist Bill Frisell" . . . While I don't necessarily think Lincoln Center should add an acid jazz department, I am concerned that these institutions keep their ears open and their feet in the streets. And I think the corporitization of this country, the world, and specifically music, is a very dangerous thing that requires diligence on the part of supporters and players. Otherwise the best any of us will be able to do is go to heavily subsidized concerts and watch corporate jazz being re-created in repertory like the classical music of Mozart or Bach. Ho-hum, and there goes the neighborhood, controlled by experts and fundraisers, professional bureaucrats. Burton calls them "jazz parasites."[12]

Baraka notes that the usual outcome of two cultures exchanging information is the creation of something new, a third entity, that binds the two cultures together as positively and primally as their two original contributions integrated each of them separately. But that process, he says, is subverted yet in America by its continuing racism.

> White supremacy in the United States is not simply philosophy, but an imposed method of social organization, because it creates an artificial and tragic social division, maintaining an aesthetic distance between the African American people and whites . . . This separation produces the classic tension of an art that is outside and inside the dominant society at the same time. It involves the same tragedy, bitter irony, national consciousness, humor, self-deprecating rage, and human heroics that have provided a line of demarcation between Irish and English literature these many years . . . At its deepest consciousness, the black liberation movement remains in sharp conflict with its enemies, even in the arts . . . Mao Tse-tung wrote the area of arts criticism is one of intense class struggle. The critical subjugation of the black arts—jazz included—by the racist U.S. critical establishment is just one more aspect of black oppression.

I am aware that many would see Baraka's rhetoric as dated and tired, whatever truth might be behind it; but those many would also dismiss the sociological events of the 1960s as the naive frivolity of youth, at best, and the dead-end or destructive idealism of arrested development, at worst. Braxton's is a music, now mature, born of and reflective of—indeed, generative to—those times; his writings, from 1985, include passages that say (as we'll see) much the same thing as Baraka. Baraka and Braxton both have been working at their respective positions in these matters through every conceivable up and down, and have demonstrated a relationship to them as to something timeless, thus always timely. As far as both are concerned, it is unlikely that whatever common critiques these two very different seminal voices in the music have articulated will fade with time rather than resolution.

What is one to think? Has Braxton labored so long and hard in obscurity because he's one of those masters dismissed in his own time because of ignorance and insensitivity, racist and otherwise; or is it just that his appeal is limited, or his music not really as important as it aspires to be? Perhaps the only possible test of the truth of Baraka's viewpoint (*vis à vis* Braxton) or its opposite is subjective: what feels right? What rings true? Which, after taking in the music and talk about it, does one have the heart and mind for?

Braxton, though his articulate outspokenness—and thus his vulnerability, and frequent exposure, to misunderstanding—has often epitomized militancy to many, yet has consistently eschewed carping confrontations, those between others or his own. "I'm tired of blaming the Europeans," he told Woodard, "because it becomes a mask for what we can change."[13]

Braxton's own words have been a large part of the picture others have painted, of course, since it was built largely on interviews with him. Even if one sets those aside, however, his media image remains full and positive. His music was the definitive force; his words about it, though as matched with the music as integrity requires, were derivative. This is an important point for those who have been inclined to see Braxton as the talker of a good line, a pretentious intellectual with more cleverness than creative substance.

Regarding the abovementioned generic category of liner notes written by a fellow artist, in Braxton's case this was Leo Smith, a trumpeter/composer who played in his earlier groups. Smith's notes to *The Complete Braxton* provide a good segue into Braxton's own writings.

Again, the match of writer and record reflects a telling irony in the dynamics between artist and media. This package was one of many in Braxton's huge recorded output that frustrated him for one or more elements that were beyond his control. In this case, it was the title; he felt it a misnomer to call less than an hour of a lifetime of music the complete anything. Yet of all the many words about Braxton cited and quoted above, these by Smith do get us closer to the real complete Braxton due to the closer proximity of their writer to him.

Context is everything. Smith doesn't say things a nonmusician writer might not say, but he does say them from a position not so detached from the personal, human experience of—and that is—his subject. Therefore, when *he* chooses to start his words with a denunciation of the typical jazz critic's ineptness with the "jazz" tradition's own heartbeat—its newest, rawest, boldest expressions, unfiltered by the jazz media's different priorities and values—it isn't the same as if a journalist did it to a fellow journalist. When *he* says that Braxton's primary contribution as an innovator has been to "open up a field of new rhythmic elements, and, through his particular solo work on the alto saxophone, to establish the 'single line' instrument (i.e., an instrument that is supposedly capable of playing only 'melody' and not so-called 'harmony') as a major solo tool, bringing the family of instruments to its truest harmonious relationship," we know that the words are not the musings of a spectator positioned somewhere safely apart from the reality to which they refer. When he emphasizes his own points of interest—such as the ultimate folly of distinguishing between/hierarchizing the tradition of one musiculture over another, or one aspect of music (such as the compositional and improvisational modes, or the various instruments) over another—we get the sense that such distinctions made by nonmusicians run counter to his (and by implication Braxton's) creative experience. When we read his offhand explanation of Braxton's pictorial titles, those so often treated as such eccentric enigmas, we feel a perspective not more eccentric but rather more sensitive and conscientious than the nonmusician's.

Unfortunately, Smith, as a fellow artist, is a rare example of fellow artists contributing as articulately as a journalist to Braxton's media image (the "Quartet" sections of Lock's book are good for that; also, his *Wire* interview with bassist David Holland).[14] Fortunately, Braxton himself has spoken up for his personal and the artist's point of view in his interviews, liner notes, and books.

Unfortunately, many readers find these writings difficult. We'll examine a representative sampling both for the alternate reality with which they counter that of the press and for the nature of the problems (and solutions) they pose for the curious reader.

・・・・・

Indeed, the most valid aspiration as well as the most urgent necessity for any writer who truly takes the social, which is to say the ethical, function of fiction seriously is not to create something at least different if not new but rather to achieve something natural to himself and to his sense of life, namely a stylization adequate to the complexity of the experience of his time and place—and perhaps with the luck of past masters, something that is more than merely adequate. Thus does the writer make his unique and indispensable contribution to good conduct: not by creating a pop-image that illustrates what is only a "conventional" conception of a Revolutionary hero, but rather by projecting an image of man (and of human possibility) that is intrinsically revolutionary. Such an image is likely to be automatically at radical odds with the status quo.

Albert Murray

If African American and trans-African intellectuals are content to let the Europeans do all the defining, then it serves them right for us to be in the mess we're in now . . . Most of the writings that have been done have been by jazz journalists or by people who aren't directly involved in creating the music. What

the musician's words

we need, I believe, are books by the composers themselves on their music. I think that's when we'll begin to clear the air and to provide a more relevant context to begin looking at this thing.

Anthony Braxton

Radano provides an appropriate opener to this subject:

> Braxton is a musician with a vivid verbal imagination, who respects the written word and its ability to communicate musical and aesthetic meaning. Braxton has found in the books of composers such as Charles Ives and John Cage an inspiration for his way of thinking and a model for his own literary work. At the same time, his prose carries particular importance because there is no precedent for it in jazz. Braxton's writings on art and culture represent a major literary achievement—the first philosophical expressions of a jazz musician.[15]

Braxton writes and talks about his music in a way that many of his most credible predecessors and peers actively disdain. In keeping with Sidran's identification of the African American jazz tradition as a modern expression of an ancient African oral tradition, it is safe to assert that jazz musicians do have a reputation for disdaining talk (and writing) about their music in favor of doing it. The literate impulse has most commonly been experienced as the oral experience's most awkward, at best, and downright toxic self-consciousness, at worst. The aversion to it taps into all the ancient tabus about revealing esoteric secrets, thus giving away (thus losing) one's power.

However, I would qualify this aversion among contemporary musicians with a few flat assertions, which I'll argue in the course and conclusion of my look at Braxton's words: (1) what they generally disdain is not words written or spoken about the music so much as those done so from a position of detachment from it; (2) Braxton has spoken and written as he has out of a conviction that language, like music, is a power that shapes reality. Insofar as he has written and spoken *defensively* (critically of the media, academia, and other societal institutions embodied around communication and concept), it's been in reaction to his perception that others were shaping his reality as an artist to their advantage and his (and others') disadvantage; and (3) insofar as he has written and spoken *offensively* (proactively and informatively about his own reality, including the specifics of his work—the vast majority of his verbal/literary thrust is offensive in this positive sense), he has used language in the way it's used in the oral rather than the literate tradition, all the while sustaining the abovementioned aversion to the latter.

It is this reassertion of language's oral root—which it shares with music— that both creates the problems literate readers have with Braxton's written (and spoken) speech and the magical power pre/non-literate people have ascribed to writing (although we should more accurately call Braxton's approach *post-*, or *super-*, rather than *pre-* or *non-*literate). This is why Braxton's writings are so valuable and have yet to be widely recognized as such. There is something there that is missing in the widely disseminated information generated by others about him and his work. That something is also in the music—but we may miss it in the music if we allow the music to be, literally, "mediated" by others. It is in Braxton's own words in interviews, but we may miss it there if we allow those words to be contextualized by the interviewer; such contextualization is, of course, inevitable, and happens whatever sincerity and good intentions the interviewer may bring. Most importantly, it is in Braxton's liner notes, and then his books—but we may miss it there if our difficulties in relating to those sources cause us to define and dismiss them as the unfortunate results of a musician presuming to write or speak when his verbal/literary facility is obviously no match for his musical one.

In any case, Braxton frames his take on tradition more completely and proactively (less defensively) in his own liner notes and unedited interviews, and his *Tri-Axium Writings*. This is the place to make the case for Braxton's own writings as the primary sources they are, for the importance of and reasons for respecting them enough to treat them as such, and, foregoing anyone else's paraphrases, for meeting the challenges they might pose to such respect.

The perceptual clash portrayed by the two different sources (of music media, above, and artist, following) begs an exposition. What are the premises underlying the music media's priorities, emphases, and value judgments? What are those of the artist? What are critics looking for? What is their information base, their perception of and relationship to it? What are the artist's intentions? What is the nature of his integrity? How does he understand that same information base (the musical traditions informing his work)? We'll look for the answers implicit in the material itself.

The Liner Notes

At times Braxton's liner notes have been as controversial as everything else about him. As his music evolved, so did his writing about it, and as the writings of others increasingly dissatisfied him, so did his conviction that his own notes on his own music would serve him better. This wasn't always a problem with record companies—for example, his notes on his traditional jazz recordings were comfortably conversational—but when he wrote about his own compositions, he brought to the documentation of their creative processes and circumstances that microscopic, idiosyncratic self-consciousness that is one of his hallmarks. Those notes were seen as esoterically off-putting by business people trying to market a product (most notably the Arista company),[16] and they then clashed with Braxton's claim of control over his art.

Braxton's maverick stance has more often than not led him to (usually European) labels less concerned with the money and more with the music; also, his success with the mainstream jazz press has familiarized its readers with his style enough to take the edge off the original strangeness of his original music. Concordantly, over time, the notes have evolved into a spicy blend of his own words and those of sympathetic and respectful (and respected) journalists of both traditional and new music (e.g., Lange and Lock). As in other aspects of his art,

Braxton has fought for and won the right to define himself and his own terms—a right the journalists and scholars certainly assert, not only regarding themselves but him as well.

Starting with the notes to traditional jazz recordings, then moving through his solo alto recordings to duos and trios, quartet performances of his own music, then creative orchestra and multi-orchestral works, the language is seen to move (parallel to the music) from least to most complex, difficult, and esoteric. Taken in this order, the liner notes provide the best entry points to the more difficult realms of the books.

The key to Braxton's daunting complexity lies in finding and staying anchored to the simple basic premises from which it evolves. His musical perspective and vision (and the writings that chart it) thus become clearer when related to their roots in traditional jazz conventions; followed from those into the creative solitude of his solo music, where he methodically works traditional conventions into his own new expressions; seen moving from that initially private universe into that of duos with other musicians; activated by the magical significance of the number three as embodied in the trio; moved into the quartet, through which the volatile trio's interactions and beginnings of an ensemble voice come into a stable structure; made to sing and speak through that voice as well as those of its individuals, in ever-larger ensembles (his "creative orchestras"); and, finally, split into several such collective (his "multiorchestral") voices careening about in the same piece.

Whether by circumstance or design, the collection of Braxton's liner notes covers all of these combinations and can be ordered so, I think, to better understand each.

On Traditional Material

Braxton's notes to *Dona Lee* are a good starting place. They are brief and to the point, and they include the elements that make Braxton both unique and challenging. They are worth quoting in full then analyzing thoroughly for the microcosm they embody of Braxton's denser notes:

> Understanding the principles used in any period of creativity is a must before one is able to replace them (understanding empirically or intuitively). Once any strong position is secured, solidifying with the whole becomes important. It is with this relationship that we are able to see the total progression as well as the significance of whatever our activity is about. Seen in this light, the music we call jazz takes on a special importance. It is in this music that the human spontaneous vibration can be attached to both the direct situation of the music and also an understanding of the total context of the environment itself . . . not to mention the fact that the whole gamut of the music is equally beautiful as well as rewarding to play. It is because of this that jazz from Louis Armstrong to Albert Ayler is new music . . . the reality hasn't really changed, only the spectacle. Our music then outlines diversion 508 and Fats Waller covers 327. The 'diversion from' is what we put our attention on.[17]

The notes conclude with a couple of dedications of Braxton's own works (with titles that look like codes from the table of chemical elements) to friends, and some chatty sentences about the album's two songs from the standard jazz repertoire, "You Go To My Head" and "Donna Lee."

The first obvious stumbling block to the informed and discerning reader is inconsistent spelling ("Dona" in two places, the correct "Donna" in another, and "Diana" instead of "Dinah" Washington). This might be overlooked as relatively insignificant negligence if it weren't for its thriving proliferation throughout the body of Braxton's writings—and for a couple of comments he made about it in interview and liner notes.

> I have found, for instance, five million different levels of criticism of my liner notes, "Did I have a comma in the right place?" "What does he mean by this particular term?" Cries of pseudo-intellectualism, etc. But in the fifteen, twenty years that I've been documenting my music, I've never heard anyone challenge some of the liner notes which have been on my own records or on the records of musicians, so-called "jazz" musicians for the last fifty years. You know, liner notes written in the most beautiful English, where the Queen herself would have approved of the structure. But articles which didn't know what the fuck they were talking about.[18]

He has also acknowledged and insisted on his spelling of "Tri-*Axium*," as opposed to the "correct" *Axiom*.[19]

This is an element of his printed language Braxton lets stand, in defiance of prevailing professional standards. His remarks about it clearly show that he is asserting a conscious disagreement with the priorities implicit in those standards. If we grant his disagreement validity—as we may feel compelled to do by the sincerity of conviction he demonstrates with this gambling of his credibility—we must allow our respect for those professional standards to be challenged. The question "Why doesn't he just get someone to proofread his work?" then expresses the same suspicion of his sincerity and competence as "Does he play so far out because he can't play correctly? Does he play time as he does because he can't swing?" and so on.[20]

In the end, if we accept his spellings—or his overall musical concept, or his rhythmic concept—we accept such "imperfections" as healthy idiosyncrasies; we grant his implied critique of our zeal for an absolute standard demanding conformity more power than that standard. (Re: professional literacy standards, we might recall the historical precedent of William Billings, who advocated that every composer be "his own Carver" at a time when spellings and word usage themselves had not yet been widely standardized, and when literary intelligence and competence weren't therefore so strictly judged by such standards.)

The next element of his style with language to challenge us might be his tendency to speak in abstractions that convolute into loosely modifying mazes. For example, what he essentially said above was, "It should surprise no one that we in the so-called avant-garde of jazz should desire to play from the conventional repertoire. From our point of view, Louis Armstrong and Albert Ayler are timeless expressions of the same song, and we are certainly not working in a vacuum apart from either of them." However, he chose to say that circuitously, making five sentences worth of assertions about the Platonic sorts of universal absolutes behind that concrete paradox ("new" musicians playing "old" music) that might rationalize it for a thinking person initially puzzled by it. (The parenthetical qualifier ending his first sentence is tacked on far past its referent as a sort of afterthoughtful explanation that "free" musicians can know how to play "straight" without formal training.) Such mazes of disjunctured asides are a Braxton literary staple, giving even the most dryly rational and organized pieces a stream-of-consciousness feel.

Sidran notes that in the oral tradition, circumlocution in speech is prized over exact definition, which is considered crude and unimaginative.[21] Braxton's speech, spoken and written, demonstrates the improvisational creativity fostered by that value.

From his maze of abstraction and sprawling syntax, Braxton blossoms into cryptic metaphor. With the sentence "Our music then outlines diversion 508 and Fats Waller covers 227?" our struggle to comprehend freezes in a flat "Huh?" If we try to look to the next sentence to clear up the mystery—"The 'diversion from' is what we put the attention on"—we're so lost we just have to pull out of the writer-reader interaction that makes reading enjoyable and fruitful and ponder long and hard. After doing so, we conclude that he was probably whimsically comparing the difficult yet playful process of making new music within a tradition to a school curriculum with classes in how to master the material (Fats Waller covers) and how to alter it (diversion). We give up the hope of understanding the second sentence conclusively but take it in as a clue or two. Who is the "we" in this sentence, the artists or the critics? Does "diversion from" mean that conventional ground from which new musical expressions launch themselves, or does it mean the process and line of their flight once they are no longer on that ground? The sentence will never tell us.

With this whole passage, Braxton seems to presume the concretes of his subject before his first words, which are abstractions of it. His statement of their concretes are unmistakably infused with the spin of those abstractions. He then gives a restatement of both abstract and concrete in metaphorical terms, for emphasis and clarity (!); then (where it loses us) a comment on all of this that is too ambiguous to really decipher. The experience is of watching his mind start to fly in midair and move faster and faster while our own, still groundlocked, must work slower and slower in order to track his flight, until finally his mind is a distant blur and ours is stopped. (Incidentally, this treatment of language is very like the process of improvisation.)

Then, having achieved that impasse, we run into a formulaic title such as *H-204 3HF/G*, and we know we are on territory bereft of referents. We are confronting someone else's private universe and wondering why we should bother learning its meanings, or if we really ever could.

Then, suddenly, we are back to mundane consensus reality, as Braxton finishes off his comments with some chatty nods to the American songbook and bebop standards, and the familiar figures of Dinah Washington and Charlie Parker.

This sketch captures in microcosm most of the elements of Braxton's writings that make them seem so daunting, but—perhaps because these notes are so brief, and written early in his career—it covers none of the (arguably) *most* daunting element: his self-coined words and terms. (The notes to *In the Tradition Vol. 1* are entirely readable, with no Braxton peculiarities at all. He states clearly his love for the tradition and desire to document its repertoire throughout his recording career, along with his original music.) If we move up to the notes for *Seven Standards 1985, Volume I* we get a taste of those in the still accessible and even palatable context of the familiar territory of conventional jazz. His first paragraph is free of them, but once we are drawn in by the thoughtful, humorous, scintillating (to music lovers) anecdotes of this acknowledged master, we encounter terms such as "alternative functionalism," "thrust continuum of post-AACM exploration dynamics," and "post-Parker continuum."

Sprinkled sparingly in a conversational essay on, again, the seamlessness of the musical garment that includes both experimental and mainstream expressions of the jazz tradition, these terms can be incorporated into the average reader's comprehension without too much trouble, though a small leap or two is presumed even there. "Alternative functionalism?" Context suggests a definition of the experimental developments in the music as including different *contexts*—e.g., deliberate evocations of psychic and meta-psychic terrain and forces, rather than simply entertaining displays of style—as well as contents. "Thrust continuum of post-AACM exploration dynamics" might translate most familiarly into "the evolution of concepts mined by the AACM," and "post-Parker continuum" into "bop" or "post-bop" (the qualifier "post" being used not merely as "after" but "along the lines of").

These, then, are the building blocks of all of Braxton's liner notes and books: a quite accessible conversational style, full of warmth and humor; a penchant for abstractions and generalized overview; a spontaneous construction of highly sophisticated, albeit idiosyncratic, vocabulary, syntax and structure; frequently oblique and unexplained metaphor and parenthetical asides; and a proliferation of graphic and alphabetic codes that seem like nothing so much as monuments of solipsism.

Now even the open-minded and sympathetic readers will inevitably ask, when challenged and taxed so, why they should, and whether they can, respond to all this as a communication begging their connection. One answer is that this is simply how Braxton chooses to phrase things conceptually accessible to and commonly used by all. Why is it not merely pretentious and contrived? Because he is a legitimate source of and participant in the realities to which he alludes. Just as journalists or academics enjoy the interpreter's authority of the realities they call "music" and "Anthony Braxton," so does he enjoy the authority of a seminal creative figure from within those same realities. If we really want to engage those realities, therefore, we'll question the nature of the ease with which we read the interpreters, the difficulty we have with the creator, and move to reverse the situation. (A clue as to the direction of that reversal: artists typically devote their typically considerable powers of articulation to the generation and sustainment of ambiguity; that ambiguity itself serves an expression and communication greater than that achieved by its dissipation into clarity.)

Before we move to Braxton's notes on his solo work, a present example of those on a more recent recording of mainstream jazz covers will provide a glimpse of the mature expression of the notes on same. Braxton's most recent liner notes often include his own and the comments of a prominent music journalist. Deliberately or not, they thus serve as models of the kind of common purpose and respectful reciprocity he has found wanting between his peers and their press, and has fought for in his own career.

A couple of things are worth noting in his notes with Art Lange to the 1990 CD *Eight (+3) Tristano Compositions 1989 For Warne Marsh*. First, his own part in them comes first and is devoid of any of the literary "problems" listed above. It is not devoid of the "conversational style, full of warmth and humor"; it reads much like a transcription of a tape of someone talking, with the fully understandable fragments, ellipses, exclamations, and rhetorical questions of spontaneous speech. In it, Braxton asserts the tradition-affirming nature of his own radical work and eschews the sociocultural and racial biases that have cast aspersions on his own passion for many white jazz artists from that tradition. The oral feel is in full bloom (we feel we're reading transcribed speech), the writer straining not at all to establish, explain, or rationalize his musical universe.

Lange, for his part, writes knowledgeably and thoughtfully about an earlier Braxton composition (the CD producer even includes its graphic-formulaic title, apart from the typesetting) that pertains to what Braxton is doing on this recording. Braxton, then, is freed from such duties to chat with us accessibly, with no difficult self-explanations or justifications. A respected voice of jazz journalism is now plying his craft to the Braxton lexicon as responsibly and comfortably as he would to that of past "controversial eccentrics" whom time has turned into central figures, such as Lester Young, Thelonious Monk, or Charlie Parker.

Solo Material

For Alto has no notes other than the diagrammatic titles with numerical formulas meant to represent each of the double album's four sides. *Saxophone Improvisations/Series F*, released five years later during the peak of his popularity, in 1976, sports a few brief paragraphs stating his purposes in doing solo music: "My saxophone music can be talked of as a language study, exploiting both the potential of the instrument and the progressions-sequence end to the formulas used to date." *Alto Saxophone Improvisations 1979/Language Music (1967)* comes with a classic burgeoning of Braxtonian verbiage. (Incidentally, that progression—from stark hieroglyph to obviously reaching language to the microscopic density of his most complete liner notes and other writings—indicates what happened generally. Braxton has said that he would have preferred not to have written as much as he has but that he felt it necessary. As with these examples, his notes and other writings started taking on their mature form some ten years after he had started working with the musical concepts they addressed, and after ten years of journalism and other writers' notes about them.)

Braxton alludes to the nature of this lag when he mentions that he was only just beginning to understand intellectually what he had known and been doing intuitively all along as a musician. According to him, the "emergence of solo activity [of this sort, his own and others] increases the dynamic spectrum of individual participation." In other words, musicians can develop their own voices and vocabularies, as he did, in the uniqueness of their solitudes (rather than, it is implied, the limits of already established common ground) and thereby have more to contribute to collective efforts. He then breaks his solo work down into six different aspects: (1) a new "language pool" (of sounds and patterns) specific to the alto sax; (2) an equal balance between notated and improvised material; (3) access to the musical expressions of all traditions everywhere in time and space (i.e., a typical solo concert might interpret standards, bebop heads, contemporary Western art music, Asian scales and inflections, and/or Tibetan chant); (4) interdisciplinary and multi-instrumental expressions; (5) entirely notated pieces, and (6) entirely improvised pieces. He declares his explorations to be in response to the exhaustion of the Western harmonic-melodic system as brought on by the work of Cecil Taylor, Ornette Coleman, and John Coltrane (in this he echoes his musical hero Schönberg, who was also enough of a traditionalist to care to *replace* that exhausted system with a fresh one, rather than just leave it for dead).

He explains his idea and method of "conceptual grafting"—a proffered mix of any premises for improvisation that can be conceived. For example, the recording includes three pieces from the tradition—a blues, a sophisticated jazz composition by Benny Golson, and an advanced harmonic *étude* by Coltrane. Their combinable conceptual grafts, if you will, might be named "that which the blues signify," or "that which Benny Golson's music expresses," or "that energy which Coltrane's later music opened up." Each of those is a consensus reality brought to life by its makers and takers. Braxton's own pieces have such essences, but he takes pains that they aren't all the same one, recycled endlessly, and that they don't reduce down to his own self-expression, rather than to the plying of a craft and art as a means to many other ends—and (perhaps more urgently to him) that they aren't perceived so.

The notes end with a paragraph on each of his ten compositions, each paragraph accompanied by line drawings representing different sounds and their shapes and movements. These are a foretaste of Braxton's five volumes of composition notes, and the stuff of many other liner notes. As such, they afford us a manageably microcosmic point of entry to that vast expanse of print and imagery.

At first glance, they seem the very epitome of dry abstraction; just the look of them evokes something scientific, the reduction of a human to his or her chemical elements. But after a few open and sympathetic readings, they become almost correspondingly concrete. Whatever interest the reader has in the process of making and hearing music at all—the mystery of a sound and its shapes, transformations, and pulses evoking mood, vision, emotional transformation—is seized and distilled from all other distractions, is focused by these blurbs and their schemata, especially if one reads them while listening. After a while, it becomes refreshing to see words and images limited to the very mechanical aspects of music to which they are adequate, and to see its other aspects—those mysteries that inspire poetic, philosophic, spiritual and political sorts of utterances—left in the silence between player and listener from which all music rises and to which it falls (though, as we'll see, Braxton's *Composition Notes* did use words to reach into such silences).

Not only do these notes at first seem abstract, they also seem impersonal, colder than we like to feel about music. But, again, after taking that impersonality in sympathetically, asking what its appeal might be to the personality who generates it, one can see in it the lightness and liberation of *trans*personality. This, it seems, is what Braxton prefers to "self-expression" as a musical motive: self-transcendence, where the music made can be measured in cosmic rather than human scales, where "cold" need not be pejorative but can bear the magnificence of a glacial terrain on some outer planet, and "hot" is not merely a human but possibly a solar, or nuclear energy. The place the human creator occupies in this *kosmos* is both transcendent (as the composer is, not merely in relation to his life's works but also, consciously and deliberately, to his life work) and immanent (as is the improviser who plays his human part in the superhuman context, just as he lives his biological life in the larger context of the planets, space, and stars).

Seen in this light, Braxton's abstraction and impersonality become, simply, shadow sides of proportionately concrete fruits and personal investments; moreover, they provide the healthy, grounding, shielding balance necessary to one who might otherwise get lost in his own density and self-sacrifice (as have, indeed, so many of his predecessors and peers in this most demanding genre in its most toxic American/Western situations).

A less subtly human touch in these "impersonal abstracts" is Braxton's dedication to a person important to him, either personally or through the person's public persona or work. These suggest that the music intended by, or resulting from his improvisations on, his own compositions was somehow an appropriate statement to make to specific people—that is, it was personal. This line from his notes to *Duets 1976*, with pianist Muhal Richard Abrams, shows how that process might work more or less generally:

> The remaining track on this record (Nickie) is actually an improvisation which was done on the spot. After listening to the playback, I felt the music we played had somehow captured something essential to this period in my life, and I appreciated Muhal letting me dedicate the improvisation to my wife.[22]

The music is made from the clean slate of freedom and spontaneity—impersonally, if you will—but something personal comes of it as a result of this Zen-like approach. Braxton discovered this dynamic early on, as we've seen, when he became fascinated with John Cage for the latter's zealous self-abnegation in the service of music, but quickly decided that his own personality was as much a part of the universe as everything else.

Moving ahead another five years (*Anthony Braxton: Composition 113*), the notes retain all the above elements but add some new ones—visuals, dramatics, and literary elements that will carry Braxton's music further toward his desired destination in the realm of cathartic collective ritual, as developed in Western art music through opera. In this move, he remains consistent to one of his solo work's primary functions: working out new ideas for larger ensembles (even though he doesn't classify this piece as part of his body of solo music, the primary function of which for him is that of "language studies" [see Chapter Five]). *Composition 113* falls, rather, under the heading of "image music." Braxton the musical scientist is now the musical storyteller (idiosyncratic spellings are included without the use of *sic*):

> It is midnight and raining at a small train station in Northern Africa and finally the old locomotive has arrived. As the smoke begins to clear from around the tracks of the engine, we can see six people boarding the train—all of whom are clothed in bulky robe-like garments with long black hoods (but our vision is obscured because everything is taking place in the shadows—so we can not see their faces). When the doors of cabin twelve are opened and the six blurred figures enter into the coach it is from this point that Ojuwain (—the believer—) must make his decision. *Composition 113* asks us to come into the world of decisions and choises—as a basis to establish fresh relationships with creative music and sound awareness.[23]

From rationalistic cerebrations we move to the mythological, dream consciousness (this piece was actually composed on a train). One finds, concurrent with this development, the appearance of human figures and real-world objects in the geometrical hieroglyphs of his titles,[24] talk of operas in progress in his interviews, and slide projections and giant puppets[25] in his projects for large ensembles. All of this turned what earlier might have seemed a clinical Cartesian posture into a Pythagorean wedding between mathematics and magic (remember, "geometry" literally means "earth measure"; it did not begin its life as an abstract universe). The African element is so primary that the adoption of Western nomenclature, idiomatic as it is, never threatens but rather globalizes it, as the poles do the world.

The Duo Notes

Braxton's readable, chatty notes for his duo date with Muhal Richard Abrams start by noting a recent increase in such combinations in improvised music. Braxton welcomes the trend, expresses his hope that it is more than a trend, declaring that "the duet situation gives the greatest possibilities for establishing an affinity relationship with another musican on a one to one basis. This is especially true of the more open-ended forms where an improvisation is directly affected by both musicians on an equal plane, rather than the 'soloist with support' situation only." He expresses his fascination with the "lower sound spectrum" and timbre of his "contra-base" saxophone.

The Trio Notes

The notes to *For Trio*, in this sampling, are a quantum leap further into Braxton's mind. Their brevity offsets their potential obscurity by functioning in print as Radano has seen Braxton's lexicon functioning in speech (as I can corroborate):

> Braxton lacked the pretentiousness I had anticipated after reading his extremely difficult prose in liner notes and published statements. In conversation his idiosyncratic language seemed more like a grassroots poetry, securely attached to his mystical perception of the world.[26]

the musician's words

Every sentence of these notes has left the realm of informal conversation merely sprinkled with such jargon; it is in full force as subject, object, and verb here in a way it is not even in the longer (but more static) notes to the original solo work, nor in those (more chatty, relaxed) to the original duo work, nor in those to traditional jazz material. For example:

> For creativity, as understood through the progressional thrust of world culture, can be viewed as activity (doing) that aligns us (on either an individual or cultural level) to the greater cosmic realness of being on this planet—having to do with helping us experience this sector in space (the universe)—in spiritual and vibrational terms, while also serving as a cosmic connector to those forces which reveal what this experience (living) could mean in its most positive state (if positive is the desired zone).[27]

An energy has entered, and Braxton is calling on his creative resources to verbalize it faithfully. The result is a kind of glossolalia of the intellect, a verbal/literary music-making not only out of language but out of the least musical use of language—that of rationalism.

How might we understand this leap in terms of the creative and musical processes we've been considering? Perhaps the leap from two to three musicians itself provides a key.

In an interview with Lock, Braxton speaks of and Lock magnifies the significance of the number three:

> L: Can we begin by talking about your philosophical overview of music? You have three primary categories: restructuralism, stylism and traditionalism.
>
> B: Three is the primary number of my generating system. Tripartial perception dynamics permeate how I've tried to deal with my music, whether we're talking of restructuralism, stylism, traditionalism; or mental, physical, spiritual divisions; or past, present, future.

In a footnote to the last sentence, Lock adds:

> In view of Braxton's reference to the ancients, including Pythagoras, it may be worth noting that in Pythagorean numerology, three is the number of knowledge—of music, geometry and astronomy.[28]

Elsewhere Lock alludes to (and demonstrates) this prevalence of three:

> Braxton talks about his *Trillium* operas, a planned set of twelve three-act operas, the acts actually being thirty-six interchangeable

"dialogues." *Trillium*, he says, has to do with "the third part of the order that I'm trying to establish: 1) my music; 2) the *Tri-axium Writings*, which is a restructural philosophical system; 3) rituals. *Trillium* is a platform to express my worldview" and will be part of a projected twelve-day festival of world culture. As *Tri-axium* had to do with the number three, so *Trillium* has to do with the number twelve. (Which in numerology also reduces to three: $12 = 1 + 2 = 3$.)[29]

The move from the personal to the transpersonal in his music is reflected in the shift in language that took place in the notes for *For Trio*.

The Quartet Notes

The macro-scope and the dynamic volatility of the *For Trio* notes—pervasive aspects of Braxton's writings as a whole—give way to the more studied, microscopic approach (an equally pervasive aspect) of the accompanying quartet recordings. In keeping with the Western art music tradition, Braxton's quartets function as both the composer's and performer's "laboratory" (and, of course, in his case composition includes improvisation): composer's/improviser's because there are enough voices to begin to realize the variety of musical patterns and structures that draw from the spectrum of voices, and performer's because they are still few enough to enjoy the self-sufficiency and intimacy of solo, duo, and trio experiences. Having moved from the (ec)static of one through the interactive of two and the volatile synergy of three, we encounter the structural stability in four that provides the core crystal for larger structures.

While Braxton's notes for *Performance 9/1/79* seem dense and obscure at first glance, they read more like a careful, detailed account of a real-world process and experience (that of conceiving and executing the quartet music) than like an abstraction of anything. They are difficult in their specialist's orientation—he assumes that his reader is probably interested enough to be aware of and to understand the contributions and significance of musical innovators from all cultures and time periods, and to see that he is carving out his own niche in that transcultural, transhistorical musiculture.

His use of the term co-ordinant (later interchanged with coordinate) for this music refers to his linking of several compositions into a single entity. It also seems to revolve around the concept that his compositional role is indeed one of a map maker for musical explorations, experiments, and expositions, both composed and improvised, more than a "paper music" writer. He makes it clear that just as a conventional composer trusts in the abilities and judgment of interpreters to render the true meaning of what he or she writes, so does Braxton trust in the abilities of improvisers to connect them to what *he* writes (i.e., improvisers everywhere and everywhen, as opposed to only those he knows and works with personally).

Braxton's aim is to make structures that trigger the most interesting, challenging, and demanding improvisations for the most dedicated and broad-minded musicians and listeners. Thus, even when he spells out and structures things the most, he leaves them elastic (e.g., he might give players a last-minute instruction to play in a different tempo than his notation calls for, so prejudgment and preparation will never be entirely possible, spontaneity always assured. In this, of course, he is solidly aligned with the tradition handed down from Louis Armstrong through Duke Ellington through Miles Davis through Thelonious Monk, to name just a few of the music's most famous synthesizers of compositional and improvisational sophistications). Or he'll leave some performance variables ambiguous while specifying others exactly within the composition itself. Vital components in the very conceptual fabric of all of his compositions, he writes, are the "dynamics" of the individual performers and the real-world situation around them at the time of the performance.

He also writes of his concept of "collage improvisation," a concept he obviously forged in his vast experience with open-ended improvisations. The concept is his attempt to keep the spirit of non-hierarchical group free play while also keeping it from swallowing its individual players in a muddy wall of sound destined to collapse (he might call it "keeping the sound-space transparent"). The collage concept puts different players on different platforms—of tempi, volume, pitch, and other specifications—from which to improvise. The effect is to save the music from degenerating into a power play of egos clamoring to be heard.

Braxton refers to the quartet as his "traditional" (his quotes) music—his link to the jazz tradition's conventional combo whereby he can experiment, but in a context familiar to his audience, his fellow players, and himself. He ends his introductory notes with the hope that they increase his listeners' understanding and thus enjoyment of the music.

Following this general introduction, he goes into details of process and production that are usually of crucial interest to a sensitized artist, but kept from the average fan as shop talk: the importance of staging and sound mechanics to the artists' musical viability; a subjective creative visualization (in the form of a diagram, in Braxton's case) of the concert as a whole as its pieces flow and segue through spacetime (this concept, which he calls the Master Progression Sequence (MPS), signals the aesthetic underpinning his coordinate system, in which each piece is networked for performance interdynamically with every other); the musical particulars of each of those pieces, and what they're intended to do or express; and the credentials and the real musicianship behind them of the players who are interacting. Braxton presents all this as of compelling interest, since it is to him; he trusts that he will have readers who won't need or desire media middlemen to decide what's of interest, relevant, or better explained otherwise.

These notes offer a key to Braxton's hieroglyphs. He shows several examples of standard notation next to his own visual versions of the same sounds. The resemblance between the two suggests a not-so-distant link between *all* of his own and conventional visual codes for sound (again, resonating with the early evolution of Western notation from abstract tracings of sound in the air).

Braxton's writing evolves through his liner notes to quartet recordings of the 1980s and into the 1990s. On *Six Compositions: Quartet (1981)* it's less ponderous and circuitous, though still microscopically technical. Both these and the notes to his LP with the Robert Schumann String Quartet comprise the sort of short analyses of each piece collected in *Composition Notes*, discussed below.

Composition 98 (1984) and *Five Compositions (Quartet) 1986* take the overview. Notes on the former give voice to the years and depths of thought he has obviously put into the respective natures of improvised and notated music. The notes are long but not dense: they are readable musings from the heart of his role as a synthesist of Western literate and non-Western oral traditions.

By 1986, Braxton can write, for his notes to *Five Compositions*, three short paragraphs summing up the musical and metamusical areas he has established for himself and fellow players with his quartet music. The many separate pieces have taken on a composite life and structure from which performances can be shaped. Like a single musician who has memorized so many tunes, riffs, and rhythms that every solo improvisation can use them all in kaleidoscopically infinite ways to make ever-fresh statements, so Braxton's quartet book can now inform his groups. His sixfold breakdown of that book's musical elements embraces extended improvisation, as developed in the "trans-African" tradition; extended interpretation of notated works, as developed through the "trans-European" tradition (re: improvisation and notation—as Braxton's way with words is a reminder that the oral is the root of the literate tradition, so is his attitude to and use of [literate] notation a reminder that [oral] improvisation is the primary, notation the secondary, manifestation of the same process); "encoded imprint logic," Braxton's description of the traditional ritualistic music of "Asian cultures"; collective improvisation; solo music; and his own structural innovations organizing the above.

The metamusical significance this musical wealth holds for Braxton the composer/thinker is expressed so:

    1. the development of a music—sound logic—system that details an evolutionary understanding of structure and vocabulary (or science and vibrational dynamics);

    2. the development of a system of thinking that allows for individual-to-group consciousness (not separate from social and political dynamics); and

    3. the development of a ritual and ceremonial platform that clarifies my own vibrational and spiritual beliefs (and my attraction to universal fundamentals).

There's a certain closure expressed here, perhaps that of a journeyman moving to masterhood. What began as a conspicuous absence then thicket of notes on this subject has become a well-defined clearing, its strangeness that of new life born more than of unrealized potential gestating. In the quartet notes, as throughout Braxton's writings, the goal of the words is to reveal and convey his reality on the assumption that his experience is simply human and therefore as potentially natural and valuable to his fellow humans.

The Large-Ensemble Notes

Relative to the quartet works, as mentioned, the works for orchestra-size ensembles and for "multiorchestras" reflect much the same position symphonies enjoy with string quartets in the Western classical tradition: the quartets show the bones of the concepts and their voices, while the large groups put on flesh and rich clothing. Economics have dictated that the quartet performances/recordings (and thus the liner notes) would far outnumber those of the large groups. Nevertheless, some of Braxton's most extensive and representative notes accompany two of the most important large-ensemble works, *Creative Orchestra Music 1976* and *Composition 82* (for four orchestras). Their importance to Braxton's musical evolution is augmented by the real-world impact they made: the first was voted Record of the Year by *Down Beat* critics in 1977, and both were put out by a major mainstream label (Arista) at the height of Braxton's popularity and success in the polls generally.

Creative Orchestra Music 1976 was Braxton's second large-ensemble recording. His notes are brief and to the point, with two paragraphs of nontechnical, readable chat and pithy notes on each of six works. He distinguishes between creative and notated orchestra music with a reference to the tradition of ensembles led by Fletcher Henderson, Duke Ellington, Charles Mingus, and Ornette Coleman, to highlight the improvisational aspects thriving therein in spite of the complexities improvisation meets in larger groups, whose size alone begs the government of notation.

Braxton offers a valuable insight into his relationship with the act of writing about his art, and his approach to same:

> It is difficult if not impossible for me to write about how I see my work in creative music, for I have never felt that words are meaningful when applied to creativity—and yet something has to be written—for many of the mis-conceptions that surround creative music are still with us today. For that reason I have written briefly on each composition with the hope that even a structural analysis can give the listener some idea as to how I conceived the compositions which comprise this record.

Those analyses don't significantly differ from his notes on pieces for smaller groups.

The later notes, to *82*, go much further. It is also a first, "the first completed work in a series of ten compositions that will involve the use of multiple-orchestralism and the dynamics of spacial activity." He goes on to speak of "multi-orchestralism" as an art and science in itself, to which he is adding his own unique contributions. Several floor plans are included, and diagrams of proposed sound trajectories and speaker placements; a human body is charted for its areas of "information approach" (places where the music is perceived or felt); the title's shape is superimposed on one elliptically zoned floor plan, the zones having colors, letters, and numbers; score page fascimiles are included, and photos of the four orchestras (160 musicians) in place; and sketches of the graphic titles of ten other proposed multiorchestral works, spanning increasingly large distances, up to star systems.

This way of music making, of course, does have a long and varied history, from medieval antiphony to turn-of-the-century battles of the bands. Such divisions of sound have usually represented the interplay between separate aspects of reality—such as the spirit and material world—or different cultures.

Early battles of the bands in St. Louis were between ethnic rival groups in parades. Two bands would approach each other from their different neighborhoods then merge ranks, each continuing to play its own piece at its own tempo in its own key. Whoever lost the thread first, to distraction by the other, lost the contest. The contests between the German and African Americans were the most heated, and the latter prevailed. One can't help but notice that their history as slaves gave them an intimate knowledge of the Western world view, and the need to reconcile it to their own to survive, while whites remained comparatively insulated from their African world view.

Braxton nods to such battles in his own neighborhood and in Kansas City as influences; he mentions the American marching band tradition, *Symphony No. Four* by Charles Ives, works by Stockhausen and Xenakis, Sun Ra's band, and parallel approaches by other cultures. The thrust for him seems to be more sensory than the conceptual one I suggested in the above paragraph:

> There has always been something special about the reality of different ensembles making music in the same physical universe space that has excited my imagination. It is as if the whole of the universe were swallowed up—leaving us in a sea of music and color.

Perhaps this vivid sensory experience is the key to understanding Braxton's penchant for synthesis, innovation, and complexity—it all makes for that much prettier, brighter noise. It's a more charitable explanation than to say he's lost in mental mazes or is pretentious, in any case. As he himself writes at the end of these notes,

> For the realness of multiple orchestra activity directly sheds light on the cross vibrational activity that takes place in everyday living (that being the realness of creative—and "real"—invention and how it is related to the very fabric of existence on this plane). For at the heart of my series of works in multi-orchestralism is the attempt to create a music that can dynamically accentuate (and celebrate) the multi-complexual—*and not complexual*—realness of life on this planet, as a means to be better prepared to deal with this sector in space, and as a factor that might hopefully be positively related to what this preparation could vibrationally and spiritually reveal about "living." (emphasis mine; Braxton's "complexities" are not affectations)

Braxton's recent liner notes, to all his music, have developed into flights of his own personal mythology, fantastic scenarios, and stories whose seed we saw in the notes to *Composition 113*. (We'll save our look at them for Chapter Nine.)

The Composition Notes

Space requires that I only synopsize and comment on Braxton's own eight thick tomes. While the variety, complexity, and development of material there could be mined much more extensively, my purpose here is to give the reader a sense of how and why to approach those books.

Braxton's books are the complete forum for the views and insights glimpsed only partially in liner notes and interviews. I recommend that a reader start with the five books of *Composition Notes*, for several reasons. First, their focus—Braxton's music—is clear and concrete from start to finish. The three volumes of *Tri-Axium Writings* are about weighty philosophical, metaphysical, and sociopolitical issues, and Braxton's idiosyncratic verbiage can inflate and stretch accordingly. Braxton's way with words works best when applied to a given musical statement of his own, at least for the new reader.

Second, recordings of the music can be heard while the notes are read. When this is done, one gets wind of *why* Braxton might use language as he does. As he says in the Introduction shared by all five *Notes* books,

> *Composition Notes* is written from the language dynamics that produced the thought process. The reality of these notes details an evolutionary thought process that involves establishing a personal relationship with given functional and vibrational perspectives. I have tried to solidify a music and idea state (forum) that respects my involvement in creativity as both an instrumentalist and composer.[30]

He uses language not as one detached from his subject, nor even as one attached to it generically—that is, he is not speaking as every instrumentalist and composer, but as one who creatively self-defines and self-actualizes through the language *about* the music as much as through the music itself.

Third, this understood, the idiosyncrasies seem less arbitrary and pretentious, less eccentric, and more fresh, creative, and centric (to the subject they fit best, their author's own creative universe; they give names to his unique, particular beasts). Once the reader finds his or her own place in that universe, learns its language, it is easier to look upon the other, less cloistered vistas of *Tri-Axium Writings*.

It is also helpful to understand that, as with his music, the seemingly impossible thickets of complexity are always couched in the contexts of simple, straightforward structures. If one scans, skims, and hovers over the text long enough to divine the structure of a given section, one can plunge into then back out of its thicket at will. After this approach is practiced and mastered, the thickets become navigable, their logic apparent, and their density accepted as that of a plenum rather than a tangle (again, just as with the music).

It is important to use the accessible, inviting elements of Braxton's books as points of entry to the less so. On the covers of the *Notes* books are simple line drawings of the sort for which he is famous. All five are of people and human-crafted settings—buildings, machinery, boats—with the Braxtonian hieroglyphic and formulaic cryptography attached to them like tabs to paper dolls.³¹ The effect is to suggest that concrete human life has its source in, grows from, numinous Pythagorean patterns and Platonic ideals. (The *Tri-Axium* covers have only the abstract patterns, attached to no such material depictions.)

Once one opens the first *Notes* book, the first encounter is with the short, straightforward and readable "Introduction." Then comes a list of "sound classifications" denoted by hieroglyphs and abbreviations of self-coined phrases. That they are there in front makes one suppose the author intends them to be memorized before tackling the notes, but they are so numerous one leaves them as a reference list to return to as needed (both Introduction and lists are in all five books). There is no "Table of Contents," and the notes begin.

Skipping through the body of the book, one finds at the back interviews both previously published and unpublished, and happily reads them as buffer zones between consensus reality and the Braxtonian reality of the notes (and of *Tri-Axium*) and their copious preliminary legends. One reads them knowing that Braxton chose them as representative of his own communications, their chronology across all five books roughly parallel to that of the compositions.

The first of these interviews, "NYC '77" in book *A*, recaps Braxton's history in music, ending with an impassioned speech about the glory and importance of not selling out one's creative vision (this at the height of jazz-critical acclaim for his most adventuresome work). Subsequent interview conversations range over the following, in the order given: critiques of Western music pedagogy, praises for recent alternatives to it; explanations of multi-orchestral music, and of his own vivid visualizations, in line and color, of music; much chatting about other musicians both long dead and alive; explanation of his understanding of time (cyclical, not linear); the global universal culture of which "jazz" is really a part, and the loss of spirituality in the West and its understanding of music, and the exciting potential of America to regain it in high culture within a century or two; explanations of his "language music." In short, a balanced, readable, interesting mix of his own artistic-cultural universe and of the larger one. (Amidst this are some pages of talk about *Tri-Axium Writings* that should introduce our look at them, below. In fact, to quote them at length will convey everything important about both their content and form in just the right [Braxton's] nutshell.)

These interviews lead to classroom lectures and materials that extend that buffer zone between Braxtonian and consensus realities by a comfortably gradual approach to the deep waters of the notes. Also included in all five books, immediately following the notes, is a "Catalogue of Works," with an "Introduction" intended to instruct musicians who would like to play those works on how to approach them. The catalogue following is 76 pages of graphic and formulaic titles with brief descriptive blurbs. A "Glossary of Terms" used in the *Notes* follows, 19 pages of the same self-coined phrases abbreviated at the front of the book. They are each defined here by a paragraph or so of somewhat difficult, sometimes also self-coined, phrases. A discography listing the works by opus number ends the books.

One is ready for the notes, aware of the keys and glossaries and understandable rationales from the interviews, lectures, and classroom instructions one has access to. But before one does take that plunge, other considerations, not encountered in the liner notes or published interview forums, arise in these books.

In a word, the reader is, as with no articles or liner notes, on the artist's turf here. Braxton is not being explained by some media person, nor edited, nor presenting his message as one of many guests of his record producer. He has written his books as one who is an acknowledged and celebrated master of his field (not that he presents himself so, but those are his credentials); he has said he has done so because those less adept but more understood were getting it wrong in essential, crucial ways. He has chosen to self-publish his books as an expression of integrity, has written and printed them at his own expense (as, indeed, he has done with his music itself over the decades, in spite of his exposure and acclaim). If a reader has these books, it is probably because he or she has gone far enough through Braxton's work, his media persona, and his own liner notes to have a sense of both promise and problems involved with tackling them, and has cared enough to pay the several hundred dollars they cost him to reproduce and send.

However, the sense of significance, purpose, and authority in these books differs from that of the previous, more public forums. The latter, remember, Braxton has both attained and eschewed in favor of this one; but unlike those public media, this one does not frame its message as controversial eccentricity. It doesn't pander to conventional ideas of readability, nor to a thousand concerns and reassuring "truths" built up by the music journalists or academics for generations. It conveys information of vital interest to both of those parties, but without assurance of or need for their acceptance or understanding. Moreover, it makes great demands on them, and the reader. Braxton, in this forum, is no longer the interesting, entertaining guest in the reader's universe, teaching, amusing, challenging like a Greek scholar-slave in a Roman household; he has fled that context, is simply grappling with principles and potentials for their own sake, and letting the reader in on the process. Like him, if a reader engages that process in this context, it must be without assurance of or need for the certainty that he and his abstractions and noises and words are worth their time and trouble—or that the reader's own are, for that matter. He is doing what he's doing at great risk and cost to himself. For all he knows, the judgment of his critics and detractors may be right in the end; he may even come to see himself as vain, pretentious, clinical, not the profound artist he aspires to be. Readers of his books must decide for themselves what value lies in them, and therefore in their own potential as self-actualizing, self-defining, creative people in their own rights. To the extent one is invested in the consensus realities Braxton eschews, one must answer the three questions his words and music inevitably provoke: "Who does he think he is? Who do *I* think he is?" and "Who do I think *I* am?"

That resolved, one tackles the *Notes* effectively. Actually, one may have already done so through the liner notes, some of which are straight from these books. For consistency's sake, we will look at the notes to one of the pieces discussed above that was not notated on its recording (*For Alto*).

The notes to *Composition 8F* might be paraphrased, perhaps flippantly, thus: the work's key premise is an unflaggingly fast-as-humanly-possible pulse; its instrumental game plan is conventional bebop tonguing giving way to low blatts and high shrieks, harmonics and multiphonics, conventional phrasings cut short by arhythmical interruptions of new phrases, large intervallic jumps between parallel motifs, and some notated patterns to trigger improvisation. In sum, the work is a mix of established ways of handling high-energy fast tempos and timbres with spontaneous mutations of them, all executed with an eye for how the oscillation between premise and spontaneity generates the musical experience validated for many by John Coltrane's sheets of sound technique, or by similar work done by the AACM.

I say "flippantly," because Braxton devotes four pages to this piece, themselves oscillating between straightforward and esoteric language, so: "I composed Composition No. 8F as a vehicle to establish a fast pulse arhythmic language platform for extended solo improvisation" (straightforward); and "The material and operational basis of the work is designed to accent the pulse dynamic implications of alternative functionalism—both with respect to procedure dynamics and (subject) focus dynamics"[32] (esoteric).

Leaving flippancy behind, a conscientious reader might turn to the book's glossary for help with, say, "alternative functionalism," or "procedure dynamics," or "focus dynamics." Not finding them there, one would have to reread and draw one's own conclusions. One might concoct this paraphrase: "I designed and approached this piece to see what playing fast and spontaneously within the context of both design and approach would produce."

And so it would go, throughout all the *Notes*. The most successful reader will be one whose passionate reaction to both Braxton's music and its influences from jazz and art music traditions has been matched by his or her intellectual curiosity about them, and whose intellectual understanding has then evolved into an intuitive and emotional-psychological second nature. This reader might well be someone who has experienced the repetitive, persistent reworking of knowledge and practice required by any discipline, whether it be a religious vocation, a marriage, an art or craft or trade, a job, or the sheer engagement of existence. He or she will be one who has embraced ambiguity and chaos with the ability to grace them with purpose and order, balancing the integrity of his or her own such ability responsibly and creatively with that of others who are doing likewise.

Finally, he or she will be open to the sheer cadences and epiphanies of these particular written words as an oral-musical rather than a literate expression. More on that later, but for now recall the suggestion that the *music be heard while the words are read*. Braxton has stated often that one of the symptoms of Eurocentric misunderstanding of "trans-African" music is its assumption that the latter is made with little or no intellectual forethought of reflection, is rather an expression of psychic and emotional holism to be taken, alternately, as sub- or superrational expression. Either of the latter takes is a mis-take, Braxton asserts, and a damaging one in a society where rationalism reigns and relegates both its "subordinates" and "superiors" to an unhealthy, imbalanced relationship with the mainstream.

Braxton (or anyone) can do nothing about this so effective as setting his own record straight, as he has proven himself uniquely able and willing, among his peers in his genre, to do, both by his writings and his self-conscious, systematic yet also spontaneous approach to his music making. The degree to which he succeeds is measured by the decline in the music—in Western culture—of the very rationalism he has taken on and reclaimed for his own creative process and goals.

Once the reading hurdles mentioned here have been overcome, the joy and interest in these books can be accessed and their usefulness as listening aids engaged. If one is blindly attracted to Braxton's music and that of his peers, these books go far toward explaining the nature of one's attraction, even activating one's access to one's own such nature and power, and singular expression.

Tri-Axium Writings

To begin to crack these books, one must go as far as scanning and skimming them oneself, finding the various points of entry Braxton himself has provided, then picking the ones that work best. As with any primary source, this one has compelling challenges and rewards unencountered in paraphrases and analyses of its content. Its importance is all the more vital in this case because one of the very reasons it exists is that its message has been paraphrased unto distortion by journalists and academics not necessarily less sincere nor sympathetic than Lock, Radano, or me. The medium is as much the message as anything else about it, and reading Braxton is an entirely different experience than reading his interpreters. Therefore, rather than submit a third summary with comments, I will quote from Braxton himself, limiting myself to suggesting more ways of making the reading easier and more understandable.

Braxton explains the title of the books so: "The name of this system of thought is 'TRIAXIUM': which is my term for gathering axium tenets from the past and present—to get to the future."[33] Here is his own summation and rationale of all three books, from an interview in *Composition Notes C*:

> They're dealing with the reality and metareality of creative music. The first book deals with the underlying philosophical basis that determines how we see world music, western art music and creative music, or what I call Trans African music. And I look at that subject at what I call three levels. I look at them in their separate contexts as level one, in their composite contexts as level two, and then there's questions and answers. And the second part of that book is transition from post-Schönbergian continuance to post-Cage and to La Mont Young. And then I look at from post-Ornette Coleman into the post-Ayler continuance. And then the same different levels with questions and answers. And then finally the next section is the post-Ayler continuance, dealing with the events that took place in the New York school in the 1960s with the AACM and moving up into this particular period. And the second book deals with social reality and redefinitions. It breaks down to aspect essence information focus, spectacle diversion continuance, and that has to do with social reality in America, how spectacle is used instead of culture. And aspect essence breaks down into how people perceive of things and the reality of our definitions. And the next section then is affinity dynamics, looking at the nature of human beings and how the reality of postulation is directly aligned with the dynamics of nature. I believe that the phenomenon of nature is more indigenous to and more real to view humanity instead of the distorted concepts we have

of what we call race in this period. So I look at those subjects in their separateness and in their composite state and questions and answers. The next subject is creative music outside America, and the first section breaks down into Germany, Holland, London, I mean Britain, and the second section deals with France, Northern Europe. For me Northern Europe was limited to only Sweden and Copenhagen because I haven't had the opportunity to travel to Norway and spend any time there ... And then Japan—I included Japan. And so then, questions and answers. The next section was the reality aspect of creative music, dealing with the performing situation of music as it relates to the media—television, radio, record companies, clubs. And then the second part of that dealt with newspapers, agents, and questions and answers. And the final section was music, creativity and politics. It looks at the events that took place in the '60s and the political ramifications of those events, and relates it to the music and tries to view the music with respect to its political dynamics. And the second aspect of that takes a look at the composite planet and what's happening in the various transitions and how that affects the music—the rise of multinational corporations in America and how this factor has affected the planet, the particulars of political changes which have taken place in this period, what this seems to forecast for humanity with respect to the music and with respect to just living. I try to take a look at the composite situation and how when you separate America and the Soviet Union and you begin to look at the smaller countries, how the effects of western expansionism is destroying many different cultures around the planet, and it's not something that's only a joke. It's something that's very real. Many people are suffering because of the nature of western expansionism. And I wrote some about the advent of nuclear technology and what this seems to pose—the negative implications of what it seems to pose. So that's Book II. Now Book III starts off with alternative functionalism and trans-information. That breaks down into black notated music, that being the whole continuum of what's happening to the methodological dynamics of Trans African music, taking a look at composers like William Grant Still, Olly Wilson, Duke Ellington's pedagogy—what that posed for the music—and looking at the music from that context. The next section was creativity and science, trying to take a look at the role of science in the music—what is the proper function for science in the music? And what is transformational science for extended creativity? The next section is—there's a level two of that: questions and answers. The next section is evolution—I'm not sure, I'm confused about the basic title of it—but I look at the reality of definitions that surround the music, the journalism that surrounds the music, and how the journalism at this point in time has been totally irrelevant to really understanding what's happening in the music because the real reality of creative music transcends the present definitions which were solidified to comment on western art music. I talk about the teaching of improvised music. The next section is popular music from the

the musician's words 177

black aesthetic, tracing the transition section from what we call rhythm and blues to the current punk rock. Actually I don't talk about punk rock, but I move up to that period. I look at music with respect to the primary projection of black creativity and the source initiation of the projection of black creativity, and how that music determines the reality of present-day commercial music. And finally, the last section, is transformation. Transformation on the physical universe level as it involves political change and social change. And then the next section is the reality of the creative woman and how that is related to what real transformation would have to be. I look at the music in terms of what I perceive are its masculine and feminine dynamics, and how there's a real need—how we have a real need as men—to try to encourage more women to become involved in the music because the music has become overbalanced from the masculine standpoint and we have suffered as a result of that. We need more input from women in the music as a means to reestablish a compositely spiritual music. And then questions and answers. That's three books. That's the subjects.

LN: That's quite a lot.

AB: Well, I worked on them for seven years, and of course there's a lot more to be said. In fact, it's Writings I, II, and III, and I'd like to hope that every four or five years I'd be able to add another book, because I think it's important for musicians to start writing. If we don't write, then we have to accept the interpretations of Leonard Feather or Gary Giddins or people who are—I don't mean to disrespect their viewpoint, but we need the viewpoint of people who are actually doing the music.[34]

The combination of macroscopic sweep and microscopic analysis, both idiosyncratically worded, makes for a read we might liken to a book by a 19th-century German philosopher on acid. That cheeky comparison reminds us that even in Western letters Braxton's literary approach has much precedent in its blithe self-definition and self-reference. Artists, philosophers, and even scientists are allowed to treat their initially subjective realities as objective, subjectively naming those realities in the expectation that both reality and name be granted objective status (presuming, of course, they meet the criteria of their discipline). Thus, Hegel develops a concept, calls it a "World Soul," and is regarded not as a self-involved solipsist living in his own private world but a wise philosopher of universal import. Sartre coins and deploys a simple word for a simple concept (existentialism) and, because it is in the mainstream context of Western arts and letters, it is taken as seriously as it was intended. Physicists speak of a "big bang" and "charm," astronomers name comets after themselves, and so on.

In America, a case could be made for the following image of intellectual racism: simple concepts with far-reaching meanings such as postmodernism, deconstructionism, and post-structuralism are constantly generated, developed, and circulated as "legal" intellectual tender—and rightly and naturally so. At the same time, equally elegant terms are applied to equally important realities by African American philosopher-musicians such as Sun Ra or Braxton, terms such as "vibrational," "restructuralism," "tripartial," "gravallic," "affinity insight," "realness"—creative artists whose work has proven them also to be profound and disciplined thinkers with important things to say—and they are regarded, beyond their "cult followings," as pretentious eccentrics who should stick to their esoteric music and leave the thinking, writing, and speaking to the real (Western literate) intelligentsia!

The short section called "Construction" prefacing all three books is worth quoting from at length, and returning to often in the reading of them.

> Since the complexity of creative music commentary involves so many different areas of inquiry, I believe the challenge of transformational journalism is to find creative ways to interpret information. It is because of this belief that I have solidified this approach to my writings. For the great thrust of creative music writings in this time period are extremely uncreative attempts at journalism, and this is especially interesting when one considers the position jazz critics have put themselves in—that being, attempting to evaluate the worth of other people's creativity . . . I have tried to construct a systematic approach that gives the greatest focus reference possible, because the seriousness of creativity demands something more than a one-dimensional viewpoint.
>
> The dictates of these books are constructed so that the reader must read through the material in at least six different ways, and the interconnection of concepts are set up so as to give maximum diversity. In other words, the reader will be able to view a given concept from as many different standpoints as possible . . . It is my hope that an approach of this nature might prove useful for establishing a more realistic look at creative music, for much of the literature I have seen on this subject seems either too simplistic or doctorial. Yet, by the same token, I have not solidified this approach as a joke, nor have I included anything in these books which was not necessary. I have tried . . . to view a given concept to the farthest point of my ability with the hope that either real understanding can come from an approach of this type, or that real intellectual stimulation about world creativity can be developed.[35]

Braxton then outlines the different (color-coded) focuses he turned on his topics. Each chapter covers a topic; Level One of each chapter examines several "regions of inquiry"; Level Two sums those up and examines them in broader contexts; and Level Three covers the same ground in a simple Q&A format through which Braxton socratically dialogues with himself. The mix of approaches, he says, "runs from open interpretation possibilities (i.e., understanding something in your own way—with respect to one's own affinity dynamics) to closed exact definitions.[36]

Throughout the book are line drawings, reminiscent of those used to analyze sentence parts and grammar years ago, meant to function as schematics of the creative and cultural processes the book tackles with words; Braxton's prefatory sections include instructions on how to understand these. Also, boldface type

the musician's words 179

highlights short sections that function as the core thrust of the ruminations preceding them.

> Thus, to really utilize this book in the way I have intended, the reader is expected to read this book: (1) completely from the beginning to the end; (2) with respect to the arguments of only one level region at a time (i.e., read only level one sections in each chapter, later only read level two chapters, etc.); (3) read the whole book interconnected with the other books in this series through what I call the integration code—which is in every section of every focus; (4) read only the isolated concepts that have been marked in bold type; (5) study the isolated terminology chart—or glossary of terms (at the back of the book)—to understand the systemic interconnection (as well as application) of these concepts throughout the total integration complex of all three books—as a means to better understand both my extended viewpoint as well as the logic dynamics of its total application, and (6) *the reader is asked to translate my terminology . . . as a means to view each focus in one's own terms: in other words, I am saying, "this is my viewpoint in this context, and these are my terms, but what do you think?—with respect to your own personal viewpoint and/or perception dynamics (in the context of my terminology—as well as your own terminology) about this same information."* Only after all of the approaches have been tried can the reader have some idea as to what I am trying to communicate—yet on this comment it is important to explain my intentions. I have not meant to imply that my understanding of phenomenon is such that one must necessarily reach for my so-called level, because to believe this has nothing to do with reality. Instead, I have constructed these writings in this manner because the realness of what I am really trying to communicate is not about "only one point of view"—or one level of transference. I believe the traditional use of so-called deductive logic has been greatly violated in this time period. What we now need is the use of every kind of information transference affinity position—whether or not it corresponds to what is now called logic. It is for this reason that Writings is constructed in the manner you have before you.[37] (emphasis mine)

The picture drawn by the writings of others about Braxton has been one of an artist important according to the terms of the new-music and jazz critical media and the academic community; the picture established by Braxton's own writings is one of an artist who ascribes the utmost importance to his potential and opportunity for critiquing those terms and stating his own.

In terms of attention, effort, and weight given their subjects, the two pictures compare rather equitably, in that Braxton's own energy and time investments in writing about his art and the sociocultural world surrounding it have been matched by those of others, who deemed the subject as worthy of books, liner notes, articles, and interviews as did the artist himself. The two pictures parallel each other quite closely in terms of focus and facts, ideas and opinions, in the sense that many of the writings about Braxton made up a forum for his own material, and many of Braxton's writings were concerned with the general music scene that is the focus of the music media.

Obviously, however, there is a big difference between the two pictures. Most people, even his audiences, know him as seen and explained and presented by others; his own liner notes and books are not widely read, nor does he seek to conform to the journalistic and academic conventions and forums that would make them so—indeed, he does the contrary. Surely this difference in mass readability would not exist if it just so happened that Braxton's writing style did conform so, without seeking to. Just as surely, it does conform to something; it has its own internal sense of logic, aesthetics, vision, and philosophical premise. If the picture drawn by journalists and academics speaks to us so much more clearly, what is it speaking to, reinforcing in us? What in that is so inadequate, even alien and offensive, to Braxton? If his writings are so compelling and self-evident to him, what about them so challenges, upsets, and confuses us?

Is it enough to say he can play but not write or speak? But then have there not also been serious doubts about his musical legitimacy? Are then his writings and music both simply best understood as the rarefied modes of a specialist who needs to be mediated—analyzed, explained, interpreted—by writers such as Lock, Radano, or I for more general consumption?

Braxton himself, as cited above, dismisses those suggestions out of hand and offers this one: his music and language both have been difficult for both media and audiences to the extent that those parties approach and receive both with expectations and value judgments he himself doesn't share (or without those he does hold). Both (his music and language) have been partially, conditionally accepted by those who do find those expectations and values fulfilled (jazz critics who appreciate his musicianship), and wholly and unconditionally so by those who respond positively to Braxton's work for reasons more concordant with his own (people who relate to their own creativity as he does to his). Braxton rejects the idea that he is much different, qualitatively, than any who might appreciate and understand his work; he would rather suggest that both music and writings are the fruits of a single-minded respect for and devotion to the unique creative vision and potential everyone has. He would say the key to connecting with his universe lies in the construction of one's own such universe—but that such constructions are virtual acts of resistance in modern globalized Western culture, and acts of faith in principles and powers neither encouraged nor facilitated by same.

The main difference between the two sources of the same information might therefore best be described as that between detachment and engagement. Whether we praise or condemn Braxton's words and music as journalists and academics, we are doing so from a position of safety from both the risks and rewards of the creative process and artistic techniques we are assessing. Braxton-the-artist has donned the writer's hat expressly because he felt this outsider's position to be the crucial deficiency in most pundits. The corresponding gesture among those of us who write is to take on the challenge of learning the music of his purview, finding our own voices and visions there, and voicing the visions by recording them, at our own expense if necessary. Then, if what we had to say after that experience changed our writing styles and contents in such a way that we could no longer make a living by our words, we must accept that.

More practically and generally, it may be most useful to think of the academic and commercial press concerned with this musical genre to be in much the same process the music itself has been and is. It has been America's "folk," "popular," "experimental," and "classical" music; perhaps our music journalism and scholarship both will become more deeply and broadly *literary* (without sacrificing existing professional standards), mythologically charged, creatively styled, and personally marked, as music is—something the subjects of its discourse can read and respond to with as much respect and creative passion as they do to the work of each other.

---

1. *New Grove/Jazz* "Braxton, Anthony," Vol. 1, pp. 147–48.

2. Graham Lock, *Forces in Motion: The Music and Thoughts of Anthony Braxton* (New York: Da Capo Press, 1988: 308–20).

3. Hugues Panassie, *Hot Jazz: The Guide to Swing Music* (New York: M. Witmark & Sons, 1936); and André Hodeir, *Jazz: Its Evolution and Essence* (New York: Grove Press, 1956).

4. Radano, Ronald. "Braxton's Reputation" (*Musical Quarterly*, vol. 72, 1986, No. 4: 505).

5. Ibid., 504, 514–15: "A survey of the literature from 1974 to 1982 shows that only two [lesser known—M. H.] critics disliked Braxton's music and wrote vituperative commentary about it. The writers for *Down Beat*, America's most popular jazz magazine, consistently spoke in his favor. Of the twenty-three Braxton albums reviewed from 1974 to 1982, eleven received the five-star 'excellent' rating, and seven the four- or four-and-one-half-star 'good' [*sic*—should be 'very good'—M. H.] rating. In *Down Beat*'s international critic's polls, Braxton took third, fourth, or fifth place in the alto-saxophone category six years in a row...and his Creative Orchestra Music 1976...won the 'Album of the Year' award in 1977...From 1975 to 1978, the years of Braxton's greatest popularity, at least fifty-six articles about him appeared in North American magazines...As critics showered him with praise, Braxton's record sales reached 20,000—a high figure for a free-jazz artist."

6. Ibid., 521.

7. Gene Santoro, "Anthony Braxton" (*The Nation*, May 8, 1989: 642–644).

8. E.g., *Coda* and *Cadence* and the more recent *Ear*, *Wire*, and *Option*. Not that these publications aren't critically discerning about Braxton, simply that they are more open to his aesthetic than the mainstream jazz press.

9. Laskin, D.L.L. "Anthony Braxton: Play or Die" (*Ear*, May 1989: 40–46).

10. Baraka, Amiri. In *New Perspectives on Jazz* (Baker, David., ed., Washington DC and London: Smithsonian Institution Press, 1986: 57–68), for this and following citations of Baraka.

11. See Ronald Radano, "Jazz Recast" (*New Musical Figurations: Anthony Braxton's Cultural Critique*. Chicago/London: University of Chicago Press, 1993: 269–76) for a good take on this ongoing controversy as it relates to Braxton's work. Also Richard B. Woodward, "A Rage Supreme" (*Village Voice*, August 9, 1994).

12. Roberta Penn, "Selling Jazz Down the River" (*The Rocket*, Seattle, Nov. 1991: 20–23).

13. Josef Woodard, "Structure, Vocabulary and Tradition: Saxophonist Anthony Braxton" (*Option*, No. 23, November/December, 1988: 61–63).

14. Graham Lock, "Still Life with Bass and Cello: David Holland in Pursuit of the Cubist Bass Line" (*Wire*, London, May 1988: 46–49).

15. Ronald Radano, *Anthony Braxton and his Two Musical Traditions: The Meeting of Concert Music and Jazz* (dissertation, University of Michigan, 1985: 458).

16. Braxton, *Creative Orchestra Music 1976* (Arista AL 4080, 1976) and *For Four Orchestras* (Arista A3L 8900) include examples of Braxton's most extensive and intensive jacket notes.

17. Braxton, *Dona Lee* (America 30 AM 6122, 1972).

18. Joe Carey, "Anthony Braxton Interview" (*Cadence,* Mar. 1984: 6).

19. Braxton, *Five Compositions (Quartet) 1986* (Black Saint BSR 0106, 1986).

20. In fact, with the advent both of the computer and more money with which to pay word processing assistants, this "problem" may go away. The question raised is why it would and should be a problem to the average literate person.

21. Ben Sidran, *Black Talk* (New York: Da Capo Press, 1981: 6).

22. Braxton, *Duets 1976* (with Muhal Richard Abrams, Arista AL 4101, 1976).

23. Braxton, *Composition 113* (Sound Aspects SAS 003, 1983).

24. The first appearance of realistic and human figures in his graphic titles was with *105A* (interestingly, also the first pulse track piece). Such figures appear on the covers of the *Composition Notes* and (rather regularly) in the graphic titles of works dating from 1983.

25. Carey; and Bill Shoemaker, "Anthony Braxton: The Dynamics of Creativity" (*Down Beat,* March 1989: 20–22).

26. Radano (op. cit.), viii.

27. Braxton, *For Trio* (Arista AL 4181).

28. Lock (op. cit.), 29.

29. Ibid., 162.

30. Anthony Braxton, "Introduction" (*Composition Notes A–E*, Oakland, CA: Tree Frog Press, 1988: ii–iii).

31. Braxton's explanation of them is that they are notes to himself that peg a visual to a musical element, one tagged with the alphanumeric formula.

32. Braxton, *Composition Notes A*, 138.

33. Anthony Braxton, *Tri-Axium Writings 1–3*, Oakland, CA: Tree Frog Press, 1988: xiii.

34. *Composition Notes C*, 645–8.

35. Ibid., 24.

36. Ibid., 26.

37. Braxton, *Tri-Axium Writings 1–3*, vii–ix.

Chapter Four

The Musician Speaks

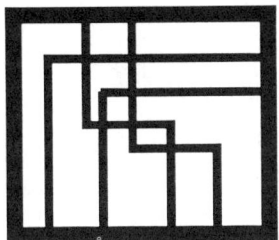

A significant attribute of writing is the ability to communicate not only with others but with oneself. A permanent record enables one to reread as well as record one's own thoughts and jottings. In this way one can review and reorganize one's own work, reclassify what one has already classified, rearrange words, sentences, and paragraphs in a variety of ways . . . The way that information is organized as it is recopied gives us an invaluable insight into the workings of the mind of homo legens.

Roger Sanjek

The trouble, however, is that when you get down to details rituals of self-expression are beyond criticism. Anything goes because it is all a matter of the innermost truth of the performer's being. Thus if his musicianship seems lacking in any way, it is not because he is working in an idiom with which the listener is unfamiliar but which has a different set of requirements, but rather because it is the best of all possible ways to express what the musician in question is all about! The self-portrait (and/or the personal signature) that emerges from the music of Jelly Roll Morton, King Oliver, Bessie Smith, Louis Armstrong, Duke Ellington, Lester Young, and Charlie Parker is not primarily a matter of such egotistical self-documentation but rather of the distinction with which they fulfilled inherited roles in the traditional ritual of blues confrontation and purgation, and of life affirmation and continuity through improvisation. Incidentally, the revolutionary nature of their innovations and syntheses was not nearly so much a matter of a quest for newness for the sake of changes as of the modifications necessary in order to maintain the definitive essentials of the idiom. *(emphasis mine)*

Albert Murray

"The historical sense," T.S. Eliot insisted, "compels a man to write not merely with his own generation in his bones but with a feeling that the whole of the literature of Europe from Homer and within it the whole of the literature of his own country has a simultaneous existence and composes a simultaneous order." The historical sense, which he goes on to describe as a sense of the timeless and the temporal together, is what makes a writer traditional, but it is also what makes him "most acutely conscious of his place in time, of his own contemporaneity" (emphasis mine)

Albert Murray

One of my beliefs is that everybody really knows everything about this planet, but they're not talking.

Anthony Braxton

Now that we've picked Braxton's own voice out of the legion, let's sum up what he has said, in his own books, about the musicultural history and issues we've examined through more conventional sources.

Braxton writes of the African American musical tradition:

> If the story of the 20th century music from the white aesthetic is in great part a story of the progression and annihilation of tonality and the evolution of process to incorporation of 20th century technological gains, then the story of creative black music would be the evolution of process as a means to cast off every remnant of the white aesthetic and re-insert its own definitions.[1]

He goes on to define that tradition[2] as the all-encompassing musicultural expression that begins with the African arrivals and includes the expressions of this century—the gospel, blues, and jazz—that have permeated the national culture so completely, and extended beyond it to the world. He states[3] that this power and influence, astonishing under the circumstances, is best understood as the result of the African American experience of, first, loss of African then enslavement to European culture. The African American culture that was forged out of loss and slavery was a forced reach to the universal personal and collective human essence that is the creative core of all cultures, beyond the surface expressions of the (lost) African or the (imposed) European-American ones. Indeed, that reach past surface to "what it celebrated in its original state" is ongoing, making for an expression at once timely and timeless, and of universal as well as specific import.

> To understand the position of American black people in western culture is to understand the path black culture had to take for expansion and survival. That path being—the composite projection of the American black sensibility must be perceived as a thrust affirming the restoration of black culture while at the same time adopting western methodological tools to do it . . . the composite thrust of American black culture can be viewed as a synthesis of the black essence umbrella with the adaptation of western functionalism as the first junction towards establishing transformation . . . with respect to the situation non-white people are in, and transformation with respect to the situation of the composite world group.[4]
>
> The thrust projection of creative black activity moves towards rediscovering the essence foundation of black postulation (i.e., what it was before the decline of black culture—what this means either vibrationally or functionally) as a means to restore order.[5]

The order to be restored, writes Braxton, is the humanization of the Western aesthetic[6]—which can only be defined by the victims of its dehumanization—and it has been struggling and in process for the last two centuries.

Louis Armstrong signaled black music's successful (because commanding the American cultural center stage) appropriation of Western concepts and instruments for these African cultural ends of humanization.[7] His was not the only such voice, but it was that of his culture that made itself most universally heard. The musical framework in which Armstrong worked ("so-called Dixieland") solidified the optimal balance and synergistic synthesis of individual and collective expression, and of composition and improvisation.[8]

As it happened, this music was alternately "popular" and "serious" (in Western terms), depending on who was writing (roughly, journalists or scholars) and in what context. But such writers, says Braxton,

> have long attempted to break down creative black music using the same systematic tools designed for western art music, with the understanding that through investigation it is possible to comment on whether or not a given participant in the music is playing correct or not correct—or even worse, 'which player is the best.' . . . the actualness of a given projection is a natural factor having nothing to do with the nature of investigation as perceived through western methodological and critical channels . . . Because the nature of the western critical alignment is based on isolating a given 'idea,' rather than experiencing the actualness of the music (which might not have anything to do with the narrowness of what in western terms is called an 'idea' . . . "[9]

In short, Braxton sees a distorted and unhealthy objectification of the music (he often describes this by saying someone "ized" this or that aspect—e.g., if you play romantically for a moment, the critics will pigeonhole you as a romantic, or will "romanticize" you [the multi-meaning can stand]) by the

Western critical paradigm, one that has run in parallel to and progressively with the music's successful incursion into the Western cultural arena.[10]

> If Louis Armstrong's music can be spoken of as the personification of black people in their first encounter with the white sensibility, Charlie Parker's activity can be talked of as the epitome of the second transformation of black people in America in the sense that his creativity not only completely utilized western techniques with a black aesthetic, but in his activity we can also see a developed reaction and awareness of the whole position of black people—in the physical and vibrational universe context . . . [11]

Braxton sheds light on this statement by stating elsewhere[12] that the music initiated by Armstrong and developing through World War II could best be understood as a *celebration* of the arrival of the African spirit in Western flesh. All America, black and white, danced to the music of the Jazz Age and the swing era. "Jazz" was America's popular music, and it had sprung from the black culture.[13] Of course, it was appropriated by white culture; the (Western) historical universal primacy of many of the black artists is so only in hindsight. Bebop was, in its move to outdo the West in the West's own technical and conceptual approaches, a reaction against this injustice (Shepp, in Sidran, quotes Thelonious Monk as describing the first bebop as largely an attempt to make a music "whitey can't play").[14] Charlie Parker and peers stormed the Western criteria for "art" music, claiming them for the black aesthetic. The dancing, both white and black, stopped, the mass appeal and popularity diminished; celebration became *confirmation* (of black culture's command of Western idioms and premises) . . . but the victory was bittersweet, exacting a price.

Parker, says Braxton, gave the African voice to Western "high" culture as Armstrong had given it to "low" (though those are Western terms foreign to the real essence of both artists). In doing so, however, he reached that much farther beyond the roots of the black church, where the expression still enjoyed more balance between male and female, mental and physical—West and Africa. This brings us to the music's next big leap, Braxton's own time, the 1960s.

"Creative Music From The Black Aesthetic" picks up this history at that point:

> The transition of creative music from the black aesthetic in the 1960s must be looked at from several necessary perspectives: (1) the incredible absorption of the western harmonic and functional arena in a time period of fifty to sixty years and thus the need to go beyond western functionalism and definitions; (2) the gradual acknowledgment among creative restructuralists that the functional arena [musical forms, instruments and instrumentation, commercial venues/contests—M. H.] of creative music did not necessarily meet their vibrational and conceptual needs; and (3) the physical universe particulars that would dictate the composite climate for social reality in the sixties.[15]

the musician speaks

Braxton develops the idea that the aesthetic in the 1960s expanded from mastery of the Western musical system to encompass the individual life experiences of the times, the potential for collective energy and awareness, and the implications of the results on American and world culture. He mentions Thelonious Monk[16] as precursor of that expansion through his idiosyncratic extensions of bop's harmonic and rhythmic potential. Charles Mingus, George Russell, Sun Ra, and John Coltrane are also cited as figures on various parts of the spectrum between Western systems and African premises who set the stage for the expansions of the 1960s.

Miles Davis, Coltrane, Ornette Coleman, and Cecil Taylor are cited as embodying most cogently their various approaches to the music's next step. When Davis initiated explorations of Greek modes as alternative harmonic platforms to song and blues forms, Braxton notes, he was tapping into an ancient musical approach at the root of both Western and non-Western cultures, perhaps extending as far back as the Egyptian seeds of ancient Greek culture:

> The dynamics of modal functionalism must be viewed with respect to what this discipline has come to solidify in world culture terms. For the functionalism that we refer to as modalism is manifested in many forms throughout earth culture—from Africa to India.[17]

If Davis opened that door, Coltrane ran through it to the world on which it opened, fusing the sensibilities of his own African American culture with those of Asian, Arabic, Indian, and African traditions. The result was a reminder of the spiritual and social force music has long been in those other cultures and had ceased to be in Western culture with the rise of secularism (and, concurrently, the slave trade). It also affirmed the power of music in African American culture; such power transcended "jazz" as either popular entertainment or esoteric art-for-art's-sake music. Going beyond, in other words, its national and "subcultural" confinements, it at once exposed the West's *lack* of a cohesive spiritual musiculture—and *offered* it one.

While modalism provided a broader cultural and historical base than the peculiarly (or recently, post-Renaissance) Western diatonic-chromatic system of making music, it was still a system imposed via the West and conformed to on Western terms—Western instruments, techniques, and systems. Coleman and Taylor took a different approach.

What Braxton calls the "affinity insight principle" refers to the way creative people can mine out their most subjective, personal private obsessions (their "affinity insight postulations") and find that they have a very public universal relevance. This approach differs from the submission of self-definition and self-expression to externally imposed rules such as chord changes, modes, preset rhythm patterns, and so on. Thus:

> The work of Coleman and Taylor can be looked at as the terminal point of a vibrational and actual phenomenon which started when black slaves were brought to America's shores hundreds of years before. In other words, the realness of their activity must be viewed

as a reconnection to source-initiation as the most important factor for re-establishing procedure and culture (unification) and also their work clarified source-initiation as a platform for re-establishing an alternative spiritualism.[18]

Just as the first expressions of slave culture were re-creations of "sources"—cultural expressions—that had been lost, rather than re-enactments of those preserved (such as other cultures have been in America), so is the music of artists such as Coleman and Taylor. This leap-of-faith-in-improvisation, thanks to the first forced one, is now a central part of African American musiculture, as time-honored and natural as is the embrace of tradition as handed down. As Braxton says often, the experience of slavery and the resources it brought out in its victims (resources its lingering effects continue to bring out), spiritual and creative resources that empowered them to survive and then move forward, are at the root of this aspect of the culture and its music.

Braxton and his AACM colleagues are seminal figures in that tradition for the role they have played in going through the doors opened by artists such as Coltrane, Coleman and Taylor. Braxton has obtained the permission and authorization, if you will, of his own culture (both African American and American generally) to brave the same sort of alienation suffered by Parker, Monk, Coleman, and Taylor—and even, to a degree, Coltrane—in hopes of leading it yet further to the African humanization of the West. Braxton has taken on the challenge by attempting to extend the continuum from the "jazz" of the current mainstream backward through early and pre-American African roots, through tribal branches to a mythico-historical Egyptian mother trunk, and through that to the primal roots of prehuman animality . . . and forward through a Western culture finally sufficiently tempered by the world around it to contribute to a balanced global culture aware enough of itself to find and celebrate its place in the galaxy (recall the music written to be performed in different star systems once humanity has figured out how to get to them—and that the ancient Egyptian religion was stellar before becoming solar).[19]

This is the vision he has allowed himself. It has been suggested to him by the very process of freely and creatively playing with the tradition's parameters—opening up and mining rhythmic frameworks, exploring textures and timbres as elements central to the music, rather than only peripheral to notes and intervals, devising new structures for improvisation, new sound-makers and new combinations of them and of conventional instruments—but it has been suggested just as forcefully by the (properly understood) tradition *within* its parameters, Braxton claims.

A certain arc can be seen from this process that is at once grounded in tradition and a leap of faith: the more Western cultural territory the African aesthetic claims by submitting to Western demands, the more Africanized the West becomes, at least potentially and in theory. In reality, the danger has been and continues to be what Braxton calls the "spectacle diversion syndrome,"[20] whereby the very real transformative forces are objectified as entertainment, or expressions with only relative rather than universal import.

The AACM might be characterized as a force that took the most extremely visceral, spontaneous, and emotional elements of the innovations from the jazz tradition—those explored in New York by Coltrane, Coleman, Taylor, and Ayler—and worked them over more deliberately and calmly, perhaps less desperately, bringing them out of the centralized, monolithic music industry and its context of arts-as-entertainment into the contexts of community, education, and daily life. Quests for a major contract and a New York–based notoriety were replaced by ideals of self-sufficiency and self-determination, small independent labels, nonprofit cooperatives, and similarly grassroots approaches—the "think global/act local" of their time and place.

Braxton's distinction in the AACM was his embrace of traditions other than African, including European, in his pursuit of a personalized, localized synthesis of all musicultural concepts and techniques. (Pianist Muhal Richard Abrams, with whom Braxton recorded some of his early trio and duo music—see Chapters Six and Seven—was the organization's guiding light. Like Braxton, his musical concept of "radical" included that word's intimations of "roots." As he has brought his music into mainstream academia, so he has gone on to administer or help direct arts-policy-making bodies such as the National Jazz Service Organization and Meet-the-Composer, to name two of the most prominent.) One cannot speak coherently about the music Braxton has cocreated with his peers in what he would call the "trans-African thrust continuum" without discussing its very place in the world. In sheerly musical terms, one can safely say that the AACM's role in that continuum has been to move through, then beyond, the Western concepts, techniques, systems, and materials central to the bop, post-bop, and neo-bop music still most widely celebrated in the commercial and academic arenas; and to develop the most African elements therein to reconnect with the non-Western experiences of community, spirituality, and nature, including those of the animals other than human (in the person of Braxton, that reconnection has also extended most consciously to the West's own such experiences, though in their global rather than narrowly Western context).

One can also see that the cultural modus operandi for fulfilling this sheerly musical function has been to carve out the niche of an art music rather than a mass or targeted entertainment. As it has happened, that niche found its first footing in Europe, then in its native America through grants and education rather than through commercial success. The path the AACM took is the logical real-world expression of the much-belabored insistence on "jazz" as America's "classical music"—and on the historical neglect of it as such. If the music that has been misappropriated, exploited, and/or so neglected has a chance at true recognition and support, it will be by redefining the culture's consensus reality so that the creative and aesthetic principles that compel the music compel the culture in the same way. The measure of the success of this approach is the culture's official sanctioning through arts funding and academic recognition first and foremost; whatever commercial success might come will then come out of, rather than before that, just as the commercial success of, say, the New York Philharmonic has derived from rather than defined its value to the culture.

This is not an entitlement approach; it takes on the market game like everyone else, and grants typically meet only about one third of a given budget. Braxton, Abrams, the AACM, and other peers operating so have risked and put all on the line for such cultural support in the same way other artists make their bids for commercial success. They have had to gamble, with no guarantees, that their work would prove relevant and appealing on such terms, thus *deserving* of such funding and support. Their gamble has resulted in some wins. Music that many a club owner, or producer, or presenter wouldn't risk $100 on has come to attract tens of thousands of dollars worth in commissions and performance fees from peers on panels formed on the premise that a society's best and most important creativity doesn't necessarily thrive or even survive in the commercial arena of arts and entertainment, at least not at first.

Braxton's music is a sterling example of this gamble. It is built on the historical experience of numerous African American artists, from Fletcher Henderson to Sun Ra, who labored on the economic fringes of the commercial arena to create American cultural treasures; from Charlie Parker, Thelonious Monk, Billie Holiday, Bud Powell, and others to Eric Dolphy, John Coltrane, Ornette Coleman, and Cecil Taylor, many of whom died struggling and some of whom continue to struggle in those fringes even as they've produced more such treasures. As for those few who succeeded both artistically and commercially—Duke Ellington, Louis Armstrong, Miles Davis—one can only wonder what even greater heights they might have scaled had they had the culture's full honor and support throughout their lives. What greater personal health for them and cultural health for the society might have resulted? Some would argue none, that do or die in the marketplace is what separates the greats from the aspirants and keeps them honest, tough, and at their best. I would argue otherwise.

As for Braxton, he has said that one of the most important lessons he learned early on was that he could starve as easily anyplace in the world as he could in Chicago. Even so, his gamble with his music is that he can starve as a major American and international artist as easily as he can as a weird, eccentric "avant-gardist." Further, for him, either starvation is preferable to "living large" as the marketplace's idea of a "jazz" musician.

Braxton's own account of the AACM[21] confirms those of Lock and Radano.[22]

> By 1967 the AACM held composer's forums where every aspect of composition—from traditional to avant-garde techniques in western art music, to the complete tradition of trans-African music—were examined. These forums were extremely important for the information that was shared by the collective membership and are directly related to the architectural concepts which later emerged through the organization. It is possible to trace all of the developments of the AACM back to this period—so great was the interchange of ideas. Moreover, while the AACM functioned as the central foundation of this interchange, each individual musician contributed his or her own research into the collective group (where the potential weight of a given direction could be evaluated or critically examined by the composite organization).[23]

He goes on to say that Roscoe Mitchell and Lester Bowie studied some of the concepts from the black minstrel groups, Joseph Jarman and Malachi Favors Egyptian and other African musics, he and Leo Smith the "reality of alternative scientific functionalism for structure" (composition), Abrams the "spiritual implications of the black aesthetic."

the musician speaks

> Among the concepts solidified in this period were: the utilization of the spectrum of sound as a legitimate concern of the creative musician—the expansion of the functional creative ensemble (no longer would a musician need to only function from one instrumental concept)—the study of timbre implications with regards to composition—research into the language implications of creative music—and finally a refocusing of the composite meta-reality of creative music from the black aesthetic.[24]

He also says that the AACM was seminal in extending contemporary percussion concepts through their use of "little instruments," though Brazilian musicians got the credit for that commercially.

The AACM's major contribution, however, was to take black music out of the context of the American melting pot and to frame it in the global picture on its own terms.

> Without doubt the greatest service that the AACM instigated would be the reexamination of black music in all of its different permutations. The AACM was the first organization in its time period to emphasize the significance of composite black music . . . it provided a backdrop for understanding and researching the significance of creative black music throughout its various time zones and the knowledge from this research has and will have a profound impact on the direction of creative music and the total understanding of black culture.[25]

The following passage argues for the AACM's preeminence even in the (admittedly more discursive) sort of stylistic preservation made so much of by the current generation of neoclassical jazz artists.

> The research done in the early sixties is also directly related to the re-adaptation of composite trans-African functionalism, and in that context the musicians from the AACM in the course of the last ten years have been found using Dixieland forms, bebop forms, no forms, as well as their own structural initiations (sometimes in the course of one concert).[26]

Braxton ascribes many of the other innovations examined above—creative solo to creative ensemble music, multiinstrumentalism, interdisciplinary and multimedia projects—not to himself but to the AACM. This confirmative connection with a community, an organization of peers, underscores further the legitimate authority of Braxton's self-described "restructuralist" role. Even his eventual independence from the AACM, in his disaffection with Afrocentric chauvinism, can be seen as the kind of individuation that is, again, part of a *tradition* of innovation. In Braxton's summation of the subject, he expresses hope that AACM will be appreciated more for the seminal role it played.

The next of Braxton's *Tri-Axium 1* chapters to add to the overview of the music is "The White Improvisor," which touches on the distortions wrought by the objectification of the music.

> At present to speak of so-called jazz is to comment on two distinctly different realities: that being, the reality continuum of the black musician and the reality continuum of the white musician—that is true even though the composite basis for so-called jazz has been designed by black people.[27]

White musicians are in large part in no different relationship to black musicians (by virtue of sharing the music) than white to black people generally, writes Braxton. The situation in music has reflected and continues to reflect the imbalanced cultural and racial clashes in America; as have Western academics and journalists, most white musicians have approached and presented the music from their own aesthetic, and have enjoyed the commercial rewards of the initial advantages in business that have come from being white, as well as a recognition and acclaim disproportionate to their contributions to the art form.

There are, however, whites who have naturally gravitated to the black aesthetic without violating or shortchanging it unduly; there are even a few who have matched it with an original white aesthetic of equal import and so played a role in shaping the course of the music (think of Dave Brubeck's influence on Cecil Taylor, or Paul Desmond's on Braxton). Nevertheless, they've been begrudged this role by champions of the black aesthetic.

> The peculiar position of the white improvisor in this cycle is not the result of black people who are angry over the composite scene, nor is it the work of what in this period is called "reverse racism" . . . the reality of the white improvisor is related to the "grand trade-off" that was solidified with the forming of America and the institutionalizing of slavery. [28]

The "grand trade-off" is Braxton's term for the deep psychological projections and assumptions that have cast white and nonwhite cultures into the respective roles they have played together in the historical contexts of the conquest and exploitation of one by the other.

> The grand trade-off is this: slowly but surely the collected forces of western culture have moved to solidify a viewpoint concerning humanity that has nothing to do with anything but maintaining the present social and political "state of things" [elsewhere[29] Braxton writes of "gradualism" as the process of selective historical revisionism that supports this viewpoint—M. H.]. In this concept, black people are vibrationally viewed as being great tap dancers— natural improvisors, great rhythm, etc. . . . but not great thinkers, or not capable of contributing to the dynamic wellspring of world

information. White people under this viewpoint have come to be viewed as great thinkers, responsible for all of the profound philosophic and technological achievements that humanity has benefited from—but somehow not as "natural" as those naturally talented black folks.[30]

This is happening now, in the music:

> Western art music is not viewed as a so-called natural thrust, but instead the solidification of a "high culture" thrust (what we now call art music)—which is to say, western art music is perceived as "more" than the "merely natural." This is also true of the white improvisor's work—for every progressional period of music from the white improvisor has always been viewed as a more "sophisticated offering" from that of their black counterparts. This is true from every period of creative improvised music, from dixieland to the present (witness any of the books written on the music before the fifties). In other words, the concept of the "grand trade-off" is not merely a hip phrase to comment on the nature of progressional continuance in the past one thousand years, I am instead referring to an all-encompassing vibrational and actual attitude that permeates the composite lining of this time period.[31]

Braxton speaks from his own experience here. While he has been acknowledged from the beginning as an important innovator and stylist by the jazz media he has never been able to make a living at his music. Worse, his many contributions as a composer to the Western art music tradition have suffered even more systemic, systematic neglect. He sees his and his peers' musical activities as the logical succession of that African American incursion into Western culture begun in earnest through Louis Armstrong; he views the frustration of it as due to the same racism and Western chauvinism that brought slavery about in the first place, making such an incursion necessary.

Braxton invited readers to match his positions with their own.[32] This might be the most logical place for me to leave off my synopsis of his and do so. As the assertion of the black aesthetic in the Western crucible has been a continued act of faith and courage, braving both rejection and misappropriation, so too can be the assertion of a white affinity insight into the black aesthetic—because the more clarity and power the black assertion achieves, the more undermined the white self-image and cultural base becomes. The sincere white improviser struggling to find his or her place in what is in fact his or her native (increasingly Africanized) American musiculture must forego the Eurocentric legacy of power and prestige (and, more traumatically, identity)—must suffer their destruction, even as the Africans suffered personal and cultural destruction in slavery and oppression. The honest and sincere white must rely on his or her own creative and spiritual resources to, literally, restructure the West on African terms, as the black musiculture has had to restructure Africa on Western terms. In taking this leap of faith, we whites can tap through to the healthy human roots of the sick Western tree (again, even as such artists as Armstrong, Parker, Davis, and Coltrane, through the conventions of Western art forms—or Coleman, Taylor, or Ayler through affinity insight—have tapped through the ravages of slavery to the healthy human roots beneath it).

For me and others, this has entailed acknowledging the primacy of Africa in American music, claiming it as my own legacy as a human being in this time and place, and reviewing my Western European cultural legacy for those aspects or potentials in it not at odds with Africa's.

On a mundane level, this position functions much like that taken by the Danes in World War II who donned the Star of David imposed as badges by the Nazis on the Jews. It blocks access to paths open to whites by virtue of their whiteness, not by a visible physical sign, but by a posture and attitude of alienation that functions just as effectively, overall. By the same token, this position also provides access to the personal and transpersonal power blacks have discovered to create their own paths by virtue not of their blackness but of the drive, skill, and genius—the universal creativity and spirit—being black in America has forced from them. Being white in America's black music can force one to those same qualities; such is the nature of America's black music.

The good news in this sacrifice of the West to Africa, of white to black, is this: we find our lives again even as we lose them. We realize all the real human potential for good and better than good that is in our own Western tradition—in literacy, in Judeo-Christianity, in our Greco-Roman legacy of arts and letters and science—in a way we cannot when overshadowed by hypocrisy and cruelty, or their flip sides guilt and doubt. Even as African America has mastered the West in (forced or voluntary) submission to it, so white Westerners can "master" the African spirits only by submitting to them. We've learned the hard way to what spiritual slavery the other kind of "mastery" leads.

Murray gives the nod to this American phenomenon:

> Precisely as white musicians who work in the blues idiom have been simulating the tribulations of U.S. Negroes for years in order to emulate such musical heroes as Louis Armstrong, Lester Young, and Duke Ellington, and such heroines as Bessie Smith and Billie Holiday, so in fiction must readers, through their desire to imitate and emulate black storybook heroes, come to identify themselves with the disjunctures as well as the continuities of black experience as if to the idiom born . . . Even now young white activists are beginning to regard themselves and their problems, with however much imprecision, in terms which are largely black.[33]

What Braxton has said in private conversation about his need to incorporate Western art music into his own I might have said (if I may re-cite it) about him and other African American musicians:

> The musicians are the ones whose hearts go out to the music, and the music takes them wherever it will, and suddenly you find yourself aligned with this guy whose life is very different from yours, but

something profoundly links you, and it's the music. It would have been very nice for me to just say "fuck Stockhausen and Cage," it would have made my life easier, but that wasn't the relationship I wanted to have with my discipline. Being open to it gives me a chance to reshape it to my own aesthetic based on whatever my needs are at the time.[34]

Braxton ends his section on the white improviser by saying that the dilemmas white and black musicians find themselves in regarding each other must be resolved, but that they won't be until they are in the culture at large, and they won't be there by blaming and excluding. He notes that the "universalist axis"—artists and people functioning within the dilemmas in a way that suggests their resolution—has been present all along, leading the way.

Some of the most readable and interesting parts of the *Tri-Axium Writings* are those on the presence of both trans-African and trans-European creative music in Europe and Japan.[35] We'll look at passages that sum up Braxton's view of Europe, since that's where he has worked the most; and on Japan, in passing, since he did make one important early recording[36] and has enjoyed some success there.

The phenomenon of trans-African creativity is nothing new in Europe, for the historical progressions related to this most basic subject have seen many so-called forms come and go throughout the last two thousand years—and Europe has always listened because, unlike America, this continent is still aware of the nature of progressional continuance and African history—not to mention that the thrust continuum implications of given projections from Africa and Asia have played a role in the motivation and dynamic implications of European postulation and acceleration . . . The most basic point that concerns this essay is that the affinity relationship of Europe's perception of so-called jazz is very much connected to Europe's total affinity relationship with African dynamics and/or its related functionalism. This interest has remained constant since the dissolution of black high composite culture and can be traced from the early treasures taken from Egypt (which can now be seen throughout Europe, in Museums or in the streets—the obelisks of Rome, for instance) to the musical instruments that were brought to Europe—on through to the later tours in the thirties that would affect European creative dynamics.[37]

The 2000-year time window is as natural to Braxton's discussion of current music as are the 20- or 40- or 70-year ones others might use in discussing the history of jazz. Ventura echoes the connection of ancient European and African spirits in the same way, postulating an unbroken line back to the ancient Eastern and Greek worlds through the African and Celtic slaves who synthesized their respective "pagan" metaphysics into the Haitian *vodou* culture that, through Marie Laveau, led to jazz.[38]

Such a deep connection speaks to the affinity and affection between white Westerners and jazz. The following does so too, but also suggests a motive for opposite feelings:

> The reality of black creativity before the emergence of bebop was perceived as a thrust alignment that simply balanced the intellectualism and complications of the post-Beethoven projectional European thrust continuum, and the realness of this balance would move many Europeans to view black creativity as a very exotic and primal continuance . . . But Europe's relationship with black creativity is much more complex than only one vibrational attitude, because while the composite affinity underlying its perception of black creativity can be viewed as patronizing in the same sense as in America, on the other hand Europe realized the seriousness of the music on a level that escaped Americans (both then and now). Europe has always viewed the composite continuity of black creativity as a signal related to the progressional greater dynamics of black culture and world change—not only does Europe remember Africa, she also remembers the nature of the transformation that put her in power. As such, the reality actualness of world change is not as abstract in Europe as it is in America because Europe has never forgotten her history—because she is her history.[39]

Mythological images of Egypt in the West have ranged from those of a high, life-giving originative to a decadent, dying, and deathly civilization. The latter (along with those of the fearsome oppressor) are enshrined in the Bible, the former fostered by archaeology and historical writings. If we postulate a West that took some three or four millennia of history from barbarism through Greek and Roman Empires, through Christianity, through the rise of Western Europe to the present to regain and consolidate, as a culture, a maturity and integrity attained by "parent" civilizations—Asian, African, Indian—over similar time spans, we begin to divine the love-hate relationship. The child needs the guidance of the parent viscerally, blindly follows it when necessary, honors it; she needs just as direly to "kill" (repudiate) the parent's example and power over her, to make and take her own way, to know it as her own, however much she follows in her parent's footsteps. This basic human fact might best frame the complex relationship between the West and trans-African music.

Braxton identifies the rise of bebop ("dynamic implications of post-Parker creativity") as a signal of a spiritual crisis in Western culture.

> By crisis, I mean that the meta-reality dictates underlying western functionalism—and postulation—had, by the late thirties, moved to function—and perceive—in strict intellectual terms, without spiritual tenets. The establishment of this vibrational position would affect the composite lining and identity of European culture—for, unlike America, which would arrive at this same position without knowing it (because there is no real understanding of philosophy in composite

America to speak of—hence, how could this country understand a crisis of identity?) . . .[40]

Just as Europe was in a position to be more sensitive to the cultural implications of bebop, so has it been to the music of the '60s.

> The nature of the impact post-Coleman creativity had in Europe must be viewed with respect to the reality position of European information dissemination—in other words, the effectiveness of the music is directly related to the fact that in Europe black creativity has long been both available to the greater public and focused on. But then, there has always been a marked difference between how black creativity is treated in Europe as compared to America. This is not to say black creativity in Europe is treated on the same level of European art music—because most certainly it isn't—but there can be no comparing the option spread possibilities for so-called jazz in Europe to the situation that exists in America. It is possible to find intelligent articles—directed towards really trying to understand the music—on every aspect of post-Coleman continuance, from the early sixties until now.[41]

He describes the experience of such understanding and reception being, from the African American musician's perspective, the visceral one of jumping from the American frying pan not into a European fire, but to a place beside it, one of warmth rather than burning. The resulting musical syntheses are thus not ideologically abstract and forced, but as tied to the compulsions of survival as their respective Western and African elements alone.

> Many musicians were starving in America because there were simply no performing outlets for their music. The question eventually became either travel and hopefully find outlets for performance, or stay in America and starve to death. It was as simple as that.[42]

In writing about how the music developed between the African American and European improvisers, Braxton describes something more complex than the simple importation/adoption of "jazz."

> Many Americans prefer to believe that Europe is dead and entrenched in the annals of the Western position: a post-existential culture feeding on the life blood of America . . . Certainly it is true that Europe was in bad shape after the second world war . . . and it is also true that improvisation—as an integral part of European art music— was practically non-existent . . . It is also true that the post-Webern movement which materialized at the end of the second war did not begin to really address the dynamics of improvisation—no matter

what word or variation they eventually settle on—until the early fifties.⁴³

In a reversal of the usual roles established by the Western discipline of ethnomusicology, the *Tri-Axium* books are essentially the ethnomusicological musings of a trans-African scholar pondering the West as "other," an other as at risk of extinction in the global cultural picture as any once remote tribe now succumbing to Western encroachment. Braxton acknowledges the new non-American versions of improvised musics but states the seminal role of African American music—not as a foreign source imposed from without onto Europe, but as a reminder of Europe's own forgotten source.

> Yet by the same token the emergence of creative music from the black aesthetic has served as the most important stimulating factor in Europe, and has dictated the re-awareness of improvisation, and its use towards an alternative thrust functionalism. In this context Europe and America are again similar—because improvised music in both countries has the position of an alternative re-generative factor . . . Creative music from the black aesthetic can most certainly be viewed as a major regenerative factor in present-day European creative functionalism, but regenerative in the real sense of the word—starting something which has stopped . . . the musical references now being utilized in Europe are no longer based solely on black music solutions in impoverished music. We now see European musicians emerging with a total awareness of their culture. Moreover, I believe we are now in a period of transition where European creative musicians are realigning their roots in improvised music from the black tradition as well as creative music from the European tradition.⁴⁴

While European respect, care, and support of art and artists generally are superior to the American situation, writes Braxton, conflicts and resentments between American and European musicians came to loom large; and large ensembles were as hard to sustain in Europe as America. While Braxton remains a presence in the European arena, his base, voice, and vision remain distinctly American.

Bringing in Japan, it's interesting to note that the two (Japanese and Western European) cultures that have sheltered and helped Braxton (and African American musicians generally) when his own American one wouldn't—people either defeated by America in World War II or, if her allies, nevertheless harmed by the war on home ground as America wasn't—are the ones in which bebop and the later improvised musics not only took hold but quickly gave way to new indigenous versions. It says something about the nature of improvisation: the power to create something from nothing, instantly. It means everything when one's world is gone, as the slaves' was, as the vanquished populace's was.

the musician speaks

> The planet expansion of post-Parker creativity can be viewed as related to the social reality implications of the Second World War— and the subsequent interest (focus) on creative black music that solidified in that period profoundly effected the vibrational creative arena of both Western Europe and Japan. This would be the period which would see the resolidification and rebuilding that took place after the Second World War . . . the progressional adaptation of post-Parker creativity in Europe (and Japan) is related to the principal interest in black postulation dynamics. This interest developed as a result of the composite projectional spread of black creative invention in the last three thousand years. The dynamic realness of this phenomenon would be of profound importance to the resolidification of post-war Europe and Japan.[45]

Also, the idea that Japan is ingeniously derivative and imitative but not original Braxton dismisses as half-baked and "probably racist."

Both Europe (Germany) and Japan were themselves, within the life-span of jazz, unarguably imperialistic and racist. America, though also those things, has also been, arguably, both humbled and energized with the new vision and strength, embodied in her music, of a non-racist, non-Western, non-imperialistic impulse from within her multicultural national identity. As it happened, that no longer (solely) white Western nation, at the height of its trans-African music's strongest mass appeal, put down the global threats of racist imperialism, then helped the vanquished rebuild and realign. Japan and (West) Germany went on to outstrip America economically.

This dynamic, fresh in recent memory, suggests a framework for other history. Egypt, which had the global power in the Western world's infancy, enslaved and oppressed the Hebrews. Europe got that power—through Greece, then Rome, then the Western countries—then came to enslave and oppress her former African overlords. That imbalance split off to America, which revolted against it (through her music, churches, social movements), then resolved it somewhat (in theory more than in practice). America then resists (both white and non-white) aggressors (including, eventually, the Soviet Union) following their own racist-imperialist impulses . . . then helps them rebuild their shattered worlds, which they do quickly and with astonishing success.

Do we see the Muse at work in this sort of power shifting? Has African culture functioned in America as a Trojan Horse full of warrior-shamans with the collective wisdom and power to save us from our own worst impulses, and force our best? The Muse in the music has its own history and purposes, seasoned with the survival of the vagaries of mortal power and suffering.

Braxton sees the spectrum of musicultural expression not as vyings for dominance but as complementary aspects of total human nature.

> For if the vibrational and actual reality of creative music from the black aesthetic has meaning for the composite realness of world culture, so too do the dynamic offerings of world creativity have meaning for western culture . . . It is important to understand that without a better awareness of Chinese or African creativity, we

> cannot know that part of ourselves—not to mention that the thrust dynamics surrounding what those forms really are, are lost to us. The move towards world consciousness is a move towards actual consciousness—the two are not separable.[46]

Finally, whatever violence and trauma have accompanied this search for equilibrium, they are not essential nor necessary to it.

> The progressional spread of creative music was not brought about from the realness of war—and/or conquering land. Rather the present situation of composite earth can be viewed with respect to how the music was conceptually-vibrationally-socially and politically desired by every sector of the planet (even including the so-called communist countries) [note that this was written before the end of the cold war—M. H.]. In every case, creative music from the black aesthetic has served as a positive dynamic factor for its host country, and while doing so also functioned as an important liberating factor for both the vibrational tone level of the country and the continuum implications of dynamicism . . . creative music from the black aesthetic has functioned as a profound regenerating factor for world culture—and in particular Europe, Japan and the Americas.[47]

Both the experience and the influence of the creative woman, Braxton asserts, has been the same as that of the African in world culture—underground, oppressed, and seminal, which is another way of saying her roots are deep and her force strong. Braxton places discussion of her near the end of his third and final *Tri-Axium* book, just before the section on world transformation. As we've seen above, his role in the music resonates with her plight through his own personal affinity (i.e., he is one of those important male voices, like Lester Young's, which itself has a healthy dose of feminine energy) as well as through the transpersonal principles of cosmic balance and justice he embraces.

Braxton criticizes not only Western culture but supposedly enlightened artists from both Western and African American cultures:

> So real is the suppression of women a fact that any attempt to understand transformation would imply a total re-shaping of society. Because one thing is clear: the most basic understanding that western society has with regard to creativity is that women are not capable of making creative statements on the same level as men[48] . . . creative music has long functioned directly in accordance to the needs and whims of masculine vibrational tendencies since the personification of this time cycle (from the beginning of this historical cycle—from early Egypt until now). In this regard there is no difference between the situation surrounding western art music today and what has transpired in creative music from the black aesthetic (there are basic differences in how the situation was established).[49]

the musician speaks

He postulates some reasons for those differences: men exclude women, women don't want to take the same creative routes as men anyway, Western sexism blocks access to viable musical careers as rigidly as racism. Braxton notes[50] that in its beginnings and at its grass roots in the church, women were and are cocreators of the music much more than in its progressively more Westernized expressions; that root is part of what needs to be reclaimed now. He says that even though Westernization has chilled women's presence, their influence is still strong in the music's premises:

> To understand the significance of the creative woman—with regard to how a given projection might be advanced—it is only necessary to examine the aesthetic lining of creative music from the black aesthetic. One thing is clear, if the functional lining of creative music reveals the most sophisticated use of "actual" participation (improvisation)—dynamic participation (improvisation and its use in different structural contexts), collective participation and spiritual participation (improvisation with regard to the cosmic forces which determine whatever there is to be determined) then quite possibly we already have some idea about the profound impact of women in creative music.[51]

Generally, Braxton attributes the moral, ethical, and spiritual thrusts of black music to women. The implication is that the male culture of the warrior, the stoic, has most suited the oral tradition's task of meeting the demands of the Western literate approach to music—but even the men who took on that task, in their most intense forays of bebop, did so with the aid of heroin and women, including (more frequently than their forbears) white women. (This would be an interesting study, one begun by Wilmer:[52] the examples of white women who functioned as allies—matrons, fans, friends and lovers—to black musicians. I suggest it might be shown that their support increased as the African "humanization" of the West progressed through the music since it began this century, and that that humanization was a palpable stimulus, through the civil rights movement, of the later women's movement.)

In sum, male sexism has excluded creative women from the music just as white racism has denied the music as a whole the respect and support due it; that exclusion is longstanding, but it has intensified with the Westernization of black music; that must be righted.

> The exclusion of the creative women has affected the vibrational dictates underlying how given thrusts of the music are perceived, and unless this suppression is corrected, there can be no real hope for either composite transformation—on a global or national level—or cosmic transformation—as a mystical and ethical restoration consideration. The significance of the creative woman is connected with the realness of world transformation.[53]

Braxton offers this view as a broadening and deepening of that which sees the history of jazz as being a century's worth of folk and popular entertainment evolving into an art form. Only part of Braxton's music fits into that scope, and the parts that do not have either been condemned by its lights or (ultimately) trivialized as a solely personal genius rooted in no such larger context.

The fourth and last section of the last of *Tri-Axium Writings'* three books is "Transformation." Its "Level One" is where Braxton's words about the creative woman fall; its "Level Two" deals with the crux of what I think of as his Millennial vision, a vision of a transformation of consciousness and thereby of physical reality itself, a vision in line with the Christian Parousia, Jewish Messianism, or any other such collective myth of collective human enlightenment within synchronous cosmic transformation. He chooses his words to get at the possible real-world modes of fulfillment for such visions.

Recalling his use of "Level Ones" as descriptions of the "local" (spacetime) manifestation of a "nonlocal" (dreamtime, mythological) "Level Two" "composite" reality, we see the suggestion of what he articulates throughout *this* "Level Two": that patriarchy, introduced to an Egypt that began with a goddess orientation, is the very soul of the Western world of disembodied literacy and transcendence; and that an establishment of the West's own spiritual *immanence*—the "return" or "arrival" of its God from heaven to earth—is one and the same as the re/assertion of collective feminine power into the global culture.

> The concept of transformation has several meanings, depending on its use, but ultimately this is the word I use to speak of vibrational-cosmic and physical universe change cycles that take place on the chemical and vibrational universe level. In other words, transformation is a phenomenon which corresponds to my belief that cosmic cycles have long played an important part in physical universe progressionalism on this planet. Quite possibly the last real transformation which determined the nature of this time period was the destruction of African civilization, and/or the decline of Indian civilization and the subsequent emergence of Western civilization as the defining agent of this time cycle.[54]

He notes that while such transformations are conceived in abstract, mythical terms that reduce them to magical, "miraculous" events—the sudden return of the Christ to begin the 1000-year reign of peace, or some New Age that comes, like Christmas morning, to the world overnight—they in fact happen more gradually and not without trauma, tragedy, death, and disintegration. As empires have risen and fallen in the past; as many clashing groups have successfully developed into cohesive empires; as the chaos of the moment has shown itself to be part of a discernible, symmetrical structure exhibiting its own life, purpose, and direction over the expanding sweep of hindsight, so that we come to speak of Stone, Bronze, and Iron ages; of pre-Christian and Christian eras; of centuries and millennia as though they were days and weeks in some life we live—as we recall and conceive our past so, so do we intuit and dream our future, which none of us will ever really "know" any more than we know such pasts, as we know our individual lives. Yet we do know this transpersonal, transtemporal, omnipresent life; we commune with it through our arts and letters both, our scientific and religious, philosophical and cultural traditions. The short personal lives we do live are framed and borne by this Muse and its forces in motion.

A "musician," then, as Braxton sees it, is one who acknowledges and seeks to take responsibility for his or her presence in that larger picture, so as to maximize its potential for human good:

> If the cosmic factors which dictate change have provided a situation that can be shaped in a number of ways, and if we are in the position to decide just what the shape will be, then that position must imply some degree of responsibility on our part.[55]

In keeping with such responsibility, he calls for a lessening of individualism as a primary motivating force and an increased sense of service to humanity as a whole; at the same time, he expresses the need for (sociopolitical-cultural) decentralization in such service, so that the needs of the individual are properly met. He notes the potential of modern communications and transportation technology to bring about the transformation to a habitable global village, citing Buckminster Fuller as a visionary of such. He declares the dominance of the white Western male agenda and spirit over so much of the rest of the world (of nonwhites and of all women: "It is possible to substitute the word 'women' in place of 'black' in almost every section of this book")[56] as intolerable, flags it as one of the specific targets of transformation. He notes the crisis in spirituality in the West, mentions the subsequent movements of Western people to non-Western religions and traditions . . . and he relates music—and other real-world phenomena—to all of this:

> The concept and existence of music and/or political reality, etc., are not factors which cause transformation as much as factors which are caused by transformation. This is a significant difference. For my opinion of transformation is not that once a given cycle is solidified suddenly everyone will love one another and all will be wonderful . . . the concept of transformation has to do with the vibrational and cosmic factors which dictate the nature underlying how change is to occur—as that change is connected to the all-cosmic considerations of "what-is." In other words, "the reality of planet progressionalism" seems to imply that given progressions function in accordance to vibrational and cosmic factors—as those factors relate to what that given time zone is about. As such, it is possible to look at the cycle that took place during the Egyptian period, the great Chinese period—the migration cycle, the Ice Age, the western cycle, etc., etc., and understand what I mean when I refer to the nature of a given transformational cycle . . . [57] I believe the present-day music journalist should be concerned about helping to solidify a more positive understanding of composite earth creativity—as opposed to the present state of name-calling and ego postulation. This is

especially important when one understands that only a small sector of the greater community has access to any medium of information transference.[58]

On that note, it is well to recall that, whether music is an effect or a cause—or both—of the transformation Braxton is discussing, it is the motivation and focus of both this book and his own. He was interested in writing and sharing his thoughts as they were inspired by the music; we are interested in them primarily as they inform and enlighten us about his music.

Armed, now, with that information and enlightenment, let us examine that music.

---

1. Braxton, *Tri-Axium Writings*, Vol. 1 (Hanover, NH: Tree Frog Music, 1985: 79).
2. Ibid., 80.
3. Ibid., 88.
4. Ibid., 92.
5. Ibid., 106.
6. Ibid., 111.
7. Ibid., 114.
8. Ibid., 115–25.
9. Ibid., 118, 119–20.
10. Ihab Hassan, "The Culture of Postmodernism" (*Theory, Culture and Society*, Vol. 2, no. 3, 1985: 119–31).
11. Braxton, *Tri-Axium 1*, 121.
12. Ibid., 122.
13. "In a highly revealing comment, Benny Carter indicated that in 1920s Harlem . . . everybody was just trying to do their thing without a great deal of thought about what was black or Afro-American or jazz . . . everybody was just trying to play what they heard, what they thought without even thinking in terms of roots" (Burton W. Peretti, *The Creation of Jazz: Music, Race, and Culture in Urban America* [Urbana and Chicago: Univ. of Illinois Press, 1992: 177–210]).
14. Ben Sidran, *Black Talk* (New York: Da Capo Press, 1981: xii).
15. Braxton, *Tri-Axium 1*, 239.
16. Ibid., 252.
17. Ibid., 261.
18. Ibid., 276.
19. See Robert Bauval and Adrian Gilbert, *The Orion Mystery* (London: Heinemann, 1994).
20. Braxton, *Tri-Axium 2*, 16.
21. Braxton, *Tri-Axium 1*, 416–442.
22. Graham Lock, *Forces in Motion: The Music and Thoughts of Anthony Braxton* (New York: Da Capo Press, 1988:.33–39); Ronald Radano, *New Musical Figurations: Anthony Braxton's Cultural Critique* (Chicago/London: University of Chicago Press, 1993. 81–131).
23. Braxton, *Tri-Axium 1*, 427.
24. Ibid., 427.
25. Ibid., 428.
26. Ibid., 428.
27. Braxton, *Tri-Axium 1*, 287.
28. Ibid., 301.
29. Ibid., 292.

30. Ibid., 305.
31. Ibid., 305–06.
32. Ibid., ix–x.
33. Albert Murray *The Hero and the Blues* (University of Missouri Press, 1973: 50.)
34. Braxton, telephone interview, April 20, 1991.
35. Braxton, *Tri-Axium 2*, 198–310.
36. Braxton, *Four Compositions (1973)* (Denon NCP 8504).
37. Braxton, *Tri-Axium 2*, 198.
38. Michael Ventura, "Hear That Long Snake Moan" (*Whole Earth Review* No. 54, Spring 1987: 35).
39. Braxton, *Tri-Axium 2*, 200.
40. Ibid., 201.
41. Ibid., 202–03.
42. Ibid., 203–04.
43. Ibid., 207.
44. Ibid., 209–10.
45. Ibid., 237–38.
46. Ibid., 278.
47. Ibid., 280.
48. Braxton, *Tri-Axium 3*, 430.
49. Ibid., 434.
50. Ibid., 444–45.
51. Ibid., 452–53.
52. Valerie Wilmer, *As Serious as your Life: The Story of the New Jazz* (Quartet Books, London, 1977: 189–210).
53. Ibid., 468.
54. Ibid., 469–70.
55. Ibid., 476.
56. Ibid., 489.
57. Ibid., 500.
58. Ibid., 493.

third arrow . . .

**in the five fingers
of the archer**

Provocation

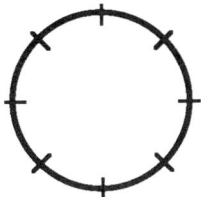 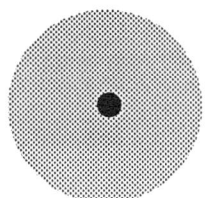

The solid circle with the (infinite) points of entry represents Braxton's roots in and covers of traditional jazz material from the American songbook and post-bop repertoire. The circle is solid, but its very integrity begs change, as an egg begs fertilization; thus the break marks. Seen as a field of quantum potential, its collapse into a quantum event is determined by an act of perception: one, rather than any other, break mark is chosen for the point of entry to the circle. Seen as the act of artistic creativity, which is chosen is determined by a given artist's affinity (as Braxton uses the term) to one break mark rather than another.

For Braxton, the circle stands for the field described in Section I: the world, earth's history and mystery, the material *he works with to make his music.*

The broken circle with the central dot represents his concept and expressions of solo alto sax music, through which he explores his own new restructurings of that tradition.

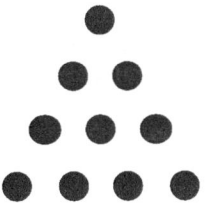

[From occult definition of] **tectractys**: *1. the Pythagorean mystery of the first four numbers (1+2+3+4) together forming ten, from which all things begin . . . 2. it became a holy symbol by which later Pythagoreans used to swear; it consists of ten dots, forming a triangle; 3. it symbolizes the beginning and the end: birth, growth, and death.*

[From occult definition of][1] **number**: . . . *8. Pythagoras: 0 = circle: a snake biting its own tail: God before creation, infinite possibility; 1 = dot in the circle: the central or circumferential fire, the beginning of creation.*

[From occult definition of] **circle**: *1. eternity, heaven, perfection . . . ; 2. universe, infinity . . . ; 3. cycle of existence: a. days: the Wheel of the Sun . . . b. seasons; c. the Zodiac . . . 4. the female principle . . . 7. correspondences: b. gods: Mercury . . .*

[From occult definition of] **egg**: *1. Egyptian hier.: a. potentiality; b. the seed of generations; c. the mystery of life . . . 4. Orphic, etc.: the typical symbol of the world; the yoke in the middle of a liquid (upper and lower waters): sun in "ether," surrounded by the vault of heaven; so: a. an egg shape with a dot in the centre . . .*

[From occult definition of] **one**: *1. unity, the Mystic Centre; 2. the Supreme Being: creative and preservative; 3. phallus, the masculine principle, activity; 4. light, revelation, spiritual unity, the non-manifest point; 5. Pythagoras: a. Essence; b. Reason; 6. Cabala: the "I am" . . . the Spirit and the Word . . . 9. psych.: a. occurs rarely; b. hermaphroditic unity of Paradise preceding the duality of good and evil.*

The point within a circle is one of the hieroglyphic signs of the Sun-God, Ra, but it is not merely an image of the solar disc . . . The earliest supreme power figured in Heaven in a masculine shape was the Power of Stability and Equilibrium, associated with the fixity of the Pole Star. This was first assigned to Anup, in the form of a Jackal; then to Horus I, to Ptah, the Great Architect, and finally to Osiris, the power that held all things in equipoise.

The Pole Star is the first fixed point within a circle, not the Sun, and the earliest Supreme Being at the head of the seven primary stars was the god of the Pole Star. Therefore we claim the Glyph of Ra to have been the Ideograph of the Pole Star at the centre of a circle . . .

The dot in the centre of a circle is equal to the point at the top of the cone that was crowned with the star at the summit.

third arrow

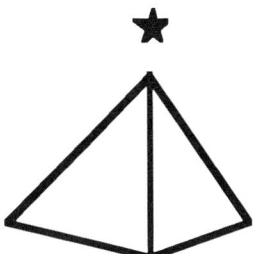

In this circle of the Pole Star there were seven gods or glorious ones grouped together in the constellation of the Lesser Bear, revolving round the Most High, the Great Judge, the All-Seeing Eye who saw by night . . .

Moreover, the Glyph is an equivalent for the Eye, and the two are co-types. Therefore it may be inferred that, as the fixed star at the centre, it was the Primordial All-Seeing Eye in the Astral Mythology. The Pole Star, considered as an eye upon the summit of the mountain, explains the Chinese name of the "Heaven's-Eye Mountain." We find the same equivalent in the States of Central America.[2]

Language is mono-dimensional and life is three-dimensional. Color and shape in music have mystical and profound implications. The only language which describes it is symbolic. My titles are contemporary hieroglyphics.

Anthony Braxton

This chapter/section is the *axis* (per the "Tri-Axium" concept) of Braxton's Muse's extension back through spacetime and forward through him; it is also, accordingly, the axis of the book's structure (as suggested by Figure I.b). Here we'll begin our direct look at Braxton and his music, that to which all preceding information has led, a look we'll sustain for the rest of the book.

Also in Figure I (a) is the first of a series of geometric symbols linked to each chapter on the music; the usages of these are mine—though, as we'll see, they overlap with Braxton's—offered as demonstrations of the way he conceives and uses his symbols to communicate as a composer musical concepts to himself as a performer and to other performers.

The solid circle with break marks represents the traditional material Braxton has recorded and performed in various contexts throughout his career; the short lines transecting the circumference, suggesting rays, represent the infinite number of ways one can express the infinite potential for improvisation within a single musical structure, or that the Muse can express itself through improvisation.

Many of the original ideas Braxton develops in his own music flow through his improvisations here, but they are set in the conventional context of the bebop improviser. The broken circle with the dot in the center represents his solo alto sax music, which, as a body, is an improvisation not only within but also upon tradition and convention.

Good symbols are polyvalent, charged with a multitude of meanings. Set in the context of the first two sections, the more solid circle also represents the world: everything the creative artist is born to, shaped by, nurtured and schooled by, and confronted with as material. It can also represent, specifically to Braxton the man, the world as female—an unfertilized egg, its obviously permeable (but not yet permeated) perimeter denoting the potential life waiting to be actualized. Specific to Braxton the (musically) modernistic scientific alchemist, it can also represent a field of potential, waiting for the creative act of per/con-ception to collapse ("quantify") it into reality. The dot is the individual, the quantum, the one from the many, the seed, the dot above the "i," the artist's unique work. (Braxton uses the circle in his notation system to denote areas of open improvisation, in keeping with the general meaning of "potential to be actualized.")

Braxton has both covered traditional material and practiced his own solo sax music from his beginnings, as he continues to do (at this writing, he has just left for Europe to record a CD of lesser-known Charlie Parker material). My sequence of presentation—of traditional, solo, duo, and so on—is not chronological, although it happens to be for this chapter, since he did cut his teeth on mainstream jazz before the innovative departures from it taken by Coleman, himself, and others. The sequence is rather conceptual, an aid to understanding the integration of tradition and innovation, the development of complexity from simplicity, in Braxton's creative vision and process.

A note on the methodology peculiar to this section is in order. The main challenge to any written analysis of Braxton's work, as should be obvious by now, is to find the habitable and fruitful ground between largely non-Western musical expression and mostly Western assessment of it. In the light of Braxton's critique of so much of such assessment, and of his own alternative literate framings of his music, I'm inclined to embark on mine with some care.

I originally developed my own writings on music as notes to myself on a subject I wanted to learn. I understood, in my formative years, this subject to be rooted in my own culture—"folk music," "the blues," "jazz," and "classical music" were *my* musics, there to learn and give my voice. Later, as a journalist, I worked those notes into a form and context which I understood as a means to teach others about this subject. Finally, most recently, I see my notes and write-ups of them as part of the Western tradition of fieldnotes and academic discourse on "the other"—even on one's own culture or self *as* "the other" (i.e., from a self-reflective detachment).

I've approached this crossroads between tradition and innovation in Braxton by presenting my reviews of the selected recordings in an only slightly edited form of the stream-of-conscious notes I take while listening to them. The process of taking such notes from the beginning has been a spontaneous creative act done in the same (oral) mode in which I play and hear the music. If part of this book's (and Braxton's) premise is that the detachment of the literate from its own primary oral mode is what has gotten scholars, journalists, and critics in trouble with this music, then such a demonstrated realignment of literate with oral seems in order. I'll therefore culminate my notes with the sort of review they typically get worked into for publication, and offer all material from notes

third arrow

to review as a microcosmic picture of the process of translating the oral/aural experience to the literate mode.

My aim in the notes is to convey the musical experience itself, to critique or define the results only as a musician might do with his or her own playing or that of fellow players, in *their* context. Before working my notes on the final (a solo alto) recording into a polished review, however, I will, on the traditional covers, revert to the literate mode to examine my own processes and assumptions in the fieldnote-taking mode. When I review my review notes, then, I will do so in the light of the disparities between the music and criticism of it, in the interests of addressing and redressing them. (To keep my primary subject developing, I will continue to weave the points I have to make about Braxton's music in with these self-reflections. Again, this self-reflection will be in the text of only this chapter's/section's musical discussion; in following chapters, review notes will revert to my authorial privacy for use primarily in the figure captions about specific musical examples.)

Chapter Five

The Solo Music's Axis (Tradition/Innovation)

I view my entire life, my entire work, in such a way as to ask myself: "How, as you become older, do you set about integrating everything that previously happened?"

Karlheinz Stockhausen

Early Musical and Personal History

Lock, Radano, and the various longer magazine interviews with Braxton are good sources for fairly detailed accounts of Braxton's childhood and young adulthood. Here I will just give a synopsis (mostly from Radano),[3] emphasizing the elements that most pertain to Braxton's traditional bases and most broadly original spins on them.

Braxton was born and grew up in the heart of Chicago's South Side to parents who had migrated there, like thousands of other African Americans of that time, from the South. Next to Harlem, the South Side was the largest and most developed arena of Northern black urban culture.

Braxton recalls his family life as relatively untroubled, and his childhood development as positive. It included a good male role model, his stepfather, who was a television repairman. Braxton's own natural intellectual gifts and introverted personality found an early object and direction in the world of electronic engineering, which he pursued happily and passionately. He was an avid reader of *Popular Science*, was especially fascinated with rocketry and with model trains (and the real railroad lore and machinery they modeled, present *en masse* in Chicago, in the railroad yards where his biological father, Clarence, worked), and conceived and sketched schemata of his own visions of high technology—both improved designs of existing devices and new inventions.

His experience of his own neighborhood's culture was filtered through this self-protective abstract inner life. It kept him from the gangs and all their emphasis on macho posturing and proving, and established a value and integrity in creative solitude. It also freed him up to enjoy the positive things about his time and place—most especially the music—in a healthy and proactively rationalistic way.

Most noteworthy here is the positive and primally personal soul Braxton associated early on with what many see as the cold, clinical field of engineering. In Braxton's case, it came with the warm, human face of a father figure; it offered itself as a field in which he could exercise and develop his own innate gifts; and it came with the promise of a professional culture with which he might connect as a step up and out from the limitations of the world to which he was born. His rapture for trains was poetic, resonant with their mythical status in the folk and blues traditions, and would inform the concept of his musical paradigm, as we will see in due course.

Following up that promise and potential, Braxton enrolled in the predominantly white Chicago Vocational High School, where he concentrated on the hard sciences and practical courses in electrical and electronic engineering. He also began his lifelong love affair with chess, quickly becoming club captain and school champion.

His access to black music was rich, naturally, given his location and parentage. His family attended a Baptist church and sang and played gospel songs there and at family gatherings. Braxton also attended Roman Catholic services, which provided an early entry point, numinous with his own youth, to the medieval sacred roots of Western music. Especially thrilling to him too were the marches performed by parade bands on holidays throughout those years.

Braxton and his brothers and friends were as passionate as most youth of their time about the popular music by both black and white groups—The Platters, Frankie Lymon and the Teenagers, Chuck Berry, Elvis Presley, Bill Haley. True to his persona as budding creator, he was by the seventh grade composing his own tunes to sing and play with friends at school performances.

His introverted, analytical side, fed through the Baby Boomers' media of television and recordings, gave him almost as full and early an access to white culture and music. By adolescence, his tastes had expanded into jazz, also both black and white; early heroes were trumpeter Miles Davis, pianists Ahmad Jamal and Dave Brubeck, and alto saxist Paul Desmond. He started learning the clarinet in school, then took private lessons with a "strict, correct teacher from the German tradition"[4] named Jack Gell, at the Chicago School of Music.

Under Gell, Braxton began to construct a foundation of concept and technique straight out of the Western European tradition. Starting from scales and exercises and elementary songs, he cut his teeth on études and sonatas by Bach and Telemann; the formal rigors of embouchure, fingering, and breathing techniques, of reading music and building a classical repertoire were Gell's staples. In this tutelage, of course, Braxton and his first mentor reflected personally the tradition that led to the early urban jazz in New Orleans and St. Louis, when itinerant German music teachers and band leaders met and taught black and Creole musicians. Again, it is important to note that his apprenticeship with Gell was the warm (if often demanding), human relationship between a fatherly mentor and a gifted, passionate aspirant. Gell, the first white person with whom Braxton formed a close bond, exposed him to the classical tradition and to white jazz artists in an inclusive context in his formative years, encouraging him to learn theory and work hard with optimism and hope for success in music.

The musical education and training Braxton got with Gell were put into practice among his fellow students in high-school and after-school jazz and concert ensembles. It was here—and, later on, in college and army bands, and informal jam sessions—that he learned to play in the sax sections of large and small groups the jazz- and concert-band repertoire of the time. His discipline and enthusiasm led him to natural positions of leadership in sections and groups, and his creative and analytical bents led him to learn theory and notation, and the understanding of structure, arranging, and orchestration necessary to compose.

By his early twenties, Braxton had become a proficient musical technician, but he felt he lacked the quality of an original voice and message, which he saw in other players around him, particularly his friend and fellow saxophonist Roscoe Mitchell. His quest for that voice and message led him to identify and sort the musical things he was and was not. This quest mirrored his early years in its strong connections between his inner and outer worlds. That is, just as the abstract concepts and mechanics of engineering, chess, and music all had their flesh-and-blood correlates in Braxton's significant others (his stepfather and chess partners, Gell, Mitchell, and others), so did those of his formal and self-education in the historical, cultural, philosophical, and sociopolitical realms. For all Braxton's introversion and autodidactic way of operating, he has always experienced his vision and growth in the context of human relationships to which many might have been less open.

For example, he speaks of getting to know and find a mutual understanding with whites who had initially been racially hostile to him in the army, furthering his access to white culture and music; he explored his budding awareness of academia's Eurocentric bias against and ignorance of non-Western music, and the information he needed to supplement formal curricula, through his own most immediate Afrocentric circles, in the context of friendships and the personal support group of the AACM; a cousin helped shape his relationship with the civil rights movement's various and related philosophies; he formed a close relationship with a Japanese woman who helped him expand from that base to a more global education in Western and African American arts and letters; his love for John Cage's music was fed and informed by a personal and professional relationship with that composer. The most original and bold innovations of his life's work, both music and writings about it, have always been rooted in the personal dynamics of relationships, never conceived and executed in the vacuum of a disembodied, isolated intellect.

Even his responses to music generally thought of as esoteric and specialized were visceral first, analytical later. As often as not, moreover, these gut responses were initially negative—such as his initial responses to Charlie Parker, Ornette Coleman, and some of Stockhausen—just as his encounters with white racism in the army had been. He grew to discern the lessons to be learned, the growth that could take place, and the solutions to the very problems they posed found beyond such shocks to his ever-evolving system.

In short, as this brief biographical sketch admittedly only suggests, Braxton's approach to music throughout his life has been informed and shaped by a basically positive early experience with intellectual discipline and abstraction, positive formative relationships with both black and white music and people, an understanding of negative experiences with both music and people as positive opportunities or catalysts for growth and understanding, and an

solo music

acceptance of less-than-ideal worldly (professional, financial, artistic) situations empowered by ambitions and practical strategies for their improvement. By virtue of his unconflicted, healthy Afrocentric orientation he has been as comfortable with the Eurocentric elements of the music. He has been able to develop his music through internal motivations and rewards in the face of external indifference and hostility. He has been able, through his comfort with intellectual discipline, to avoid the pitfalls of addiction and general instability (and their shadow sides of rigid dogmatism) so many of his peers suffer from the emotional dynamics of race and creativity in a conflicted and pedestrian world. Finally, he has had a solid base of joy and wonder from youth on which to build and stay in touch with through the difficulties his music has encountered in the marketplace.

A Braxton-like "biogram" might best capture this uniquely American picture of successful traits and strategies for survival and success in a pluralist society with classist, racist, anti-intellectual, and anti-cultural dynamics:

Fig. 5.1: We recall from Fig. I.b the tipped hour-glass shape—an ancient symbol for the finity of a lifetime, and for the perpetual round of creation and destruction between material and spiritual realms—to evoke another

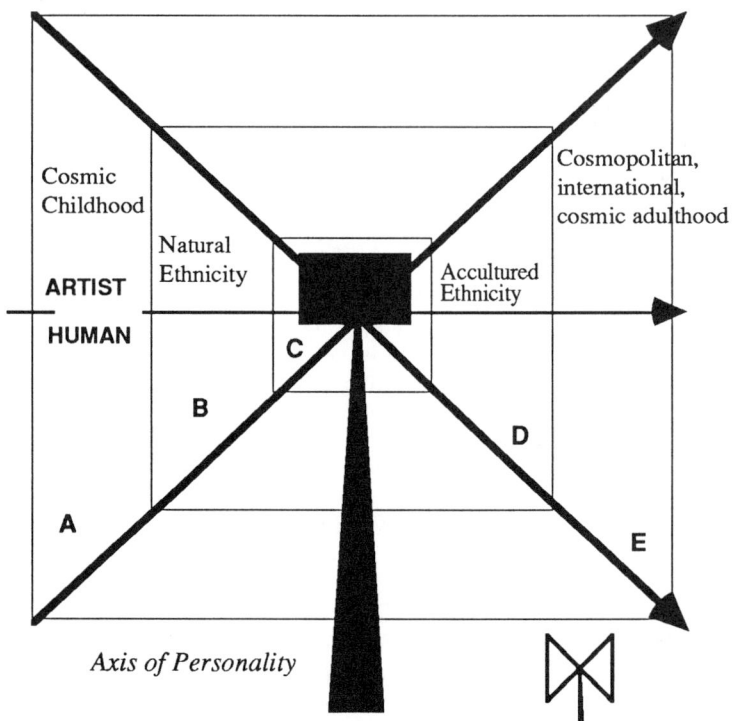

(Ancient Egyptian symbol for battle-ax)

image/concept: the personal armor, weaponry, and cunning Braxton developed to get through America's minefield—and her Dream—to his place in the larger world and universe.

The child is born to undifferentiated humanity, which is informed and shaped by his ethnicity, which is informed and shaped (and challenged) by the American culture of multiethnic compromise, to then come to a point of mature personal identity. That identity then expresses itself and eventually finds its place in the largest possible world of relationship to everyone everywhere and everywhen. It does so first through that most personally constricting but potentially leveraging national cultural base—i.e., if one wants to become a musician, he cuts his teeth in the American academic and commercial arenas for a long time before attempting to change them to better suit and serve him. The first step of such change is to assert his humanity—to differentiate it—including the ethnic/cultural identity he experiences from "the inside," however much the Western Eurocentric context in which he developed his first (public) musical identity may have perceived and experienced it from "the outside." He finally gets through all that to discover his global identity.

Area A is the simple human birthright of a happy, healthy childhood; it is the soil for Area B's flowering of one's healthy ethnic identity, which in turn can empower one to conceive one's path through Area C, one's birthright as a functional American citizen, with all the promise and potential that implies. One's personality then has what it needs to reverse the journey back to one's now differentiated (individuated, then re-integrated) humanity.

Not all, by a long shot, of course, make it through so neatly; one can imagine various distortions on this design that would fit real people who are so "cosmic" they can't resolve the tensions relating to their national or ethnic identities, or so stuck in the national or ethnic sectors that they don't function well with the rest of the world around them. Braxton's swim up this stream has been fraught with the frustration and poverty that came with going against the aesthetic and cultural currents of his times and places—but it has also made for the splashes of excitement and discovery that make such swims worthwhile to him and those of like mind. Such a biographical profile goes far toward explaining the staying power of the musical paradigm he has developed to compose and improvise from, and the power and authority of his music in general.[5]

Covers of Traditional Material

The objective of artistic experimentation, whether in the case of the individual or of an entire aesthetic school or movement, is to develop a device with which to render the subtleties of contemporary sensibility. The maximum communication of these subtleties, however, is achieved only to the extent that rhetorical innovations become a part of the natural mode of expression of the

solo music **217**

time. The lasting results of avant-garde experimentation always become inevitable-seeming parts of the grand style of the mainstream of discourse.

Albert Murray

Recordings Analyzed

In the Tradition, Vols. 1 & 2 (Inner City IC 2015 & 2045, 1974); with Tete Montoliu, piano; Niels-Henning Orsted Pedersen, bass; and Albert "Tootie" Heath, drums.

Seven Standards 1985, Vols. 1 & 2 (Magenta MA 0203 & 0205, 1985); with Hank Jones, piano; Rufus Reid, bass; and Victor Lewis, drums.

Six Monk's Compositions (1987) (Black Saint BS 120 116-1, 1989); with Mal Waldron, piano; Buell Neidlinger, bass; and Bill Osborne, drums.

Eight (+3) Tristano Compositions 1989 (Hat Art CD 6052, 1990); with John Raskin, bari saxophone; Dred Scott, piano; Cecil McBee, bass; Andrew Cyrille, drums.

Braxton, then, established in his youth the working base in Western European musical concepts and techniques, and in the African American jazz idiom they helped spawn, on which he later built his own original work. Perhaps "base" is the wrong word; more accurately, he made sure he understood the history, musical mechanics, and premises of both Western and African American music before he presumed to build his own alternative systemic and structural bases. While he would often seek to dismantle and restructure those musics with his own original contributions, it was only and always so (as will be seen repeatedly throughout the material presented here) in affirmation of the spirit he saw it housing and sought to house himself.

Traditional jazz material—statements of and improvisations on American song forms—is peppered throughout Braxton's solo recordings of original material, as we'll see and consider through those reviewed below. However, recordings devoted wholly to "the tradition" are sporadic exceptions to his rule, overall. These recordings reflect his concept of "Group Musics," as outlined in Fig. 5.2, designated "musics that seek to further the value systems of the group" and "to honor the masters from the past."

I. Line Forming Logic

    1. Monophony—(drones) (static)
    2. Monophony—(melody)(active) . . .

. . . XLL. GROUP MUSICS
       a. march music
       b. musics that seek to further the value systems of the group
       c. to honor the masters from the past

Fig. 5.2: From Braxton's classroom materials about his musical paradigm, an outline called "Tri-Metric Modeling." This three-page outline essentially roughs out his musical consciousness from its simplest (I.1., above) to its most sophisticated aspects (XII, "Image Musics"). XIII ("Group Musics") places that individual consciousness in a community/historical context.

His own such musical statements fit in with his convictions, also cited below, that concepts such as "innovation" and "avant-garde" are Western impositions on the unbroken continuum of the trans-African music of which he is a recent participant. He makes these traditional covers in essentially the same spirit that he composes, performs, and records the music most unique to him. Even though Braxton's first recording devoted entirely to traditional material was his fourteenth—some six years after the first releases of the original material that defined his public debut—he had been playing and improvising on tunes and big-band charts since his adolescence.

The recordings made in the 1970s do have some Braxton original touches. He plays the contrabass clarinet on two fast bop war-horses for high horns, Miles Davis'/Charlie Parker's *Donna Lee* and Parker's *Ornithology*, as well as on Mingus' *Goodbye, Pork Pie Hat*, and the spontaneous free *Duet*, the two less awkward vehicles for that instrument by conventional lights. He departs from the very well traveled playlist of staples from Miles Davis, Parker, Mingus, Billy Strayhorn, and the American songbook with a rendition of Warne Marsh's *Marshmallow*, not (like all the others) a typical spontaneous "first-contact" jam session tune (which this was, by the way. The producer called him to fill in for an ailing Dexter Gordon).

Lock is a good book source for the connections Braxton makes in their full interview sections between the tradition and his own music. While Radano provides thorough background on Braxton's traditional influences and looks at their effects in his compositions,[6] he doesn't focus on Braxton's actual covers of traditional material. Some comments Braxton made in interviews about the subject might be the best transition from the more extensive expositions of his liner notes and writings pertinent to the subject (see Chapter Three).

In a 1974 interview with Ray Townley, the latter articulated the implied and express biases for the "avant-gardist" and against the "traditionalist" in reviews by Litweiler and Martin: "The atmosphere during a Braxton concert borders on that of 'serious' or classical music. At the same time, the historical link with traditional 'jazz' pervades the show like a disreputable grandparent—you know he's left his mark but you don't want to mention his name in public."[7]

Braxton was then quoted explaining that his and his peers' music was born of the same spirit that had originally generated the then radical/now traditional musics of Parker and Coltrane; only the surface expression, along with the times, had changed.

Some 15 years later, discussing his then recent release of Monk tunes with interviewer Shoemaker, Braxton referred back to his first recordings of standards.

> If I had not made a record of traditional material they would say I can't play traditional material. If I make a record of traditional material they want to call it old-fashioned. If I develop my own

concept of rhythmic logics, it's not swinging. If I play using Charlie Parker's language they say I'm just another guy following Bird . . . I have always been excited by the tradition. The [*In the Tradition*—M. H.] recordings with Tete Montoliu . . . during that period you were put down for playing that kind of material. Now we're at a point in time where the opposite is true. You play something perceived as separate from the tradition and it is automatically viewed in a negative light . . . We were viewed as renegades, trying to violate the tradition, as opposed to restructuralists who understood that, however beautiful the music was, change was a universal law . . . Somehow, the positive implications of the music got distorted under the weight of social and political dynamics, and also to decisions that were made in the jazz business and journalistic complex.[8]

Generally, throughout his extensive interviews in the media, Braxton has maintained the position that he grew up on mainstream jazz records, has always embraced their tradition, and has seen his own work as in line rather than at odds with it. Perhaps the investment of his mature passion in the most quirky and difficult "standards" by Monk and Tristano—themselves quantum creative leaps beyond the American songbook and better known jazz heads of Braxton's earlier recordings—was the reach he needed to make, finally, to meet the jazz press in that territory halfway between (its idea of) "tradition" and "avant-garde."

The musical examples I've chosen to review comprise a selection informed by my own keenest responses to Braxton's recorded work, his judgment of what recordings have most fully realized his own intentions, and the media judgments as to which were most important and successful. What is interesting about reviewing this and subsequent chapters' selections, each spanning 20 years of recordings, is the encapsulation of the artist's development each provides. We know what initial promises were kept, what problems resolved and how, what weaknesses strengthened, and what difficulties overcome.

The following quote from Ullman came to my mind upon hearing the three recordings of traditional material. Braxton is describing to the author his childhood feelings of alienation:

Many of my friends learned the concept of hip. I never could quite be the right kind of hip. I never seemed to follow the same track that everybody was following, even if I wanted to. I'd be trying to be like everybody else, but it never quite worked out. So I grew up feeling somewhat unhappy about being on the planet and not quite understanding what I was dealing with. I don't want to paint a picture of the child who is miserable, but I recall growing up with an intense desire to figure out what I was really dealing with. I was and still am very affected by the physical reality of black people and what minority people are dealing with in this country.[9]

Somehow, all three of those things—the awkward alienation, the intense desire to figure it out, and the hunger for justice for the oppressed—loom particularly large for me in these recordings. Braxton's playing often sounds restless and ill at ease; at the same time, it sounds comfortable with that discomfort, determined to bear and get through and beyond it to a better place. This mix of steady and restless, sure and hesitant, rough and graceful works as a perfect musical metaphor for the poignancy of second-class citizenship in one's own country. Standards done smooth bop-style had become the "field-hollers-brought-into-the-house" by the time Braxton started his apprenticeship; as mentioned above, he had already made the many initial recordings that defined him as one of the new "field hollerers" by the time he made the first of these traditional dates. Inevitably, he would bring to them bits of the new musical ground he had broken—would, as Archie Shepp, for example, did around the same time, re-infuse that housebroken bebop with its original field energy—however diligently and humbly he submitted to its conventions.

Some final observations, to fully prepare the reader for the experience of reading review notes, especially those more extensive sections on the solo sax material: like that of reading Braxton's writings, it is both an exciting yet, after awhile, a frustrating experience. Both excitement and frustration are those—of real, unmediated life, and of the oral tradition's participation in it—literacy has arisen and evolved to manage. The literate readers will most likely engage this mode with interest in its power to evoke experience through description, its immediate access to spontaneous insights, its spontaneous poetry; they will quite soon, in proportion to their literate sophistication, tire of the repetition, the lack of self-reflective development, the dominance of the mundane. I suggest that this is the same experience literate listeners and critics encounter when they read Braxton's writings—which are wholly submitted to the oral experience of the music and the oral mode of speech—and when they hear his music. Indeed, it is the experience *homo legens* and his *mondo legens* encounter in life itself. I suggest, however, that the realignment of the literate with the oral experience is possible, desirable, indeed necessary to the world today; the process of fieldnotes-to-write-up is offered here as a microcosm of that realignment.

Therefore, one last suggestion: listen to the selected cuts while reading the notes.

In the Tradition Vols. 1 & 2, 1974

> *Marshmallow*—phrasing has a certain flatulent feel to it, but also moments of singing, synced rhythm & inspiration; like the voice of wood, then sometimes a breeze. Angular, choppyblocky for bop idiom (not so with pianist Tete, who also responds to AB's [Braxton's] sudden leaps alertly).

> *Goodbye, Pork Pie Hat*—Bass pedals bowed, contrabass (cb) squawks, bass string harmonics, slap tongue, air & keys, hornhonk, multiphonics, doggy yips—pure Braxton eeriness . . . foghorn sounds, sea creatures & gulls crying, circling, wind & bowed bass: a sacred space of that of a few minutes as intro; then head, bass-contrabass duet—"free" playing is spiritual often because it comes to

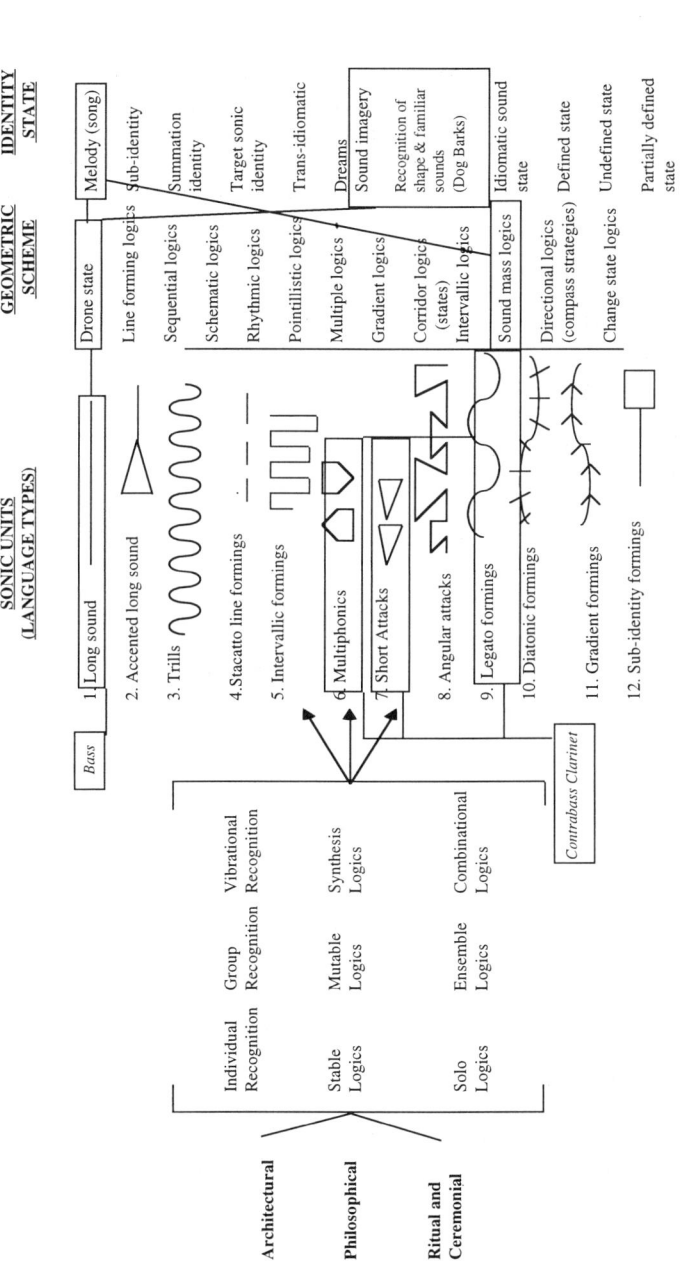

Fig. 5.3: *Goodbye, Pork-Pie Hat* (duet)

that sacred space and lets what is be & arise, the chaos-death, then gives it life-order . . .

Ornithology—medium tempo; while the timbre is obviously unusual in this context, this horn seems suited to AB's wide-open pitch and rhythmically sporadic phrasing; its highs speak more humanly, and its lows ground AB's flightiness more earthly. Something ancient and deep in the psyche is suggested by these deep reeds. Fig. 5.3: See Fig. 5.5 for the mostly blank template from which the above and the other "paradigmatics" are derived.

What's New—back to the clattery phrasing, disjointed; the head keeps pace with the changes, but as though it were hanging on the body by a thread; then linear phrases give way to sudden screeches, squawks, blatts, phrases that stop dead in the middle of their logic, pick up again to start a new logic, explode or shatter it to break its monotony.

Again, that bass-contrabass free duet (2d piece on both LPs); chirps, harmonics, air-&-keys;

Body & Soul—resonant w/ though not reminiscent of the Desmond approach to this tune; rather light frisky lope-along phrasing giving way to flurries and furies, sudden soaring singings hi, then lo warbles.

Donna Lee—same hit as Ornith; not breakneck. It's like these big deep instrus make his bounces more fleshy & resilient.

My Funny Valentine—ballad; sweet, lyrical alto; yet ever raggy & loose, rarely in the pocket. Like, this isn't really his path; like visiting the relatives at Thanksgiving & being bored but half-part of the scene.

This is the record (Vol. 1) he dedicated to the Roche Pharmaceutical Co. due to the difficulty of the last couple of years that turned him to Valium, just before Arista and big rise in polls. Interesting that that rise came right after these trad dates. Feel of him on these dates is lackadaisical, disjointed, not what you'd call seamless, on alto, better on cb, best in 2 free spots.

Seven Standards, 1985

Joy Spring—mercurial, jumpy, loose, stilted; very apt and adept at sketching the changes & blowing on them vertically *à la* late-bop

Trane, only like half there, then into his own flights & climaxes. Uneven. Wound tight, not relaxed. Eager, sincere, enthusiastic, not urbane—but worldly, in his ease with that position. Oddly his jumpiness often seems to work better in ballads (*Spring Is Here*); that timeless quality . . .

You Go to My Head—he loves to romp & frisk with the improvisatory invention; the emotion is assumed, implicit, covered by others, an ambiance he accepts as a given rather than works on generating; it's that quicksilver mind he's into, at least on this musical universe; his relationship to mainstream jazz is truly secondary, like, say, Stravinsky's to Rimsky-Korsakov's—thus, so strong is his identity as the torchbearer that his role as the sax stylist-soloist, when he most submits, is that of one champing at the bit to get to new territories. That traditional people respect him validates that role. Tete bends to it; pianist Hank Jones tolerates it; drummer Max Roach (who had violent negative reactions to Ornette at first) joins in it, all according to their own lights & talents—they in effect express their solidarity with AB's claim that he, for all his roughness & strangeness, is in their tradition. (One could possibly hear AB as not cutting it in this context, or, alternately, being held down by players stuck in the straight ruts.) Like Duke did with Trane, who was humble & wanted to play straight & maybe re-take a taping; but Duke said no, was happy. AB was the youth in 1st traditional recordings, then journeyman here, then master in those below. Doctoral equivalent wd be to have his own orig work find widespread popular acceptance, even while it's in the process of evolving, as Duke & Trane enjoyed. No reason to think that won't happen over next 2 decades, in just the way most ideal to him.

Eight (+3) Tristano Compositions 1989

Two Not One—head stated like it probably was originally in '40s-'50s (same wild fire feel, not the rotes of notes); a flowing, thoughtful line on a song form. Solo starts like cartoon character realizing he's suspended in midair (off the cliff of the head), then falling (the alto solo is the fall enjoyed & turned to a downspiral glide; bari more of a meaty screaming struggle). Rhythm section stays in bop/time groove pocket throughout; horns blow on duo, grounding each other the most each has been grounded in this tune, making the piano splash with them. That interaction is what the tune did.

317 E. 32nd Street—pitch and phrases hover; he doesn't want to become one with time like swimmer with a river, wants rather to skip stones across it, tread the water with light spasms that keep him afloat where he can see the view . . . bass solo, drum brushes, piano

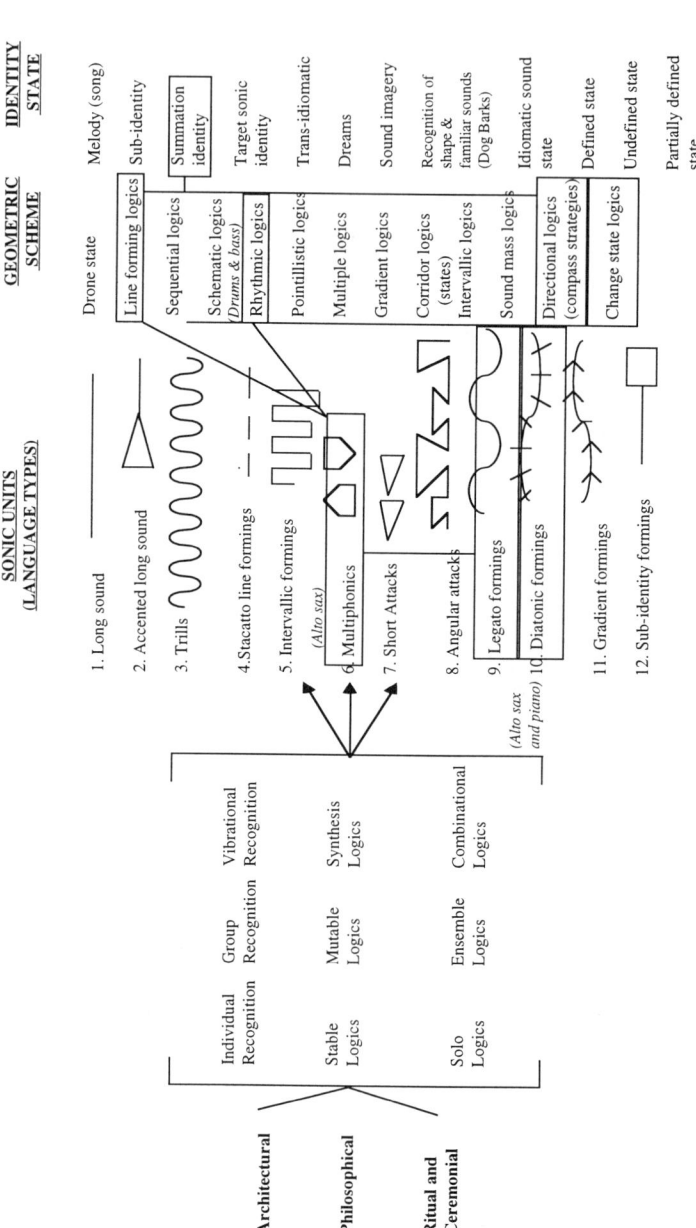

Fig. 5.4: *Victory Ball* (quintet)

puts us back into the Jazz Club (where are the clinks of glasses?). Touching base. Horns splash around again du-etifully free; reminiscent of Gerry Mulligan & Paul Desmond, more raggedy jagged, but no less a clean sync.

Dreams—alto/piano . . . head like French chamber music; piano-comp alto solo; AB's rhythm so like rain flurries fluxing, responsive to winds and walks of piano, riffing on them (give him an inch he always takes two miles) . . . (then turns around to connect with his partner) . . . piano same swing only less triplets, sixteenths, etc. flurry, more 8th-note curve: alto wind and water, piano earth and water, chiming in together on last phrases of in & out heads.

Lennie's Pennies—most challenging, a warm-up chorus of 2-sax blowing, into head as fast and mercurial as a solo, then solos as likewise as head. Changes are mundane, but this time Braxton lets that distract him not at all, in the pocket of his own conception & Trist's at once, totally. Bari tears it up Shepplike; a minor blues with sprung phrases & rhythms.

How Deep is the Ocean—just a flute blow on changes (the one standard didn't get stated, lines on it laid right off the bat). Flute has that wide-eyed wonder sound of Dolphy, open, cool instrument but hot breath, breathless statements . . . nice.

Victory Ball—head another killer. solo more floats and flurries, then certain rhythmic slashes through uncertain-sounding pitches, till they get certain in regular warbles and shriek phrases bridged by bits of scales. Piano's triplets and runs more tight with 4/4 pulse. But however awkward Braxton can feel he's always comfortable with his place there, and is covering the notes and stringing them with his own rhythmic logic.

Sax of A Kind—this lyrical rubato, German cabaret tragicomic sound here fits his sound and approach like a glove (it's SteveLacy-like); done like a Brax composition, with piano tones percussing and sustaining harmonically free, horns doodling timbres and phrases.

Lennie Bird—bop medium up . . . AB's solo (after Jazz Club moments) . . . hmm . . . this funny stilted way he has feels like a result of viewing the chords as they change, from above (the eye of heaven looking down on the pyramid's peak), raining on them light or heavy as desired, rather than flowing with their horizontal wendings through beats.

Six Monk Compositions, 1989

Brilliant Corners—tone querulous; twisting in the wind of higher tempo/octave—tone, with pianist Mal Waldron on Monk, has different context than Trist: again, that German cabaret feel (Monk's tunes much closer to that than to American songbook; changes more like the Expressionistically shivery, stark drama punctuating short pithy statements (Kurt Weill, Billie Holiday, Abbey Lincoln—Schönberg) than like a flowing storyline with an obviously transcendent arc.

Skippy—like Bird on KoKo; anyone who ever doubted Braxton's intimate connection with the blues & song form & highest bop treatments thereof because he started out in youth beyond those and sometimes sounds ill at ease with them in earlier recordings should be on a desert island with this cut. Both Mal and Braxton have technique born of music as much as vice versa.

My most immediate goal with these notes is mnemonic. The words I choose, the cadence and punctuation, are determined primarily by my need to relive the musical experience. Descriptions of musical mechanics are fashioned so as to do that more than for any value they carry in the abstract.

Sometimes these descriptions blossom into metaphor and simile (e.g., "sea creatures & gulls crying, circling, wind & bowed bass: a sacred space"). As do the technical descriptions, they are meant to signal my subjective experience—in this case, a visual fantasy actually experienced—not an assessment based on objective premises.

After several of these vignettes, patterns become evident, and my awareness of them leads me to interrupt my mnemonic sketching and reflect spontaneously on this or that meaning I am perceiving (or conceiving—or both) through the music. I notice these reflections seem to emerge most at the end of each recording.

I am not trying to do anything *other* than a conventional music review. I am accepting my own personal and cultural connection to the Western literate mode in faith that it is adequate and equal to this task, part of which is research and homework on and affinity for a subject. I am allowing myself to hear what I hear and make of it what I will; yet my hope is that my subjective experience, articulated well, will find a common objective American ground with that of the African American aesthetic and intent at this point in the culture's history, and offer praise inspired by successful intent and criticism likewise based on the artist's own standards.

In these recordings, I felt that in Braxton's style which critics have called a lack of swing, awkward; I also saw his brilliant flashes. In summary, the listening experience suggested to me the process he might have gone through on a different level in his early development that led to his first expressions beyond the tradition. Improvising in conventional contexts so extensively that the forms and other premises cease to challenge and satisfy even as the improvisations on them suggest new such patterns that *will* do so is a common experience of innovators (those of Parker, Coleman, and Coltrane are well documented, and

solo music

touched on above). It is just the experience these recordings suggest to me. Braxton started out an able but restless voice in the first set of recordings, moved with more confidence in that restlessness through the even more conservative sound of the second, and found the richest mother lode of both black and white veins from which to finally mine his own most viable synthesis of tradition and innovation in the third and fourth.

As a critic, I find I am on the very safest ground—safe being that where I don't feel haunted by the charge that, as a *white* critic, I may be violating and missing the point of the music—when I take the biggest risk. That risk entails leaving the realm of supposedly objective, impersonal journalism and scholarship for that of unabashedly personal, subjective creative writer, as much as possible. In converting the raw notes to their publishable form, I try to keep the imagery and cadence in my language that subliminally triggers—not necessarily articulates—my own immediate experience with the music. My hope and intent is that it will trigger something equally sub- and super-conscious in the reader, above and beyond its literate rational mode. In this, I feel the product that is the writing can reflect the process that makes the music: words, like sounds, are kicked around without intent or organization of meaning so much as for their power to evoke and suggest, to trigger something; they are worked and reworked to, in the end, expressly articulate that nonverbal/nonmusical *something* they stirred up in those who generated and received/responded to them.

Solo Alto Innovations

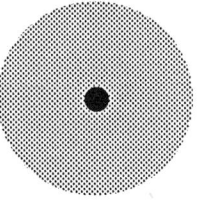

The circle (egg/field of potential) is now broken (fertilized/collapsed to a new material point) by the artist's original spin on tradition. Both circle and point have been compelled by their own freedom and self-sufficiency to embrace the death of same for the sake of their synthesis: a new life.

[From occult definition of] eye*: 1. general symbolism: 1. sun: . . . a. Egyptian hier.: sun-gods: Horus, Ra, Osiris; b. = the eye of Horus: the other eye he had lost in his eternal fight with Seth (Saturn), who had lost his genitals; 2. knowledge: a. Egypt: iris + pupil = 'sun in the mouth' = the Creative Word . . . 3. understanding (sacred fire) . . . abode of the mind . . . 4. judgment . . . 5. authority . . . 6. care . . . 7. life . . . b. Egypt: in a creation-myth, man was born from the eye of Ra; c. "From women's eyes this doctrine I derive: They sparkle still [always] the right Promethean fire; They are the books, the arts, the*

academies, That show, contain, and nourish all the world" . . . *8.* orb, world . . . *15.* vulva: *Lat. euphemism: 'pupilla' = the pupil of the eye, and 'little child';* *16.* testicles: *euphemism, which entered many myths . . .*

[From occult definition of] **reed**: *1.* music: *a. Syrinx ("reed") was changed into a reed to escape being violated by Pan; he then cut reeds at random and made his Pan-pipe, which later Hermes sold to Apollo as his invention . . . 2.* the human voice (or writing), *exposure of secrets . . . 3. royalty, established power . . . 4.* weakness: *a hollow man as a thinking reed . . . 5. resilience: pliancy (in a storm) . . . 6.* divine protection: *in magical escapes the fugitives often throw a reed behind them, which becomes a wood entangling the pursuer . . . 7. vulva, woman, fertility . . . 8. Christian:* humility, *justice . . . 9. lightning, life . . . 10.* death: *a. material for arrow-shaft; b. the Field of Reeds: (Egypt) the hereafter, a region of perpetual Spring, over which Osiris rules, and situated below the Western horizon . . .*

Implicitly, experimentation is . . . an action taken to insure that nothing endures which is not workable; as such, far from being anti-traditional, as is often assumed, it actually serves the best interests of tradition, which, after all, is that which continues in the first place.

Albert Murray

Recordings Analyzed

For Alto (Delmark DS 420/1, 1968): *8A, 8F, 8H, 8A/B, 8D, 8C, 8G, 8B.*
Alto Saxophone Improvisations 1979/Language Music (1967) (Arista A2L 8602, 1978/1979): *77A, 77C, 77D, 77E, 26F, 77F, 26B, 77G, 26E, 77H.*
Solo (London) 1988 (Impetus Records IMP LP 18818, 1988): *106C, 118F(+99G), 138C, 99C, 138E, 99I.*

Braxton calls his solo alto music "language music." The way he uses the word "language" is as people do when they say "the language of the blues," or "the language of love": the particular voice with which particular sound events speak. The more general usage of the word would present trills, for example, as a *part* of the language that is music; Braxton calls them a "language type" in their own right, a field within which (compositional and improvisational) statements and conversations can be made. "My saxophone music," he told Townley, "is nothing more than language systems . . . which allow me to enter new areas."[10]

Braxton made his first big impact with the 1971 two-record set *For Alto*, a solo sax recital of his own compositions. If he had recorded solo a full set of standards or song-form-based jazz heads, the solo situation in itself would have been a bold move, but not without some promptings from both Western and African American traditions. Seen through the latter, it is a move resonant with the ancient and still current pattern of a collective voice splitting itself into an individual expression winging on the wind of the supportive background of the collective, then reuniting to do the same through another individual voice. One sees this pattern in nonhuman primate behavior, in countless tribal rituals around the world, in the call-and-response and testifying dynamics of churches (dynamics mirroring the Hebrew psalmist and congregation, or the Greek protagonist and chorus), and in the cycle of ensemble and solo statements in the many musical traditions.

In European art music, solo recitals of single-line instruments are common in academia, less so in concert halls. If we include bowed strings with polyphonic instruments, such are of course much more common in solo, as also in jazz. Pianos, harps, guitars, bowed strings are built to yield not only melodic song but also harmonic and percussive expressions.

Not so horns. In Western tradition, a solo statement, accompanied or not, has mostly served to showcase mastery of technique and conformity to classical standards of tone, pitch, timbre, and rhythm without the shield or crutch of other players. In jazz, that same performance concept has applied, only the standards have been different. Most markedly, tone, pitch, timbre, and rhythm have functioned differently. Horns constructed in the West for Western musical systems and conventions have been used against their grain, as it were, for African expressions. Growls, speech-like sounds, squeals, non-chromatic intervals, and other such effects have been a part of the African American musical lexicon from the beginning. Wind instruments are closer to human voices than strings, keyboards, or percussion and have the volume and penetration to function as lead and solo voices over the drones, chords, and rhythms of the latter.

The art of improvisation, of course, is also showcased in jazz solo "breaks" (the formalized cadenzas of classical music were also improvised not so long ago). The longer one's inspiration and invention last, the longer one's break may last, increasing the excitement when the ensemble finally starts to play again.

Braxton, in developing an unaccompanied solo *persona* for the alto sax, is simply taking this part of the music a step further. It is a step that evokes interesting speculation about the indisputable roots of the music and their potential fruits, and the forces working both for and against their flowering.

Consider more familiar solo situations. The piano has the strongest history, both in jazz and classical traditions. It is an instrument born out of the peculiarly Western premises of equal temperament and chromaticism, and can mine thoroughly their musical potential. It is also a percussive instrument. From Scott Joplin to Cecil Taylor, its excitement has lain in its capacity for maximizing Western harmonic and African rhythmic possibilities at once. It has functioned as the best middle ground for the American musical synthesis in solo, enjoying also its comfortable and crucial role in the rhythm section in ensemble.

Strings and percussion have traditionally played their roles in that section, soloing, of course, but never, like the piano, alone for long. Horns have been at the more Western end of the spectrum in their statements of theme and variations; on the other hand, they have also covered the most African nonpercussive expressions with their abovementioned vocal simulations. If piano, then, is a soloist's middle ground, horns have embodied both Western and African extremes at once. Horn players have not been pressured to serve timekeeping functions; they've left that to drums and bass while they've developed the facility and invention necessary to spin melodic statements over a pulse. They have not been expected to underpin the Western harmonic *kosmos* of their own improvisations; chordal instruments (piano, guitar, etc.) have done that while horns have been free to couch the most far-flung growls, vocalisms, mute effects, and other aharmonic statements in that harmonic context. Western technical facility and invention on the one hand, African pitch and rhythmic implications on the other, and the freedom, authority, and permission to expand on the music's more basic elements as far as one's personal voice and genius can take one have defined the special province of the horns.

In claiming that province as solo territory, and in charting it with both his own and (as he has throughout his solo work) traditional material, Braxton made explicit and brought to synthesis many aspects theretofore implicit and disparate in the mix, which might be stated thus: (1) traditional, composed, and improvised musical statements are interwoven through the same oscillation between creativity and discipline at work in all music; (2) the extremely African elements uniquely served by the Western horn—timbral and vocalist texturings—stand as well on their own, at the center of a Western-style recital, as they do on the middle ground of African pulse and Western harmony provided by the rhythm section or its equivalent accompaniment; and (3) the extremely Western elements uniquely served by the Western horn—technical facility and invention within the chromatic scale—can be as well informed by the African rhythm-sound universe in a solo context as they are on the platform of that middle ground we call the rhythm section.

The horn in the jazz tradition has thus developed from that middle ground a voice that encompasses its world's farthest poles. Before Braxton, solo music was primarily developed in the "safest" middle ground, through the piano. Accompanied horn solos, from Louis Armstrong on, stretched out to the poles only while "safely" (middle-) grounded; they cut loose into such "polar" expressions (of either European or African extreme) without accompaniment only momentarily—scouts getting their first glimpses of the new American musical synthesis in brief forays, returning to the familiar negotiated territory quickly. Braxton left familiar territory in order to further the logic of its own growth, to make the wilderness beyond it tomorrow's familiar territory.

It seems no accident that the innovations considered his own most radical can be traced to the role of the horn in the American musical synthesis of Europe and Africa. As both composer and instrumentalist, he is known for his relocation of music's rhythmic center from a regular pulse to the infinite variety of patterns that have traditionally been improvised over it anyway; his relocation of its central harmonic structure from the song form to the infinite variety of patterns that have traditionally been improvised over it; his relocation of its melodic arc and voice from the Western lines and tonal conventions to the infinite variety of melodic patterns and timbral colors that have traditionally been improvised over them.

The very word "over" suggests some of the extramusical sociopolitical dynamics reflected in the tradition and Braxton's contribution to them. The musical hierarchy that conceives (African) rhythm, chords, and root tonal centers as on the "bottom"—the "background" accompanists, or musical slaves—and (Western) melody, invention, and virtuosity on the "top"—the leaders and stars—is a reflection of Eurocentric sociocultural hierarchical dominance; musically, it became an imbalance many players in the 1960s quickly tired of as it became apparent to them. An alternative aesthetic favoring one pole over another—for example, the Westernization the music has undergone in its academic contexts, or the rejection or downplaying of Western elements imposed now and then from the Afrocentric side—is often tempting, but rarely satisfying for long. Braxton's vision has avoided such muddying from the first. At the same time, it has consistently stirred the mix of fear, disdain, confusion, misunderstanding, and rejection, on the one hand, and excitement, hope, support, and recognition, on the other, that has typically been provoked in America by voices (both black and white) from "the field" in those (both black and white) invested in the life of "the house."[11] (Even more complex in Braxton's case, his embrace of the European extreme—in his adoption of the literate tradition's notating, concertizing, cataloguing, systematizing, and writing about—gave Afrocentric and "jazz" purists plenty to put down as "cold" and "clinical"; at the same time, his plunge into the African extremes alienated Western people who were just coming to terms with the middle ground, and were unable to discern between passionate authenticity and compulsive shrieking beyond its pale.)

This is not to say that Braxton was the only or even the "best" to do any or all of this. The point is that this is what he has set out to do with his solo music, and—like Armstrong, Parker, Coltrane, and other innovators before him—what has been so offensive to some and exciting to others, has solid, discernible roots and precedents in the tradition from which it grew and, like an air-borne spore, at once left and carried with it.

These two poles of Africa and Western Europe were decidedly defined by *For Alto*—and so were the two extreme responses of rejection and acceptance in the media. Reviewer Joe Klee gave it (the highest possible, excellent) five stars, comparing its concept to Bach's work for solo cello and violin, articulating pithily the problem he had in finding criteria for any rating at all, then falling back on those of his own subjective responses.[12]

Fellow (white) altoist Phil Woods, on the other hand, in a Blindfold Test with Leonard Feather in that same year,[13] panned it viciously, summing it up with the statement that "there's a lot of primitives that play and get a lot of exciting music." While we might take his response purely in aesthetic rather than racial and/or cultural terms, it echoes many of the assessments by white jazz players of black peers throughout the history of the music.[14] At the same time, it is also mirrored within the African American circles by that of Miles Davis to Ornette Coleman and Cecil Taylor, for example.[15] Again, the dichotomy between "house" and "field" blacks (and their respective white allies) captures the uniquely American dynamic in this response better than any clear lines between the two races-cultures. For the most part, however, the thrust of the information about Braxton's solo music from articles and liner notes by others intended for general and specialist consumption over the more than 20 years of its development shows that the rationales, intents, and executions of the artist have been, overall, understood, well received, and passed on.

Braxton himself discusses his solo work generally in liner notes; its place in his musical system as a whole is indicated on Fig. 5.5. More specifically, he has written about the various compositions he has made for solo alto in his *Composition Notes* (I'll include the latter with my "fieldnote" reviews of his solo alto music, below). The broad viewpoints common to Braxton's and the media's understanding of his solo alto music are: (1) it functions as his "sketch pad" for the concepts and methods he employs to construct his music for all instrumental combinations; and (2) it replaces Western aesthetic and American pop and jazz premises for improvisation with a variety of sax-based (timbral, rhythmic, extended technical) and conceptual (dynamic, register, metric, melodic-harmonic) premises/frameworks. These are alternatives to the Western harmonic and African American rhythmic conventions of both concert music and jazz.

Braxton outlines the musical system he has worked out largely on the "laboratory" of his alto sax as highlighted in Fig. 5.5. From various readings and private conversations, I would explain this schematic, reading from left to right, so: His music can be understood in terms of its *Architecture*, or form; its *Philosophical* (and historical and cultural) contexts (as expressed in *Tri-Axium Writings*); and its personal and group spiritual context (*Ritual and Ceremonial*), that which a composition or improvisation really, functionally comes to *mean*, in a given performance. Each of these aspects—architecture, general philosophical base, and specific identity—itself has access to the nine different aspects in the long brackets; a given construct (of music or writing) will focus on and develop any one or a succession of them.

For example, *Tri-Axium Writings* presents its information in three different sections that represent stable, mutable, and synthesis logics as Braxton conceives them. By "stable" he means something specific and concrete, such as a given idea, belief, or notated piece of music; by "mutable" he means the area of generality that might give rise to such a specific, such as the field to which a given idea belongs to, or the belief system, or the musical system that produces a given statement; by "synthesis" he means, naturally enough, what results when any two or more self-sufficient such areas, stable or mutable, are combined (such as, in his own scores, notated sections and open improvisational sections). Soloists and ensembles execute these patterns; individuals and groups recognize and experience them; intuitions and dreams, collective myths arise from the syntheses made by every possible combination, feeding what Braxton calls "vibrational recognition."

In Braxton's music, these statements are built from within the twelve "sonic units (language types)" listed and drawn; any one of these languages can be used to form itself into any of all the "logics" described under "geometric scheme"; any of those transcendentally emergent patternings of a given language can carry any of the meanings, or perform any of the functions, listed under "identity state."

The diagram should be understood as a modular system of switchable tracks through which a given musical thrust—a player, a piece—moves like a railroad train of several cars (the different areas comprising it. Braxton consciously associates his delight with this system with that primal childhood fascination with trains).

To say much more at this point—to try and pin down exactly what those statements and their meanings are in words—seems inadvisable. Most are self-

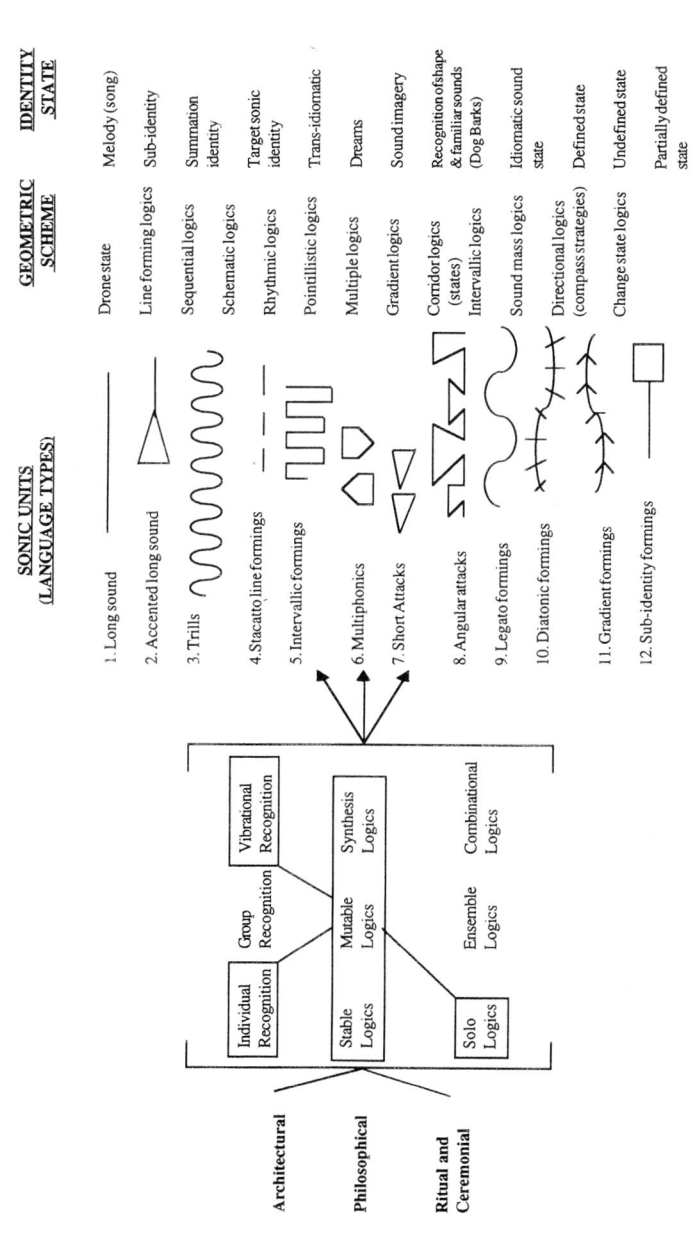

Fig. 5.5: Solo Alto ("language") *music*

evident; the others may best be explicated by our encounters with Braxton's music (those we miss here the reader can, hopefully, recognize in other encounters with the music) and his own words about it. First, however, it might be useful to point out the way this system can relate to the sort of traditional jazz material we've already examined.

Take a tune such as *Donna Lee* (see Fig. 5.6). It is of a structural (*architectural*) interest to musicians and music students; it has the general sociocultural and *philosophical* thrusts of post-war New York black urban America, expressed in bebop; and every different performance of it by various artists at various times in various situations has (*ritual and ceremonial*) meanings as unique as fingerprints to the individual and collective psyches involved. The mix of those meanings includes epiphanies—"vibrational recognitions"—that are greater than the sum of their components.

When an improviser starts to solo on *Donna Lee*, he or she might hit upon one of the twelve language types—say, diatonic formings (a natural one for bebop). In a simple, straightforward rendition, that way of manipulating sound might lend itself to line-forming logics (another typical bebop result) and end up as a primarily melodic statement—an alternate tune to *Donna Lee*'s chord changes, even as *it* was the bebop alternative to the standard *Back Home in Indiana*. If this many aspects of something as complex as a complex bop head can be captured by such a simple linkage within Braxton's table, imagine the soundworlds some of the other more complex connections might map—then imagine mapping such worlds generated by *combinations* of players, rather than just one.

This system is what he worked out for himself as the beginning of a conceptual and practical "road map" to inform his improviser's and composer's imagination. He has done it in the jazz-traditional context of his role as an improviser, shaping it from the actual experience of learning and making that music in the real world on its highest professional and cultural levels. His charting of such a complex of sub- and super-rational processes so meticulously and yet succinctly in a literate format effects a demystification of African oral-traditional dynamics that have largely been esoteric from a Western literate viewpoint. It also forces Western literate paradigms and criteria that have forced themselves on African American expressions to accede to the authority of the latter, or at least to compromise with it. Finally, Braxton's system, so charted, stakes its own claim to its own authority in the culture, one commensurate with the African American tradition's real significance, and one with more relevance than the classical tradition of Europe to the current American culture.

Back to words. (Braxton's liner notes to his solo recordings are the first and easiest source of his words on them; for those, see Chapter Three.) Since we are now considering Braxton's original compositions and notes thereto, an interesting alternative to the "review of review notes" used above on the standard material suggests itself. The intent of that double review was to build a bridge between oral and literate mindsets with the alternating planks of my one typical reviewer's spontaneous creative and then reflective rationalistic processes. In keeping with the same intent, I will yet take a slightly different approach with the three sample solo recordings. I will take my notes (marked "MH") before reading Braxton's (marked "AB") on each piece, and then scan (in underlined sections) his for points that most pertain to the hypothesis that his work should

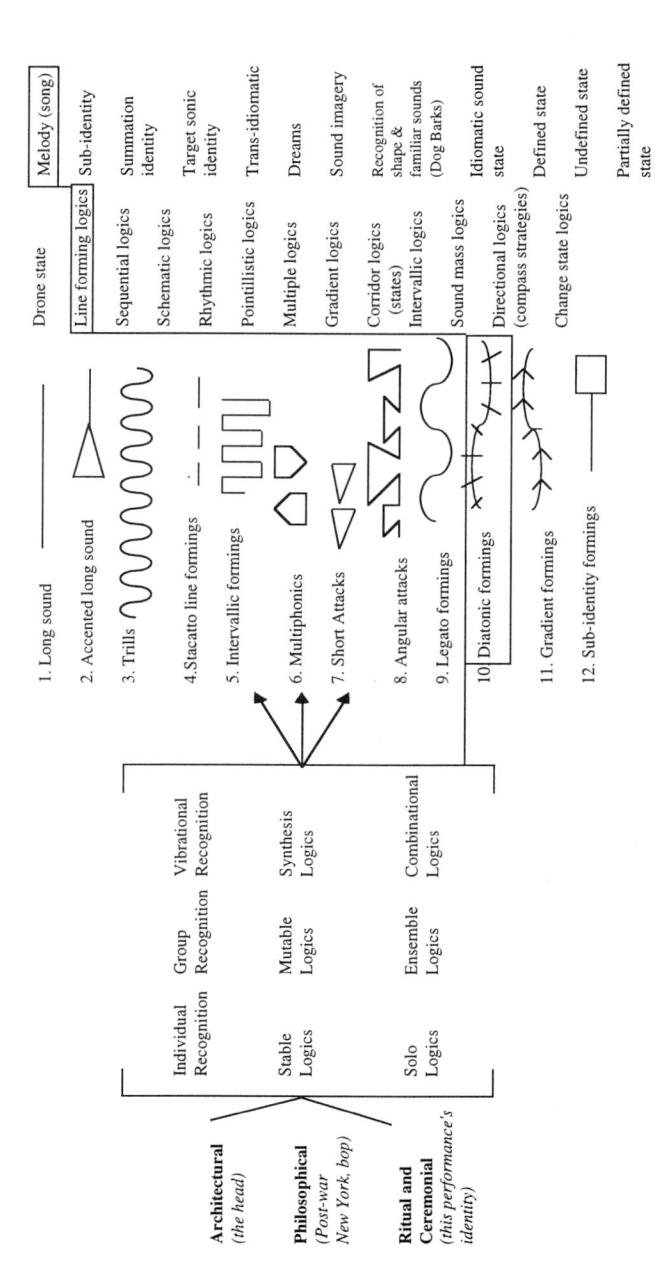

Fig. 5.6: *Donna Lee* (alto sax part)

be understood, discussed, and accepted as a *centric* musicultural synthesis rather than an *eccentric* personal statement. Instead of putting the two sets of his and my comments on the selected pieces in two different sections, as was done for the traditional material, I will weave them together piece by piece, to best establish their common ground (and that of oral and literate worlds).

For Alto

1. MH (*8A*)—short prelude. lyrical, atonal statement, gracious opening.

AB—Composition No. 8A ... was not conceived to generate any of the modern language devices that we now associate with what is called new music (i.e. complex rhythms or extended timbral devices) but rather ... to participate in the challenge of traditional construction (and idea formation) from an open improvisational context. The instrumentalists in this context are challenged to create a music whose moment linear nature develops with open invention. The design of this material is non-harmonic and non-thematic and the dynamics of its invention must also adhere to those same qualities ... . The first performance of Composition No. 8A took place in Chicago at Lincoln Center. This concert would be the first exclusive concert of designed solo music for the creative improvisational instrumentalist (on a single-lined instrument with extended improvisational materials).[16]

The focus here is Western, a departure from (harmonic/melodic) system, but not from the music traditionally made from same. The phrases use notes from the chromatic scale, outlining simple rhythms. This brief rendition serves as familiar common ground into the most radically experimental second cut.

2. MH (*8F*)—fast extended: letting the fingers fly and the embouchure squeeze and squeal. superfast phrases, crashing into low blatts for ground, back up to mid-range quickies ... up and down, timbre increasingly rough—then superhigh, dash down to lo, honk-like two-notes, more phrases. Rhythmic energy, adrenalin trigger, clear out all the cobwebs: solo version of group energy music. fast sixteenths, slashed by crashes to bottom. frenetic oratory ... into quieter, pitter patter between sudden tonal grounds, random pitch. pause: percussive lows, fingerings that ripple off the tongue as it were like glossolalia ... gather up into the steam of primal scream, woman scream, or animals freaking ... occasional sax chromatics for the human male (intellectual) touchstone. more intricate stitchery with the diatonic needle ripping out to multiphonic STOPS, SHRIEKS, GROWLS, back into rhythm of riffing on speed and fight AND flight (like the intensity of Trane and Pharoah, then the blistery runs of notes, always chopped into phrases the size of pants at a dead

run, climaxing into high horror screams, plateauing back to complex rhythm of a running body (breath, limbs, innards all maxing out), end on blatt.

(Since I have already extensively discussed Braxton's notes on this piece in Chapter Four, I will skip them here.) *The writing and reading of my notes involve much more adrenalin and alertness to the moment than did my notes on the traditional material. The listening experience here is more like a bucking bronc than the comfy auto ride of the jazz heads. If I were to write these up into a review, I would pass most of them on intact, then end with just that reflection, and the judgment that unlike many players who might try this sort of thing, Braxton rides the bronc with, if anything, more aplomb and mastery than he brings to the driving of the car.*

3. MH (*8H*)—soft slow trills, like the prelude, modernistic intervals and romantic sax pitch bends . . . music out of overtones the axe is built for . . . dynamic swells, turning flutters into warbles into hard metallic oscillations; polarizing lo thrashes with hi fluffs, finding upper middle ground, dashing low again, riffing up and down the horn easily.

AB—Composition No. 8H is designed to focus on the dynamic implications of trill sound techniques as an infrastructure device to define extended improvisation . . . This is not to imply that Composition No. 8H is only an exercise for trill execution—because it isn't. The reality of this effort is constructed as a medium slow pulse vehicle that utilizes conventional linear phrase development. Composition No. 8H is conceived as a melodic (ballade) type of music that gives the instrumentalist a traditional context to use as a basis for language improvisation . . . for the challenge of this effort is not to create a restructuralist music but rather to create a substantial music that adheres to the dictates of traditional formation—in its construction and development of materials . . . Too often we have come to view the challenge of restructuralism as the only aspect of participation worthy of pursuit—but this viewpoint cannot be correct. The real challenge of extended participation involves coming to terms with the composite music in all of its dynamic aspects—whether we are referring to traditional, stylistic or restructural projections. To really move into the future is to understand more about the past and the realness of this viewpoint must also be reflected in the music.[17]

Again, Braxton emphasizes the traditional premises and influences underlying this, his first most controversially, "radically" innovative recorded statement. The relaxed pace and cadence of my notes reflect the music. He took

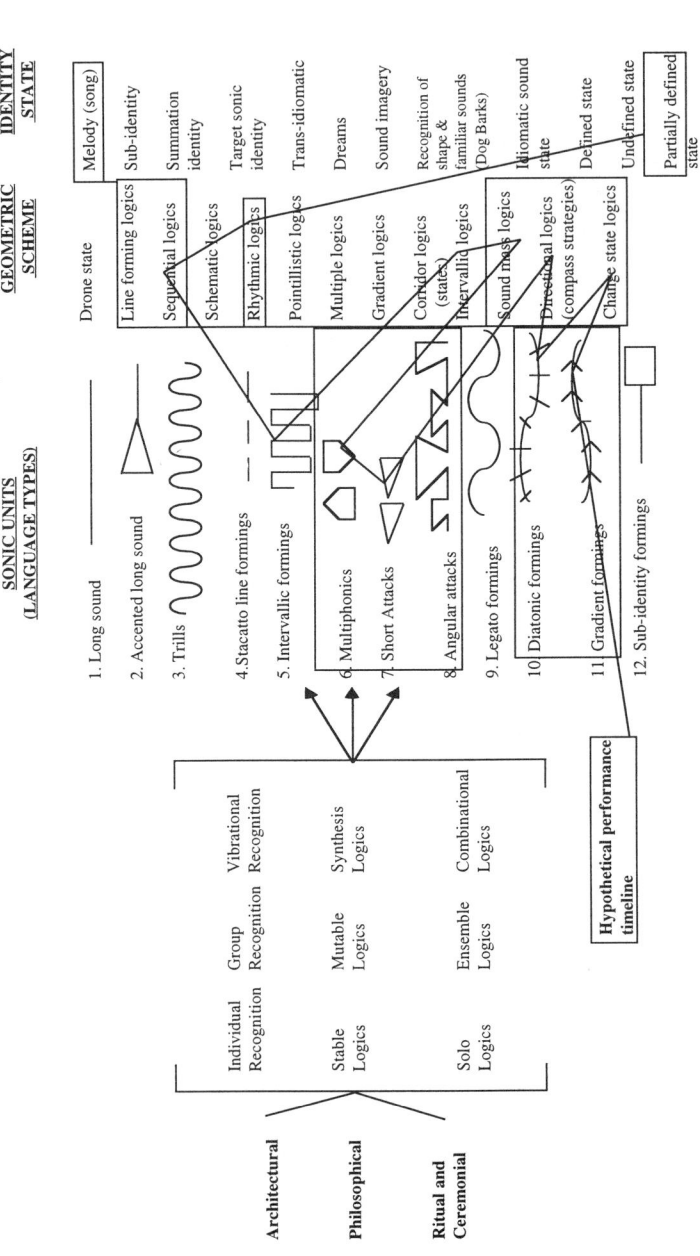

Fig. 5.7: Composition 8F (solo alto)

solo music   **239**

one musical convention—trills—and played around with them leisurely using a largely conventional musical vocabulary rather than forging a new one, as in 8F.

> 4. MH (*8D*)—soft, slow, half-step/whole-step, rubato; thoughtful, moody, a slow whisper middle register, breathy, suspended chain of intervals . . . silence . . . plaintive attacks, air blown through horn . . . hiss, hush, sigh . . . harmonic overtones . . . half steps connected by various intervallic spaces, tonal phrases floating like dust motes in sun . . . shadows . . . flows and delicate rhythms, falling into keys clattering like soft percussion . . . long tones held softly . . . grace notes jazz style . . . then into lower register more; the world Desmond inhabited, floating free of pulse, free of harmonic logic in theory but not always in practice. roving tonal centers more than none at all. and then more than centers—strong, welling tonal soliloquies that define the spacey fragments that came before them as that feeling of emptiness and "agreeable sorrow" that echoes in the sound of a horn player practicing in some room alone on a down, lazy, stop-time day. it starts out disoriented and fragmentary, sad and empty, with that soft warm phrasing and dynamic flux and American feel of jazz, then gathers momentum and clarity and form into a Statement. On this side-length piece, the musical rationale for long stretches of silence and soft ramblings becomes clear by the end: it climaxes into a lovely lyrical flowering that could only have grown organically out of the soil of that meditation.
>
> AB—Composition No. 8D is conceived as a slow pulse vehicle that emphasizes the extended ballade implications of traditional material. The solidification of this effort establishes a unique context for solo music invention—and opens fresh perspectives about time and space . . . The reality of this structure is constructed to emphasize the dynamics of silence as a natural occurrence. This has been done in accordance with the breakthrough of the post-Webern continuum. There are no fast improvisational sections in Composition No. 8D, in fact the reality of this effort is designed to keep any accented postulations from developing. What remains instead is a music that emphasizes its own terrain—that is, a music whose space is more important in many ways than its notes. This is a space with music poured in as opposed to a music that needs a space to happen in. Ideas in this context seem to simply float in and out of the space of the music without a unified time/space continuance. The reality of this phenomenon moves to create an extended ballade-like music that appears to start and end but in fact is simply "there"—in that space of time . . . a performance of this work is designed to open the listener and instrumentalist to the dynamics of non-motion.[18]

What strikes me first about my notes is that, true to the music, they started out as a fragmentary stream of consciousness, but gradually coalesced into a coherent, cohesive statement. What strikes me about Braxton's is, again, his anchoring of his most experimental-sounding (this piece is reminiscent of something by John Cage, until the end, when it blossoms into a pretty ballad) pieces to a traditional context.

> 5. MH (*8C*)—relaxed rhythmically, intense timbrally (high squeaks, low squawks, multiphonic middles)—this whole piece sounds like it's made of the "wrong" notes or sounds jazz players hit on the run, then stop to dwell on and incorporate.
>
> AB—Composition No. 8C is designed as a ballade structure that calls for the use of traditional linear improvisation. The challenge for the creative instrumentalist in this context is to create an open ballade improvisation that is not afraid of the traditional continuum of the music . . . My decision to utilize the ballade sound-world as a basis for creative generation has to do with my belief in the composite tradition of the music. Too often we are ready to simply discard given aspects of the music because of the mis-directed urge to create something new (even though in actual fact there is no such thing as "real new"). The effects of this dilemma have moved to distort the dynamic implications of creative music—as well as the challenge implications of creative participation. Composition No. 8C is composed as a vehicle to affirm traditional idea and material development. *This is true even though the context of its working space on the surface seems to be non-traditional.*[19] (emphasis mine—M. H.)

Again, tradition. Only the last line gives a hint that something that sounds unlike a regular ballad might have occurred. Braxton's experience as an artist was obviously to make something familiar to him and everyone out of materials not so familiar—a house out of "found" materials, such as cans and tires, rather than wood, but still a house.

> 6. MH (*8B*)—long tones attack/decrescendo, various durations, snowballing into sudden attacks on neighboring notes . . . violent dynamic flux . . . then the harsh attacks/intervals/timbres become like forceful, bold energetic brush strokes of a yet-subtle big picture (to experience what I mean, try this exercise, brass or reeds players: improvise a duet with this piece, or similar pieces that seem to be random noise more than thought-out statements on thought-out premises, within the traditional parameters of harmonic resolution, tonality, and timbre. I find that my own such duets have a synchronous and synergistic logic and vitality that wouldn't exist if I were playing with an unschooled novice who'd picked up the horn and started making any sounds he could.)

AB—The thrust of this work laid the ground work for what I now call Language Music and in doing so affected the composite dynamics of *all future material and operating premises (and focuses)* . . . Composition No. 8B is composed as a language vehicle for pointillistic extended improvisation. The "stuff" of this work involves the isolation of short phrase fragments juxtaposed in opposition over rapid and extreme dynamic shifts . . . The conceptual dynamics underlying Composition No. 8B can be viewed from several different contexts: (1) the nature of its overstructure and material use, (2) the use of infrastructural micro-phrase placement material and (3) the use of dynamic opposition.[20] (emphasis mine)

Both of these notes take on their real significance with an actual hearing (and, as I suggested, playing) of the music. As he indicated, this piece charts new territory especially well; yet, as I discovered when I felt compelled to play with this one more than the others, it completely incorporates traditional territory, implies it with its deep structure while explicating *the new terrain tradition* implied *when it itself was explicit.*

This recording shows well, with these notes, the literally revolutionary process—a turning over of the soil of tradition to prepare it for his creative seeds of fruits not new in kind but in crop—of Braxton's innovative music.

To change with the recording and vary the reading flow, I will switch the reading order of Braxton's notes and mine (I took my notes before reading his on both recordings).

Alto Saxophone Improvisations 1979

This recording shows the solo music almost a decade later, released by Braxton's most widely distributed label during the time of his most mainstream visibility and popularity. Also a double album, the whole package, with its extensive illustrated liner notes by the artist, bespeaks a legitimacy and significance more present as a hopeful boldness in the first solo album. Braxton and others had been doing solo concerts since *For Alto*, and Braxton was clearly the torchbearer of the new practice.

1. AB *(77A)*—The most apparent factor that holds this work together is the nature of how given idea fragments are mashed together in a somewhat reverse development situation. The dynamics of this piece also utilize extreme intervallic leaps—which is to say, the idea construction of this work is both varied and complex in that the actual "stuff" of the music has nothing to do with development but instead deals with the constant collision—or in most cases interruption—of fragmented constructions[21] . . . Composition No. 77A is a system of thinking that gives fresh insight into the moment dynamics of sound postulation. The reality of this process can be viewed as a Charlie Parker–John Coltrane–Albert Ayler language

continuum that has been reversed and coupled with the tendencies and explorational particulars of the post-Webern/Stockhausen continuum of the music . . . 77A is a response to all of these masters of musical thinking . . . The use of intervallic shifting in . . . 77A has to do with the use of great sound register changes as a means to find a new path for line extension . . . Intervallic shifting in . . . 77A can be viewed as a "material ladder" that allows the instrument to extend a given perceived sound line statement.[22]

MH—tight tone & phrasing, medium-up feel, forays into lo & hi, volume flux; fragments, slipstreams to hi liquid sounds, plunges to timbral gashes . . . machine-gun phrases short and shorter linking lyrical pearls, harmonious gems, first-cast stones . . . fragmentary: interruptions of thought, sidetracks to explore, then back to the main run up and down the horn; one learns exactly what one is saying only when one has spoken nonsense long enough to make sense of it . . . climax of medium-up figures of discrete notes into sound blurs fluxing, & super high note.

In his notes, Braxton is not so consciously anchored to tradition generally now, but focused on current voices of disparate traditions for their synthesis. My notes are limited to evocative descriptions, groping for meaning in them (again, reflecting the music?).

2. AB (77C)—Composition No. 77C is a work designed to deal with the dynamic possibilities of a major third diatonic phrase (i.e. CDE, DEF, EFG, etc.) . . . The work was conceived as a horizontal sound continuum that provides a unique context for creative exploration. In this sound universe the instrumentalist is given a three-note diatonic principle that forms the moment to moment fabric of the music. This is a linear sound state environment that only contains suggestions about the "moment." Composition No. 77C was conceived as a material forum that emphasizes "loop" shapes as a basis for creative invention. A given version of this work should establish a kind of loping music that "curls" through the sound space. This is accomplished through the use of a diatonic three-note process that permeates the composite personality of the music. To experience what this phenomenon means is to enter a song-like music state that expresses itself "in bright lights" (sounds) (because this is a kind of wistful music).[23]

MH—triplets, exercise-book–like, letting them take on their own life in the fingers as the mind cuts in now and then with soft, sweet comments of song. Sounds like a French Impressionist diversion . . . phrasing/vibrato that sound informed by Euro concept of "jazz," "sweet" and "hot." Explorations are determined by the lilting rhythm, the tone it evokes on the triplets and lazy up and down—like being a kid swinging on a sunny day, happily wandering/returning mind . . .

but not sappy—it gets studious and sophisticated just as it's starting to feel sappy. Sense of a planned, not arbitrary ending to this and many of these rambles.

Again, Braxton's notes reveal a more concrete sense of his own new musical worlds—more visual and fewer traditional referents—than For Alto's. *My notes, too, seem to pick up more concrete visual and emotional suggestions from the music.*

> 3. AB *(77D)*—Composition No. 77D was conceived . . . to emphasize the use of slap tongue and positioned sound shape considerations. My first awareness of slap tongue sound possibilities came in 1971 from master saxophonist Ben Webster. In fact Mr. Webster taught me personally how to make a slap tongue sound on the alto saxophone. Ever since that experience I have attempted to provide material and structural operatives for slap tongue dynamics—so that I could better establish a relationship to what this device could mean in the forward spread of my own creative awareness . . . I remember the first time I heard Charlie Parker's and John Coltrane's music—it was the actual sounds they extracted from their instruments that first caught my attention. [24]

> MH—slap-tongue, bits of high squeaks, low mutters—like a little dog and a bigger one having conversation and the hiccups. The pops define a rhythmic field that the other sounds whip and wiggle around in like balls in pinball . . . discourses feel like dogs struggling with human speech, with wisps of floaty melodicphrase. Planes coming in for a CRASH landing . . . medictrucks with WWII German sirens scurry to them; whimpers that would be for pain in real life (not art)—slap tongue out.

Braxton's focus on tradition remains fixed on specific masters, this time through his personal connection to one. What he says (about Webster, Parker, and Coltrane) and what he played suggests that an innovator's relationship to tradition allows him to view its moments/aspects of subjective inspirations objectively, then choose which to pursue subjectively. The sounds players make in the course of making music are largely incidental, even unconscious, to them, like speech mannerisms or styles; Braxton's use of such material focuses consciously on it as musical ends rather than means or side effects. He objectifies it for his own subjective musical statements.

> 4. MH *(Red Top)*—hearing a blues like this sounds like so many snatches of musicians playing on the street alone, or practicing in places audible from the street; breaks into double-time romp, slightly screamy, back into more relaxed lope after a chorus, then up again. It sounds more thoughtful, less reactive, when alone. A warm feeling, not lonely.

Such solo renditions of standard material (others from this date were Along Came Betty *and* Giant Steps) *show its roots, in a solitary player working out musical patterns, problems, and potentials on his horn.*

> 5. AB (*77E*)—Composition No. 77E is built from five notes (G, Ab C, D, Eb) basically and was designed as a vehicle to make *shakuhachi* [Japanese bamboo flute] type music. (I have long been interested in this kind of approach.) There are three basic treatments in this version: (1) the basic statement of material with respect to the five-note row, (2) the use of this same concept with the addition of circular breathing and (3) the fragmented use of given figures . . . Here is a forum to recall the greatness of Trans Asian and African affinity dynamics—and the wonderful projections that have come into existence from those areas. Composition No. 77E takes a five-note principle as *a basis to re-investigate the concept of harmony* and open material formings . . . Composition No. 77E is a performance state that seeks to emphasize fixed sound and scale materials as a basis to create a music (state) that contains few operating variables. *It is fashionable in this time period to confuse the amount of materials that make up an intention as more important than its assignment. This is especially apparent in light of the present-day wonder of "abundance."* Composition No. 77E was realized as a discipline that could help shed light on the process and phenomenon of creativity. The challenge of making five sounds come alive as a reality context involves establishing a broader concept of application and selection . . . Composition No. 77E is an opportunity to connect with the vibrational offerings of those old great master musicians (thinkers) from days gone by. *We cannot go into the future without their help . . .* I consciously tried to think about the great Asian master musicians and "what they might have played" in the music. This was necessary because I had no idea what to do—or what to play. I also tried to approach the music with respect to what I had been hearing on my records of Indian music or Chinese music.[25] (emphasis mine)

> MH—pentatonic, Asian motif; bent, drawn out, plaintive . . . circ breath, long tones linking runs up and down, gradual emergence of the rhythm suggested . . . back to rubato feel; has that Asian sensitive probe of silence and stillness, then tonic.

This time the self-limitations on improvisation are extreme (five notes; the anchors to tradition on For Alto *were general, conceptual, allowing for much diffuse activity), underscoring this recording's more specific focus on* both *traditional sources* and *original treatments. Braxton has clearer, more developed things to say on narrower, more defined premises. He also has faith in the magic of music to reveal its esoteric secrets through the exoteric reconstructions of the "musical anthropologist."*

6. AB (*26F*)—Composition No. 26F is based on the concept of a repetition continuum. That being the use of repetition and the gradual change of events by either adding a given element to the basic idea scheme or taking away a given element . . . In this work shapes are presented to stabilize the focus of the music—but in the process of providing that function are instead transformed . . . Ideas in this context are established, repeated and gradually transformed through the use of either additive phrase splicing (that hook on to either the beginning or ending of a given phrase)—or diminutive phrase splices (the reduction of some aspect of a given musical focus—idea). The use of this technique moves to solidify a very special reality of procedure operatives—having to do with the breath of a universe that refocuses on how its own continuity is to be maintained (worlds of elements that are shifted and shifted—yet hung together by common material particles that in the beginning seemed unimportant.) To really experience this phenomenon is to better understand the position of a given idea function—or sound function. This is so because the reality implications of . . . 26F reemphasize the role material dynamics play in establishing how we heard ("what we thought we heard"). In this universe of sound a sound (or sound fragment) that seemed either unnecessary or "extremely supportive" (and on its own, musically not very interesting) suddenly becomes the center of a reforming universe then opened up right before our eyes. This is the magic of . . . 26F . . . It is important for the instrumentalist to recognize the nature of this work so that its use can be positive (and positively given and received). The fact is a performance of . . . 26F is a physical phenomenon that must be correctly approached (and for the right reasons). This work was not composed for any abuse on any level. All of these matters are intended for musical purposes. *A stabilizing pattern that has to do with each instrumentalist observing his/her own affinity and vibrational nature as a means to know what the body needs and when.* Idea patterns are needed so that the performer can relax without attempting to "push" when there might be no "push" left. *It is important to listen to one's own forces so that higher intentions can be realized*[26] .(emphases mine)

MH—tritone toggle, spawning similar toggles of other intervals: seeds of minimalism, suggested by technology of horn as minimalism is suggested by that of computers (sequencers). Regular rhythmic phrases splintering off into their own intrinsic irregularities (chaos). Those suggesting new intervals/actions/rhythms to be attacked spontaneously, then allowed to flourish up and down the register/time as they feel like doing. Repeating a motif until it becomes robotic, losing it to one's humanity, replacing it with the next motif more human at that time. Something really organic and seamless emerges: expressions that might have sounded forced if approached differently.

The music here is functioning as a mantra for meditation. Braxton's disclaimer of its possible harmful effects, and assertion of respect for its power, is a cogently considerate expression of awareness of the volatility of any attempt at synthesis between the African American spirituality of immanence and the Western one of transcendence. Again, he shows his respect for the power of the exoteric to convey the esoteric, this time in his own piece. This is why he takes form so seriously.

What my notes tried to but didn't quite capture is that this piece shows an extraordinary integration between the "mindless" rote of a catchy phrase turned over and over unthinkingly and the mindful music that can arise from consciously trying to sustain rather than shake off or go beyond its monotony.

> 7. AB (77F)—Composition No. 77F is a ballade forum for extended improvisation that was composed circa 1976. The concept of this effort calls for a relaxed and flowing kind of music that floats through the sound space. This is a sound environment structure that provides terms for open linear improvisation and "story telling." . . . 77F was conceived as a light melodic phrase statement that could initiate a ballade improvisation. In the course of a given day I hear about five to twenty quick "would be" songs of this nature. That is, a quick phrase statement or fragment that somehow takes on a "life of its own" (something that kind of "stays on one's mind") . . . In the past twenty years (since 1965) I have always tried to maintain room in my life for special melodic line shapes (and "references") because this is part of "who I am" (and how I hear "sound") . . . 77F is an excuse to become involved in the wonder of ballade and perceived melodic improvisation. When I think of the realness of Johnny Hodges and Paul Desmond—and how the beauty of their line perceptions transformed my whole life, I can only be thankful for the concept of the music. This intention is at the heart of . . . 77F . . . This work is offered as a vehicle to activate one's own "life feelings" and sound thought—an idea particle that might be relevant as a basis to extend from.[27]

> MH—sounds like a ballad, likely improvised from the first: tentative, uncertain, except in feel (relaxed, wending, winsome, spiralling into rapt breezes) . . . then into full-blown rapture, like walking pleasantly up a hill then getting to the view of the summit.

Braxton's keener focus on his relationship to tradition here takes on a look at the processing he does of this sort of music as it permeates his mind from without. He's clearly more focused on that process than on the material, putting it at the core of the piece, with the material on the surface.

> 8. AB (26B)—Composition No. 26B is constructed to deal with the dynamics possibilities of staccato long and short sound movements . . . 26B consists of 5 primary construction criteria that serve as regions of exploration. Those criteria are (1) the use of

multiphonically integrated phrase types (2) the use of multiphonic high sounds as an isolated section (3) the use of dimensionality, (4) the use of quick register changes—from very high to very low and (5) the changing rate of attacks as a means to establish dimensionality . . . The first criterion—the use of multiphonics . . . with this approach the instrumentalist is asked to utilize the voice in the "seat" of his/her sound as a secondary idea approach factor—to be considered in the moment nature of the music. What this means is that the staccato long sound can be used as broad canvas—that emphasizes its own separate nature as well as a multicomplexual universe that contains many new kinds of sounds (floating in and out of the "fish bowl" nature of this approach) . . . The second criterion involves the use of high note multiphonics as an isolated focus to be explored . . . I would ask each interpreter to create a very special universe with this section—"create a music that does nothing and yet holds our attention." *When this is done correctly (understood) then the listener will recognize my words as true* . . . The third criterion of . . . 26B's language intermix involves the use of dimensionality as a procedure device to open the floor of the music. In this new world, sounds and phrases are seen as separate from their linear interconnection—or continuous flow. This state of being is brought about through the use of extreme dynamic shifts—from note to note or phrase to phrase . . . The fourth criterion of this work contains the procedure dictates of the previous section and emphasizes the use of register changes as a factor that creates a "bubbling like" universe (that changes parts— material—as opposed to specific phrases).[28]

MH—lines made out of repeated short notes; atonal feel, rhythms like a coin or pencil tapping to rest on a drum head. forays into florid phrases, then dutifully back to premise. his determination to make music out of this premise posed seems to stoke his intense adherence/return to it. it started out lightly, relaxed; but he attacks it with increasing force, getting into extensions, multiphonics, rhythm apparently as expressions of that force. the music that gets made is not from the florid phrases so disconnected from (though inspired by) the premises; it's rather from full engagement with the premises . . . eventually, the engagement relaxes, ends on a halfway florid statement yet totally crafted out of the premises.

The words both of us grasp at here seem more music-specific than with earlier pieces. Braxton's intentions and designs seem to become clearer to him over time, moving his ruminations from the general to the particular; the restless energy of the music seems to reflect and trigger that move in my notes.

9. AB *(77G)*—Composition No. 77G is based on the whole tone scale and utilizes the eighth note as the primary language factor . . . To experience . . . 77G is to enter a sound universe of even long

sound pitch elements. This is a perceived linear sound state context that allows for lyrical and gentle improvisations.²⁹

MH—augmented scale patterns resolving into phrase fragments. going right into improvisation, returning to whole-tone riffs often. this can't help but evoke French Impressionism; Braxton's relationship to that sound is clearly personal (his idiom informed by his stays in France?). Trane's use of the whole tone scale was much more martial/regal, less wistful/lyrical (though Braxton's way with extensions is more martial, and Trane's use of standard ballad material more from his lyrical side. Interesting, in that the musical premise most new yet idiosyncratic to each artist is the one that brings out the warrior spirit, while the idioms handed down from before—seemingly less personal than the new ones each artist generated—were the vehicles for the more personal lover's spirit).

Also interesting is the thought that Braxton's affinity for the European tradition is more than abstractly aesthetic, is informed by the acceptance the culture over there offered him when he couldn't find work in America. Such a personal/emotional affinity would fit in with abovementioned warmth and humanity he weaves into his relationship with abstractions.

10. AB (*26E*)—Composition No. 26E utilizes intervallic shifts as a means to establish its working language. By intervallic shifts I am referring to the execution of a given figure in several registers of the instruments—or in several permutations . . . In . . . 26E phrases are approached from at least two different criteria—that being the higher and lower part of the shape . . . Intervallic phrase shifting in . . . 26E has to do with the establishment of arc like shapes in two basic portions of the "sound field" . . . The low register use of . . . 26E involves establishing the realness of shadowlike phrases—that are presented like a mask that never fully reveals its true identity. In this world of music the listener is given entry to new worlds of vapor and mystery. Wind instruments are expected to achieve this state through multiphonic sound clusters that tear away at the fabric of the music.³⁰

MH—chromatic fragments, hi & lo, horizontal lines fluttering in space, sewn together now and then vertically . . . ladderlines . . . steppes of sound . . . speed within slowness . . . after awhile the vertical connections between the stepped figures take over; then he goes back & forth between vert. & hor.; more-than-ornamental flourishes get suggested, non-chromatic (but also non-diatonic) harmony/melody emerges from the various chromatic patterns; good dynamic flux and natural developments. great instigator of Western-style (Flight-of-the-Bumblebee) virtuosity.

Braxton's notes move from the technical to the poetic, even as mine do, here and elsewhere. That move tells me we're meeting each other halfway; his "clinical" approach is not divorced from the non-rational aspects of music, but is developed so thoroughly in order to establish new non-rational aspects. My attempt to record sheerly sensory impressions until they suggest subjective images, rather than review his music according to preconceived values, is matched by his own strategy of generating that sensory data until it creates his own subjective context.

> 11. AB (*77H*)—Composition No. 77H is designed to deal with the dynamic possibilities of trills. This work utilizes several types of trills—from the chromatic and diatonic trill to the intervallic trill to the extreme intervallic trill ... To experience this work is to enter a melodic and forceful sound continuum that breathes in several different presences and timbres ... The instrumentalist is asked to ... paint a music of trills or at least paint a ballade state of soft and active sounds that makes use of trill sound line shapes as a primary ingredient in the sound space. This material is to be placed in a song-state-like sound environment that makes use of living material coordinates and strategies.[31]

> MH—a trill, swelling & resolving ... suggesting statements ... do a trill, take it into the statement it wants to make, go back to another trill to find the next statement. Like many of B's pieces, this puts a premium on unhurried, thoughtful rather than urgent, gripping statements. These can all also be compared to Western études, but ones that always include creative as well as technical premises; to always be consciously working on the technical and conceptual premises of music, but to never do so without also making music with them ... this breaks from close trills into wide trills, with the low and high notes doing counterpoints ... then ascending half-step trills for tension, then out.

Most important is the insight that Braxton's pieces are like Western études not only for musical improvisation as well as technique, but for creativity itself.

Perhaps, at this point, the reader will think that one or two of the above couplings and commentaries would have sufficed to make the central points—such as the comparability of Braxton's informal (though careful and analytical) use of the written word and that in my own review notes. In fact, there are many more pieces and sets of notes that could have been included that would have displayed even more variety of concept and expression. As it is, this one set of selections shows Braxton's resonance with Webern, Stockhausen, the French Impressionists, blues, post-bop structures, extended Afrocentric techniques/effects, Asian music, "sweet" ballads, and Western pyrotechnics. Having just some of even more musical vocabularies (the march, or ragtime) in the Braxton lexicon on one solo recording personalizes these disparate influences—ithat is, unifies them into one voice (i.e., both *universalizes* and *personalizes* them all equally). Including that whole array of (verbal) notes similarly takes that personalization-universalization out of the (esoteric) realm of music and into that (once esoteric, now more mundane realm) of text (transcribed speech).

Solo (London) 1988

For the final example of a solo recording, I will include both my notes and a final, polished review such as I might submit for publication. I will follow that with reflections (in the light of the oral-literate, Western-African clashes examined throughout this chapter) on the process of putting the notes into such a form.

As I have been doing, I will include Braxton's notes on these most recent pieces—but instead of excerpting from copious written passages, I am drawn by his material into simply representing his notes in facsimile here, as figures (5.8). They are clearly *performance* notes, verbal cues and triggers meant to engage an improviser with the composer's vision; they retrospectively define the thousand-plus pages of previous notes as such. This is what Braxton turns to the written language for: provocation more than evocation, inroads to the wilderness of the music more than lookout points from someone else's highway that afford the most choice views of it.

As a critic in the Western tradition, I am trying here to acknowledge those inroads as new highways and byways, to learn from the artist who scouted them how to navigate them and map and stake them out for public use—and, hopefully, with the artist, to respect and work with the wilderness rather than conquer and appropriate it for yet more Western-style "development."

> *106C*: Sounds like a big, open room, a saxophonist practicing advanced études. Up and down the horn sounding like two or three things: 1) the fulfillment of Adolphe Saxe's most European dream (France is the birthplace of the saxophone) of chromatic/overtone technique; 2) a minimalist's fondest sequencer dream sprung into human, acoustic incarnation; 3) a finger-dancing circle breather's most eminent satisfaction, with the regular brushes with single low notes snagged from the arpeggial cascade, like heavy round stones on a riverbed, 4) a horngrowler's dream, with the honks and other rough sounds that satisfy something so left out by the instrument's purities and facilities; 5) the harmonizer's dream, with those Slominsky-like patterns that turned into "sheets of sound" in Trane's horn (and something that includes same here). This piece just knocks me out. It has all those elements in a seamless stream.
>
> *2d hearing*: runs, then with ornaments; into new pattern, fumbling till it flows, tagging on lower notes, then higher ones on the fly . . . into smeary distortions (multiphonics) like a plane into a cloud. After awhile, the low notes can almost sound like a detached bass line, the

high like solo horn figures, while the midrange principle patterns sound like a chordal field. This is an anthem of tonality, vital with that edge of fourths and half-steps that makes for the thrill of Hindemith, George Russell, McCoy Tyner. AB's outdone himself as both composer & player with the elements executed & synthesized here with such skill & sophistication . . .

1. 'DOG BARKS'
2. ('you must become the dog')
3. GROWLS
4. Barks
5. repetition (focus) logics (or 'Whimpers')
6. Have fun (look for images for imitation)
7. long additive growls
   a. (w/ additive multiphonics
   b. (w/ voice) + HOWLS
8. Small dogs (light sounds)
9. Medium dogs
10. heavy dogs
11. 'Fighting' sounds
12. 'Playful' sounds

Fig 5.8: Composition notes for 99G.

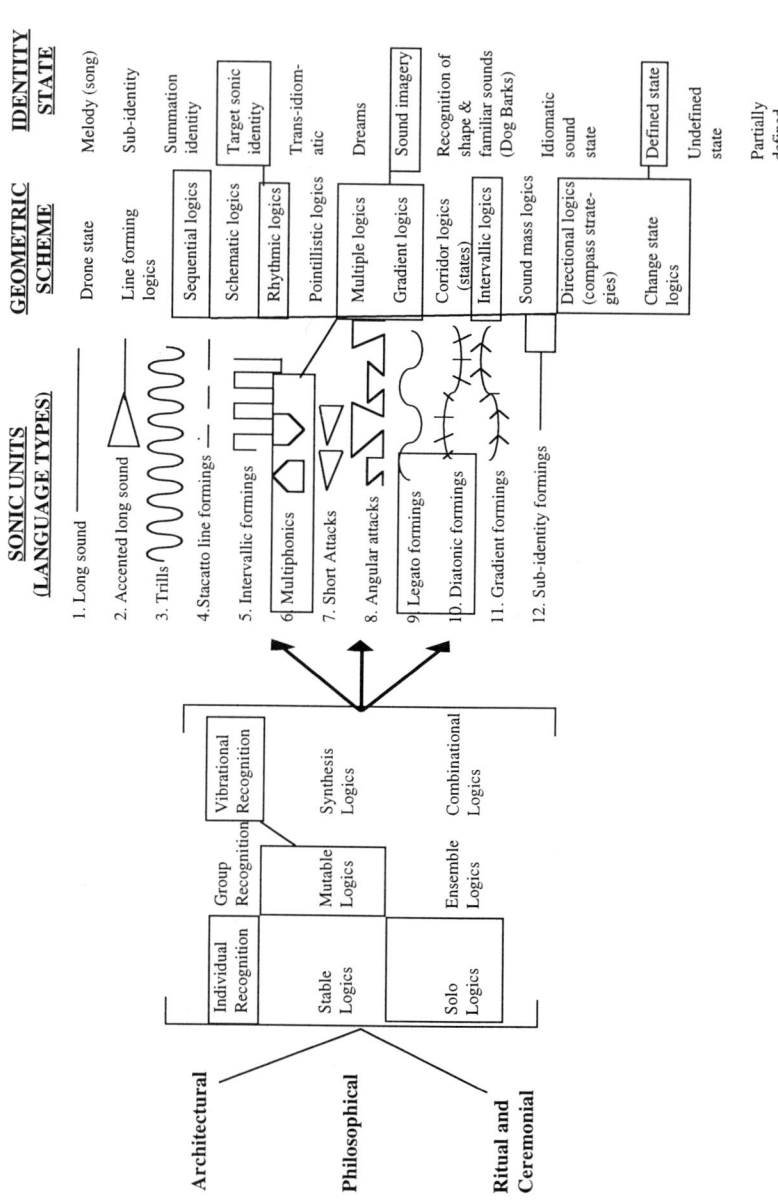

Fig. 5.9: Composition 106C (solo alto)

118F: Multiphonic & growled tones strung out into phrases like someone humming absent-mindedly while working or something . . . Frankenstein in a lighter moment . . . into dog-like sounds, amazingly realistic; high yips, low woofs, vocalish whines, all intruded-on ever so subtly by the sax's own voice.

138C: Long tones, mastered for most burnished sounds; tritones, octaves, minors, half-steps, all slipping through wistful, sober statements.

Invitation: Going back to the traditional phrasing and improv platform feels like a way of lightening/loosening up after intense focus of originals: "let's just relax and blow," run through changes, linger on patterns & feelings they suggest/generate. When AB does his own pieces, a lot of energy goes into both statement and exposition of his premises; on tunes like this, he's flying around on automatic more; quotes *Giant Steps*; lotta rhythmic (fast 32ds) riffing; somehow that always seems more static than how Bird did it, even when the notes are the same. When he does sing & soar, it's into snatches of phrases emerging out of this rhythmic (as opposed to harmonic/melodic) riffing. like the pitches are secondary to their rhythms, especially in low reg . . . 99c: careening about between slowing & speeding of phrases, and purity & distortions of timbre, & loosening/tightening of pulse

138E: Soft, restrained volume, jaunty, hints of Fletcher Henderson's sax section . . . ricky-ticky feel, tonal, melodic, up into high keening thing, keys clattering with the same playful rhythm

Impressions: modal framework suited to AB's oscillation between rhythmic riffing and timbral raptures; they both handle the modal stasis well. Harmonic palette as drum, pitches as its mallets.

99I: A big slow vibrato, moving through multiphonics, different tones. Ayler-like.

Naima: Plaintive statement of tune, unfolding downwards into solo. Very brief, appreciative yeahs/applause.

Mock-Professional Review Based on Notes

With *Solo London (1988)*, Anthony Braxton has brought to glorious fruition the seeds he planted more than 20 years ago, with the groundbreaking *For Alto*. This recording of solo alto saxophone music covers with seasoned panache and substance the ambitious spectrum spanning virtuosity and soul, originality and tradition, and informal and formal brilliance posed with such confidence and humility by that first musical coup.

The curtain rises on *106C*. An obviously advanced saxophone (perennial) student is at practice in a soundspace suggesting the high ceiling of an acoustically live studio, perhaps in some old French *maison* mere miles from the 19th-century warehouse of instrument maker Adolphe Saxe. The diatonic scales and *arpeggios* he plays would take that ingenious inventor's breath away. "This," he might say, "is the facility and fire of the music of my world given flesh and blood." Braxton is an Everyman of the saxophone as an instrument of Western virtuosity, chromaticism well-danced, overtones blown to a life of their own.

As the *étude* continued with no pause for breath, Saxe might have held his own. Braxton's mastery of circle-breathing gives the West an Indian cast, turns within moments the aspiring pyrotechnician into a *bona fide* snake charmer. Then Africa makes her appearance: low notes snagged like toothy fish from the arpeggial stream, or like rough, round stones from its silty bed, high smears of phrases wriggling on the end of a fly-cast line. More Africa, now with its American voice, growls in the multiphonics like some bear roaring through a cloud of bees. All these splash about in that European stream of Slominsky-like patterns Coltrane turned into sheets of sound, taken here by Braxton as only one of several equally important elements in the mix.

This piece bears the fruit of years of study and practice made second nature, ideas made music. Braxton the composer here makes a minimalist's mouth water, and Braxton the instrumentalist does it with the human organism of his body commanding an acoustic wind instrument, rather than with his isolated brain commanding a computer's sequencer. The minimalism of disembodied cerebration becomes the maximalism of full-bodied, as well as mindful, engagement.

Braxton makes it sound so offhand and easy—but then it is only the latest word in a life's work of such synthesis. The technique and harmonic concepts on display here serve as the means to an end, as such things should do in music. That end *is* synthesis—of Western harmony, Asian monody, and African rhythm and timbre. His midrange *arpeggios* become, as trance sets in, a Western chordal field that would have made Hindemith proud; his low notes take on the rhythmic, root-tone life of a bass line; his high flourishes the statements of a solo improviser. An amazing tonal parade, complete with excited barking dogs.

Said dogs take over the parade on the next cut. Braxton's use of "conceptual grafts"—the combination of two pieces into one statement—joins *118F* and *99G* to effect a meeting between Frankenstein's monster and his frisky pup in a lighter moment. The lumbering, growling buzzes of the former and uncannily canine sounds of the latter showcase Braxton's dogged determination to make music out of the mundane. The saxophone's own voice colors and intrudes upon these with just the right measure of subtle control.

138C is one of several short pieces that showcase musical premises just long enough for them to become music. Long tones are mined for the most burnished of tones, slipped through tritones, octaves, minors and half-steps to end in wistful, sober statements; *99I* considers the potential of slow vibratos moving through multiphonics and moods derived from Albert Ayler's influence; *99C* puts the stretches and contractions of tempo first explored by Charles Mingus into the service of elastic rebounds between timbral purity and

solo music

distortion, pulse and space; *138E* is a restrained bit of whimsy that sounds like the ghost of Fletcher Henderson's sax section, with its ricky-ticky feel; *Naima* states a plaintive theme then a wistful reflection.

The latter is one of three contemporary jazz repertoire covers. Another by Coltrane (*Impressions*) and the standard *Invitation* round them out. In the context of a Braxton solo concert, such recitations seem to yield more between than in their lines.

Invitation, the first standard on the album, placed at the end of the first side, serves to unwind both player and listener from the intensity of focus and imagination the originals require. The familiar conventional phrasing and theme-and-variations format puts invention and emotion on automatic through familiar territory. The message that does jump out from between the lines is that Braxton's "straight" solo style has been shaped by—or did it shape?—his experiments with pulse. His way of stating a fast bop phrase such as Bird might have made ranges from a Morse-code-like feeling of stasis to the more swinging, singing peaks we're used to in bop. The absolute value of linear development is clearly called into question by said stasis. From a swimmer on the river of (musical) time, Braxton turns himself and his listeners into fishermen with hip boots, looking for the most inviting spots.

Impressions, a solo staple for Braxton, is a perfect vehicle for this approach, for its modalism. Improvisers began turning to neo-Greek modes in the 1950s as a way to escape the Byzantine complexities of harmonic changes. The challenge has always been to make a solo statement that carries itself somehow, since the harmonic/melodic framework around it is standing still. Playing melodically is one approach. Braxton tends to build to melodic statements from rhythmic platforms; his use of the lower register suggests the harmonic palette as drum, with pitches its mallets. Then, when he rhapsodizes up into the higher with a more song-like section, as often as not he also turns his timbral palette into a drum too.

This record features a fine and comprehensive exposition of Braxton's solo music by Graham Lock, the preeminent Braxton chronicler. Like so much of Braxton's recent work, this music and these words about it serve as the best entry points to the body of work this artist has produced over the last two decades. All dues are paid, seasoned authority applied, and awareness shining bright after leaps of faith into the dark. Five stars—not a rating, simply a worthy visual image for this record.

• • • • •

Since a central stumbling block in his personal career and in the development of African American music generally, by Braxton's own estimation, is Western journalism's basic misunderstanding and misappropriation of it, the processes that turned the material from the notes into the review deserve more attention than they can get in one chapter. I hope in reflecting personally and briefly on them, however, that the reader will make more of them than I will articulate and apply that to his or her own experiences of music and writings about it.

When one is taking notes on a listening experience, one writes as one might easily and spontaneously speak. When one writes the notes into a review, one adopts a voice that has (typically) been trained for years in professional journalism and academia, a voice used primarily on paper, for publication. As one works with that paper voice over time, it can serve the ends of the more immediate voice in the notes effectively and comfortably, but it is definitely something one must ponder and practice long and hard for it to do so (not so the notes—mine have functioned as they do now since I started taking them in adolescence, though hopefully they have matured in responsivity and insight along with me).

In short, reviews such as this are on the crest of a wave of a tradition of arts and letters; that tradition is assumed in the froth of the crest, implicit in every word choice, transitional phrase, assessment, and explanatory image. What makes it succeed, for me, in the end, somehow lies in a sincere bluff: one says what one has to say as though it were the inevitable viewpoint of any educated, thoughtful person. This is a bluff because much from the tradition may be clamoring to dismiss and criticize any departure from same; but it is sincere when one commands that tradition well enough to inform *it* of the things outside it, rather than be informed of them *by* it. This knowledge and command comes gradually over years of trying to reconcile the rational and creative in both oneself and the larger world, and (in the case of Western writers) the Eurocentrically (however American) scholarly and journalistic and the Afrocentric (however American) musiculture in the world. The goal is to bring the two together rather than set them against each other, to let both blossom and neither overshadow. It is achieved by a willed perception and then careful articulation of what is there. What is there is not only the mythology of jazz dating from Buddy Bolden, nor the discourse of jazz scholarship and journalism dating from Hugues Panassie and André Hodeir, nor the more general cultural orientation and information of Western-educated readers and writers—what is there is also one's own (reader's or writer's) sensory experience and creative imagination, sensitivity to "the other" (to oneself, for that matter), courage, charity, and "citizenship of the world." Those *facts* are as present and can be as compelling to any critic as to any artist. The ideal critique will be one that stirs readers as much, or at least in the same way, as the artist's music might have, one that furthermore might stir the artist as his or her music stirred the critic, elicit the respect due one who understands, even if it criticizes (indeed, one that contributes to the artist's insight and growth when it does criticize).

We looked at the traditional jazz influences and precedents in the context of Braxton's work in that idiom. Moving into his solo work has taken us from Braxton the conventional "jazz musician" to Braxton the innovative composer in the Western (both American and European) art music tradition. Moving next into his duo work shows that new voice in dialogue with others.

---

1. See p. 19 for explanation of "occult definitions" (Ad DeVries, *Dictionary of Signs and Symbols,* Amsterdam/Holland: North Holland Publishing Co., 1974).

2. Albert Churchward, *Signs and Symbols of Primordial Man: The Evolution of Religious Doctrine from the Eschatology of the Ancient Egyptians* (London/New York: E.P. Dutton & Company, 1910: 325–26).

3. Ronald Radano, *Anthony Braxton and his Two Musical Traditions: The Meeting of Concert Music and Jazz* (University of Michigan, 1985: 39–63).

4. Ibid., 47.

5. L. Hudson and B. Jacot's study (*The Way Men Think: Intellect, Intimacy, and the Erotic Imagination*, New Haven & London: Yale University Press, 1991) looks at the preoccupations of selected prominent thinkers and artists with abstract thought and creative imagination as rooted in the basic wound of maleness. The results of these preoccupations—in the arts, sciences, and letters—are seen more as oysters' pearls created by the exacerbation of that wound unhealed than as healing resolutions. Braxton's grasp of his work's (and musical tradition's) role as the "Africanization/humanization of the West" is rather an example of the wound healed by the "body's" (Cartesian dualism) own "antibodies" (non-Western metaphysics, such as vodun). "I think, therefore I am" becomes "I am, therefore I think."

6. Radano (diss.), 158–79.

7. Townley, 13; "Record Reviews," *Down Beat* (Litweiler review), June 5, 1975: 18; and "Braxton[8]," *Down Beat* (Martin review), Apr. 1987: 43-48. See D. Adams and A. Goldbard's "Grass Roots Vanguard" (in *Art in America*, Vol. 4, no. 70, 1982: 24) for a refreshing discussion of what non-Western musicultures have to offer those questing for the West's leading edges.

8. Bill Shoemaker, "Anthony Braxton: The Dynamics of Creativity," *Down Beat*, Mar. 1989: 21–22.

9. Michael Ullman, "Anthony Braxton" (in *Jazz Lives*, New York: G.P. Putnam, 1980: 203.

10. Townley, 12.

11. See Bruce Perry, ed., *Malcolm X, The Last Speeches* (New York/London/Sydney/Toronto: Pathfinder Press, 1989: 28–30) for the source of this particular metaphor.

12. Joe Klee, "For Alto" (*Down Beat*, June 24 1971: 18).

13. Leonard Feather, "Blindfold Test: Phil Woods" (*Down Beat*, Oct. 14 1971: 33).

14. See Peretti; also Braxton's "The White Improvisor" (*Tri-Axium 1*: 283–317).

15. The antipathy Ornette Coleman and Cecil Taylor (to name the two most widely known examples) have provoked in black listeners and peers has been widely documented in media coverage of them (e.g., Troupe [indexed under both of their names] and Goldberg). Charters (58) captures the deep-seated nature of this antipathy to genuine genius in recounting an African tribal custom: "It was perhaps their cleverness that had been part of the reason the griots had been so feared in earlier times, and why when they died their bodies had been left out in the forest to rot."

16. Braxton, *Composition Notes A*, 118–119.
17. Ibid., 150–51.
18. Ibid., 128–29.
19. Ibid., 126–27.
20. Ibid., 120–22.
21. Braxton, *Composition Notes D*, 158.
22. Ibid., 160–62.
23. Ibid., 174–75.
24. Ibid., 185–88.
25. Ibid., 190–200.
26. Braxton, *Composition Notes B*, 218–23.
27. Braxton, *Composition Notes D* , 205–09.
28. Braxton, *Composition Notes B*, 197–01.
29. Braxton, *Composition Notes D*, 210–12.
30. Braxton, *Composition Notes A*, 210–16.
31. Braxton, *Composition Notes D*, 221–25.

fourth arrow . . .

**whistling through the
air of the future**

Convocation

Having spent so much time establishing Braxton's performance and conceptual bases in the jazz tradition, and his Western-style composer's voice and vision as defined by his solo alto work, this might be the logical point to reflect on just what *he* established with both. This point, because it marks the first confirmative incursion of the "real" world (i.e., that of a musical "other") to what might have remained a predominantly private universe.

We've noted Braxton-the-"jazz"-improviser's restless thrashings against the constraints of conventional song-form structures; we've traced the steps he took into more musical freedom through the freedom from musical input from others, as a solo performer. We've established that the areas he charted there were expansions of both African and European ends of the American musicultural spectrum.

We might note here that his odyssey might have ended here. If he were more the eccentric than the universalist, he might have developed himself as a conventional jazz stylist who also made more adventurous experimental solo recordings. Other musicians might have appreciated the latter but seen no entry point to their own participation; he, for his part, might have tried to stake and claim his exclusive rights to that solo territory (like Jelly Roll Morton claiming to be the inventor of jazz) and (in his own mind) fenced others out from it. The proliferation of ensembles from duos to multiorchestras to give bloom to the musical universe that budded in the privacy of solo work attests to and reminds us of an important point about Braxton's role as an American composer: his processes, voice, and vision have not taken place in a vacuum but have been part of an historical and grass-roots activity shared with other musicians from the first. His value and genius have come not so much from inventing new concepts and techniques as they have from taking seriously enough to personalize and codify those he shared with his peers, to mine and develop their potential relevance to the broadest-based musiculture over time.

A somewhat fresher path to explore from here, however, starts in Braxton's compulsion to synthesize Western literate and African oral elements to the degree that he has. His system of ordering his musical works—by number, by time and place, often by instrumental combination—serves more than organizational needs. It is similar to the system the Western literate/classical tradition uses with the composers of its canon. That word's evocation of sacrosanctity is intentional. For those who embrace and celebrate it, the literate tradition literally lifts its heroes and their time-bound world views out of cyclical time and into the timeless and transpersonal immortality of history. History is literacy's supermagnification and comprehensive preservation (Braxton would call it an "identity summation") of orality's myth and legend, and it brings an authority to Western culture that is still numinous with power, however Africanized it has become. Indeed, part of Braxton's contribution to that Africanization is his honoring of that peculiarly Western numinosity by claiming it neither as foil nor as lesser or greater, but as *match* to his own measure of the African oral tradition's different—and in his hands, complementary—numinosity. This is important because the authority and power of Western culture have been contrary to the intent and spirit of the oral tradition, have run the toxic gamut of repression, oppression, exploitation, misappropriation, and slights and damages more well intended but still paving the road to hell. Orality celebrates itself in the moment, cyclically, in performance, always transitory, always renewing; literacy historicizes, fixes what is important into a medium, sets up a mental sacred space in which to celebrate itself through its codes (scores, books, choreographs, scripts). The physical performances, however vital, are almost secondary to their primary blueprints in the way matter has been seen as secondary to spirit in the West.

These two traditions have met head on in America, have clashed, have learned to respect and feed each other, and are evolving so healthily, if still turbulently. Literacy has, generously and naturally enough, shifted its focus from, say, Beethoven to Louis Armstrong, as evident in the body of scholarship and honor granted the latter—but such glory through history is not the same thing as glory in time, and one of the cruellest aspects of the Western experience is the way the two become confused and imbalanced, both by those who seek and those who can confer both. Armstrong (and Beethoven, for that matter) lived for glory—happiness here and now, a response commensurate with their gifts—in their moments, as well as the ages. Had the balance been better, Armstrong might have grinned a bit less and Beethoven might have gotten married.

Braxton's synthesis is just as full of both moment and ages. He has worked out a music that can draw on all the rich potential of the transitory moment, per Africa and the other oral traditions—and he has granted it all the numinous power and authority conferred by the Western literate ritual called history. In doing so, he has shown that the one thing need not be done at the expense of the other.

Numbering and otherwise cataloguing his music, seen in this light, doesn't sterilize or rigidify or deflate it; it rather reflects that overarching consciousness, both personal and the transpersonal one of (oral) Muse and (literate) history, that both engenders and forms not only individual pearls but the string that makes them a necklace. The oral tradition has its shadow side too; one *needs* the empowering and pleasant self-consciousness of consistent purpose in the making and living of one's shifting, fleeting life. To the listening, Braxton's meticulous documentation brings a context that can be felt as a good light shone on (what it reveals as) a good darkness (neither good always being pleasant). What's more, as we'll see in Chapter Eight, the opus numbers and graphics themselves, as charged with a history of mythical meaning as more conventional verbally descriptive titles, add up to a corpus that resembles a body indeed—a living organism more than the sum of its organized parts, with hints of an intelligence and personality beyond that of the artist's conscious control.[1]

The duo—and the trio, quartet, and other combinations, and indeed every other aspect of every musical event—are neither arbitrary nor random in real time, and need not appear to be to retain their souls' freedom. Rather, such meticulous definition and documentation gives the fullest access to that freedom. And, as that aspect called "ensemble" attests, in the chapters covering their various sizes, those souls in Braxton's musical universe are embodied far beyond the flesh of his own idiosyncratic performances of his own music. That's what makes him, in the end, more the composer than the performer.

Chapter Six

Duo Music

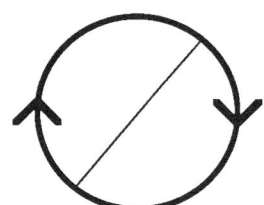

[Example of a] **Tri-Metric caption:**

1. *The egg has healed the rift made by the sperm and is taking on the integrity of the new life; the seed* qua *seed (the dot in the circle) is dissolved in that life. That life has started to grow from the feeding motion of the nutrients on the lining of the egg.*

2. *The quantum is interacting with another such on the same (standing) wavelength (literally, in physics terms) as itself; their interaction simulates an "orbit" around a(n implied) "nucleus" of their field of mutual attraction, to move from the atomic to the molecular level of matter.*

3. *Braxton's duo music results from the shifting interplay between him and his partners; both lighter line and bolder arrows denote the discrete motion of the points of their statements, now here, now there, a discretion so fast it is experienced as continuous.*

[From occult definition of] **number***: 8. Pythagoras: . . . 2 = broken line: polarity, resistance, primordial matter . . .*

[From occult definition of] **two***: 1. polarity, diversity, dualism, (conjunction of) opposites: positive/negative, life/death, man/woman; twins . . . 3. primordial matter: a. nature as opposed to its Creator; b. Mother Earth as Magna Mater, or womankind in general; 4. the stillness of equilibrium, but also inception . . .*

duo music

[From occult definition of] **twins**: *1. general: A. they represent two opposites, which, in the end, have a synthesizing, complementary function, e.g. life/death, sunrise/sunset, bad/good, hunter/shepherd, vertical mountain/horizontal valley, etc . . . .b. fertility kings . . . B. most famous twins are children of an immortal father and a mortal mother (the "hieros gamos" between heaven and earth), e.g . . . .Castor-Pollux . . . C. as secondary deities they are usually in the service of a supreme deity; D. they often appear in animal form . . . 2. they are generally considered to have special powers, which give them an awe-inspiring numinous quality.*

Form is at its best a meaningful assortment of oppositions—light and dark, fast and slow, serious and comic, orderly and chaotic. Without this dynamic formal interplay, the sublimest vision and the earthiest realization are equally empty of power. The artist who cannot establish a context of expectation can never surprise. The artist who cannot compel seriousness can never command irony. The artist immune to violence is incapable of peace. The artist who cannot repeat cannot vary.

Robert Grudin

I've chosen the following recordings and selections to represent the music Braxton specifically improvised, wrote, or altered for specific duos. Were I doing a comprehensive review, more duets under other musicians' names and those featured throughout recordings by trios, quartets, and larger ensembles would afford a much larger field than this handful. This review is meant rather to bring Braxton's definitions to that duo context conventional to both jazz and Western art music traditions.

Duo (Emanem 3313/4(RI), 1974): open improvisations, with guitarist Derek Bailey.

Live at Wigmore (Inner City 1041, 1974): open improvisations, with guitarist Derek Bailey.

Trio and Duet (Sackville 3007, 1974): *The Song Is You, Embraceable You, You Go To My Head*, with bassist David Holland.

Duets 1976 (Arista AL-4101, 1976): *60, 40P, 62;* and an open improvisation post-titled *Nickie,* with pianist Muhal Richard Abrams.

Elements of Surprise (Moers Music MOMU 01036, 1976): *64, 65,* with trombonist George Lewis.

Duets With Anthony Braxton (Sackville 3016, 1977): *40Q, 74A & 74B,* with reeds player/composer Roscoe Mitchell.

Birth & Rebirth (Black Saint BSR 0024, 1978): open improvisations, with drummer Max Roach.

One in Two, Two in One (Hat Hut 2R06, 1979): open improvisations, with drummer Max Roach.

For Two Pianos (Arista AL 9559, 1980, released 1982): *95,* performed by pianists Frederick Rzewski and Ursula Oppens.

Four Pieces (Dischi Della quercia Q28015, 1981): *101,* with pianist/composer Giorgio Gaslini.

Open Aspects '82 (Hat Art 1995/96, 1982): open improvisation, with synthesist Richard Teitelbaum.

Six Duets (1982) (Cecma 1005, 1982): *6A & 6N; 23J; 69A, 69B, & 69P*, with bassist John Lindberg.

Duets 1987 (Ratascan 002, 1987): *86, 134(+96), 40D(96, 108B)*, with percussionist Gino Robair.

Kol Nidre (Sound Aspects 031, 1988): *85 & 87*, with reeds player/composer Andrew Voigt.

Duets, Vancouver 1989 (Music & Arts CD 611): *136, 140(+112+30), 62, 116*, with pianist Marilyn Crispell.

As it happens, Braxton's recorded duos range the spectrum most broadly from the jazz to the European and American concert and experimental traditions. His work as a soloist in the traditional recordings examined above suggests the music of this spectrum as much as "jazz" solos can. He hints, quotes, borrows ideas; a player can always sound like Debussy for a moment, or Stockhausen, or Lester Young or Charlie Parker or Ornette Coleman—or she can explore her own original ideas that transcend the conventional context without leaving it—while soloing on a song.

As an unaccompanied soloist, she can do the same, and more, by isolating those fleeting snatches into their own pieces and working them out there—but one voice is static, however ecstatic. Braxton, although a virtuoso instrumentalist, sees himself primarily as a composer, especially in his solo context; this is signaled by several aspects of that context. For one thing, he has always been utterly unselfconscious about uneven instrumental execution; much of his solo and duo music has the feel of someone practicing rather than presenting a rehearsed piece. He's typically more overwhelmed by the concepts he's working on than he is by his own executions of them.

Also, in a context that would seem to invite variety, he, although a multiinstrumentalist, limits himself to his least exotic, most familiar alto sax. Braxton the instrumentalist is the surface, Braxton the composer the core. Variety on the surface would distract from focusing on the veins he's trying to mine at the core. His alto voice is his most natural and developed; he can forget about it while he concentrates on the new things he wants to say. When an audience might hear a rather offhand sax riff or two, Braxton is having detailed inner visions of its numinous structure. A quick throaty growl might imply a cloud of multiphonics that he imagines textured by a whole orchestral section. The solo alto experience is thus suggestive, evocative; we catch the excitement of invisible large worlds imaged in a visible small one.

The duo situation opens up that closed universe. He's no longer interacting solely with his own abstract premise and/or the echo of what he just did. He's taking those new things he wanted to say, in the full array of his many instrumental voices, to the table to converse with like-minded (and like-mined and mining) partners.

Braxton's recorded duets pretty well cover the spectrum of possible combinations, those being his single-line with another single-line instrument (other reeds, trombone); with drums and other percussion; and with keyboard, plucked, and bowed polyphonic instruments (piano, synthesizer, guitar, bass). He allows himself the whole range of reeds he plays: those lower than baritone in the saxophone and clarinet families; the tenor clarinet; flute; and alto and higher among the saxes. In addition, he has put out one recording for two pianos (Ursula Oppens and Frederick Rweszki) as a composer only. As mentioned, duets are also sprinkled throughout his recordings for larger combinations and on dates led by others, but we'll focus here on recordings fully devoted to the duo and released under his name, perhaps glancing at a few others in our looks at larger ensembles.

There are interesting ranges other than that of different instruments defined by the spread of recorded duets. One such range, the most conventional, is that of American songbook standards, with bassist David Holland. The time Braxton worked with Holland inspired several compositions specifically for sax and bass, which he recorded with other bassists (and other instruments) over the years, and which he explained with his notes. A selective scan of such a work or two, from their roots in his traditional covers with Holland, will continue our thread between tradition and innovation here.

That line suggests another promising insight. Braxton has done duets with two figures he looks on more as mentors than peers: drummer Max Roach and pianist Muhal Richard Abrams. He has also done a number of them with artists he would certainly consider peers (Holland, Roscoe Mitchell, pianist Marilyn Crispell, trombonist George Lewis). Finally, he has recorded with younger players whom he obviously considers peers but who would more likely, to varying degrees, look to him as a mentor (Andrew Voigt, Gino Robair, perhaps John Lindberg, perhaps Crispell and Lewis).

Something about this range resonates with Braxton's own "Tri-Axium" concept: the past informing the present creating the future (it also fits with the oral tradition's intergenerational personal transmission of culture). It sheds that much more light on Braxton's deep affinity with tradition, his subsequent comfort with the demands of the innovator's role, and the staying power of his music. We'll see how much of that light we can shine as we look over the duo music.

Another aspect of the *Tri-Axium* motif has been made accessible by the sheer amount of time Braxton has been prominent in the public arena. The three-decade arc of his career can be traced through (though, of course, not reduced to) three discernible stages: (1) the early years of open, free exploration and innovation, roughly mid-1960s to mid-1970s; (2) the middle years of solidification and codification of the innovations into systems and structures, packaging them for general public consumption, roughly mid-1970s to mid-1980s; and (3) the evolution and development of those systems and structures into increasingly musical yields, proving Braxton's power and vision and ever-wider relevance, reshaping the musical arena, roughly mid-1980s to the present. This process mirrors the *Tri-Axium* in the way its second stage draws upon its first to create its third.

The instruments being coupled in a given duet frame another perspective: what history in Western, African, and American music does a given coupling have? What musical characteristics has it defined? How is Braxton's work related to both (history and musical territory)?

Another range reaches from wide open free improvisation (with Roach, with guitarist Derek Bailey, and with synthesist Richard Teitelbaum) to the carefully predetermined notated and orchestrated compositions. As we did with Braxton's traditional covers, we'll look at the open sessions as fertile breeding and seeding grounds for his original compositions.

Then there's the range between experimental improvisers/composers from Europe (Bailey, Gaslini, Rzewski, Peter Wilson), European America (Lindberg, Crispell), and African America (Abrams, Lewis, Mitchell). This spectrum is interesting for the musical specifics it gives to the notion of Braxton-as-synthesist of Western and African spirits, a notion that remains abstract when derived only from his or others' words.

We'll weave in and out of all these ranges, let them loom invisibly to manifest at points, as we move through our look at the duo music.

The duet part of *Trio and Duet* is a good starting point for a number of reasons. It comprises the most traditional duets Braxton recorded, the three standards with bassist David Holland. Along with that most traditional *material*, the *combination* of bass and horn is probably the most on-center duo possible in terms of making a jazz statement because of the way the bass both roots a rudimentary harmonic structure and counterpoints with melody, while at the same time defining the pulse so explicitly. A chordal accompaniment is more natural for rubato ballads and can mimic the traditional bass role and voice as well, but the bass certainly defines the center of the music with more historical and sonic authority and resilience. Percussion/horn or horn/horn duos veer away from that American center into their respective African and European flanges of it. (It's interesting to note, in the light of this traditionally central role and voice of the bass, the number of compositions generated between Braxton and Holland that he went on to record in duo not only with bassists but also [as we'll see] with percussion and another horn, corroborating the idea of the bass as center to those flanges.)

After nodding to Braxton's pioneering role in the modern solo context, Lange[2] discussed the history of the duo in jazz, likewise attributing seminal contributions to its modern development to Braxton. That development, he noted, lay primarily in changing the hierarchical soloist-over-accompaniment situation to a counterpoint of equals: melody, harmony, textures, and rhythm were accessible to both players, and neither was locked into a fixed structure of those elements (Braxton himself wrote, "There is no such thing as a duo if both instrumentalists can't have the same ability to direct the focus of the music").[3]

On this particular recording, two of the cuts (*The Song Is You* and *You Go To My Head*) do in fact adhere to such convention, with Holland laying down roots and walking through chord changes under Braxton's statement of and solos on the head; only with *Embraceable You*[4] do the two move into a more plastic freedom from both hierarchy and structure. Lange alludes to Lee Konitz[5] on the two "inside" pieces and Eric Dolphy and Richard Davis on the "outside" one. "Both Braxton/Holland and Dolphy/Davis collaborations," he writes, "see the duet as a musical tug-of-war, each side giving slightly, surfacing and taking the lead, then rescinding."

Two of Braxton's most recent duo recordings—with Robair and with Voigt—feature compositions originally conceived during the time of *Trio and Duet* for Holland and him. In his notes on one of them, Braxton too nods to the Dolphy/Davis duos, and others. *Composition No. 85* (with Robair) is a good example of Braxton's conscious first steps away from traditional to innovative ground in a sax-and-bass context. It was written in 1977 for Holland and Braxton

duo music 267

to perform, and was conceived as a medium-tempo vehicle to showcase and further the language and spirit of bebop. "I recall the duet recordings of Eric Dolphy and Richard Davis or with Charlie Mingus, or John Coltrane and Rashied Ali as a point to think about in this work."[6] He also mentions the lines of Count Basie and Charlie Parker.

The expectations for improvisation are similar to those ascribed to a bebop treatment of a standard song form, only that form is replaced by written phrases floating on (and directing) waves of open improvisation. Braxton's six pages of words about this piece in essence add up to a mix of poetically, theoretically, and technically reaching language that tries to inspire and direct the performers onto musical ground that is new but at the same time accessed through the familiar traditional territory—as bebop itself originally was.[7] (*23J*, dedicated to T.S. Eliot, is similar to *85*, a bop-like linear statement over an even pulse stretching into Coleman's extensions of tonality. Its recorded duo version is with bassist John Lindberg.)

86 and *87*, also conceived *circa* 1977-1978 as duets with Holland, represent conscious quantum leaps into still greater realizations of that particular duo's potential. Both, like *85*, were conceived specifically for the duo.[8] *86*, recorded in 1987 with Robair, was inspired by the concepts and dynamics activated by the music of both Webern and the AACM, and Ornette Coleman and Stockhausen: atonal, arhythmic moments of sound sculptures suggesting improvisations along similar lines. The forward rhythmic motion and linear developments of bebop are left in the other universe of the preceding piece; here, the players are not racing alongside each other and quipping on the run but are rather sitting still, "facing" each other and speaking the "words" that arise from that stillness.

87 quantum leaps still further. Here, Braxton has written out much more than in the previous two pieces: 25 "structural points that stick together to form a reality context."[9] The notated phrases are meant to suggest extended improvisations, but the number and complexity of them show Braxton's desire to anchor the most far-flung freedoms of those with his own composer's vision. Sections and transitions are orchestrated and explained in the notes so as to estab-

Fig. 6.1a: From *85*.

Fig. 6.1b: From *86*.

Fig. 6.1: Embraceable's *(Fig. 6.1c, next page) free-floating time, snatched fragments of the head, extreme intervallic trills, blatts/overtone squeals, growls, interrupted logics — and regular jazz phrasing too — demonstrate extended techniques/concepts in a conventional context, to show how the traditional gives rise to the innovative. Through 85, 86, and 87 — all written as duets with Holland a few years into their regular collaborations — some of those extensions are developed into pieces in their own rights. (Interestingly, given his affinity with Cage, Monk, Desmond and Miles Davis, Braxton's paradigm has no category for the element of silence, which is used to very tasty effect on 85; the duet (with Voigt) almost sounds like two tracks of a master tape isolated from other tracks of a rhythm section. 87 too plays the silences; the dynamic flux is less the usual tension-and-release than it is like Morse code: premise/improv, dot/dash, this/that, a statement then a flurry out of it. Phrasing that sometimes sounds clattery on alto sounds just right on the lower horns.*

lish and integrate that vision completely with the process of improvisation explored in solo and duo.

This relationship between spontaneous improvisation and Braxton's charts is clearly stated in his notes to both *86* and *87*.[10] Variations on this explanation of his composing process come with the notes to most of his works. Braxton has said in conversation that he typically composes as he improvises: by opening himself to the ideas that come through most clearly, immediately, and strongly. Whatever personal and conceptual influences and affinities he claims are assimilated and left "behind" consciousness by the time he enters the creative process.

In fact, these three pieces demonstrate something about Braxton's unique significance as a composer (see Fig. 6.1). They were directly inspired by and for the bass/sax duo with Holland, traditional expressions of which are documented by the three standards on *Trio and Duet*. From such conventional sessions, Braxton set about trying to codify, organize, and control the spontaneous variations on fixed parameters that typically occur in them. Those

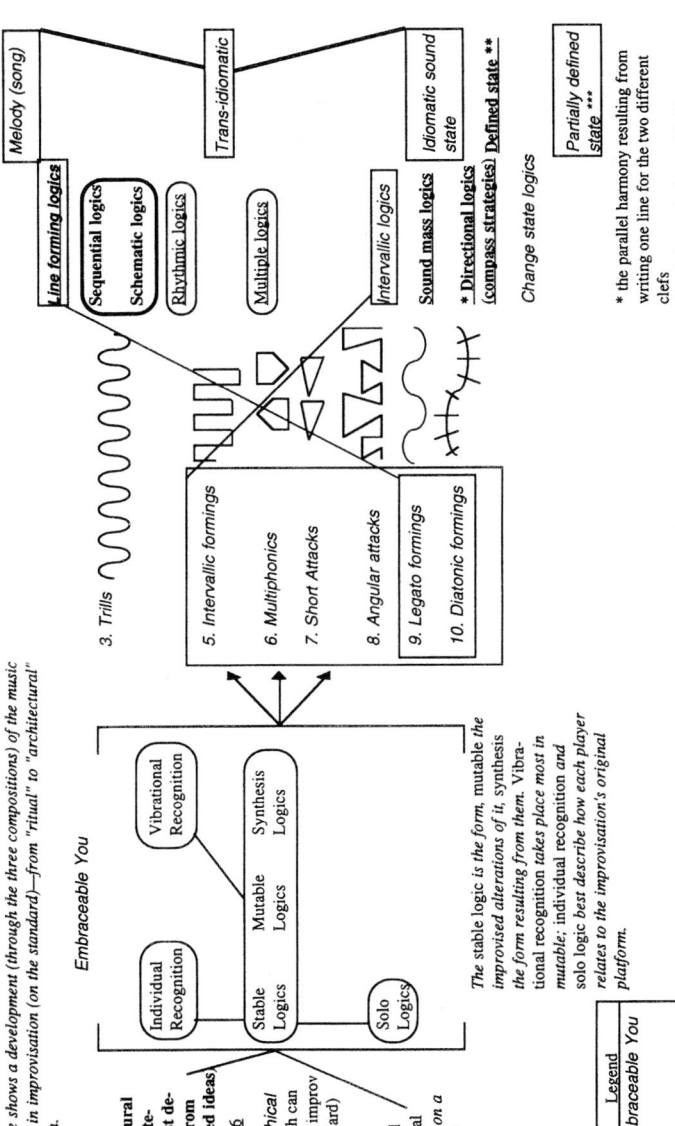

Fig. 6.1c: Comparison of *Embraceable You*, 85, 86, and 87.

improvisations are holistic in nature, as mentioned above; within a given "jazz solo" the musical concepts and expressions of the whole world can pass through the choruses kaleidoscopically, now sounding like a classical or romantic, an impressionist or serialist composer; now like the blues, now like a gamelan, or a raga, or a Native American chant, or a Western post-serial textural tone poem. With each of these successive three pieces, Braxton notated more with the goal of improvising more on more, and that both more consciously and more variously.

Other modern composers (Cage, Stockhausen) have perhaps integrated spontaneity and chance with orchestration as well as anyone, but who else has mastered and mined the transcultural musical potential of the art of improvisation as forged within the African American tradition so completely and consciously? Who else has tried to pursue the most sophisticated utterances of the oral tradition's process (performance that mines a seemingly simple and fleeting premise's immanence for its most profound and timeless transcendences) and to devise their equally sophisticated literate expressions?

Another piece for collaboration with Holland, originally for flute and bass and later expanded for quartet, reappearred in its original duo state in the 1992 release with European bassist Peter Wilson (see Fig. 6.2; Lock[11] examines some details of this from one of Braxton's lectures).

69P, recorded in 1982 with bassist John Lindberg, was written in 1976 with inspiration provided by pianist Cedar Walton's heads for the Jazz Messengers in the early and mid-1960s. The first section is a good example of a device Braxton takes quite seriously and explores diligently, often taking it from other cultural contexts: repetition. As a composer (as we saw in his solo material) he has frequently acknowledged and exploited the mantra-like potential of repetition to unlock the energies and insights of focused meditation; musically, these are expressed in the improvisations his repeated "mantra" (musical phrase, rhythm) triggers. Along similar lines, the second section is inspired by the rhythmic and melodic meta-mantra that courses through Native American music.

duo music

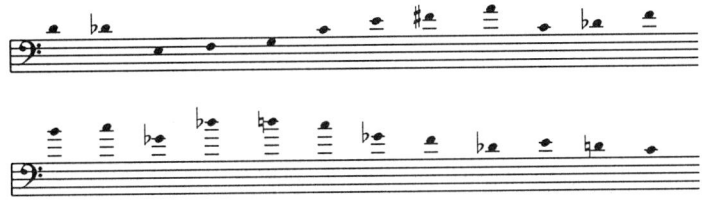

Fig. 6.2: Bass part to Braxton's *40A*.

Fig. 6.2: This piece works especially well as a trigger to Braxton's best work on flute, an instrument that has always challenged him. The mood set by this particular figure seems as important as its technical aspects to its nature as "flute-challenger": ominous, lumbering, night-lightning, foreboding--good horror-movie soundtrack. Much of Braxton's music has this feel, as though he's scaring up the monsters in his psyche for the power they might bring to meet, in this case, the dread beast—FLUTE! (Aa-aa-g-h!!). This kind of piece both enacts and represents engagements with mystery, as a protest singer will do with a political position, or a ballad singer with love. Braxton is a composer who, like Bach, unaffectedly musicalizes philosophical or metaphysical conundrums, or mathematical/physical ones, and the emotions and passions that come with the intellectual and spiritual life.

This piece allows for one person to support the other in solos rather than improvisational counterpoint. It ends on sopranino, after flute (a rise in brassiness, perhaps a reward to the flutist after his struggles). There are two or three themes/motifs being repeated here, and several sections. Circular breathing is used for some of the cycled lines.

The rest of the material recorded with Lindberg was originally composed for quartet. The natural reduction to bass/sax duo, and the equally easy expansion in the other direction, underscores again the central stability of this combination.[12]

6A (1968) is from Braxton's stable of marches. He writes in his notes that it has been around long enough to have proven amenable and yielding to a number of different performance approaches originally unforeseen.[13] His comments about the relationship of this music's themes and structures to players' improvisations on it are telling, and typical of many of his composition notes:

The most basic criteria I have applied for music in this category (extended quartet music) is that a given composition must establish a "procedure or vibrational space" for the ensemble as well as the musicians. In other words, compositions from this category must have relevance on several different levels—as opposed to functioning only in the context of a "head" or theme (to be played and left behind).[14]

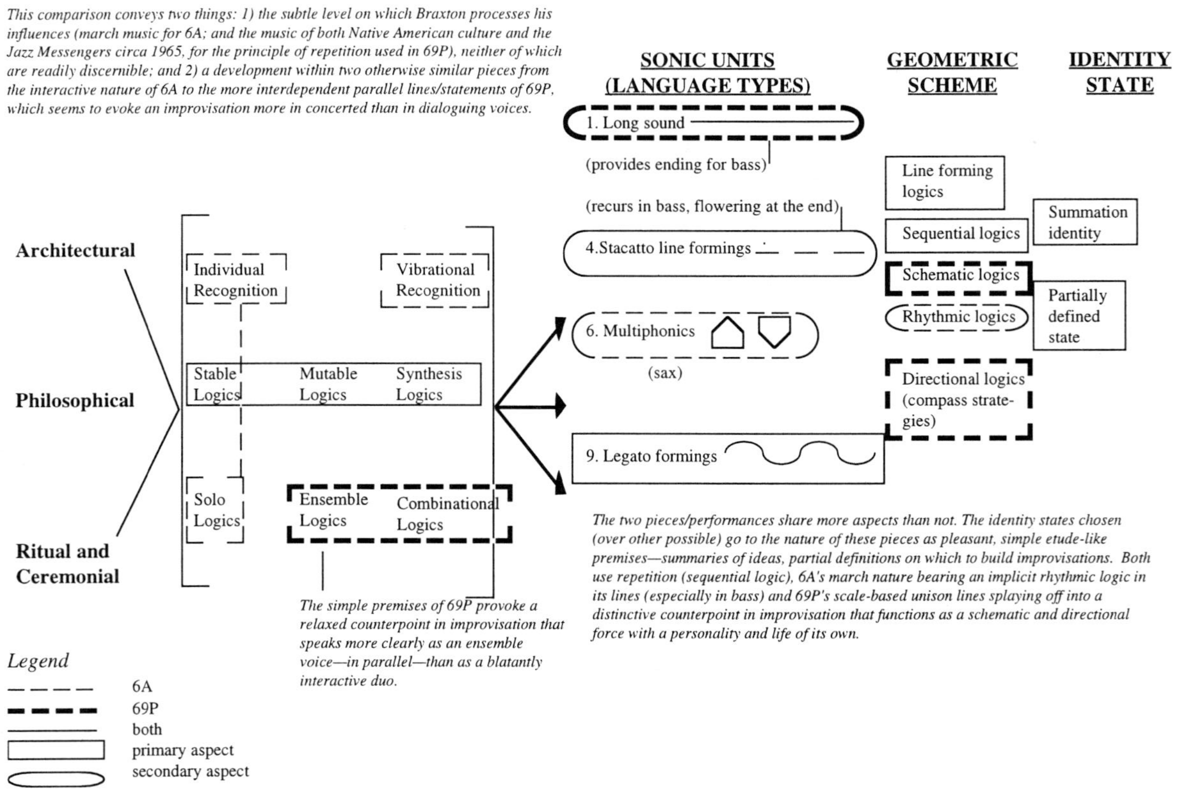

This comparison conveys two things: 1) the subtle level on which Braxton processes his influences (march music for 6A: and the music of both Native American culture and the Jazz Messengers circa 1965, for the principle of repetition used in 69P), neither of which are readily discernible; and 2) a development within two otherwise similar pieces from the interactive nature of 6A to the more interdependent parallel lines/statements of 69P, which seems to evoke an improvisation more in concerted than in dialoguing voices.

SONIC UNITS (LANGUAGE TYPES)

1. Long sound
(provides ending for bass)

(recurs in bass, flowering at the end)

4. Stacatto line formings

6. Multiphonics
(sax)

9. Legato formings

GEOMETRIC SCHEME

Line forming logics

Sequential logics

Schematic logics

Rhythmic logics

Directional logics (compass strategies)

IDENTITY STATE

Summation identity

Partially defined state

The two pieces/performances share more aspects than not. The identity states chosen (over other possible) go to the nature of these pieces as pleasant, simple etude-like premises—summaries of ideas, partial definitions on which to build improvisations. Both use repetition (sequential logic). 6A's march nature bearing an implicit rhythmic logic in its lines (especially in bass) and 69P's scale-based unison lines splaying off into a distinctive counterpoint in improvisation that functions as a schematic and directional force with a personality and life of its own.

Architectural

Individual Recognition

Vibrational Recognition

Stable Logics

Mutable Logics

Synthesis Logics

Philosophical

Solo Logics

Ensemble Combinational Logics

The simple premises of 69P provoke a relaxed counterpoint in improvisation that speaks more clearly us as an ensemble voice—in parallel—than as a blatantly interactive duo.

Ritual and Ceremonial

Legend
- - - - 6A
▬▬▬ 69P
▭ both
▭ primary aspect
⬭ secondary aspect

Fig. 6.3: 6A and 69P, two duo compositions (performed with John Lindberg) widely separated in time and development but similar in feel and concept.

This says something about the schizoid way notation and improvisation had come to be practiced among jazz artists. The notated aspects came to be seen in the 1960s as superfluous, obsolete Western literate conventions still lingering around the real music that happened through (pan-African, oral) improvisation. Indeed, the whole "free" movement in the music was in part seeking freedom from *any* literate premises, and for complete oral spontaneity. Braxton was one of the primary pioneers of that freedom, and therefore in the best position to know its need for compensatory balance. His approach, one of its earliest expressions represented here, was rather to elevate—or to reclaim the original elevation of—the notated aspects to better match the improvisational. Western musical and cultural premises were simply not adequate to the music African America had made from them, but form and symbolism in general—as many would discover the hard way, and as Braxton knew from his beginnings—was essential.

6A's connection to march music sounds tenuously implicit; improvisation dominates. What *69P* sounds like is a meandering conversation around scale patterns, in the clarinet/arco-bass voices. Again, the connection to Native American music is subtle. Both are in keeping with Braxton's way of extracting/abstracting essence or premise from an influence and subsuming it in his own personal spin.

69A (1977) is a simple structure open to extended improvisation; perhaps because of that, it is also part of Braxton's "coordinate music," which comprises such structures in a modular fashion to be interlocked together or embedded in more complex structures in a variety of combinations (more on that in Chapter Eight). Typically, Braxton's notes try to evoke the challenge and process of making profound music out of not particularly daunting premises. The *69B* notes are similarly technical on one level and mystifying on another—until they're read in tandem with the listening experience.

69B is a lighthearted piece with a cheeky ending. Phrases declare themselves, improvisations noodle out relaxedly; the music is over in a matter of minutes. But look at Braxton's notes on it:

> The first section (A) of the work establishes the basic material and phrase particulars of the music . . . The second notated section (A1) elaborates on that same material—emphasizing longer sound material as a basis to establish thematic generation. There is an apparent change in the material focus in the third section . . . because of the tempo and material shift in sections one and two, but in actual fact section three (B) only realigns the terms of the material. This is so because section three utilizes those same principal elements already established in the earlier sections . . . but in a different context (that being with the use of a march music foundation) . . . The fourth section (C) reestablishes the material construction of section one in an extended sense as a basis to set up the coming material changes that take place in Section D . . . Section D activates the use of an open sixteenth note staccato (line) figure played by the string bass under the solos in the music. This secondary influence is a major operative that affects both the vibrational dynamics of the music as

well as each instrumentalist's extended improvisations . . . Section C2 then is an extended recapitulation (to solidify the language dynamics of its material before extended improvisation). The use of these various devices provides a dynamic platform for creative music exploration.[15]

Excerpts such as this typically describe music that unfolds in a matter of minutes; accordingly, their density and difficulty, and "pondering time," are swallowed in the listening experience as neatly as a leaf incorporates the complexities of its veins. All five volumes of the *Composition Notes* might be seen as one long Zen koan referring to the ineffability of the compositions' music. A reading of them in tandem with a listening to their recorded performances effectively "re-wires" the language, visual, and audial processes of the reader's neural networks to attune them with those of the artist.

The horn/bass duo music examined here, as suggested in Fig. 6.3, is reflective of what he's doing more recently (such as with bassists Peter Niklas Wilson and Mario Pavone). Improvisation and notation serve each other as equals, usually in dialogue; each piece is usually characterized by a simple idea being "kicked around" (as Braxton says) leisurely to tease out all its complexities. The bass—more than keyboard, percussive, or wind instruments—bears a relaxed grounding that shows in this tributary of Braxton's compositional flow.

With Keyboard

Getting back to Lange's *Coda* review will move us into the next duo field, that of horn and piano. In addition to *Trio and Duet* (featuring the standards with Holland), Lange also reviews *Duets 1976*, with pianist Muhal Richard Abrams. A propo of the duo's abovementioned new-found egalitarianism, Lange observes that while Abrams had recorded before, his instrument's traditional supporting role had obscured his talents. "In the past Muhal's role was mainly as a base for the soloists . . . On this album he is able to step out of the background and become an equal voice in dialogue with Braxton." Lange reports with approval and praise the Braxton compositions and Scott Joplin and Eric Dolphy covers here and the way the artists handled them, including Braxton's work on the clarinet and contrabass sax. (Braxton's own notes to this LP are discussed in Chapter Four).

If bass can be called the center of the jazz-traditional rhythm section, piano is surely the Western European flange of it (while African American pianists have always developed the instrument's percussive potential along Afrocentric lines, that potential remains intrinsically implicit and secondary; hitting a string doesn't make it a drum).[16] Further, if Braxton and his AACM and other peers tangled the conventional horn/bass hierarchy so that both were equals rather than one the support of the other's flights, they similarly redeemed the keyboard from its dual destiny as chordal/rhythmic wallpaper and self-sufficient (thus noninteractive) solo voice.

Such constraints loosed, the tension a polyphonic instrument will inevitably bring to a monophonic one stems from the former's ability to make more than one sound at once; speed and facility, as well as a less linear and more informed sense of the making of intervals, result from the single-liner's attempts to weave in linear time a match to the tapestry a chord can present in the whole cloth of a moment.

As mentioned in Chapter Two, the piano plays a particularly important role in Braxton's musical history. His love for the solo piano music of Fats Waller, Schönberg, and Stockhausen inspired him to conceive of his own instrument, the alto sax, as "his piano" for his solo music. His first scored work (1968) was for solo piano. No instrument provides quicker concrete access to Western musical systems of harmony/melody and orchestration and voicing.

Braxton's pianistic partners on duo recordings have included Abrams, the Italian Giorgio Gaslini, and longtime quartet member Marilyn Crispell. (His two-piano work for Ursula Oppens and Frederick Rzewski is of a somewhat different nature, of course, and we'll examine it in a different context). The contexts established by these three duos personalize three major wellsprings of Braxton's art: the "trans-African" and "trans-European" cultural streams (especially as both have evolved in America) and the feminine in nature and culture. We've already looked at them in the abstract and, somewhat, in the solo alto music, but here is where we can look at their musical personalizations not only in Braxton's private universe but in the interactions with others at large.

Braxton on Abrams:

> Muhal Richard Abrams has produced a body of necessarily relevant creativity that must be dealt with in the eighties. The thrust of Abrams' work can be traced back to the time zone of the fifties—from his involvement with hard bop, to the founding of the experimental band, to the theatre work he contributed in the sixties, and to the inspiration he provided for all of the musicians in the AACM. Muhal's piano music is like a history of black music—encompassing every area and period of black music, yet offering something that is uniquely different at the same time. This is a musician who has worked with master musicians in every period of black creativity—from Dexter Gordon to Eddie Harris, from Max Roach to Clifford Jordan. I believe Muhal's contribution to creative music represents one of the significant offerings of the post-Ayler continuum.[17]

Braxton writes of his *40P* (written as a duo for Abrams and him; see Fig. 2.8):

> The weight of a given statement in this sound space has to do with life tenure and purpose . . . The notated material that comprises this work is purposely light and to the point (as it should be for works of this nature) . . . a return to the basis of "the old"—as a means to refurbish vision and rekindle energy.[18]

The words "atonal line structure" provide a good springboard to *Compositions 60* and *62*. Braxton invokes the person of Coleman again, but also Schönberg, which brings the trans-European into the picture with the trans-African. Here's where we can see the Braxton synthesis made to meet its core challenge.

As mentioned above regarding Schönberg, his work repulsed early audiences more for its perceived barbarism than for some sort of artificial futurism. Arguably, his introduction of *sprechstimme*—speech-song—was even more of a shock to diatonicism than the switch from diatonic hierarchies to chromatic symmetries. After all, the latter still fell within the twelve even measurements of the octave around which Western instruments have evolved. *Sprechstimme* worked with the entire pitch spectrum of the octave, not just the twelve discrete increments (not to mention the fact that it stressed music's integration with the spoken word). The point here, however, is that its expressivity does not reduce down to what Braxton would call its "science": the charting and codifying of its movements. The power and poignancy of, say, Jessye Norman's brilliant performance of Schönberg's *Erwartung* does not lie in some ingenious emotionalizing of what is primarily a mathematical beauty (as some might argue—also mistakenly but perhaps more easily—about an interpretation of Bach, or of Charlie Parker). Both composer and performer succeed when they convey not only their own most intricate certainties but also the mystery that surrounds them.

The common ground of atonality between the trans-African and trans-European borders their disparate approaches. Western music absolutized tonality, incarnated the musical soul into it; the 20th century's foray into atonality similarly absolutized the shadow side of that incarnation. The soul can remain at home in neither "place," though both have *their* place. The physical aspect of sound that suggests tonal systems (sound-as-wave, and the overtone series) reflects that of other physical systems, from stars to quanta; but atonality is a reminder of the *mutability*, the more general potential, the confusion of the boundaries and definitions of such living systems, such as those of biology, or of psychic archetypes. Further, the appropriation of *both* tonality and atonality for expressive purposes by a human artist is an image of the overarching and unifying presence of the transcendent in such systems (Hermes, recall, is lord of boundaries and roads, and regulator of their traffic).

Atonality has been more a part of the constantly worked soil of African music than, as in the West, some repressed shadow side. African and pan-African musics typically include moments of Western-style melody and harmony interspersed with casual asides lapsing into atonal vocalisms and noise, much as a speaker fills his talk with "uh" or "you know": mulch for the thinking process. Having been suppressed in the West under a tonal formalism for so long, much of this century's European atonal expressions have had the feel of one long "uh": no tension and release, no sense of purpose (as, for that matter, have some of the recent European "free" players Braxton's worked with, more on whom ahead).

Trans-African rushes into atonality have also been a liberation from that Western repression, but have carried the opposite extreme, that of a scream: all tension with no release, an intensity over the line from purpose into obsessive compulsion. Braxton's has been a tempering voice in this imbalance:

> This is an extended forum that fluctuates from a notated (controlled) to improvisational (open) sound environment—as a means to provide unique options for post-AACM exploration dynamics . . . a chain structure that contains seventeen different shifts of state in its conceptual and material design . . . deliberately designed as a non-personal structure that seeks to "forward" the affinity dictates of creative music in its most basic sense . . . no thematic or even primary material factors in this work—that can be used as a "cause" for creative involvement (or "centering"), nor does the work contain secondary sound references (or motifs) that provide an expanded sense of linear or vertical sound references . . . nine material components that intersect (as a sequential operative) with eight blocks of improvisation (directives) . . . a complex string of non-personal material and affinity objectives that gives fresh challenges for participation.[19]

The notated sections express three different musical approaches:

> 1) sound attacks and unison phrase groupings, 2) that plus isolated single phrase material 3) repeated phrase (and/or sound) component structures . . . This is a cold universe of sound that doesn't take one's feelings into account (that really doesn't care about your feelings!)[20]

Braxton emphasizes the impersonality—or transpersonality—of the work not only directly but in his clinical description of its structure and its "spirit of collectivism." The recorded performance of *62* is a tour through the atonal premises the composer has orchestrated, but the distinguishing feature of the listening experience is neither those orchestrations nor the improvisations on them. The latter aren't conceived as virtuosic displays or statements, and they aren't felt so. What is felt is the abovementioned trans-African intensity held in restraint, rationed out carefully until it bursts in some improvisational flurry, then gathered back into check. The actual sounds might have been scored and made in an academic concert of atonal music, but the feeling "between the sounds" here is what is unique. In the course of conscientiously ruffling and rumbling the piano freed from rhythmic grooves, harmony or melody, of making random-sounding noises, jagged intervallic leaps in unison and counterpoint, there emerges the *feeling* of a jazz musician, blowing not on chord changes or modes but on the given soundscape. The effect is of the atonal fragmentation being pulled together, made to sing and even swing in its own way. It is as though the spirit that survived the West's glaring, shadowless floodlight of rhythmless rationalism and predetermined formalism is now taking on its proportionately cold shadow side of nihilistic chaos, is seeing to it that the premises of anarchy yield, in the artists' hands, the dream rather than the nightmare.

60, "part chamber music, part sound environment,"[21] is similar in nature but lighter, more facile, more of a showcase for command and catharsis, with its whorling vortices of sound ridden like whitewater rapids by rafters avoiding tonal centers as rocks on which they might crash. This trans-African spin on atonality makes for a good segue into the trans-European connections Braxton made in his duo recordings.

It's interesting that Braxton's taste for Schönberg and "free jazz" innovators both started up in the army, through which he made his first trips out of America. His subsequent early success in Japan[22] and his gradual steady build-up of a European following place him squarely in the tradition of expatriate African American jazz artists who find more understanding and support abroad, especially in Japan and Europe, than at home. What's pertinent to the chronicling of his music is the visceral, give-and-take nature of his relationship with the European audience and its culture. He didn't go there at his leisure in an insulated bubble of "jazz" that would never pop; he rather went, still in his formative years and struggling to survive, after floundering in America, to engage in the process of forging his music from the world in which he found himself there. As such things go, the process had its ups and downs, but led to expressions and directions uniquely responsive to his situation and contemporaries *there*. Perhaps Braxton's openness to and affinity for the modern European composers and for Western conventions of scholarship and aesthetics is better understood as the natural human response to a hospitable culture than as pretentiousness or obsequity. Then too, where better to further the Africanization of the West in America than at its European cultural headwaters?

One result of this in the duo field is Braxton's *Composition No. 101*, for himself and pianist-composer Giorgio Gaslini. Released in 1981, it came at a time when Braxton's presence in the American jazz marketplace and media was declining, after a success in the polls and the recording scene that was remarkable, given the market-riskiness of his material.

Gaslini had explored the improvisational potential of twelve-tone music in his own work;[23] Braxton had mirrored that with his need to express and develop his own improvisational tradition in literate terms. This need is reflected both in his score for *101* and his notes on it (see Fig. 6.4).

101 is a work from what I see as the climactic prime of Braxton's *ouevre*, the "Golden Peak" period spanning *Compositions 95* and *105B* (full discussion of this in Chapter Eight). His notes on it capture something of the high, rich synthesis of fixed and open principles and practices it achieved:

> Composition No. 101 is a notated improvisational state that is midway between both notated and improvisational disciplines. My decision to move in this direction was based on the importance of establishing a discipline context from the expanded solutions that emerged in the post-Ayler continuum of the music. This is important so that the devices that emerged in that period can be forwarded into the future.[24]

Fig 6.4: "To enter the universe of . . . 101 is to work in a field of tall long trees (of glass) that established a prism of angled sheets (that gives us fresh insight into the world of music").[25] *Braxton is reaching for the kind of "oral painting" McKenna describes. "The nature of a given event formation of . . . 101*

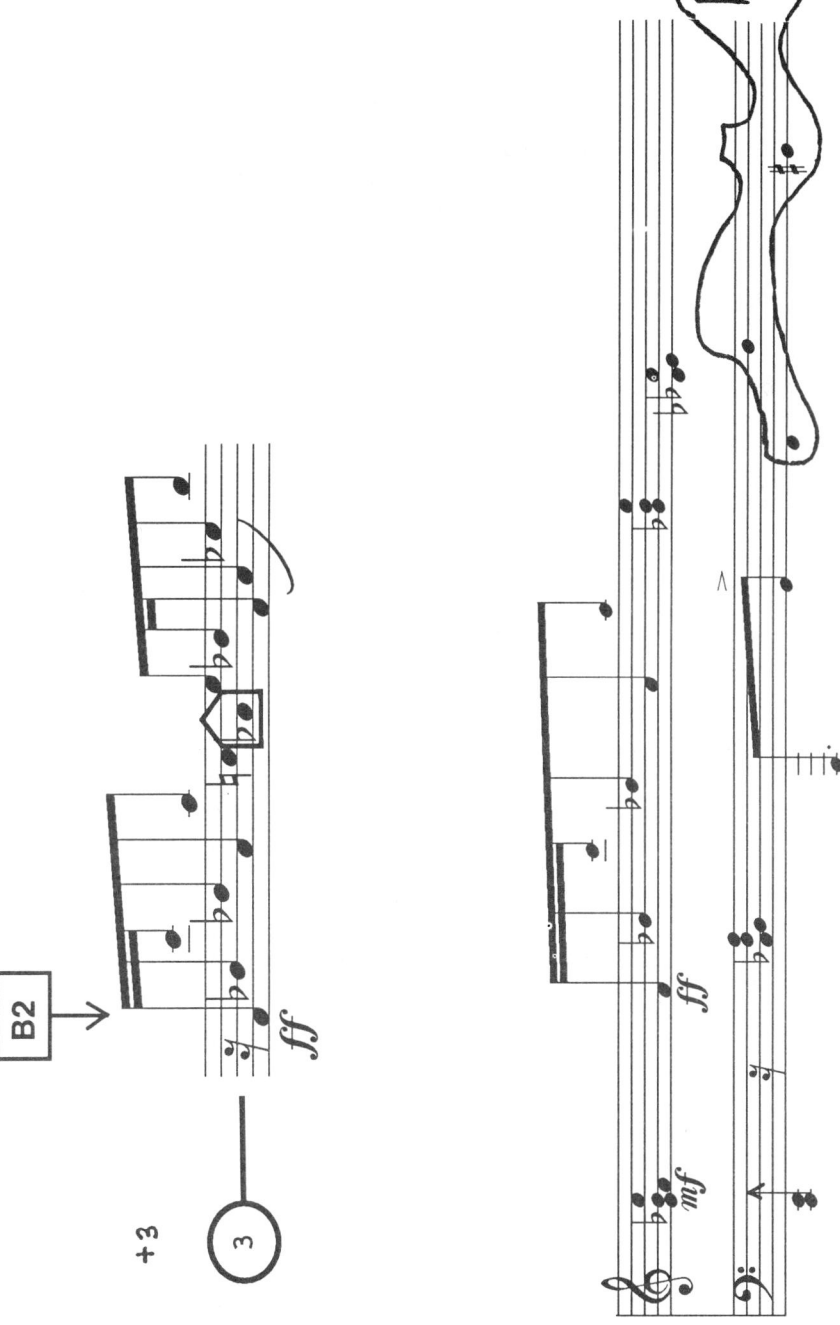

solidifies in the same sense of changing cloud formations that appear and reorganize in seconds—yet the actual vibrational character of the work is more rigid than mutable:"[26] *(that which looks most freshly spontaneous and original comes only by dint of both composer's and performer's real struggle with solid principles).*

In this example, typically, the "+3" refers to the number of beats the improvisation will span; the latter is qualified by the circled "3," which specifies something about timbre or pattern (via numbers listed in a legend at the front of the score). The "cloud" shape outlining the notes shows how such shapes (usually without notes inside) developed from standard notation.

This work seems as daunting as any, certainly any duo, in a hearing unaided by the score; in the hands of the conventionally trained music student, however, the latter is easily followed, and easily yields insight into the process of the music. It becomes clear that it is for musicians sophisticated in Western reading, improvising (through the jazz tradition), and theory; more importantly, it is for such musicians with a passion to explore and experiment with such skills. In that sense, it is esoteric and specialistic. But a listener who develops such traits in disciplines other than music may well be the one to respond to it as the musicians do: those in other arts, or sciences or letters, might find in it the music that will complement, inspire, or otherwise enhance his or her own work.

Here, as in much of his writing, his drive to explain/document reads like a cultural survival instinct: he seems often to be saying, "Get that oral tradition's peaks down, don't let them fade or be misappropriated."

This work, like most of Braxton's, was written for a specific person and performance; its success as what it purports to be—a synthesis of the post-Schönberg European and post-Coleman/Ayler/AACM musicultural continua—lies in the commitment of its principals to their own unique visions and paths. This is the key to understanding why Braxton's music has been difficult to many whom one would think might know better. Many are equally committed to their chosen paths—to classical music, to jazz—without necessarily being, *à la* Billings, their own Carver. Tepperman points out, in discussing the similar success of what might be called Braxton's similar synthesis with the post-Webern/Stockhausen continuum defined by guitarist Derek Bailey,[27] that altoist Eric Dolphy was the only figure in the Third Stream attempts to bring the classical and jazz traditions together who really brought it off. It was Dolphy's deep connection to the universals underlying both traditions that did it, and most other peoples' lack of same, adherence only to surface distinctions, that failed the synthesis. Many have stumbled on this aspect of Braxton's work as too abstract, detached from the emotive drive of the jazz tradition. But to him what may have begun as an abstraction has long since taken on its own concrete significance and feeling, as a result of commitment and work. An *idea*, such as "Third Stream"—or, for that matter, "jazz," "classical," or even "music"—is not enough to carry meaning and life through time; a soul must be given to it. This work and this duo is rich with such soul.

99, like *101*, is also within the Golden Peak period of the first Ritual and Ceremonial music. The former is a solo alto piece, part of which he recorded as a duo with classical pianist Marianne Schroeder. The dialogue of the recording includes both solo and duo statements by each; Schroeder's mercurial feel and the

duo music

elegance of her dynamic flow yet has a bite that suits this music; Braxton alternates between the same classical European technique and concept and his own postulations of post-Trane/Coleman/AACM statements. The implied affinity between both musicultural worlds is undeniable and effectively demonstrated. The recording is something of a flowering of Braxton's earlier work with the Robert Schumann String Quartet, Frederick Rzewski, and Gaslini.

Reviewer Bill Shoemaker wrote of Braxton's recent duo recording with his regular quartet's pianist Marilyn Crispell that

> Crispell's . . . gifts as a composer/improviser, combined with her bracing conservatory-correct technique, account for a command of Braxton's music that no other pianist has as consistently demonstrated. Her pace-setting performance on the non-stop *Duets Vancouver 1989* has a palpable energy. It's this quality that prompts occasional comparisons to Cecil Taylor; but, throughout this program, Crispell's motivic orientation and tactical use of clusters, crossovers, and percussive octaves are clearly her own.[28]

The words "woman of substance" come to mind when listening to Crispell: "substance" for her command, facility, responsiveness and force; "woman" for her poise, lack of abrasive edge even in her most boldly cacophonous and rhythmic moments, the refined sensibility she brings to the music. Yet, that said, there's nothing about her playing, nor about the music Braxton has given her to play, that unmistakably identifies her gender. That musical fact, coupled with Crispell's line of response to Lock's questions about her feminism,[29] say much about the nature of this dynamic in Braxton's musical universe.

Both Braxton (see Chapter Four) and Crispell express a sensitivity to women as subjects of male oppression in manifold ways . . . but both are also uneasy with feminism as a movement, in the same way Braxton has always been uneasy with organizations and movements predicated on blackness. Both rather seem to express the truth that "living well is the best revenge," and are impatient with the victim posture, are rather proud of themselves as free people with the power to make their own choices, take on the challenges that are there, and reap the rewards and accept the responsibilities. Both seem extremely connected with the power of the feminine and the African, but not in a defensive or uncomfortably self-conscious way. They display this mutual connection in their musical rapport: it's a musical meld between a white woman and a black man such as one can't picture between mutually exclusive chauvinists, however their mutually exclusive chauvinisms might mirror each other.

As Lock's passages (and many Jungian therapists/scholars) indicate, there is no clear line between feminine and masculine, any more than there is between black and white, when it comes to the personal level of specific men and women. Nevertheless, it is possible to speak qualifyingly of a balanced dynamic between the masculine and feminine as expressed in one person (or culture) of either gender, between two of the same gender, and between two of opposite genders. (Indeed, we may be getting to the heart of the duo here: the yin-and-yang of and in nature and culture). Thus, we can see examples of men or women (or cultures) who are unhealthily intense (compulsive-obsessive, aggressive, addictive, etc.) or soft (indecisive, spaced-out, addictive), and, in duo, who carry that imbalance into the relationship and act it out either in conflict or oppressive symbiosis. Examples abound in all art forms of the human toll taken by such imbalances; in American pop-jazz-entertainment journalism/culture, the examples of Lester Young (in the film *Round Midnight*) and Billie Holiday (in *Lady Sings the Blues*) have been made into stereotypes of them.

Braxton's own drama has been to come into his own in an intensely male and Afrocentric milieu, to wake up to the destructive imbalances of same, and to take the necessary corrective measures. In musical terms, these were simply his acceptance of European musiculture and of that potential of the music for silence, gentleness, ambiguity, and rest, as well as the constant eruption of fiery screams and streams of notes.

Both Crispell's and Braxton's comments about feminism and the feminine are from the point of view of people determined to find and express their identities ultimately in their humanity rather than their race or gender. They fully embrace both of the latter, but don't stop there; they go through them as aspects rather than seats of their beings.

Perhaps the most interesting indication of this in Braxton's music is how similar the three duos with pianists sound. Nothing in the compositions played with Abrams, Gaslini, or Crispell identify them unmistakably as the composer's collaboration with the "trans-African," "trans-European," or "feminine" (recall Green's quote in Chapter Two about Lester Young blurring the lines between black and white sounds). The variations in personal styles are subtly distinct, naturally, but not categorically disparate from each other in the way they sound.

Recall, again, Young's deep distinguishing traits: the ability to sustain a constant stream of ever-changing ideas, outlasting players who seemed at first to have more force. The stamina itself is a picture of a male energy suffused with female power; so is the intellect and imagination that doesn't dry out and lose itself in abstraction—though it may well lose a few less grounded listeners there. Braxton's music with and for Crispell, and her own fulfillment therein, are fruits of the same rich male-female affinity and balance shared so naturally by Holiday and Young (the real people, not the movie fictions), and by a precious few other gender dyads in the music to this day.

Before leaving the world of the piano in the duo context, we enter two new worlds: that where Braxton is present only as a composer, not a player; and that of his "Ritual and Ceremonial" compositions.

Braxton's work throughout the 1970s might be seen as the "scientific" period of his music. It was then he established himself as one who was serious about building and codifying a new musical vocabulary and paradigm from the ground up. His recorded work covered everything from traditional jazz covers to all combinations from soloists to large ensembles performing his compositions and spontaneous improvisations. His work was about building a musical vocabulary, a compositional approach that embraced, synthesized, and personalized the concepts coming from every variation of human cultural consciousness. This process was more concerned with collecting, building, rebuilding, and arranging tools—sounds, rhythmic patterns, structures, isolated musical problems, and solutions—than it was with identifying and realizing the grand truths they could express. Not that each piece of music didn't have its own new life—Braxton is not an étudist—but for the most part it was a life sufficient unto itself, a musical universe in an aggregate of them, the aggregate yet to reach the critical mass leading to congregation.

Composition 95, written in 1980, marks the beginning of the Ritual and Ceremonial compositions, which we might think of as the first blossoms of the plant that began in seed with Braxton's first notated work, for solo piano, and with the first of his own sonic sketches on the solo alto. These would find their full blooms through the multimedia, interdisciplinary works for large ensembles and visuals, or dancers, or theater artists, and then through opera, where his mature focus has come to rest.

The extramusical particulars of this work—its visual aspects, and the metamusical truths they're meant to express and convey—are as composed as the sounds themselves. It was written for two performers whose gender, race, and other visible aspects are shrouded in a hooded robe. Each of the two figures are to enter the sacred space of the stage while playing a melodica (in the recording mix, their sounds come from opposite "directions"); they meet in the middle at the two pianos. They play the work, then leave as they came on, the melodicas fading into silence.

I offer the following from Braxton's Composition Notes with observations meant to amplify what they're expressing.

> The reality of Composition No. 95 is constructed to utilize the dynamics of both music and theatre and the meta-reality dynamics of this work have been constructed from spiritual intentions . . . By the terms ritual and ceremonial music, I am saying that the meta-reality dynamics of Composition No. 95 were conceived with extra-vibrational intentions—having to do with my belief that the challenge of transformational creativity in this time cycle must involve "postulation" as related to both world culture and its extended "all spiritual" dictates, as well as what those dictates signify about participation.[30]

Many musicians, especially improvisers, feel it presumptuous to define or explain—to postulate—any intent behind the making of their music. The feeling is often "let the music speak for itself and do its own work, and leave its 'meaning' up to the individual listener." Braxton has no qualms about such defining or explaining; indeed, he feels it his responsibility to, in a cultural milieu notorious for missing or misappropriating the point of, the music.

> Composition No. 95 is a vehicle for understanding that the *vibrational and physical universe particulars of a given focus are changing and as such, the spirit should be made aware and prepared.* I have written this work because of my belief about the seriousness of "change cycles" and what this phenomenon poses for living (and time/space). Composition No. 95 is composed as a statement about this phenomenon and the performing of this work is ritual because the seriousness of its meta-significance (purpose) is about spiritual

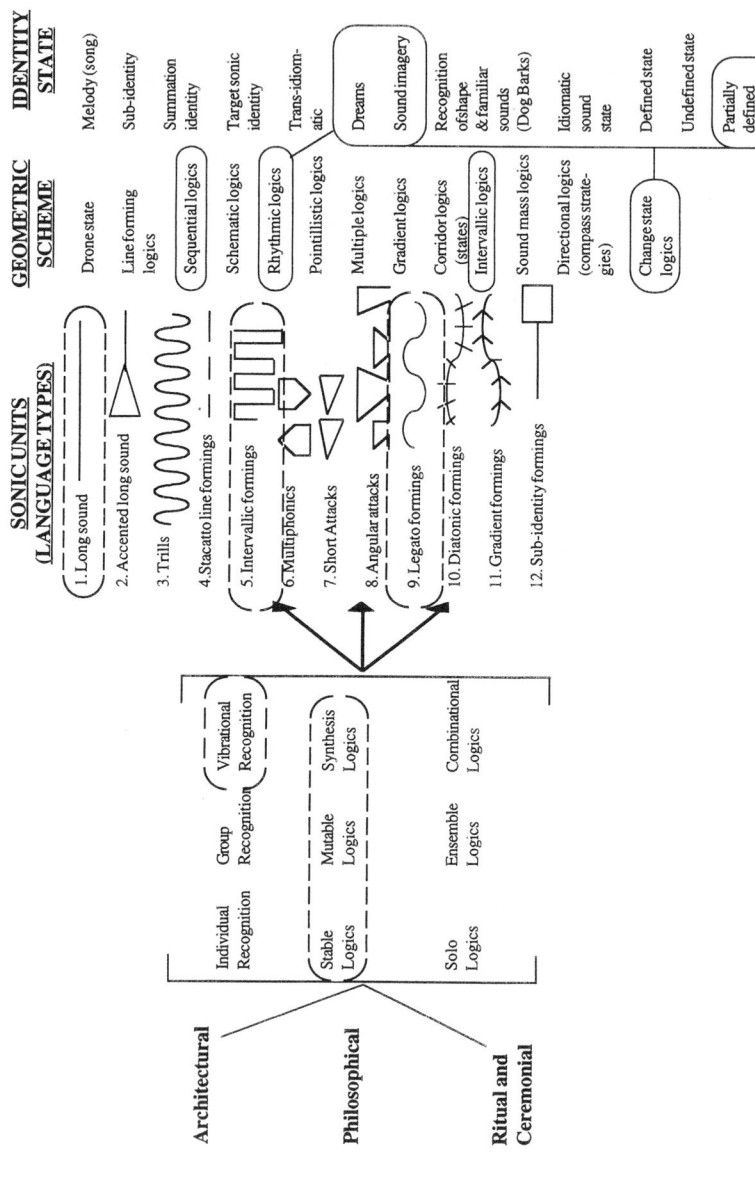

Fig. 6.5: 136 (duet). This piece suggests no lines connecting most elements because of the floating feel of both instruments (flute and piano) and the dynamic of these particular players (Braxton and Crispell)—until the very end (also right of page), when the soprano sax comes in, and the concepts get harder along with the sound.

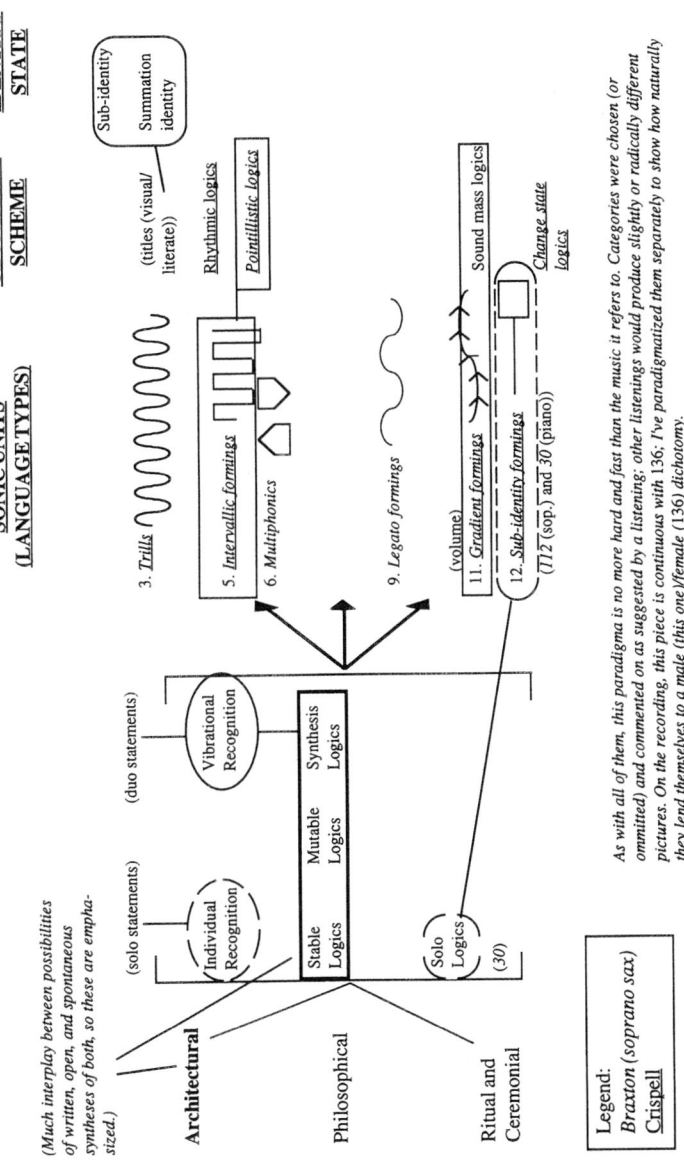

Fig. 6.6: 140 (112 + 30)

matters. This work is designed to be performed for any context that involves vibrational and/or physical universe change, as that change concerns spiritual matters—for instance, DOCUMENTATION (i.e., the rise and fall of a given culture), WARNING (of an impending change), CELEBRATION (of a given focus or postulation), ACKNOWLEDGEMENT (i.e., of the change of the season, etc.). My original intention when composing this work was that I sensed and felt that the next immediate cycle in social reality promises to be extremely difficult [this was written when Reagan succeeded Carter as U.S. president; more broadly, it preceded the collapse of the U.S.S.R.; most broadly, it is in the shadow of the pre-Millennial period, mythically imagined as chaotic and destructive, but ultimately positive—M. H.]—*and there is danger in the air* for all people and forces concerned about humanity and positive participation. Composition No. 95 is composed as a vehicle to alert the spirit about serious change . . . Composition No. 95 is my first attempt towards solidifying a ritual and sacred music.[31]

After laboring intensively with Braxton's language for some three years now, I've found it to be the doggedly persistent language of a man dialoguing with his own "cloud of unknowing," to borrow from the medieval Christian mystic. I found my own attempts to understand it rationally to be my own blind forays into my own such cloud. What couldn't be grasped and decoded in a single straight reading, however, gradually worked on the psyche to produce its own light. What was initially a reading experience swallowed in chaos and mystifying convolution is now a point of entry to a private inner life with a strong connection to the outer consensus reality. This particular passage reads loud and clear to me, then, at this point, as the expression of an artist whose own *inner* world has reached a critical transformational point—an artist whose power is such that such an inner transformation is properly perceived as a change in the *outer*—social, cultural, and physical—universe, at least potentially, because, as such an artist, Braxton has an inner life that finds its fulfillment not in the secrets of its own privacy, or in a narrow personal/familial realm, but in the fullest, most universally public expression. As such an artist, his own subjective secrets, idiosyncrasies of language and musical style—"eccentricities"—are offered as those of the universe itself, as validations of those of each of us. Braxton's speech and music, once yielded to with the same faith patience, devotion, and conscientiousness that went into them, yield the same spiritual and creative fruits in reader/listener, just as they are intended to do, by demanding that much. They express and bring about what they mean to in the same measure as is brought to them.

This isn't to say that this one composition serves all such enlightenment up on a single plate. The work is more significant as the first of many much more developed approaches to such works than it is as a masterpiece towering over a more mundane field.

Braxton's musical notations and the improvisations they inspire in duo take on the highest subtleties of the most sophisticated concepts and practices of European, American, and African American art musics; the dynamics of culture,

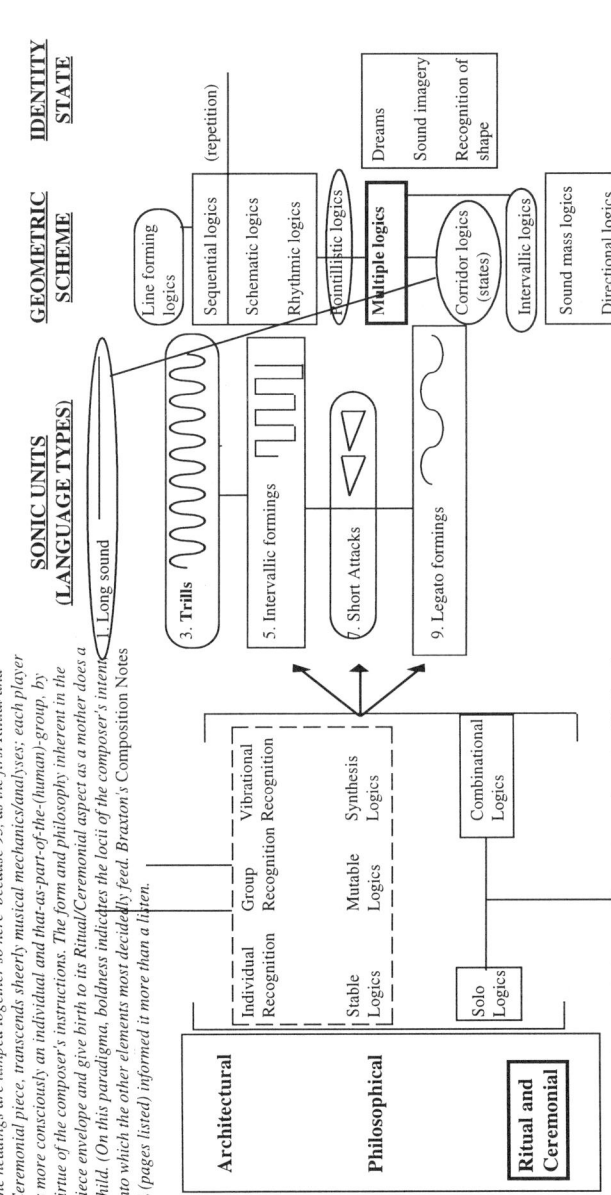

Fig. 6.7: 95—the first of the "Golden Peak" pieces, in which Braxton's composer's voice came into its own in the culmination of so-called jazz/classical syntheses he'd worked with for a decade and a half. This first Ritual and Ceremonial piece (performed by Ursula Oppens and Frederck Rzewski) is a precursor to later works that would incorporate mythological imagery through theatrics, narratives, and visuals.

race, and gender are addressed consciously as a part, rather than ignored as a violation, of the art (through the "Philosophical" and "Ritual and Ceremonial" aspects of his paradigm). These musical and metamusical forces—charted in their Philosophical aspect in Chapter Four, through the *Tri-Axium Writings*—appear quite sweepingly and starkly in the duets with piano: the trans-African stream with Abrams, the European with Gaslini and Rzewski, and the American and feminine/transformational with Oppens and Crispell.

Without Notation

The three streams (trans-African, trans-European, and co-gender) through which these examples of notated works flow also flow through several duo and trio recordings of spontaneous and open improvisations.

Note that this is the first mention of such "free" music; the solo work (and the duo work examined so far), while exploratory and experimental and improvisational, has also been structured. Braxton, of course, has played in open and spontaneous sessions from early on and was seen as one of the major forces in "free" music—but most of his recordings are of compositions. The ones that aren't provide a glimpse into the process that inspires and suggests his compositions, and informs his composing processes and criteria.

With Percussion

[From occult definition of] **drum**: *1. call to war: a. attribute of Mars . . . b. the "instrument of honor": loss of a drum in battle = loss of regimental colors . . . 2. communication: a. call for help; b. vehicle for the Word and Tradition; c. warning . . . 3. dispenser of evil spirits: from of old the most sacred and magical instrument; 4. according to its shape: a. the form of an hour-glass: Inversion and relation between two worlds; b. round: the image of the world, and the feminine: with the sticks as phalloi: androgyne . . . 5. according to its sound: masculine; 6. induces ecstasy: for religious or fertility purposes, since it is related: a. to the Creative Word; b. to thunder as a precursor for fertilizing rain.*

The two duo recordings with drummer Max Roach embody the trans-African stream and move us from duets between mono- and polyphonic instruments into those between horn and percussion. No keyboards impose harmonic fields; no bass lines insist upon tonal centers; the African and European extremes of the jazz tradition face each other on a field uncluttered by middlemen.

The most obvious and well-known recording comprising precedents devoted to this combination is perhaps that of the Rashied Ali/John Coltrane duets.[32] The unrelenting rhythmic intensity of that 1967 recording was nonetheless balanced by the exceptional inventive lyricism and mercurial finesse of both artists; Braxton and Roach are rather free to relent, to explore other climes. The blues, fast bop, the ballad, and standard swing feels are all covered here, though free of any imposed structures. The payoff for a bop-schooled master like Roach is clearly the opportunity to let his mind wander and associate freely in a familiar

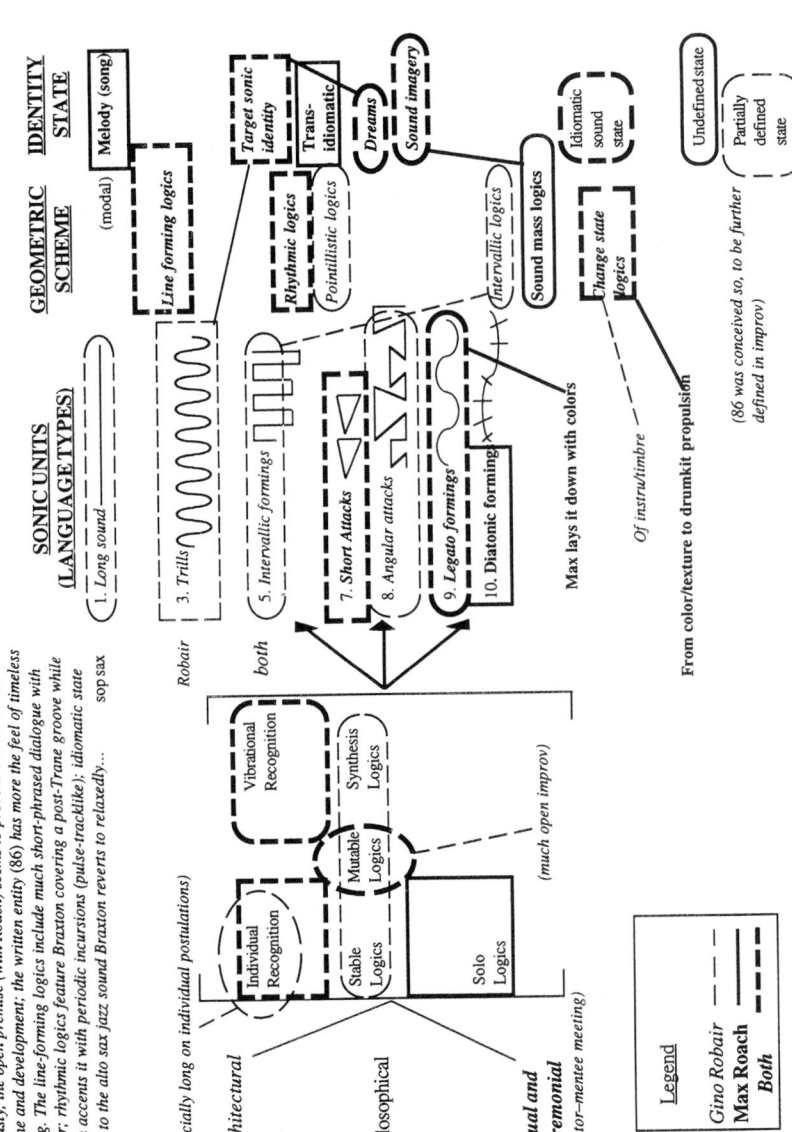

Fig. 6.8: First 5–10 minutes of *One in Two* (with Max Roach) and 86 (with Gino Robair)

language set free from its usual contexts. Braxton's contribution is blessed with the confirmation of the traditional roots he claims (often against the resistance of those who don't see them). Further, Roach gets to explore a sound-world his own peer/mentor Charlie Parker eyed longingly but never got to: rhythmic texturings such as one finds in the music of Varèse, whom Bird admired and wanted to study with. Roach's expansion from the drum kit into bells and other percussion, while it has become standard practice for post-bop percussionists, is in his hands another of the tangible links between tradition and innovation so important to Braxton.

The linkage is reversed in the only other horn/percussion duo recording, with Gino Robair. Here, Braxton is the elder whose innovations have become validated, codified, assimilated over time; Robair is the younger aspirant. The equal access to all musical aspects and roles, the kaleidoscopic and relaxed relationship between improvisation and composition, the pastiche nature of each piece are all in place as standard practice. The Braxtonian egalitarian democracy extends even to the teacher-student (which Robair literally was, at Mills College) relationship, through an equal mix of Braxton's and Robair's pieces (this compositional mix, incidentally, is standard practice on most of Braxton's duo recordings). The *Tri-Axium* principle's integrity holds in this past-present-future thrust of the recorded horn-percussion duos.

With Guitar

That ubiquitous dialectic finds yet another expression in the duo recordings with British guitarist Derek Bailey. Whether one ascribes the "past" tag to African oral roots and the "present" to European literate fruits, or the past to the Western classical approach and the present to African American spins on it, the "future" postulated by these duos is a rich tangle of both that speaks volumes about their relationship. A scan of the literature on them will suggest further comments.

Martin Davidson observed in his liner notes to *Braxton & Bailey: Live at Wigmore* that new global communication was de-provincializing, thus universalizing, music, offering it transcendence from ethnic and nationalistic identities. He saw historical significance in the recording's musical conversation between artists making serious statements in, respectively, the African American milieu as voiced most recently by Ornette Coleman and Albert Ayler, and the Western vocabulary forged by Anton von Webern and John Cage (as distinct from, incidentally, Gaslini's Schönbergian language). Another reviewer[33] likened the sound of this duo to that of Bessie Smith with guitarist Eddie Lang, Braxton and Smith being the earthy, grounding force and Bailey and Lang functioning more mercurially and on the edge.

Tepperman's *Coda* review, mentioned above, is developed a bit further along these lines. He evokes the figure of Eric Dolphy as one who made some of the first moves to unite the jazz and classical traditions, in his work in the Third Stream movement of his time, and sees Braxton as carrying that start well on its way. He defines the African American approach to improvisation with words such as "driven," "linear," "emotive"; he also invokes Webern in describing Bailey's music as an exploration of pitches, timbres, intervals, and timing, of moments strung together. Tepperman delighted in the growth of the music's spirit over the course of the recording. What he wrote resonates with Braxton's own words about one of his compositions having to do with the musicians' occupying the same space without killing each other:

> There is something inexplicably beautiful about listening to these three performances in chronological order (not as they are on the disc), as if you were watching a child grow, as bit by bit the pair learn more of each other's arts and bend to each other. In "Excerpt from Rehearsal," at one end, you find intense pressure, almost hostility as if each man felt an irrepressible urge to overtake and dominate the other. The other end of the continuum . . . merges many passages of delicately interwoven but strongly alive beauty.[34]

Litweiler's 1975 review of *Duo* is more critical of the chemistry that occurs between the two:

> Occasionally a true sense of duet emerges, the ringing or harp-like or muted plucked sounds project just the right feeling and momentum. But Braxton, in free space, has always proven difficult to work with, and on the basis of this concert Bailey may be an equally problematic performer.
> Bailey's playing tends toward stasis, and whenever Braxton breaks into a guitar solo to accompany, Bailey is often too ready to assume a background role, forcing Anthony to assume leadership. Thus the collection is a series of Braxton solos, about equally long, on all his woodwinds . . . Late in the first set, Bailey directs a sonorically imaginative sequence, followed by a well-taken abstract "classical music" duet, but most of this LP has leader Braxton echoing himself, Roscoe Mitchell and Joseph Jarman. The second set is far more successful. The flute, and the structured clarinet sequences work, Braxton's wide alto clarinet (?) leaps are striking, and an alto sax solo achieves an extended organization and variety of content that becomes the high point of the two records. The fusion of plaintive sounds and fierce leaps on clarinet is almost as rewarding and, to me, a more remarkable achievement.[35]

What stands out in all this is the tangling of roles traditionally played between Africa and Europe. In America, the Western influence has provided the linear, progressive framework, and Africa the sense of time as cycling stasis in rhythm, of timbres and textures and pitches strung together in spontaneous moments. Especially through Braxton's time and place and person (his role in the AACM in the 1960s), those traits had blossomed into freedom from their Western frameworks; contrary to Tepperman's descriptors "emotive" and "driven," Braxton's detractors often decried his music as cold, clinical, static—the charge leveled so often against modern European art music. Yet it's true that in these duets Braxton is covering what structure there is ("areas of improvisation," broadly and vaguely defined—the compromise between Bailey, who didn't want to play anything notated, and Braxton, who didn't want to play completely spontaneously), and has the less static, more linear and emotionally expressive voice. The tension noted above, in the use of atonality in improvisation with Abrams, is in full force and stark contrast here.

This duo in fact illustrates the character of the meeting between the African American innovators of the 1960s working in Europe and their European counterparts. The former came with a consciously Afrocentric energy and approach; the latter responded to that as to an oasis on the desert their own Western culture had become. The music they made, and made into a movement that thrives today—on labels such as FMP, Incus, Intakt, hat Art, hat Hut, and others—eschewed predetermined structure entirely, and doggedly mined the *realmusik* potential of the farthest extensions of sound-making techniques and trance-inducing repetition. As they made and mined the music so, the trans-African thrust brought out more of the Western elements it had taken on in America—harmony and melody, notation, control of as much as abandonment to more and more of the spirit—to then return to America with something much more realized as an art music than as an experimental music. Braxton's experience has been a prime example of this, but others of his peers (e.g., Leroy Jenkins and Julius Hemphill) have had similar experiences, coming to function in the United States as composers getting grants and commissions, writing operas and chamber music, bringing improvisation and other traits of their idiom into the mainstream of American culture.

A vital exchange took place in this move that was initially an economic exile. The African Americans had an energy and approach that the Europeans needed unalloyed; the Europeans gave them a forum. European culture was the source of the Western elements the African Americans had been working with in America, was more vitally and distinctly Western than its American branch. "The West" in Europe not only proved more responsive and responsible to the African American aesthetic at Braxton's point, it also proved to be a point of entry into its American incarnation in the seats of culture not granted earlier African American music.

Getting back to the Lange review of *Trio & Duet*, another stream might be added to the three just examined, from Braxton's collaborations with electronic musicians, most notably synthesist Richard Teitelbaum: the electronic high-tech, space-age, computer culture electronic music evokes.

Since the early days of the sounds developed by electronic composers, synthesizers have been mainstreamed into pop and New Age musicultures. Their use in what Braxton would call creative music remains undeveloped relative to acoustic sound-makers, but Braxton, with Sun Ra before him, is definitely one of the artists suggesting and starting that development. What Lange wrote of Teitelbaum in the trio context applies equally to the *Open Aspects* duos: "He can play chords which reinforce the harmonic basis for soloists, he can play percussive rhythmic patterns, he can add unusual timbral effects to the density of the sound collage." Whereas Sun Ra's theatrical and lyrical imagery might be said to have brought an African human cast to the white Western technology of space travel, Braxton's background in electronic engineering and subsequent schemata and notations for his music rather personalizes the electronic age as it might be confronted on the earth. His alto voice is as undaunted by the coldness and impersonality as it is underwhelmed by the charm many encounter in that confrontation. He rather brings a warmth and vitality to the table, and a comfort with, if you will, carbon-based feelings of inadequacy. His use of the synthesizer on the CD *Eugene (1989)* shows the electronic voice's assimilation into his musical vision over time (more details on that in Chapter Nine). Computer and electronic technology is only recently becoming a major factor in Braxton's music—most tellingly, now that he has access to or can afford the necessary equipment, on a major campus, and through a regular salary. In sum, the synthesizer has begun to function in Braxton's hands and circles as a fulfillment of the promise of earlier strategies such as shoveling coal and manipulating balloons (for microphones to tape their sounds).

These duo recordings (and those of other combinations, mostly the Company recordings) of open improvisations showcase an important aspect of Braxton's composing processes. As the solo alto music served to sketch his ideas, these more unstructured collective events serve to suggest them. A musical architecture arises spontaneously from the subconscious interactive mix between players; he selectively transcribes and develops its details; the improvisational ideas they trigger are also written out into pieces. True to his conscious synthesis and the larger spirit of the African American tradition, and unlike many of his European or "jazz" peers, Braxton has never been satisfied with a music that polarizes improvisation and notation, subsumes one in the other, or embraces only one or the other. The whole music is in the mix of the two constantly informing and interacting with each other. In combinations beyond the solo, the interchange of voices and visions can start to happen, and to feed the solitary musicmaking.

With Another Horn

[From occult definition of] **horn**: *1. the difficulties with the symbolism of the word "horn" mainly arise from the fact that the horns of animals and the musical instrument are the same word, and of the same origin . . . 2. power, strength, fertility: A. related to all the Sun (and Earth or River)-gods: a. in Paleolithic paintings; b. on the altars . . . to represent the strength of the Bull-god Yahweh . . . B. moon-goddesses: a. related to Venus: at the Venalia in Cyprus heifers with spreading horns, covered with gold, were sacrificed . . . as "cornuta" she was especially revered in Egypt falling in with Isis-Hathor-Io and all the Moon and Sea-goddesses . . . connected with female humidity through the Moon . . . the moon-horns of Isis shot forth gleams of light . . . a reference to the phallus . . . 4. salvation, immortality . . . 5. protection, asylum . . . [in folklore, often a symbol of both fertility/potency and cuckoldry, including the madness and rage caused by the latter, associated with the cries of a rutting animal.]*

The two-horn duos serve well this chapter's wrap, for their place in the jazz tradition and in its newest spins. Like the solo alto concept, a recording of two unaccompanied horns, out of the various duos possible, was another concept taken seriously and developed in the AACM. Duets between single-line winds are a staple in Western conservatories, defining the art of counterpoint from the beginnings of polyphony. Their place in the jazz tradition is a singularly exciting one: the (accompanied, except in breaks) duos, both cooperative and competitive (actually, both at once) between virtuosi on the same kind of instrument. Virtually every other duo combination expresses more of an anchor/flyer dynamic. Two horns, especially of the same kind, make for a most immediate synergy and dialogue. Recall King Oliver and Louis Armstrong, Coleman Hawkins and Lester Young, Dizzy Gillespie and Charlie Parker, Gerry Mulligan and Paul Desmond, Warne Marsh and Lee Konitz, John Coltrane and Pharoah Sanders, Don and Albert Ayler, Steve Lacy and Steve Potts, Ornette Coleman and Don Cherry—and Anthony Braxton and Kenny Wheeler, or George Lewis, or Roscoe Mitchell, or Evan Parker, or, more recently, Andrew Voigt.

In the case of the Braxton unaccompanied duos, in the terms outlined so far, the interest and excitement lies in these two most Western voices taken over to speak the most African messages. Again, we can see some of the same broad streams. Parker and Mitchell are the trans-European and trans-African, respectively, enjoyed between peers; Voigt and Lewis represent the same two, only with the more American cast of a new generation, and with more of the mentor-student than the peer-peer dynamic.

Elements of Surprise, with trombonist George Lewis, is a particularly successful record on several levels: it showcases the trombone, an instrument with which Braxton has demonstrated a unique affinity; its playlist works exceptionally well as a unit; and the Lewis/Braxton synergy is exceptionally rich.

The modern trombone probably has the most direct connection to the ancient roots of Western instruments. Its slide is a pre-valve invention, allowing it a natural access, like the voice, to the whole continuum of pitch between octaves. Its range is wide, spanning a middle ground with frequencies close to those of the human voice: it can rip up to the cry of an elephant or down to the growl of a lion, or it can speak with the calm, measured tone of a man or woman. It was the first instrument allowed into the church with singing voices in Medieval times.

In the jazz tradition, it has played a role closer to the rhythm section than other horns, both because of its low register and its relative lack of facility. It has moved easily from associations with the comic and vulgar to the smooth-as-silk sublime. The scope and sound of this brass horn cover territory Braxton got to by extending his technique on his reeds, and by extending himself to the whole range of reeds. Braxton's work with Lewis and, later, Ray Anderson, in both duo and quartet contexts, worked that relatively underworked ground as thoroughly as he and others have worked the more common sax/sax and sax/trumpet veins.

Lewis has a combination of power, energy, humor, and finesse on his instrument that sees and raises Braxton's own. We hear him first on Braxton's *Composition 64*, a showcase for his wide-ranging virtuosity and invention. Braxton writes of *64* that it was

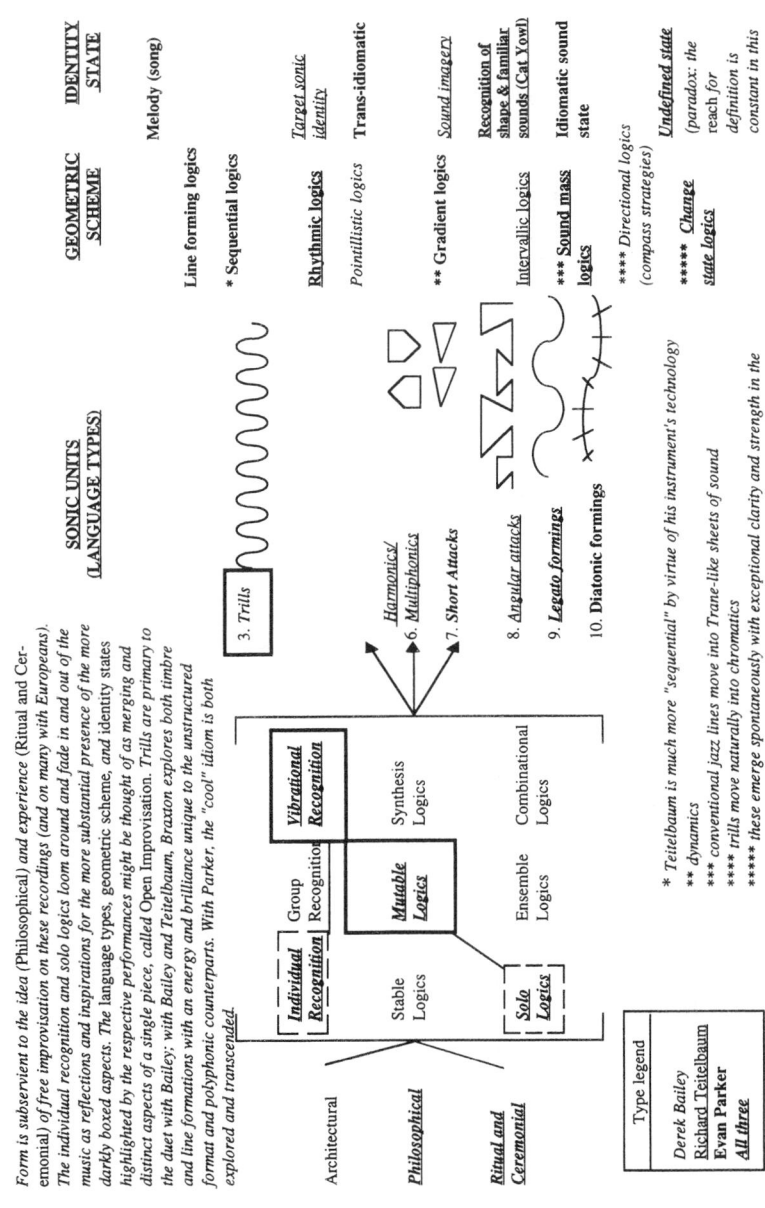

Fig. 6.9: A comparison of three open improvisations (one each with Derek Bailey/guitar, Richard Teitelbaum/synth, Evan Parker/alto sax).

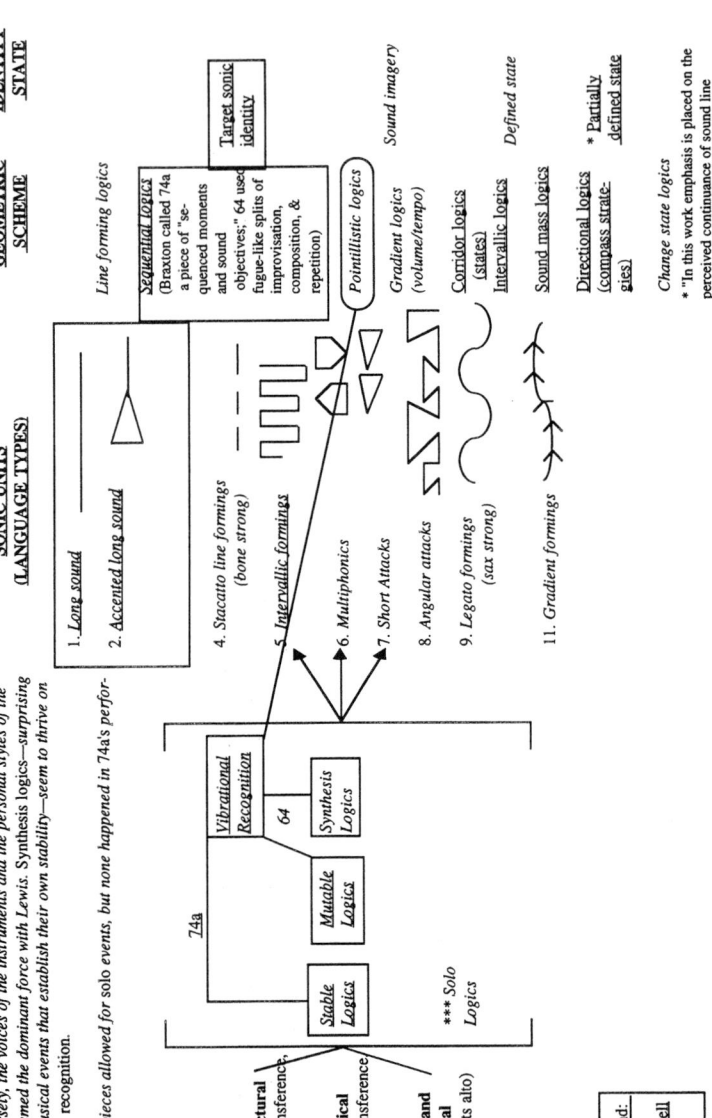

Fig. 6.10: Comparison of duets with George Lewis (64) and Roscoe Mitchell (74a)

> constructed as a platform for language music investigation . . . to emphasize repeating long sound (lines) sounds . . . In the first context of this approach long repeating sound lines are used as a phrase generating shape that pushes the music (invention) into the open space of the music (interpretation) . . . Four-note sound line patterns are . . . a generating device that establishes focus for improvisation.[36]

At times one plays long sounds while the other dances and skitters over them like beads of water and oil on a griddle; at others both trade attacks on the same long sound to get a phase-shifting rhythm going, then make lines from that; there's a slow unison section and several fleeter phrases written for the players to target (1) as both release after the tension of a long tone and tension after the unchecked release of open improvisation, and (2) as an entry point into a new sort of improvisation.

The piece has seven sections, each generating a slightly different kind of improvisation; the solo virtuosity of each radiates from conservatory-correct to Africreative, and the duetting done is a splashing needlework of "bone and alto color. In a nod to "the sonata form . . . dear to all of our hearts," the last section echoes the first.

The duo treats Charlie Parker's *Ornithology* in much the same way, turning it inside out texturally, rhythmically, and harmonically during the improvisations to flap in their strong wind. Positioned as it is between *64* and *65*, the duo's treatment of it demonstrates the common ground between the bebop conventions and Braxton's. *65* is a brief, evocative statement conceived for extended improvisation, but is played only as written here, serving as an encore (you can hear Braxton say to Lewis "just the piece," and Lewis answer in this live recording). Like *64*, it is written to mine the duo context:

> It is important that the uniqueness of duo interaction is carried forward into the next cycle of the music. The discipline challenge of improvisation in the future will involve the widest possible viewpoints about sounds and images . . . This is a platform for two creative instrumentalists to explore the moment and its secrets.

Braxton alludes to saxophonist-composer Benny Golson's approach to musical structure—"a structure that changes personality in the course of its composite form (even though it doesn't always seem apparent on the surface)"—as a model for that of *65*. The basic thrust of this work is cast as a medium pulse structure that is "brittle" in character and design. Clipped rapid phrases are common in this terrain and so is the use of call and response phrase constructions. The pulse is plastic, and the dialogue is more parallel than interactive. Lewis plays with a Harmon mute that brings the brass of the trombone sound closer to the throaty growl of the reed. Braxton dedicated the piece to trombonist Ray Anderson, who often played the same role (and music) as Lewis, in a distinctly different voice (more on that in Chapter Eight).

Like much of Braxton's work, especially for duo and trio, *65* is not intended—as is, for example, *64* and many other pieces—to grip, captivate, and excite. It is lighter and more relaxed than that, part of a "creative salon" or chamber music, something of pleasure for both players and listeners to include in an evening's typical setting without intruding unduly. This is another aspect of his music that takes it out of the conventional, current realms of "sensational entertainment" and "profound art" as spectated by passives, and puts it closer, in Western tradition, to the medieval and Renaissance making of such music in both court and home, a tradition that has evolved around pianos and guitars, bowed strings and voices in European and American homes.

Fig. 6.11: From 74A, *written for a Mitchell-Braxton duo. The three dotted peaks represent a passing back and forth of the held long tone.*

The duets with Roscoe Mitchell swing fully into that spirit. Of all of Braxton's duo "twins," Mitchell is perhaps the most "identical." Where others might run through Braxton's material like frisking horses, this duo meanders like a quiet brook fed by two sources but making them one in it. The fire of clash and brinksmanship with Lewis, Voigt, Bailey (and Evan Parker—see Fig. 6.9), Roach, and Abrams—a dynamic informed by differences in generation, instrument, race/culture—gives way to the intimate introspection of brothers pondering over a chess game. As he does only in his duets with Crispell, Braxton plays a lot of flute here—the one of his many instruments identified as specifically feminine in occult lore, and the one he claims is most challenging for him—to fine effect. The methodical steps away from common jazz and classical ground of his duets with Holland, Wilson, and Chick Corea[37] give way to direct leaps into "outside" material (such as high, chirping overtone play). Still, in contrast to the duets with Parker (and, somewhat less so, Steve Lacy, also on Company recordings) even the most "out" of these with Mitchell sit in the background in a way the others don't. Of all his duet recordings, this early one (logically enough) has the feel of his early trio and quartet recordings with fellow AACM pioneers: exploration by scouts who have learned to work together comfortably.

In fact, Braxton doesn't have any one partner with whom he has made a famous duo (as those mentioned above to open this discussion of the two-horn duos). These widely varying statements within this broad range haven't been a central focus of his career in that way, in the way both his quartet and large-ensemble work have been. Duos and trios both have generally functioned more as fertile exploratory ground for, or isolated slivers of, the quartet and large-ensemble music, which, like the solo music, has been more controlled by and more imbued with Braxton's personality, presence, and vision.

duo music

Like Ellington, Mingus, and other composers, Braxton the composer wrote much of his duo music with specific artists in mind. Of those, all but Gaslini, Rzewski, and Oppens were artists he had a chance to work with on an ongoing, if sporadic, basis. Curiously and significantly, *101* for Gaslini and *95* for Rzewski and Oppens stand as compositional culminations of the principles he had worked with over the years in his pieces for all combinations from solo to quartet.

[From occult definition of] **Gemini***: A. general: 1. the 3rd sign of the Zodiac . . . 2. represented: a. two lovers, a man and a woman; the sign is related to the perfect Hermaphrodite . . . c. the hour-glass: perpetual inversion . . . B. 3. all twins: celestial/mortal; black/white, etc.; 4. any harmonious ambiguity, any apparent paradox . . .*

[From occult definition of] **hermaphrodite***: 1. creation: a. the God of Creation, linked with the Gemini-type . . . c. Adam before the feminine side (Eve) was taken out of him . . . 2. integration: the union of opposites, connection with the number two applied to humans . . .*

[The Egyptian god] Thoth is predecessor to the European gods Hermes (Greece) and Mercury (Rome); and to the African gods Esu (Yoruba) and Legba (Fon), the last of whom crossed the Atlantic in the slave ships and survives as Papa Legba in Haitian voodoo mythology and as Papa La Bas in the hoodoo mythology of the United States. Thoth is credited with the invention of magic, alchemy, writing and mathematics; as Hermes Trismegistus he played a vital role in the European Renaissance . . . as Mercury he is astrological ruler of Gemini, birthsign of both Sun Ra and Braxton.

Graham Lock

Anything we can talk about we can also talk about and prove its opposite— as a Gemini you must be aware of that!

Anthony Braxton (to Lock)

It is no surprise that Braxton would be led to develop such a keen definition of the duo. The creative self-*mythos* he draws on includes his astrological sign of Gemini, which is that of the twins. This sign images one of his persona's major motifs, that of the synthesist who can accept, encompass, and mediate polar opposites others experience as impossible conflict or schizophrenia.

Braxton's instincts led him to develop his solo music, in part, so as to have something original and coherent to say in collective situations. The duo is the first of such, a conversation of equals, a context in which self-sufficiency must learn to yield to interdependency, in which issues of power and dynamics of dominance and submission must be faced and resolved to mutual satisfaction. Duos define poles, conduct conversations, more than any larger combinations.

Braxton has shown himself to be hungry for the broadest variety of metamusical trysts (between tradition and innovation, Europe and Africa, male and female, oral and literate, old and young—between, simply, two equal but uniquely original voices) made possible by musical common ground. This balanced, egalitarian modus operandi on duo recordings extends to the compositional as well as the instrumental duties: he typically splits the bill with his own and his partners' charts. The timeliness and value of such resolutions to the wars between the races, sexes, cultures, and generations—between each member, most broadly, of a global community of clashing individualists—is obvious.

The duo context is a logical one to use to speak to an aspect of Braxton some might see as pretentious and forced: his loose, vague connections of his musical paradigm with those of physics, computer science, mathematics, or systems analysis. If such affinities *were* forced—if he consciously made his music from rational constructs mirroring those others—they *would* be pretentious. But the creative tolerance of dichotomies that lies at the heart of much of postmodern thought, in the urgrund common to a host of specialisms, are simply there for anyone to see in Braxton's music-seen-as-successful. The way he's contrasted sound with silence; reduced, ordered, and mastered sounds down to their most elemental nuances; strung them together into sentences of music; strung these sentences into paragraphs and stories, monologues, dialogues, and collective statements; interwoven, inter-embedded, and interlocked many such statements into "systems of chaos" with discernible intrareflective and transcendent organization—all this does mirror, and analogize, the amazing complexity computer technology has woven from the simplest binary system, and the startling finds of the new science of "chaos."

Less rational, more metaphysical, is the way his work mirrors new-physics concepts. The oral tradition is like the river that no literate ladle can capture; native peoples who have suspected photographers of soul murder, note-taking Western anthropologists as spectators rather than livers of life, fencebuilders as vandals rather than stewards of earth are expressing their oneness with life's flow. But the literate impulse, however undermined, will not be denied. Dams, fences, and geometrical gardens and cities will be built, roads and boundaries charted and imposed, slices of life written down, and music recorded and notated. History will be made and written; cultures will be self-conscious.

Western literacy and non-Western orality have plumbed mutual demonization; in America, they've been forced to reach for higher terms. Their best dynamic suggests that of complementarity in the new physics: reality is *both* particle and wave, *both* motion and position—*both* composition and improvisation, *both* oral and literate—but never either at once. Once this is understood and accepted, the dynamic between the two states is experienced as the dance it is rather than a fight for control. Surely we see by now that paradox is not only tolerable but good, that one side or the other will never prevail absolutely, that the hierarchies are tangled rather than fixed, and that the demonization is self- as much as other-destructive. Mutual exaltation of "the other" by "the self"—whoever happens to be playing each role—is precisely the road to the unity between both.

No other artist in Braxton's milieu resonates so keenly and so consciously with these concerns of his time, and nowhere does he do it so directly, poetically, and starkly as in the duo context.

1. Such as researchers into the physics phenomenon of "chaos" find in statistical runs documenting stock market fluctuations; see James Gleick, *Chaos: Making a New Science* (New York: Viking, 1987).

2. Art Lange, "Record Reviews: *Trio and Duet, Duets 1976*" (*Coda*, February 1978: 18–19).

3. Anthony Braxton, *Composition Notes D* (Hanover, NH: Tree Frog Music, 1988: 370).

4. The only pop song to appear on any Ornette Coleman album (see John Litweiler, *Ornette Coleman: A Harmolodic Life* (New York: William Morrow and Company, Inc., 1993: 87).

5. *The Lee Konitz Duets* (Milestone OJCCD-466-2 [MSP-9013], 1967) is an excellent display of the art of the duo as practiced by one of Braxton's main influences.

6. Braxton, *Composition Notes D*, 340.

7. Ibid., 343–45: "This is not a work to play one's exercises on or 'coast' in the illusion that no special efforts are needed to exist in this sound space. Composition No. 85 could not have come into existence without the actualization of be-bop—but the work itself is not be-bop (just as Charlie Parker, and the masters who developed that music, were not playing be-bop)."

8. Ibid., 348, 370: about *86*: "In this work, two instrumentalists are allowed to enter into a series of moments and sound strategies that give fresh insight about duo interaction (and sound thinking)." About 87: "I constructed this forum as a dynamic sound space structure that positively exploits the duo context so that each instrumentalist can have an opportunity to function in 'immediate' form space (that is perceived as 'involved' in the forward thrust of the music.)"

9. Braxton, *Composition Notes D*, 368.

10. Ibid., 356, 367.

11. Graham Lock, *Forces in Motion: The Music and Thoughts of Anthony Braxton* (New York: Da Capo Press, 1988: 325).

12. Braxton, *Composition Notes A*, 41.

13. Ibid., 43.

14. Ibid., 41.

15. Braxton, *Composition Notes C*, 454–6.

16. However, to hearken back to the medieval Africa-Europe connection, it is interesting to recall the centrality of the struck string—the monochord—to the conceptual roots of Western music.

17. Braxton, liner notes to *Duets 1976* (Arista AL 4101, 1976).

18. Braxton, *Composition Notes C*, 138.

19. Ibid., 380.

20. Braxton's "really doesn't care about your feelings!" rings as his answer to those who have called his music itself cold and clinical. Consider it in the light of the following passage, from R. J. Stewart's *The Spiritual Dimension of Music: Altering Consciousness for Inner Development* (Vermont: Destiny Books, 1987: 64): "Whereas modern culture certainly claims music as an art, at its best, or as a commercial product in its lowest form, our ancient predecessors used it in a way which is often incomprehensible to the modern mind. It was accepted that music epitomized certain natural laws, not only of physics, but of the metaphysics from which physics was derived. This belief was not in any way limited to an 'emotional' or 'creative' application of music, but depended upon the premise that physical emission of sound was an outer and audible agency of an inner and transcendent power. The composition of music was irrelevant to this interpretation, as was personal artistic merit of

'originality,' the very qualities prized so highly today." Braxton: "The challenge of structures of this nature is the excitement of establishing a seamless continuity of sound and material ideas to create a transcended music state (entity) . . . Extended improvisation in the work is carried out in the spirit of AACM collectivism—that being participation without respect to any one role or function (each participant has the flexibility to react to whatever is perceived to be 'the point' of the music)."

    21. Braxton, *Composition Notes C*, 367.

    22. *Four Compositions (1973)* (Denon YX 7506) won Japan's *Swing Journal*'s Gold Disc Award, as well as an Oscar from the French Jazz Academy in 1973.

    23. Gaslini's *Tempo e Relazione* (1957) was a pioneering attempt to synthesize the jazz tradition and the twelve-tone system.

    24. Braxton, *Composition Notes C*, 137.

    25. Braxton, *Composition Notes E*, 142.

    26. Ibid., 149.

    27. Barry Tepperman, *Coda*, February 23, 1976.

    28. *Down Beat*, November, 1990.

    29. Lock, 179–88.

    30. Braxton, *Composition Notes E*, 1–24.

    31. Ibid., 3.

    32. John Coltrane, *Interstellar Space* (Impulse 9277, February 22, 1967, with drummer Rashied Ali).

    33. Barry McCrae, "Braxton, Bailey & Company—the art of ad hoc and ad lib" (*Jazz Journal International*, July 1977: 22–3).

    34. See Lock (240) re: improvised music as an arena in which conflict can take place and be resolved nondestructively.

    35. John Litweiler, "Record Reviews" (*Down Beat*, June 5, 1975: 18).

    36. Braxton, *Composition Notes C*, 18–25, for this and the next four citations.

    37. Not discussed here, but a good example of several Braxton/Corea duets on the Circle recordings is on *The Complete Braxton* (Freedom 400112/3[RI], Arista-Freedom 1902, 1971). Note how distinctly Braxton's written line matches Corea's own highly distinctive style, as well as his own such saxophone style.

Chapter Seven

Trio Music

[From the occult definition of] **number**: ... *8.* Pythagoras: ... *3 = equilateral triangle: active unity of duality, source and prototype of all that has been created* ...

[From the occult definition of] **three**: *1. divine: threefold divinities: A. Egypt: a. the phases of the sun: morning (Horus), noon (Ra), setting (Atun); b. the first division of the Great Goddess: Isis as sister-bride, mother, and layer-out; B. Graeco-Roman: a. the three worlds: Zeus (heaven, with 3-forked lightning), Poseidon (sea, with trident), Hades (underworld, with 3-headed dog) ... C. Christian: a. Father, Son, and H. Ghost (or, feminine Wisdom) ... 3. perfection, completion, sufficiency: a. beginning, middle, end; b. sun: East, Zenith (South), West: birth, culmination,* death [emph. mine] ... *e. the dynamic equilibrium of the action of unity upon duality, or the growth of unity within itself ... 4. creative, masculinity: a. the creation of spirit out of matter, action out of passivity: b. the formula of the Creation of the world ...*
5. spiritual: a. the ternary as symbol of the intellectual or spiritual world: synthesis; b. solution of the dualism-conflict ... d. through the pyramidal shape three is related to Fire: Purification and Illumination ... 7. man and human relations: a. the elementary nucleus: man, woman, and child; b. physical, mental, and spiritual life, etc.; c. Pythagoras: mediation, atonement, completeness; d. thought, action, emotion; e. religion, law, love ...
12. correspondences: a. "The Artist," controlling the talented ... c. Zodiac: Gemini ... 13. psych.: a. solution of a conflict; biological synthesis; childbirth; b. often seen as a conscious-spiritual value, lacking the One of the unconscious to make the Whole of Four: the triangle can be seen as the half of

the diagonal square: together they are at once polarity (2 triangles in opposition) and the conjunction of Wholeness (cf. Chinese Yang-Yin); three thus represents masculinity (or the animus in the female), whereas Four is femininity (or the anima in the male) with subconsciousness included . . .

In the Egyptian Stellar Mythology, Shu, standing on seven steps, first lifted up the heaven from the earth in the form of a triangle, and at each point was situated one of the gods, Sut, Shu, and Horus. The number 3 was a sacred number, because it represented these three. They are the Trinity in its very earliest form, which was Stellar.

In some of the oldest papyri and monuments we find the original triangle of Horus I . . . with the apex downwards . . . It is in the form of this triangle that Shu lifted up the heavens, standing on the top of the "Seven Steps," and the apex of the triangle rested on them.[1]

Of the one comes two, and of the two three. And from the three come ten thousand.

Lao-Tzu

The "male" triangle's solidity denotes the beginning of the integrity of the new life (its three points as father, mother, and fetus). It is the first construct of points to accede to the planar two-dimensionality of the circle: new life first feeds on but then feeds the world.

The shadow definition of the "female" (downward pointing) triangle denotes the early lack of gender differentiation in the fetus, and the lingering vestiges of the opposite sex in the maturity of that differentiation (male is solid here because it's Braxton we're discussing). The juxtaposition of the inverted triangles inside the circle is also an ancient symbol for the balance of male and female; and of heaven (from earliest Egypt, female), earth (male), and underworld (circle, source of both). Here it can also stand for the emergence of the actual from its potential.

In Braxton's music, the trio has most often functioned as a volatile, fertile base for experiments that he developed into more established, codified procedures in the quartet music. It figures a liminal place, a gestation, halfway between many "thises" and "thats." He also uses the figure of the triangle (pointing up) in his scores to denote sections of written material he wants the player to alter improvisationally somehow, without departing too far from it; he uses the inversion of that triangle to signal a lock: i.e., "stay in and work whatever chord/line/language system you've established at this point." These sections generally function as transitions between "circle" spaces (open improvisation) and "square" sections, or blocks of notated material to be played as written.

The trio music contains, of course, the solo and duo dynamics charted in Chapters Five and Six.

Duos define poles, symmetry, conversation, consensus or conflict; the trio introduces middle ground, compromise, politics, democracy, synthesis, the beginnings of collective. Groups of singers will find both musical poles and middle ground naturally, organically, led by their own nervous systems (witness the spontaneous octaves, fifths, and triads that occur in the spontaneous chants and songs from traditions across the racial and cultural board). From Medieval polyphony to Native American chant to the early American shapesingers of the "sacred harp," from the multiphonic chants of Tibetan monks and Mongolian singers to the glossalalia of white and black American Pentecostalists, and the impromptu choirs of strictly non-instrumentalist churches—wherever people pool their voices, the same architecture of tonality's intervals tends to form. It may be understood as coming forth from atonality, and atonality may be felt ever looming around and interpenetrating it, but it is clearly an order as primal as any chaos.

The first step to leading such music-making groups, to composing their voices into a particular statement, is to organize the people and empower them to access, control and direct their own collective process. Only when a composer's statement becomes the performer's does it truly come to life for the composer.

For Anthony Braxton, that process goes back to orchestrating doowop sessions on street corners and making up childhood R&B tunes; his trio works (especially the very early *6E* and the mature *76*) exemplify, on one level, exquisite developments of those youthful efforts; his verbal and written instructions likewise stem from those he used to impart the simpler musical strategies and concepts. The trio is where the process moves from one-on-one interactions and parallels to collective organization. It is a volatile structure in its lack of symmetry, moving ever from the three-in-one trinity of a chordal field to the more pointed expressions of its internal duo and solo potentials.

In discussing Braxton's liner notes for trio music (Chapter Four), we spoke in terms of numerology and astrology. We should probably address, briefly, the role of such knowledge systems classically defined as occult. In the context of his work and Muse, they are traditions that resonate with the intuitive experiences of much of humanity—certainly artists and mystics. In the 1960s, of course, those of Braxton's generation were unabashed in their embrace of those experiences. Since then, the thrust of the culture has been to eschew them as naive and superficial, otherworldly; however, they have also matured through the corroborative explorations of Jungian psychologists, quantum physicists, and others among the more substantial and credible of New Age intelligentsia. Like that of the latter, Braxton's work is grounded in the West's traditional concepts and techniques of his field, while also successfully reaching areas that reconcile those concepts and techniques with others once considered their antitheses. Those who have avoided coming to terms with the sociocultural and musical implications of such "occult" wisdom by relegating it to the youthful vagaries of either the ("primitive" human) race, a ("lost") generation, or an individual—or to the (relative) wackiness of "woman's intuition"—may eventually find Braxton's music (or at least the concepts it incarnates) a stumbling block they ignore not only at their own psychic but also intellectual peril.

Braxton's trio music itself falls into three (over three decades) periods, most naturally tagged early, middle, and late. It figures prominently in the early period (from the late '60s to the early '70s) as a combination of choice, with the solo, to showcase innovation (the quartet took over that role in the later two periods). Even when a fourth instrument appears, it often functions more as extra color (percussion), or as a polyphonic voice (piano) that can dialogue with and reflect the polyphony of the trio, than as one that redefines it as a quartet (e.g., *Three Compositions of New Jazz*, or *Four Compositions [1973]*). (Braxton says his quartets can be seen as trios with floating "others"; a concept most obvious in the earliest and the latest quartet work.) As with the duo music, the recorded examples range from very fixed to very open premises, the latter mostly in the Company 3 recordings.

The middle period, from the middle to late 1970s, sees a working-out of those fixed premises into full-blown scores at once playful and committed to the ground they're breaking (our examples will be 36 and 76). Some principles most fully developed in the quartet music are worked out here.

The later period (from the 1980s to the present) exhibits a stateliness of formality, a Western chamber-music style of relaxed clarity, a maturity only latent and implied, naturally enough, in the earlier work. On the theoretical level, Braxton's whole system, as realized in the quartet format, is just as well defined here.

The Early Period

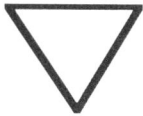

The Yoni Yantra or triangle was known as the Primordial Image, representing the Great Mother as source of all life . . . As the genital focus of her divine energy, the Yantra was adored as a geometrical symbol, as the cross was adored by Christians.

The ceremony of baptismal rebirth often involved being drawn bodily through a giant yoni. Those who underwent this ceremony were styled "twice-born" . . . [2]

In Egypt the inverted triangle was a hieroglyphic sign for "woman," and it carried the same meaning among the gypsies, who brought it from their original home in Hindustan . . . In the Greek sacred alphabet, the delta *or triangle stood for the Holy Door, vulva of the All-Mother Demeter ("Mother Delta").*

Most ancient symbol systems recognized the triangle as a sign of the Goddess's Virgin-Mother-Crone trinity and at the same time as her genital "holy place," source of all life. The triangle represented the Virgin Moon Goddess called Men-Fer, archaic deity of the first Mother-city of Memphis . . . Concerning this, Oriental sages said: "The object of the worship of the Yantra is to attain unity with the Mother of the Universe in Her forms as Mind, Life, and Matter . . . preparatory to Yoga union with Her as She is in herself as Pure Consciousness . . ."

trio music

The triangle was everywhere connected with the female trinity, and a frequent component of monograms of Goddesses. To the Gnostics, the triangle signified "creative intellect."[3]

The symbol we'll use for the early period of trios (late 1960s to early 1970s) is the inverted pyramid. Egyptian architects conceived this as an underground mirror image of their actual constructions. It is also an ancient symbol for the female.

Braxton's music from this period is at its most structureless, spontaneous, improvisatory, and experimental, as he searched for his composer's voice within the creative free play and reflection of the AACM. He uses the inverted triangle in his notation—which we'll examine fully in Chapter Nine—to denote sections combining such free play (the circle) and written-out parts (the square).

Selected Early Period Recordings

Three Compositions of New Jazz (Delmark DS–415, 1968): *6E, 6D,* and (Leo Smith's) *The Bell* (with multiinstrumentalists Smith and Leroy Jenkins).

Silence (Freedom FLP 40123, 1969): same personnel as above, no Braxton compositions.

Familie (Birth NJ 008, 1972): open improvisations with vocalist Jeanne Lee and reeds/vibist Günter Hampel.

Creative Construction Company recordings (Muse MR 5071, 5079).

Company 3 recordings, open improvisations with guitarist Derek Bailey and saxist Evan Parker (Incus 23 & 28; and 29 & 30 [also CD 07]).

Town Hall 1972 (CD: Art Union TKCB-30108): *6N, 6(O), 6P*, with bassist David Holland, percussionist Phillip Wilson (except on *6P*); and multi-instrumentalist John Stubblefield, percussionist Barry Altschul, and vocalist Jeanne Lee (on *6P*).

Four Compositions (1973) (Denon YX 7506): *23N, 23P, 23M, 23(O)*, with pianist Masahiko Sato, bassist Keiki Midorikawa, and percussionist Hozumi Tanaka (on *23(O)* only).

Three Compositions of New Jazz

Braxton's *6D* and *6E*, with Leo Smith's *The Bell*, made up this recorded example of the music newly born from his work with the AACM. *6D* bears the seeds of the "collage" approach, or "conceptual grafting": a juxtaposition between the trumpet, sax, and violin (Ornette Coleman's three instruments) of "independent phrases"—later he would juxtapose whole compositions so—and between the piano and that trio of single-liners (though they all play several instruments, mostly for a splashing variety of colors).

6D showcases speed, intensity, and extended improvisation. It suggests an open collective improvisation generated by three restless horns simply trying to signify their ambiguous energy, which are joined in progress by a pianist who has been listening to them enough to mirror and magnify their collective statement to up the ante, working his own on the fly into support for their improvisations.

In fact, such a process was initiated by Muhal Richard Abrams on this piece, which inspired Braxton to develop the piano's role "as soloist as well as 'total rhythm section.'"[4] As conventional piano comping serves to ground improvisers in their harmonic-melodic and rhythmic platform, and to spur more creative construction thereon, so does Abrams remind the trio of their new platform: individual expression within a constant *expansion*—not metric/harmonic containment and control—of rhythmic and tonal fields. The piano's magnified reflection of the music Braxton was trying to orchestrate between monophonic instruments would prove a staple in his music, in contradistinction to the earlier monophonic (linear, male) experimenters from Marsh to Mulligan to Coleman to Ayler, who more usually felt constrained by the piano's polyphonic (holistic, female) tyranny. This use of the piano speaks nicely to the way polyphonic solo piano music inspired him to conceive a monophonic solo music for his alto sax. A step further, it sheds light on his primarily monophonic concept as a composer, in which harmony—indeed, pitch—figures as much as the color of a heart pumping blood as of the abstraction of a ratiocinating mind. (Next chapter we'll consider the piano fully as a feminine force to the masculine one of Braxton's horns.)

Braxton describes *6D* as a single repeated block of "independent phrases"—i.e., phrases written for each single-line instrument independently of the others—with the piano providing "an arhythmic generated foundation ... over which all of the solos are postulated." The tempo is "fast to fastest." He identifies this study in writing "independent phrases" as a direct outgrowth of the AACM's "working theater of the collective creativity," which had developed as the interaction of a free-for-all continually trying to pull itself together in the context of its freedom. To begin to conceptualize and notate this process in Western terms, Braxton mirrored with this effort the heterophony of medieval Western music (and early jazz) in which a vertical harmony and horizontal counterpoint in accord with same was at first incidental to the composer's focus on successive juxtapositions of independent melodic-rhythmic lines. Looking forward, the seeds of his later major structural devices are here: pulse tracks in the piano, and the inter-nested "coordinate music" (see Chapter Four, "Quartet Liner Notes") in the independent phrases.

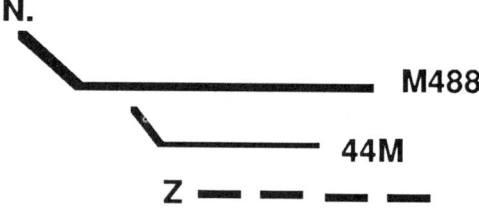

Fig. 7.1: Graphic representation of 6D (the music has been lost). This simple graphic conveys the structure of the horn trio, whose concept is similar to Mingus' Self-Portrait in Three Colors. The piano part, which came later, isn't represented in the graphic.

Composition 6D *is an excellent entree into later more complex expressions of its principle. The piano's role is not that different from the way pianos comp during conventional jazz solos: angular, syncopated harmonic jabs from outside the melodic-rhythmic nitty-gritty of the solo space. Braxton's later pulse tracks are simply extended schema of such attacks, a raising of the music's "floor" from the vital but monotonous basement of heartbeat-like even pulse to the first story of the house, where life is more interesting. His independent phrases free the people living there to speak as they will from within their individualities, spontaneously, unstifled by rigid household rules and decorum. To his audience, the creation and performance of such pieces demonstrate responsibility to, rather than abuse of, that freedom.*

6E (dedicated to Eric Dolphy and Louis Armstrong) is a platform similarly close to the AACM's pioneerings. What is showcased here, much like in a street-corner "doo-wop" harmonization, is the voice as an instrument, a concept initiated in jazz by Armstrong's *scatstimme* (to paraphrase Schönberg). More, the piece makes the statement (as do Braxton's notes)[5] that both the voice and its extensions in horns signal talents as deserving of acknowledgment and respect in their most unschooled as in their most schooled expressions. Braxton offers the piece as a bridge between the two states, to overcome their mutual hierarchization: "the whole of Composition No. 6E's dynamics are aimed at this same challenge—that being greater involvement with respect to what one can do."

Outline (for comp 6E)

```
    1. the integration of voice into the texture of the
music
    2. expanding the dynamics of the musicians'
challenge
    3. written in 4 sections A1(A2) B A
       A1 basic use of voice w/ counterpoint like
situation
       A2 extension of materials
       B  whistle & pointillistic section
       A  repeat of first section

    4. for open improvisation
       a. utilized with little instrus
       b. w/ solo possibly inside

    5. sounds have no particular meaning
```

```
    1B. using the voice creatively w/ respect to normal
speaking voice & vocal sound possibilities

    6. performances in Chicago & Paris

    7. written as I heard it in my head
```

Fig. 7.2: The notes above were informed in performances by the AACM's way of filling sections described as "open . . . with little instruments," for example—but any beginners could inform them so in their own way. Braxton's notes invite the most open and reaching improvisational sections, calling on solo, duo, and trio dynamics together.[6]

The effect of hearing these three non-"professional" singers scat around spontaneously with a concertizing air is, in fact, much like that of Schönberg's first presentations of *sprechstimme*, or Cage's use of orchestrated silence, or Armstrong's scatting must have been for many. Anyone can speak/hum/whistle/be quiet aimlessly—but is it art? This piece rather begs the question, "Anyone can make art—but is it life?"

Actually, *6E*, as recorded, works very well as an oral/aural primer in basic-to-advanced musicality, somewhat along the lines of simple Renaissance rounds, Bach's *Inventions*, or Bartók's *Mikrokosmos*: something a student can have fun with and learn from in a highly musical context. It meets both advanced and beginning listeners with a range encompassing the first vocalized musical impulse to the first contact with an instrument to the mature mastery of technique, creativity, and intellect. It umbrellas this range from simple to complex instruments and from inexperienced to sophisticated use of them under one compositional concept. It invites the listener to do likewise. Imagine a commercial and critical arena where the criteria for success operated not on the listener's detached and pre-programmed judgment of but rather his or her own access to active engagement with music making—or, indeed, with his or her own extramusical life's dreams. This piece belongs in such an arena. Its importance lies in its suggestion that the wandering, unconditioned mind—which, of course, is essential to creativity—can be as valuable and worthy of respect as the formally trained one.

Silence is worth a mention for the fact that it includes no Braxton compositions, rather one each by the other two trio members, Jenkins and Smith. The music sounds like something Braxton might have conceived during that time—Cage-y, dadaistic—and it was put out under his name (come to think of it, a record called *Silence* under Braxton's name with no Braxton compositions on it, and with obvious Cage traces, is quite the (post-Cage) compositional statement). The point of mentioning it here is both to relate Braxton to and distinguish him from others of his time and place doing what he was doing. While many of his AACM-era peers would distance themselves from his music, others shared and mirrored his approaches. Yet players/composers such as Mitchell, Abrams, Smith, Jenkins, or percussionist Steve McCall seldom came under the same fire from critics and peers.

My sense of this fact is that those others stayed within the realm of personal statements one could take or leave; Braxton offered his as universal principles within a system. This is a tricky business, especially in its early stages. Bach comes to mind as someone who likewise was accepted as a genuine, gifted musician but who also encountered resistance and indifference from employers and peers, many of whom thought him to be overly intellectual, emotionally dry, and overbearing for writing out so many notes that other composers left to players' improvisation. Bach's way of overcoming this resistance lay in his superabundance of musicality, a constant churn of performance, improvisation and composition, a constant personal-universal synthesis of his own German traditions with those of France, Italy, and England; deadlines, family life, the never-ending cycle of music/survival with its highs and lows, periods of plenty and scant. Bach, Beethoven, Brahms, Berg . . . and Braxton. It scans.

The European incarnation of this American AACM trio was the Creative Construction Company (CCC), with whom percussionist Steve McCall became an occasional fourth member. Recordings of this period develop further the "art-as-life-as-art" Cagean pieces that contextualized all sounds (Braxton's modified garbage cans, balloons, shoveled coal) and contexts (street noises, birds, raked leaves) as music. As he realized the concept of quartet-as-trio-plus-floating-other obviously at first then more subtly in later years, so with this early concept of melding music with life. The subtlety of the former lies in the fact that all his groups are made up only of floating others, in the sense that their musical roles are completely interchangeable; the latter, in the fact that his intended instrumental and the unintended non-instrumental sounds of the world around him are not distinguished from each other in his music.

6H, from *This Time*, is an example of the work on the most direct line to the mature musical universe. Recorded by the trio, it was conceived (and performed) for an optional percussionist (McCall, here) and pre-recorded tape. Like most of Braxton's early work, this was designed for extensive open-ended improvisations. Looking back from his *Notes*, he called it "a major step in the formulation of alternative composition tenets for my later compositional growth (and focus)."[7] The four-part structure includes (1) solo statement/basic germ, (2) ensemble unison statement of extended phrases, (3) extended counterpoint, (4) written material to be played "within the improvisational fabric of the music." *6H* is a post-Coleman/Webern/AACM exploration of solo, duet, and trio possibilities. The work's pivotal role lay in the new improvisational directions its structure and lines suggested.

The CCC made a few records important in hindsight, but Braxton's music was even less well received in Europe than America (that situation would soon reverse; see Jost for both negative European criticism (of CCC) and the beginning of its turnaround, in response to the Circle quartet). In *Familie*, an improvisation with no compositional platform, the music, curiously, sounds more conventional than that triggered by Braxton's compositions.

Several reasons for this come to mind. The players (Braxton on multi-reeds, vibist-reedsman Gunter Hampel, and vocalist Jeanne Lee) are newer to each other than the AACM trio members; are using the "open space" to get acquainted, tentatively, on broad familiar common ground, as people do at first; and one of them is a woman.

It opens with a free session in the low reeds, segues gracefully through a more intense animal-like section, some spacey atonal virtuosity between clarinet and vibes follows, some sweet vocals arrive at the fore. It then moves into bright, urbane yet homey jazz and winds down through rubato meanders: professionals enjoying themselves as amateurs. It's a good example of how the open space, treated with care, could feel its way democratically and interactively into structure through its freedom. Even the Braxtonian animal-like "out" parts stand more like discourse in than escape from the overall framework.

This group would blossom through three pieces Braxton went on to write for a concert with it at New York's Town Hall. *6N* is an uptempo AABA head with structural diversions (into vamping repetitive phrases and canonic motifs) built into it, and structural digressions (out of the metric framework) taken in performance. The trio (with drummer Phillip Wilson and bassist Dave Holland) functions more like a conventional jazz quartet than the AACM/CCC trios did, and this piece would become part of the quartet book. It still serves to set up long, post-Coleman (for their regular meter, instrumentation, and melodic chromaticism) improvisations. The trio is muscular and vigorous, and Braxton the young sax virtuoso is in full force, the composer clearly his humble servant. His playing demonstrates the influences from Desmond to Parker to Coltrane and Ayler in a way that offers them as healthily integrated aspects of a well-rounded personality.

6N segues into a brief reading of *6(O)*, a balladish, written duo between the bass and sax, colored with percussion. The piece was new at the time of the concert, and Braxton writes in his *Notes*[8] that it went on to evolve its own development, suggesting a distinct sort of improvisational space in which it would sit as a statement between improvisational parentheses (as opposed to the usual in-head/out-head parentheses around the improvisation).

6P is a two-side-long showcase of Lee's conventional and extended vocal techniques. In the early 1970s, this long and varied piece stands in hindsight as precursor and groundbreaker to the work of later female vocalists (such as Ursula Dudziak, Terry Jenoure, Irene Aebi, Tina Marsh, and Flora Purim) of the then new music that was initially an overwhelmingly male province. Braxton the composer rises grandly to the task, orchestrating long sections of restrained lyricism for the instrumentalists to support Lee's voice at its most introspective, even writing a poem for her to sing.[9] The restraint finally gives way to a correspondingly volcanic sax outburst which nonetheless is always transparent enough (despite the addition of another percussionist and multi-reeds player) for Lee's own such eruption to join the more outgoing, boisterous ride, even keeping her position at the center of the piece. The widest range of reeds, from contrabass clarinet to flute, mirrors beautifully Lee's own command of her most mannish lows and most womanish highs. As a platform and catalyst for the music everyone made, a precursor to the extensive use of text in Braxton's later work, and a statement of the female vocalist's place in and mastery of the new musical arena, *6P* is a breathtaking marvel.

At the end of the spectrum opposite this spirit of international, co-gendered, civilized gentility in *Familie* and *Town Hall* lies the Company recordings, including a trio version (*Company, Vol. 2*, Incus 23, 1976), of Braxton's collaborations with the new European free players of the time. Saxophonist Evan Parker and guitarist Derek Bailey bring a well-worked duo of their own to these sessions, and the music that results is a glimpse at the beginnings of what has blossomed into a European network of improvisers who adamantly distinguish themselves as definitive voices in their own right, in contradistinction to a European history of following the African American lead.

As some AACM members[10] earlier bristled at the suggestion that their experiments took cues from avant-garde Western music, so would the European free players assert their originality in response to the African American peers whom their culture embraced, and with whom many of them played. Braxton has always taken a firm position above such battles, and his comfort with the role of empowering as much as haggling with "the other" can be heard in this trio, as in the duos with Bailey.

The free play of this music is more defined, more extreme and intense in gesture, more redolent with crazy rapport—more everything—than that with Hampel and Lee. The latter is a perfect example of how open improvisation can fertilize composition; this trio rather storms composition like a hill to be taken and plants the flag of free improvisation with the warrior's wild and bloody panache—an action about which Braxton, of the three, clearly has the most mixed feelings.

Bailey's guitar suggests a Brazilian *beribeau* biting out streams of sprung rhythms, Parker's sax a rusty hinge on a shutter banging in the wind. Braxton and Parker together tend toward a language of nasally clucks, with sudden moments of harmony; insects, ducks and other fowl are evoked in the human syntax and textures. The pulse is thin-to-nonexistent, contrary to that between Braxton and Lewis, Abrams, or Mitchell even in their longest atonal, arhythmic stretches. As if in reaction against both Western compositional traditions and African spins on it, no developments complicate the tonal expressions, no pulse unifies and contextualizes their undeveloped complexity. They reel forth more like automatic writing than like glossolalia, and while Braxton's more mercurial, wound-tight side is provoked, his is still the voice with the softest, least jarring edge. If this music is Western European in character, it suggests a pre-literate, hunter-gatherer Europe in which the drum figured only slightly in the shamanism, next to the taut string and harsh reed. Braxton's voice often seems to long for the drum, and the timbres, pitches, and other musical elements to which it gives rise.

In any case, both *Familie* and Company poles of this trio range take the male and female wildness of both African and European cast and put them into the artistic context of live and/or recorded artistic performances. Sensitive restraint in the first and unleashed obsession in the second both push, from different directions, Braxton to the middle ground of composition as, respectively, catalyst and container; and of improvisation as reiteration of, as much as innovative spins on, tradition. Again, as in *6E*, the effect is to showcase the spontaneous romps of the spirit in the "open space"—the Wild Man and Wild Woman, in all their humanimality, interacting nonhierarchically—in the most formal Western literate, classical contexts of score and concert.

Braxton wrote the *Four Compositions (1973)* from the *23* series (*M*, *N*, *O*, and *P*) to fulfill an invitation from Nippon Columbia to record and perform for Japanese audiences. The musical result was a refined summation of the trio-plus-piano approach more chanced upon earlier. The artistry of his Japanese collaborators (on bass, piano, and percussion) made for an expression still adventurous and fresh but with fewer volatile and uncertain parts. It prefigures the chamber music-like feel of his later quartet period, after the more conventional jazz style from the Circle through the two-horn groups of the middle period. The showing this recording made in the Japanese and European marketplace (Japan's *Swing Journal*'s Gold Disc Award, and an Oscar from the French Jazz Academy) prefigured the blossoming of his mature music in the global more than the American arena.

The Middle Period

Horus and Sut had been twin-builders of the heaven and the founders of North and South (South first by Sut) . . . Shu followed with the new foundation in the equinox, which was double—East and West . . .

. . . this triangle was the first hieroglyphic for the name of Sut or Set, but after the great fight[11] *it was associated with the name of Horus I . . . [From the peak of the pyramid] Shu lifted up the heavens with his hands, hence the base of the triangle above . . . From the base of the triangle thus lifted up, the square of the heavens was afterwards worked out . . .* [12]

The triangle set on its base is an ancient symbol for both mountain and male. Walker speculates the origin of this usage in the Caucasus Mountains, from whence came the Indo-Europeans to conquer the southern peoples and establish the first patriarchies among them. She suggests that the pyramid and mound structures throughout the ancient American and Eurasian and Egyptian cultures may have been simulations of mountains to evoke the male fire god in flat lands.

We take it as a symbol of Braxton's middle period of trio music (mid-to-late 1970s) because that was when the early sketchy premises for extended open improvisations—as in the *6* series above—gave way to more elaborate orchestrations based on the dynamics and potential of those improvisations. If the latter were relatively passive gestures to attract the active inspiration of, and possession by, the Muse, compositions such as *36* and *76* were rather active constructions offered as houses, temples, where Muse and musicians might meet and linger, and commune at length.

Selected Middle Period Recordings/Cuts

Trio and Duet (Sackville 3007, 1974): *36,* with trumpeter Leo Smith and sysnthesist Richard Teitelbaum.

trio music

For Trio (Arista AL 4181, 1977): *76*, with multiinstrumentalists Roscoe Mitchell, Joseph Jarman, Douglas Ewart and Henry Threadgill.

Composition 36 takes up the flip side of *Trio and Duet*'s three standards with Holland. Braxton wrote it for his reeds, Leo Smith's trumpet, and Richard Teitelbaum's synthesizer, right after he had composed the run of solo piano pieces taken up by most of the *30s* (see next chapter's Insert 8.1 for a breakdown of Braxton's *oeuvre* into instrumental/ensemble types). Indeed, Teitelbaum's *electronic* keyboard personifies the mystery of the "floating other" to the Braxton-Smith duo with its futuristic (especially in 1974), space-age timbres as much as with the polyphonic voice it shares with the piano. Braxton describes *36* as a musical expression of the act of per-/conception itself, the experience of consciousness splitting into subject (listener) and object (music). The following Braxton notes on the piece are a fascinating foray into the mind of the Muse manifested in music:

> On the material level the "idea" "phenomenon" that led to the creation of Composition No. 36 could be viewed from the context that connects to the phenomenon of "winking" and how it affects what we calibrate in our own minds about the nature of what happened when we experienced "something". The phenomenon of winking as it relates to this viewpoint can be equated with the use of a primary (central) sound point with interference and/or opposite focus criteria that are attached through the use of "grace note" sound devices (to re-shift the focus dictates of the music). When this principle is established in Section B . . . we (the instrumentalist and listener) are given a tool that unlocks the nature of what the experience ("the music" and "listening" to music) is . . . This is a soundscape that sings in its own way—but not of sadness or joy—of nothing.[13]

Consciousness as the twins of subject and object, "winking" as their act of self-per/conception, of collapsing the universe-wave into matter's particle, of Prometheus stealing fire, of Beethoven shaking his fist at heaven, of James Brown finding his best dance steps against rather than with the flow of the pulse, of Dylan Thomas' "do not go gentle into that good night," of the crossroads in the dark night of the soul, where the nothing of the mystic meets the Something of her God, to yield the New Thing of life unfolding on the material plane.

> Composition 36 can move to manifest itself as a Schönbergian type of romanticism one moment and suddenly give us impressions about Ornette Coleman"s "pools" of "silent universes" (the "sad" aspects of his ballade musics".)

Braxton calls it

a 3-part structural world that attempts to incorporate collective and solo extended improvisation . . . a slow pulse interactive continuance that borders on the concept of the ballade . . . for post-Webern/AACM creative instrumentalist . . . with three notated and two improvised sections.

The piece opens with long synth sounds shifting slowly around on what Braxton calls the music's "canvas screen."[14] The trumpet and clarinet in unison enter with a somber, sad, elongated melody, pitched high and pitching intervallically; the synth wind keeps blowing, defining a clean loneliness, that of an astronaut outside his ship in space. The unison of the horns gives way to a gentle split into separate lines; some percussion barks, then each horn wings into sudden flurries. The synth responds with some space-bird's chirps, liquid bells, radio noise. The horns peek cautiously back in, blow, but then stop to listen, then blow again—back and forth between virtuosic bursts and listening. Then we're back to a written duet over the solar wind, reaffirming the common ground. This evokes a First Contact between "I" and "Thou," "one" and "the other."

Braxton wasn't alone, of course, in bringing the synth voice into jazz or post-jazz contexts; Sun Ra had consciously used it as a reflection of the space age, and it was quickly working its way into pop and fusion music. The context Braxton set for it, as a composer, was informed by his love of Stockhausen and other electronic composers in the Western concert tradition; he embraced the air of depth and introspection associated with the instrument there, in his work with Musica Elettronica Vita, Teitelbaum, and, later, composer Todd Barton. He differed from Sun Ra in that he didn't claim to be from Saturn—but he was certainly ready to seek, receive, and communicate with anyone who was. He differed from the commercial artists in his disinterest in electronic and computer technology as Bigger and Better Toy. He brought the plaintively organic, post-jazz acoustic improviser's voice into dialogue with the disembodied nervous system of the avant-garde electronic composer.

The synth drops out at one point in the piece, leaving the horns-twins to recollect and reflect on their encounter with the other. Braxton takes on a reverb echo and Smith slap tongues and fingers valves, as if trying to reiterate and reflect on the electronic utterances to each other. The synth jumps back in with gusto, tearing up the music texturally, matching the thrust of the bass clarinet. The tact of first contact has given way to the force of real concourse. The synth disappears again, and Smith makes balloony sounds through his mouthpiece, then plays some percussion with a pulse—Africa, finally at home while lost in space. Braxton solos on contrabass clarinet, grounding Smith into a longheld tone, which pulls Braxton into the trumpet's range via the clarinet. As if successfully re-evoked by the horns, the synth comes in for one last deep tone, a floor on which the flute and trumpet state a unison figure. "Finally 'these matters' are brought to 'acceptance' (in the world of sound). This is a sound world of slow moving sounds that finally face into the night," Braxton writes.[15]

Lange praised *36* as a composer's, as well as an improviser's, statement. He lauded the players' skill in establishing the rambling type of "imaginary landscape" which Braxton composes so brilliantly . . . The important thing in this type of delicate, architectonic structure is not soloistic concepts, but rather group interplay within an exquisitely scored formula. All three performers here carry out their parts with extreme empathy and brilliance . . . The variety of remarkable voicings throughout the piece label it a success on any level you care to measure it.[16]

His comments corroborated Tepperman's liner notes: "Despite the kaleidoscopic textures of individual passages, the performance soars to an irresistible power in which individual contributions are virtually superfluous." Both writers point up the nature of the trio consciousness as the potential for group dreaming, collective consciousness, and teamwork, and they support Braxton's compositional approach as engaging and developing that potential.

Part of the greatness of great composer/arrangers in jazz—from Fletcher Henderson to Duke Ellington to Gil Evans to Charles Mingus to Sun Ra—has been their ability to establish their own voices through distinctive orchestration. But an even greater part is the way they've managed to incorporate the original voices—the inner composers—of their improvisers within that orchestration, to evoke them with it. Braxton joins those ranks of masters for his ability to do that in an area of the music in dire need of it. Unbridled freedom was proving a bore at this point, yet older compositional strategies weren't an adequate bridle—and how can you go back to the old farm once you've broken free?

How dire the need—and how difficult the task—is evident in the long fallow period the musical ground Braxton and others broke in the 1960s and 1970s has since endured in the main musicultural arena. While such ground broken by Parker, Coltrane, Miles Davis, and even Coleman was worked and cultivated immediately by peers and succeeding generations, Braxton's has proven too foreboding for many to deal with. But, again, what looks difficult and/or unyielding from a distance often proves less so when engaged, especially as the old ground, as all ground finally does, unquestionably needs a rest.

Thirty-six plus one opus numbers after *36 (73)* brings us to the very next composition (unrecorded) scored specifically for trio; three opus numbers after that—or (an occult-traditionally sacred number) 40 after 36—we meet *76*, something of a watershed work. Two different versions of it, by different musicians, are the sole fare on *For Trio*, one of Braxton's better-known and distributed Arista recordings, which was released at the height of his critical and popular fame (1977).

Both *73* and *76* were crafted to fulfill the opportunity to play and record with AACM cohorts Joseph Jarman and Roscoe Mitchell, *73* being written for and performed with them at The Kitchen in New York. *76* is essentially a full blossoming of and progression from musical and metamusical premises and principles tackled in *73*:

• multiinstrumentalism, as a kaleidoscope of timbre and instrumental voice: each of the players must play at least nine different instruments; passages are written in nine different colors (ten including black) to indicate which instruments to play (black indicates a free choice);

- a chain of "102 multiple phrase grouping components and 25 unison grouping components"—short written phrases (in 19 notated sections) cued in by one of the players to serve as entrances to, exits from, or parallels or supports to solo, duo, or trio improvisations (24 designated);
- an equal amount of time allotted to notated and improvised sections, and a blurring of their obvious distinctions. Braxton wanted to engage the musicians with material and each other in a way that would draw them together "vibrationally," rather than isolate them into different musical roles and routines.

> The excitement that generated this work involves the interaction and inter-effect (and inner reality state) of multiple phrase construction alignments (as this phenomenon establishes "a way of relating to sound and thinking—feeling"). This is a music that "comes together"—sometimes joined by a common intention (as in the case of frozen sound line constructions that serve as unison—agreement—devices for moment and composition dynamics) and goes apart (depending on the needs of the moment). To experience this forum is to encounter a "developed" state of being that extends throughout the whole of its structural form. At no point in the music does Composition No. 73 totally release its instrumentalist from the confines of its structural (moment) agenda.[17]

Braxton was able to package *For Trio*, as all of his Arista recordings, with extensive, lavishly produced liner note inserts, with his *Composition Notes* on the work and color graphics of parts of its score. His mix of post-bop and original material in solo, duo, and quartet contexts had proved to the jazz community (by its criteria) that he was no flash in the 1960s avant-garde pan. His use of his success, through the five-record Arista contract, was to put forth his own most innovative and ambitious—and market risky—work. The bold move paid off when *Creative Orchestra Music* won the 1977 Record of the Year award from *Down Beat*.

For Trio is a look both forward and back: back (70 opus numbers) in its evocation of the trio recordings with AACM colleagues Smith and Jenkins in Europe and the States—similar sound and approach, same circle of colleagues; and forward in its solidification of new composing procedures that thrust the improvisers more into the composer's realm, foreshadowing the thrust of his later period (from the 1980s, starting with 95).

Most obvious of these is "modular notation": scored phrases floating on the page rather than moving sequentially through it. Performers are pre-routed, or route and cue themselves, in any number of combinations and orders through the phrases, reading them down then briefly improvising on them, then moving on.

> The reality of this forum was conceived as a dynamic sound continuum that emphasizes the collective interchanges of its composite ensemble—rather than the "wonderful" soloist . . . There are no extended solos in this work, nor does it attempt to impress us with

> "momentum" (so that "one might pay attention"). This is a slow unfolding procession of events that affirms one central attitude and presence . . . Moments in this sound world come together from nowhere and disperse—from its own logic. There is no development at all in . . . 76, and the work also extends from an impersonal material basis.[18]

While Braxton has always expanded the performer's role far past anything specified by most composers/arrangers, the structures with which he has done that demonstrate an evolution from relatively rigid to relatively flexible. His earliest pieces were not that different from jazz "heads," in the way they denoted a statement to be recited in sequence through a beginning, middle, and end, then directed players into open improvisational sections, then brought them back to restate the head exactly. Later structures were more like suites of written sections that didn't necessarily develop from or restate each other, spelled by improvisations—but still straight shots to read through.

By 73, he had broken the sections down into cued phrases, and mixed written with improvised sections. With 76, he further broke up the order of the sequence of phrases—much like the cubist painters did with visual elements—into the interconnecting modules. Decisions about development that he had made in the process of composing could now be made by others in the process of improvising.

> 76 would move to clarify the direction my work has taken me in the last 10 years, and also give insight as to what this work will mean when translated—and integrated—into the composite metareality of world culture (after the transformation of this period).

He isn't looking for the place the culture has reserved for successful "jazz" artists, or "classical" artists, or "experimental" artists; he is looking for his music to transform that culture, to suggest to it new contexts wherein the new musical worlds he had himself moved into could be opened up to others as well. While his modules (playable both backward and forward), routing, and array of soundmakers widened the player's already wide option spread, his many tight, close linkages between improvisation and notation called for just as much responsibility as freedom. He likens this to Japanese brush painting: an infinite variety of free and spontaneous executions—devoted actions—of an infinite variety of fixed abstractions to convey with evermore discipline evermore distilled and deep essences. He likens the music to both astrology (through "color as an occult force") and science, evoking their common ground in system and discipline that spans macro- and microcosmos in an "aspiring, not complacent . . . interdisciplinary spectacle."

The first version, with Henry Threadgill and Douglas Ewart, evokes the meandering chamber brook of the Braxton-Mitchell flute duo, this one rolling over the rocks of Ewart's percussion. One of the flutes magically transforms into a sax barking away the gentleness, then the other into an answering clarinet. Then, like hunters just behind their heralding dogs, three voices signal the arrival of the humans. They intone and noodle much as in *6E*, only more maturity and mastery course through both voice and instruments now. They yodel, scream, call out for response; their instruments try to imitate their flurries.

If *6E* was the youthful splash in mother earth's secret swimming hole, *76* is very much the reunion with it ten years later by the old gang. Unexpected relationships constantly occur—such as that between percussive clatter and vocal riff—that feel spontaneous; but so do synchronicities that may or may not be orchestrated. One can never tell what's written and what's improvised. Free will or predestination? Human or some higher intelligence? Past or present, young or old self? Paradox in Paradise, twins entwined . . .

The second version, with Mitchell and Jarman, is even more active and bold, defining a wider range of reeds and vocal dynamics (from whispers to screams). Moments of rarefied atonal counterpoint and conservatory correctness give way to shocking shrieks and growlings: some extreme of cold keeps meeting its counterpart in heat. Although it is much more labyrinthian than, say, *6P*, or *36*, its mercury is running in *76*'s channels with just as much control and balance, even as it rises with the heat of freedom and invention.

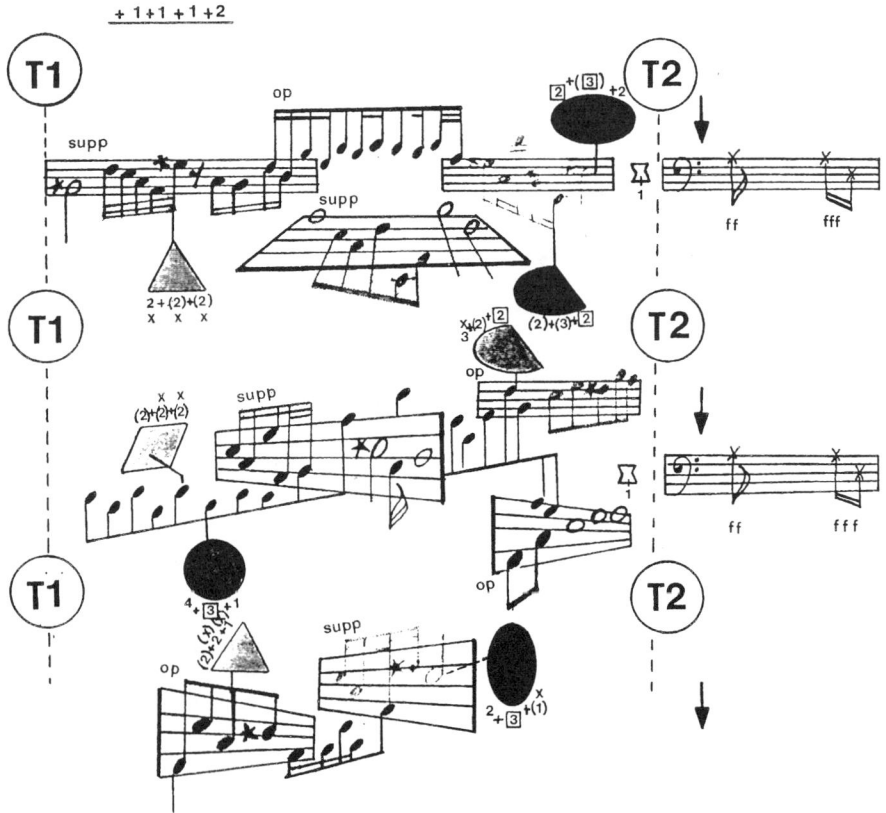

Fig. 7.3: From score of 76. The use of perspective here gets at Braxton's concept of his music as a three-dimensional painting, and prefigures the virtual

reality of computer technology that interests him so much now. It also recalls the introduction of perspective in Western art—roughly concurrent with the late medieval music that staggered its lines in such a way that each "stood" in the soundspace independently from even its nearest neighbors, suggesting therein a third dimension. It seems no accident that this was also the time the Copernican concept of the cosmos—that is, the more accurate one—finally took hold in the West.[19]

Another aspect of *6E* is expanded here: the placing of the most primal, visceral, unschooled impulses into the loftiest formal contexts and restraints. Mammalian roots and space-travelling thought are the unified twins in this piece. Anyone who has ever intuitively thought of the Lascaux cave paintings, the medieval European cathedrals, the music of Louis Armstrong, and the physics of Albert Einstein all as expressions of the same human genius will appreciate *76*.

Reviewer McCrae mentions the primacy of textural relationships over counterpoint, and harmonies "beautifully conceived" through that approach, and single lines that "dovetail in a highly organized manner." He notes how two different sets of players demonstrate the distinctively Braxtonian universe in terms of individual players who are equally distinct, both from him and each other. "While it might transcend jazz it is music that shows that John Cage's theory of 'chance' can be used very effectively by jazz men."[20]

The concept of modulars, in particular, is a microcosmic foreshadow of his mature coordinate system of linking not just phrases but each of his more than 200 compositions together both as compositional statements and as improvisational platforms. That concept is one of his original devices for achieving something profound and important on the metamusical, as well as musical, level: the integration (per Stockhausen) of "all that came before." That is a picture of successful perseverance and development through time, and of a healthy integration of life's many paradoxical—and potentially mutually destructive—universes: the legion of voices, psychic archetypes, stages, periods, personalities, and circumstances that either make or break a person or a life. One's childhood can kill one's maturity, or vice versa; one's kindness and strength, mind and heart, body and soul can all kill each other in the subtlest ways and at the height of their respective passions; one gender can kill another in the very act of trying to love; air, water, fire, and earth—the stuff of life—can destroy each other; Scorpio can either sting or heal all its fellow signs and itself. Such poles must bond in common ground. The word "religion" comes from the Latin "ligare," meaning "to tie together" (as in "get your shit together"). This is the realm of the trio.

> This is a spiritual work that is concerned about spiritual matters. Moments in this sound state are like brief occurrences that float in and out of the time/space. In this fantasy events are moving so fast that it "appears to be slow" ("and we are caught off guard"). Moments . . . form and dissipate in brief light flashes that give no sense of linear continuity ("and expectations"). To experience 76 is to enter a "temple of sound" that calls out for our sense of well-being. There is no

happiness or sadness in this space—only "the experience" . . . Here is a theater piece that is cast in stone and etched in the course of music history . . . By establishing this feeling 76 is in effect realigning a kind of ancient chant context ("as in a monastery or closed time/space") back into our consciousness . . . It's time to get ready for "the past" (and the "vastness" of existence).[21]

"No feelings"—they are part of the wheel of life and death—"only the [transpersonal] experience" beyond the wheel. "Etched in the course of music history," because the oral tradition's spoken word has a power and finality and authority every bit as valid as its written counterpart in the literate tradition.

76 represents a return to the definitive trio zone of Braxton's youth in the AACM, the zone that provided fodder for the trio-plus-floating-other (the "other" being piano, originally, as in *6D*) concept he forged from the more traditional framework of his pianoless quartets. It seems significant that he would return to this ground that had lain relatively fallow through the 1970s, almost as if to re-engender his peculiar vision by "returning to the scene of the crime" before moving it to its more mature "locale." It also has the feel of a personal evocation of the past—in youth—that resonates magically with a similar transpersonal evocation, that of the (human) race's youth.

Both of these resonances are amplified by the fact that the first trio work from his later period—*Composition No. 94*—immediately precedes *95*, his first Ritual and Ceremonial piece.

The Recent Period

These versions of the hexagram are variations of an ancient symbol for the union of male and female, and of heaven and earth, in the world. In Tantric Hinduism, the upward-pointing triangle, for male, is called *vahni*, or fire; the "female" triangle is *shakti*. In mystic Judaism, it is *shekinah*, the feminine aspect of God. "A man aspiring to mystic wisdom had to become a 'bridegroom of Torah,'" writes Walker, "for the law was embodied in a maiden."

We can invoke the hexagram to stand for the late period of Braxton's trio music, beginning with *94*. The relatively open (female) approach of early works such as *6D* and *6E* and the more structured (male) directions taken in *36* and *76* are integrated dynamically in such works as *94* and *107*.

trio music

After [the upward-pointing] triangle was assigned to Horus we frequently find them blended together in this form

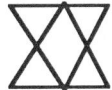

... or in this form

as we find among the oldest Mexican Indians, and those of Central America and Australia. These two triangles, thus depicted, we find, as may be seen in Egypt, Assyria, Mexico.[22]

Selected Recent Period Recordings

Compositions 99, 101, 107 & 139 (Hat Art CD 6019, 1988): with pianist Marianne Schroeder and trombonist Garret List.

7 Compositions (Trio) 1989 (Hat Art CD 6025, 1989): *40D, 40G (+63), 6A, 40J, 110A(+108B+96)*, with bassist Adelhard Roidinger and drummer Tony Oxley.

94 is an unrecorded work for three multiinstrumentalists that has been performed in concert by trombonist Ray Anderson and, alternately, synthesist Richard Teitelbaum and guitarist James Emery. Braxton wrote it in 1980 for a European tour, just before his (compositional) breakthrough with *95*. Like *76*, it consolidated and expressed summarily some concepts he had been playing with loosely, laying the groundwork for their more established use in the work to come.

> The creation of this work was approached as an integration context that demonstrates a unique adaptation of various visual and symbolic processes that have been developing in my music in the last ten years . . . 94 was conceived as a forum of open shapes (clouds) and flows (relationships) that is "filled by the music"—as opposed to a work that is conceived for a particular instrumentation to express a fixed (empirical) idea (that can't be changed).[23]

These "clouds" look like just that (see Fig. 7.4a), floating on the staff amidst the notes and the more geometrical shapes. Unlike the symbolism of the latter, about which shortly, the liquid formations, as he also calls them, are meant as "tracings" of notes low and high, and enclosures of short duration, pitch ranges within which one improvises sketchily. The concept effectively suggests a sound event as a quantum wave potential rather than limiting it to the discrete points (particles) of Western notation. The latter are retained for their part in a relationship with the clouds, much as the Newtonian physics was subsumed in Einsteinian.

> All structured pitches (events) inside the shape configuration are to be blurred from the normal sound nature of the instrument—so that the resulting sound decisions (creativity) are fitted into a shape of static sound occurrences that emphasize the primary sounds of its notated pitches. This approach is akin to having a pianist use the pedal of the instrument throughout all events inside the shape form . . . The challenge of this process for the instrumentalist involves the interrelationship between establishing a linear long sound phrase statement (in the shape of the notated "global" in the score)—whose ingredients all contain one moving idea plasma . . . that must also interact with staccato or pointed (or "accented") sound points (notes) that are outside of—or under, over or in between—its shape contour.

Fig. 7.4a: Example of Braxton's "clouds" of improvised sound, a staple of his work (from *94*).

trio music

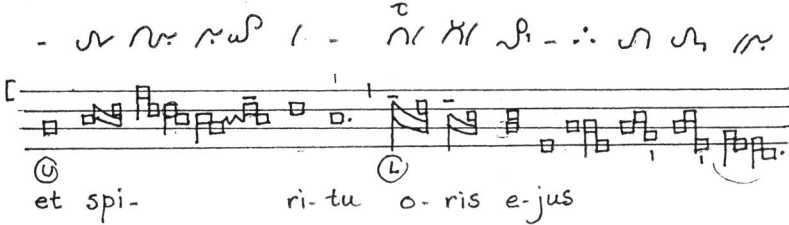

7.4b: A square-note line from Obrecht's mass, under its earlier neumed version (see Chapter Two). Like the neumes, the ligatures referred more to a pitch range than discrete notes.

Fig. 7.4: Braxton's concept, again like that of medieval Western music, is more about a pitch range than a series of discrete notes. The long slides up and down in 7.4b are called "ligatures," and even though modern musicians have tended to read them as shorthand renditions of running notes, they weren't necessarily sung so originally.[24]

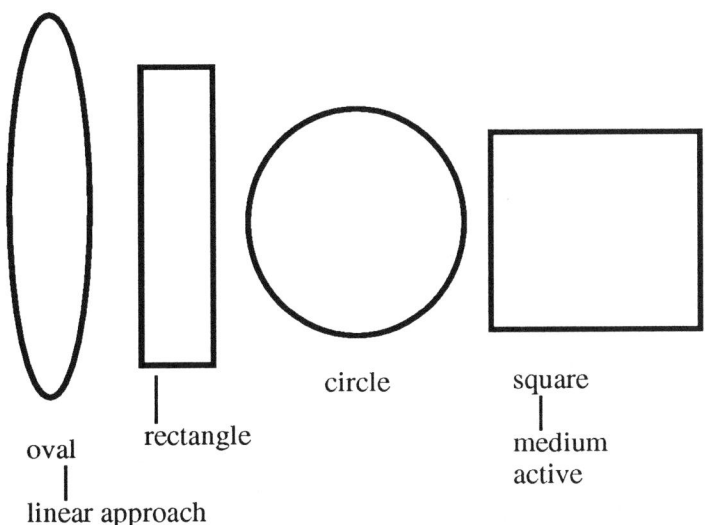

Fig. 7.5: From the composition notes to 94. Braxton would appropriate these and similar geometric symbols—the circle, square, triangle (both inversions), and diamond—to function as what he calls "road signs" signaling "territories": open improvs (circle), notated sections (square), "transitional" sections combining those "fixed and mutable logics" (male triangle), "plateaus"

where an improvised pattern is "locked" into place (the female triangle, sometimes written on the page, often spontaneously signaled manually by Braxton conducting), and areas of pulse (diamond). This use of the symbols is on or around the staff, as are clef signs, time signatures, or dynamics in conventional scoring; on the staff, with the extended line, they refer, along with other shapes, to the actual soundstream. The symbols' meanings vary slightly from piece to piece, even performance to performance, but have tended to be consistent over time in this usage of them in reference to his paradigm, as opposed to a particular musical event.

The more geometric shapes are also conceived as delineations of improvisational sections, only "a given phrase form image is to be approached with 'harder edges' in between its sound movements—to create a more 'constructed' kind of line shape character." Whereas the liquid formations are typically moments mixed in with conventional notation, these shapes more often stand alone on a staff, with a timeline leading down it from their right sides, to suggest the overall shape and nature of a longish open improvisation section. The character of a given shape would be largely determined by the player, but the composer expected whatever it was to be distinct from that of another such shape, and to be consistent with itself throughout a piece.

As was *95*, *107* is significant as a highly refined African spin on the most rarefied (atonal) extensions of Western tonality. Included in that significance is a performance by classically trained pianist Marianne Schroeder, known also for her interpretations of Stockhausen and other modern composers. Braxton on various reeds and trombonist Garrett List make up the trio.

Reviewer Terry Martin explicates that significance so:

> It may be further cause for reflection that amongst these recordings, clearly documenting the amazing breadth of Anthony Braxton's artistic enterprise, at least this set of ears finds more satisfying improvisational and expressive values in his transformations of another tradition than his work within what is regarded as standard jazz practice.[25]

Art Lange, in the liner notes, makes much the same point. Both, as jazz reviewers, are keenly sensitive to the distinctions between "jazz" and "classical" as genres, though by now Braxton's confusion of the two is no longer a problem, at least to them. Listeners grounded in Braxton's traditional jazz and classical training and study for whom it never was so might turn the usual question around. Instead of "Is it jazz? Is it contemporary concert music?" in regard to *107*, one might direct the question to (what history, through the media, has defined as) jazz and classical music. Do such terms and their associations really do the music and its possibilities justice? Have they ever?

Lange also notes that *107* itself forces qualities of trust, empathy, conscientiousness from the group in that much of the written music is nebulous (the shapes). Braxton describes the piece as "an elastic sound continuum that establishes a series of checks and balances for three creative instrumentalists . . . Each instrumentalist in this work is expected to solidify a united family consciousness."[26]

trio music

Trombonist List, in sharp contrast to Braxton's longstanding trombone partners Ray Anderson and George Lewis, brings a conservatory correctness to the formal aspects of the piece, and the same stateliness even to the improvisations. The Muse's gentle side prevails here, though over the exceptionally wide range of each of the instruments speaking. Their discourse is always both meaty and floaty, stretched over five sections stressing five different pulses. Harmony and counterpoint, though no more vertically conceived than in earlier works, is beginning to occur spontaneously in increasingly frequent and fresh expressions, like a newborn infant, still unnamed, displaying glimpses of its unique personality.

Braxton called *107* (dedicated to fellow composer-improviser Bill Dixon) "A dry and glass-like sound universe that sculptures its events into the forward space of the music." He describes the piece's "four operating principles" as suggesting the "three-plus-floating-other" pattern: three fixed and one open premise, the former comprising linear, pointillistic, and cluster note arrangements, the latter

> the use of extended improvisation approached free of any structural or language directives—based on each instrumentalist's relationship to him or herself. With this operative a given designated or 'arrived at' improvisation is reshaped from a conscious decision to change its appearance (or its surface materials)—and this consideration was conceived as a safety valve that allows for smooth exchanges and emphases. I wanted to include this operative so that . . . 107 can be of interest to improvisers and interpreters from every musical and projectional persuasion—because each musician has something special to offer the music (by virtue of one's existence). This is so because the reality of this effort proposes a fresh landscape context for creative interaction and consciousness—that includes the tendencies of Trans European and African sensibilities.

Fig. 7.6: Two systems from 107. *Apart from sections where the tempo is halved or doubled,* 107's *pages read down in a very straightforward way (the score is easy to follow to the recording, and the symbols and shapes are learned quickly that way). In fact, for all the unfamiliarity and difficulty a page like this seems to convey, the flexibility between pulse and meter, key/clef and pitch, graphic signals and their meaning—all amply conveyed, with more, by Braxton's presence as conductor or performer (à la oral tradition)—make for a read-down and improv session much less demanding, once into it, than a simple conventional performance of a bebop tune. The melodic-harmonic-metric structures are less rigid, the phrases shorter and more self-sufficient, the improvs thus too, and more varied.* 107 *is, both in sound and the experience of the players, the quintessential chamber-music trio in the Western sense. In the American African sense, it is just as satisfying as a session of creative freeplay. A telling difference: exists whereas the body movements of a non-improvising trio serve to cue each other into sync with each other according to the score, those of these players improvising rather "inform the score" with the musical event of the moment, pulling each other in and out of it with their inventions.*

The first section is active, with much back-and-forth between notation and improvisation; the second is more pensive, slow. "Improvisations in this sound state," Braxton writes, "are frozen portraits based on the contour of visual phrase shape statements." The third section resumes and extends (quickens, stretches duration of) the improvisational activity of the first, so the "music can breathe." The fourth—a floating pointillism of plucked piano strings—develops the ballad feel of the second section. "In this context the use of long linear line statements interjected with isolated multiphonic sound clusters opens up the space of the music—so that the music doesn't turn into a love song (smile)." The fifth does take it as close to a love song as it gets, summing up the spirit of the two slower sections with its phrasing and balance, only speeding the tempo up a bit. Braxton's soprano sax duets with Schroeder capture the lyrical heart of this work.

107, in sum, is a sensitive piece of composing designed to optimize the individual and group improvising potential of players highly trained and skilled in the most sophisticated Western concepts and techniques. Moreover, the way its five sections counter and prefigure and develop each other serves as an entry point to a new level of Braxton's body of work, a level we'll enter and stay on through the final examples of his trio work and the next two chapters.

Theme and variations—development of pitch logic—is, of course, a staple form in both Western art music and jazz. Braxton has worked with it some, mostly in his earlier work, but it fell by the wayside as an area of interest in his maturity. However, the underlying principle invoked by the concept—the principle of cyclical repetition—has swelled in his music from micro to macro levels. For example, while a melodic-harmonic structure and pattern is not something he finds useful to work as a composer for improvisers—he sees that approach as having been mined fully by past masters—an ambiance evoked by a section's tempo, phrasing, or his language devices *is* something he will repeat and build upon, as in *107*, in the same cross-referring way as theme and variation. Likewise, though he won't set up a steady metric state to vary creatively, he will recycle his own rhythmic patterns—the pulse tracks (more about which next chapter)—in a manner subtle and sophisticated enough for his taste.

These are Braxtonian musical expressions of the universal phenomenon of repetition, variation, and mutation in nature we call evolution. They correspond to the AAB form in the blues, or the AABA American song form, where A is repeated, usually altered slightly to place an emphasis somewhere in some way, and where B functions both as inevitable yet surprising outcome of and as contrast to A, leading back to it after having recast its identity or meaning.

We saw Braxton's working of this process begin in the juxtaposition of independent phrases into compositional sections that exhibited development (in *6D* and *6E*). By *36* and *76* he was describing such development in poetic, dramatic terms: "winking" and sounds "that finally face into the night" (*36*); and "a theatre piece etched in stone," "as in a monastery" (*76*). Like words that build sentences that build paragraphs that make stories, Braxton's composer's consciousness rises through the levels of notes, phrases, sections, and—finally—whole pieces made from the materials of both African and Western traditions. What it rises *to* is a system of networking all his pieces, from the first to the latest, so that their players have access to any one of them from within any other. This is the "coordinate music system" described in Chapter Four; we'll explore its traditional precedents and the way he uses it here and in the next chapter. *7 Compositions (Trio) 1989* affords us a glimpse of it in the trio context.

7 Compositions (Trio) 1989 includes five by Braxton, a standard, and one by percussionist Tony Oxley. Braxton's five are actually eight (*40D*, *40J*, *40G*, *63*, *6A*, *110A*, *108B*, and *69J*), but he offers five of the eight in combination with each other so as to form two compositional statements comprising two and three pieces together (*40G(+63)*, and *110A(+108B+69J)*). Their intra-relationships are loose, players typically dipping into the material for improvisational fodder, or reading it at their own pace; Braxton asks only that they stay tuned and sensitive to the collective sound as they use his work to shape it. As Lock writes in his notes, "This use of 'collage form' and 'multiple logics' has played an increasingly important role in Braxton's music in the 1980s, culminating in his 1988 declaration that all his compositions, and all the parts of his compositions, can be played, simultaneously, all together or in any combination."

Most of these pieces were originally written for two-horn quartets; Braxton plays alto, C-melody sax, clarinet, flute, soprano, and sopranino here. The absence of the piano and presence of bass and drums brings this trio (of three men) into a focus in sharp contrast with that of *107*. Here is the active, fiery side of the Muse, in a post-Coleman jazz group.

The pieces also span the length of Braxton's *ouevre* at that time, from the 1968 *6A* to the 1984 *110A*, through points in between from the *40*s and *60*s. The pieces are positioned so that their interaction and flow—unbroken throughout, except between *6A* and *40J*—stand naturally as a mobile display of a slice of personal and musical history taken out of sequential time to suggest the evolution of a lifetime in an hour's worth of music. The musical effects of this chance-ridden procedure recapitulate their more determined forbears, from the early juxtaposition of independent phrases in single horns; of environmental noises with improvisations; of extended rhythmic patterns, notated, and improvised blocks; to pieces played simultaneously by different orchestras. The musical results of "collaging" echo the loose heterophonies, compared in previous chapters, of medieval *organum* and antiphony, early jazz, black and white American grass roots religious services; and the polyrhythmic feel of African and polytonal and atonal sound of 20th-century European and American music. The standard *All The Things You Are* complements this concept perfectly with its title.

This use of his material has become the norm in Braxton's mature recordings and performances. Like virtually all of his music, it has its traditional precedents and expands on them in a way methodical and logical enough to follow into a new area and define it clearly. That area in this instance is, simply put, time beyond history.

Bob Dylan (of whom Braxton considers himself a fan) has said that "songs are just parts of one big symphony"; critics often say of great artists that they are trying to make the same movie, or write the same book or play throughout their life's work. To keep us in the broad example of the pop song, think of the scholarship that grew up around the recurring, evolving, cross-referring imagery of Dylan's music (itself as much derivation from the folk and blues traditions as definitively ingenious spins thereon). When John Lee Hooker sings that he's "a man" who can "rock you all night long," he's saying one thing in his youth that may mean the same, but also much more, in his old age.

In jazz, quotation of songs that were popular in the past, riffs of one's peers, even of childhood ditties, all disgorged from the subconscious in the creative process, is standard practice. It serves as a way of touching base with one's roots, one's formative influences, to establish a context for one's new and original statements. The reworking of one's own material is also a common practice, the grounding there being that with one's own continuity, ever-solidifying the base as new building takes place.

The downside of the process, of course, is stagnation in old ruts, cliché slavery, development that is arrested by old laurels. That's why the "integration of all that came before" is a challenge, rather than simple automatic accretion. The key lies in aligning that which always changes with that which is always fixed: *Composition 6A* is one thing in 1968, in the 23-year-old artist's hands, and quite another—yet also the same—in 1989, when he's 44, with other collaborators, in a different world. Braxton, like Dylan, could be seen as an oldies, nostalgia act for hippies and Afrocentric militants trying to mummify their youthful past—but such a view overlooks much. Indeed, both are dismissed as such by those who themselves are stuck in time.

Acknowledging, rather, the personal and artistic success of his coordinate system's integration of fixed past with mutable present unfolding into sited future, we see its transpersonal counterpart: it is a musical microcosm that is also magical, in the traditional shamanic sense, in its evocation of the past, present, and future of the whole of humanity, and of the planet.

This magical-musical process is part of the churn of music in individual and collective consciousness. In the African American tradition, it occurs time and again, all over the spectrum; the thing called most "modern"—Louis Armstrong's "hot" style in his day, Lester Young's "cool," Charlie Parker's "hip," Ornette Coleman's "free," John Coltrane's and Albert Ayler's "energy music," the AACM's "Great Black Music"—has actually been the most *timeless* thing. All those expressions had to labor under a modernist aesthetic imposed upon them by the Western paradigm of the time (and of time). But all were reaching more deeply into the collective subconscious, thus further *back* in time, with the very same reach they were making through their presents into the future: through gospel and blues, through work songs and field hollers, through primal African rhythms and, in Braxton and others, through ancient musical systems and concepts unearthed by modern scholarship and communication, and recast through modern intuition—but as omnipresent as lost and found again, wending through the culture in an infinity of disguises.

This capture of time in the musical mobile of his life is what he means by the *Tri-Axium* concept, his personal artistic reflection of history and prehistory as a single moment, or a cyclical spiral, in relationship to which humanity is both transcendent and immanent.

Anyone who has gone far enough into love to re-enact (both roles of) the parent-child dynamic with one's lover has lived the concrete truth of this cyclical spiral. Anyone who has gone the next step, and actually produced and raised a child, knows how the experience reconnects one with one's own childhood. Finally, anyone who has gone through the midlife crisis of retro- and introspection and managed to age into a second childhood knows this truth in full bloom. People strive for psychic and spiritual integration and balance by recalling and reflecting on their childhoods, the personal mythology of their dream life, the journeys they began in their youth, the words of wisdom, and the negative examples, they've inherited. What one experiences and achieves on the personal level resonates with that of the race and the planet, quantifies it that much nearer to the point of its critical mass.

This is what places Braxton and his work—indeed, the thrust of African American musiculture throughout the 20th century—in the postmodern, rather than the modern camp to which they've often been assigned. They have, in fact, been modernism's pithiest critics, leaders of the charge against it even as they've been seen as its standard-bearers. This ingenious "double agency" gives us one more definition to throw into that yet-to-be-filled bag we call postmodernism: it is the West's transcendence of its distinction of itself from the rest of the world, of its peculiar history, into its recollection of and reconnection with that world as a nurtured and nurturing part of it. Transcendence is neither denial nor blurring nor compromise nor violation of the thing transcended; it is a flowering, a reconceptualization of some whole, intact, as a part of some greater whole. African American culture has been European America's nagging reminder of that greater whole, and in Braxton it has nagged with an extra measure of the pointed articulation of genius.

Lock's liner notes, citing Braxton's *Composition Notes* on *6A*, say that "a given composition must establish a 'procedure or vibrational space' for the ensemble . . . as opposed to functioning only in the context of a 'head' or theme (to be played and left behind)." Lock's explanation of that with examples of songs that function in African sociocultural contexts (work, play, love, war) grounds the music in that same definition of postmodernism (something that could be called "pre-modern" or "a-historical" just as effectively).

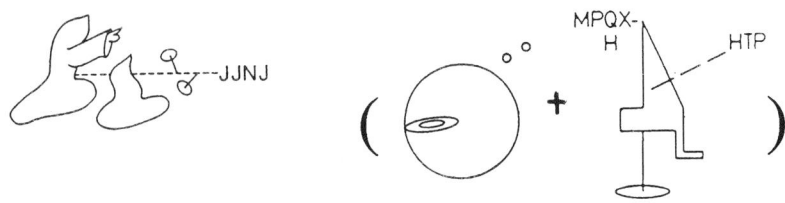

Fig. 7.7: [Graphic titles of] 110A(+108B+69J). *Note the small circles attached to the hooded figures, the circles within circles orbited by circles of the pulse track (108B), and the angularly winding shape, with letters, growing from the circle of the earliest piece. All this speaks of the way Braxton conceives of music as a creative force generating the form and life of an increasingly self-aware reality. The concrete grows from the abstract, becomes sentient, then looks back on its own mystery-shrouded sources. Compare this picture to the following by physicist John Wheeler, of what he calls the self-synthesizing nature of the universe.*[27] *Stemming from the quantum physicists' findings that the material universe—spacetime—is contingent upon perception of it, Wheeler conceives of all science and knowledge as contingent on cosmogeny, of the Big Bang* qua *Big Bang as contingent upon the (time-transcending) perception of it by the sentience that arose from it, so:*

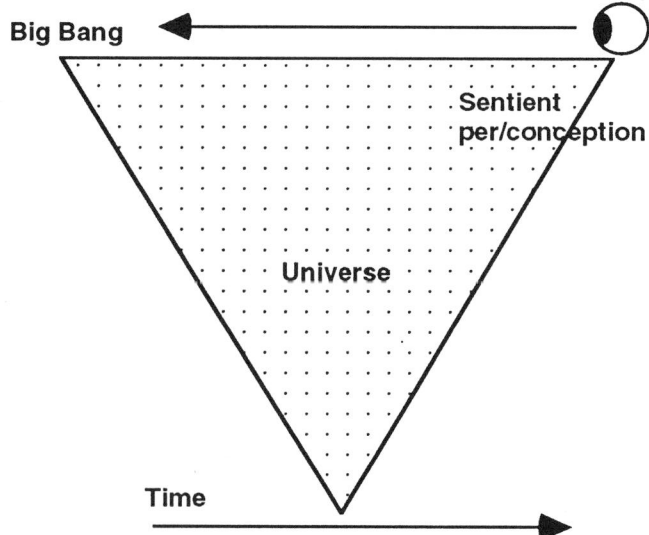

> Musically, this "coordination" of three pieces, one being a "pulse track"—a repeating sequence of notated materials interspersed with brief (five-to-ten-second) spaces for improvisation—offers alternatives to the usual chordal field of vertical harmonies, or (writes Braxton) "an attempt to integrate horizontal structural formings into the forward space of the music."

The graphic title of *110A* recalls the two hooded figures Ursula Oppens and Frederick Rzewski represented in performing *95*; a larger one is pointing out the way (of the music) to the smaller. Human figures had just appeared in Braxton's graphic titles at the end of his "Golden Peak" (*95* through *105B*: see next chapter) of compositions, in the titles of his first pulse tracks—another sign of the major transformation his work underwent at this point.

Braxton's notes on *110A* call it

> a light (small) structural platform that seeks to provide a focus for extended improvisation (and ensemble character) . . . This is a kind of song structure that winds its way into the space of the music to create the sensation of "blowing winds and trees" (on an island experiencing a rain storm) . . . The tradition of creative music is full of structures of this type—works that are made up from a few "golden" phrases to create a riff or "life"s focus." All of these matters are directly related to the wonder of creativity—and the fact that sometimes a very sparse effort can produce great abundance.[28]

· · · · ·

The late Miles Davis (another Gemini, Stockhausen fan, and fellow bandleader to Braxton's major collaborators Holland and Corea) was asked by biographer Quincey Troupe what he thought the future of music would be. "Shorter phrases," he said.[29] His comments about his drummer Tony Williams, and about the gifts African American players generally brought to the music making, cap this chapter best. Williams was so dynamic and fresh, Davis said, because his father had started him playing drums when he was a young boy; the rhythms he had developed since then were combined from the thousands of little patterns he had developed throughout his life of (literal) play. The "brothers," Davis said, brought to the music all kinds of tricks and secrets they learned together as children.

Braxton's process of making musical innovations is in just that spirit of wonder and play, and he has sustained its continuity back to the first thrills of his childhood. The complexity is something that just comes with enough time and persistence, but its primal impulse is the same simple childhood spirit of unabashed play, increasingly simplified and liberated with maturity, whether it's responding to the epiphanous moments of Webern, Coleman, or Cage or the grand forevers of Schönberg, Stockhausen, or Coltrane.

The trio music shows the liminal space between such play in individuals and that of groups. From here on, we join the artist in that play in the place beyond time, where time is made.

1. Albert Churchward, *Signs and Symbols of Primordial Man: The Evolution of Religious Doctrine from the Eschatology of the Ancient Egyptians* (London/New York: E.P. Dutton & Company, 1910: 308–315).
2. Barbara Walker, "Yoni," in *The Woman's Encyclopedia of Myths and Secrets* (San Francisco: Harper & Row, 1983).
3. Ibid., "Triangle."
4. Anthony Braxton, *Composition Notes A* (Hanover, NH: Tree Frog Music, 1988: 52–56).
5. Ibid., 57–61.
6. Ibid., 61.
7. Ibid., 71–74.
8. Ibid., 99–101.
9. The text:

> The real became us too
> everything we felt when living
> and fallen memories
> knowing that we had no voice
> as life receives a gift unknown behind a day
> the truth of our past.
>
> Actualities in finding nothing
> holding to prefabricated time slots
> waiting for contemporary mind cards
> we lost our dream.
>
> The real became us too
> offerings that went untouched
> destined to belong
> knowing that we had no voice
> watching as the world collides
> after all we've said and done there.

10. See Ekkehard Jost, "The Chicagoans" (*Free Jazz*, Grasz: Universal Edition, 1974: 163–79), and Leslie Rout's "The AACM: New Music (!) New Ideas (?)" (*Journal of Popular Culture*, 1/2, Fall 1967: 128–37).
11. Emphasis mine; see Walker's links between the "Aryan" invasion of ancient Egypt, the pyramid as simulated (volcanic?) mountain in a flat land, and the followers of Horus.
12. Churchward, 313.
13. Braxton, *Composition Notes C*, 17–23, for this and next two citations.
14. Ibid., ii.
15. Braxton, *Composition Notes C*, 17–23.
16. Lange (*Coda*).
17. Braxton, *Composition Notes D*, 42–62.
18. Ibid., 136–54, for this and next citation.
19. Thanks again to Jon Barlow for pointing this out.
20. Barry McRae, "For Trio" (*Jazz Journal International*, September 1978: 20–21).
21. Braxton, *Composition Notes D*, 136–54.
22. Churchward, 313–14.
23. Braxton, *Composition Notes D*, 457–71, for this and the next two citations.
24. Again, credit goes to Jon Barlow for this suggestion.

25. Terry Martin, "Braxton[8]" (*Down Beat*, Apr., 1987: 43–45).
26. Braxton, *Composition Notes E*, 286–301, for this and the next four citations.
27. See Plate 1 and notes thereon in Wheeler's *Between Quantum and Cosmos* (New Jersey: Princeton University Press, 1988: 2, 614). Wheeler's diagram reverses the position of subject and object, and distinguishes the thinness of one from the thickness of the other, but my version is faithful to his concept.
28. Ibid., 350–52, this and next citation.
29. Quincey Troupe, *Miles Davis: The Autobiography* (New York: Simon & Schuster, 1989: 393).

Chapter Eight

Quartet Music

[From occult definition of] **three**: ... childbirth; *b. often seen as a conscious-spiritual value, lacking the* One *of the unconscious to make the* Whole of Four: *the triangle can be seen as the half of the diagonal square: together they are at once polarity (2 triangles in opposition) and the conjunction of Wholeness (cf. Chinese Yang-Yin); three thus represents masculinity (or the* animus *in the female), whereas* Four *is femininity (or the* anima *in the male) with subconsciousness included.* (emphases mine)

This familiar religious symbol is commonly called the Star of David. Robert Graves discusses it as Solomon's Seal, something the ancient Hebrew king himself derived from Egypt.

The Seal seems to have sanctified a divine marriage in countries which originally worshipped a Supreme Goddess rather than a Supreme God, but in which (by a compromise between matriarchal and patriarchal custom) the executive side of government had been entrusted first to a lover chosen by the Queen to act as her temporary vizier, and then, after a political revolution, to her husband as a permanent King reigning with the God-monarchy, the sacred marriage had been celebrated at the annual vintage Feast of Booths or Tabernacles, between the Hebrew King, representing the Bull-god El (who had been brought down from the North by the Hittites) and the virgin chosen to represent the Canaanite Mother-Goddess Ashera ...

Yet Solomon's Seal meant far more than an announcement of a public lovefeast; when examined closely it proves to be a statement of man's dependence on woman for his well-being, most applicable wherever man is equated with the Sun as power and energy, and woman with the Moon as wisdom and healing.

An ancient architectural rule insisted, we are told, that every pyramid should rest on an inverted one of the same proportions. This concealed pyramid plainly

quartet music

represented the power of the Great Goddess by whose divine mercy each Pharaoh reigned, and whose secret authority he acknowledged by a ritual marriage nominally with his own sister but (to avoid incest) with, it seems, a cross-cousin. The shape of the upper pyramid recorded the Pharaoh's domination of the upper world: at his installment he had shot four arrows with his full strength to the north, south, east and west, and a fifth straight up into the air. But the lower world remained under the Goddess' power, because from the depth of earth rose hidden waters, also sacred serpents and mice, and oracular wisdom. Unless the Pharaoh honoured his goddess wife as royally as she honored him, the magic of the double pyramid would fail and their joint empire be overtaken by misfortune.

The six points of the Seal represent a multiplication of the female or lunar number, three, by the male or solar number, two; so do the six points of the double pyramid. Moreover, the double pyramid has eight sides, which is two to the power of three, a figure symbolizing increase . . .

Nor was Solomon's Seal merely a dynastic charm. As a two-dimensional sign for the double pyramid it laid down the basic law for all true-love-alliances. This law may be framed in English as "Man does, Woman is!": which does not deny women their right to activity, but confirms their power to restrain male activity within the bounds that, their intuition warns them, are needed to restrain genocide. In traditional West African monarchies, no King, although in theory absolute, still dares do anything in defiance of his Queen Mother's tearful protests: "My son, my son, you are killing us." But without any such love understanding—and in the civilized world the conspiracy between money, politics and science grows daily more threatening to human survival, nor can any women put an effective brake on male government—we are already on the brink of moral ruin.[1]

Walker traces the history of the Seal to ancient Hinduism, picking up its history in medieval Spain.

The Cabala was developed by the Jews of Moorish Spain after the crusades brought eastern Goddess worship into their ken. Cabalists used the hexagram as Tantric yogis used it, to represent the union of God with his Female Power, Shekina, the Jewish form of Shakti-Kali. As Shakti was the essential soul of any Hindu god, so Shekina was the essential soul of the Cabalistic God. As in all religions of the Divine Marriage, Cabalistic Judaism discovered man and woman to be earthly images of God and Goddess; and sexual union of mortals naturally encouraged its like in the supernatural realm. Therefore sexual intercourse was "a sacramental act in the service of a God and his consort (or perhaps vice versa: a Goddess and her consort)" . . .[2]

[From occult definition of] **four***: A. the earth, the material world: 1. terrestrial order; 2. space: a. the cube; b. the square, = Mercury: Lord of the World, the Sower of all things; bc the four-stringed sistrum: the 4 regions of the world, seasons, etc.; 3. the limits of the minimum of totality; 4. the 4 main directions of the compass . . . the intersection of the cycles of heaven and earth . . . the four horses are the four elements: a. fire: the fastest, shining horse, with*

on it the signs of the planets and constellations; its hot breath sets the manes of "air" on fire; b. air: a little slower: lit up on one side only; c. water: still slower: it drowns the earth with sweat; d. earth: turns round and round ...

C. the human situation: *1.* reason: a. rational organization; b. the realization of an idea . . . *2.* tangible achievement; *3.* the figure 4 = phallus + vulva (= androgyne = fertility) . . .

D. divinity: *1.* most ancient peoples had a supreme god of four letters, forming the tetragrammaton: e.g. Zeus, YHWH . . .

E. psych.: *1.* wholeness: the masculine triangle + its opposite counterpart (= unconsciousness and femininity) seen as a square cut diagonally . . . *2.* the functional aspects of consciousness: thinking–feeling–sensation–intuition; *3.* concentration . . . *6.* any well-ordered space and structure . . .

H. special mythical meanings: *I.* Egypt: a. the celestial number: the four columns holding the sky . . . c. the four sons of Horus; *II.* Hebrew . . . b. universality + divine equilibrium; c. an extremely important number in all visionary and apocalyptic literature . . . *III.* Greek-Roman: *1.* Pythagoreans . . . b. reminds us of God and his Infinite Power in the arrangement of the universe: Harmony = God; the first mathematical power generating virtue; c. squareness, justice, earth . . . *5.* the oldest tools (Stone Age Man): a. warfare: e.g. the arrowheads, which were later often considered as "fairy weapons" . . . cleavers, handaxe, etc . . . .

There is an octagonal heaven which may be formed of a double square. There were four gods of the four corners; four consorts were assigned to them at the second four corners or half cardinal points. Twice four points are equivalent to a double square. The square may thus be doubled like the double triangle to make an octagon, as the octonary of Taht, the Moon God. The eightfold way is equal to the square when doubled and blended in one figure.

The Japanese have an eight-forked road of heaven. A four square sign named Tesennu or Khemenu—i.e. No. 8 in Egyptian. Four sides of Egyptian Pyramid. Four corners Assyrian Pyramid = four sides and four corners = a double square or cube 8, = a double square and circle—i.e. eight half cardinal points ... Triangle added above with three gods at the corners.

This has precisely the same meaning as the Double Triangle.[3]

quartet music

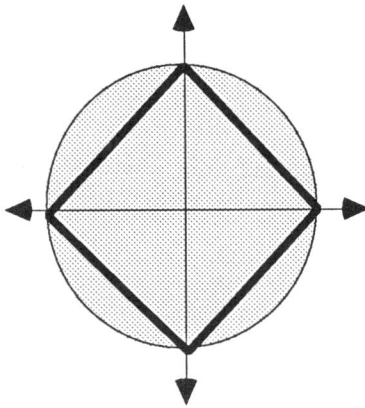

The child is born; and the quanta wave potentia have been activated into particular events that have combined to form new matter. The undefined perimeter of the circle denotes the presence of the fertilized egg—of the formerly integrated world of potentia (musically, the information of traditional material) used to make the new life—in a state now subsumed in that life (as we see parents in their children, and past in present in future). The solid line of the diamond indicates the independent, integrated life of the new individual (or, in this case, art); the arrows have switched from circle to diamond because that's where the forces (in motion) have moved to. They denote the creative act; the music now plays its maker.

The diamond position of the square denotes the nature of its volatility; it is not static, however solid, the forces must keep moving to realize its stability. This position also signals the balance between male and female achieved: each of the triangles has a symmetrical mirror image, three couples dancing (the four single and two doubled isosceles) around, in, and through the diamond/square of the quartet.

Braxton uses the diamond shape in his notation as a "road sign" to denote the music's heart—pulse; he uses the square to denote notated blocks to be played exactly as written.

In Braxton's music, the above citations go to his use of the quartet as the most stable and complete structure for working out his musical vision and system, in several ways:

1) *instrumentation*—it covers both African and Western and masculine and feminine poles of the American middle ground as voiced by the instruments (see Chapter Six). The groups with piano, both from his very early and most recent quartets, use the most conventional instrumentation in the most Eurocentric and feminine (what he would call post-Webern, post-Cage, post-Schönberg, post-Stockhausen) ways (the trio-plus-floating-other, the holism of the field of sound, and the inter-independence of the coordinate system's operation); the more traditionally radical combination of two horns, bass, and percussion usually covers the more masculine (linear, tunnel-visioned, hierarchical in its solos-with-support, rhythmically driven), jazz-familiar sound-and-pulse ground (post-Parker,

post-Coleman, post-Ayler). That line between the two types of groups isn't hard and fast, but discernible;

2) *number*—it combines solo, duo, and trio dynamics, as defined heretofore, within its own "largest" symmetry, and surveys and charts the ground for larger ensembles;

3) *tradition*—even Braxton calls it his most commercial, familiar context that links him with the jazz audience;[4] it is also the combination of choice—in the string quartet—for composers and the most serious listeners in the European tradition.

Not surprisingly, then, the body of quartet music displays the transcendent aspects of Braxton's *oeuvre*—or perhaps we should say the immanent aspects of that of his Muse—in a way the solo, duo, and trio work, by comparison, only suggests. This (the book's eighth, this section's third) chapter is therefore the climax of the book's (fourth) section; as such, it brings us through the four-chambered heart of Braxton's work.

Before delving back into the music, however, it would be well here to get our bearings. We've covered much ground in the contexts of the other combinations, and have transcended a bit more of it with each chapter. Imagine each chapter as a step up the pyramid in progress; what do we see looking back and down, around us where we are, forward and up?

First, we need to recall that although we've been charting chronological developments of Braxton's music within each chapter, we haven't done so between the chapters; traditional jazz groups didn't evolve into solo, then duo, then trio, quartet, and large ensemble musics through linear time. Braxton has worked all these combinations and their concepts all along, juggling his real-world opportunities and inner visions as best he could, letting them feed and inform each other's growth; the development between the chapters is primarily a way to grasp the progression from simple to complex in his music—but it also suggests something of his experience in moving between the various situations from solo to collective.

His quartet book is by far his fattest, his quartet recordings most numerous, with press coverage to match. To continue tracing his development as a composer as above, through works selected to represent the whole 30-year arc would require a second volume, or would leave out much. Fortunately, it would also go over ground already covered well enough—the musical elements and approaches, and the metamusical associations Braxton has evoked and invoked with them. We are thus free to move "up" from looking at the "trees" (of individual compositions) to the whole "forest" (alphanumeric series) of which they're a part.

Insert 8.1 will help us do that. It organizes Braxton's opus numbers sequentially and in relation to the recordings on which they appear. We can refer to the musical traits of the 6 *series* as a block, rather than those of each piece, for the broad overview.

But, in fact, we have done that all along without organizing the music so densely, every time we've drawn conclusions about the way the music did develop over time through selected compositions. Insert 8.1 does improve that process, but its greater usefulness lies in what it displays about the *non*musical dynamics at work through Braxton's music, and what those suggest about the *meta*musical forces in its motion.

quartet music

We touched on these forces toward the end of the last chapter, in noting the numerological dynamics between some of the trio pieces' opus numbers ($6, 6^2, (6^2)2+1, 6^2+40, (6^2+40)+3^3, (6^2+40)+3^3+13$; that is, *6, 36, 73, 76, 94,* and *107*). These dynamics are not something Braxton has ever planned or paid much attention to. Much of what he has said in print and private interviews is consistent with an awareness of them—of a synchronistic universe charged with its own meaning and creative intelligence—as background, but not with an interest in predetermining and/or manipulating them. Indeed, he would more likely shun that as stifling and trivial, or beyond his province. Nevertheless, such patterns between the trio material's opus numbers carry a "charge" one with an eye for numerology will readily appreciate; their counterparts in the quartet are so much more plentiful that we couldn't trace them in all their detail here. However, to stop and view *some* of them, in the whole body of work, from our new, more distant view of that musical forest, will give us a sense of something important to our consideration of the music itself (especially next chapter): the sense of the invisible, metamusical "terrain" such patterns may be mapping—the footprints of the Muse moving through that terrain—and the corresponding nature of Braxton's approach to rhythm and meter.

Note the four (note the number) series devoted mostly to quartet works, numbered *6, 23, 40, 69.* Those particular numbers themselves are supercharged with mystical and mythical associations. It may seem to casual (and cynical) observers that every number is equally significant to those looking for such meanings, and that therefore none are. In fact, the numbers 1 through 10 are so—thus they have long entries in dictionaries of symbols and images such as the one used here (de Vries)—but beyond that only a few stand out. De Vries covers all of the four just cited except 23 (which comprises 6's multiples, and is the ninth prime number), yet it too has similar associations.[5] The "identity" of 40 appears throughout the Bible and other ancient mystical texts; 69, in lore a "lucky number," survives in common usage as both astrological (Cancer) and sexual symbol.

There are 17 numbers between each of the first three of these series numbers, and 29 between the last two. Seventeen is the seventh prime number, 29 the tenth. So after three intervals measured by the seventh prime number, an interval measured by the tenth such occurred before the *69*s capped the four series.

The *6* and *23* series each include letters *A* through *P*, totaling 16 letters; the *40* and *69* series run *A* through *Q*, 17 letters. Sixteen is four squared, that plus one is 17; 1+6=7, 1+7=8 . . . all of which is of aesthetic interest, if nothing else, in the way not only the numbers but their proliferations in sets resonate with the musical concepts of the trio-plus-floating-other and other triangle-derived concepts of the square.

Continuing on these lines just a bit more, we see that seven numbers after 69 is *76*, the watershed trio work; three nines after 69 (which is three 23s), two tens after 76, and we have *96* (which is twice three 4^2s), the seminal work for large ensemble that pops up in all combinations, especially quartet.

Insert 8.1: Braxton's works cross-referenced with recorded performances. Think of this as a picture of the crossroads where the composer's inner world (best depicted by his Catalogue of Works) and the outer world have met. The transcendent patterns of the former trace the message of the Muse through the artist in time; those of this insert show that message as it has been willed and forced to unfold through the world with which the artist had to deal.

Type legend: SOLO, duo, *trio*, **quartet**, *LARGE ENSEMBLE*; (covers/collaborations)
Braxton compositions   *Braxton recordings*

Mostly quartets
4	The Complete Braxton 1971 (Arista/Freedom 1902)
5	Willisau (Quartet) 1991 (hat ART CD 61001/4)
6A	The Complete Braxton 1971 (Arista/Freedom 1902)
	Six Duets (1982) w/ John Lindberg (Cecma 1005)
	Seven Compositions (Trio) 1989 (hat ART 6025)
	Quartet (Coventry) 1985 (Leo 204/205)
6C	The Montreux/Berlin Concerts (Arista 5002)
	Dortmund (Quartet) 1976 (hat ART 6075)
6D	*Three Compositions of New Jazz (Delmark 415)*
6E	Three Compositions of New Jazz (Delmark 415)
6F	This Time (Affinity 25)
	Chick Corea: Circling In (Blue Note 472)
	Circle: Paris Concert (ECM 1018/9)
	The Montreaux/Berlin Concerts (Arista 5002)
6F	Donaueschingen (Duo) 1976 (hat ART CD 6150)
6G	B-X°-NO/47A (Affinity 15)
6H	*This Time (Affinity 25)*
6I	The Complete Braxton 1971 (Arista/Freedom 1902)
6J	The Complete Braxton 1971 (Arista/Freedom 1902)
6K	The Complete Braxton 1971 (Arista/Freedom 1902)
	(VIENNA ART ORCHESTRA: FROM RAG TIME TO NO TIME)
6L	The Complete Braxton 1971 (Arista/Freedom 1902)
6M	The Complete Braxton 1971 (Arista/Freedom 1902)
6N	*Town Hall 1972 (Trio 3008/9)*
	Six Duets (1982) w/ John Lindberg (Cecma 1005)
6(O)	*Town Hall 1972 (Trio 3008/9)*
	Braxton/Pavone: Duets (1993) (Music & Arts CD 786)
6P	Town Hall 1972 (Trio 3008/9)

Solo
8A	FOR ALTO (DELMARK 420/1)
8B	FOR ALTO (DELMARK 420/1)
8C	FOR ALTO (DELMARK 420/1)
8D	FOR ALTO (DELMARK 420/1)
8F	FOR ALTO (DELMARK 420/1)
8G	FOR ALTO (DELMARK 420/1)
8H	FOR ALTO (DELMARK 420/1)
8I	SAXOPHONE IMPROVISATIONS SERIES F
	(INNER CITY 1008/AMERICA 30 AM 011/2)
8J	SAXOPHONE IMPROVISATIONS SERIES F (AMERICA 30 AM 011/2)

8K	*This Time (Affinity 25)*
10	Willisau (Quartet) 1991 (hat ART CD 61001/4)
15	Splatter/Debris: Jump or Die (Music & Arts CD 843)
16	RECITAL PARIS '71 (MUSICA 2004)
17	(w/ Robert Schumann String Quartet [sound aspects 009])
20	Joseph Jarman w/ Anthony Braxton: Alone Together (Delmark 428)
	ENSEMBLE (VICTORIAVILLE) 1988 (VICTO 07)
	Willisau (Quartet) 1991 (hat ART CD 61001/4)
	Twelve Compositions (Music & Arts, CD 835, 1993)
21	Joseph Jarman w/ Anthony Braxton: Alone Together (Delmark 428)
22	The Complete Braxton 1971 (Arista/Freedom 1902)

quartet music

Mostly quartets_____

23A	New York, Fall 1974 (Arista 4023)
23B	Live at Moers Festival (Ring 01010/11)
	New York, Fall 1974 (Arista 4023)
23C	New York, Fall 1974 (Arista 4023)
	Willisau (Quartet) 1991 (hat ART CD 61001/4)
	Splatter/Debris: Jump or Die [Music & Arts CD 843]
	Twelve Compositions (Music & Arts, CD 835, 1993)
23D	Live at Moers Festival (Ring 01010/11)
	New York, Fall 1974 (Arista 4023)
(+108A)	Splatter/Debris: Jump or Die [Music & Arts CD 843]
23E	Live at Moers Festival (Ring 01010/11)
	Five Pieces 1975 (Arista 4064)
23F	Live at Moers Festival (Ring 01010/11)
23G	Five Pieces 1975 (Arista 4064)
	Performance 9/1/79 (hat Hut 2R19)
	Quartet (Coventry) 1985 (Leo 204/205)
	Willisau (Quartet) 1991 (hat ART CD 61001/4)
23M	Twelve Compositions (Music & Arts, CD 835, 1993)
23H	Five Pieces 1975 (Arista 4064)
23J	The Montreux/Berlin Concerts (Arista 5002)
	Dortmund (Quartet) 1976 (hat ART 6075)
	Six Duets (1982) w/ John Lindberg (Cecma 1005)
	Quartet (Birmingham) 1985 (Leo 202/203)
23K	Dona Lee (America 30 AM 6122)
23L	Dona Lee (America 30 AM 6122)
23M	Four Compositions (1973) (Denon 7506)
(+10)	Willisau (Quartet) 1991 (hat ART CD 61001/4)
23N	Four Compositions (1973) (Denon 7506)
(+112, 108A, 33)	Willisau (Quartet) 1991 (hat ART CD 61001/4)
23(O)	Four Compositions (1973) (Denon 7506)
23P	Four Compositions (1973) (Denon 7506)

25	CREATIVE MUSIC ORCHESTRA (RING 01024/5/6)

Solo_____

26A	SAXOPHONE IMPROVISATIONS SERIES F
	(INNER CITY 1008/AMERICA 30 AM 011/2)
26B	SAXOPHONE IMPROVISATIONS SERIES F
	(INNER CITY 1008/AMERICA 30 AM 011/2)
	SOLO: LIVE AT MOERS FESTIVAL (MOERS 1002)
	ALTO SAXOPHONE IMPROVISATIONS 1979 (ARISTA 8602)
	(w/ Robert Schumann String Quartet The Montreux[sound aspects
009])	
26C	SAXOPHONE IMPROVISATIONS SERIES F (AMERICA 30 AM 011/2)
26D	SAXOPHONE IMPROVISATIONS SERIES F (AMERICA 30 AM 011/2)
26E	SOLO: LIVE AT MOERS FESTIVAL (MOERS 1002)
	ALTO SAXOPHONE IMPROVISATIONS 1979 (ARISTA 8602)
	(w/ Robert Schumann String Quartet (sound aspects 009)
26F	SAXOPHONE IMPROVISATIONS SERIES F (AMERICA 30 AM 011/2)
	SOLO: LIVE AT MOERS FESTIVAL (MOERS 1002)
	ALTO SAXOPHONE IMPROVISATIONS 1979 (ARISTA 8602)
	19 [SOLO] COMPOSITIONS, 1988 (NEW ALBION 023)
26G	SOLO: LIVE AT MOERS FESTIVAL (MOERS 1002)
26H	SOLO: LIVE AT MOERS FESTIVAL (MOERS 1002)
26I	SAXOPHONE IMPROVISATIONS SERIES F (AMERICA 30 AM 011/2)
	(w/ Robert Schumann String Quartet (sound aspects 009)
26J	SAXOPHONE IMPROVISATIONS SERIES F
	(INNER CITY 1008/AMERICA 30 AM 011/2)

_____

29	Braxton/Pavone: Duets (1993) (Music & Arts CD 786)
30	(Frederic Rzewski: First Recordings [Finnadar 9011])
	Quartet (London) 1985 (Leo 200/201)
	Quartet (Birmingham) 1985 (Leo 202/203)

	Various: Music from Mills [MC001]
	Five Compositions (Quartet) 1986 (Black Saint 0106)
	Duets, Vancouver 1989 w/ Marilyn Crispell (Music & Arts CD 611)
	Willisau (Quartet) 1991 (hat ART CD 61001/4)
	NYCO: FIRST PROGRAM IN STANDARD TIME
	[NEW WORLD/COUNTERCURRENTS DIDX 80418-2])
	Quartet (Victoriaville) 1992 (Victo CD 021)
	Twelve Compositions (Music & Arts, CD 835, 1993)
31	(Frederic Rzewski: First Recordings [Finnadar 9011])
	Quartet (Birmingham) 1985 (Leo 202/203)
	Five Compositions (Quartet) 1986 (Black Saint 0106)
32	Quartet (London) 1985 (Leo 200/201)
	Willisau (Quartet) 1991 (hat ART CD 61001/4)
	NYCO: FIRST PROGRAM IN STANDARD TIME
	[NEW WORLD/COUNTERCURRENTS DIDX 80418-2])
	Twelve Compositions (Music & Arts, CD 835, 1993)
33	Quartet (Birmingham) 1985 (Leo 202/203)
	Willisau (Quartet) 1991 (hat ART CD 61001/4)
34	Six Compositions, Quartet (Antilles 1981)
	Willisau (Quartet) 1991 (hat ART CD 61001/4)
36	*Duet & Trio (Sackville 3007)*
37	New York, Fall 1974 (Arista 4023)
	(ROVA Saxophone Quartet: Beat Kennel [Black Saint 0126])
38A	New York, Fall 1974 (Arista 4023)

Mostly quartets_____

40A	Six Compositions, Quartet (Antilles 1981)
	Willisau (Quartet) 1991 (hat ART CD 61001/4)
	Eight Duets Hamburg 1991 (Music & Arts CD 710)
40B	Dortmund (Quartet) 1976 (hat ART 6075)
	Six Compositions, Quartet (Antilles 1981)
	Willisau (Quartet) 1991 (hat ART CD 61001/4)
40D	Seven Compositions 1978 (Moers 01066)
(+108A, 108B)	Anthony Braxton/Gino Robair: Duets 1987 (Rastascan 002)
	Seven Compositions (Trio) 1989 (hat ART 6025)
	(Splatter/Debris: Jump or Die [Music & Arts CD 843])
40E (+40D)	(Splatter/Debris: Jump or Die [Music & Arts CD 843])
40F	Dortmund (Quartet) 1976 (hat ART 6075)
	Performance 9/1/79 (hat Hut 2R19)
	Seven Compositions 1978 (Moers 01066)
	Quartet (London) 1985 (Leo 200/201)
	(ROVA & Anthony Braxton: the Aggregate, live [sound aspects 23])
40G	Six Compositions, Quartet (Antilles 1981)
(+63)	Seven Compositions (Trio) 1989 (hat ART 6025)
40I	Performance 9/1/79 (hat Hut 2R19)
	Seven Compositions 1978 (Moers 01066)
40J	*Seven Compositions (Trio) 1989 (hat ART 6025)*
	Willisau (Quartet) 1991 (hat ART CD 61001/4)
40K	The Montreux/Berlin Concerts (Arista 5002)
40L	Willisau (Quartet) 1991 (hat ART CD 61001/4)
40M	Live at Moers Festival (Ring 01010/11)
	Five Pieces 1975 (Arista 4064)
	Willisau (Quartet) 1991 (hat ART CD 61001/4)
40N	The Montreux/Berlin Concerts (Arista 5002)
	Quartet (Coventry) 1985 (Leo 204/205)
40(O)	Live at Moers Festival (Ring 01010/11)
	The Montreux/Berlin Concerts (Arista 5002)
	Dortmund (Quartet) 1976 (hat ART 6075)
	Quartet (London) 1985 (Leo 200/201)
	Quartet (Birmingham) 1985 (Leo 202/203)
	(ROVA & Anthony Braxton: the Aggregate, live [sound aspects 23])
	(Splatter/Debris: Jump or Die [Music & Arts CD 843])

quartet music

Mostly duos

40P	Duets 1976 w/ Muhal Richard Abrams (Arista 4101)
	(Splatter/Debris: Jump or Die [Music & Arts CD 843])
40Q	Roscoe Mitchell: Duets w/ Anthony Braxton (Sackville 3016)
	Roscoe Mitchell: Snurdy McGurdy and Her Dancin' Shoes (Nessa 20)

Mostly large ensembles

41	*(BRAXTON/BARRY GUY/LONDON JAZZ COMPOSER'S ORCHESTRA: ZURICH CONCERTS [INTAKT 4/5])*
45	*(W/ THE NORTHWEST CREATIVE ORCHESTRA: EUGENE (1989) [BLACK SAINT 120 137-2])*
	CREATIVE ORCHESTRA (KÖLN) 1978 (HAT ART CD 2-1671)
48	(Splatter/Debris: Jump or Die [Music & Arts CD 843])
48	**Twelve Compositions (Music & Arts, CD 835, 1993)**
50 (+53)	(Splatter/Debris: Jump or Die [Music & Arts CD 843])
51	*CREATIVE ORCHESTRA MUSIC 1976 (ARISTA 4080)*
	CREATIVE ORCHESTRA (KÖLN) 1978 (HAT ART CD 2-1671)
52	Six Compositions, Quartet (Antilles 1981)
	Quartet (London) 1985 (Leo 200/201)
53	(Splatter/Debris: Jump or Die [Music & Arts CD 843])
55	*CREATIVE ORCHESTRA MUSIC 1976 (ARISTA 4080)*
	CREATIVE ORCHESTRA (KÖLN) 1978 (HAT ART CD 2-1671)
56	*CREATIVE ORCHESTRA MUSIC 1976 (ARISTA 4080)*
57	*CREATIVE ORCHESTRA MUSIC 1976 (ARISTA 4080)*
58	*CREATIVE ORCHESTRA MUSIC 1976 (ARISTA 4080)*
	CREATIVE ORCHESTRA (KÖLN) 1978 (HAT ART CD 2-1671)
59	*CREATIVE ORCHESTRA MUSIC 1976 (ARISTA 4080)*
	CREATIVE ORCHESTRA (KÖLN) 1978 (HAT ART CD 2-1671)
	(W/ THE NORTHWEST CREATIVE ORCHESTRA: EUGENE (1989) [BLACK SAINT 120 137-2])

Mostly duos

60	Duets 1976 w/ Muhal Richard Abrams (Arista 4101)
(+108C, 96)	Quartet (Birmingham) 1985 (Leo 202/203)
62	Duets 1976 w/ Muhal Richard Abrams (Arista 4101)
(+30, 96)	(Various: Music from Mills [MC001])
	Duets, Vancouver 1989 w/ Marilyn Crispell (Music & Arts CD 611)
63	**The Montreux/Berlin Concerts (Arista 5002)**
	(BRAXTON/BARRY GUY/LONDON JAZZ COMPOSER'S ORCHESTRA: ZURICH CONCERTS [INTAKT 4/5])
	Seven Compositions (Trio) 1989 (hat ART 6025)
64	Elements of Surprise w/George Lewis (Moers 1036)
	Donaueschingen (Duo) 1976 (hat ART CD 6150)
65	Elements of Surprise w/George Lewis (Moers 1036)
	Braxton/Pavone: Duets (1993) (Music & Arts CD 786)
66	**Twelve Compositions (Music & Arts, CD 835, 1993)**
67 (+147, 96)	Willisau (Quartet) 1991 (hat ART CD 61001/4)
69A	Six Duets (1982) w/ John Lindberg (Cecma 1005)
69B	Six Duets (1982) w/ John Lindberg (Cecma 1005)

Mostly quartets

	Quartet (Coventry) 1985 (Leo 204/205)
	Willisau (Quartet) 1991 (hat ART CD 61001/4)
69C	Performance 9/1/79 (hat Hut 2R19)
	Quartet (Coventry) 1985 (Leo 204/205)
69D	(Splatter/Debris: Jump or Die [Music & Arts CD 843])
69E	Performance 9/1/79 (hat Hut 2R19)
69F	Performance 9/1/79 (hat Hut 2R19)
	Quartet (Coventry) 1985 (Leo 204/205)
69G	Performance 9/1/79 (hat Hut 2R19)
	Seven Compositions 1978 (Moers 01066)
69H	Seven Compositions 1978 (Moers 01066)
	Prag 1984 "Quartet Performance" (sound aspects 038)
(+31)	Quartet (Birmingham) 1985 (Leo 202/203)
69I	Splatter/Debris: Jump or Die [Music & Arts CD 843]

69J	*Seven Compositions (Trio) 1989 (hat ART 6025)*
69J	**Twelve Compositions (Music & Arts, CD 835, 1993)**
69K	Seven Compositions 1978 (Moers 01066)
69L	(Splatter/Debris: Jump or Die [Music & Arts CD 843])
69M	Seven Compositions 1978 (Moers 01066)
	Four Compositions (Quartet) 1983 (Black Saint 0066)
(+33)	Quartet (Birmingham) 1985 (Leo 202/203)
69N	Six Compositions, Quartet (Antilles 1981)
69(O)	Four Compositions (Quartet) 1983 (Black Saint 0066)
	Willisau (Quartet) 1991 (hat ART CD 61001/4)
69P	Six Duets (1982) w/ John Lindberg (Cecma 1005)
69Q	(Dave Holland: Emerald Tears [ECM 1109])
	Four Compositions (Quartet) 1983 (Black Saint 0066)
	(Splatter/Debris: Jump or Die [Music & Arts CD 843])
71	*(W/ THE NORTHWEST CREATIVE ORCHESTRA: EUGENE (1989) [BLACK SAINT 120 137-2])*
74A	Roscoe Mitchell: Duets w/ Anthony Braxton (Sackville 3016)
74B	Roscoe Mitchell: Duets w/ Anthony Braxton (Sackville 3016)
74C	(Splatter/Debris: Jump or Die [Music & Arts CD 843])
76	*For Trio (Arista 4181)*
77A	ALTO SAXOPHONE IMPROVISATIONS 1979 (ARISTA 8602)
77B	SOLO: LIVE AT MOERS FESTIVAL (MOERS 1002)
	(w/ Robert Schumann String Quartet The Montreux[sound aspects 009])
77C	ALTO SAXOPHONE IMPROVISATIONS 1979 (ARISTA 8602)
	19 [SOLO] COMPOSITIONS, 1988 (NEW ALBION 023)
77D	ALTO SAXOPHONE IMPROVISATIONS 1979 (ARISTA 8602)
	(w/ Robert Schumann String Quartet The Montreux[sound aspects 009])
	WESLEYAN (12 ALTO SOLOS) 1992 (HAT ART CD 6128)
77E	ALTO SAXOPHONE IMPROVISATIONS 1979 (ARISTA 8602)
	(w/ Robert Schumann String Quartet The Montreux[sound aspects
009])	
77F	ALTO SAXOPHONE IMPROVISATIONS 1979 (ARISTA 8602)
77G	ALTO SAXOPHONE IMPROVISATIONS 1979 (ARISTA 8602)
	19 [SOLO] COMPOSITIONS, 1988 (NEW ALBION 023)
77H	ALTO SAXOPHONE IMPROVISATIONS 1979 (ARISTA 8602)
82	*FOR FOUR ORCHESTRAS (ARISTA 8900)*
85 (+108B, 30)	Quartet (Birmingham) 1985 (Leo 202/203)
	Anthony Braxton/Andrew Voigt Duo: Kol Nidre (sound aspects 031)
86 (+32, 96)	Quartet (London) 1985 (Leo 200/201)
	Anthony Braxton/Gino Robair: Duets 1987 (Rastascan 002)
	(BRAXTON/BARRY GUY/LONDON JAZZ COMPOSER'S ORCHESTRA: ZURICH CONCERTS [INTAKT 4/5])
	Willisau (Quartet) 1991 (hat ART CD 61001/4)
	Twelve Compositions (Music & Arts, CD 835, 1993)
87 (+108C)	Quartet (Birmingham) 1985 (Leo 202/203)
	Anthony Braxton/Andrew Voigt Duo: Kol Nidre (sound aspects 031)
	Braxton/Pavone: Duets (1993) (Music & Arts CD 786)
88 (+108C)	Quartet (Coventry) 1985 (Leo 204/205)
(+108C)	Five Compositions (Quartet) 1986 (Black Saint 0106)
90	(Splatter/Debris: Jump or Die [Music & Arts CD 843])
91	*(w/ the Northwest Creative Orchestra: Eugene (1989) [BLACK SAINT 120 137-2])*
92 (+30, 32, 139) (+108C, D)	*NYCO: FIRST PROGRAM IN STANDARD TIME [NEW WORLD/COUNTERCURRENTS DIDX 80418-2]*
93	*(W/ THE NORTHWEST CREATIVE ORCHESTRA: EUGENE (1989) [BLACK SAINT 120 137-2])*

quartet music

GOLDEN PEAK

95	(For Two Pianos (Arista 9559])
96	Composition 96 (Leo 169)
	Quartet (London) 1985 (Leo 200/201)
	Quartet (Birmingham) 1985 (Leo 202/203)
	Quartet (Coventry) 1985 (Leo 204/205)
	(Various: Music from Mills [MC001])
	Five Compositions (Quartet) 1986 (Black Saint 0106)
	(BRAXTON/BARRY GUY/LONDON JAZZ COMPOSER'S ORCHESTRA: ZURICH CONCERTS [INTAKT 4/5])
	ENSEMBLE (VICTORIAVILLE) 1988 (VICTO 07)
	Anthony Braxton/Gino Robair: Duets 1987 (Rastascan 002)
	Willisau (Quartet) 1991 (hat ART CD 61001/4)
	4 (ENSEMBLE) COMPOSITIONS 1992 (BLACK SAINT 120 124-2)
97C	*Compositions 99, 101, 107 & 139 (hat ART 6019)*
98	Composition 98 (hat ART 1984)
99B	19 [SOLO] COMPOSITIONS, 1988 (NEW ALBION 023)
(+97C, 117E, 117H, 118H)	*Compositions 99, 101, 107 & 139 (hat ART 6019)*
99C	SOLO (LONDON) 1988 (IMPETUS LP 18818)
99D	WESLEYAN (12 ALTO SOLOS) 1992 (HAT ART CD 6128)
99E	19 [SOLO] COMPOSITIONS, 1988 (NEW ALBION 023)
99F	WESLEYAN (12 ALTO SOLOS) 1992 (HAT ART CD 6128)
99G	SOLO (LONDON) 1988 (IMPETUS LP 18818)
99I	SOLO (LONDON) 1988 (IMPETUS LP 18818)
100	*(W/ THE NORTHWEST CREATIVE ORCHESTRA: EUGENE (1989) [BLACK SAINT 120 137-2])*
	4 (ENSEMBLE) COMPOSITIONS 1992 (BLACK SAINT 120 124-2)
101	Giorgio Gaslini/Anthony Braxton Duo: Four Pieces (Dischi Della Quercia 28015)
	Compositions 99, 101, 107 & 139 (hat ART 6019)
(+31, 96, 30)	Five Compositions (Quartet) 1986 (Black Saint 0106)
	Willisau (Quartet) 1991 (hat ART CD 61001/4)
105A	Four Compositions (Quartet) 1983 (Black Saint 0066)
	Prag 1984 "Quartet Performance" (sound aspects 038)
	Quartet (London) 1985 (Leo 200/201)
105B (+96)	Quartet (Birmingham) 1985 (Leo 202/203)
	Willisau (Quartet) 1991 (hat ART CD 61001/4)
	Twelve Compositions (Music & Arts, CD 835, 1993)

Solo

106A	19 [SOLO] COMPOSITIONS, 1988 (NEW ALBION 023)
106C	19 [SOLO] COMPOSITIONS, 1988 (NEW ALBION 023)
	SOLO (LONDON) 1988 (IMPETUS LP 18818)
106D	19 [SOLO] COMPOSITIONS, 1988 (NEW ALBION 023)
(+170B)	WESLEYAN (12 ALTO SOLOS) 1992 (HAT ART CD 6128)
106G	WESLEYAN (12 ALTO SOLOS) 1992 (HAT ART CD 6128)
106J	19 [SOLO] COMPOSITIONS, 1988 (NEW ALBION 023)
(+106M)	WESLEYAN (12 ALTO SOLOS) 1992 (HAT ART CD 6128)
106M	WESLEYAN (12 ALTO SOLOS) 1992 (HAT ART CD 6128)

Beginning of Coordinate System

107	*Compositions 99, 101, 107 & 139 (hat ART 6019)*
	Willisau (Quartet) 1991 (hat ART CD 61001/4)
108A	Prag 1984 "Quartet Performance" (sound aspects 038)
	Six Compositions (Quartet) 1984 (Black Saint 0086)
	Quartet (London) 1985 (Leo 200/201)
	Five Compositions (Quartet) 1986 (Black Saint 0106)
	Anthony Braxton/Gino Robair: Duets 1987 (Rastascan 002)
	Willisau (Quartet) 1991 (hat ART CD 61001/4)
	(Splatter/Debris: Jump or Die [Music & Arts CD 843])
	Quartet (Victoriaville) 1992 (Victo CD 021)

108B	Prag 1984 "Quartet Performance" (sound aspects 038)
	Six Compositions (Quartet) 1984 (Black Saint 0086)
	Quartet (Birmingham) 1985 (Leo 202/203)
	Anthony Braxton/Gino Robair: Duets 1987 (Rastascan 002)
(+86, 96)	*(BRAXTON/BARRY GUY/LONDON JAZZ COMPOSER'S ORCHESTRA: ZURICH CONCERTS [INTAKT 4/5])*
	Seven Compositions (Trio) 1989 (hat ART 6025)
108C	Quartet (Birmingham) 1985 (Leo 202/203)
	Quartet (Coventry) 1985 (Leo 204/205)
	Five Compositions (Quartet) 1986 (Black Saint 0106)
	Twelve Compositions (Music & Arts, CD 835, 1993)
	NYCO: FIRST PROGRAM IN STANDARD TIME [NEW WORLD/COUNTERCURRENTS DIDX 80418-2])
	Quartet (Victoriaville) 1992 (Victo CD 021)
108D	Five Compositions (Quartet) 1986 (Black Saint 0106)
	NYCO: FIRST PROGRAM IN STANDARD TIME [NEW WORLD/COUNTERCURRENTS DIDX 80418-2])
	Twelve Compositions (Music & Arts, CD 835, 1993)
110A (+108B)	Prag 1984 "Quartet Performance" (sound aspects 038)
(+108B)	Six Compositions (Quartet) 1984 (Black Saint 0086)
(+108B)	Quartet (Birmingham) 1985 (Leo 202/203)
(+108B, 69J)	*Seven Compositions (Trio) 1989 (hat ART 6025)*
110C	Six Compositions (Quartet) 1984 (Black Saint 0086)
110D	Six Compositions (Quartet) 1984 (Black Saint 0086)
112	*(W/ THE NORTHWEST CREATIVE ORCHESTRA: EUGENE (1989) [BLACK SAINT 120 137-2])*
	Duets, Vancouver 1989 w/ Marilyn Crispell (Music & Arts CD 611)
	Willisau (Quartet) 1991 (hat ART CD 61001/4)
113	COMPOSITION 113 (SOUND ASPECTS 003)
114 (+108A)	Prag 1984 "Quartet Performance" (sound aspects 038) .
(+108A)	Six Compositions (Quartet) 1984 (Black Saint 0086)
115	Six Compositions (Quartet) 1984 (Black Saint 0086)
	Quartet (London) 1985 (Leo 200/201)
116	Six Compositions (Quartet) 1984 (Black Saint 0086)
	Quartet (London) 1985 (Leo 200/201)
	Duets, Vancouver 1989 w/ Marilyn Crispell (Music & Arts CD 611)
118A	19 [SOLO] COMPOSITIONS, 1988 (NEW ALBION 023)
118F	19 [SOLO] COMPOSITIONS, 1988 (NEW ALBION 023)
	SOLO (LONDON) 1988 (IMPETUS LP 18818)
	WESLEYAN (12 ALTO SOLOS) 1992 (HAT ART CD 6128)
118H	*Compositions 99, 101, 107 & 139 (hat ART 6019)*
119D	WESLEYAN (12 ALTO SOLOS) 1992 (HAT ART CD 6128)
119E	*Compositions 99, 101, 107 & 139 (hat ART 6019)*
119F	WESLEYAN (12 ALTO SOLOS) 1992 (HAT ART CD 6128)
119G	19 [SQLO] COMPOSITIONS, 1988 (NEW ALBION 023)
119H	*Compositions 99, 101, 107 & 139 (hat ART 6019)*
119I	19 [SOLO] COMPOSITIONS, 1988 (NEW ALBION 023)
120D	*ENSEMBLE (VICTORIAVILLE) 1988 (VICTO 07)*
	Splatter/Debris: Jump or Die [Music & Arts CD 843)
121	Quartet (London) 1985 (Leo 200/201)
122 (+108A)	Quartet (London) 1985 (Leo 200/201)
(+108A, 96)	Five Compositions (Quartet) 1986 (Black Saint 0106)
(+108A)	If My Memory Serves Me Right (West Wind 04)
	(Splatter/Debris: Jump or Die [Music & Arts CD 843])
124 (+96)	Five Compositions (Quartet) 1986 (Black Saint 0106)
(+96)	Quartet (Coventry) 1985 (Leo 204/205)
129 (+40F, 40(O])	(ROVA & Anthony Braxton: the Aggregate, live [sound aspects 23])
131	Five Compositions (Quartet) 1986 (Black Saint 0106)
	If My Memory Serves Me Right (West Wind 04)
	Quartet (Victoriaville) 1992 (Victo CD 021)
133	Splatter/Debris: Jump or Die [Music & Arts CD 843)
134 (+96)	*(BRAXTON/BARRY GUY/LONDON JAZZ COMPOSER'S ORCHESTRA: ZURICH CONCERTS [INTAKT 4/5])*
	(W/ THE NORTHWEST CREATIVE ORCHESTRA: EUGENE (1989) [BLACK SAINT 120 137-2])
135 (+41, 63, 96)	*(BRAXTON/BARRY GUY/LONDON JAZZ COMPOSER'S ORCHESTRA:*

quartet music 349

	ZURICH CONCERTS [INTAKT 4/5])
	Willisau (Quartet) 1991 (hat ART CD 61001/4)
135	Twelve Compositions (Music & Arts, CD 835, 1993)
	Braxton/Pavone: Duets (1993) (Music & Arts CD 786)
136 (+96)	Anthony Braxton/Gino Robair: Duets 1987 (Rastascan 002)
	(BRAXTON/BARRY GUY/LONDON JAZZ COMPOSER'S ORCHESTRA:
	ZURICH CONCERTS [INTAKT 4/5])
	Duets, Vancouver 1989 w/ Marilyn Crispell (Music & Arts CD 611)
138A	19 [SOLO] COMPOSITIONS, 1988 (NEW ALBION 023)
138B	19 [SOLO] COMPOSITIONS, 1988 (NEW ALBION 023)
138C	19 [SOLO] COMPOSITIONS, 1988 (NEW ALBION 023)
	SOLO (LONDON) 1988 (IMPETUS LP 18818)
	WESLEYAN (12 ALTO SOLOS) 1992 (HAT ART CD 6128)
138D	19 [SOLO] COMPOSITIONS, 1988 (NEW ALBION 023)
138E	SOLO (LONDON) 1988 (IMPETUS LP 18818)
139	*Compositions 99, 101, 107 & 139 (hat ART 6019)*
	Willisau (Quartet) 1991 (hat ART CD 61001/4)
	NYCO: FIRST PROGRAM IN STANDARD TIME
	[NEW WORLD/COUNTERCURRENTS DIDX 80418-2])
	Quartet (Victoriaville) 1992 (Victo CD 021)
140	Twelve Compositions (Music & Arts, CD 835, 1993)
140 (+112, 30)	Duets, Vancouver 1989 w/ Marilyn Crispell (Music & Arts CD 611)
(+147, 139, 135)	Willisau (Quartet) 1991 (hat ART CD 61001/4)
141 (+20, 96, 120D)	*ENSEMBLE (VICTORIAVILLE) 1988 (VICTO 07)*
142	*ENSEMBLE (VICTORIAVILLE) 1988 (VICTO 07)*
	(Splatter/Debris: Jump or Die [Music & Arts CD 843])
147	*2 COMPOSTIONS (ENSEMBLE) 1989 / 1991 (HAT ART CD 6086)*
	Willisau (Quartet) 1991 (hat ART CD 61001/4)
	Quartet (Victoriaville) 1992 (Victo CD 021)
148 (+108A, 139, 147)	Quartet (Victoriaville) 1992 (Victo CD 021)
151	*2 COMPOSTIONS (ENSEMBLE) 1989 / 1991 (HAT ART CD 6086)*
152	Eight Duets Hamburg 1991 (Music & Arts CD 710)
153	Eight Duets Hamburg 1991 (Music & Arts CD 710)
154	Eight Duets Hamburg 1991 (Music & Arts CD 710)
155	Eight Duets Hamburg 1991 (Music & Arts CD 710)
156	Eight Duets Hamburg 1991 (Music & Arts CD 710)
157	Eight Duets Hamburg 1991 (Music & Arts CD 710)
158 (+96)	Willisau (Quartet) 1991 (hat ART CD 61001/4)
(+108C, 147)	Quartet (Victoriaville) 1992 (Victo CD 021)
158	Twelve Compositions (Music & Arts, CD 835, 1993)
159	Willisau (Quartet) 1991 (hat ART CD 61001/4)
(+131, 30, 147)	Quartet (Victoriaville) 1992 (Victo CD 021)
160 (+5)	Willisau (Quartet) 1991 (hat ART CD 61001/4)
160	Twelve Compositions (Music & Arts, CD 835, 1993)
161	Willisau (Quartet) 1991 (hat ART CD 61001/4)
	Quartet (Victoriaville) 1992 (Victo CD 021)
163	*4 (ENSEMBLE) COMPOSITIONS 1992 (BLACK SAINT 120 124-2)*
164	*4 (ENSEMBLE) COMPOSITIONS 1992 (BLACK SAINT 120 124-2)*
165	*COMPOSITION NO. 165 (FOR 18 INSTRUMENTS) (NEW ALBION 023)*
170A	WESLEYAN (12 ALTO SOLOS) 1992 (HAT ART CD 6128)
170B	WESLEYAN (12 ALTO SOLOS) 1992 (HAT ART CD 6128)
170C (+77D, 99F)	WESLEYAN (12 ALTO SOLOS) 1992 (HAT ART CD 6128)
170F (+138C, 106G, 119D, 99D, 119F)	
	WESLEYAN (12 ALTO SOLOS) 1992 (HAT ART CD 6128)
170G	WESLEYAN (12 ALTO SOLOS) 1992 (HAT ART CD 6128)
170H	WESLEYAN (12 ALTO SOLOS) 1992 (HAT ART CD 6128)
170I	WESLEYAN (12 ALTO SOLOS) 1992 (HAT ART CD 6128)
171	Twelve Compositions (Music & Arts, CD 835, 1993)
174	*COMPOSITION NO. 174 (LEO RECORDS CD LR 217)*

That will serve as a glimpse of such patterns in the quartet work; others interested in these lines might dissect the whole *corpus* so, finding (what we can call) these wave patterns, particularized by and between these and solo, duo, trio, and large group works. We can leave them alone here, after drawing a couple of conclusions from them.

The first is a reminder that these patterns are not mere abstractions; if they have occult lore attached to them at all, it's because they've been noticed in nature, in countless forms. Such forms are easy to track with the first ten digits (e.g., our ten fingers and toes) but they exist on subtler but just as concrete levels for the numbers that seem more abstract (e.g., the seventh prime, in the 17-year larval cycle of cicadas—which was symbolic to the ancient Greeks of unmoderated slavery to the Muse of song—or the tenth, in the more cultural serendipities so farcically explored by Shea and Wilson [see footnotes 5, this chapter, and 17, Chapter Ten].

In musical terms, Western tradition has reflected the most sophisticated such patterns in its evolution of pitch logics: tuning systems, modes, harmony, diatonics, modulation, counterpoint, serialism all invoke the authority of concrete complexities in nature for the meaning they bring to pitch relationships—keeping the rhythmic logic strictly metered at the simple levels of two, three, and four. African systems have rather developed their sophistication in the rhythmic patterns; cycles of 17 (for example) beats juxtaposed with, subdivided into, and/or multiplied with those of a range of other numbers form a polyrhythmic norm that develops against a tonal simplicity that corresponds to the (post-classical) Western metric one. The two traditions have always been shadows of each other in that sense, both dwarfing and dwarfed by each other, offering and demanding much accordingly.

Schönberg pushed the pitch logics (we might call them the gravitational intrigue of tone) to their conclusion, making them into a rocket capable of escaping their own gravity field. His students Berg and (especially) Webern explored their possibilities in the free fall of space. Cage transcended them entirely (ironically, from the earth) with his discovery, through the *I Ching*, of the principles they (and their African rhythmic counterparts) were expressing: the numerological synchronicities noted above are the symmetries and synchronicities chance (or, again, per current physics, "chaos") gives rise to, including the chance of cosmic and biological evolution. Cage's music was the West's window re-opened onto such chance/chaos and its patterns, relatively forgotten after the Renaissance; he (literally) went out of his (ego's) way to showcase that rediscovery, to make it both his work's frame and centerpiece.

The problem with that, for Braxton, was that the patterns beg meaning and engagement, they don't stand alone well, just as a finger pointing is not as interesting as what it's pointing at. He found this out on his terms when he saw first the glory in unstructured spontaneity (in both Cage's and his own and others' music), then its limitations. He was interested in a Muse who sought the company of equals, not doormats, not perpetually empty vessels it must perpetually fill with itself, to the satisfaction of neither.

Such musings do bring us to the heart of Braxton's music, that which he calls its "gravitational intrigue." His musical universe is built on that center of gravity commonly called the down beat; the intrigue lies in the dance that tries, on the "up," or "and" of that "down," to bounce away from its "gravity," to float above and fly around it as skillfully and expressively, as fast and far, as gracefully and stilly as one can, before swooping back to its inevitable attraction. The meter is usually based on 4 and 8, the latter often used to "recalibrate" the down to where the up was, as the earth's poles shift their magnetic fields every few eons. The units per bar (i.e., 2/4, 3/8, etc.) seldom go above 9, usually stay between 3 and 5, the defining parameters that suit their composer's phrase-making mind. Some pieces have no metric structure at all, but they still have down beats, each of which he cues, with (written) clues about how to handle their "ups" (i.e., directed improvisations that usually span a part of the 2 to 10-second range).

That's it in a nutshell: a dance stepped by the reader/improviser, choreographed by the composer for fellow reader/improvisers, variations on an infinitely cycling, infinitely various down-up dynamic through which the music breathes and pumps its blood. It may be as simple as a quarter note placed on beat one of a 4/4 bar or as complex as a string of lurching pitches subdivided into triplets that are further subdivided into septuplets, with grace notes, rests and accents, all crammed into an impossible spark of time somewhere *between* the up and the down. Or it may not be notes at all, rather some cluster or field of sound, but it all leads to and from the down-up, down-up of the metronome as all musicians know it, and of the heart as all people know it.

Braxton routinely leads not only his professional but also his student ensembles into and through their own intrigues with the gravity of the down, defiances of it, pursuits of it, swan dives into it. As his excitement in conducting grows, he starts counting out loud, shouting the figures out for players to catch, squeezing instructions between them, like some speaking foghorn over a pitch-black, roiling sea: "Target that down, saxophones, feel it in your body: onetwothreefourfiveDOWN! put 5-over-1 in your elbow, the 3/4 pulse in your foot, so you're free to think ahead to what you're going to do when the 7-over-3 moves from the 3/4 to the 1/8 bar . . . DOWN and-ee-up da-DOWN! I'm not hearing that DOWN there, people. I know it's a rest, but if you don't feel its gravity, you can't bounce properly into the phrase on the UP: (down)-AND boob-lee-ya DOWN!. Forget the pitch, don't even try to play the figures yet—just give me good strong downs, all the rest will fall into place from that."

That proves true. Probably half of his students are unaware of his achievements in the music; he's seen as a sweet, funny guy whose Principles of Improvisation class is built around his own difficult, bewildering music few hope to crack, much less master, upon first sight. Within a few rehearsals, however, it's clear that the music is as much fun romp as demanding discipline; he exudes warmth, cheer, respect, and genuine interest in each of the players. They respond like mountain goats, newborn, stumbling around on the highest, trickiest ridges, clumsily trying to match his adult mastery of them . . . then, always on the run, slowly but surely beginning to do so. Every footfall has to happen, to be exact, to follow from and lead to the others, to become increasingly sure, and soon they just do. All skill and energy is engaged, and the view is breathtaking.

But does this analogy fit the literate situation of reading Braxton's scores? Mountain goats aren't given maps of the exact steps they must take to becoming the guide and model for their own newborns. Wouldn't the oral-traditional process of imparting concepts and organizing group statements through playing (rather than charting) the music, through verbal and body language, match the analogy better?

It would if Braxton wrote his notes to be executed exactly, or harbored his own standards to which he held the improvisations. In fact, the mountain is the literate tradition, his scores its high, tricky ridges—and we goats have come from the ground of the oral tradition, below, from which this mountain rises and to which it descends. We climbed here, learned to frolic here, but our life here is the same one lived throughout the earth, continuous with it, not chained off from it.

Braxton composes as he improvises (much more at the piano—and, increasingly, MIDI keyboard—than with his sax, these days) in the same inspiration. The process is to romp and splash in sound, to explore its labyrinthian possibilities as much as its sheer force, then to transcribe the results. Anyone who has developed that process, along with facility on an instrument, knows one can spontaneously play a much fancier figure than one can sight-read from a score. Yet anyone who has developed sight-reading, and mastered difficult material, knows *that* process as one which imprints *that* material on one's mind, heart, and soul, so that it becomes one's song as surely as it was originally the composer's. But Braxton is an improviser writing for improvisers; a somewhat different end is desired.

"Once I've documented the origin identity of a piece," he says, referring to a score as written, "I prefer my groups to alter it, to kick it about." In other words, the written material is there to provoke players to come up with their own music in the process of trying to execute Braxton's. When they do get to the point of executing it exactly, Braxton asks them to alter it, to improvise on it.

The first thing to go is the pitch—the notes as scored on the page. He exhorts people to develop a feel for the rhythmic contour, to orient themselves to the downs and ups of it—really, to swing those, in the classic jazz sense. Once they've established the "targets" they can actually hit on a sight-read, even if those are only the beats themselves, with neither pitch nor rhythmic subdivisions, the latter will begin to come closer into reach. For Braxton, locking into a pulse, then juggling two or more of them together—as anyone does when she taps one rhythm with her foot and another with her hands; or as dancers do when they express three different rhythms with arms, hips, and legs—is the key to making pitch decisions, in improvising, composing, or sight-reading. At first, the rhythm distracts, consumes, possesses, and obsesses one, but eventually, with hard work, it falls into place. When it does, the time that has been sweeping the player away like a river seems to rush by him while he stands fast. In that position, picking pitches out—to play, to write down, or to read—becomes an art like fly casting, or like a frog lazily or avidly snatching flies out of the air.

This rhythmic bedrock in Braxton's music is not always apparent to the ear alone; what's heard often (though not always) sounds like it has no pulse—as a house looks like it rests on the ground rather than on its foundation. Therein lies the intrigue: the finding and the shaking of the pulse inside out, as a dog does his toy. If the music is only read, in a score, the pulse is there in the abstract, but is such a complication of conventional scoring that its physical expression will probably not be divined. But if one reads the score while hearing the music, one begins to understand—only begins, because much of the music, of course, is improvised. If one sees Braxton play with his quartet, or conduct an ensemble, one *sees* the rhythmic ground in his body, sees him swinging it with all his heart and soul. Best of all, if he is conducting one in one's own performance of his music, one begins to swing so with him oneself. The spiritual and aesthetic experiences he rhapsodizes about in his writings become one's own, through the music, their mystery a part of one's own history.

In medieval Western Masses, the process of composing and performance was very similar to such a Braxton piece (for large ensemble). The parts were written from a master melody with little regard for how they fit together with each other vertically; they were sung to a master pulse, the *tactus*, which was not necessarily conducted. In the course of a piece, the *tactus* would be subdivided into shorter durations, variously tied and accented, to create the effect of an increase in tempo; notes, alternately, would be held over several beats to effect a "slowing," or sustaining of the beat. The pulse had to remain steady for these tactics to be effective. The group would choose their *tactus* by finding the singer with the most command over his own temperament, one who got neither too excited during the busy nor lulled during the stiller parts. The pulse chosen would be that of his or her heartbeat.

What medieval composers left to chance was much of the vertical harmonic and rhythmic texture; the musical world of Bach would begin to "clean up" and order this a few centuries later. Braxton leaves much of his own music to the chance of improvisation and interpretation, but both of those processes presume a mastery of the material, starting with the pulse, moving to its subdivisions, then to its pitches, then to improvisations impeccably rooted in that material. Those unschooled in his work might not discern the difference between a reading by a player who has mastered and is taking her own liberties with it and one who is merely bluffing or struggling with it, but Braxton and anyone else who has taken the time and trouble to learn his music inside out can discern that difference.

This particular approach is a different process from composing from tonal systems (modal, diatonic, serial), or from systems of chance operations (anything from throwing dice to working the *I Ching*, or picking out the meaningful patterns in "chaos," such as the numerological play above), or putting a musical-conceptual frame around ambient noise or some other slice of "nonmusical" life. Those are all *parts* of Braxton's approach, but his music, like life, is more than their sum. His badge of honor as a composer is that he makes his music as inspiration compels, never resting on the patterns and systems it generates as—predictable, unengageable—sources of generation themselves.

Even so, the periodicity with which he orders all his pieces into the one coordinate system is a macrocosm of each component piece's own metric structure. As such, it is more the articulation of wild freedom and rapture than a dry librarian's dream, or a classicist's canonization of the past. Again, the past is a part of Braxton's present and future, but not their determining aspect. The term he uses to capture the living dynamic of anything—a person's spirit, a collective spirit, a musical work, a life's work—is "tri-metric" (or, most recently, "tri-centric"). The tri-metric dimension can be figured as past-present-future, or matter-mind-spirit, or (per his paradigm) Architectural/Philosophical/Ritual-and-Ceremonial. This usage itself is another of his "celebrations of the number three."[6] And, as the microcosm of an artistic statement reflects its maker's mind, so its maker's life reflects the macrocosm from which it issues. This is the stuff of myth and religion, Braxton's access to that level of consciousness—inspiration, possession—where "a thousand years is as a day and a day as a thou-

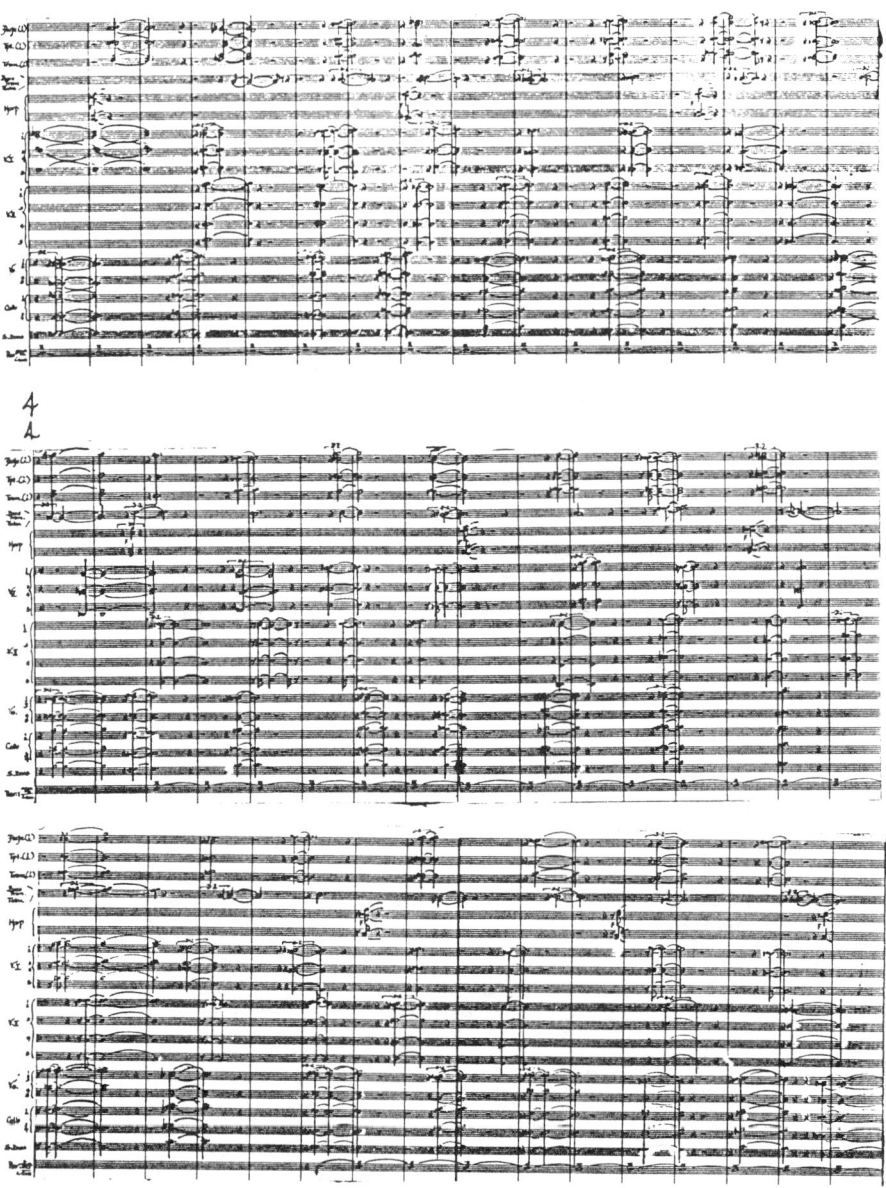

Fig. 8.1: From Braxton's 82 (For Four Orchestras, composer's score). *The galaxies of notes and numbers emerge from, defy, and fall to pulse like stars and planets splinter off from, incarnate, and return to the black-hole implosions and Big Bang explosions of gravity. "Let that DOWN swallow you up. Let Nixon be Nixon," as Braxton recently told a student having trouble finding the beat.*

sand years,"[7] and to active participation in its mythical drama in Millennial time.

This approach, this "gravitational intrigue" within this "coordinate system," demonstrates that our most extreme compulsions to organize, rationalize, to (literally) mediate knowledge and knower, to name and tame the beasts, need not be feared as stiflers of life. They aren't that strong. In fact, they enhance and proliferate the healthy chaos, as pruning does a tree. This is a model to inform the dynamic of any communication, especially the troublesome one—man and woman, old and young, race and race, culture and culture, individual and group—away from the trouble and toward the love. (At this point, the reader might benefit from a review of Braxton's own liner note writings on the quartet music presented in Chapter Four.)

As the numerological symmetries and synchronicities in Braxton's *oeuvre* display, at the very least, designs and coincidences beyond his conscious control, so do some aspects of the music itself which he did control. That is, he had some say in what musicians, what instrumentation, what playlists would make up his recordings; but some of those things were also determined by who was available when, and which of his compositions they could play best. Also, Braxton made his choices in time, and he based them on his personal needs and opportunities of the moment; he couldn't foresee the future, so as to set it up through present choices. He didn't say to himself, "Over the course of my lifetime, I will construct a body of work in accordance with numerological dynamics worked out beforehand; I will compose X number of solo, duo, trio, and quartet pieces on a timetable and schedule that accords with the metamusical dynamics of their respective ensemble characters; I will do three years with a piano in my group, then four with another horn instead, then seven with both; I will compose certain pieces I'll never record and others that will evolve through many recordings. Between the tenth and twelfth year I will compose my greatest work, then build upon that for the rest of my life."

What actually happens is that the artist follows the Muse and the Muse has its own designs; the artist becomes increasingly aware of those, ponders, marvels—but they propel and respond to him only incidentally to his pursuit of his own designs, of simple personal growth and balance in time. Otherwise, he's a moth swallowed by the flame; the Muse flares up brightly for a moment, but the dance in the air of the artist's beating wings is over.

Staying with the broad view with an eye for such patterns is more a means than an end; our end is to look at Braxton's music, but we can do that in many different frameworks. In fact, we've framed his one music a bit differently with each chapter; at this point, we're well enough grounded to take that broad view, and use those patterns so, for quick snapshots of some of the "forces in motion." They are:

- the flow of instrumentation through sets of groups;
- the flow of compositional concept, in series and pieces, through those sets;
- the flow of the personal voices articulating those concepts through the groups' personnel; and
- the merging of the flows into the most current quartet recordings as integrated compositional statements.

quartet music

We can zoom in on these flows through the more general early-middle-late construct already used (see Insert 8.1): the *6*s and *23*s, from the late 1960s/early 1970s, form an early period; the *40*s and *69*s, from the mid to late 1970s, a middle period; the *80*s up through *96* to *98* run through the late 1970s to the first Ritual and Ceremonial piece (*95*) and weren't recorded until well into the 1980s, which mark the first transitional flowering of the mature quartet music as a coordinate system, into the recent period.

The first set covers the widest conceptual range between radically experimental (1), collaboratively dynamic (2), jazz-traditional (3), and compositionally developed (4); the second covers both high (trumpet) and low (trombone) brass with Braxton's full range of reeds; the third is a flowering of the mature music in both trio-plus-one and conventional rhythm-section quartets; the fourth contains (for my money) Braxton's most exciting and interesting horn partner; and the fifth his mature quartet.

Arranging them in a flow of circles and triangles through time suggests other attributes:

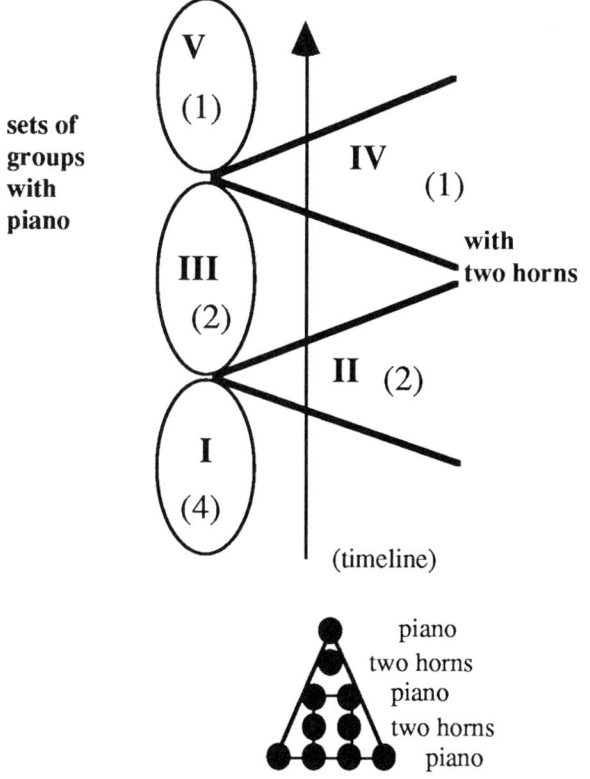

Fig. 8.2: This flow of instrumentation through time is just one of many examples of the balance between the masculine and feminine approaches to the Muse found throughout Braxton's work; the progressive division from four to one suggests the evolutionary refinement unfolding therein. The other graphic (a

quartet music 357

slightly altered tectactrys) shows that dynamic as crystalline entity in, more than liquid flow through, time.

The three ovals denote groups with a piano, the two triangles the two-horn groups. The piano expresses the feminine force field: historically, it goes back through the harp and lyre to the bow that couches the arrow, sings in harmony or friction with another bow or as pitched percussion in response to blows. The piano presents the harmonic field as a range of discrete notes that can sound all at once. The horns are male, phallic, monophonically linear, pitched to cover both a continuum of tone and its discrete notes, like a voice can do; two or more together can cover the harmonic field that one player can cover on piano. The drum, pulse, encompasses both genders.

We used this gender dynamic in the last chapter to frame the development of the composer's vision in time: female energy prevails when the players are trying to evoke, seduce the Muse with relatively open experiments, to then run loose in the cathartic inspiration of its possession; male energy prevails when they take command and build the structure of their own desire and design to house the Muse, inviting it to come and go as it will. Braxton has always oscillated between the two approaches in an interactively fertile dynamic, and in many different ways. His relationship with the piano is a prime example of this dynamic.

Part of his original musical rapture was for solo piano; he forged his own concept for solo alto sax in homage to that rapture because he didn't feel he could master the piano as well as the sax. The languages he developed on the sax moved its voice away from the Western linear one into fields of sound and percussive effects—his "languages" of trills, multiphonics, rapid and extreme intervallic leaps, pointillistic punctuations, clusters, attacks—that, like an arrow stretching the string of a bow, stretched a monophonic wind as far as possible toward a polyphonic string instrument. His first notated work was for solo piano; he has used the piano to compose from the first; the instrumentation he has settled into for his mature quartet music included the piano (played by a classically trained woman); and he himself has taken classical lessons in and begun to play the instrument publicly lately, with student groups, in standard jazz treatments of the American songbook and bebop material (his sound therein is not "straight"; however, its pan-tonal, pan-rhythmic sweeps do stay anchored to the conventional structure, in keeping with the "gravitational intrigue" spelled out above). As with the flute—the only of all his winds that occult lore frames as feminine—piano has loomed as a challenge beyond the direct reach that worked for the saxophone family. He has met that challenge indirectly, by composing for ensembles of horns what he couldn't play on the keyboard; and obliquely, with patience and persistence in the face of little yield, over time.

Personnel

Focusing on the personnel of the groups, we see another, more detailed flow informing the picture of the composer developing through time:

> **(I)** 1. from the same AACM territory as the early trios; piano and percussion serve as the floating other—texture, color—to the other instruments, when there is polarization at all; mostly, the field is

open and wide, the sound ranging through a broad flux of instruments; contextualizes Braxton's statement as part of the collective's;

2. distinctive voices converging on each other's alternating terms; Braxton is more the (representative) voice of the previous collective than one in it; the others speak the language of his pieces with voices fluent in other languages, as he does theirs with his own; contextualizes AACM/Braxton voice as one in a larger discourse about which direction the culture's mainstream of the music will take;

3. similar to group 2, only Braxton more in leadership role; playlist, instrumentation and use of it contextualizes Braxton's music as an aspect of the jazz tradition;

4. similar to group 3, only the leadership role more pronounced, the composer's own vision and style more prevalent;

(II) 5. a refinement on group 2, with Braxton taking the music in his direction, whether or not that would prove to be the mainstream's; brass voice mostly high (trumpet) and refined even when low (George Lewis' trombone); Braxton's leadership intensifies toward power and art of delegation: i.e., he conveys rather than imposes his vision as something that can serve his collaborators' own creative originalities, as well as his;

6. similar to group 5 only earthier, funkier;

(III) 7. Braxton's system's mature quartet statement in its bud (through male trumpet/reeds/bone trio and female piano); his leadership role subsumed in a collective process now completely defined by his vision, and completely at the service of the improvisers;

8. that same conceptual maturity in, as with Circle, a group of distinctive voices functioning more as collaborators from parallel universes meeting in one of them (Braxton's, here) than as regular denizens of that universe at their usual play;

(IV) 9. my favorite of Braxton's two-horn quartets, with George Lewis, with whom he also shares composer's duties; and

(V) 10. the mature quartet—the traditional one of piano, bass, and drums/percussion—in full coordinate-system flower.

Compositions

△ beginning ☐ middle ⊙ climax ⏃ eternal denouement

6 23   40 69   Golden Peak   Coordinate System

The 6s: a variety of premises ranging from the most radical to the simplest innovations on standard jazz and concert-music premises and practices—brainstorming together with the Muse;

the 23s: a grounding of that creative spectrum in more command, less chance, a more muscular sound and more narrowly sited, detailed vision—laying the foundation;

the 40s: an expansion of structure from more or less cohesive blocks of statements in symmetrical relationships to improvisations to strings of written sections and improvisations developing out of, rather than mirroring each other—rooms on the foundation;

the 69s: an intensification of that approach, with improvisational and written sections increasingly knitted together, their boundaries blurred within a piece—a second story built;

96, 98, and 105A&B (Golden Peak): all the principles at work in the series—structural, improvisational, harmonic-melodic, textural, rhythmic, philosophical—come together into these single pieces. A human family has moved into the house with all their possessions, and encountered the Spirit of the House there;

the coordinate system: new pieces after this point usually act as parts of strings of 3-5 pieces ranging from the beginning—the family is going about its life in the house, infused with the spirit after encountering it.

Fig. 8.3: Throughout the numbered quartet series, Braxton worked on music for other combinations, three of which (solo, duo, and trio) are included within the quartet. As they thus informed it, so did it inform the work he did for larger ensembles, serving as the most-worked format and a stable, developing structure for his ideas for collective music.

The lighter sections of the line of each series denotes its presence in *potentia* in the creation of the others, and their ongoing overlap on recordings; the bold sections denote their realization in time, culminating in the all-embracing coordinate system that locks them together within one statement. The quartet recordings after *Composition 98* are generally those of Braxton's most recent and longstanding quartet. What is fresh and intriguing about them is no longer some new concept developed from some old one (though that does happen with new compositions), but rather the latest spin on and arrangement of—synthesis of— existing or familiar musical territory. Most of the quartet CDs from the mid-1980s stand as single statements that anticipate the musical mythologies of Braxton's most recent music, for large ensembles (see next chapter).

Quartet Recordings Examined

The Complete Braxton (Freedom 400112/3[RI], Arista-Freedom 1902, 1971): *6K, 6J, 6A, 22, 6I, 4, 6L, 6M;* with pianist Chick Corea, bassist /cellist Dave Holland, and percussionist Barry Altschul.

Dona Lee (America 30 AM 6122, 1972): *23L, 23K;* playing alto and soprano sax, flute, and contrabass clarinet, with Michael Smith, piano; Peter Warren, bass; Oliver Johnson, drums.

Town Hall 1972 (CD: Art Union TKCB-30108): *6N, 6(O), 6P;* with bassist David Holland, percussionist Phillip Wilson (except on *6P*); and multiinstrumentalist John Stubblefield, percussionist Barry Altschul, and vocalist Jeanne Lee (on *6P*).

Four Compositions (1973) (Denon YX 7506): *23N, 23P, 23M, 23(O);* with pianist Masahiko Sato, bassist Keiki Midorikawa, and percussionist Hozumi Tanaka (on *23(O)* only).

New York, Fall 1974 (Arista 4023): *23B, 23C, 23D, 38A, 37, 23A;* with trumpeter Kenny Wheeler, bassist Dave Holland, and percussionist Jerome Cooper (except on *38A* and *37*); saxophonists Oliver Lake, Julius Hemphill, and Hamiett Bluiett (on *37*); synthesist Richard Teitelbaum (on *38A*); and violinist Leroy Jenkins (on *23A*).

Quartet Live at Moers Festival (Ring 01010/11, 1974): *23B, 23E, 40(O), 40M, 23F, 23D;* with trumpeter Kenny Wheeler, bassist Dave Holland, and percussionist Barry Altschul.

Five Pieces 1975 (Arista 4064): *23H, 23G, 23E, 40M;* with trumpeter Kenny Wheeler, bassist Dave Holland, and percussionist Barry Altschul.

Montreux/Berlin Concerts (Arista 5002, 1975): *40N, 23J, 40(O), 6C, 6F, 40K, 63* (same personnel as above).

Dortmund (Quartet) 1976 (hat ART 6075): *40F, 23J, 40(O), 6C, 40B;* with trombonist George Lewis, bassist Dave Holland, and percussionist Barry Altschul.

quartet music

Composition 98 (hat Art CD 6062, 1981); with trumpeter Hugh Ragin, trombonist Ray Anderson, and pianist Marilyn Crispell.

Performance 9/1/79 (hat Hut 2R19): *69C, 69E, 69G, 40F, 69F, 23G, 40J*; with trombonist Ray Anderson, bassist John Lindberg, and percussionist Thurman Barker.

Six Compositions, Quartet (Antilles AN 1005, 1981): *40B, 69N, 40A, 34, 40G, 52*; with pianist Anthony Davis, bassist Mark Helias, and percussionist Ed Blackwell.

Four Compositions (Quartet) 1983 (Black Saint 0066): *105A, 69M, 69(O), 69Q*; with trombonist George Lewis, bassist John Lindberg, and percussionist Gerry Hemingway.

Prag 1984 "Quartet Performance" (sound aspects 038): *105A, 110A, 114, 69H*; with pianist Marilyn Crispell, bassist John Lindberg, and percussionist Gerry Hemingway.

Quartet (Birmingham) 1985 (Leo 202/203): *110A(+96+108B), 69M(+10+33+96), 60(+96+108C), 85(+30+108D), 105B(+5+32+96), 87(108C), 23J, 69H(+31+96), 40(O)*; with pianist Marilyn Crispell, bassist Mark Dresser, and percussionist GerryHemingway.

Quartet (Coventry) 1985 (Leo 204/205): *124(+30+96), 88(+108C+30+96), 30, 23G(+30+96), 40N, 69C(+32+96), 96* (drums), *69F, 69B, 96* (bass), *6A* (same personnel as above).

Quartet (London) 1985 (Leo 200/201): *122(+108A), 40(O),* collage, *52, 86(+32+96), 30, 115, 105A, 96* (percussion), *40F, 121, 116* (same personnel as above).

Five Compositions (Quartet) 1986 (Black Saint 0106): *131, 88(+108C), 124(+96), 122(+108A+96), 101(+31+96+30)*; with pianist David Rosenboom, bassist Mark Dresser, and percussionist Gerry Hemingway.

Willisau (Quartet) 1991 (hat ART CD 61001/4): *160(+5)+40J, 23M(+10), 158(+96)+40L, 40A, 40B, 161, 159, 23C+32+105B(+30), 23M(+10), 40M, 67(+147+96), 140(+147+139+135), 34A, 20+86, 23G(+147+30), 69(O)(+135), 69B, 107(96), 101, 23N(+112+108A+33)*; with pianist Marilyn Crispell, bassist Mark Dresser, and percussionist Gerry Hemingway.

Quartet (Victoriaville) 1992 (Victo CD 021): *159(+131+30+147), 148(+108A+139+147), 161, 158(+108C+147)* (same personnel as above).

Early Quartet Music

The 6 Series

The groups that recorded the 6 series, from earliest to latest versions, consist mostly of the same three players (Braxton, Holland, and Altschul), with one spot turning over between three others (Corea, Wheeler, and Lewis, plus some extras on *Town Hall*). The exceptions to that are the CCC players who did *6F, G,* and *H*, released in the same period as the trio renditions of the first recorded 6s, *E* and *D*. Two points: these 6s were early quartet statements still close to the AACM-experimental trio frameworks, and their evolution over time was within a continuity of core players (primarily the European players; the AACM alumni would regroup occasionally for duos and trios, but wouldn't form the working quartets).

6G wasn't one that Braxton has recorded again, but its premises have evolved as much as those of compositions he has. Those premises resonate with the Cagean influence: the blurring of boundaries between art and life, the incorporation of all sounds and their arrangements, even those not generated by the composer, into a composition. (I say they resonate with, not stem from, Cage because, as Braxton says in the liner notes, this approach is part of the jazz tradition). Braxton's early trio and quartet works and performances pursued these premises unself-consciously, with panache, in keeping with the times (1968-1970).[8] After that, his recordings and performances became less "happenings" of this sort and more the conventional presentation of works to an audience. The concepts themselves have remained central to and have evolved through those works, but not as they did through those of Cage and others following his lead. It was in 1970 that he told an interviewer what his differences with Cage's approach were,[9] and the directions his music took from that time reflected those.

6G is an extension of the *6E* concept (see Chapter Seven), in its use of ("so-called") nonmusical material—balloons—for its "material dynamics." The players were given balloons, to inflate, deflate, rub, and otherwise manipulate while next to a microphone. The resulting soundscape ranges from earth rumbles to buzzing mosquitoes; within that terrain, each of the instrumentalists also shows his virtuosity as a soloist, both in written (Colemanish) and improvised parts; and the timbral/instrumental variety is noteworthy. (Also, on another piece from the record, Braxton recites his own dadaistic poem.)

The musicultural forces resistant to this early approach were more subtle and complex than hindsight might suggest. On the Western hand, you had classical avant-gardists looking at the art of improvisation as shallow, showy assertions of ego; on the new Afrocentric purist hand, it was politically incorrect to invoke the authority of the Western composer in order to steal from the realm of collective spontaneity (i.e., it was okay to bring balloons for everyone to play, but perhaps not to instruct them to play them in the context of a musical event for one to then claim as one's own "composition"). As for the Europeans, many of them were looking to African American music as a shot in the arm to their own declining culture; they were less interested in seeing what they considered "sick" (overly cerebral, no longer vital) embraced for its own healthy universal aspects. It was these dynamics that may have affected the fate of many of the *6*'s (those recorded only once) and of the thrust of Braxton's early music generally. That thrust can be traced, through the *Composition Notes*, directly from the *6*s to new works, but little of it survives intact through continued recordings of the *6* pieces themselves, as it does in the other series.

6F is an exception to that. Like *6A, C,* and *N,* it would be performed and recorded again over the next decade; in fact, it was recorded the most (four times), and its musical significance matches that attention. It was the first of the Kelvin Series of improvisations based on "repetitive phrase generating structures . . . a phrase-based repetition structure that establishes a fixed rhythmic pattern—with open actual pitch possibilities based on suggested contour." The material was repeated, altered, staggered by the four instruments, then the shape of the line improvised upon. Braxton called this his "first attempt to move into the world of repetition and pattern thinking."[10] The Kelvin pieces would eventually lead to the pulse tracks, which would come to function as a rhythmic alternative to melodic-harmonic approaches to pitch generation. This Braxtonian alternative is not so radical for its emphasis on rhythm—plenty of Afrocentric approaches demonstrate that—but it is so for its conscious assertion and exploration of pulse, and patterns and cycles thereof, as a systematic generation of pitch logics.

This is a "system" neither Braxton nor scholars of his work has rationalized, as pedagogues have the Western (diatonic and chromatic, including jazz) systems of composition and improvisation. Whereas its rhythmic patterns do not correspond *analogically* to pitch statements, it is nonetheless a system, just as those evolved from pitch relationships are systems, with a system's self-sufficient internal logics and dynamics. Instead of assuming pitch statements to be extracted from an abstract field of possibilities floating somewhere apart from the rhythm, the improviser assumes them to be generated by it. This is, in fact, a natural process, one that goes back to McKenna's and others' thought about the common ground of music and speech: we systematically choose pitch in relation to the rhythm and cadence of our speech all the time, intuiting immediately in ourselves and others what pitch and manipulations of it convey, evoke, and/or facilitate what emotional affects and rational matrices. Furthermore, although speech's rhythm and cadence is largely determined by its emotional and rational contexts, the optimum relationship between meaning, affect, and verbal means is neither hierarchical nor even divisible; it is, as Braxton might say, "tri-metric," one of nature's living triune phenomena.

In speech, of course, we gravitate toward pitch ranges (albeit close ones) rather than notes; Braxton's use of the cloud-like shape notation to suggest moments in such ranges reflects this fact. So does the fact that many of his pieces, especially the later ones for large ensemble, have such distinctive and consistent pitch identities even though much of the pitch is determined by the performers. Braxton's pieces have poetic and mythological imagery and meaning surrounding and emanating from them (see next chapter) through his intent and vision; players typically pick up on that and get into it with him.

The primary goal of both this and the more abstract conventional form of pitch selection is satisfaction of artist's and listener's needs and desires; analytical understanding of that satisfaction derives from it, though that too is a satisfaction in its own right. The rational understanding and analysis of rhythm as pitch determinant is there to be mined from Braxton's improvisations and scores, and from the improvisations of those he plays with and writes for—but that is another book, or whole body of literature, well worth the writing. It is enough here to declare it as another of those phenomena not created so much as brought to the light of more conscious control and communication by the composer within his work.

Braxton called *6F* (dedicated to Stockhausen) an arhythmic phrase used to anchor "multiimprovisational participation."[11] On *This Time*, it has the feel of an active mind wandering freely yet purposefully, unhampered by any overwhelming emotional affect (including the "energy" that dominated much of the genre at the time). Harmonies are spontaneous and close, the two horns and violin often sounding as one; rhythms are primary and orchestrated.

The evolution of *6F* through two Circle versions and one by a two-horn variation of that group documents the way his music and its players can grow in each other's "hands." The *Circling In* version is more realized than *This Time*'s, mostly because the quartet concept itself is more clearly and widely defined and mined by these players; that is, they speak with four very different instrumental and personal voices, covering a broader and more dynamic range (and range of dynamics, for that matter). The contrast extends to their racial-cultural and national identities; the music seems to reflect all the contrasts, calling on the proficiencies of each and the rapport of all, both of which abound. The tentative, gradual transitions of the CCC give way to immediate and stark, yet warm and relaxed, motions between fixed and open drum sections, when Altschul offers a single long cymbal swell in stark contrast to the written pattern. This and other such usages of free improvisation serve as sonic areas in which listener and player can contemplate the unfamiliar fixed parts until they're learned and second nature. The percussion, cello, and reeds play more variations than did the CCC on the pulse pattern.

Back at the scene of *This Time*'s crime, the live *Circle: Paris Concert* version makes the previous performance sound like a conservatively restrained rehearsal. The rhythmic premises *are* second nature here and matched with melodic, harmonic, and timbral/textural fills that in turn magnify the rhythmic patterns far past what's written. The players are giving the all of a live, superstar performance of mastered material.

Almost a decade after *This Time*, some interesting harmonic development has crept into the *Montreux/Berlin* version. It goes much farther out with its improvisations; sometimes the bass and drums hold close to the pattern, with the horns acting more as complementary color. Braxton's first improvisation, on contrabass clarinet, is loosely anchored over the drums; his puppy whines are joined by George Lewis' snuffles and grunts, both moving in and out of the rhythm. A hot drum solo follows, then all four are in, noodling into a walking groove . . . then another written part, walky, swingy, punchy. Extended collective and solo improvisations continue to weave through romps through the written material; the overall effect of the piece has become very Felliniesque, showing how Braxton's most individualistic work, however contrived and awkward it might seem at first, succeeds in moving into areas staked out by other originals with its own original voice, without compromise or imitation (other pieces evoke Schönberg, Webern, Ives, Stravinsky, Stockhausen, and Weill, as this one does Nino Rota). Pulling this off is rare—Stravinsky's later work moved so into Schönberg's territory—and it happened here only after much time and work.[12]

6C is another oft recorded over time, in collage with newer work, and another with a Felliniesque (a result of being in Europe?), circusy feel. The two recorded versions are of live performances in Europe from around the same time (1976), though Braxton had written the piece in 1967 (so the players were familiar with it). The differences in the two versions are pronounced but seem due more to the whim of the moment than any transformations the music itself had undergone. The *Dortmund* version opens with a session in the bush: animals, including humans, making the noises of their physical and mental life. The head comes in with humor and color, and the bass and drums stay close to the two-beat throughout, horns moving in and out of a Dixie-ish feel for the phrases and improvs. Braxton didn't develop the rhythmic figure, as in the Kelvin, but both Sousa's and Coleman's influences are apparent, the first in the rhythmic drive behind the pitch selections, the second in the nature of those selections.

Montreux/Berlin takes the piece right into its circusy bass line under noodling horns; the theme is slightly faster, more densely stated, not quite as fleshed out and relaxed as in *Dortmund* . . . although after the head on this version, it actually slows, by halving the two feel into an expanded groove. The space opens up for more low blatts and other spontaneous effects; extended improvisation, mostly a hold-that-tigerish horn duet over rhythm, leads to more noodlings, then a fade-out, with no restatement of head.

6K shows another aspect of the composer's flexibility, to add to that through time (*6F*) and place (*6C*). It's a unison line written for Corea and Braxton's soprano sax. Notice how it synthesizes their two very different concepts and styles; it sounds like something either one of them could have written for a duo with the other. (Corea, in fact, is the dominant voice in the dialogue.)

6J, from the same record date, opens another area Braxton would return to and develop throughout his quartet music. "All of the postulation moments in . . . *6J* are framed with silence and the general continuum of this phenomenon moves to create a static space with its own separate laws."[13] It sounds bleak, stark, poignant, sad, lonely. Static. "Each performance has opened my awareness to the importance of musical space and 'non-development' postulation. The strength of this approach has served as an important direction for my music—as well as an important color for my quartet book." The range of activity in this and other such pieces is actually greater than those with more tension and release. More things happen, from open improvisations between different combinations; more instruments, with more timbres and techniques; sections of interactive counterpoint alternate with chordal accompaniments to single lines. It's as though the silence is saying "show me what you've got," then always having the last and definitive word, in the unsettling, challenging way it does in a life open to contemplation as well as action.

6A is the first catalogued quartet piece, written in Chicago in 1968; it too has been recorded often over time (see Chapters Six and Seven). Conceptually, Braxton calls it another first—"one of my earlier attempts to solidify a language platform for creative music," long before he used the term "language music." Several of the language components are easily discernible—gradient logic in the *accelerando/ritard*, diatonic formings in the 10-note scale, the rhythmic logics of the basic two feel and the 9/4 phrase. The most recent (*Coventry*) version is a relaxed, easy treatment, a quick glance back at the beginning of it all.

6B is the only *6* not recorded, written in 1967 for a Chicago club gig: a Colemanish vehicle for quartet-context soloing, something to suit the occasion (musically similar recorded 6s are *N*—see Chapter Seven—and *I*). Written in 1971 for a London performance, *6I* stands as Braxton's compositional entry point into the Parker-through-Coleman line of the music: "*6I* was a turning point in my creative growth and future direction. This work would play an important role in reawakening my awareness about tempo structures and traditionalism in general."[14] It sounds like straightforward jazz, yet with Braxton's signature—a medium-up groove over a walking bass, two horns playing a symmetrical, cyclical head with interrelated motifs, the whole thing a brief and simple kernel for extended blowing. The choppy atonality, intervallic jags, and offhand harmonic weave give the music away as Braxton's, but his move toward the common jazz ground was prescient of the *23* series, which would establish the connection of his more experimental and original concepts with the mainstream tradition.

Fig. 8.4: Consider this line of notation and the graphic with Chapter Six's paradigma of 6A and 69P, to get a sense of Braxton's sensitivity to (and need to capture) the multidimensional aspects of music with his work.

6L, dedicated to Paul Desmond, pairs Braxton's soprano again with Corea's piano, this time in a traditional ballad, Braxton style. A stately, regular procession of chords leads into an atonal statement of "two melodic phrases structured in a canon response pattern as a basis for extended improvisation"[15] Braxton's *Notes* exhort improvisers to play within the context of what he wrote: "a dirge-like music that breathes very slowly with linear melodic-like musical phrases . . . too often the extended continuum of restructuralism seems overly preoccupied with abstraction and pandemonium at the expense of real creativity." His own solo moves around lyrically in groups of thirds; the piano moments begin to manifest less regularly, and he plays a bit more out, though still with restraint and a dynamic flux, coming to rest in his initial intensity level, after bubbling out of it.

The ballad format is one of the least explored in his early music, and one which seems to have called to yet also challenged and frustrated him, much as the piano and flute, among the instruments he plays, have done. He has left the door open to the ballad and experienced a few inspired visitations by the Muse there. Indications are that he may grow into it as age brings him more to express in that format. (*6M* is another, spontaneous and self-absorbed solo shot at the ballad; you can hear the moody frustration with the format in the honks. Like *8D* [from *For Alto*], it evokes John Cage's feel for chance and silence.)

The *Town Hall 6*s (*N*, *O*, and *P*, see Chapter Seven) were written for and played by Holland and Altschul in various combinations with the others. Both *O* and *P* include further excursions into the ballad space, probably the most successful—*O* because it was couched effectively next to the greater mastery of *N* and of transitional improvisations, and *P* because it was given to Jeanne Lee to vocalize and verbalize (see footnote 9, Chapter 7). The group of six players actually defined a quartet structure, of (1) two horns, (2) a vocalist, (3) a bassist, and (4) two percussionists. Lee's rendition of Braxton's poem, and the responses it evoked from the others, probably stands as a prophetic voice of Braxton's ballad music, in seed, as it may unfold over the course of his life. A vital part of its interest lies in the way the piece seemed to just have to take off, finally, into the nervous energy of the latter faster part—and the way Lee found her place in that, just as the men had found theirs in the ballad. The male-female dynamics here are akin to those in Polynesian dances in which the men dance with legs spread, to convey strength, and the women with them close together, to convey grace, the total effect being an integration of the two qualities.

The period of the 6 series encompasses that of what Radano called "studies in iconoclasm": early (1967-1971) compositions that are reaching away from many (not all) elements of the jazz tradition and falling more within the province of the postmodern experiments of the concert music of the time, as defined by Cage and others. Radano's discussion of these works (e.g., $6G$) is interesting both for the musical specifics and the cultural-historical context it establishes.

When viewed as an integrated, cohesive entity unto itself, and then as the first of the four series through which the music evolved toward a level of conceptual and practical sophistication not fully reached until *98*, the 6 series displays (as do the others) aspects that set but don't restrict it to a certain time period and a certain point in Braxton's evolution as a composer. I find this fact useful in conveying the way the Muse really works through the artist in time, and the way it makes its statements timeless.

For example, the sound and feel of the recordings of these works range from the 1960s free-form sound splashes of the AACM/CCC sessions (the trio recordings, *This Time*, and B-X^O) to something much tighter, more realized, or even just different (*Town Hall*, the Circle recordings, *The Complete Braxton*, the later recorded versions). Braxton, however, was doing pretty much then what he has done all along: orchestrating improvisation for a wide and flexible timbral palette on a variety of musical premises. This composer's vision and method have been doggedly consistent and straightforward from the first; the improvisers', Braxton's, and all his collaborators' treatments, have been a continuously evolving realization of that vision and method, informing it so as to move it from one discrete fixed point to another. The 6s were firsts, but they weren't onlies. They were, and continue to be, followed by more attempts at the same goal: to compose a crosscultural, transhistorical, and cogender-specific body of work built on and for the process of individual and collective improvisation.

What they may have marked most significantly to Braxton's development is the loss of whatever innocence and naiveté he'd had about the music business and his future in it. He had studied long, hard, and earnestly and was breaking through with media attention, recording opportunities, and collaborations with well-established jazz stars; he was finding and cultivating his own voice, contributing fresh possibilities to the traditions he'd embraced and loved. His youthful enthusiasm for his work (and naive expectation of its reception) is wonderfully captured by his half-serious, "I thought *Three Compositions of New Jazz* would top the charts and sell a million copies!"

In fact, his early work's ecumenical, experimental approach, seldom fashionable to the jazz *cognoscenti*, nor paid much attention by the academic vanguardists, has developed unfazed by their agendas—but it's also been supplemented and protected by qualities that came into play as artist and art matured. Braxton went on to claim even more popular and critical success through the next three series and ten years . . . and a proportionate loss of more innocence and naiveté about the value of such success.

Looking down the composition/recording list, one gets an idea of the real-time tie between compositional concepts and recording/performance/workshop opportunities, the first such being the weekly AACM workshops. A burst such as the *8*s, in 1967, fuels two solo recordings and one solo cut; the need for variety and personal distinction and a balanced range within the unity of the burst dictates the different musical premises each *8* explores. Some pieces from this period were not recorded until 1992, and then by an ensemble other than that originally intended (*5* and *10*, both for solo piano). They too develop specific, distinct premises, as do the works yet to be recorded from the same time. Those premises include:

> *1* (solo piano): conventional and "visual" (graphic) notation put, together, to the service of improvisational platforms inspired by the music of Webern (intervallic), Coltrane (chordal), and Coleman (linear);

> *2* (any four single-line instruments): conventional notation developing chordal potentials, sonic analogues to astrological dynamics, and improvised cadenzas;

> *3* (any eight single-line instruments, piano, and two percussion, one inside the piano): notated linear and pointillistic soundscape for improvisation; early example of "creative" (improvised) chamber music;

> *4* (five tubas): extreme ends of sound spectrum; rhythms written but pitches left open; a slow pulse, with silence/space meant to effect "another level of awareness" than development brings; timbres, range, pitches, left to each player, as well as the freedom to play any of the five parts. "The interpreter in this context cannot merely coast along without any involvement in the music because the strength of a given performance . . . is not separate from the invention each musician brings to it;"[16]

> *5* (solo piano): three different premises/sections, each based on a (Braxtonian) language component;

> *7* (orchestra): sound density, neither pitch nor instrument specified, rhythmic and structural extension of *4*;

quartet music

8A–K (solo alto sax): a variety of premises (see Chapter Five for samples);

9 (four amplified shovels): electronic treatment of sound of coal being shoveled;

10 (solo piano): visual notation;

11 (creative orchestra): visual notation (interesting that a concept was developed first in solo piano then large ensemble; this has become his favored strategy with the advent of the MIDI sequencer's "exploding music" capacity);

12 (woodwind quintet): fixed notation/flexible time, open pitch/fixed rhythm, fixed notation/intervallic shift of a phrase;

13 (four single-line instruments): pointillism medium and slow, unison rhythm/open harmony;

14 (solo alto), a grab bag of language music and procedures;

15 (four tubas, later any four instruments): visual notation, timed orchestration of same;

17 and *18* (string quartet): visual notation, chance arrangement of pages;

19 (100 tubas): orchestrated into four different parades of 25 each, weaving, converging, and interacting musically and spatially with their own logistics of motion and its sound effects;

20 and *21*: explorations of single-line duo and electronic possibilities intended for meditation and personal spiritual development;

22: an open interpretation of a remembered/lost piece originally written for quartet; overdubbing of four of Braxton's soprano sax tracks made possible a new transcription, and another of those Braxton innovations of the time (foreshadow of saxophone quartets to come, first through another Braxton recording [see Insert 8.1], then in the person of the World Saxophone, ROVA, Billy Tipton Memorial and other such quartets).

To always examine the structure and particulars of each composition any more than this would be to marvel at the microscopic world of each snowflake and so miss the beauty of the fall. That beauty is evinced by Braxton's repeated assertion throughout his *Composition Notes* that his pieces are conceived as his improvisations, in the unchecked inspiration and imagination of the moment, not in impositions of systems or conventions; that they nonetheless give birth to such systems (structures, sound parameters, motifs, and patterns) and can include such conventions; that those systems, conventions, and innovations are offered not as masters nor as slaves but as friends and collaborators with the inspirations of musicians who would engage them; and that such performers are free, as the composer has been, to let the engagement go where it will all paints a picture of a composer firmly rooted both in and beyond the moment and his own role. It is a music that respects the reality and the harmony of both the fixed and the fluid nature of life.

While Braxton intended this creative storm of musical activity as a sort of grass-roots composer's invasion of jazz and improviser's invasion of Western concert music, and while most of it was well reviewed, it might have gone the way of a failed, dated experiment had it not been carried further. The 23s comprise Braxton's next step toward survival and place in the world for his inner vision.

The 23 Series

Along with the continuities of discipline in his own compositional and performing practices, the personnel on Braxton's quartet recordings throughout the mid to late 1970s had the same core as the Circle group (Holland and Altschul, with Wheeler, on *Quartet Live at Moers*, *5 Pieces*, *Montreux-Berlin*), and featured guests from among the AACM/CCC peers (Jenkins and Jerome Cooper, on *New York, Fall 1974*). This is important to remember when trying to understand the nature of composing for improvisers generally, and when trying to understand Braxton's own written explanations of the process. The telepathy that develops between longtime intimates has helped produce the personality of the small-group and big-band improvised music from that of Louis Armstrong on up through groups as different as those of the Marsalises and Sun Ra. What might seem redundant, self-evident, and/or esoteric both in Braxton's work and in his notes on same has developed largely in the context of players with whom he'd developed increasing complexities and profundities signaled by increasingly subtle, nuanced exchanges within well-traveled channels of communication.

The two exceptions to this personnel in the quartet recordings of this period demonstrate nicely the other side of that coin. *Dona Lee* and *Four Compositions (1973)* each show Braxton's ability to function as a globe-trotting leader of pick-up groups, to begin to carry and convey his quartet music as part of the common currency of improvisers in the traditional context of that ensemble, free from any homeboy clannishness. Both European (actually, expatriate American) and Japanese quartets would foreshadow his later touring quartets, which would be formed less as the Circle/CCC/AACM parties of peers scouting new terrain, and more as members of his own highly select, directed, and focused surveyors, led by him to chart that terrain.

Although the 23s are part of an unbroken continuum with the 6s, then, they too afford a good window onto a certain distinguishable phase of the Muse's development. Braxton is launching himself in earnest in this period as a leader, captain of a group with a specific mission and destination. The success he came to enjoy in the jazz world during the 1970s would bear witness to this earnestness, but it would also prove to be mere stops along his (and his Muse's) way.

quartet music

Compositions 23K through *P* were written in 1971, and *A* to *J* between 1973 and 1975 (the temporal disparity is due to the imposition of much of this ordering system back through time onto pieces originally titled only graphically and/or formulaically). *23K*, originally written for Circle, was made to peg an open collective improvisation featuring a variety of Braxton's horns in various combinations with the others. Soprano sax, then flute swirl lazily with a spacey piano, brushy drums, thoughtful bass . . . pianissimo . . . the subconscious finally speaks, through the contrabass clarinet—the same sort of sacred space as on the free cuts of the *In the Tradition* recordings. The alto extracts the theme from the middle of that space; then the spirit of the music intensifies, then fragments pointillistically and runs down. Each player is alone, after flowing together in a stream.

23L is a monophonic line structure for any instrument(s), entirely written, played by bass, soprano sax, and piano in unison, with the drummer malleting cymbals. Sounding like a modern Gregorian chant, it is Braxton's meditative evocation of "what has been lost from the ancients." He likens it to an alternative muzak, "Music that seeks to re-awaken . . . a music for reflecting and life space."[17] He takes pains in his notes to caution the reader against seeing it as an attempt on his part to say something uniquely new to the world.

Braxton calls *23M* a "gravallic etude." It is a post-bop extended line *à la* Mingus or Coleman, yet with no stems or metric divisions to dictate its emphases. In a reversal of his rhythmic generation of pitch, Braxton wanted to see this arrangement of pitches find their own weight/gravity in a given performance (see Fig. 2.12c). This one is traditional in its walking bass, vamping piano, and soloists over support. The later brief appearance of *23M* on *Willisau* serves to establish a pulse and swing context after a lot of floaty, lurchy music, into which a piano rendition of *10* and a gritty, swinging sax solo are grafted.

The musical thrust of *23N* is "multiple forms," or several types of music to improvise on in one piece—"a childlike melody, a medium-pulse post-Schönberg relationship complex, a march and a language design construction on one note"[18]—intended for collective rather than "individual solo investigation." It was inspired by Mingus' use of ballad, Latin, two-beat, and other styles all in one piece. Braxton states what he calls the fairy-tale motif on the clarinet with the piano and bass; then all (this is a trio) blow atonally on the quarter-note pulse. The meld is active in all its parts: Braxton cooks, the piano chords appropriately atonally, the bass interacts right up front with both arco and pizzicato. Clarity, cleanliness, and balance are exceptional, as though the music were being born with none of the usual anxiety or violence, or tentativeness—very chamberly, no brinksmanship. Again, 20 years later on *Willisau*, the piece forms the "primary identity" of a collage of later works, setting the old stage briefly for them to declaim their new lines upon.

23O, another scored trio with an open percussion part, is the last piece on its LP, making for a tasty climax of tasty trio fare that felt more like a quartet's, even as some of the earlier quartets felt more like trios. Radano notes,[19] validly enough, the likeness of the phrases and their rhythms here to serialist compositions—but the bass note/pulse Braxton laid down as those figures' pivot is what distinguishes both his process and its product here from serialist pieces; the scored figures are not the heart of the work, are rather notated salutes to the mind in improvisational flight. To put them at the center of the concept, or to look to them for a systematic mediation of the creative impulse, would be to miss the point of Braxton's music. Braxton states that point: "*23(O)* is designed as a multiple structure (ABA) for open improvisation involving the composite reality relationship of group interchange." No solos are designated; "Rather the challenge . . . goes to the very heart of the improvisational discipline: that being, moment interaction and vibrational directives."[20]

Fig. 8.5: From 23M. *The three-note sets bracketed serve as both destination and springboard in the line.*

Braxton dedicated *23P* to Muhal Richard Abrams. It too is a slow, solemn, open improvisation leading to a written statement, all in that same sacred space that moves through Braxton's music like prayer over time: the contrabass clarinet speaks right from the depths, the piano strums recall their primal origins in Egyptian harps, horsehair pulls harmonics from the bass, the flute comes in with the written music, then improvises, then returns to the low voice of the contrabass clarinet, with the bass, to state the piece again: Braxton's aim was "to achieve a very solemn texture that was also spiritual."[21]

Braxton's words about this piece, following, pertain to the points made about *230*, and across the board of his *oeuvre*:

> Generally the act of composing is viewed as a complex science that must involve hundreds of decisions and thousands of notes, chords and diverse rhythms. And indeed the last three hundred years have seen many great works and achievements in creative notated music—involving compositions that sometimes stretched for more than five hundred pages. Yet by the same token, the nature of present-day life participation has moved to place much emphasis on the peripheral activity that surrounds the creative act and little curiosity about what that activity was designed to be utilized for. For this reason it is important to constantly re-examine one's relationship with process—because in the final analysis the music—intention—is more important than how it's done. Composition No. 23P was conceived with this in mind—that being to establish a reality context with the fewest possible extraneous controls (so that music can happen).

Very lovely music does happen here. Braxton is really using the craft of composing, in the context of his own African American tradition, to achieve a pristine communion indeed resonant with Japanese culture. Gemini's ruling Muse, Hermes, is lord of roads and boundaries; he crosses them all as naturally and gracefully as he defines them, neither compromising nor violating his own identity nor the ones they contain. This piece is an example of why the record for which it was written won awards from Japan to France (forget about America—for the moment). It is sensitive and serving, not imposing or coercive or self-serving in its mastery.[22]

23A, from 1973, is the "most out" (and last) cut on the B (and most out) side of *New York, Fall 1974'* (the A side was very much in the jazz pocket). It's a ballad statement couched in a free improvisation that sounds farther removed from it than do improvisations on the faster pieces from their themes. Composers have always been most challenged by the ballad form, improvisers even more so. Ornette Coleman met both challenges more consistently than not in his new musical terms; Braxton does so in the same way for fast and medium pieces, but his improvisations on the slower ones often have a yearning, lost feel to them, as though he's looking on what he wrote from a distance he's trying to cover. Then again, many of his ballad lines—like this one—themselves feel that way. The timbres and conversational interactions between muted trumpet, bass harmonics, and contrabass clarinet well serve this piece (dedicated to Billy Ekstine), which itself well serves the album as a haunting reach past the hard-driving rhythmic romp of Side A.

23B is the first cut on the same album: very jazzy, fast, post-Mingus/Coleman conceptually, setting the tone for the A side (see Fig. 2.11). It appears a year later, after the album had been out and well received, on *Live at Moers*, in a more developed version.

After the head, Braxton solos first, relaxed and fluid over a fast walking bass and drums. The jumpy, choppy way he often phrases may be an occupational hazard connected with continually meeting new concepts and material; it seems to disappear both in moments of inspiration and on long-familiar pieces, however quirky. That's the case here. He floats, bites, intensifies gradually, shortens his phrases from streams to bursts of ideas. The solo itself is long, but the interest doesn't flag. Wheeler's trumpet finally jumps in with him, quotes *Donna Lee* himself, atonally. Wheeler's approach to atonality is that from bebop, which is to turn notes previously defined as passing tones or extensions into the center, only now they're farther out from that center than in Parker's time. The two horns together suggest the Coleman/Cherry sound, at first, but it moves from there into squeals, and then into the choppy/jumpy phrasing—as if the tryst with the known is itself another way to the mystery. Braxton then takes the improvisation without Wheeler to an extended plateau that climaxes suddenly when Altschul drops out to leave Holland and him to a duo. He gets back to the head by quoting *Donna Lee* again; Altschul's solo following refers at length to AACM devices—slide whistles, a clown horn honk, little percussives. Braxton noodles leisurely back in, using the half-note figure as an entry, then spools the piece out. The brilliantly reined and led brilliance of these virtuosos prefigures the genius of *Composition 98*.

This tune may well have been conceived in the middle of a solo on *Donna Lee*, which was part of Braxton's playlist back then. It stands as one of the classic expressions of the early two-horn quartets at their best, those (and the material) that picked up and extended the "harmolodic" lines laid down by Coleman in his own similar ensembles. The audience's delighted visceral engagement with this music is a strong and obvious part of it.

The two versions of *23C* elegantly demonstrate the relationship between the quartets without and with piano. *23C* is a jaunty succession of phrases telescoped through successive repeats, with an overall effect reminiscent of Stravinsky's *Ragtime for Eleven Instruments* or *L'Histoire du Soldat*. The trumpet and flute unison of *New York, Fall 1974* gives way to that between flute, piano, marimba and bass on *Willisau*. The dynamic between Braxton and Crispell is clear in the transparency of *23C*, and the open improv leading to it. If he submits the jazz tradition to European art music conventions, she does the opposite; the result is a stately mix of polish and roughness, like burnished gold. If the two-horn quartets with Wheeler, Lewis, and Anderson stand as Braxton's mature response to the liberation from Western harmonic tyranny effected first by Coleman, the piano quartet with Crispell seems his equally serious response to the reclamation of harmony as musical means, rather than stifling end, effected by Cecil Taylor.

23D is one of Braxton's most accessible pieces along post-Colemanish lines; the melody suggests chord changes, even though none are included (which is the case with all, even the most conventional-sounding, of his work). Curiously, Wheeler seems to avail himself of this accessibility more than the composer himself, who plays at the same sort of remove in the solos as on some of the *In the Tradition* cuts. As a quartet, however, the group syncs up more for creative sectional-type statements than conventional ones, even on these more conventional *23* charts (as opposed to the more parallel read-downs/run-throughs of forms and solos on their four tracks—rhythm, root, chords, melody—conventional quartet players typically do). The *Live at Moers* version has a similar feel as the *New York*, only less eclectic and experimental with pulse and texture, more hard-driving down the post-Coleman/Ayler lines. The audience response is ecstatic.

Litweiler called *23B* and *D*, on *New York*, "a genuine triumph ... In the past an emotionally indecisive artist who avoided frightening ambiguities with, alternately, studied abstraction and surface passion, Braxton is discovering personal resolutions in the 'total spontaneity' aesthetic."[23]

If the *23*s on the A side of *New York* take the Coleman line of the Coleman/Ayler (two-horn, pianoless) train, *23E* switches to the Ayler line. Braxton dedicated it to Ayler and intended it as an intense engagement of the implications of "free energy music."[24] Again, the audience response is wildly approving; seldom is it less on Braxton's many live recordings, contrary to his reputation as an esoteric and inaccessible eccentric.[25]

Both *Moers* and *Five Pieces* versions feature the horns playing what stands as a beautifully conceived and crafted anthem to freedom in unison over increasingly agitated bowed bass drone and brushed drum improvisation. The horns join in the agitation after the melody, skirmishing briefly and rapidly; Braxton switches to contrabass clarinet, Wheeler to harmon mute, Altschul to silence and little and exotic percussion as the post-Coleman/Ayler intensity shifts into more relaxed and various post-AACM modes. Braxton evinces his responsibility to the piece's freedom with a sustained pitch of imagination and interest in its potential, moving through to their ends the ideas that come up, pacing himself through them to the point where they cascade with a momentum both breathtaking and manageable. This is the sort of piece that could have started out with high aims and fallen far short in other hands; Braxton shines as the leader of this rigorous but heady expedition he also planned. Lake called it "Quite extraordinary," adding, "it might be the most extreme example yet of the dichotomy between jazz and contemporary classical in Braxton's music."[26]

Palmer's liner notes to *Five Pieces* are worth quoting for their insights into Braxton's composing process:

> Braxton calls the compositions themselves schematics. By this he means that a composition is a kind of diagram suggesting the kinds of improvised things that can happen within it. He also emphasizes that these are not merely compositions, but compositions for particular players, in this case the exceptionally gifted members of the quartet. "Composition for the contemporary improviser," he adds, "has to do first with determining a particular type of flow and, second, with defining the actual languages involved."

23F is a buoyant, happy-go-larky swing between high and low registers, into a more jagged swing through a clarinet solo over bass and drums. Braxton explains this piece as residing in the pocket of the post-bop, trans-African tradition, claims that as his own, and declares how important it is to him to participate in and further it.[27]

The four recorded versions of *23G*, spanning almost two decades, afford another interesting glimpse at how a piece can develop through time. This one, in fact, also reaches back, to the first Kelvin (*6F*), in concept. It isn't one of the Kelvin pieces, but it shares their use of rhythmic patterns as platforms for improvisation. The horns play a set of atonal bop-like lines in unison, with a medium-up swing feel. Only the drums and bass aren't keeping the time of that swing groove for/with the horns, are rather accenting it arhythmically. The horns' lines are in one tempo, over the "time-shifting gravallic basic" of the bass and drums in another, a line the horns both speed and stretch, playing here support-for-soloists roles. Braxton ascribes his use of minor seconds to Monk and Steve Lacy; this piece's oddly accented rhythm is also Monk-like, reminiscent of his *Evidence*. The *Performance 9/1/79* version is similar to this first one from *Five Pieces*.

Fig. 8.6: From Braxton's 23G. The chromatically shifting eighth-note runs are based on a germ of four eighths and one quarter-note rhythm (bracketed). The pulse is fast, explicitly so in the upper voices but implicit except at the "sound attacks" notated here in the bass line. See also Fig. 2.1c.

By *Willisau*, Marilyn Crispell is playing open, parallel harmonies to Braxton's melody, then moving into material from *30* while he improvises, the rhythm lurching through *23G*'s topography of accents. Then, in the *Coventry* performance, the piece also serves as third in three steps back in time and evolution: (1) *124*, written with an integrated pulse track (and a use of minor seconds similar to *23G*'s); (2) *88* collaged with *108C*, the kind of splicing Braxton did as he was developing his finished pulse track concept through pieces entirely devoted to it, such as the *105*s and *108*s; and (3) the energetic headwaters of the mature pulse track river's more languid sophistication running through the later works: *23G* as originally conceived, an atonal bop groove running parallel to an exaggeration and isolation of the sorts of accents, or punches, the rhythm sections of the music have traditionally spiked the piece's regular pulse with in practice.

The later versions, in these juxtapositions with other pieces, showcase an aspect of Braxton's approach to composition that he shares with several who crossreference some new musical statement with an earlier one of either their own or another composer's.[28] The musical effect is a recalibration of perception of both the new and the old. The coordinate system, in the light of this tradition, functions as more than an arbitrary linkage of material for improvisation (although, as we'll see, even that "more" isn't its primary function).

23H establishes terms for open collective—as opposed to extended solo—improvisation. Its lightly designed, extended monophonic line is offered "to vibrationally provide structural marking points for its interpreters and to stimulate them into looking 'for other focuses.'"[29] *23I* is an unrecorded piece with a few simple premises (some melodic, some rhythmic, some primary and some secondary) meant to evoke the feel of Spanish and Latin American music (one of his few such) within the context of Braxton's extensions of jazz improvisational conventions.

23J is another straight-ahead Ornettish jam, with three hot solos over rhythm. In his notes, Braxton explains that the head functions more to suggest, then give way to, the feel/phrasing/rhythm of the improvisations than to serve as a theme for variations. (Braxton's notes are alternatives to orthodox pedagogy, but they do pursue the same goal: scholarly understanding and musicultural documentation, as well as performance instruction.)

The *Montreux/Berlin* LP, Braxton's last quartet LP for Arista, released at the height of his popularity, got a five-star rating from *Down Beat* reviewer Neil Tesser. His words about Braxton's partnership with George Lewis (who played on the *Dortmund* version of *23J*) capture what made their two-horn quartet the one that served the composer's ends most definitively:

> [Lewis is] a front-line member whose idiosyncratic voice is as fully innovative, and as frighteningly virtuosic, as the leader's . . . The difference from Kenny Wheeler is almost that of passive empathy versus an active, challenging sympathy among partners . . . Braxton's longtime rhythm team of Altschul (who combines abstract sensibilities with an almost atavistic understanding of mainstream drumming) and Holland (simply stated, the best bass player in the world today) . . . this music comes closest, of all of Braxton's recent recordings, to crystallizing the large-scale implications of his art. Author Robert Pirsig (*Zen and the Art of Motorcycle Maintenance*) has examined our great societal dichotomy between the rational and romantic mindsets, and offered solutions; Braxton, with the intuitive comprehension of artistic endeavor, seems to me to be bridging that dichotomy in a manner that can be exemplary.[30]

The *Dortmund* version is a little faster, hotter, more fluid than the *Montreux/Berlin*, with the same solo order (with Lewis in place of Wheeler). Lewis is running on rocket fuel, and Braxton is playing at his most fiery, to a screaming audience.

The *Birmingham* version is, again, the first by a quartet with piano. Crispell harmonizes here much as on *23G*, extending the chords into a comping approach appropriate to the harmolodic, ametric post-Coleman handling of a regular walking pulse. If her part were isolated and transcribed, it would probably function perfectly as a pulse track composition.

The *23*s have lasted from their own time into Braxton's current music more than the *6*s. This may be for much the same reasons many aspects of the 1960s now seem dated, at least in the form they took then. While it's true that Braxton has often swum against the cultural tides toward his own artistic goals, it's also true that he has stayed open to them, engaging them cooperatively when possible. His music during the 6 series was very much in tune with the 1960s; the thrust of the 23s was similarly attuned to the way the Baby Boomers turned, in the 1970s, from the wild activism and experimentalism of the 1960s to tend more conservatively to their own domestic gardens, and to negotiate with, rather than confront, the world. The 23s incorporated the musical advances made through earlier experiments, but they did so in the context of a strong statement of solidarity with the jazz tradition. Braxton the composer was very much at the service of Braxton the torchbearer of the jazz saxophone legacy, and the groups he led then played to his areas of strength rather than vulnerable aspiration.

The Circle group embodied both the promise and the fatal flaw of the 1960s: the brightest and best coming together to conceive and deliver their disciplined etchings of freedom's glories, to change the (music) world—then falling apart in a clash of egos and visions. Braxton salvaged this experience by building his own group from Circle's core, leading it through his particular vision, learning leadership as stewardship rather than power trip. He was rewarded with media attention, critical acclaim, mainstream recording contracts; he got married and started a family just as the world seemed to be opening up for him. The work he did as a composer in this period was fueled by the feeling of this success, the prospect that his creativity would be taken seriously and supported. The 40s and 69s encompass that period, in the mid to late 1970s. Before we look at those, however, let's run through some more of the creative snowfall between the series.

Between 1972 and 1974, Braxton composed

> *24* (orchestra; this and all such we'll examine next chapter): the third in the L-C-J series,[31] which explore notated music as a platform for improvisation, to discover the interactions that arise between the many coexistent improvisations on the fixed material;

> *25* (creative orchestra): in response to a performance opportunity (in contrast to *24*, which was self-generated, and has never been performed);

> *26A–J* (solo alto sax): the recorded juxtaposition of many of these with 17, for string quartet, suggests that the harmonic nature of the latter is more textural than contrapuntal, like that of a single voice with the overtones sounded rather than resonant;

> *27* (orchestra): further development on *24*. "With this work I have continued to participate in my love of sustained material in multi-dimensional time spaces—to work on 'musics' for large canvases."[32] This is a musical approximation of being in a crowded room where everyone is talking at once. Braxton's poetic descriptions in the notes are often verbalizations of the subjective experience the music is exciting in him. For example, "This is a music of universes being created 'while other worlds are disappearing'—'there are suddenly

many events being presented, and then only strangers' ('who were more important than we had earlier perceived'). All of this takes place under the veneer of pointillism . . . " I find this a poignant signal of the experience of serving the Muse in the midst of one's own mystification. He just wanted to compose music in his life, had no idea what he was getting into, could only hope it would eventually find its audience;

28 (dancer and six musicians): important in its prefiguring of growing interest in "world music ritual and magic functions" (opera, theater, dance);

29A–E (small groups): a series of quick and simple notated premises charged with enough meaning to Braxton and his fellow improvisers to inspire sustained improvisations;

30–3 (solo piano), first recorded by Rzweski, then Crispell in later quartet collages;

34 (quartet): a six-note figure with twelve permutations used as springboards into open improv;

35 (trio): one of three pieces conceived for a specific performance (with Rzweski, Braxton, and a tubaist), based on 3 "'music types' (sound environments)" presented 3 times "(to show the spectrum of possibilities that exist for creative music) . . . Composition No. 35 is another structure that extends my involvement with extended improvisation. Since 1965 I have focused attention on the role of improvisation as we move into the next stage in earth progressionalism. I believe the significance of this discipline will be extremely important as Western information dynamics moves into its own next cycle (and focuses)";[33]

36 (two horns, one synth): see Chapter Seven;

37 (saxophone quartet): three of the (yet-to-be) World Saxophone Quartet (*sans* David Murray) recorded this first with Braxton;

38A–B: more little pieces for any instrumentation meant to evoke much improvisation on slight but pithy material;

39 (orchestra): first use of "regulated notation," or a replacement of scored meter with arrows—cue symbols—pointing down from above ↓ the staff to notes and phrases. This is Braxton's way of keeping pulse but making it flexible, so that he can conduct it according to his interactions with the players.

The Middle Period

The 40s and 69s

It took Braxton about six years (1968-1974) to write *Compositions 1* to *39*; *40* to *94* took another six after that. The *Six Compositions* version of *40A* (which originated as a duet with Holland) affords a rare glimpse of Braxton on tenor sax. The piece is a confluence of four soloists improvising on disparate and staggered material; when all are finally in a collective jam together, each fades in and out of center stage as the briefly "featured" soloist.

The structure here is not the first such in his work, but it is a good example of the way he would increasingly write for quartets. Whereas the 6s and 23s most typically had one statement, maybe with an A section repeated and bridged by a B, from which improvisation would issue and to which it would return—like a typical jazz head, though usually closer in intent to the improvisations it engendered—the later pieces would be more like suites. In *40A*, the structure is ABCD: A is a theme, B a scale pattern, C a new theme that is "the culmination of all of the previous sections as well as the platform for their extended implications," and D is where all the improvisations begun separately in A, B, and C come together to make their statement. The A soloist (piano) is working with a ballad, the B (bass) a faster tempo, the C (percussion) a synthesis of both, and the D (saxophone) links up with what the percussionist is doing at that point. Each soloist is to "exemplify some aspect of . . . 40A's principle construction."[34]

40B is a medium-up line that evokes aspects of Mingus, Parker, Tristano, Coleman, and Dolphy, with Braxton's own signature in the jagged, jumpy intervallic contour. The *Dortmund* version is as satisfying a sequence of solos by Braxton, Lewis, and Altschul as any jazz jam can produce, but the *Six Compositions* version has something special. This group, with drummer Ed Blackwell and pianist Anthony Davis, is a one-record collaboration between like-minded but independent players (as opposed to Braxton's own regular working group). The overall effect is of a pick-up band of greats relaxing with some Charlie Parker or Monk tunes. Braxton sounds as relaxed on his music as he did kicking around standards in duo with Holland; Davis and Blackwell bring a hip panache to it that dispels all overtones of awkwardness, or pretentiousness, as though Braxton's music were as comfortable a part of their repertoire and vocabulary as anyone's. In this sound space, Braxton's "eccentricity" has finally found its home in the jazz lounge, where he's riffing his lines, with not a bit of controversy.

In the same spirit, it is also refreshing to hear Marilyn Crispell play like a jazz pianist, on the *Willisau* version. Braxton blows long and hard on what we might call this post-jazz vehicle, with Crispell comping him closely. Her thorough exposition of the piece's intervallic contour's rhythmic and harmonic

quartet music

implications is, naturally enough, more Braxton-attuned than Davis', but, again, the feel here is that we are beyond (a successful) experiment and into a well-wrought addition to tradition.

40D is a rich source piece for Braxton's use of harmony. Its polytonal fanfares over rhythms make for a big, pushy sound, rushing into open solos that take on the moment like a fast car on a dead-end street. The contrasting complements of smooth legato and quirky march lines indicate the control over and detachment from the screaming catharsis that make it interesting as art. He's doing here what artists admire: getting in and making his point, then getting out again in a graceful and timely way. He's also doing that in a ("free jazz") voice notorious for its proclivity to monotonous self-indulgence. "Composition 40D has been an especially valuable structure for my quartet music growth and dynamics. I have relied on this structure for many different chords throughout the whole of the late 70s . . . The work has long been one of my favorite for extended solo interpretations, and it works equally well as a collective environment experience."[35]

40F is another of those evocations (albeit supercharged) of Brecht, New Orleans, and Fellini. Its structure is ABAC1C2D, played as written to open up into improvisations that return to it. It explores chromatic patterns, repetition, and juxtapositions of same. As with many of the structures that extended from A and B into more sections, B, C, and D are expositions on or extrapolations from some aspect introduced in A: in this case B adds harmony to A, C suspends two phrases over A's chromatic pattern, and D expands that pattern in another pitch range.

When the momentum of this piece is secure it demonstrates, on all four recorded versions, what kind of "pocket," or context, such material can establish for improvisation. The fast insistence and persistence of even eighth-note rhythms naturally provoke a soloist to gushings of even faster sixteenth-note phrases spiked with accents opposing the even pulse; the unrelenting sequence of half-steps similarly inspires its bursts and lines of chromatic connections infinitely varied from the half-step that are strong, sustained, and musical. One finds oneself tripping musical statements off of one's tongue that are clearly being unlocked by the composition, and that would be impossible to read or even come up with on less challenging improvisational platforms. Braxton's notes call for the written material to be used only in "an extended sense," in improvisation; what that means in practice is that it is there to kick around and draw from, but not to restrict or, ultimately, define the improviser's musical statement. Ray Anderson turns in one of his exemplary trombone renditions on *Seven Compositions*, mastering his spirited bucking bronc of a horn as surely as Lewis masters his own fine stallion. By the *London* performance, with Braxton's most current quartet, this piece takes its place in the fabric of a long set after a gradual rise in excitement from slow and soft playing—a perfect demonstration of the musical efficacy of the coordinate context. The written material is both mastered and "kicked around" by all in just the way Braxton likes for his music to be.

Braxton's notes to *40G*—a ballady, slow, bluesy piece (on which Blackwell just breathes with those cymbals)—give another insight into the way form was evolving in his work. The piece is

> one long extended phrase executed in unison by the total ensemble
> ... [simple enough—yet] ... the composite form of the work is
> ABA and the material structure of that form (as a given phrase
> grouping interacts with its composite idea) is A (A1) B C D (D2) E
> F/F B C D A (A3). What this means is that the material basis of the
> work is an extensive network of interrelated ideas and tendencies ...
> of seventeen phrase groupings in two sets of nine and eight each.[36]

In other words, within what might at first appear to be a simple, single integrated line, there is an ABA structure; within that, there are phrase patterns that break up into their own subdivisions—both variations on and oppositions or additions to—that structure. The process that leads to such a statement is the creative process of composing/improvising, a direct engagement with the Muse; the rational analysis comes later. Braxton's mind can simply wander farther and farther down the logical extensions of his ideas as he becomes more familiar with its workings; yet this piece suggests those suite-like extensions as branchings from a single taproot, rather than, say, an endless proliferation of spider plants from a shoot. And that suggests depth, rather than mere glib facility, of intellect. The unrecorded *40H* is a similarly simple premise broken down into, or zooming in on, the microscopic complexities of its components. *40I* is just a light, playful march, constructed to be easy to learn and blow on collectively, oscillating with a boisterous joy between the march and open interplay.

40J displays another aspect that would take on more life in Braxton's mature music: notated music requiring no improvisation to establish its concept. In this piece, the four parts are written as independent from each other, and the material is repeated and "recentered" (changed timbrally) throughout the repetitions. *40J* is a good example of why Braxton's complex use of metric notation is organic rather than contrived: the phrases, conceived and executed in the inspiration of "moment time" determine the metric changes and divisions, not the other way around. Braxton calls this "a peaceful yet rigid sound universe whose personality establishes a vibration—as opposed to a 'fixed phrase' (that can be sung forever) ... a terrain of sound space that only 'touches' on what it could really be" via improvisation.[37]

These extensions of forms happening in the *40s* were mixed with pieces with the structural simplicity more common in the *6s* and *23s*. Braxton has used some of those more as musical marking points in a coordinate set than as entries into improvisation. *40L* on *Willisau* is a good example of that. The effect of ending a long run through the arduous *96* with *40L* is that of solidifying the busy-ness and intensity into a spacey flow and float that is calm and serene, yet still active enough to pique the interest to its end.

40M, like *40H*, displays Braxton's trans-African voice. Repetition and variation on simple rhythmic and melodic patterns serve such a voice well in this piece, as in many such; accordingly, I'll quote Braxton's notes on it to reiterate with still more force some points I've already made about the *40s*.

> After the basic idea of the work was understood each succeeding
> moment was inspired from its immediate predecessor moment. This

> is so because ... 40M was composed in moment time without any overstructural devices—in either its form specifics and/or harmonic decisions—as the process of the work was establishing itself (that being the moment decision that took place to create the music).[38]

This quote captures the relationship between "linear" and "cyclical" in Braxton's approach. An overstructure defines a cycle; spontaneity free of the cycle describes a line. But spontaneity within certain parameters begets another cycle, defining what "felt" (to the creator) like a line in relation to the cycle of its parameters (one begins to puzzle over the old free will vs. fate debates). The *Five Pieces* version of *40M* consists of a nervous, jumpy sax solo, marked by a calm strength in the two horns taking it out. The *Willisau* version is strong, calm, and lively throughout, a Coltrane-like energy carried and furthered perfectly by the whole group.

40N, on *Coventry*, makes for an apt exit from the abovementioned string of three pulse track pieces: a minor/atonal phrase-grouping over a bass drone, inspired by Indian music (see Fig. 2.2c).

We come to the end of the *40*s, a propos of pulse tracks, with *40(O)*, a Kelvin piece from the early 1970s. Braxton describes this as "69 notes in 6 different phrase groupings in a time field of 24-1/2 beats"; and as "arhythmic," to emphasize "different weight shifts" (sound as accents, dynamics determinants): a "design intended to surprise all involved."[39] Entrances/accents suggest shapes (form emerges); "the dynamic implications of this forum extend into infinity" because of the options of repetition; open pitch, harmony, and dynamic contour; give and take of nuance; timbral colors, and different instrumental combinations.

Such Kelvin pieces are designed to induce the same sort of benign possession of a dance trance people typically enter through simpler rhythms in those of us who find the latter only partially satisfying, for whatever reason.

> It will be important to stay open to the widest possible informational and vibrational stance—and this is especially true in this time period (with the acceleration of electronics and microelectronics). Everything must go forward—including our perception about who we are ... 40(O) was composed as a response to what this means.[40]

The three recorded versions of *40(O)* cover the Stravinsky-ish sound of many of the Kelvins (*Montreux/Berlin*), and the relaxed assimilation of complexity as a context for the most primal statements (*Dortmund*).

What shall we say to summarize the *40*s? The innovations peculiar to them include extensions of form, suggested by a bleeding of the improvisational into the compositional process. They also include conceptions of written material as statements complete unto themselves, not only as platforms for improvisation, statements that can frame, reflect upon, other compositions and improvisations. Whatever musical ground was covered by earlier work, of course, is part of the *40*s ground.

Fig. 8.7: From Braxton's 40(O). After conducting students through 15 or 20 repetitions of this Kelvin piece, they play (and a student conductor conducts) it as easily as a conventional jazz head and start taking improvisational liberties as easily.

Braxton's work after the 40s

> *41–2, 45–6, 51, 55–9,* and *63* (chamber and creative orchestras): see next chapter;

> *43* (five or six instruments): a series of 27 groups of phrases meant to suggest the thrust of improvisations, triggered by 21 different cue points for one of the players to signal, and cut off by silences planted to induce reflection on the music in both listener and player;

> *44* ("traditional quintet" of two upper voices, piano, bass, and percussion): concepts/devices similar to those in *43* explored in three parts successively subdividing into six (A, B^1B^2, $C^1C^2C^3$); Braxton set up a deliberate synthesis of his two-horn and piano quartet concepts in this one piece (in *43*, the core group was a trio, with bass, percussion, and piano options);

quartet music

47 (quintet): another piece in which Braxton consciously expanded from his usual quartet format, in this case to three upper voices over bass and percussion instead of his usual two; again, he's exploring the "time cue points" of phrases conceived in "moment time" on which to improvise for designated brief durations;

This "cut-off and pause" sign begins to appear often, as does the conducted cue point above each of a series of timed sound events.

48 (two upper and two lower voices, piano, percussion): a slow tone poem intended to slow/stop time, allow for examination of the moment, be a dreamlike "door from one state to the next"; the pitches/clefs are open, improvisation minimal and close to the music, and time cues again employed;

49 (1–20 musicians with or without dancers): created for a 1975 performance with Merce Cunningham; built upon Braxton's language music options/routes; the players proceed through designated time durations from one language area to another, visualized as circles connected by lines, and by other graphic devices; this piece prefigures much of his later music, visualized as virtual road maps (see next chapter);

50 (two instrumentalists and two synthesists): 52 timed cues, to be performed backward or forward; each cued event is a premise as simple as, for example, one note with a dynamic flux; the range of them covers, conceptually, Braxton's language material, repetition, solo/collective dynamics, open sections, notated material, and chords;

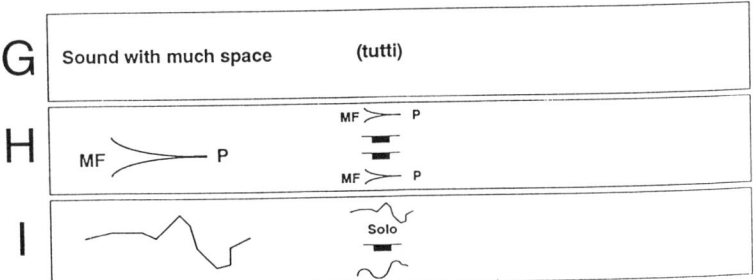

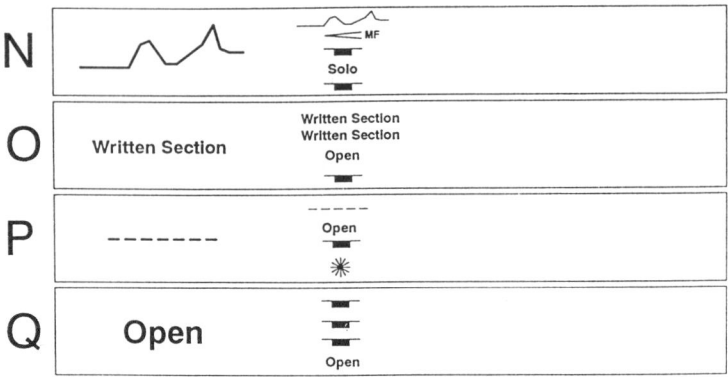

Fig. 8.8: From *50*.

52-4 (quartet): *52* is a typically Braxtonian atonal, arhythmic, intervallically jagged theme (an A section repeated three times) that generates derivative sections (B, C, C^2); *53* is built on couplets of notes ranging the pitch spectrum, conceived as "sound that rhythmically creates the impression of 'a sound reflection' (seen in the water and 'sometimes from the water'), in seven interrelated sections"; and *54* focuses on the percussion as the defining voice in the duration and cutoff of the pieces, the snare drum "snatching up" each cued moment and the bass drum "spitting it out."

60-2 (duos with Muhal Richard Abrams, see Chapter Six);

66 (trio): designed to explore dialogues between upper and lower voices; a slow ponder on a light construction that paved the way to the Braxtonian chamber-music feel of *107* (see Chapter Seven);

67 (quartet): a chirpy tonal phrase repeated endlessly unto endless permutations; the recording of this is a wonderful demonstration of how far a simple premise, strictly observed, can lead past the strict observation;[41]

68 (horn/bass/drums trio): a brief mixture of unison and multiple phrases meant to inspire similarly woven improvisation.

This part of Braxton's creative snowfall led him to devise ways to literally seize (and freeze) the moments he had begun to put under his microscope in the *40*s expansions of forms. The increase of cueing rather than metric structure and the cutoffs and silent pauses between phrases were especially moves toward both more control and more spontaneity, ways of stopping so as to redirect, reflect

quartet music

on, shape the flow of time down predetermined lines and on impulse both. The concept may be paradoxical in the abstract, but these devices and recordings show their concrete life.

The 69s

In keeping with the goal of fewer trees and more forest, as we ascend, we'll forego a look at every one of the 69s separately, going through them instead for the broad strokes and points key to Braxton's development as a composer.

Generally, by now the written material can best be understood as having evolved in the way and degree that it did in order to keep up with the highly developed needs and skills of the improvisers. The expansion on simple ABA-based structures into strings of sections spun from one or two of them continues here. As written statements, they seem to establish the kind of fixed imprint the players both can handle and need in order to improvise music that matches their atonally melodic and arhythmic complexities. The sense of an awkward distance between the feel of written premises and improvisations on them often found in earlier work is fading.

69B and C are good examples of this growing synergy. Both are tricky little mazes of abstraction that could ensnare many an intrepid but unprepared player into lost wanderings or boorish blunders. Braxton and family are so familiar with such musical spaces that they now flow through their crystalline intricacies without smashing a single detail, and with a warm, human voice that can move into moans of bliss, screams of terror, and thundering orations of fury as the spirit moves. (Braxton's group with Ray Anderson, Thurman Barker, and John Lindberg seems particularly well suited to this wild abandon in a highly charted, controlled context. Though all are in command of Braxton's music, neither is so in a precious or fastidious way, neither as jazz nor new-music artists, all are having as much fun with it as he.) Especially on the later recordings, the 69s have become home bases, or "primary territories," that ground still more complex and otherwise ambitious statements.

On the other hand, later recordings of *69C, H,* and *M* demonstrate another relationship between primary and the "secondary territories" of the solo piano pieces (*31–3*) in the parentheses. Many might wonder just why Braxton has felt the need to string his compositions together and juxtapose them in the web of the coordinate system. The musical experience is at the crux of it, and these collages of 69s and 30s exemplify that. The *Coventry 69C*, for instance, tears through its rhythmic drive in stark contrast to Crispell's relatively static chording from *32*. The effect is of a split screen, with rushing traffic on one side and a person walking leisurely down the sidewalk on the other (it's also another expression of the gender dichotomy, in its juxtaposition of drive and stasis). This and all such couplings go back to Braxton's love for the "multidimensional soundspace" that he expressed in connection with Ives' *Symphony No. 4*. The musical payoffs seem to be a combination of stimulus and space: stimulus in the parallel universe's challenge to one's focus on one's own, and space in its unconcern with same. Both seem to spark a fire and freedom in the treatment of the 69s that would have been harder to extract from within its own confines.

Fig. 8.9a: From *69C* and *32* (played simultaneously).

quartet music

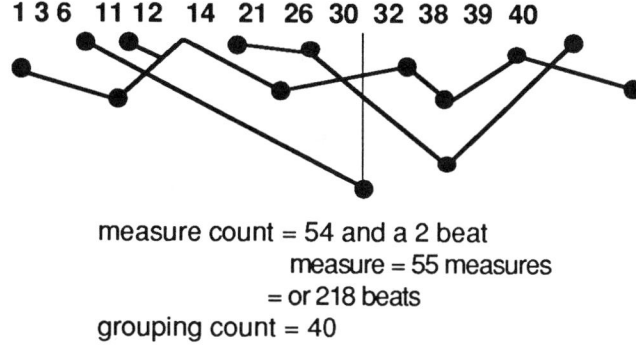

measure count = 54 and a 2 beat
measure = 55 measures
= or 218 beats
grouping count = 40

Fig. 8.9b: From *Composition Notes C*, p. 467.

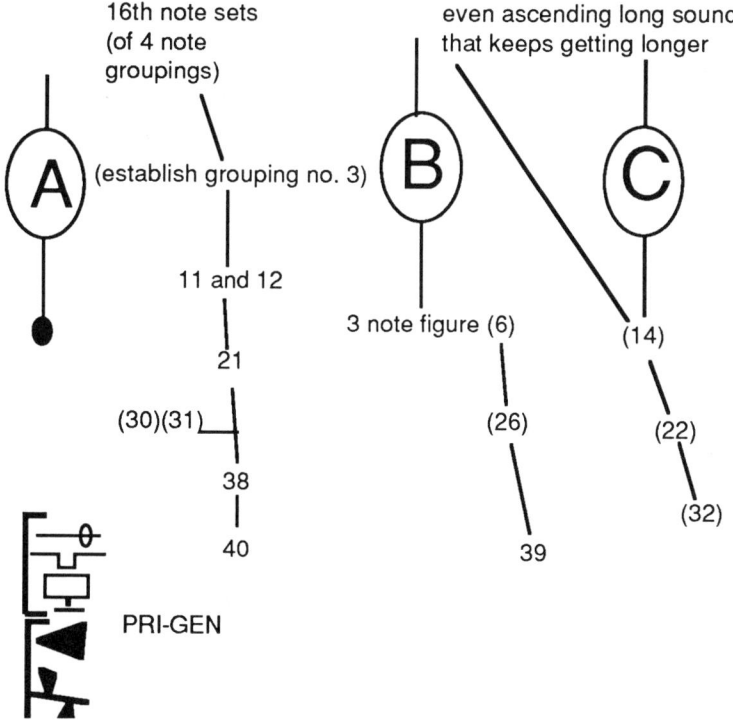

Fig. 8.9c: From *Composition Notes C*, p. 464.

Fig. 8.9: Braxton improvised/composed the material for 69C (a) and then spliced segments of it together (b) to form its three sections (c). The result is a post-bop piece with post-Ayler deviations from it (written parts can be played any time during improvs). This concept of manipulating blocks of time is shared by such composers as Cage and Stockhausen; the difference here lies in the performers' vocabulary of jazz-rooted improvisation. 32 (a) is like a lady walking down the street next to her more friskily prancing man (69C).

69E is notable for its introduction of "dimensional notation," a kind of harmonic hocket technique. Braxton writes of it, "All of the musical parts in this system are constructed from one cell complex (and in a given performance every part can be interchanged as desired). The excitement it held for Braxton lay in its evocation of the collective improvisations of early jazz: "The thrust of this approach to creativity encourages the most balanced group involvement since dixieland music—and this should not be lightly viewed."[42]

Fig 8.10: From 69E. Notice how much like solo piano music this is. Players enter at various points and play the phrases and long tones as they will. The variety of instruments desired, the flexibility of execution and the focus on the space and silence in pointillism is what puts this piece in the post-AACM continuum.

69G wasn't recorded as part of a collage, but Braxton's notes about it reveal something else about the aesthetics behind his coordinate system, and the way he structures the flow of performances and recordings. It's a post-Coleman atonal/boppish line he crafted for the "master progression of the performance" in a festival situation, where the music was more ambient than demanding of any focused attention, as at a concert. He placed this piece in consideration of larger flow, rather than leaving his playlist to "what feels good at that moment." Think that way long enough, and you come up with the coordinate system, in which all statements, however self-sufficient, have to serve the aesthetic thrust of their network of relationships.

While the musical patterns increased in complexity, the composer's and players' mastery of them transformed them into simpler visualizations. The webs of cascading notes and accents in *69H* swoop up to shoot off into improvisations entwined around pillars of octaves, like ivy around a tree. Braxton would try to describe such pictures in his notes, or render them with his titles. He would leave minute technical descriptions behind in favor of these and other allusions to the metamusical patterns he was sensing. The phrases of *69H* were etched in the music like crystals. Jagged kinds of rhythms are matched with long sound streams (that are like breath in the phrase statements) to complete a kind of agreement that never took place.[43]

The *Prague* version serves as the perfect exit from a set marked by the most free and reaching musical exuberances on the most basic, even childlike premises—an interesting strategy for this music in that part of the world. The *Birmingham* version benefits from the abovementioned splitscreen effect of stimulus and space. Braxton also expressed his desire for many pieces from this time that they stand up as compositional statements as well as they do as platforms for improvisation, even though that's what they were composed to be. He was maintaining the balance of the synthesis between the two processes.

69K is an unrelenting run of eighth notes set up as a scan of pitches which the player is meant to emphasize alternately each time through its cycle; *69M* and *N* are couchings of atonal bop, ballad, and circus-band phrasings within sweeps of "curved" lines; *69O* and *Q* are both suites of written and improvised sections, "interrelated stories." All are pithy, fluid blends of improvisation and notation on the wide variety of premises and permutations thereof that constitutes Braxton's signature.

The nine years (1968-1976) marked by these four series saw the particulars of Braxton's development as a composer unfold in a publicly successful way. The star that was on the rise in the 1960s shone with the fulfillment of its potential in the mid to late 1970s. By the end of the 69s, he had also refined his composer's game in solo sax (and piano), duo, trio, and large-ensemble contexts, the techniques and concepts stemming from each informing and overlapping all.

Musically, the series might be seen as a progression most directly from Ornette Coleman's overhaul of the jazz quartet instrumentation and music. Where Coleman left Western harmony and meter behind—in the music he wrote and improvised, in his more melodic use of bass and drums, and his eschewal of a keyboard or guitar—Braxton's early quartets and quartet music took a track with two parallel rails down Coleman's road.

The first rail was into the trio-plus-floating-other, where the "other" might be a chordal, percussion, or bowed instrument; harmony was reclaimed (even as atonality expanded), but more as an epiphany of melody and rhythm, as texture and color, than as the generative matrix of system and meaning it had become for the West. The melodic/contrapuntal ground Coleman had broken with his two-horn quartets was still claimed and worked by Braxton, but his freer use of harmony took the burden off of that ground. This rail ran through the most experimental 6s for both AACM/CCC trios and those-plus-one, leading to the horn-trio/piano recording of *Composition 98*.

The second rail ran through the Circle recordings and *The Complete Braxton* to the mature two-horn and horn-piano quartets with bass and drums. It reconceived those standard jazz configurations so as to have it all—post-bop, post-Coleman/Ayler (two-horn), post-Coltrane/Taylor (horn-piano), and post-AACM (multiinstrumental, any combination)—in the way it used the piano as both single-line and atonal chordal voice, and shuffled all the instruments around into a variety of combinations and improvisational contexts.

That second rail might be seen as the one of the two with the "charge," running the train on into the 23s. Their written sections strongly evoked Coleman's pianoless, driving music, especially in their first recorded versions; just as strongly, they opened that sound up into even more expanded fields in their improvisational sections.

By the 40s, and into the 69s, the written sections were showing the influence of those expanded improvisations. Braxton's structure, syntax, and concepts evolved to accommodate the things that would happen in improvisation—the unplanned but meaningful ways motifs and rhythms would cycle through and mutate, the little skirmishing moments of synchronicities and silences that would arrange themselves in the unpremeditated course of a jam, the private dream images and psychic dramas that would arise in improvisation and suggest themselves as the music's "meaning." Braxton used these to inform and develop his approach to composition.

This feedback loop between the two processes is key to understanding why his music evolved as it did, why it was as exciting as it was—and, perhaps, why it suffered the neglect it did after 1977, when it went on from the highest critical acclaim and (relative) commercial success to its even higher musical pinnacles, in *Compositions 96* and *98*, only to find itself alone there. As Radano chronicled,[44] Braxton's star, arguably the brightest of the 1960s innovators, waned from 1978 on, in America anyway. He would continue to hold the top spot on *Down Beat*'s clarinet polls into the 1980s, but his role as a jazz vanguard standard-bearer was, it seemed, over.

What happened to him then might be understood best in the broader sociocultural context of the times. The cultural and political discourse initiated by the countercultural movements of the 1960s had progressed through Watergate and the Ford administrations to, at the height of Braxton's success, the election of Jimmy Carter. The Carter administration embodied for many the mature, responsible mainstreaming of the thrust of those movements, just as Braxton's work did the most radical aesthetic revolutions in jazz. People let that spirit have its turn at the wheel, in both Braxton and Carter then, after disillusionment with the other options.

We know what history followed: twelve years of Reagan and Bush, and a commercialization and neoconservatism in jazz, both of which drew much of their power from a new generation. The swing of the pendulum back through the Clinton presidency, to continue the parallel, may include a similar resurgence of Braxton's music in the culture, as signaled by Radano's and this book, by his recently tenured position at a major university (a mainstream affirmation), and—the crown—the award of the MacArthur "genius" grant.

Be all that as it may, Braxton's music did reach what I've been calling his Golden Peak and claim and work it as part of his new musical ground, during the time spanned by *Compositions 95–105B*, in the early 1980s. It was then that the house he'd built and moved into to meet the Muse got its first serious visitations thereby; after that, the life of the music would manifest as recapitulations of that meeting, and as a unifying integration of "all that came before."

Before we get there, however, let's quickly survey the ground covered between the 69s and 96s.

quartet music 393

70 (five instruments): for Braxton's quartet with Lewis, featuring Muhal Richard Abrams. This unrecorded work, performed at Carnegie Hall during the Newport Jazz Festival of 1976, has expanded the ABA structural scope up to letter P! Lines evoking the sound and spirit of, and leading to, collective improvisation are pegged throughout those sections on a teaming of piano and percussion within sporadically stated sustained trills. Braxton's notes are worth quoting for their insight into his music's anarchy-within-consensus aesthetic, and its life beyond music: "Participation in this sound forum necessitates that each individual be responsible for his or her own statement—in its isolated and separate sense—rather than leaning on another person's invention. This is important because in . . . 70 there are 'moments' where suddenly 'you are out there by yourself' (which is to say, whatever one plays—creates—he or she must 'mean' it on its own, without respect to 'what someone else might do' to affect it). The reality of this phenomenon strikes at the heart of extended improvisation and self realization."[45] It also strikes at the heart of the nature of the creative işolation which, compared to the 1970s, the 1980s would prove to be for Braxton.

71, 78, 82–83, 89, and *91–93* are for creative and traditional orchestras; *72A–H* and *85–88* are duos with Holland (the *Coventry* quartet version of *88* is virtually divided into duets, and collaged with other pieces); *73, 75–76,* and *94* are trios, *74A–E* duos with Mitchell; *77A–J* are pieces for solo alto, three of which Braxton orchestrated for a string quartet; and *79–81* are three-horn trios plus pianist Abrams, four unrecorded works scored for a Chicago club date that were inspired by the Count Basie sound. All of these either include or are like material and periods we've examined or will examine in other chapters. They're characterized by Braxton's reunion with old AACM cohorts, as well as continuing associations with members of his own post-AACM groups. His composing is developing in the context of performance opportunities that increasingly include large ensembles, after the success of *Creative Orchestra Music 1976*. It is developing in the light of affirmation from the public jazz scene, whatever detractors he might have had there, and of a big commercial outlet (Arista) and its contractual deadlines. This is a period when the artist is neither starving nor neglected—which means he's breaking even and is able to work—and is thriving creatively in response.

84 and *90* are worth some special attention here, for some traits that would blossom in *96* and *98*, traits that show why the quartet music, more than the others, is such a natural window onto the whole system and body of music.

84, from 1978, is a "visual shape score" for any number of instruments. The players are given nine shapes and twenty language types. As in *42* and *78*,[46] *49* and others, the shapes are meant to function as symbols of the sound worlds, only here he has the players choose which shapes will represent which (up to four for each shape, to make for interaction between languages). His notes indicate that he's trying to provoke in his players their own experience of such visual-audial connection and creativity—even a mystical experience—rather than imposing his on them.[47] The piece is dedicated to Picasso, and a dancer (another eye-addressing signal) is optioned.

> Composition No. 84 consists of fourteen pages of symbolic shapes that can be utilized as a basis for creative exploration. The work consists of nine shapes, each of which can be utilized as a language music context variable (mixture) that can be integrated into the composite shape complex. Each symbol in the visual formation is a matrix factor that solidifies some or one isolated material operatives as a basis for language and sound focus. Composition No. 84 is constructed in conjunction with the spread of language music sound directives and strategies. I conceived this discipline as a forum to place language music material coordinates so that the thrust of this structural method can expand. A given interpretation of this work involves matching a given symbol with one of twenty language music operatives (that are included in the score) . . . The nine shapes of No. 84 are:

Fig 8.11: All of any number of players read from the same complete score of 84, of which this is a page.

90, from 1979, is a "graft structure for any instrumentation" conceived and designed to direct volume dynamics and improvisational "patches" within a collective jam (Braxton's attempt to counter the problem Stockhausen mentioned of "free" players staying at the top of their volume and intensity ad nauseum). The lines denote held long tones, their breaks silences, their flux volume; the broken circles denote improvised solos (four on each page). Each page is cued by a conductor, and conceived as a step further into the musical universe the composer sees in this premise's potential; each player reads his or her part from the complete score.

Braxton's notes recall the "sonic pictures" the *Ayahuasqueros* tribe, of McKenna's study, created together: "Composition No. 90 is a meditative discipline that asks its interpreters to *extend themselves into a single consciousness (that can execute given sound shape variables as a unified ensemble—and intention). This is a dream world sound state* that attempts to establish single and multiple sound occurrences that give fresh definition to the fabric and focus nature of the music. A given performance of the work moves to solidify a 'cloud-like' music state that contains positioned short improvisational statements (that 'sit' inside of the 'swells' and 'lobs' of its material environment)."[48] (emphasis mine)

What's happening here is a shift of the focus up from his music as patterns and arrangements of notes and rhythms onto a level that transcends and subsumes those as the components and syntax of its own shape and flow. He has experimented with such concepts and techniques all along, but now they are falling into their proper relationship with the way he has also been using Western notation all along. The latter might well describe a certain aspect of the *Ayahuasqueros* tribe's chants, but not the thrust of it as they experience it. So it is with Braxton's music. His growth led him here to represent directly the "music beyond the notes," to acknowledge it not as his private universe but as something not only possible but imperative to wake up in others and to share.

This reconception of the eye as a processor/instigator of sound resonates with the way it's used as an occult symbol (above the pyramid) and its prominence in Egyptian art generally, and the occult lore associated with it (see Chapter Five). It recalls the feminine dynamic—an eye comprises concentric circles that take in "arrows" of light—as one to be reckoned with in music as in life. In this, in fact, it is like the ear, only up from the energy level of sound waves to that of light waves, both of which reduce to molecular-to-subatomic particles jostling each other in wave patterns. The ear represents the evolution from aquatic sensors of vibrations in water, used by sea creatures to orient themselves correctly to the currents and gravity field—to get their bearings and equilibrium[49] (thus the inner ear's importance to our sense of balance). Music sheerly on the level of sound hitting the ear is a watery world, with all that that means to our evolution as watery creatures. Light, that which called us out of the sea, is the more subtle vibration, best borne in air; a music made on that level (such as the *Ayahuasqueros'*) will always contain the world of sound, as we contain our fluids, as the Einsteinian contains the Newtonian universe, and not the other way around. (In fact, this goes to another mythological image called on by both Braxton and Stockhausen to explain their respective musics: the coming of the Aquarian Age, following the Piscean. The latter is about life within the water; the former, Aquarius, images the *bearing* of that water within a skin, a transcendence of it as medium.) Braxton's development up to that "light" through that "sound" level over time on the terms of his written work—in paradoxical tandem with his immediate access to it, as both player and composer, from the beginning—is in keeping with this concept (and with the way the speed of light is literally timeless; indeed, his music's treatments of time themselves are likewise in keeping with it). His conscious and purposeful engagement of the potential of that light/visual level, once he got there, is marked by what he calls his Ritual and Ceremonial music, the first of which was *95*, in 1980, as we've seen.

96, the second such, has assumed a seminal role in his music generally, and in his recorded quartet work specifically; *98*, though only recorded once, is charged with the same potent musical magic. Neither was written for quartet but both have served to define consummately that dual-aspected essence it's exhibited from the first. Both are part of Braxton's Golden Peak. Let's look at what that is before examining those pieces.

The Golden Peak

The image of a Golden Peak draws on the "golden section" in music, a mathematically symmetrical structure that serves as a sort of cornerstone from which to expand; the Golden Mean in architecture, first associated with the pyramids, is a similar concept. Radano quotes Braxton as saying he used a golden section in three of his works from what I'm calling his Golden Peak.[50] However, I use the image here in connection with a sequence of ten works which I see as charged with the essence of Braxton's whole body of more than 300 (by now) works.

Notice the pattern of blocks in his recorded work up to 95: *4* through the *6*s are mostly quartets (the few trios quite close to some of those quartets in concept); the *8*s are mostly solo music; *10* through *25* are mostly quartets (with some duos expanded to quartets and quartets reduced to duos); *26*s are for solo sax; *30*s are keyboard oriented, *40*s are quartets, *41* to *59* are mostly for creative orchestra, *60*s are mostly duets, *69*s are quartets, *77*s are solo alto, *80*s are quartets (even *82* is for four orchestras), and *90* to*93* are for large ensembles. Quartet and solo alto blocks dominate; trios and duets almost look like rest stops; and creative orchestras appear in a block in the middle and one at the end. Braxton has worked one context after the other, usually overlapping, but typically blocked out so in response to recording and cataloging needs.

The Golden Peak block, defined by *95* to *105B* (see Insert 8.1), is marked as much by its heterogeneity of such contexts as the others by their homogeneity. Moreover, each of the pieces—for solo, duo, trio, quartet, and creative orchestra—is a full flowering of one or more aspects of Braxton's music as developed through the earlier blocks. The first Ritual and Ceremonial piece, and all that meant to Braxton artistically and personally (as examined in Chapter Six), sums up his relationship to piano music, to the male-female dynamic, to occult "perennial wisdom" and its links to science, to visual and dramatic elements of theater, to Western-traditional harmony and notation, and to his Africanizations of same. *101*, as we saw in Chapter Six, is a similar apotheosis of some of these dynamics.

96, the second Ritual and Ceremonial piece, does much the same thing in an orchestral[51] context. As we'll see shortly, like *95*, it has the same "science-magic" thread, the male-female thread, the visual-theatrical cast, the Europe-Africa/literate-oral syntheses. *98* is the quintessential synthesis of Braxton's use of notation and improvisation, and its structure resonates with occult patterns and systems in the same way. *102* is a theater piece constructed along musically similar lines (see next chapter) that features four giant puppets that represent mythological archetypes.

105A–B are the first composed pulse tracks, Braxton's rhythmic alternative to structures of harmonic matrices (chord changes) as bases for improvisation. To put a rhythmic pattern in the context of the compositional-statement/improvisational-platform he'd developed served to canonize, in Western literate terms, the African oral heart of this trans-African music that had been defined and codified—shortchanged—by those terms for so long. Significantly, for the first time, human figures appear in the graphic titles of these pieces, and would proliferate in those to come.

The other pieces in the Golden Peak are charged with similar significance to their predecessors, solo, duo, and trio statements overlapping with each other. It's as though the separate voices and conversations that had taken place earlier had all converged here for a party, between 1980 and 1984. Then, once they had gotten acquainted, they began networking, through the coordinate system, into associations that would grow new musical entities greater than the sum of their parts.

This was also the period in which Braxton finished his *Tri-Axium Writings*, lost his Arista contract, and found most of his work, as some ten years before, in Europe. He continued to use the solo alto format to develop original ideas to bring to collectives, and to keep his instrumental fettle honed; the duo format to dialogue with other musical minds; the trio as a chamber-music context in which to leisurely kick around concepts in a three-way conversation; and his mature working quartet as both the composite of all those and the cornerstone of the larger collective statements (indeed, the quartet structure itself works as a Golden Mean of all the ensembles).

Past the Golden Peak, developments in the work might best be captured here in the framework of one of those developments itself: the setting of pieces from all parts of the whole body of work into sequences and collages that stand as one unbroken musical statement—or maybe two, as many recordings were of two live sets broken by an intermission. Quick overviews of a few such recordings will give a sense of the thrust of such statements, affording us the opportunity to light on the occasional new development an individual piece might bear. First, however, *96* and *98* require our attention.

Braxton wrote *96*—a number rich in both threes and fours—for orchestra and four slide projectors, for a New York performance George Lewis had arranged. He dedicated it to Stockhausen. "I conceived this effort based on the changes that took place in my extended quartet music structures in the late seventies."[52] He goes on to specify the increase of "collage improvisation"—his version of the collective jam, in which each player improvised on different platforms from the others—as being a musical reflection of a real-world phenomenon that engaged him most deeply as both composer and human being. *96* was a major move into notated music suggested by such multiimprovisations.

The different instrumental sections comprise the independent statements set into motion to create what rhythmic topography and sonic texture they will; in that, *96* is like a quartet with members playing independently. (Of passing interest: Braxton scores thickly for many woodwinds, better matching the strings and brass in timbre and volume, a value not inherent in traditional orchestral instrumentation.) Within each instrumental section, the lines are more in sync, and are constructed

> To adhere to the phrase construction tendencies of my alto saxophone solo music (and the general construction tendencies that have solidified through the continuum of post-Parker language dynamics). The use of arhythmic phrase statements in 96 seeks to implant those structural gains into the next cycle of notated pedagogy . . . I have attempted to structure what could only be called a fast-to-medium

pulse post-saxophonistic solo music for both the wind and string sections.

Recall the recorded juxtaposition of solo alto music (from the 26s and 77s; see Insert 8.1) with the string quartet (*17*) as a clue to the process behind the layering of these sectional parts. Braxton again alludes to an analogy from the bop world to explain it:

> [*96* is] n extension of the "super sax" approach to executing Charlie Parker solos—the only difference in this case would be that all events in the work were written as an affirmation of "what I was hearing" (rather than what Mister Parker was hearing).

But of course the Supersax arrangements—harmonizations of Parker solos for saxophone ensembles—while they indeed may have been close to what Parker "was hearing," were also written according to the rules of harmonic logic that go straight back to Bach. Braxton wrote his harmonies based on what he heard as ruled only by the twelve chromatic options.

This is one major point of interest in *96*: it might be described as post-Schönberg, for its atonality; as post-Webern, for its static essence (it is essentially one long fanfare of moments strung together and juxtaposed); as post-Stockhausen and even post-Cage, for its structural and metamusical premises and identity; but, as far out along those lines as it sounds, the essence of its generation is best grasped in the image of an alto saxophonist practicing alone, and making explicit all the implications of Charlie Parker's most ingenious chromatic spins on the diatonic field, and of his most ingenious polyrhythmic extensions against the basic pulse of meters of 3, 4, and 8.

Braxton's students and professional collaborators experience this firsthand. The process of learning *96* entails mastering a seeming infinity of phrases made as though by shaking up the chromatic scale in a jar and throwing its notes out onto the staff like dice. Any one of the phrases might be isolated and judiciously grafted into a bebop chart, especially after Braxton has conducted everyone through them a hundred times, like a drill sergeant in boot camp, until they can throw them off as casually as he. Braxton calls for his players to master an equally endless and irregular stream of rhythmic subdivisions on a beat that is meant to swing just as Max Roach still would if one of his moments were extracted from that bebop chart and placed in a score by, say, Varèse.

This goes to the heart creative process as a *muscle*: the static flow is in the even pulse and the diatonic tendencies of the chromatic field; the actual music comes from a wrestling match *against* both flow and tonality. The arhythmic atonality is not set into the separate peace of an orderly serial universe apart from tonality's and pulse's life in nature, is rather wrenched from the guts of a tonal groove. And yet, once so wrenched, Braxton expects it to make up its own flow and groove, as relaxed and nonreactive to bebop as bebop ultimately was to swing. He expects it to *swing*, on the up and the down of the pulse, in just that way. Braxton both alludes and speaks to this:

This is a music of opposition tendencies that powers its way through the space of the music ... the super-charged nature of collage event occurrences in this context is an intense experience that places a degree of stress on both the instrumentalist and listener. To balance this phenomenon I have positioned five-minute fermata sections of static sound movement behind each material section so that the propulsive momentum of the music can relax (before the next "push").

These areas of sustained tones are gorgeous foreshadowings of the best of the meditative New Age electronic and minimalist music that would emerge during the 1980s. Within such textures, as Braxton observes, the use of dynamic flux staggered between the sustained notes brings out timbral and harmonic, even rhythmic, aspects more subtly than the active parts.

The number four is central to this grand piece recorded mostly by quartets: four "independent voice continuum logics" (winds, brass, strings, and harp) wend through four basic sections, each divided into four structured areas, making a total division of sixteen.

There are also 16 musical languages which correspond to each structured area in the composition—as well as 12 visual shapes (plus variations totaling 16) that are integrated into the infrastructural mechanics of the music. As such, a performance of ... 96 is an affirmation of its numerological equivalent—number seven [1+6].

There are also four types of "phrase groupings"—the "language" approaches Braxton the solo altoist takes to determine the myriad of actual notes that flesh out the skeleton of a given structure—(1) the arhythmic constructions of chromatic phrases, discussed above; (2) chords (or his more delicious "sound beams"); (3) intervallic intrigue; and (4) pointillism. These strategies serve four different "structural operatives"; (1) long linear statements, (2) short ones, (3) staggerings of those two, and (4) "pockets of 'positioned involvement'."

Braxton collaborated with his wife Nickie, who took photographs of (twelve) religious symbols from all over the world, and of the same shapes and patterns as they occur in nature, double-exposed together.

The reality of this project was conceived as a vehicle to celebrate the composite interrelationship between dynamic symbolism and positive world change—as a given consideration sheds light on (living) and as a given consideration sheds light on primary information about living ... I believe the challenge of the next cycle is not separate from a reinvestigation and resolidification of all information and creative disciplines. This is necessary because present-day specialization has in many cases moved to distort the composite realness of creativity (and what a given function—variable—could mean in its most real context). (emphasis mine, to recall the continuum between sound and light, above—and, concordantly, between music and the universe as a

400

whole, as Braxton was experiencing it explicitly through these Ritual and Ceremonial pieces of the Golden Peak. His words are prescient of the rise of the interdisciplinary field of cultural studies in academia)

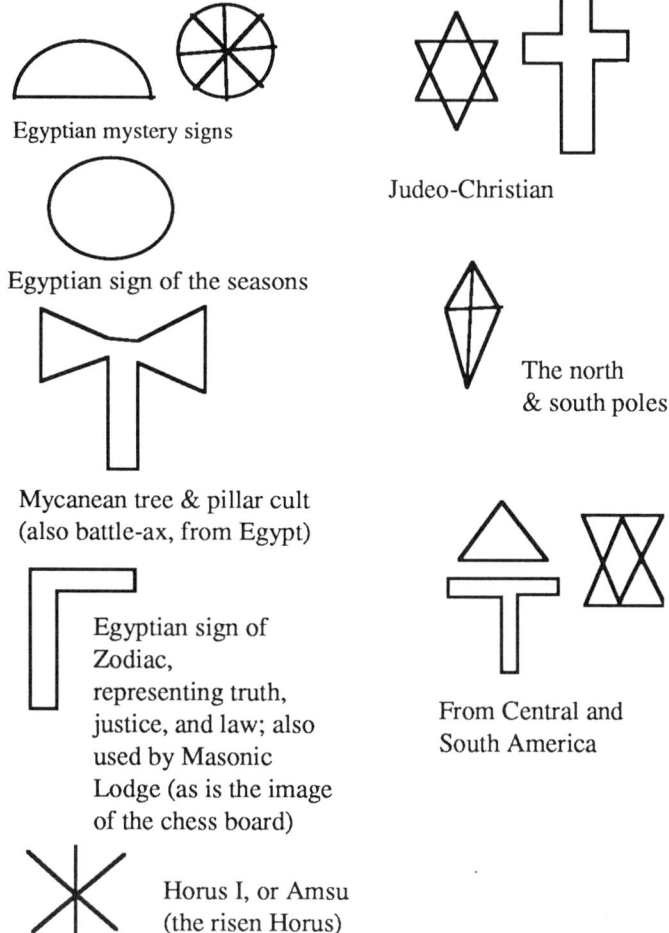

Egyptian mystery signs

Judeo-Christian

Egyptian sign of the seasons

The north & south poles

Mycanean tree & pillar cult (also battle-ax, from Egypt)

Egyptian sign of Zodiac, representing truth, justice, and law; also used by Masonic Lodge (as is the image of the chess board)

From Central and South America

Horus I, or Amsu (the risen Horus)

Fig. 8.12: The twelve religious symbols that formed the visual component of 96 (Nickie Braxton's slides of man-made and natural occurrences of them were projected on four screens during the premier performance). The score pages show

quartet music

the two extremes of actively changing and sustained pitches that characterize this piece at the crux of Braxton's work.

The simultaneous static and active nature of 96 is similar to that of a hologram, which is an interaction between laser light and visual information whose parts are the sum of its whole, as it were. Other analogies might be the permeation of the same DNA (deoxyribonucleic acid) information throughout an organism, or the binary code throughout an artificial intelligence, the basic components here being pulse and chromatics. Lock quotes Braxton as saying 96 is the primary source pool for the collage approach. Braxton calls the "stable neutrino" notation of 96 similar to "genetic material" which "defines the space of the music" (also similar to the way a hologram works, containing all the information from which the image is built in every part). He likens it to DNA, a deep structure/seed that emerges subtly throughout the music. 96 itself evolved from collage improvisations on several pieces as a "multiple line" orchestral work that unifies all the many dimensions, then is itself fed back out as one of several pieces in a collage: as, indeed, a unifying piece.

Lock notes:

> The philosophical impulse behind this music is a vision of synthesis which Braxton again relates to contemporary physics (and ancient mystics): i.e., to a perception of the universe as an inseparable network of energies or degrees of vibration, and specifically, to the scientists' current "move to create a 'unified state' which demonstrates a scientific and vibrational synthesis of forces that allows for physicality and the phenomenon of existence."[53]

The truth of this is demonstrated by the way parts of 96 are used so much in quartet contexts, where they function as particularly life-giving parts of a collage: they function well as both stimuli and contrast to other pieces (as on *Willisau* and *Five Compositions*), transitions from one space to another (as on *London*), one voice in a conversation (as on *Birmingham*), and the primary territory (*London*), all because 96 captures the very essence of Braxton's mind at work and at rest, and in the context of the radiant heights of his own spirituality and creative vision.

To really appreciate the different but comparable brilliance and power of 98, here's a suggestion: get a recording of one of Louis Armstrong's Hot Seven groups that has a lot of interplay between trumpet, clarinet, and trombone, with the piano also in the mix. Then listen to something similar between, say, Ben Webster, Lester Young, and Roy Eldridge, with Mal Waldron; then Lennie Tristano with Warne Marsh and Lee Konitz; then something from a similar Mingus-led combination; then a Miles Davis thing from *Birth of the Cool*, then *Kind of Blue*. Then check out something from Ornette Coleman playing more than one instrument, with other horns, but no piano (like *Free Jazz!*). Then get Cecil Taylor in a duo with Jimmy Lyons (no drums or bass), then in performance with the Chicago Art Ensemble. Finally, listen to 6D, Braxton's piece for three single-liners and Muhal Richard Abrams on piano . . . and then 98. Then, go back to Ives, Stravinsky, and Schönberg and work your way up through a similar ladder of forbears in 20th-century post-tonal American and European art music.

If *96* is about picking all the wildest musical herbs, roots, and spices to mix and fix (notate) into the most exotic and nutritious dish, *98* is about preparing and fertilizing the richest notational soil into the garden beds that will yield the wildest, yet also most cultivable, of those flowerings.

Braxton toured Europe with this 52-page-long piece scored for four winds, two brass, and piano in 1981; a double LP recording of two performances, one live and one studio, came out in 1984. The actual personnel on tour and record both were four: Braxton, trumpeter Hugh Ragin, trombonist Anderson, and pianist Crispell. Its graphic title is an abstract stylization of a telescope, which says something about the way it magnifies, zooms in on the process of writing and playing written music, then improvising on it, then running out of "things to say" and having to scour the heavens for more premises on which to improvise.

Braxton's liner notes are also his *Composition Notes*[54] and open with a statement about the way his long career as an improviser has led him in the directions he has taken as a composer. Those, he says, entail more control over the improvisational process than is afforded by simply writing a theme to function as a door to endless, open improvisation. He bemoans the lack of a sociocultural understanding of the kinds of musical issues that compel him as a deficiency in the collective spiritual life.

The piece is structured into seven sections, based on seven different visual shapes; different tempos, timbres, and line configurations distinguish the sections. Its musical excitement lies in the way it sounds so wildly spontaneous yet controlled and in sync at the same time.

The discussion in last chapter of *107*, for trio, could almost be repeated for *98*.[55] Its musical points of interest are the same: the shapes used as "road signs" that bring a certain cast to an improvisation (e.g., diamond for pulse space, the sign for multiphonics), the cloud-like shape notations suggesting the "aura" of a sequence of notes, the cue points, the mix of traditional and idiosyncratic notations, and of improvisation and notation. *98*, of course, was the first of these paragons of Braxton's chamber repertoire, as distinct from the music that evolved through the more conventional jazz quartet formats. Where *107* had a relaxed conservatory feel to it, *98* sounds as down and dirty, and as sharp, as ferrets in the earth (in the horns); yet that wild, gritty virtuosity is grounded, like yang in yin, in Crispell's equally elegant, alert pianisms.

The holistic magic of the Golden Peak continued through *103*, another (unrecorded) Ritual and Ceremonial piece. Seven trumpets are arranged on risers to play and improvise within notated music inspired by "Spanish architecture and decorative visual imagery . . . as a tribute to the wonder of South American bravura trumpet playing . . . crossed with the post-Webern continuum."[56] (Lester Bowie and Leo Smith are also named as influences; this is actually Braxton's post-AACM creative "Brass Fantasy," curiously the only one, given his penchant for march music.) A taped recording of a bullfight sets the stage, which includes a backdrop of a stadium. Perhaps most noteworthy for Braxton's future theatrical conceptions (his "image musics," mythologies, and operatic settings of his own texts) is his notion of the "emerging musician dancer." Braxton, like many musicians, himself dances, in place, when he plays. Miles

Davis, influenced by rock artists and aided by technology that freed him from a stationary microphone, improvised his own organic, mercurially mobile choreography in his later work. Stockhausen's prancing, costumed players in *Montag aus Licht* offer another image of this concept, which has lately blossomed in Braxton's mature work from the seed of *103*.[57]

The Golden Peak ends with Braxton's first pieces with an integrated pulse track, *105A & B*. The listening experience of this revolves around marching eighth notes or underlying solos, mostly between the sax and piano . . . while the drums go off into their own explorations of the less symmetrical pulse track, and the bass bows and floats in a slower part of the pulse track than the drums. The four hang together in those roles during the written music, but split into their four separate "screens" during the open middle section. The marching eighth notes here splay off into quick improvisational flurries, cycling back and forth between piano and clarinet like a round, while the bass and drums continue with the pulse track. The pulse track constitutes a cyclic pattern, like a Kelvin piece repeated, but the pulse track pattern is a shorter loop than the framework as a whole, so that it repeats in staggered sequences, avoiding a too-predictable periodicity.

The effect Braxton was after was of extended solos over support, but he wanted the support to be more that of a percussion solo than a timekeeping groove, or of a bass-drums duo interacting free of such a groove. He instructed the duo to play vigorously, each as if alone in solo, as opposed to walking gingerly to accompany something "more important" (the soloist). The concept recalls John Coltrane's duets with Rashied Ali, or the way Elvin Jones played in the quartet generally. In keeping with the gravity metaphor, Braxton conceived the pulses in a pulse track as planets—the "downs," gravity wells—in a solar system, around which improvisers orbit and dance. (That such metaphors come so naturally to him as appropriate to concepts many would see in more abstract, less grandiose terms, says something about the experience of a musician getting swallowed up by the music. It is in the creative trance and experience where down beats do loom like the very gravity of the universe, upbeats like aerospace flight, sounds like multicolored stars and visions.) Like *96*, the whole concept and technique is what Braxton would call "oppositional"—not a "go with the flow" kind of music, either for the pulse trackers or the improvisers.

The first recorded version of *105A*, with the dynamite mix of Lindberg and Hemingway with George Lewis, was a knock-your-socks-off full LP side. He has used it since then as a set opener, uncollaged with others, something that packs a punch and can sustain its force, an uncluttered focus for excitement and interest that unfolds at a muscular but measured pace.

In sum, Braxton's Golden Peak wraps up and solidifies musical as well as the metamusical concepts, mentioned above, that had been kicking around in looser forms throughout the two decades previous. Rhythmic experiments started with Kelvin structures and *23G* blossomed into pulse tracks; the "creative chamber music" explorations started in solo piano music; multiinstrumental duos, trios, and quartets blossomed into *95, 98, 101, 103*, and *107*; solo alto music made its appearance through *99B* and *E*; the most jazz-traditional extensions on chromaticism and pulse that formed the bulk of the quartet music blossomed into *96*; and the visual, mythological, and occult associations, the racial, gender, and cultural conflicts/resolutions, including those between notation and improvisation, weaving through all of his music blossomed into a new coherence and completeness in all the Golden Peak works.

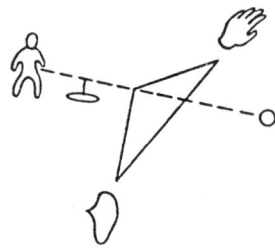

Fig. 8.13: From 105A, *the first graphic title with a human representation, to the first pulse track piece. "I wanted the operational space of the music to be exciting and powerful—with the use of strong bowed improvisational statements within (and without) the structural point operatives of the music. In other words play hard! (Be completely wild if necessary—but please no pianissimo here.) All of these works are to be played vigorously with conviction. If you can't believe in the process (music) then leave it alone."*

The latter aspects, actually, would go on to new heights, in the large-ensemble music to come. The various creative and traditional orchestral works before the Golden Peak blossomed, like the other strains, in the Golden Peak, through *96, 100,* and *102*; however, the large-ensemble music would find their own fullest flowerings later. By comparison, the other ensemble strains, while certainly retaining life, integrity, development, and force of their own, can be seen to have peaked conceptually, in a sense, in the coordinate system. There they would come as close as they could, through the interconnections and juxtapositions, to approaching the scale and scope of the larger works. In fact, that seems to be the context to which Braxton purposefully brought them, in his subjugation of every small-group piece's musical statement to the network it formed with every other, and to the symphonic aspiration of their whole. This can't be said of his later large-ensemble music; each piece there more typically stands alone, distinct in its identity from the others, however many levels it may have within it, some even grafted from other pieces. A quartet concert or recording after the Golden Peak might well be likened to the split screen of a TV set; but, relative to that, the corresponding large-ensemble event must be likened rather to a "virtual reality" computer program, where the (greatly expanded) multiple voices of the music are both set free in and unified by the cyberspace

quartet music

(indeed, this is Braxton's own metaphor for his most recent and ambitious music).

With that glimpse of the next chapter's field, then, let's end this one with a walk through the quartet music's gathering of solo, duo, and trio dynamics into the coordinate system as if they were the foothills we must cross in our approach to the real peaks—not this writer's fanciful golden one—of Braxton's version of ancient court and temple music. In the foothills we begin to sense ascent, new air, something new in it—life above the vale, then above the treeline, then into the climes where mythical figures cavort through their mythical dramas in the mythical cities and wilds created for them, wreaking both their elemental havoc and vital magic on the mortal realm below.

The Recent Period

I take my cue for the best approach to the recent quartet work from Braxton's "performance flow chart" concept, first made public in the notes to *Performance 9/1/79*. I invoke this for its conceptualization of a performance/recording as an integrated musical statement, rather than a sequence of disparate ones, with its own shape, flow, and dynamics, however those might be conceived.

To start with a simple example, *Four Compositions (Quartet) 1983* features the first recorded version of *105A*, taking up the whole A side; side B includes three *69*s (*M*, *O*, and *Q*), linked and balanced to much the same effect as the one newer piece. The MPS statement here includes a compare-and-contrast symmetry between two distinct periods, and suggestion of the earlier one as a trinity and the later a unity.

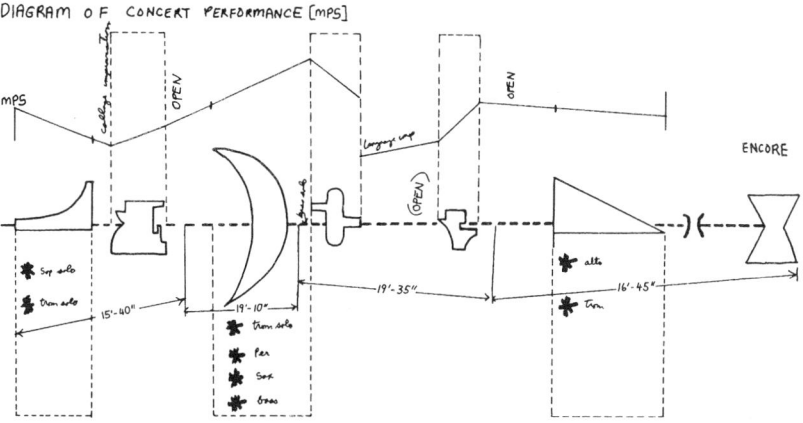

Prag 1984 (Quartet Performance)

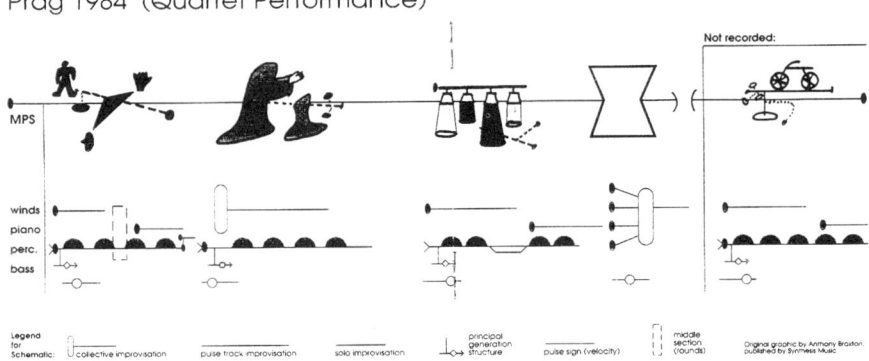

Fig. 8.14: The first MPS, from the liner notes to Performance 1/9/79 *gives simple, general shapes to the pieces; the second, a few years later, is conceived with the graphic titles themselves.*

Moving, a year later, to *Prague* (and from the two-horn quartet with Lewis to the horn-piano group with Crispell), Braxton says in his liner notes of this live performance that it marked the beginning of his quartet's shift into the coordinate-systemic approach to playlists; he notes the extended use of pulse tracks and "isolated notated solo materials (for each instrumentalist . . .)" as the first move of that shift.

105A, as noted above, serves to open this new approach up in the most forthright, relaxed way. *110A* extends the relaxed feel, taking it into the first open collective improv, a measured dialogue that breathes through its balanced interplay. This performance is like a long cadenza, with floating chords and meandering lines, into the childlike étude that is *114*.[58]

quartet music

Fig. 8.15: Braxton: "The reality of this effort [110A] can be viewed as a small drawing that establishes creative definition—for vibrational agreement. This is a kind of song structure that winds its way into the space of the music to create the sensation of 'blowing winds and trees' (on an island experiencing a rain storm) . . . an uncomplex structure that emphasizes linear metric sound changes . . . the tradition of creative music is full of structures of this type—works that are made up from a few 'golden' phrases to create a riff or 'life's focus.' All of these matters are directly related to the wonder of creativity—and the fact that sometimes a very sparse effort can produce great abundance."[59]

Despite tuning problems, the clarinet and piano impart a fresh innocence in their unison runs through a simple C scale, realizing improvisational abundance and complexity from compositional spareness and simplicity. The pulse tracks continue (at increased velocity) as the rocky floor of the music; over them, piano and clarinet lilt in and out of the scale into the farthest reaches of their free improvisational bag: a demonstration of the continuum, within the reconstruction of tonality, between those two musical poles.

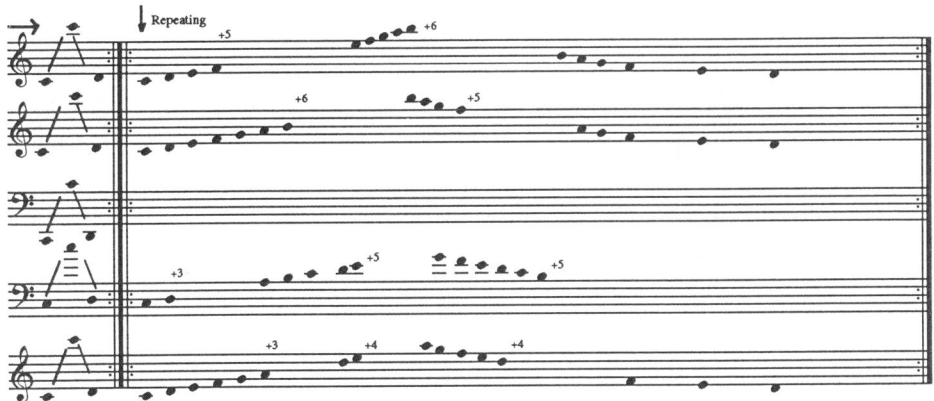

Fig. 8.16: From composition notes to 114, " . . . a revolving world of repeating scale and time parameters for creative improvisation . . . a scale world universe that emphasizes the use of metric linear even moving eighth note sounds that creates a linear & multiple sound context . . . to create a wall of moving sound beams (shapes) that gives a fresh sense to the tonal experience."[60] *The score page is a picture of simplicity and purity, like the first plainchants, suggesting (one of many possible) post-tonal tonalities.*

69H is an interesting finish to this recording on several levels. Its graphic title suggests a nuclear reactor; combined with the ominous percussion and dark bass sounds of its opening, Chernobyl (which happened two years later) is prefigured. Only in passing, though; the meat of the music continues the theme of "most out" from "most in." The scale of *114* is quoted again during the initial opening improv; when *69H* is finally stated, the dichotomy between Braxton's fleet Webernian phrases and simple repeated long tones carries the performance's more-with-less motif, so starkly presented throughout, into a rich farewell.

Five Compositions (Quartet) 1986 showcases Braxton's piano music a bit more than most quartet playlists. It opens with *131*

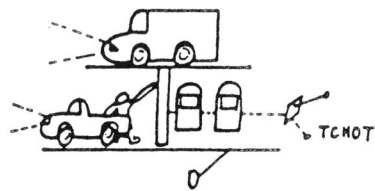

Fig. 8.17: Conceived as a busy gas station, a florid new piece (131) *with conventional solos over accompaniment.*

88(+108C) follows, one of many examples of the duets with Holland coupled with a new pulse track. *124(+96)* and *122(+108A+96)* are more fresh statements, moving through adventurous improvisations into a pronounced lyricism, coupled with the ubiquitous *96* and another new pulse track. *101(+31+86+30)* takes the lyrical momentum into a soft, mysterious ballad journey through Braxton's piano universe—*101*, for Gaslini, and the two *30*s for Rzewski—collaged with Dresser playing from one of the Holland duets.

The arc of this album, then, serves to showcase its special guest, pianist David Rosenboom, who ends it with some thoughtful dialogue and a major solo.

The Birmingham *playlist*

> 69M(+10+33+96) (primary = older quartet piece)
> 110A(+96+108B), (primary = new quartet piece)
> 60(+96+108C), (primary = duo originally with Abrams)
> 85(+30+108D), (primary = duo originally with Holland)
>
> 105B(+5+32+96), (primary = new quartet piece, with built-in pulse track)
> 87(+108C), (primary = duo originally with Holland)
> 23J
> 69H(+31+96), (primary = older quartet piece)
> 40(O) (Kelvin)

The three 2-CD sets (*Quartets London/Birmingham/Coventry 1985*, from the tour chronicled by Lock's book) solidify these patterns governing the practical treatments of pieces within the coordinate system. The overarching pattern is the division of pieces into "primary" and "secondary territories"; the

quartet music   **409**

former head up the cut's title, the latter are in parentheses. In practice, this denotes a few different approaches.

Take *Birmingham* as a representative sampling of them. One approach has the whole group playing in the primary territory together—usually on a piece originally scored for quartet, old *(69M, 69H)* or new *(110A, 105B)*—then going into what was originally an open improvisational space, but now armed with music to read and improvise from. Crispell's secondary parts are usually solo piano pieces (the *30*s and some of the numbers up to 10); Dresser and Hemingway are usually off into pulse track pieces (mostly *105*s and *108*s); and Braxton, Dresser, and Hemingway all three frequently (Crispell occasionally) play from *96*.

Another pattern has Braxton playing duo music with Crispell or Dresser *(60, 85, 87)*, usually in unison and with some harmony, while the other two play a pulse track to go with it. Then there's the usual presentation of a piece without any others tacked on *(23J, 40(O))*. Each approach has a certain effect, makes a certain statement within the MPS.

Birmingham, for example, shows how a trip to the musical wilderness can make for renewed appreciation of the city and comforts of home. Its grafts of new and old pieces, including pulse tracks, foster improvisations and recitals that essentially double, triple, and quadruple whatever demands were made on both players and listeners before; by the same token, it multiplies the opportunities for engagement. The MPS statement of these two disks is a demonstration of what kind of new matrices new and familiar material can form to support group and individual improvisations, and how those matrices can make charts that once seemed complex and quirky turn into simple riffs by comparison. The music up to *23J* is like a first trek through rugged terrain, complete with inclines of scree, off-trail climbs, rushing water crossings, long hikes, and careful compass-and-map work—not a walk in the park. But *23J*, and *40(O)*, both maddening little things to get our mind/ears/instrument around at first, now greet us like old friends, eager to let us tell them all about our adventures in the wilds, over a hot cup by a cozy fire in their written and improv spaces.

London, the tour's first concert, has an MPS that hints at the limits of the quartet's envelope in its reaches for the larger ensemble sound and scope. The playlist is dynamic, well conceived, and well executed. *121* and *122* more or less frame the sets; both works embody new concepts Braxton called "signature logics," phrases repeated by all throughout improvisations, like winking night lights on a ship at sea. *40(O)* emerged like a lifeboat from that ship seamless and cool, *52* washed it ashore in an excitement of drums and piano, and the first set's last three pieces gradually dried the music off and calmed it down into a relaxed, tasty sway through tempo flux.

The second set opened similarly to *Prague*, only the more relaxed and better instrument situation showed in the music. Braxton's solo on *105A* was quite conventional; oftentimes in his later work he sounds like he wants to relax and play with traditional phrasings and ideas, but with evermore radically new supports and interactions coming from the other musicians. This piece plays around with both simple premises and sudden flurries, then gives way to a percussion solo on *96* material. Curiously, when Hemingway solos from *96*, as he frequently does, he slows that most frantic and dense piece down to a tenth its original speed. That makes for one of those hushed sacred spaces that everyone eventually gets in on in a reverent open improv—from which *40F* appears. *40F* is a familiar story for all to kick around and rehash with vim and grace. Then come the linchpin segments of this particular MPS.

121 is a long notated piece for piano, two single-line instruments, and optional percussion. It marches along through an atonal, pulse-tracky field, the piano's parallel harmonies in unison with the sax line, for a hypnotically long time. In this constant cyclical motion, it has the feel of the all-notated works for orchestra; its interest is in the relaxed, out-of-sync jostle of the "unison," and in the way it sounds thinner and thinner as it increasingly succeeds in suggesting a sound beyond what it really is. When it finally ends, Braxton erupts with a solo sax improv that recalls his finest, most monstrous "free" fettle, as raised on the old Company recordings with the European gang. It also recalls something he said in a recent class, after working the ensemble through a lot of demanding notation: "Let's just play for awhile; too much notated music is bad for your head!"

The beast in the music roars, growls, moans, screeches, then whimpers, alone; then the others come in soothingly, causing Braxton to take up his flute. The sound turns to lace curtains fluttering in the breeze, shutters blown on creaky hinges, the breeze turns to a wave . . .

. . . and we are back at sea, where we started, in *116*, a piece built from three different pulse tracks. It unfolds into improvisational (more, unlike *121*, than compositional) displays rich with virtuosity and sensitive interplay. This piece shows the range of the piano role in Braxton's mature quartet. Crispell often plays in unison with him like another horn; she also moves outside of time with her harmonies-as-color, taking on the role of "other" in trio-plus-floating-other. When she solos, she leads the music through ground thoroughly informed by Braxton's solo piano music.

The MPS of these first disks is still touched with that thinness of affect, overall. It's as though they'd gotten an eyeful of the vastness of musical vistas afforded by the new plethora of written material (brought on by the coordinate approach and *121*) and were at once full of it and not yet up to it. The pulse tracks and octaves in *116*, however, made for a strong conclusion, ending on a note of hope for the next visit to this island.

Coventry, the last concert on the tour, has an MPS that balances the flow of compositions in much the way *Four Compositions (1983)* did, with newest material (including the new juxtapositions of old material) in the first set, and three *69*s and two solos from *96*, mostly uncollaged, dominating the second. *6A* ends the two disks, functioning as a target for the arrow of time shot back through this whole tour of the newest music to the first catalogued piece for quartet.

124 was actually written on the tour and debuted in Liverpool. Its written material is a scant platform along the lines of *96* (superextensions on bebop chromatics and pulse), meant for extended improvisations. Dresser and Hemingway cover its built-in pulse track, while Braxton blows and Crispell covers the "other" space of a solo piano piece; then Braxton couches Crispell's solo with some *96*.

This piece points up particularly well the way the coordinate approach expands on heterophony, as do medieval Masses and early jazz both, as a desirable route to unity. It sheds its musical light on the still prevalent ensemble modes—of the division of musical labor into the different instruments, and the resulting hierarchies (albeit, at best, rotating ones)—as codependent, in the negative sense, by comparison. Braxton's screaming, heady sopranino solo gets an energy and freedom from Crispell's comfortable detachment in *30*, and Dresser's and Hemingway's contentedly busy constructions in their own space that is simply unique to Braxton's music. The more typical obsession with mutual, simultaneous group catharsis in such energy and freedom is, this proves, only one of several options, and not necessarily always the healthiest (most musical).

88(+108C+30+96) comprises several relaxed sonorous duos. The four carry on these differently coupled conversations simultaneously, each couple oblivious to the other, moving in and out of awareness of the whole sound they're making; sometimes only one person carries it. Then a flurry leads to a piano solo on the same *30* that was moments ago part of the split coordinate screen: jagged, abrupt phrases, with which the alto soon syncs up like an old friend, squawking casually, hitting at *23G*'s sound attacks so as to cue the bass and drums in on that piece. When all are ensconced in the primary-secondary matrix of *23G(+30+96)*, after piano and sax state the line, Braxton solos nice and rough. After a percussion solo that winds things down, *40N*, a slow, reverent homage to the music of India, ends the set.

69C(+32+96) is a simple romp for everyone. Braxton gets to blow, Crispell hovers in her alternate piano universe like some Chagall angel, the pulse premise is simple and exciting. After all the complexities of the first disk, there is a great hunger for such a session, reflected keenly in its expression.

Hemingway's solo on *96*—again slow, static, and calm—has become part of the MPS statement after hearing it on all three CD sets. He does plenty of more vigorous playing, but rarely in a solo. This is another distinguishing feature of the mature Braxton quartet: the drum solos don't function as showy display of the music's rhythmic heart, or of virtuoso percussionistics. They rather state the music's pulse topography with care, thought, and humility, in a way John Cage would appreciate.

That gently marked silence leads well into *69F*, a dreamy, open line, a soft unison of sax, bowed bass, and low piano sounds, as gentle as *C* was fierce, falling into a three-note riff in the bass on which to improvise.

69B goes back to the up-tempo jazz jam, an oscillation back into wild catharsis—still crazy after all these years. The animals, the humans, then the angel Muse, all chasing each other around and howling in the spirit wind.

96 comes back in a bass solo, like some perpetual-motion machine that deigns to let you wind it up (so as to make you feel useful). Finally, *6A* arrives like a balanced, relaxed conversation between fluid clarinet and well but loosely defined piano and bass. All are stopped by an ending that hangs in the air like Ives' unanswered question.

The energy of this last concert had a better balance and flow to it than the first, but there was still that thinness, along with more suggestion of its nature. It is the thinness of air on the heights. Our lungs are gulping to their capacity yet expecting more; our ears are still plugged with water appropriate to the pressure of the lowlands. It is our eyes, on which the light, colors, and shapes of the music beat like a drum, dragging our other senses along in the wake of their visual rapture. By *Willisau*, our ears have popped, our lungs strengthened—and our view suddenly taken our breath away, as we round the bend out of the foothills into full view of the mountain.

Willisau is a 4-CD set recorded—half of it live and half in the studio—six years later in (the Alpine country) Switzerland. It stands as a stable expression of the music still in volatile process at the point of the three British concerts. The mountain Braxton had begun to scale through the post-Golden Peak large-ensemble music is in full, splendid view here.

The first sign of that view is the presence of stories attached to the latest works. "I see two people walking down the street, beautiful trees in the fall, snow, winter coming. They're thinking about their lives, trying to have some hope for the future even though it's always complex." So Braxton wrote for *160*. Musically, the premise is as simple as a sigh: a two-note descension repeated, ornamented, built upon, pitched variously by everyone in turn. The piano music from *5* complements more than counters this poignant, lyrical sigh, voiced so well by the clarinet and arco bass; percussion is the "other" here, a pastel colorist. The improvisers' constant return to the premises, their interactive referrals to it, recall the riches yielded by *98* and *107*: this quartet, in the coordinate system and "story music," has found its own way into the creative chamber music universe of Braxton's African (*98*) and European (*107*) cast.

Another feature of this breakthrough is the incorporation of breaks—beginnings, endings, and pauses—so essential to those quintessential syntheses of notation and improvisation. The music of the unbroken plain of the British tour (probably recorded without breaks to cut costs) is now set off into five separate tracks on each disk, marked by discernible boundaries. This reflects both the discrete flow within *98* and *107*, and that within and between most large-ensemble pieces, the difference here being that 12 of the 20 tracks are collages or sequences. *40J* is recited here to take out the statement *160* began. *23M(+10)* goes into a long sax, then piano solo on the line's quirky thrust.

The primary territory of *158(+96)+40L* marks a development from both signature logic and pulse track techniques Braxton called the "C[onnector]-class" pieces. Each player is given a variation on overlapping written material, with improvisational sections delineated by a (different) number of beats that stays constant throughout. The result is a stream of staggered improvisational and notated statements that merge, clash, and echo throughout a churn of music that is always moving, on the edge, but also stable, never crashing to regroup, and never regimented to avoid such a crash. The advance here doesn't lie in phrase making, but in how best to arrange phrases for the freshest, most stimulating dynamics between notation and improvisation both individual and collective.

96 (its harp part) functions here as a piano statement. *40L* acts as an exit all four go through with dispatch, as with *40J* on the first track.

40A is a nice step into the flute-and-arco bass space. Dresser bows harmonics in a same-range duet while (!) covering the bass line. Crispell's solo is present and intent, a refreshing change from the splitscreen effect of the piano-as-other. *40B* ends the first disk with a jazz jam sublime.

The second disk's MPS closely reflects that of the first: another story piece leads off, followed by another C-class piece, followed by two *23*s typically collaged, and ending on another jazz-feel *40*. The blend and lyricism established by each disk's MPS, followed by the rich and stable mix of cohesion and freedom in the C-class piece, capped by the grounding of the familiar, including

quartet music

the most unabashedly jazz-traditional, fills and thickens aforementioned thin air like a gust of something impossibly warm and tropical blowing down from the snowy peak.

Fig. 8.18: Graphic title to 161. Wrote Braxton on the liner notes: "Suddenly you see three guys in the pool room, having fun, talking about their feelings of pessimism for the future. Yet these three guys are very strong and we can still have hope for them."

This new element of story—here, just a few words in the liner notes; later it would blossom into libretti and stream-of-conscious mythico-fantasies to be sung and spoken with the music itself—is the key redeemer (integrator) of "all that came before." The works themselves are connected, through the collaging, sequencing, and MPS; the blend of which they're capable flowers (musically) in the soil of these images that take them out of a splitscreen pastiche of statements and into the unifying three-dimensionality of a picture worth a thousand such pastiches.

Braxton, for a change, plays the role of floating other on the seven-note cycle of *67(+147+96)*; he mans *67*, then *147*, on three different instruments, while the trio plucks and tears apart the music. *140(+147+139+135)* seems a precursor to the C-classes, with its crowing, one-to-two-note patterns and staggered lines. Braxton really declaims and signifies on his horn on this piece in his trans-African way. Piano, then drums, dominate the intense dervish of *34A*, which is built on a figure one note less than *67*'s. *20+86* is two parallel duos: *20* is gentle, soft, contemplative, running parallel to the more active *86*. Several solos spot the soundscape, all low-key and low-register. *23G(+147+30)*, bop line over the prototype pulse track, is another good blowing session for Braxton, the trio texturing around him (when Crispell solos, her phrasing is a lot like his, but not when he's playing).

The fourth disk, then, rounds everything off with an MPS that, after warming up in some familiar *69* territories, moves through *107* and *101*, the major trio and duo scores that aren't a regular part of the quartet book. The quartet as (successful) chamber music, one that brings in the best traits of the best chamber pieces and sets them into the quartet instrumentation, history, and approach, is the metamessage here. *23N(+112+108A+33)*, with the feel of *Three Blind Mice*, takes it out on a whimsical, mischievous note.

The images Braxton uses to talk about his quartet music's coordinate system—mostly of trains with interchangeable cars on switchable tracks, running on parallel tracks in the same or opposite directions, splitting and rejoining; and of maps and territories, road signs and zones—say much about his goals as a composer-improviser and the experiences he's having with others and trying to cultivate. Primary is the role train mythology has played in his personal life. Chicago is the real Grand Central Station of the country's railroads. Braxton's father Clarence worked for them, and he grew up fascinated by them. His organizer's mind memorized the many different lines and their routes; his childlike wonder led him to collect and build his own model train sets in his youth, then with his own children. On the level of musical mythology, this personal passion resonated with the charged significance trains took on in the blues and early jazz tradition; on the level of metamusical mythology, Braxton's close link through Gemini to Hermes, Thoth—tricksters, thinkers, creative magi—means proximity to the Lord of the Roads, of the crossroads, where the multitudes from the whole one world's extremities converge, to clash and converse. The passion to both define and cross roads and boundaries, to confute then restore consensus reality, to guide and conduct souls from one place to another, to unify the farthest-flung diversity without violating or compromising any part of it: this is the wellspring of Braxton's music. To enter it as a player is to become aware of the relativity of one's own imperatives, to see how they naturally cooperate with those of others even when out of sync with or opposed to them. It is to find oneself, at the heart of one's most distinctive individuality, to be part of a human totem structure outside of time and space, or of an Egyptian picture that tells a story with a lot of little images, or of a medieval Mass (literally) of melodies both oblivious to and aware of each other.

This experience is in all the music we've looked at so far—but in the creative and traditional orchestra music and operas, it makes those examples look like sectional rehearsals.

---

1. Robert Graves, *Difficult Questions, Easy Answers* (London: Cassell, 1972: 176–79).

2. Barbara Walker, "Hexagram" (*The Woman's Encyclopedia of Myths and Secrets,* San Francisco: Harper & Row, 1983).

3. Albert Churchward, *Signs and Symbols of Primordial Man: The Evolution of Religious Doctrine from the Eschatology of the Ancient Egyptians* (London/New York: E.P. Dutton & Company, 1910: 22).

4. See Radano, M.R. *Anthony Braxton and his Two Musical Traditions: The Meeting of Concert Music and Jazz.* University of Michigan, 1985: 161. Radano's book (*New Musical Figurations: Anthony Braxton's Cultural Critique.* Chicago/London: University of Chicago Press, 1993) doesn't focus on the quartet as does this dissertation, but it conveys much the same picture in its look at all of Braxton's music from the 1970s. For a good summation of his perspective on the quartet, see 162–79 and 255–58. Lock fills in the quartet details from the 1980s.

5. See Robert Shea and Robert Anton Wilson (*The Illuminatus Trilogy,* New York: Dell, 1975: 111–13) for an informed and creative romp through 23; also Thomas Crump's "Music, Poetry and Dance" (*The Anthropology of Numbers,* New York: Cambridge University Press, 1990: 103–14) for general background.

6. See liner notes to *Two Compositions (Ensemble) 1989/1991* (hat Art CD 6086); hear also Sun Ra's lecture on the number's significance as the earth's position in line from the sun (talks on "The Possibility of Altered Destiny," on the CD *Sun Ra Arkestra/Live From Soundscape,* DIW-388). For general corroboration, see Dorothy Sayers, *Mind of the Maker* (London: Methuen & Co. Ltd., 1947) for her (characteristically) magnificent Western discourse on the number. A propos of which,

triplum meter in medieval music was described as "perfect" meter, duple as "imperfect." The reason was theological, owing to the perfection of the Trinity (Western attempts to notate the "swing" of trans-African music have resorted to triple meters such as 6/8 and 12/8 as more accurate than duples such as 2/4 and 4/4). Also: Western medieval music theory was itself "tri-partite," in its divisions of *Musica Instrumentalis* (music's material/mechanical aspects), *Musica Humana* (its human-soul aspects), and *Musica Mundana* (its transcendent, spiritual aspects).

7. 2 Peter 3:8.

8. Radano frames these as "iconoclastic early works" (diss., 135–260; also book, 180–268).

9. Joe Carey, "Anthony Braxton Interview" (*Cadence,* Mar. 1984: 13).

10. Anthony Braxton, *Composition Notes A* (Oakland, CA: Tree Frog Press, 1988: 62–66).

11. Ibid., 62.

12. See, for example, *Threni: Lamentationes Jeremiae Prophetae* (London: Boosey & Hawkes, 1958).

13. Braxton, *Composition Notes A,* 80, for this and next citation.

14. Ibid., 77.

15. Ibid., 86–89, for this and next citation.

16. Braxton, *Composition Notes A,* 184–92.

17. Braxton, *Composition Notes B,* 105–11.

18. Ibid., 99.

19. Radano (diss.), 228–31.

20. Braxton, *Composition Notes B,* 130–3.

21. Ibid., 134–37, for this and next citation.

22. Actually, this piece and two of the three others on this record were performed by a trio, though written for quartet. The sound of the album stands as a fine early example of the chamber music essence of Braxton's trio music.

23. John Litweiler, "Record Reviews" (*Down Beat,* June 5, 1975: 18).

24. Braxton, *Composition Notes B,* 47–56.

25. This sort of disparity between review and event was still alive and well in Peter Watrous' 1993 review of an appearance by the quartet at New York's Knitting Factory (*New York Times,* late NY edition, Nov. 15, 1993: C18): the room was full, the response great, the review a bust (its thrust: Braxton is stuck in the dated, obsolete 1960s, joylessly, grimly). The operation was a success, but the patient died in the media's hands.

26. Steve Lake, "Jazz Records" (*Melody Maker,* July 27, 1974: 49).

27. Braxton, *Composition Notes B,* 57–62.

28. See Mike Heffley, "Sounding Old, Sounding New" (*Chamber Music,* December 1992: 26-36), especially on Margaret Fabrizio, for examples of Braxton's contemporaries doing that. It is, of course, a common practice among 20th-century composers, including Ives, Carl Orff, Respighi, Stravinsky, and Vaughn Williams, to name some of the better known.

29. Braxton, *Composition Notes B,* 75–9.

30. Neil Tesser, "Montreux/Berlin Concerts" (*Down Beat,* August 20, 1977: 22–23).

31. Braxton, *Composition Notes A,* 9.

32. Braxton, *Composition Notes B,* 224–42.

33. Braxton, *Composition Notes C,* 11.

34. Ibid., 62.

35. Ibid., 73–78.

36. Ibid., 89–93.

37. Ibid., 108–12.
38. Ibid., 125.
39. Ibid., 136.
40. Ibid., 132–36.
41. It is also a refreshing affirmation of the creative improviser working the same sort of material minimalist composers propose as desirable negations of same.
42. Braxton, *Composition Notes D*, 478–84.
43. Ibid., 499–504.
44. Radano (1985), 93–134.
45. Braxton (*Composition Notes C*), 553–572.
46. Braxton's two "Cell Structure and Language Design" pieces; see next chapter.
47. Braxton, *Composition Notes D*, 332–8.
48. Ibid., 408–16.
49. See the first of Yehudi Menuhin's four-video series on the evolution of the ear from the sea.
50. Radano (1985), 415.
51. Note Lock's distinction between traditional and creative orchestras, from *Composition 96* (CD LR 169) liner notes.
52. Braxton, *Composition Notes E*, 26–90, for this and the next eight citations.
53. Lock, *96* (CD) liner notes.
54. Braxton, *Composition Notes E*, *Composition 98* liner notes (hat Art 1984, 1981).
55. In fact, both *98* and *107* are part of the same series, along with *75* and *94*. See Lock's notes to the CD reissue of the LP (hat ART CD 6062).
56. Ibid., 185–209.
57. He mentions in Lock the correspondence of movements and gestures in occult lore to color, astrological sign, and other such aspects of the total human being (222–4), and is interested in pursuing such connections in his future work with singers and players who move about on the stage.
58. Braxton, *Composition Notes E*, 350–52.
59. Ibid., 401–08.
60. Ibid., 350–52.

Chapter Nine

Large Ensemble Music

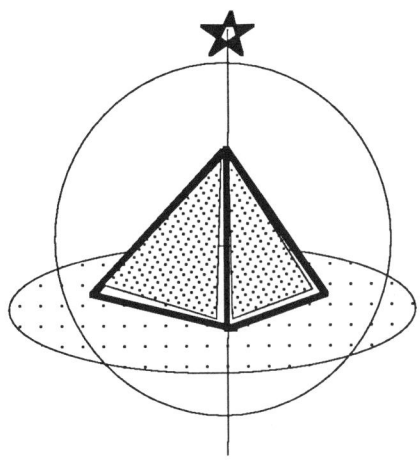

[From occult definition of] **number**: ... Pythagoras: ... 5 = five-pointed star ... ; spirit (1) having power over matter (4); 6 = six-pointed star ... : structural unity of the cosmos and e.g. man: both are built on three main principles; 7 = equilateral triangle inside a square: divine power in material form (a high Initiate and Divine Messenger); 8 = octagonal: 4 + 4: order in matter, justice, harmony, friendship; 9 = the treble triad: the extent to which numbers can go: all others are embraced, or revolving in it; 9. Cabala: a. the Creator (Ainsoph) = 1, married to Zero (0), which produced the numbers two through nine; b. the numbers 1–10 represent the Descent (Fall) of the Eternal Spirit into the world of phenomenal manifestation.*

The shape of the upper pyramid recorded the Pharaoh's domination of the upper world: at his installment he had shot four arrows with his full strength to the north, south, east and west, and a fifth straight up into the air. But the lower world remained under the Goddess's power, because from the depth of earth rose hidden waters, also sacred serpents and mice, and oracular wisdom. Unless the Pharaoh honored his goddess wife as royally as she honored him, the magic of the double pyramid would fail and their joint empire be overtaken by misfortune.

Robert Graves

The solidity of lines within the structure denotes its full, three-dimensional presence in the material world; the lighter lines outside the structure represent the planes of three transecting circles: the potentia of the artist's creativity; that of culture, tradition, history; and that of the archetypal realm of the Muse. The child is the man, and he stands at the peak of the structure's ascending crossroads, where he meets with heaven and earth. The structure will crumble back to earth to become soil again, in time, but that time may be a long one.

Anthony Braxton's music for large ensembles includes works for "creative orchestra," which is his extension on the American big-band tradition; for traditional orchestra, in which improvisatory elements may be minimal, and the concepts informing the score more extensions on the European orchestral tradition; for multi-orchestras; and for operatic ensembles. All of these pieces, from the first one (*25*, from 1972), exhibit links, especially in their structures, to the patterns and designs of nature, culture, and mystical perception invoked here, links much more obvious than those in most of the other music. They also generally function as an umbrella vehicle for the distinctive dynamics of all the smaller groups as described here, often weaving them together as if the large ensemble were an aggregate of solos, duos, trios, and quartets of various sorts. They've exploited the performance potential of visuals the most, and—most recently—of poetry and myth, as part of the music.

In the large-ensemble work, the saxophonist-composer is more typically the conductor-composer; his instrument is now the group, and he plays it in a much more hands-on way than do conventional conductors or bandleaders. His stock of hand signals is more aligned with the art of chironomy, as depicted on ancient Egyptian murals of musical performance and figuring large in the development of Western music theory and notation.[1]

There really is a palpable element of the "inner child" let out to play by the adult in this part of Braxton's music, especially from the Golden Peak period on. *102* is for giant puppets reminiscent of Sesame Street characters on an Olympian scale; the stories that go with some of the later works have the feel of juvenile fiction (adolescent boys adventuring around in the wilderness, or in a science-fantastic city). Braxton often explains his scores to his (mostly young, student) players as best understood by the image of linkable-detachable cars of trains moving around switchable tracks; he often seems, in the thick of rehearsing a piece, like nothing so much as a kid running his model trains around the system of tracks he's designed and decorated.

The financial and logistical difficulties of large-ensemble projects that made them sparse in earlier years are finding some resolution more recently, just as the music itself is blossoming most through large ensembles now. Braxton's fairly new role as educator has given him the opportunity to present his musical philosophies, concepts, and techniques to young people.[2] In his own unique synthesis of the oral-traditional (mentor-mentee interactions that lead to learning through osmosis and imitation) with the literate-traditional (transmission of information through media such as scores, books, and recordings), this quintessential maverick of difficult esoterica has ended up at the heart of the grassroots academic mainstream, where he may define and design curricula. He trains and rehearses his own student ensembles to perform his most challenging work at a nearly-to-fully professional level, grooming the best for professional projects. Digital technology makes for CD-quality recordings of live performances; he also gets commissions from and travels to other schools in his academic network. This and the various collectives and other professional ensembles around the world interested in performing his music under or independently of his direction familiarize musical communities beyond his own with his work in a hands-on context.

Another direction, also facilitated by his access to the personal and physical resources of a large university, is through computer, MIDI, and interactive visual technologies. One of his current long-range goals is to get his musical paradigm, systems and materials into a computer format that will allow him to work with it just as he always has, only infinitely more efficiently and quickly. He envisions interactions with texts and visuals therein, and hopes to explore the area of virtual reality as the computer's grandest simulation of the kind of altered state he (like the *Ayahuasqueros*) experiences when he visualizes, mythologizes, "geographizes" or poeticizes his music. The technology is especially exciting for its potential to simulate the kinds of fantastic operatic productions of Braxton's most recent music.

The male–female polarization is subsumed here in the spectrum of family, as is the African–European one. There are simply more parts contributing to a whole greater than their sum at this point. Braxton's own childhood and adult family dynamics comprise a mix of African and European backgrounds; his music reflects that as deeply as anything else.

Generally, Braxton's work might be distinguished by its purposeful exploration of the inner world. Many composers write their music to celebrate things in the outer world of culture (e.g., Anthony Davis' treatment of the figure of Malcolm X, or Philip Glass' of Ahknaten), to express/communicate their own voice/vision/opinion (e.g., Laurie Anderson), or their sociopolitical views (Steve Reich) or—more typically—to make a sheerly musical statement. Braxton writes music primarily for creative improvisers to engage in their own spiritual growth, and that in a collective context; the listener is expected to be immediately sensitive to that experience by osmosis, the players to have faith in their ability and diligence in their attempts to convey it. The abstract purpose of each piece is usually declared (e.g. *56* : "For the participating instrumentalist this work can be viewed as a series of involvements that necessitates patience and growth").[3] Such functionalism complements shamanic cultures that have certain songs to tackle certain problems and develop certain powers, as well as that religious strain in the West from Hildegard through hymnodists through Holiness sects examined above.

Braxton's most recent story pieces provide the best entry point from the last chapter back into the music. We'll look at them as through the eye of heaven, stepping from there into their worlds as much like he does as possible. Each step "down" will lead from more to less recent work, finally to ground again, where the whole *ouevre* can be viewed as it stands in its world.

Large Ensemble Recordings

Creative Music Orchestra (Ring 01024/5/6, 1972): *25;* with fourteen players.

Creative Orchestra Music 1976 (Arista 4080): *51, 56, 58, 57, 55, 59;* with twenty-two players.

For Four Orchestras (Arista A3L 8900, 1978): *82;* with four symphony orchestras.

Composition 96 (Leo 169, 1981): with The Composers and Improvisors Orchestra; thirty-seven players.

Ensemble (Victoriaville) 1988 (Victo 07): *141(+20+96+120D), 142*; with reeds player Evan Parker, trombonist George Lewis, trumpeter Paul Smoker, vibist Bobby Naughton, bassist Joelle Léandre, and percussionist Gerry Hemingway.

Eugene (1989) (Black Saint BS 120137-2, 1991): *112, 91, 134, 100, 93, 45, 71, 59:* with the Northwest Creative Orchestra; sixteen players.

Two Compositions (Ensemble) 1989/1991 (hat Art CD 6086): *147, 151*; with the Ensemble Modern Frankfurt (*147*) and the Creative Music Ensemble (*151*).

Composition No. 165 (for 18 instruments) (New Albion NA 050, 1992).

Four (Ensemble) Compositions 1992 (Black Saint 120 124-2): *100, 96, 164, 163*; thirteen players.

171, 165, 151, 147

Actually, *171* is for solo piano, but it serves the thrust of this chapter—in the way *96* (for large ensemble) served that of the quartet chapter—so well that I'm going to open with it. In fact, it may find its way into a large-ensemble expression sooner than other such pieces the composer generates on the piano. Braxton is exploring the use of MIDI keyboards on which to compose in the way he's usually done on the piano; once a score like this is in the computer, the push of a few keys can change it from solo piano to large-ensemble piece. This one lends itself to that especially well, for its visual and dramatic elements.

171 sums up Braxton's musical journey on many levels. Like his first composition, it is for solo piano, the body of work for which, in both Western and African American traditions, inspired Braxton to conceive, begin, and develop his own body of work through the alto saxophone. Both text and visuals of this piece act as metaphors for that body of work. A full performance would feature several maps from the score (one is pictured in Fig. 9.1) projected on a screen at the back of the stage, with people pointing out the routes as they come up in the text. The pianist speaks the lines of the text as he (Frederick Rzewski has performed and privately recorded part of the piece) plays both the music and the role of Officer Crumpton. The performance includes an imaginary press conference and simulated guided tour of a mythical park system and its many regions. The numbers of the routes roughly correspond to Braxton's real compositions; the imagery and commentary he applies to the natural scenery metaphorically speaks of his music as a whole.

165 has no text spoken in its recorded performance, but Braxton's liner notes constitute a story set in Norfolk, Virginia, 1937. He weaves in and out of a narrative about Ben and Jonathan, two teenage cloud gazers wandering about the countryside, to make his comments on *165*: a "sound world that breathes like the clouds and paints a soundscape alive with *balance*."[4] The boys get lost in their cloud gazing; shapes are shifting and minds projecting when Ben's mother calls. He's in trouble. She knows he's out there, and he's supposed to be home.

large ensemble music 421

He "climbs under an oak tree"; he knows she'll be mad, but he laughs, and runs off into the woods with his friend.

Night falls, and they get lost there; lightning strikes, trees burn, earthquakes hit. The boys are remorseful for getting off the path, not doing their share of work at home. They have charts of the terrain (parts, score), they follow the clouds (chords) to try and divine direction. "'Don't rush it,' cried Ben, 'it'll come in its own time. In *Composition 165*, moments float in and out of the sound space—yet there are target recognition states. This is a sequential event continuum that places equal emphasis on sound and space.'"

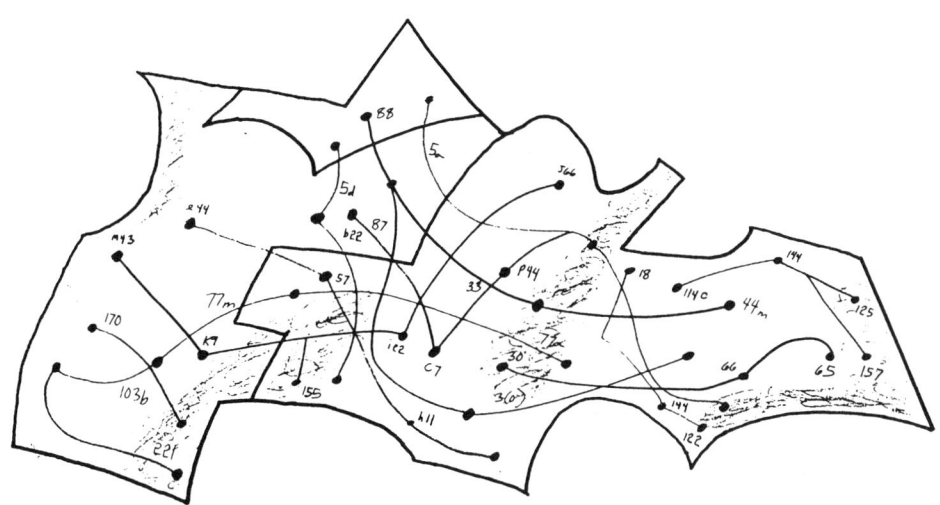

SOUTHWEST TRI-STATE REGION

Fig. 9.1: Map and text to go with 171, for solo piano. One might fancy the map of the South West Tri-State Region as a close-up of one of the typical shapes from Braxton's titles and scores. A suggestion to future researchers: the harmonic personality of this piece—the intervals and chords he chooses, and the way he orders them—displays a rapid development of longstanding harmonic aspects (still in place in music as recent as ten or fifteen opus numbers earlier) that is striking enough to merit some serious analysis.

The boys continue panicking and running, barely escaping death. They peer at their charts with their flashlights and finally hear the familiar voice (signature logic) of Aunt Sadie in one of the "cloud configurations." The boys find their way home in the landscape of their lostness. "'Safe again on the PRINCIPLE SONIC LANES,' Ben says. 'Thanks to the cosmics for the experience of living and for the ability to make a mistake and be forgiven—and even helped! Thank heaven for hope and redemption. The phenomenon of manifestation is the greatest gift of all.'"

German bassist/composer Peter Niklas Wilson's liner notes to *2 Compositions* describe the experience of rehearsing and getting both *151* and *147* into shape, with little lead time. His account could have been mine, regarding *Eugene (1989)*; it brings to mind the scene in the film *Straight, No Chaser*, in which the musicians in Thelonious Monk's band are complaining that he doesn't let them see his new music until the last minute before a performance. In fact, Braxton states that strategy, in the "Introduction" to his "Catalogue of Works,"

large ensemble music

as a way of keeping the edge and adrenalin flow, of allowing for surprises. Unexpected adversities are certainly a common part of the tradition of improvisation. In Braxton's case, the combination of his conducting and the very metric nature of even his most challenging scores is usually the lifesaver.

Braxton's part of the liner notes describe two guys who are speeding (through the music) so fast that a cop pulls them over and runs a check on them. "'Yeah, people, you've really done it this time. I hope your explanation will be broad and expansive because there is the possibility of 'complexity.'" They discuss the soundscape in terms of repeating lights and circles, a city of twenty tall chrome buildings (a Braxtonian image for chords or clusters if I ever saw one), a "major but not mega" airport: a Grand Central type of place, where many lines converge, with a lot of signposts. Again, Hermes is the lord of the roads, especially the crossroads; he's also lord of thieves: the two guys try to bolt (blow free of form), but Hermes is also the *psychopomp* (cops) who guides souls through chaos to order. The two guys think they've escaped the piece, but the cops—who have a "pan-system authority"—direct them *via* loudspeaker to pull into a "rest area."

This read is funny; it's also reminiscent of the images and (like the music) the "cut-up" technique of writer William Burroughs. "*Composition 151* is a trimetric structure that will serve as a 'primary identity territory' in the geo-sonic designs of post-nuclear/architectural/modeling . . . an 'all purpose adapter structure' that can connect/channel twelve different pathways through its greater metro areas . . . an E-class prototype. *In this soundstate, the individual looks for the transparent corridor/layer as a means to view a freshly unified theatre of form/relationships/alliance.*" (my emphasis: this is a keen description of the process triggered by the high synthesis of notation and improvisation in performing a piece like this. It seems you're always reading and always improvising, simultaneously—with so many others doing the same thing. The experience is much like driving or walking down a busy city street, where the channels and rules are simple and broad, but the interactions within them complex and demanding of focus). The sophisticated sound of the ensemble work depends on no displays of intensity or virtuosity, rather of a just reading and a sure, pithy improvisational responsiveness.

Bill Shoemaker's contribution to these notes, entitled "A Wake-Up Call," gives the nod to this new literary direction in the music:

> The complete spectrum of Braxton's activity, then, can be seen as an endeavor in semantics. Not semantics in the narrow sense of grammar, but as it's used in semiotics, the theory of signs—semantics as the study of signs in relation to what, or how, they signify. It is the interrelationship of Braxton's compositional methods, especially his lexicon of non-traditional notation, his prolific writings, particularly the somewhat recent advent of narratives accompanying scores, and his ever-evolving visual titles for his compositions, that not only enriches the experience of Braxton's music, but begins an articulation of the extra-musical implications of Braxton's work.

147 exhibits the numerologically rich structural design common to most of the large-ensemble works. It's for sixteen ensemble instruments and three solo clarinets; it comprises "three sorts of textures in spacially symmetrical arrangement, making up a seven-part form in the scheme $A^1B^1C^1A^2B^2C^2A^3$." The three A's form blocklike parallel motions in the woods and strings, altered suspended chords mutating into sudden sound swirls, over harp and percussion pulse track-like punches. The two B's feature groups of brass, harp, and percussion working three-tone statements over busy woods and strings, conducted flexibly; the two C's are open improvisations. Each of the solo clarinets are improvising freely throughout from different written parts.

Verbally titled *When Chancey Speaks, The Number 3 Changes "Lights,"* *147* is part of the Trillium series of operas ("Chancey's Hall of Mirrors," Braxton writes in the notes, "and the character Chancey are images in the tri-partial Zakko sound/thought stories (myths). The complete 'Hall of Mirrors' fantasies will be included in the stories of Zakko/Ashmenton/Kim (to be published before the year 2000)").[5] It is the piece, depicted in Chapter Two (Fig. 2.5), that chanced upon the *Close Encounters* theme, floating above the musical fray like one of Braxton's "signature logics." The strings sound like buzzing electric wires on crosses, the three clarinets like birds on those wires (doing a lot of supersax-like three-part harmony lines, written or improvised, we can't tell by ear; by eyeing the score we see it's both); the brass and percussion move like cars and machines down below. Peter Wilson, again the noteswriter, quotes Braxton about his desire, since the 1960s, to develop a music that incorporated the musical universes of Coleman, Ayler, (Cecil) Taylor, Coltrane, Cage, and Stockhausen.

In Braxton's notes, a 90-year-old man is talking:

> I can still see Chancey in the background—in between Zakko and the chorus line . . . his "reviews" were always first-class acts—and of course, it went on all night . . . an image sound state that seeks to reawaken our respect for the number three . . . a change station structure that contains nine switching paths for the "Zakko Sound Galaxy" region of my sound/works . . . a smooth sound environment that opens up into 12 "blue" lights moving into space. Suddenly, there are stars that swirl into the "clouds of the formings." . . . an image music that allows for creative exchanges between three solo clarinets and chamber orchestra . . . It was Chancey who first talked about the changes in the music (especially the importance of corridor structures, as a way to extend nuclear inter-connection architectural dynamics). I told him even then—leave it, Chancey, leave it, Chancey! Don't let the Feds get into this! You know how hard those people are!

The music critic becomes the literary critic at this point, discussing musical devices in the light of text, as one does with opera. Braxton's choice of names, images, and settings—Chancey, the wilderness, the city, Depression-era Norfolk, maps not only of public-access but forest-ranger roads—constitute a way of conceptualizing and discussing his own music that draws on mythological

large ensemble music

images with roots as deep as the Bible and the writings of Augustine (the wilderness, the city) and with fruits as fresh and charged as the science fiction and fantasy literature of our own time. Interpretations are there to be made—Chancey is indeterminacy; Chancey is Braxton; the feds and cops are cultural conservatives, or the human impulse to freeze the living Muse in stone—and remade as time, perception, and perspective flow through the fixed images of the fancies. One senses a circle charged with its continuous connection with those who imagined the gods and angels—from Nut, Sut, Thoth, Isis, Osiris, and Set; to YHWH and his four archangels, and Satan, moving and acting in history and nature; to Zeus, Diana, Pluto, and Hermes cavorting back and forth between the world and the realms of Hades and Olympus; to Father, Son, and Holy Spirit, presiding over the heavenly Jerusalem—that have shaped our own collective memory and culture.

Eugene (1989)

One of the most delightful aspects of performing this live recording at a university music school was the stir it created among the music students and faculty. Except for a handful, none of them (shockingly) was aware of Braxton's music beforehand, even among (more shockingly) the jazz students. What they saw was a man conducting in a very subtle, controlled manner—broken only by two rather brief solos on his alto sax—music that to them sounded utterly spontaneous, volatile, wild, and eerie. For a week afterwards they were asking the one faculty member who played with us (the late Ed Kammerer) what the parts and scores looked like, and how such sounds *could* be notated and conducted. These eight pieces, then, I can discuss in the context of my own experience of putting the band together, copying and distributing parts, holding sectional rehearsals before the event, and working with Braxton to rehearse and perform the pieces in this and one other concert. (My comments incorporate material from Braxton's composition notes on the pieces.)

The eight pieces we did (plus patches of *96* dispersed throughout them) made up a cross section of Braxton's work from 1975 to 1985—good, solid musical vehicles, with little in the way of the metamusical statements of either Ritual and Ceremonial or story pieces (*100* is from his Golden Peak period, *112*, *91*, and *93* near it—the period in which his Ritual and Ceremonial work started taking off—but, while we did link up the two sets of four pieces with *ad hoc* "corridor structures," the audience for both concert and recording had none of that sort of extramusical information).

Fig. 9.2: From trombone part to 112, *to be used with list of "language musics." This is a good example of how simple and conventional much of Braxton's music is, especially in individual parts, the complexity of the sum arising from the improvisational options and relative independence of lines.*

112 is a "post-Mingus/Oliver Nelson"[6] piece written for a specific group (the NDR Radio Studio Orchestra of Hamburg) to showcase its talent and diversity. That is, it was written for the ensemble more than its featured soloists. It opens with a sax sectional inspired by Basie, quickly adding other such similarly swinging (though a-rhythmic) sectionals to make a complex cross-current of them. It goes from this into pulse-track cycles designed to underpin collective, duo, and solo improvisations. The overall feel is swingy and boppish, even though the percussion was told not to keep the time, to play with an open feel, since the pulse track established the desired "groove."

Section A of *112* features the sax section; this was one they rehearsed a great deal before the gig. Braxton was particularly impressed with Thom Bergeron's alto sax solo, which he praised as setting up a context for the rest of the whole concert. This stuck in my mind as being similar to Abraham's blessing of Jacob disguised as Esau, in that the power of a "word" (music) in the oral tradition is such that it shapes reality and can't be "taken back" or erased once its force is in motion.

Much of the density and convolution in the ensemble sections resulted from throwing together multiple lines with no consideration for their vertical stacks; some of it was due to undetermined pitches left for us to pick. The relaxed, diffuse pulse made it easier to play than it might sound. My solo went with the pulse and treated the harmonic thicket as the One Big Chord I could "rhythmelodicize" from; it was offset by another horn reading a part of *96*.

In *91* we really got to enter the Braxtonian world. Each of the columns under the numbers with the plus sign he conducted in the time signature

large ensemble music 427

indicated. Clefs and keys were up for grabs; the shapes were to be interpreted as we pleased, as outlines of notes, or phrases, or abstracts of textures or colors. Braxton described this as pointillistic sprinkles of sound that swirl into extended improvisation, a piece to emphasize "the 'inner life' of sound particles"; he pictured figures as "vertical columns in space, islands on water," in "a 'thin' universe constantly changing size and motion . . . consciously designed to call on the skills of both classical and trans-African player," in an oscillation between the post-Webern and post-AACM continuum.

Obviously, the success of a piece like this required more interpretive and creative skills from the players than many other pieces might have; this group of players was mostly made up of middle-aged professionals who had worked together in different situations and combinations since their student days. We had all followed new, adventurous music and experimented in private sessions, but rarely in gigs; most of us were working straight-ahead jazz and classical performers. Braxton was, again, particularly happy with Todd Barton's work on the synthesizer. We all agreed it showed how a synth could be used—as a sort of hyper-texturer—in this music.

Braxton's first solo, on *91*, was with some written material from another piece he gave the pianist. The bowed bass solo work immediately following was one of those several impromptu segues he conceived with us on the spot to span the different pieces.

134 was the real take-off piece. That half-stepped triplet figure at its core was played at staggered and varying speeds, creating the feeling of a gyroscope spinning then lifting off the ground; the solos had rather the stability of the half-step in a steady two. The tension between steady two and volatile three, in the rhythm, and the ominous mystery of the half-step interval itself, generated the piece's excitement. The bari sax improvised over trombonist Tom Hill's reading of a *96* part.

100 was a garden of delights. The score was much like *91*'s (was in fact an extension of *98* material)—a myriad of events built on fixed and open premises—only busier, while at the same time more eternal. That is, it seemed to go on forever, with no tension, but plenty of vibrancy and variety; as performers, we got to pull out all our wildest, freest ideas in a framework of teamwork and collective purpose that called on the same skills as any piece scored for a trained ensemble. *100*, for whatever reason, *felt* exceptionally good to do (perhaps because it is at the very midpoint of the Golden Peak, and is the only one of them recorded by a large ensemble).

Then there was *93*: that wild opening with the synth, the sectional attacks, the drums, and the high smear of a sax solo . . . resolving into those tonal harmonies, then back to synth-land, then sectionals. They felt good to listen to, but the playing of them was really very conventional. This was mostly a showcase for the soloists featured, though one with its own integrity.

45, after a brief opening built on a whole-step interval much as *134* was on a half-step, got into a grand interchange between Charles Dowd's timpani and Braxton leading the saxes in a sort of buzzing mush of trills; then a traps solo followed; the vibes (also Dowd) proved to be a singularly effective voice on this piece and the program generally. The sax unison sixteenth-note riffs that got us into the rhythm vamp were a killer, and took some rehearsal. Jeff Homan's soprano solo conveyed, again, that lumbering, ominous thing Braxton can evoke

428 large ensemble music

with his gestures; and Mike Vannice's tenor madness was a cry straight back to Albert Ayler's first such. All hands were heavy on this minor Russian march-like piece, satisfyingly so, as you can tell from the audience's response. Bassist Forrest Moyer broke through to his finest reaches for this piece's dénouement.

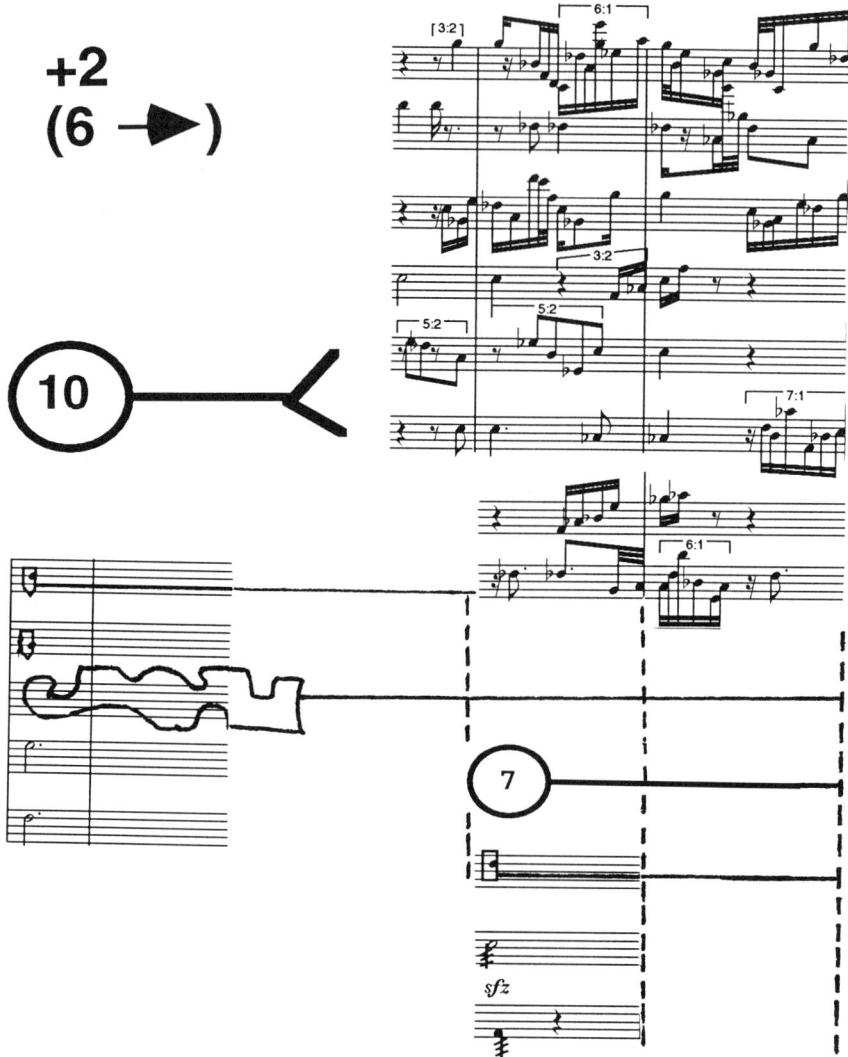

Fig. 9.3: From 100. Braxton likened this "post-Webern/Taylor" piece to an ant colony, where you can see the world in situ *through the glass case.*

71—I can almost hear Rod Sirling's voice over the opening to this one, welcoming us to another dimension. More long-rehearsed workouts were required for the sections, but again a simple rhythmic and bluesy bass-root (logically enough, by now, a variation on both half- and whole-tone intervals) platform

large ensemble music   **429**

was employed. I wonder if these pieces were designed and/or chosen to maximize virtuosity without taxing it, given the pick-up band nature of the situation.

My solo played with the idea of a timepiece; I felt myself (like Buster Keaton) to be in a giant mechanized clock, trying to get in sync with (or stay out of the way of) gears and other moving parts that could either kill me or give me a ride to safety.

The clock stopped, got rewound in the last two sections of sectionals, and ran down just as it should. For the most part, this concert was very much about tension and release. Lock[7] compared it to the *Creative Orchestra Music* album for its variety of usages of the big-band format. Its pieces, however far out and Braxtonian they sound, are not that far from the mechanics more typical of such a format; the difference lies in the sounds, line construction, creative spirit and imagination, and historical knowledge of the music that Braxton expects his performers to bring to the open sections. We even ended on the same piece (*59*) that ended the 1977 *Down Beat* Album of the Year, a piece that showcases the conductor—as a creative manipulator of the ensemble—as much as the two saxes that duoed together.

Another delightful aspect of this performance was what the musicians had to say about it; descriptors such as "religious experience," "highest musical experience," and the like were common. Particularly gratifying were expressions from Portland and Seattle reviewers that praised it not only as an evening of good music, but as the community/regional celebration we hoped it would be.[8]

102

"It is my hope to become involved in the world of children and family-centered music (types) in the future—because all of these matters are related to positive world change."[9] So Braxton wrote right around the time his own family was newborn, as well as his music, through the Ritual and Ceremonial transformation (which included *102*). "A given interpretation of Composition No. 102 establishes a forward music and visual state that is intended for both children and adults."

Bird Man, Sun Goddess, and Robot Man are the 25-feet tall puppet characters (whose movements and operating specs are in the score) enacting a "two-hour celebration of movement and creative interactions that places the listener in an imaginary setting (as if in a dream state or cloud setting)." The organizational principles of the piece seem to reflect a childlike thrust (as opposed to, say, *96*, which is similar in form and scope but which seems very much the "adult" piece, with its Promethean thrashings and Minoan mazes):

> Every language system in . . . 102 is approached with respect to what it poses to the principle two-note (sound) operating sequence that opens the very beginning of the music. To visualize that relationship is to see the two-note principle as a fire that contains dancing figures that twirl in the proximity of its "light." . . . Collage formings in this world of sound establish the projection of independent line spirals in the space of the music.

430 large ensemble music

In other words, the same material rotates throughout different sections—three principal time/space parameters housing nine principal language strategies, and timbral and focus specifications in six different "language systems" (chords, phrases, staccato lines, chromatic lines, grace notes, and metric constructions)—of *102*.)

> All of us have been (and still are, for that matter) children. For that reason I have asked that all puppet characters be constructed as exciting moving figures—but not scary (or too scary for young children). This is so because the experience of this effort was approached as a positive offering to all children—everywhere.

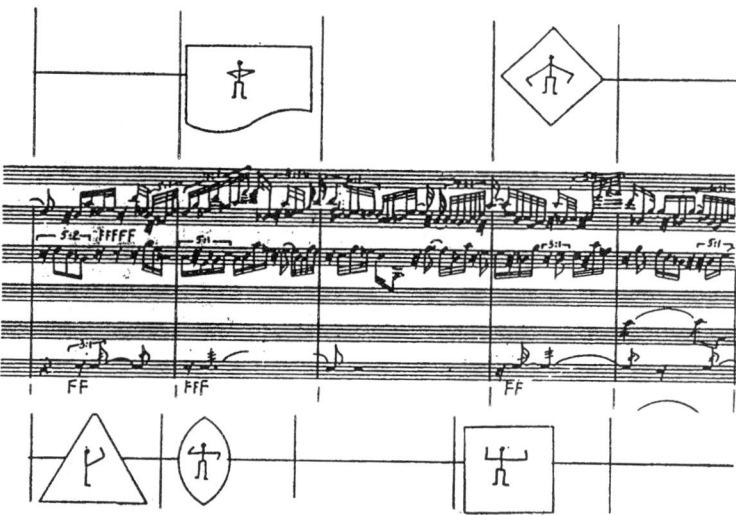

Fig. 9.4: 102 runs on three of each of the following: flutes, oboes, English horns, soprano clarinets, clarinets, bassoons, trumpets, percussion instruments, and low brass; and strings and piano. As in some of his trios+piano, the piano is used here "as an ensemble as well as soloist operative that is used to balance (and in some cases generate) the nature of the music." Also like many of them the piano part was written after the collage structures for the other instruments. Repetition of lines within a time/space section of them is also used.

The stick figures in various poses reflect Braxton's interest in the idea of gestures and poses as having mystical/symbolic meanings. He now looks with relish to the day he can program his computer to respond (with sound and visuals) to video images of such positions, caught in the real time of performance.

82

The music for large ensembles requires the most support from the world. One can't make the kind of stone soup often possible with smaller *ad hoc* situations; one needs money and/or in-kind help from one's community, one's audience. To get to this scale, one's work has to be important to more people than the artist and a few kindred spirits. In the big-band tradition, that importance came from people's desire to dance and hear what they knew both showcased and extended. In the experimental-music tradition, when it finally does come, it comes because enough people with enough money and other resources relate to an artist's work not as his or her private compulsion but as a fruitful departure of the common public consciousness into something new.

In Braxton's case, this necessary confirmation took the form of a friend with a knack for organizing and producing (see *Creative Music Orchestra*, below), the Arista five-recording contract (see *Creative Orchestra Music*, below) and, for *82* for four orchestras, a National Endowment for the Arts grant. In all three cases, Braxton chose risk over conservative investment, producing his own most adventurous work as the most generous, responsible, and conscientious response to the gestures of support and good faith.

The four orchestras in the grand event that is *82* define four corners of a space which surrounds the audience. Their quadraphonic effect is splintered by the motions of the rotating chairs seating the forty musicians in each orchestra, and the music is scored to pass from orchestra to orchestra "midstream." The liner (for the live performance, program) notes feature a chart of the human body as a collection of sound-receptor zones, alerting the reader to his or her whole being as ear—and to those parts of it targeted as such by composer and players, at least conceptually, in their various strategies for sound projection. Every bit of the performance space—the audience's body surfaces, the floor, the air—is part of a three-dimensional "magic circle" (sphere) partitioned into elaborate and graceful curves, currents, and colors designed to receive or carry sound. The complexities of the score, daunting as they seem, break down to layers of relatively straightforward strategies—information moving from orchestra to orchestra; trios, duos, and solos; different "languages" juxtaposed in one block of sound; metric options ranging from a synchronization of to a disparity between all four orchestras, including the degrees between; and the (Mingus-inspired) "accordion" timespace (gradual speeding and slowing of tempo), and conductor-controlled rubato passages—all mixed together variously. The most daunting complexities, most peculiar to this piece, stem from its attempts to project and target all strands of the plethora of mass and individual sounds with laserlike precision— one of those Braxton conceits that succeeds fully if it achieves only a fraction of its ambition. This mining of space for its acoustic dynamics of spirituality is another of Braxton's links with medieval Western music, as Lange notes in his five-star review of this work.[10]

82 is the first in the series of multiorchestral works Braxton conceived for different locations stretching from cities to star systems. It reflects the plenum of some huge gathering of nomadic tribes into a temporary, transient city, with hundreds of groups of musicians playing within overlapping earshots, a thousand conversations and independent activities occurring at once—colors, order, chaos, humanity, all in the simple presence and moment of itself.

> The realness of multiple orchestra activity directly sheds light on the cross vibrational activity that takes place in everyday living (that being the realness of creative—and "real"—invention and how it is related to the very fabric of existence on this plane). For at the heart of my series of works in multi-orchestralism is the attempt to create a music that can dynamically accentuate (and celebrate) the multi-complexual—and not complexual—realness of life on this planet, as a means to be better prepared to deal with this sector in space, and as a factor that might hopefully be positively related to what this preparation could vibrationally and spiritually reveal about "living."[11]

78, 42, 41

The unrecorded *42* (1974) and *78* (1977) deserve a mention for their unique expressions of Braxton's musical evolution. They are both entitled "Introduction to Cell Structure and Language Design" and are essentially the first classroom/workshop materials Braxton developed to teach students how to think about and perform his music.

> Composition No. 42 consists of four cards of cell structure notation, two sections of traditional notated material and one set of language sheets for each participating instrumentalist. (The attending audience can also be given one language sheet if desired.) The four cards of cell structure contain twenty-six structural time parameters that indicate what groupings and/or specific instruments are to be activated for each given parameter.[12]

Two traditionally notated sections—a bright march and a slow, darker part—complement Braxton's infusions of his "languages" into interconnected "cells." The sound types are "1) [a long tone, starting on] concert A [then moving to other pitches], 2) an accented long sound, 3) trills, 4) staccato long sound, 5) high sound types, 6) low sound types, 7) moving sound cluster, 8) use of air or other part of instrument, 9) specified sound type and 10) curved sound type." Their numbers are placed in circles (the cells) and played as charted. (Braxton still puts these in his classroom band book, to be used for practice and warm-up improvs he directs with hand signals.)

large ensemble music

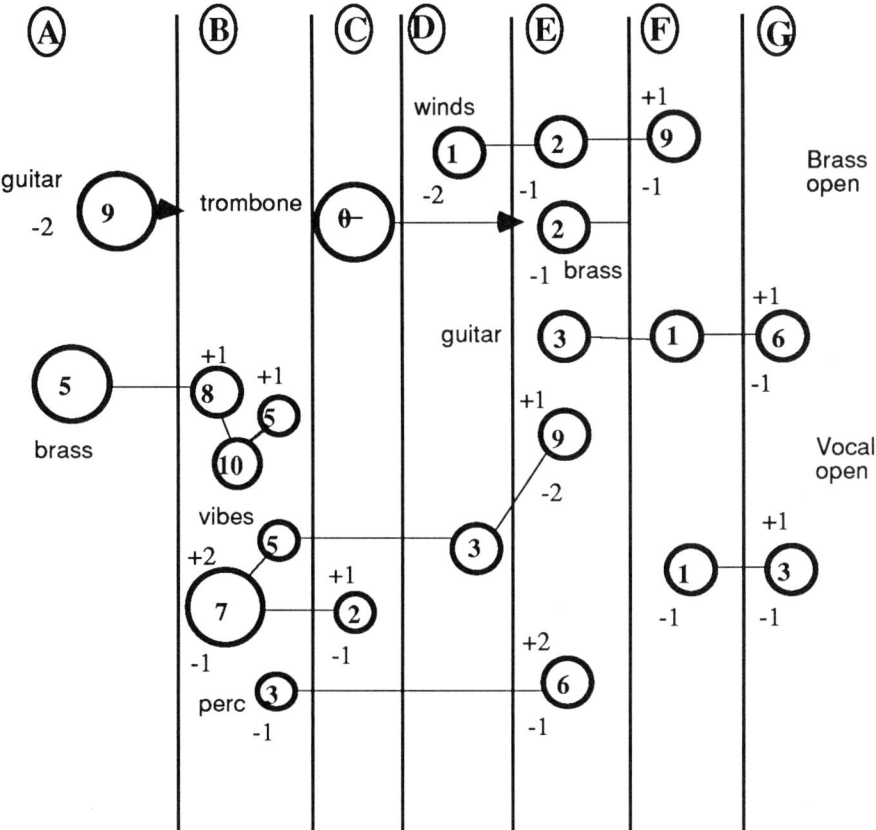

Fig. 9.5: Braxton: "A given performance and/or use of this material involves interpreting [it] with respect to its language and procedure specifics—as it is written (positioned) in the score. The twenty-six structural components that make up the cell structure system of notation is the master structure and composite score of Composition No. 42." [13] *This layering and flow of circled numbers is from 42's score. Like early Western neumes, it presumes command of an orally transmitted musical vocabulary. Braxton writes of it, "The reality of this material has to do with how it can be substituted into any musician's working vocabulary as a means to broaden one's focus and exploration scan."* [14] *A similar chart of 78 extends this from 42, wherein color becomes a factor Braxton conceives as a catalyst to "the creative act and how this discipline is viewed by the ancients."* [15]

Braxton describes this system as an extension on his earlier "conceptual grafting"; it is an organization of sound away from fixed pitches and pulse but into timbral and timed events. Each player is given freedom of choice of pitch and interpretation of the language, but is still constrained by time and timbre (language) for the sake of the collective.

> The concept of cell structure in this context involves creating a given fixed and open time space as a means to provide an expanded context for participation. For this purpose I have designed a variation of language music notation that incorporates new responsibilities for both the individual and collective ensemble (i.e. like the use of material specifics that are not cued by the conductor that still must be collectively executed by the composite ensemble from vibrational agreement).[16]

42 was designed as "a door into the world of visuality . . . of sound shapes."[17] The complexities of lines and layers roiling together throughout much of his work are absent here.

In workshops, he leads the ensembles first through the language sheet, cueing by number, letting players get a feel for each, dividing each up between groupings and individuals; then he paces them through the "cell structure," with its notated sections. The piece is very much like an ensemble version of his solo alto music's system of language musics. *78* extends the concept through the addition of shapes other than circles (that function as symbols) and of colors. Improvisatory modes are more specified.

Immediately before *42*, Braxton wrote *41*, the sixth in what he called the

> L-C-J series of interrelated structural types. All works from this category seek to transfer material and conceptual elements from extended improvisation into workable specific re-system types to serve as structural theorems for notated (empirical) music strategies . . . another attempt to apply some of the changes reshaping my instrumental language viewpoint into a frozen notated state.[18]

The piece is a string of four traditionally notated sections spaced by three more open (but still specified) ones, each of which proceeds conceptually from the other in a developmental way. Braxton notes its similarities to serial music, but stresses its freedom from formulism.

Creative Orchestra Music 1976

Between those pieces came the material that went into this Record of the Year for *Down Beat*'s 1977 critic's poll. Braxton took umbrage in an interview at the suggestion that this was his first excursion into writing for large ensemble.

> [It] wasn't a change in direction. It was merely my first opportunity to have large ensemble music on record. Because of that I decided to put three compositions on each side of the record to show a cross-

> spectrum of what I would like to do with that medium. I say "like to do" as opposed to "did" because the compositions were very short and I had only two days of rehearsal time. In fact, we didn't even have two days, we rehearsed the day before, and then rehearsed in the afternoon and recorded in the evening. I'm very happy with the record.
>
> I wrote the music in the studio each day. But my point is that I was able to do that album so I did it—it's no more than that. I'm happy with the music but it's no great milestone in terms of my life. It didn't happen because I became so inspired that it changed the direction of the music.
>
> In fact, it's part of a logical continuum, that being the thrust of my work.[19]

The opener, *51*, is the most conventional harmonically and rhythmically, a fast, brash, and boppish romp down "post-Henderson/Ellington" lines. The metrical structure is symmetrical throughout, and the solos, sectionals, and full orchestrations are tight and muscular, inspiring like-minded solos. Braxton compares his sax sectional, again, to the Supersax model, a group that featured his main man, Warne Marsh, and prefigured the recent spate of sax quartets Braxton kicked off with his own *37*. His intent here was for

> a highly charged work . . . that reawakens the "session" period of swing and bebop continuance—so that we can remember the "excitement" that has always been associated with creative music . . . This is a big band music that relates to the toughness of the big band era (spirit)—as a forum to "shout" about the strength of positive creativity and (growth).[20]

The contrast between that active energy and *56* is stark—and instructive, especially in the light of Braxton's notes. This is a classic example of the static aspects of his music many have less patience with than he obviously does; what one must keep in mind is how exceptionally active, busy, and energetic is so much of Braxton's work. In the light of that, the *lack* of fairly large "rest areas" such as *56* would be the more intolerable imbalance. Braxton's words about this piece go to the meditative heart of all such faces of his music, which, if anything, are deepening and broadening as he matures:

> A slow pulse environment . . . not a complex work that contains thousands of notes and/or precision multi-structures . . . nor does 56 seek to provide terms for extended individual solo realization . . . rather the work is conceived to establish a way of perceiving sound distance and inner purpose . . . as it concerns the composite ensemble (rather than "the glorious soloist") . . . in this work objects (thought) are *moving so fast it appears to be slow—or the slowest* . . . Perceived events in this sound environment seem to drift into the sound space almost lifelessly . . . a sea of drifting sounds that flows into the greater space of the music . . . not separate from the post-

Webern and AACM continuums of creative music . . . "no pulse". . . (silences) . . . *All of this material is presented as a means to enhance the 'act' of involvement. This is a "secret" for the instrumentalist and listener alike.* "Listen to the one who had the best opportunity but did not take it." . . . a world of light flashes—and deception . . . Collective improvisation is valued in this work because the nature of this context transcends what any one person can do (or know). Improvisation in this context is not about who you are (or aren't, for that matter), rather . . . 56 was conceived as a crack in the sound space—into the void. *There should be no excitement in this world of sound, nor should we be disturbed by some fellow's impression of who he wishes he were . . . 56 has no time for our feelings—at all!* The challenge of involvement for this context moves into the "moment spot" of the time and the realness of intention . . . *For the participating instrumentalist this work can be viewed as a series of involvements that necessitates patience and growth.* . . . Too often in this time period we tend to confuse movement and excitement with "real"—and this is not always the case. In this work I wanted to construct a clear universe of sound sculpture that can be entered *without any kind of fear or discomfort.* There are no perceived "varieties" that give recompense to those who want to "show us something about themselves" . . . 56 is a haven for those of us who might need to lean back and compare notes (every once in a while).[21] (emphases mine)

58 and *57* are "creative" yet light treatments of specific, simple traditional gestures, *58* a march (dedicated to Sousa and inspired by his *Stars and Stripes Forever*) and *57* an atonal ballad. The march is half conventional and half "out," the latter through its staggering of rhythms (which make for an effective pulse track for solos), wide-open solo improvs, and some undetermined pitch and duration of sections. The ballad is a texturally colorful collective statement rather than solo vehicle (though it does have the feel of the duo music with Roscoe Mitchell, who plays flute with Braxton's contrabass clarinet here, along with others on vibes, marimba, piano, and brushes). A, B, and C sections define the music lightly through parts of the group, then more heavily in the final D tutti part. "I conceived this material in terms of how it visually looked (sounded) moving across the space of the sound canvas," Braxton wrote.[22]

55 takes us back to the heart of the big-band world, this one inspired by Ellington and Mingus, and

> indebted to the last 100 years of creative African master thinkers and restructuralists in its attempts to establish "blocks" of structural involvements (in between solo sections or time/space) and in its language components and science (vibrational and structural types) applications.[23]

large ensemble music

It has the feel and sound of post-bop swing in its brass sectionals, sax sectionals, vamp patterns, background lines under solos—all an "explosive excitement positively intended."

The piece grew from four basic premises that themselves grew directly from the composer's experience as improvising instrumentalist: (1) extreme intervallic distances, to distort the perception of continuity:

> The reality of this approach moves to solidify a state of "indecision" as to the overall effect of a given note (phrase) decision—and what this means is that I myself am always surprised about "what happened" in the music. In other words the use of intervallic contour shifting moves to create an attitude about music that is more important than "is it right or not?" . . . How we integrate our past (and the past of humanity) into future decisions will determine the success of the future (or if there is to be a future);

(2) repetition, as developed in Kelvin and Cobalt (less conventional, more complex and idiosyncratic) material, is used under the extended solos; and the interplay between sections is as much an instrumentalist's as a composer-arranger's treat (generally, while Braxton's music demands much in the way of selflessness and sensitivity to the group, even in its wildest flights, it rewards those traits with equal opportunities for virtuosity and self-expression, over the course of a piece or a program); (3) open solo space—but the spirit is bop, so players are expected to be able to "bop" in a post-Colemanish way:

> The structural elasticity of 55 does not represent innovation in any sense of the word—for the reality of "open performance options" comes from the world community.

This goes back to the comments in Chapter Two about improvisations traditionally and transculturally being extensions—freshenings—on a pleroma of simple, familiar traditional material. Braxton mentions Henderson and Basie as recent American models of this process; and (4) linear (horizontal) development and musical thinking. As usual, he stresses that 55 was done in "moment time," spontaneously:

> 55 is not an affirmation of a fixed theorem (that glorifies some mathematical theorem) nor did the work happen by chance. Rather the final realness of this structure involves the integration of improvisation and preparation—and as such these matters can be discussed.

59 ends both this recording and *Eugene (1989)*; its effectiveness as a climax lies in its mix of flexibility, simplicity, and directness, and showcase of the duo dynamic at its most exciting (a special treat from this Mitchell-Braxton duo, which is more typically unsupported and subdued). Braxton identifies the piece as

"post-Stockhausen/AACM"; the former for its simple isolation of, focus on, and working over the improvisational parameters and attitudes developed by the latter. The score is a series of punches, pitches mostly open, cued in by a conductor and splayed off into chords and new accents through his spontaneous signals; the conductor in effect functions as a third player in a trio with the two featured solo reeds, his instrument being the ensemble. The piece has even more potential than many to create something new on the spot, and that in the most visceral, accessible terms.

Creative Orchestra Music's playlist—especially with the validation of a major commercial recording contract's *carte blanche*, rewarded by a mainstream magazine's Record of the Year award—stands as a celebration of American culture in the tradition of court musics from around the world and history, especially those that give a new voice and words to time-honored myths and songs.

25

25 is something of a "First Symphony" of the "new music" of the time (1972). It is dedicated to Ornette Coleman, and was done right around the time Braxton was living with Coleman. Braxton credits his longtime friend Kunlé Mwanga for providing the opportunity to produce and record the work. Braxton and Mwanga were together in Paris (Braxton's second time there), Braxton bemoaning the lack of opportunities in America for creative music generally. Mwanga countered this pessimism with an invitation to Braxton to state his most ambitious creative project. Braxton responded with "the creative orchestra—because large ensemble projects are practically impossible when you have no money and can't pay musicians for every rehearsal." Mwanga supplied the concert opportunity and the musicians.

At that point, no post-AACM orchestral versions of creative music existed on record, and there had been few live ones. "Since I realized my next opportunity to work with a creative orchestra might be in the year 2135, there was no reason to hold back any ideas I had been thinking about for this context." He wanted to show what was possible and, hopefully, inspire more such efforts.

He describes *25* as a multistructure of 12 "units," labeled A through L (actually 13, since G has 2 parts), for 13 instruments. Each unit, designed to suggest improvisational premises and timbral areas, interlocks flexibly with the others; the whole is conceived to fill up a whole program, to be one unbroken statement (in this, *25* prefigures the coordinate system, and the Master Progression Sequence). In other words, whatever statement the Muse might have to make on a given evening through a given *program*, this *piece* is meant to facilitate alone.

Section A directs air through horns, and keys and valves to be tapped for their percussive effects. Braxton invokes a

> cloud-type terrain . . . mist . . . a living breathing universe—we are dealing with the concept of the "Glimpse": . . . what it signifies about "other matters"—"dimensionality with smoke" or "driving in the snow."[24]

large ensemble music

It sounds something like a nighttime jungle scene—the chimps of our very first chapter chattering softly with nightfall. The flute and oboe come in over that with seven notated phrases conceived not as themes to develop but as catalysts launching improvisation.

B starts as a flute/oboe/muted trumpet trio improvising collectively. A soprano/piano duo comes in to take the pulse and vitality up from a soft and reflective collective statement into a stronger, more vibrant and interactive improvisation. By C, we've gotten to the tuba and drumsticks, and a second, more forceful notated section.

C itself is a medium–fast fanfare under a very up-and-out tenor solo.

> Brass structures . . . like steel beams over the floor of the music (sounding as if strung tightly over the foundation of one's imagination) . . . like a call to arms (although that was not my intention at the time. I have always reacted positively to brass and brass ensemble music and this structure was written with the historical significance of creative brass music in mind.)

The ancient martial roots are evident, however, along with the more recent feel of a New Orleans parade. A hot drum solo leads into a hot piano solo.

> I wanted in this section to establish a platform for post-Ayler improvisation dynamics . . . in the interrelationship and reality between all percussion, bass, and piano.

An unaccompanied piano solo makes some atonally nervous forays into those dynamics, then makes them more gossamer, less edgy.

> What is needed . . . is the creation of a super charged reality state to be secured for the purposes of generating the "vibrational path" of its soloist. On top of this energy wave in the soloist—in the position of having to play music: having the opportunity for "life statements"—without any extraneous factors in terms of either time parameters or harmonic expectations.

D goes to ground with a notated 10-phrase unison melody for contrabass clarinet, tuba, and string bass.

> The basic effect of this material moves to create a dark world in stone that is carved—as opposed to its elaboration in improvisation, which is murky (as if in a void) . . . There are two images for this section—that of the night and of the struggle towards learning who you are; and of the light (which looks different from what you "thought you'd see").

It gets into a real dog-whiney pathos, after a poignant lonely trumpet: the shadow as dark as the earlier sections' energy was bright.

E takes refuge from such stark darkness in the activity of 44 linked phrases in staccato and longtone language, read independently and at different speeds by each player: "a multiple universe of sound that includes openly applied fixed material." From there we go into 225 balloons to be inflated, rubbed, deflated, and/or popped: a civilization of insects waging their Great War! The soprano sax, bass, flute, and tenor voices scream, then settle into loose conversational improvs over the insects.

Like a great homecoming, F embraces tempo and works up a boppish jam.

> I included this section because of the special love that I have long had for this context . . . It is fashionable in this time period to simply dismiss the traditional criterions which have been utilized from time period to time period as information that doesn"t adhere to "what is perceived" as the most advanced. This attitude extends into every area of world culture—and its resultant effects have not been positive. I believe that the science and devices underlining the composite music are necessary—"all relevant"—regardless of period, focus, or time zone. It is really a question of understanding how to give the illusion of "newness" (or really-freshness) that is important. Real growth can only be based on a foundation.

I think of F as the last "day" of this work's (world's) creation, when the human soul arrives. Braxton describes its thrust as "post-Coleman . . . couched in the traditional thrust and weight of one million (and some) previous travelers who have taken that same route." The soloists, he says, should "be angry at something." There are no traditional harmonic or voicing patterns, but the pulse and line constructions would be familiar to jazz improvisers. The drums take it out.

If F is the sixth day, G is the next day, of rest and assessment: "A Christmas tree in music, with lots of glitter and stardust; (G^1) and (G^2) comprise "a meditation-like music, establishing a world that changes yet goes nowhere . . . akin to walking to the rain with giant lights of dark beams that seem to go on and on . . . In establishing this approach I have extended the research involving monophony and extended phrase construction." From this point we're going beyond the world completed by Coleman.

H and I are, respectively, unaccompanied tenor and tuba solos; Braxton's only premise for them is that the players make them "as honest as possible." He intended them as a contrast to the full orchestra "so that its particulars are not simply taken for granted." When it comes back in (J), it's with gradually shifting sustains (à la Penderecki), the piano soloing over them as they rise and fall in halfstep pitch and pulse and volume. The effect is of unsettling tension, something suggesting a spacetime warp. A trumpet solo makes for an ensemble voice recalling Ives' unanswered question.

The two horn solos of H and I are answered in K, by two percussion solos. Braxton specified slow pulse exchanges:

large ensemble music   441

I did not want for this duo to degenerate into either a cutting context or simply "the destruction hour"—"with sticks." Rather, Unit J was perceived as an open space where sounds could happen (and even do what *it* wants to do) without being so important. The more we look at time the more possible it becomes to not let the excitement get in the way of learning—and to not let the learning get in the way of being excited. (emphasis mine—the Muse is "it").

This early conscious use of the drums so prefigures a broad swath of Braxton's later work, which is virtually distinguished by it (see Chapter Eight, on soft, arhythmic drum solos).

L ends the piece with a cacophonous sound mass conceived as black: the creative plenum/void of the universe that both emits and swallows all colors and sounds.

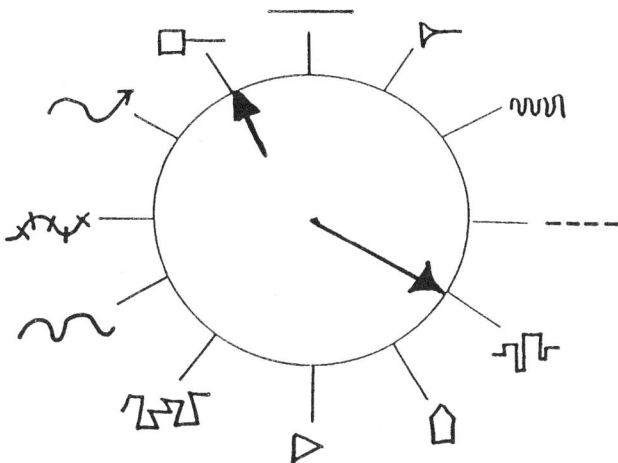

Fig. 9.6: Hot off the press, this is the beginning of one of Braxton's latest versions of his system's diagrams. The languages can be indicated with the "clock's" hands; he's talking about superimposing a triangle and a square to make, with the circle, the tri-metric device. Imagine it in a computer, dimensionalized into virtual reality and in its finished version with the system's geometric schemes and identity states, capped off with a recorded composition

and an operatic drama set up for interactive musical-mythical dialogue with you . . . and you begin to play this game.

That this look at Braxton's work for large ensembles is perhaps more the survey than the analysis seems appropriate for several reasons. One, it seems advisable to leave the reader piqued enough to want to know more, rather than exhausted (especially after last chapter). This part of Braxton's music would justify its own book, for its complexity of content within simplicity of organization, and the principles and mythology it engages and embodies.

Also, it is the part of his work that is most current and in process for him, largely because of the increased opportunities to have it played, and the ease with which computer technology can generate it. Braxton's most current and also long-term focus is to explore the possibilities of that technology, including its visual ones. He's greeting the advent of virtual reality as a match made in heaven for his approach to music. His strategy for the immediate future is to compose solo piano pieces on MIDI keyboard that can be blown up into orchestral and operatic works in the computer.

The path begun with the inspiration of Fats Waller's and Arnold Schönberg's solo piano music has come full circle here, and it is as full as a world with its own creations.

---

1. See Lise Manniche's *Music and Musicians in Ancient Egypt* (London: British Museum Press, 1991) for its indexed references to chironomy; see also discussions of Western notation's roots in hand gestures in Chapter Two.

2. In this, he is reflecting the career of one of his role models, the bandleader Frank Johnson (see Chapter Two).

3. Anthony Braxton, *Composition Notes C,* (Hanover, NH: Tree Frog Music, 1988: 319–30).

4. Braxton, *Composition No. 165 (for 18 instruments)* (New Albion NA 050, 1992).

5. *120D*, as performed on *Ensemble (Victoriaville) 1988* (Victo 07), is an example of how Braxton and the best of his collaborators can take this most recent—and most adventurous—of Braxton's work and still work it, without stating the text, into their own most burning music.

6. Braxton, *Composition Notes E*, 369–85.

7. Lock, *Jazz* (London, 1992: 57–8).

8. Gary Bannister, "Eugene 1989" (*Earshot Jazz*, September 1992: 14).

9. Braxton, *Composition Notes E*, 152–85, for this and other on *102*.

10. He mentions the Renaissance/baroque antiphonal choirs, and similar works by Gabrieli, Bach, Mozart, Bartók, and Henry Brant; compares Braxton literately to Stockhausen and Schönberg; alludes to lucidity and transparency in spite of ambition; and declares Braxton "at the forefront not only of instrumentalists, but of composers of every classification. No longer can he be pigeonholed as a 'jazz composer.'"

11. Liner notes to *For Four Orchestras*.

12. Braxton, *Composition Notes C*, 163. Roscoe Mitchell recorded part of *42* as "March" on *Snurdy McGurdy and her Dancing Shoes* (Nessa N-20, 1980).

13. Ibid., 163–64.

14. Ibid., 165–66.

15. Braxton, *Composition Notes D*, 254.

16. Ibid., 170.

17. Ibid., 175.

18. Braxton, *Composition Notes C*, 149; also, from 160, "Composition No. 41 was the first chamber orchestra work of mine to be publicly performed. In fact this work was the first large notated work of mine that I ever heard—and as such the realness of this experience will always have a special place in my memories" (recorded with Barry Guy's London Jazz Composer's Orchestra [Zurich Concerts, Intakt 4/5]).
19. Braxton, *Composition Notes C*, 596.
20. Ibid., 264.
21. Ibid., 320–21.
22. Ibid., 331–38.
23. Ibid., 302–18, for this and all on 55; also see Fig. 2.10.
24. Braxton, *Composition Notes B*, 160–93, for this and other 25 references.

fifth arrow . . .

In the Eye of the Bull

Chapter Ten

The Music's Muse

Flesh tells what spirit tells, but spirit knows it tells.

Charles Williams

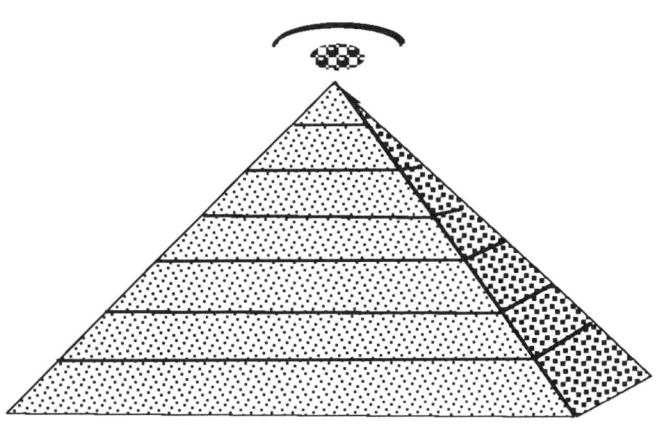

The word "music" has come to us from the Greek mousike *by way of the Latin* musica. *It is formed in Greek from the word* mousa, *the Muse, which comes from the Egyptian, and the Greek ending* ike, *derived from the Celtic. The Egyptian word* mas *or* mous *actually signifies generation, production, or development outside a principle; that is to say, formal manifestation or the passage to act of that which was in potency. It is composed of the root* ash, *which characterizes the universal, primordial principle, and the root* ma, *which expresses all that generates, develops, or manifests itself, grows, or takes on an exterior form.* Ash *signifies in innumerable languages unity, the unique being, God, and* ma *applies to all that is fecund, formative, generative; it actually means "a mother."*

Thus the Greek word mousa *(Muse) has applied since its origin to every development from a principle, to every sphere of activity where the spirit passes from potency to act and clothes itself in a sensible form. In its most limited application, it is a manner of being, as the Latin word* mos *expresses it. The ending* ike *indicates that one thing was related to another by similitude, or that it was a dependency or an emanation of it. One finds this ending in all the Northern European languages, written* ich, ig, ic, *or* ick. *It is connected to the Celtic word* aik, *which means equal, and comes from the Egyptian and Hebraic root* ach, *symbol of identity, equality, fraternity* ... [1]

[From occult definition of] **Muses**: *1. originally the Great Goddess in her incantatory aspect (v. Great Goddess, serpent, etc.); 2. then the first division into Three took place: Meditation, Memory, and Song, who watched over (blessing or cursing) incantations; the Muses are the offspring of earth and the Graces of heaven (Bucolic Vestinus); 3. finally the fragmentation into nine took place (v. Multiplicity), with emasculated Apollo supervising them* ... [2]

[From occult definition of] **music**: *1. religious: (related to fire and smoke) a. in the O.T. . . . the most effective trance-inducer among the nabis ("prophets") . . . 4. creative: a. Harmony rising out of Chaos: b. creation caused by pre-Hellenistic goddesses with lyres; c. often connected with the foundations of cities . . .*

10. Rough Music: a. needed when the balance of nature (Fate—Themis—"Justice") had been upset by an offense (especially sexual); processions were formed of people with anything that could produce loud sounds (kettles, pans, etc.) in order to scare off the spirits of ill-luck evoked by the offense . . .

[From occult definition of] **Mercury**: *1. the Heavenly Messenger: "Hermes" = "interpreter," "mediator": a. as psychopomp he announces death and accompanies the soul to the Underworld; b. he controls the nervous system (the nerves as messengers) and sleep; c. he brings out the Graces in spring as the fertilizing god of nature . . . 2. as a male Hecate he is god of the roads: a. often triform: with three heads (= directions and potentialities); b. he safeguards the roads . . . b. he is the protector of animals: the ram (or lamb)-carrying Hermes as Good Shepherd . . . the power of the Spoken Word, scattered about the universe; (later) the immanent and transcendent god in the world . . . he bargained with Apollo over the lyre and flute; b. eloquence . . . science, art, skill: the inventory of the lyre . . . strategy, cunning: he stole Apollo's cows as a child, which also made him a patron of thieves, frauds, gamblers, etc.; 7. the paragon of manly grace . . . in God: the Holy Spirit; b. in man: conscience, sometimes intelligence; c. the male principle . . .*

But perhaps above all else the blues-oriented hero image represents the American embodiment of the man whose concept of being able to live happily ever afterwards is most consistent with the moral of all dragon-encounters: Improvisation is the ultimate human (i.e., heroic) endowment. It is indeed; and

fifth arrow: bull's eye

even as flexibility or the ability to swing (or to perform with grace under pressure) is the key to that unique competence which generates the self-reliance and thus the charisma of the hero, and even as infinite alertness-become-dexterity is the functional source of the magic of all master craftsmen, so may skill in the art of improvisation be that which both will enable contemporary man to be at home with his sometimes tolerable but never quite certain condition of not being at home in the world and will also dispose him to regard his obstacles and frustrations as well as his achievements in terms of adventure and romance.

Albert Murray

Anthony Braxton is a seminal figure among Western musical innovators who are drawing on the global (especially, in his case, African) roots of the international Western cultures, finding there the common primal ground from which to move into a present and future of timely reconciliations of timeless conflicts.[3] His/their approach isn't so much a conscious application of past patterns to modern contexts as it is a free play of the creative imagination from its traditional base into what is new and original. As it develops, it leads the artist to that which it resembles throughout time and space. Its own life, larger than the artist's personal imagination and idiom, becomes apparent in this network through time and space. Jungian concepts such as racial memory and collective unconscious are suggested in these resonances between personal and historical expressions. Ethnomusicologist John Blacking wrote:

> When people talk about creativity in terms of Muses and inspiration, they invariably refer to processes of unconscious cerebration such as Schönberg discussed in *Style and Idea* (1951). They are, in fact, talking about ways in which the human mind works in its "natural" state, unfettered by social and cultural conventions. They are talking about cognitive universals that all members of the species have in common . . . Thus musicians reared in mutually incomprehensible cultural traditions may use a common device which, because it is based on a universal mental structure, can resonate with listeners unfamiliar with the cultural or musical idiom. To do this, they must reach beyond the convention of their particular society to the universal mental processes of the species, beyond the stage of lip-service to conventional definitions of self (in terms of social status) and others (in terms of ethnic and other groupings), to an understanding of their common humanity and the reasons for variations in behavior.
>
> This is how the most personal composers can have the most universal appeal: they communicate to others at the level of the innate; they begin with cultural conventions, but transcend them by reorganizing their sound structures in a personal, but basically universal, way, rather than slavishly following culturally given rules.[4]

If a discussion of Braxton's work in millennial and metaphysical terms seems grandiose or essentialistically meaningless, then, we can remind ourselves that they are not unique to him. In the African traditions, not only presumption of but direct engagement with a transcendent realm—"peopled" with particular entities with distinct roles and personalities, and distinct relationships with both their own kind and humankind, from outside time—is the given and the goal of a musician. This engagement in the pan American/pan-African cultures has taken place in the context (among others) of Africanized Christian theologies and mythologies, including that of the Pentecostal/Millennial descent/return of the Holy Spirit/Messiah. Moreover, a musician so engaged is simply a person who does music to some degree or other, not some breed apart from the other modes of "worship." Music and musicians are everywhere and everywhen. As a trans-African man in the Western world of America, along with all that means, Braxton is fulfilling his role in the world to which he was born. The role itself is transcultural and transhistorical—we've examined his playing of it as means to that universal end, just as he plays it so.

Having done so, what should we say about it? How shall we name the *loa* riding his "horse," and what is it saying to us?

This is the way to start talking about it; people in a *vodou* ceremony discuss the spirits so, identifying them and their messages after a visitation and possession. Church people given to comparable rites talk about the Spirit coming into the group and having a particular feeling, and specific information is associated with a given presence.

If we were to apply our most current and general understanding of such things, in Western terms, to the music in which Braxton has developed and works, we might say, for example, that to talk about the music of Debussy, Miles Davis, or Lester Young, is to talk about the archetypal Lover;[5] or of that of John Coltrane, the King. We could speak of Mingus in terms of the Warrior, and perhaps Stockhausen, Cage, Parker, and Coleman as Shaman-Tricksters. Using this line, we would have to give Braxton (like Schönberg) the position of Magus, hands down: the one who spells things out, the spirit of knowledge, of context, the web within which all the other Muses find their proper and optimum place in relation to each other, the systembuilder, the wizard of alchemy and student and master of all its details. Lover, King, Trickster, and Warrior are all there too, but it is the Magus who stands at the fore in this body of work, and those who want or need their own particular session with that spirit would do best to turn to it for that.

Who does need the Magus? What redeems his role from that of mere cerebrator, one never preferable, most of all in music, to those of Lover, Warrior, and the others? Without the Magus, the others don't know how to direct themselves, they get sick, their energies get misplaced; the Lover loves wrongly the wrong thing for the wrong reasons in the wrong seasons, the King and Warrior get too soft or too hard and likewise misdirect and misspend their energies, the Trickster becomes a facile fool.

Music is a language with roots, like those of speech, in both inner and outer worlds. Those who learn it well and uniquely in order to master self-expression inevitably encounter the deep and simple roots of *its* (global) family tree; the musical equivalents of word origins, evolutions, and migrations and transmutations between peoples are there to unearth as they are in language. The

fifth arrow: bull's eye 449

more they are so unearthed, the more they reveal a history of consciousness and ideas, as well as a natural history. In the first two chapters I tried to trace the broad outlines of this history as suggested and evoked by Braxton's music and words. Before adding details, smoothing rough spots, and tightening loose ends for a summary, I recall (an altered) Fig. 3.1—the tipped hour-glass/battle-ax figure—as the most fruitful visual framework for all such summaries. It lends itself to the dynamic between Muse and artist, and the dimensions from personal to cosmic thereof, on which we can hang this summary discussion.

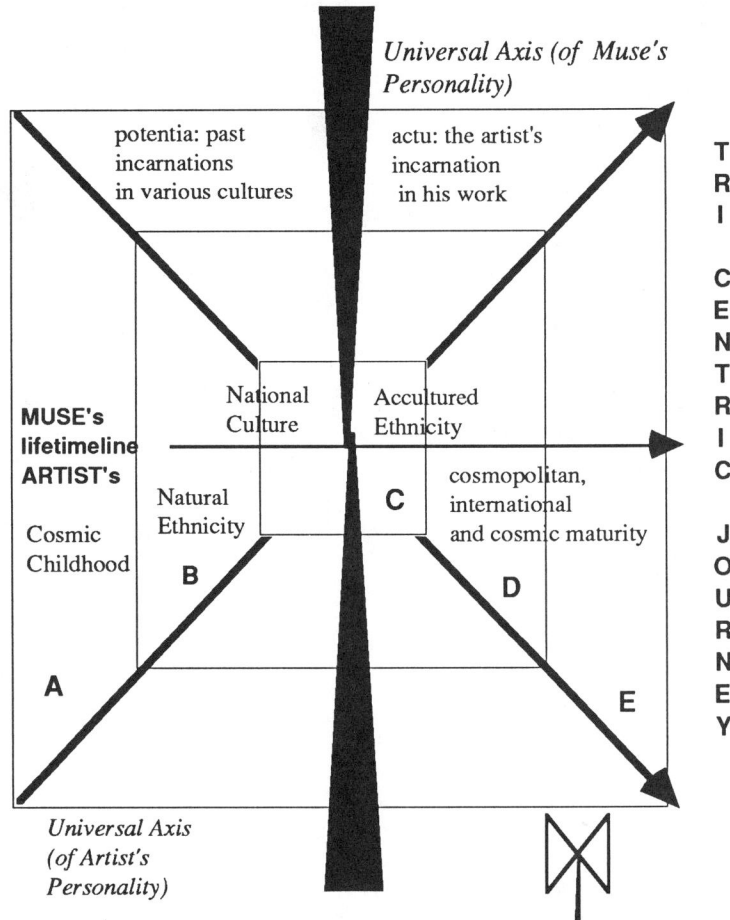

(Ancient Egyptian symbol for battle-ax)

Fig. 10.1: A picture of Braxton's place on (what he calls) the Universal Axis of creative and spiritual people engaged with their Muse throughout time and place.

Time

Fig. 10.2: Titian's The Allegory of Prudence[6] *is built from the artist's self-portrait and those of his apprentice and son. The three portraits represent old age, middle age and youth—past, present, and future—respectively. (The motto above it, in Latin, translates as "Learning from the past, the present acts prudently lest it ruin future action.") Beneath them is a three-headed animal (wolf/lion/dog) known in Renaissance times as a symbol of time. The beast dates from early Egypt, first appearing as companion to the sun god Serapis. The Roman scholar Macrobius wrote about it: "The lion's head . . . denotes the present, the condition of which between the past and the future, is strong and fervent by virtue of present action; the past is designated by the wolf's head because the memory of things that belong to the past is devoured and carried away; and the image of the dog, trying to please, signifies the outcome of the future, of which hope, though uncertain, always gives us a pleasing picture."[7]*

fifth arrow: bull's eye

Continuing the look at taproots, what *musical* phenomenon is special to Braxton's work, in relation to his chosen milieu (experimental music consciously synthesizing both the jazz and Western concert music traditions)? What overarching aspect of the music suggests the most to a look such as we've taken, to make it more (magically) efficacious than (musically) affected?

As Leo Smith said in the very beginning, it is his work on *time*. Time, as expressed in rhythm and meter, has been the most difficult aspect of the African musical presence in America for Westerners to grasp and master; in Braxton's work, the difficulty has been magnified, as he has been doggedly determined to engage with the most challenging parts of that difficult area. The Western legacy of philosophic and scientific literature about time[8] is relevant to the essence of Braxton's music, beyond its sheerly musical mechanics. Everything about his work—his "tri-axium" philosophy of past informing future; his ongoing integration of his current and planned work with his earlier work; his way of always talking about "time zones" and "cycles" in a way that describes equally, with little distinction, historical eras and bits of a personal life; and his equally constant way of referring to "the next thousand years" as though he were going to be at that party and is looking forward to it with great relish—all of this stems from a particular relationship with time that we associate with shamans and mystics and artists in their trance.

Braxton's musical contribution has been to restructure the rhythmic field, to *systematically* expand it from the narrow constraints of regular pulse and synchronicity between elements, of symmetrical patterns of same, into more evolved organisms that draw more flexible, mutable, multi-leveled *improvisational* lives from more evolved *compositions* of the metric-rhythmic aspect.

Considering music as sympathetic magic, the effect of this approach—especially, naturally enough, when it perseveres long enough in time to develop—is to take consciousness out of the "wheel of life and death," beyond its cycles of heart-beating moments, days, weeks, years, decades, and generations into the Eternal Moment (and all that takes place there).

Relative to the Western musicultural tradition, this gesture transcends the historical constraints that have distinguished between and set against each other the souls of oral and literate folk, thisworldly and otherworldly, Africa and West. Roving free of these constraints, our memory links up with the Western branchings from the taproot of the ancient shamanistic animism of both Africa and Europe, reclaims the common ground and initiates discussion there as to where to proceed next.

A respect for and healthy relationship with the fourth dimension of time is as essential to survival and life beyond survival as that for and with the three dimensions of space. If we hurtled through space as recklessly as we do through time, we would drive ninety miles an hour down a dead-end street, would wander blithely in front of that which would mow us down from behind or beside, would lie down without a thought of the possibilities of standing and walking upright, and would hurl ourselves off a high cliff oblivious to the concept of crash. If we perceived and maneuvered within time as easily, gracefully, and automatically as we do in space, we would see every beginning and end of everything from every point. We would discern the loves, friendships, and alliances that benefited us from those that didn't as instantly as we discern a hot stove from one that is safe to touch. We would discern the causes of all dilemmas and their resolutions from that which merely appeared to be so, and act accordingly. Music does offer a way to such a relationship with time, and Braxton has taken on that way and worked it in his own music. I suggest that his music and the words he has been compelled to write and speak grow from his experience of this work.

Global

Return with me to the discussion of entoptic images found in both prehistoric African and European cave art. In the BBC program *Images of Another World* (see footnote 11, Chapter One), the point was made that sensory deprivation and sensory overload both lead to the same altered state in the nervous system that generates, first, the (universal) entoptic images and, when the state intensifies, the (culturally specific) deeper hallucinations of realistic images. We have every reason to believe that the people of the North (who painted in the caves at Lascaux and others) generally favored and developed the path of deprivation, while those in the South went instead for overload. Much of the European cave art is deep in chambers where the shaman could well have lain in silent darkness, entered his or her trance, then envisioned and made, by firelight, his or her art. This experience may be the taproot of the predominance in the West of the otherworldly God (even Plato's classic image of the relationship between *nous* and *phenomenon* takes place in a cave, as did the prophecies of the oracle at Delphi), of asceticism, of individualism, of the demonization of this material world and those who revere it.

The more southerly ancestors of the Bush people, on the other hand, had the impetus from climate and geography to prefer the route of sensory overload— that brought on by the most riotous and organized sound, rhythm, dancing, and general interaction with nature and community. The shamans found their solitude at the core of community at its most active, saw and expressed their visions there, dispensed their power there. The earliest historical religions and cultures developed there, from that "way of affirmation," in that hospitable environment. Egypt's celebrated preoccupation with death can be understood as its expression of the proper end of a life celebrated fully past such overload.

Braxton's music begs and suggests musings such as this because it embraces, orders, and honors both affirmative and negative paths, as if he indeed knows from experience that they lead to the same place. Tapping the common end of these two radically disparate means that have clashed so violently throughout history, and are still doing so, he suggests their reconciliation and the fruitful synergy of their global expression. The healthy person has plenty of room and need in life for both sound and silence, celebration and meditation, self and loss of self. So the healthy people and planet.

Blacking's book (see footnote 5, this chapter) is a commentary on the work of Percy Grainger, a pioneer in the field of ethnomusicology who forged a serious argument for a universal "world music" early in the century. Many of his observations pertain to Braxton, especially those on the relationship of intellect and form to feeling and content, music as a sociopolitical as well as a spiritual force, and the nature of creativity. These issues come to the fore, it seems, when one is seeking the feelings that survive transcendence of a given personal and

fifth arrow: bull's eye

cultural context, since emotions are typically so much more rooted in these contexts than is pure cerebration; and since the creativity that does transcend usually does so by embracing more, rather than fewer, personal and cultural contexts. A few of many such observations from Blacking will give a representative sample.

On the creativity:

> Geoffrey Crankshaw"s remark about lifting the particular to the universal has relevance in so far as people"s creativity has been shown to relate to their ability to live beyond culture and not for culture, and to have an open view of human relationships . . . Creativity, as distinct from exploratory behavior, seems to require what the psychologist Milton Rokeach (1963) called an "open mind," and Edward de Bono later (1969) described as "lateral thinking." Rokeach demonstrated that the ability to think creatively and to construct new forms is a function of personality. People low in ethnocentrism reveal a comprehensive cognitive organization, while people high in ethnocentrism reveal an underlying narrow cognitive organization. Thus the most "open mind," and hence the highest degree of creativity, belongs to those who see cultural experience in the broadest terms . . . As Constant Lambert said at the end of *Music Ho!*: "The artist who is one of a group writes for that group alone, whereas the artist who expresses personal experience may in the end reach universal experience."[9]

On intellect and emotion:

> Technical virtuosity and depth of expression are not incompatible or contradictory if they are conceived as complementary processes, and if we remember that there is what Susanne Langer called 'a life of feeling' . . . which is influenced by the public images of culture . . . It is important to treat feeling as a rational function, as Robert Witkin points out in his important book, *The Intelligence of Feeling* . . . and to recognize that 'emotion is essentially a purposive, creative state' which 'raises, transforms and symbolizes' . . . as Carl Jung has argued. It is not helpful to draw distinctions between the emotional and the cognitive . . . [10] [and] We are moved to creative and reflective thinking as a result of greater intensity of feeling.[11]

On music as a sociopolitical force:

> Karl Marx actually knew that art forms, especially when re-used, are "ideological disguises" . . . This general principle has been proved correct again and again, but I take issue with the notion that "in the first instance, the work of art honestly proclaims its ideological message," whilst "in its survival state, the original becomes a fake

and a prop of what Marx calls "false consciousness"" . . . Musical progress cannot be separated from political progress, nor political freedom from musical freedom . . . Under the subheading "The Tyranny of the Composer", Percy Grainger wrote, "The fact that art music has been written down instead of improvised has divided musical creators and executants into two quite separate classes, the former autocratic and the latter comparatively slavish . . . though the state of things obtaining among trained musicians for several centuries has been productive of isolated geniuses of an exceptional greatness unthinkable under primitive conditions, it seems to me that it has done so at the expense of the artistry of millions of performers"[12]

These two paragraphs sum up nicely the applicability of Blacking's and Grainger's vision to Braxton:

> Nevertheless, in every society there are some musicians whose compositions and performances are considered to be more original and more generally affecting than others. There is also the paradox that the more individual and personal composers are the more universal may be their appeal. One common explanation for this is that individuality and personal dominance are the most important human attributes, and the keys to cultural progress, and that in the universal struggle for survival, the less able will recognize and applaud these qualities in others and be thankful for the security that they afford. This is not the place to demolish the "great man" theory of history and music, except to point out that it tends to reduce communication in society to a process of domination and submission, with aggressive leaders and passive followers, so that musical performance becomes a matter of display and showing off. It also ignores the cooperative basis of tradition and invention, as well as the facts of creativity.[13]

The West

I'll make this short and to the point: consider Braxton's role as a figure in the *Western* musicultural drama as one whose work succeeds in the deep synthesis between improvisational-oral and compositional-literate to which he aspires. Consider him therefore to be as important to that drama, begun in our Western consciousness in the chants of the Middle Ages and stretching through Bach to Stockhausen, as the latter and other such figures he admires.[14] Consider his critics and detractors to be in the position of Theodor Adorno *vis-à-vis* Stravinsky, whom Adorno saw as a clever but trivial maker of pastiche and musical illusions. Finally, to place Braxton in the Western pantheon with an identifiable persona, see Leonard Bernstein's final lecture in the Norton Lecture series at Harvard.[15] Replace the name "Stravinsky" with the name "Braxton," and the name "Adorno" with the category "Braxton's critics," and presume the field of "turn-of-the-millennium world music" in place of "turn-of-the-century Western music," and see how it scans with the information presented here.

Braxton has much more personal affinity with Schönberg, Stockhausen, and Cage in that latter field than with Stravinsky, but I see parallels with Stravinsky's work and persona (not the least of which is their Gemini aspect) that are striking, and begging of inquiry.[16]

National

Musical language, consciousness, and ideas serve a different purpose than their verbal and literary counterparts. The latter have branched off into the purely mental experience of literacy.[17] The musical experience, on the other hand, puts written and spoken language in the musical *context* (of lyric, poetry, declamation, theater); it puts the artist's and listener's mental experience in the context of performance, utterance, gesture, and dance. It affords a collective the opportunity to come together and create, express, explore, and celebrate its persons and shared myths and creative potential.

Braxton is trying to put the experiences that literacy has made the most sheerly, profoundly, and far-reachingly mental—those of abstract thought—into their correspondingly extreme physical contexts. This move to claim the highest ivory towers of the West for grass-roots African ends is wholly consistent with the thrust of the "jazz" tradition; those towers are where the power is, and in America Braxton is one who has proven he belongs in their most recent extensions.

The historical move by African Americans to master Western idioms has often been characterized by competitiveness, clannishness, and attempts at intrigue. As they have tried to find their rightful place in a racist culture (including its music business and academia) that exploits and misappropriates rather than acknowledges, learns from, and honors and rewards their music and its artists and thinkers, they have had to be defensive. From early trumpeters, such as King Oliver, who covered their fingerings with handkerchiefs, to the beboppers trying to make a music "whitey" couldn't play, to the cultural black nationalists of the 1960s (and their current counterparts), that trend has been strong. Braxton has decidedly not participated in it; yet his openness and sharing of "secrets" has presented that much more starkly that which remains an enigma in America: the African as Westerner, as primal Westerner, as primal, centric American, calling the West, in America, to realign with its own professed principles and myths.

Regarding the West *as* America, Moore writes of Charles Ives' time and atmosphere:

> Romantics, and Victorians after them, gravitated toward music as best exemplifying the spiritual potentials of art. Since Plato, Western philosophy has been cognizant of music as an art uniquely abstract and uniquely affective. The paradoxes of Romantic and Victorian aesthetics grew and prospered when seeded in music: the art of emotional mathematics.

Schopenhauer placed idealist philosophy at the service of music. "Music is . . . by no means like the other arts, the copy of Ideas . . . but the copy of the will itself, whose objectivity the Ideas are. This is why the effect of music is so much more powerful and penetrating than that of the other arts, for they speak only of shadows, but it speaks of the thing itself" . . . A passage from the American music critic Lawrence Gilman merges Schopenhauer's idealist philosophy with the language of Christian devotion: " . . . The musician is . . . privileged to pass beyond . . . to the Platonic 'eternal archetypes' . . . For music, alone among the arts, can deal with those essences of which even ideas and concepts are projections . . . this is the Holy of Holies of all loveliness."[18]

Moore's image of Ives and his colleagues as nineteenth-century *centennial* prophets resonates with Braxton's own subjectively personal (yet informed) mythological relationship with the coming *Millennial* shift:

The fate of their redemptive culture rested on a future whose solid foundation it was the calling of centennial composers to construct. As Yankees and as Victorians, their progressive task was nothing less than to shape the future. Ives viewed "his music as an expression of theology and political thought," writes David Noble. "The rise of all to the spiritual out of the profane was how Ives defined the years of progress from 1900 to 1917." . . . The centennial composers huddled at the edge of their wilderness, the terrifying and seductive twentieth century. Like their Puritan ancestors, they were called to an errand. Through their art they must invest the future with sacred meaning.[19]

When we move from this global/millennial field of time to the American-historical (national) level of the musiculture, we begin to see the real-world expression of our own particular dilemmas and resolutions. We see in the music how the myths and rituals of Christianity and *vodou* met and interacted, clashed and synthesized over time into the first expressions of a real, inclusive American universe in the music of Ives and in the beginning of jazz. We looked at the supportive roles that Europeans, European and African Americans both, men and women, have played in that emerging American musiculture. We've seen the microcosm of it in Braxton's musical universe.

Speaking in the context of an American culture still in the process of forming, it is clear that the Muse's message in Braxton might go something like this:

America, like the world, houses all peoples. *None* of them—not the African, not the European, Asian, Latin nor Native American, not the woman, man, nor Jew nor Muslim nor Christian, neither the individual nor the group, not the composer nor the improviser, nor the oppressor nor the oppressed—will be happy or functional or strong until they *all* are. None (and all) of us are saints and/or demons; all of us have turned not only on each other but on ourselves since as far back as we can remember. History is a *civil* war's battlefield, *within* races and genders and nations and religions as much as *between* them. No one agenda may prevail over another, and all must find and/or forge their mutual enhancements together. Time doesn't stand still nor run like a broken record; yesterday's song is just that, and as long as we cling to it we get yesterday's tired old dilemmas and their limited parameters. Today and tomorrow, as yesterday's children, honor their parents by finding and being *themselves*. The passions we feel against each other *as* "others" must be transformed into passions *for* each other as complementary expressions of the same (American/androgynous/global/personal) self. Otherwise we'll continue to take turns savaging each other and ourselves as we have all along.

When one voices this message at one's Muse's behest, as Braxton started doing in his youth, it can empower one, ring loud and clear and righteous—but it may also come easy, cost little, and remain safely in the realm of abstract idealism. As it becomes clear to an artist (and his or her audience) that it is the Muse rather than oneself speaking, it also becomes clear that one is free to quit saying and living by and listening to it when it becomes difficult or painful to do so. But as one continues to engage the Muse, it also becomes clear how the ideal may take on reality through one's own being and life, and thus in the world. As it does become more real, turning away becomes less the option. Again, we're speaking here of a property of time: the strangest, most difficult place can become home, over time, as the most familiar and comfortable can become alien and hostile. How Braxton's work is perceived often says much about the perceiver's own engagement with Braxton's particular Muse and its message; it is obvious to anyone seeing him perform that the artist's own relationship to his music is the opposite of bloodless, clinical, or abstract.

Ethnic

To consider the Muse's aspect in the context of the African American community, especially in the immediate present, is to encounter the most disturbing and painful dilemma. As I write, the burning issue there is violence and crime among young males; Louis Farrakhan and the Nation of Islam are at the center of an ongoing controversy in the media; books and movies by and about African American men from youth to middle age, are offering a variety of testimonials to the rage, pain, and frustration encountered from the urban streets to the corporate glass ceilings of America. Spike Lee's movie about Malcolm X, the Rodney King beating and the ensuing riots in Los Angeles, and the O.J. Simpson trial are still fresh in recent memory.

For Braxton, this is virtually the same historical moment as its 1960s counterpart. As it was then, his interest in it is that of an open, thinking person with all the passion and compassion that comes with the territory of survival against daunting odds.

In terms of his music and the role it has taken on in its milieu, Braxton's response to this ongoing and deep dilemma has been extreme in both directions at once. His music's voice has from the first included the fire of the rage and moan of the pain and frustration core to the African American situation—but it has also cultivated the sunny gentleness and intrepid joy of (it must be said) love for the Western culture that many of his peers denounce as the source of that dilemma. This position of his has been attacked all along by the African American intelligentsia and fellow musicians for being something of an equivocating sell-out, the Tommish betrayal of the race.

Let's treat four points about that before we move on to finish, with the "personal" and "cosmic" aspects of our "biogram":

• rage and anger are healthy when directed at the source of one's problem—but when they grow to consume the person/community generating them, something is wrong. Furthermore, when wielded by the powerful, they are abuse; when by the powerless, self-destructive and impotent folly. Their health lie in their energy, in how it can be harnessed and put to creative, positive solutions. Strength and courage lie in one's ability to turn the fire into ice into life-giving water and air, not to burn one's enemies, self, and world; and

• responsible upward mobility from second-class to first-class citizenship is healthy, but when one's inner vision, options, resources, and freedom—one's soul—seem to narrow in proportion to one's access to more of someone *else's* vision/options/freedom—the world—something is wrong. A move from the "field" to the "house" is just that; it isn't a wrong move, but a narrow one. Let the house stand, and let the masters share power with the slaves—but the field is wide and yielding. Let new and better houses be built there, by and for neither masters nor slaves, and let a thousand gardens bloom;

• anyone who stakes their claim to humanity—especially at the expense of part or all of the rest of humanity—in accidents of birth such as gender, race, culture, nation, and even temporal position (i.e., one's historical position) is, Braxton's Muse suggests, still in cosmic kindergarten. And the "universal axis" comprises people from across the board of place, time, and humanity who will be happy to make that known in no uncertain terms, and to lead the way through the higher grade levels; and

• a chain is only as strong as its weakest link. America as a nation and culture can't afford to ignore the suffering of its people any more than a man with an overtaxed heart and high blood pressure can afford to keep eating, smoking, drinking, and stressing to the strains of his own blind and stupid compulsions.

Personal/Cosmic

As the biogram suggests, there's a point where the personal and the cosmic—Muse, music, and musician—stand in the world as one and the same. It is at that point not only that the most difficult questions get asked, but also answered. What is truth? How do we discern prophecy? How do we discern true from false prophecy (for "prophecy," read "art")? How do we tell the profound and significant from the trivial and deluded person or spirit? Which information should we ignore and which build our personal and cultural lives on?

fifth arrow: bull's eye

Braxton has paid his dues in the real world of spacetime; his music is out there doing its work as surely as that which perpetuates materialistic greed, racial chauvinism and enmity, blind conformity and mediocrity, and reactionary politics and aesthetics. The Muse has proven as benign as demanding; the artist did have his struggle, but he survived; his family life survived, his music is well documented, his professional position is secure. The burning issues that have made him a(n unwilling) figure of the same sort of controversy surrounding most artists of genius who die neglected, then enrich others in their death, are in a sense no longer his because that's a rap he beat. The issue now is what we as people, and as a people, might gain in terms of our own psychological and emotional, spiritual and creative lives by engaging the services of his Muse in his work and honoring it accordingly.

The cosmic and personal both are impossible to speak *about* without also speaking from *within* them. The cosmically personal is what is, what one can't escape, the self that says things like, "I'd love to sell out if only I could, but this is it, this is me, even if they kill me for it." No one could have done Braxton's music but him, and if it didn't exist, someone would have to invent it. That's where its authority lies; all the other realms of identity—national, cultural, ethnic—can be denied or shaped by choice, but death is the only thing that alters life there.

Questions of context and content have been inseparable and equally significant in this book. In the course of looking at musical examples, we encounter issues of context immediately: professional critics and scholars, fellow artists, and Braxton himself all operate from premises and definitions that share some common ground but also (frequently disputed) borders between mutually exclusive territories. The researcher's task is to take all primary and secondary sources into account and present them in new lights that in turn shine on the music they address.

My finding was that this music and the very written and spoken language that refers to it in Western journalism and scholarship are much more integrated in the (primary sources' and the music's own) oral tradition than in the (secondary sources') literate one. That fact alone makes a strong case for a critical perspective and framework built on the primary source of Braxton's writings—both the *Tri-Axium* books for their explication of the traditional bases he is working from, and the *Composition Notes* for the contributions he is making to those bases. To understand and express in the literate mode, as I am doing here, the need for this more oral approach is only a signpost; the thing itself is embodied in the music and in Braxton's writings and speech. His music has been more than sufficiently acknowledged, but not necessarily on its own terms. His writings were his attempt to convey those terms in terms awkward to the musician, those of literacy. Artist and his oral-traditional base have thus met his audience, critics, and their literate-traditional base halfway, so there can be no excuse or misunderstanding. So far, his books and notes have been acknowledged too, by a few dedicated specialists, but they have not been engaged so far as to change the rules of engagement themselves from literate toward oral. Perhaps the music has been so engaged, to a degree, but not to the extent that it has itself engaged the literate West.

My research and collaborations have sensitized me to the subconscious and intellectual uses to which American cultural "whiteness" and "blackness" can and have put each other.[20] My attempt here has been a co-creative rather than a race-free, culturally weighted, or pseudo-objective rationalistic dream. Many of Braxton's and my primal personal and musical influences were both white and black because (in our case) we are both Americans from urban centers. This emerging American identity looms larger in Braxton's work than in that of many because he consciously cultivates it. Traditions steeped in distinctions—"jazz," "concert music," "American Independent/experimental"—are what Braxton has sought to synthesize, not simply confound or superficially manipulate.

The oral tradition develops different skills and acuities than the literate, carries different values; to be really faithful to this music (and thus fulfill Western standards of literate scholarship), critics and scholars will have to make shifts as painful and awkward to them as their literate mode has proven to those making the music. Once that shift is made in regard to Braxton's work, the extent to which he is working within and embracing the broadest, most inclusive—most American—traditional base becomes clear; the logic of his own innovations according to traditional criteria then compels, bespeaks a cyclical nature that both deepens and furthers tradition. When it is misperceived as the "avant-garde" of a linear evolution, it cannot convey its magic to the perceiver, just as the trunk the blind man feels can not convey the whole elephant. The musical (and its correlative cultural) realities of fifty years ago—the neo-bop climate dominating the culture, the marketplace, the academy—remain the order of the day because they are all the literate mode (and its current musical counterpart, the diatonic-chromatic system) can handle. The culture has frozen there in fear and confusion because the next step looks like a leap into a non-Western void.

But it is not. It is a leap into an American plenum, scouted, staked, and already developed for habitation by Anthony Braxton.

---

1. Fabre D'Olivet, *Music Explained as Science and Art and Considered in its Analogical Relations to Religious Mysteries, Ancient Mythology, and the History of the World* (from the 1928 edition of Jean Pinasseau, Rochester, VT: Inner Traditions International, 1987: 90-2).

2. For a nice current wrap on women's musical traditions in the West (mostly) from ancient times to the present, see *Rediscovering the Muses: Women's Musical Traditions* (Marshall, Kimberly, ed., Boston: Northeastern University Press, 1993).

3. See Heffley, "Sounding Old, Sounding New" (*Chamber Music*, December 1992: 26-36), for a sampling of such artists.

4. John Blacking, *A Common-sense View of All Music: Reflections on Percy Grainger's Contribution to Ethnomusicology and Music Education* (Cambridge: Cambridge University Press, 1987: 33-34).

5. The reader will recognize these as Jungian terms (see Moore and Gillette, and Shinoda-Bolen, footnote 41, Chapter One); they aren't suggested rigidly, as each of these musicians has elements of all the different "Muses," but shows an extra measure of the one mentioned.

6. Reprint photo from the National Gallery in London.

7. From Erwin Panofsky's *Meaning in the Visual Arts* (New York: Doubleday, 1957: 153), quoted in Grudin, 11.

8. A less ambitious and perhaps more refreshing dip into that pool is provided nicely by Grudin's book. As he points out, Mnemosyne (memory, a function of time) is the mother of the Muses. Sidney Bechet called jazz "the remembering song."

9. Blacking (1987), 42, 126.
10. Ibid., 74–75.
11. Ibid., 64.
12. Ibid., 104, 107, 108.
13. Ibid., 33–34.
14. Dudley Young (xxxii–iii), our source of the "chimp music" in Chapter One, says something about Beethoven's last piano sonata that goes to what I'm trying to say here: "This piece is a wonder of sanity regained, also a prophecy: after some initial argument melody returns gracefully to its home in the human body, and the syncopated rhythms point amiably and unmistakeably forward to ragtime and the jazz age. As he leaves the stage, this last of the European grandmasters quietly announces that he has concluded (consummated and killed) a musical life that had begun in medieval plainsong. As Vico would say, it was time for a *ricorso* to primitive beginnings, and Beethoven tells us here that we should look for it not in Wagner's Europe but in the southern states of America, where the chanting equivalent of monastic plainsong would be the Negro "holler" that had come from West Africa . . . the jazz that evolved from holler and folk music has housed as best it could the wandering soul of the twentieth century, and I know of little genuinely life-enhancing music from our time that is not jazz-based . . . Although much of our jazz became old and unhappy some time ago, leaving us once again spiritually adrift, with 'no direction home' in important respects, its origins offer most of us a more accessible meditation 'in the meantime' than does plainsong. In the beginning is the holler."
15. Leonard Bernstein at Harvard, "The Poetry of the Earth" (*The Unanswered Question*, the Norton Lectures: Columbia M4X 33032: 1973).
16. Stravinsky's music reached back to primeval roots; his complexities of rhythm and harmony result from layering independent simplicities; he was accused by Adorno of being a facile fraud, a clever artist of the pastiche; he synthesized disparate historical and philosophical streams of the music (classicism and modernism, tonal and atonal), to name a few of the most obvious parallels. Also, he said this: "Music is given to us with the sole purpose of establishing an order in things, including, and particularly, the coordination between man and time" (John Blacking, "Percussion and Transition," *Man*, N.S. 3: 314). The fact that Braxton's music resonates with both Stravinsky's and Schönberg's goes to his role as synthesist of opposites.
17. See Anne Carson's *Eros: The Bittersweet* (New Jersey: Princeton University Press, 1986) for its brilliant evocation of the exhilarating and unsettling impact of literacy on ancient Greek (bardic) consciousness.
18. M.S. Moore, *Yankee Blues: Musical Culture and American Identity* (Bloomington: Indiana University Press, 1983: 48-49).
19. Ibid., 63.
20. See Toni Morrison's *Playing in the Dark: Whiteness and the Literary Imagination* (Cambridge, MA and London, England: Harvard University Press, 1992: 65) for her point that American notions of freedom (like, I would point out in this context, ancient Egyptian and Athenian) are predicated on the social institution of a slave class. Braxton's refusal to play this Africanist role of foil to the white self-image has estranged him from the expectations both of the latter and of the African American community. He has languished as an artist in spite of consistent diligence and discipline, critical and scholarly acclaim, and important contributions. He has in this demonstrated the truth of Morrison's observation that African humanity can get obscured by a culture that appropriates it for its own cultural identity, yet fails to bestow that identity on its very source: "In what public discourse does the reference to black people not exist? It exists in every one of this nation's mightiest struggles.

The presence of black people is not only a major referent in the framing of the Constitution, it is also in the battle over enfranchising unpropertied citizens, women, the illiterate. It is there in the construction of a free and public school system; the balancing of representation in legislative bodies; jurisprudence and legal definitions of justice. It is there in theological discourse; the memoranda of banking houses; the concept of manifest destiny and the preeminent narrative that accompanies (if it does not precede) the initiation of every immigrant into the community of American citizens. The presence of black people is inherent, along with gender and family ties, in the earliest lesson every child is taught regarding his or her distinctiveness. Africanism is inextricable from the definition of Americanness—from its origins on through its integrated or disintegrating twentieth-century self."

Appendix

Laughable error and profound discovery are born of the same freedom.

Robert Grudin

The slapstick protagonist, like the jam-session soloist, is either nimble or nothing. Moreover, of all the storybook heroes he is perhaps the most comprehensive as well as the most sophisticated archetype of the "successful" individual...His definition of integrity, for instance, is much more complicated than that of the tragic hero. Thus he is less vulnerable to the fatal flaw of pride...he values his mission, responsibilities, blessings, or long-range aspirations so highly that he can withstand any embarrassment and can even regard humiliation as a passing episode (which incidentally gives him useful information about his adversary's pride).

Albert Murray

Basically, if I had one paragraph to explain myself and my work, I would say that I simply hope that anyone who hears my music or reads an article about me will be moved to re-examine things and establish perspectives that aren't found in the media. Re-examine for yourself what is happening because there are many wonderful things happening in musical creativity that are being choked by alien definitions by people whose intentions are separate from those of the music, and it's hurting the culture. Braxton is not that weird—I grew up in the culture and have experienced many of the same things everybody else has. It's just that my life's work is about creativity, and I have pursued a path that is not sanctioned. But that doesn't mean that the path is not valid...
  I'm tired of being controversial, though I see it as a validation . . . I don't want the controversy anymore. I just want to be involved in my life and present that which I have worked on and am working on . . . I would just like to show people—young people especially—that creativity is a pursuit worth devoting your life to.

Anthony Braxton

Partial versions of Anthony Braxton's *Complete Catalogue of Works* are included in the books of Lock, Radano, and Wilson. The following (from *Composition Notes*) provides the next best thing to having the composer on hand to conduct and explain the mechanics and spirit of his work, and how best to approach it.

INTRODUCTION TO "CATALOGUE OF WORKS"

The body of "musics" that make up this Catalogue of Works represent the "best I could do" when confronted with the incredible gifts of beauty that the Masters have given us in the phenomenon we call music. I perceive this effort as an evolving MULTI-LOGIC sound universe that demonstrates sonic unification on three primary planes of perception dynamics—abstract realization, concrete realization and intuitive realization. All of these matters are part of the wonderful world of sound wonder and beauty—I am so grateful for music and the "act of thinking about music/feeling." Life on earth would be impossible without music—our species could not exist without love and compassion. All of these matters are related.

The construction of this body of works has been my main preoccupation since 1967 and as such it is my responsibility to present this material as correctly as possible—THAT IS: it is important for the reader to understand the overcontext that gives this material its "perceived meaning" (LIFE). This is necessary because all of these works are part of one organic sound world state—and all of these efforts seek to affirm my life experiences: that being, what I have learned and experienced in my actual (REAL) life—as perceived from my value systems—rather than from imposed social and/or political values. This difference is important and must be taken into account or real penetration (insight) into this material could be "complex" (smile). As such, I would like to establish a general overview about this material for future musicologists and musician/interpreters so that any person interested in my work will have some idea of my values and "way of being." My comments in these notes will apply to every composition in this catalogue—and will encompass all additional entries I hope to add. Indeed, I am really commenting on the aesthetic tenet axiums of my music system/platform (life).

The most important feature of the body of material that must first be understood is that this information represents the vibrational fluid and atomic structural ingredients of one dynamic sound state (intention). That is, I have approached this material with respect to my needs as an instrumentalist as well as composer. With this effort I have tried to erect a "perception context" that respects and allows for both disciplines (improvisational/fluid musics and notated/stable musics) to exist and evolve—as unified and independent realities (with its own secrets and particulars). I have designed this material as an affirmation of "SOUND" AND MUSIC SCIENCE—as a response to the great African, European, and Asian men and women who have clarified the profound "beauty" of that which we call music. There are no words to adequately express

appendix

my gratitude to the heavens for the fact of "reception and definition." Music is profoundly interwoven into the total experience of existence.

There are four fundamental postulates that must be understood about this material if my objectives are to be respected (or understood), that being:

I. All compositions in my music system connect together

II. All instrumental parts in my group of musics are autonomous

III. All tempos in this music state are relative (negotiable)

IV. All volume dynamics in this sound world are relative

Let me clarify:

A. a) All compositions in my music system can be executed at the same time/moment. That is, this material in its entirety can be performed together as one state of being—at the same time (in whole or in part—in any combination). This option is the aesthetic conceptual/vibrational/fulfillment of my music.
    b) Shorter works can also be positioned into larger works—into any section of a given "host" composition.
    c) Isolated parts from a given structure can be positioned into other structures—or one structure—as many times as desired.
    d) Any section (part) of any structure can be taken and used repeatedly by itself or with another structure—or structures.

B. a) All instrumental parts in these groups of compositions are changeable—that is, any instrumental part can be used by any instrument—or instruments. Or any section from a given structure can be spliced out and integrated into another structure. What this means is that the harmonic reality of a given structure has vertical, linear, and correspondence realities (logics) that transcend any one plane of definition. All notated pitches in this music state involve only the primary imprint reality of a given form—as viewed from its origin/identity instrumentation. Every part can also be utilized (or "adopted") by any instrument or instrumentation. In other words, every solo piece can be an orchestra piece—in any order or sequence. Every orchestral instrumental part can be taken away from its "identity territory" and used by itself or with another piece or pieces.
    b) A given performer or group of performers can take any part of any composition (or compositions) and use that material

as solo or combination material. A given performer can sequence parts of different compositions into one music/type for one musician or for as many musicians as desired. Structural material used in this manner becomes a reservoir of structural and conceptual possibilities—including traditional interpretation.

C. a) All tempos in my music system are relative. That is—the initial "indicated" tempo of a given composition is only a point of definition for the unified imprint state of that work and is not intended as the only option. What this means is that the "life" of a given structure in this system has limitless possibilities—"settings" or "colors."

b) Every composition in this music world can be executed in any tempo—in the same way that a composition of Duke Ellington's can be played as a ballad or as a fast piece. Primary tempo designations are also included so that the interpreter can have every option available.

c) Each composition contains open duration spaces where time/space adjustments and parameters can be treated creatively.

D. a) All volume dynamics in this universe of music are relative. What this means is that volume adjustments can be made when two or more given instrumentalists perform (execute) different compositions together.

b) Each person can respect his or her physical and vibrational particulars when dealing with the physical demands (and challenges) of the music.

c) Performers are encouraged to look for "affinities" and "composite sound states" based on the collective dynamics of the ensemble. All of these matters will affect the music in every way.

The reality of this system seeks to establish fresh concepts about structure (FORM) and participation dynamics. What this means is that architecture and vibrational properties in this sound world are designed to establish **1) an individual reality context** (i.e., solo manipulations and strategies); **2) a collective or ensemble reality context** (i.e., interactive strategies for large and small ensemble groups); and finally, **3) a correspondence reality context** (one that establishes the interconnection logics—"WORLDS"—between structures).

I would also like to make four additional comments about this material to hopefully give insight into those things I would want any person interested in my music system to know about.

My comments are:

a. Have fun with this material and don't get hung up with any one area.

b. Don't misuse this material to have only "correct" performances without spirit or risk. Don't use my work to "kill" young aspiring students of music (in other words—don't view this material as only a technical or emotional noose that can be used to suppress creativity). If the music is played too correctly it was probably played wrong.

c. Each performance must have something unique. I say take a chance and have some fun. If the instrumentalist doesn't make a mistake with my materials, I say "Why!? NO mistake—NO work!" If a given structure concept has been understood (on whatever level) then connect it to something else, something different—be creative (that's all I'm writing).

d. Finally, I recommend as few rehearsals as possible so that everyone will be slightly nervous—and of course put in "emergency cues" just in case anything goes wrong. Believe me there will be days when nothing works at all. Also try and keep the music "on the line" to maintain the "spark of invention," and be sure to keep your sense of humor.

Good Luck,

Anthony Braxton
Mills College 1988

P.S. (and please don't make the music too "cutesy")

Sources

Books

Adorno, Theodor. *Philosophy of Modern Music*. New York: The Seabury Press, 1973.

Apel, Willi. *The Notation of Polyphonic Music 900–1600*. Cambridge MA: The Medieval Academy of America, 1961.

Bacon, Francis. *New Atlantis*. Cambridge (Eng.): University Press, 1919.

Baker, David, ed. *New Perspectives on Jazz*. Washington, DC and London: Smithsonian Institution Press, 1986.

Bauval, Robert and Adrian Gilbert. *The Orion Mystery*. London: Heinemann, 1994.

Ben-Jochannon, Yosef. *Africa, the Mother of Western Civilization*. New York: Alkebu-Lan Associates, 1971.

Blacking, John. *A Common-sense View of All Music: Reflections on Percy Grainger's Contribution to Ethnomusicology and Music Education*. Cambridge (Eng.): Cambridge University Press, 1987.

Bleibtreu, John, *The Parable of the Beast*. Macmillan: Toronto, 1968.

Boggs, Vernon W. *Salsiology: Afro-Cuban Music and the Evolution of Salsa in New York City*. New York: Excelsior, 1993.

Bolen, Jean Shinoda. *Goddesses in Everywoman: A New Psychology of Women*. San Francisco: Harper & Row, 1984.

Braxton, Anthony. *Composition Notes A, B, C, D,* and *E*. Hanover, NH: Tree Frog Music, 1988.

_____ *Tri-Axium Writings 1, 2, & 3*. Hanover, NH: Tree Frog Music, 1985.

Cage, John. *Empty Words: Writings '73–'78*. Middletown, CT: Wesleyan University Press, 1979.

Carson, Anne. *Eros: The Bittersweet*. New Jersey: Princeton University Press, 1986.

Chailley, Jacques. *40,000 Years of Music: Man in Search of Music*. New York: Farrar, Straus & Giroux, 1964.

Charters, Samuel. *The Roots of the Blues: An African Search*. Boston/London: Marion Boyars, 1981.

Churchward, Albert. *Signs and Symbols of Primordial Man: The Evolution of Religious Doctrine from the Eschatology of the Ancient Egyptians*. London/New York: E. P. Dutton & Co., 1910.

Cole, William. *John Coltrane*. New York: Schirmer, 1976.

Crouch, Stanley. *The All-American Skin Game*. New York: Pantheon Books, 1995.

Crump, Thomas. *The Anthropology of Numbers*. New York: Cambridge University Press, 1990.

D'Olivet, Fabre. *Music Explained as Science and Art and Considered in Its Analogical Relations to Religious Mysteries, Ancient Mythology, and the History of the World.* From the 1928 edition of Jean Pinasseau, Rochester, VT: Inner Traditions International, 1987.

Davis, Francis. *In the Moment: Jazz in the 1980s.* New York: Oxford University Press, 1986.

_____ *Outcats: Jazz Composers, Instrumentalists, and Singers.* New York: Oxford University Press, 1990.

De Vries, Ad. *Dictionary of Symbols and Imagery.* Amsterdam/Holland: North Holland Publishing Co., 1974.

Diop, C. A. *The African Origin of Civilization.* Chicago: Third World Press, 1978.

Fleischer, Oskar. *Neumenstudien: Abhandlugen uber mittealterliche Gesangs–Tonschriften.* Leipzig 1895, Berlin 1897, Berlin 1904.

Fox, Matthew, ed. *Hildegard of Bingen's Book of Divine Works, with Letters and Songs.* Santa Fe, NM: Bear & Co., 1987.

Gaume, Miriam. *Ruth Crawford Seeger: Memoirs, Memories, Music.* New Jersey/London: Scarecrow Press, 1986.

Gaustad, Edwin S., ed. *History of Religion in America to the Civil War.* Grand Rapids, MI: William B. Eerdmans, 1982.

Gleick, James. *Chaos: Making a New Science.* New York: Viking, 1987.

Goldberg, Joe. *Jazz Masters of the 50s.* New York: Macmillan, 1963.

Goswami, Amit, with Richard Reed and Maggie Goswami. *The Self-Aware Universe: How Consciousness Creates the Material World.* New York: G.P. Putnams Sons, 1993.

Graves, Robert. *Difficult Questions, Easy Answers.* London: Cassell, 1972.

Gray, John. *Fire Music: A Bibliography of the New Jazz, 1959–1990.* New York/Westport, CT/London: Greenwood Press, 1991.

Green, M. *The Reluctant Art: The Growth of Jazz.* New York: Horizon Press, 1963.

Grudin, Robert. *Time and the Art of Living.* New York: Ticknor & Fields, 1982.

Hodeir, André. *Jazz: Its Evolution and Essence.* New York: Grove Press, 1956.

Hudson, L. and B. Jacot, *The Way Men Think: Intellect, Intimacy, and the Erotic Imagination.* New Haven & London: Yale University Press, 1991.

James, G.G.M. *Stolen Legacy: the Greeks Were Not the Authors of Greek Philosophy, But the People of North Africa, Commonly Called the Egyptians.* New York: Philosophical Library, 1954; reprinted San Francisco: Julian Richardson Associates, 1976.

Jost, Ekkehard. *Free Jazz.* Grasz: Universal Edition, 1974.

Koestler, Arthur. *The Slepwalkers: A History of Man's Changing View of the Universe.* New York: Grosset & Dunlap. 1963.

Kofsky, Frank. *Black Nationalism and the Revolution in Music.* New York: Pathfinder Press, 1970.

Küng, Hans. *On Being a Christian.* New York: Doubleday, 1976.

Lee, E. *Jazz: An Introduction.* London: Kahn & Averill, 1972.

Leonard, Neill. *Jazz: Myth and Religion*. New York/Oxford: Oxford University Press, 1987.

Litweiler, John. *The Freedom Principle: Jazz after 1958*. New York: W. Morrow, 1984.

_____ *Ornette Coleman: A Harmolodic Life*. New York: William Morrow & Co., 1993.

Lock, Graham. *Forces in Motion: Anthony Braxton and the Meta-Reality of Creative Music*. London: Quartet Books, 1985.

_____ *Forces in Motion: The Music and Thoughts of Anthony Braxton*. New York: Da Capo Press, 1988.

Lovejoy, Arthur. *The Great Chain of Being: A Study of the History of an Idea*. New York: Harper & Row, 1960.

Lott, Eric. *Love and Theft: Blackface Minstrelsy and the American Working Class*. New York: Oxford University Press, 1993.

MacNulty, W. Kirk. *Freemasonry: A Journey through Ritual and Symbol*. London/New York: Thames & Hudson, 1991.

Maconie, Robin. *The Works of Karlheinz Stockhausen*. London: Oxford University Press, 1976.

Malcolm X. *The Last Speeches*, Bruce Perry, ed. New York, London, Sydney, Toronto: Pathfinder Press, 1989.

Manniche, Lise. *Music and Musicians in Ancient Egypt*. London: British Museum Press, 1991.

Maslow, Abraham. *Toward a Psychology of Being*. Princeton: New Jersey: Van Nostrand, 1962.

McKenna, Terrence. *The Archaic Revival*. San Francisco: Harper, 1991.

McKinnon, James, ed. *Antiquity and the Middle Ages from Ancient Greece to the 15th Century*. Englewood Cliffs, NJ: Prentice-Hall, 1991.

Mellers, Wilfrid. *Music in a New Found Land*. New York: Hillstone, 1964.

Mezzrow, Mezz and Bernard Wolfe. *Really the Blues*. New York: Random House, 1946.

Mingus, Charles. *Beneath the Underdog: His World as Composed by Mingus*. New York: Knopf, 1971.

Moore, M. S. *Yankee Blues: Musical Culture and American Identity*. Bloomington: Indiana University Press, 1983.

Moore, Robert and Douglas Gillette. *King, Warrior, Magician, Lover: Rediscovering the Archetypes of the Mature Masculine*. San Francisco: Harper, 1990.

Morgan, Robert P. *Twentieth-Century Music*. New York: W.W. Norton & Co., 1991.

Morrison, Toni. *Playing in the Dark: Whiteness and the Literary Imagination*. Cambridge, MA, and London, England: Harvard University Press, 1992.

Murray, Albert. *Stomping the Blues*. New York: Da Capo Press/Plenum Publishing, 1976.

_____ *The Hero and the Blues*. University of Missouri Press, 1973.

Panassié, Hugues. *Hot Jazz: The Guide to Swing Music*. New York: M. Witmark & Sons, 1936.

Panofsky, Erwin. *Meaning in the Visual Arts*. New York: Doubleday, 1957.

Peretti, Burton W. *The Creation of Jazz: Music, Race, and Culture in Urban America*. Urbana and Chicago: University of Illinois Press, 1992.

Radano, Ronald. *New Musical Figurations: Anthony Braxton's Cultural Critique*. Chicago/London: University of Chicago Press, 1993.

Russell, Robert Jay. *The Lemur's Legacy: The Evolution of Power, Sex, and Love*. New York: Jeremy P. Tarcher/Putnam, 1993.

Sanjek, Roger. *Fieldnotes: The Makings of Anthropology*. Ithaca & London: Cornell University Press, 1990.

Sayers, Dorothy. *Mind of the Maker*. London: Methuen & Co., 1947.

Sheldrake, Rupert. *The Presence of the Past: Morphic Resonance and the Habits of Nature*. New York: Times Books, 1988.

Sidran, Ben. *Black Talk*. New York: Da Capo Press, 1981.

Smith, Bill. *Imagine the Sound No. 5: The Book*. Nightwood Editions, 1985.

Stockhausen, Karlheinz. *Towards a Cosmic Music*. London: Element Books Limited, 1989.

Thompson, Robert Farris. *Flash of the Spirit: African and Afro American Art and Philosophy*. New York: Random House, 1983.

Thomson, Virgil. *Twentieth-Century Composers: American Music Since 1910, Volume I*. New York: Holt, Rinehart & Winston, 1971.

Troupe, Quincey. *Miles Davis: The Autobiography*. New York: Simon & Schuster, 1989.

Ullman, Michael. "Anthony Braxton," *Jazz Lives*. New York: G.P. Putnam, 1980.

Vecellio, Tiziano. *Titian: Paintings and Drawings*. Vienna: Phaidon Press, 1937.

Wheeler, John. *Between Quantum and Cosmos*. New Jersey: Princeton University Press, 1988: 2, 614.

Williams, Charles. *Taliessin Through Logres*. Grand Rapids, MI: William B. Eerdmans, 1974.

Wilmer, Valerie. *As Serious As Your Life: The Story of the New Jazz*. London: Quartet Books, 1977.

Wilson, Robert Anton and Robert Shea. *The Illuminatus Trilogy*. New York: Dell, 1975.

Young, Dudley. *Origins of the Sacred: The Ecstasies of Love and War*. New York: St. Martin's Press, 1991.

Articles

Adams, D. and A. Goldbard. "Grass Roots Vanguard," *Art in America*, Vol. 70, no. 4, 1982: 24.

Albertson, Chris. "Braxton's Basics," *Stereo Review* (review), Aug. 1985: 71.

Bannister, Gary. "Eugene 1989," *Earshot Jazz*, September 1992: 14.

Bergstein, Barry. "Miles Davis and Karlheinz Stockhausen: A Reciprocal Relationship," *Musical Quarterly* Winter, 1992: 502–25.

Blacking, John. "Percussion and Transition," *Man*, n.s. 3.

Carson, Tom. "Greece is the Word: Afrocentrism and Its Discontents," *Village Voice*, April 16,1996: 20-21.

Carey, Joe. "Anthony Braxton Interview," *Cadence*, Mar. 1984.

Davidson, Basil. "The Ancient World and Africa: Whose Roots?" *Race and Class*, Vol. 29, no. 2, 1987: 1-16.

Feather, Leonard. "Blindfold Test: Phil Woods," *Down Beat* (review), Oct. 14, 1971: 33.

Gioia, Ted. "Jazz and the Primitivist Myth," *The Musical Quarterly*, Vol. 73 no. 1, 1989: 130-43.

Hassan, Ihab. "The Culture of Postmodernism." In *Theory, Culture and Society*, Vol. 2 no. 3, 1985: 119–31.

Heffley, Mike. "Turtle Island String Quartet: America's String Savers?" *Chamber Music*, Spring 1991: 26–29.

_____ "Sounding Old, Sounding New," *Chamber Music*, December 1992: 26-36.

Henschen, Bob. "Anthony Braxton: Alternative Creativity in This Time Zone," *Down Beat*, Feb. 22, 1979: 18-20.

Klee, Joe. "For Alto," *Down Beat* (review), June 24, 1971: 18.

Kostakis, Peter and Art Lange. "Conversation with Anthony Braxton," *Brilliant Corners: A Magazine of the Arts*, no. 4, Fall 1976: 53-99.

Lake, Steve. "Jazz Records," *Melody Maker*, July 27, 1974: 49.

Laskin, D.L.L. "Anthony Braxton: Play or Die," *EAR*, May 1989: 40-46.

Levin, Michael and John S. Wilson. "No Bop Roots in Jazz." Reprinted in *Down Beat*, February, 1994: 44.

Lewis-Williams, J. D. and T. A. Dawson. "The Signs of All Times: Entoptic Phenomena in Upper Paleolithic Art," *Current Anthropology*, Vol. 29 no. 2, Apr. 1988: 201–17.

Litweiler, John. "Record Reviews," *Down Beat* (review), June 5, 1975: 18.

Lock, Graham. "Still Life with Bass and Cello: David Holland in Pursuit of the Cubist Bass Line," *Wire*, London, May 1988: 46-49.

_____ "Jazz," *Wire*, London, 1992: 57-8.

Lynch, Kevin. "Anthony Braxton: Solo Live at Moers Festival (Ring 01002)," *Coda* (review), Feb. 1978: 18.

Mandel, Howard. "The Color of Music." Reprinted in *Down Beat*, February, 1994: 44.

Martin, Terry. "Braxton[8]." *Down Beat* (review), Apr. 1987: 43-48.

McRae, Barry. "For Trio," *Jazz Journal International*, September 1978: 35.

Metcalf, G. "Black Folk Art and the Politics of Art." In *Art, Ideology, and Politics*. Balfe, J. and Wyszomirski, J., eds. New York: Praeger, 1985: 176.

Mitchell, Charles. "Record Reviews: Anthony Braxton," *Down Beat* (review), Oct. 7, 1976: 20.

Penn, Roberta. "Selling Jazz Down the River," *The Rocket*, Seattle, Nov. 1991: 20-23.

Radano, Ronald. "Braxton's Reputation," *Musical Quarterly*, Vol. 72, no. 4, 1986: 503-22.

Reagon, Bernice Johnson. Foreword to *Reimaging America: The Arts of Social Change*. O'Brien, M. and Little, C., eds. Philadelphia/Santa Cruz: New Society Publishers, 1990.

Rout, Leslie. "The AACM: New Music (!) New Ideas (?)." *Journal of Popular Culture*, 1/2, Fall 1967: 128-137.

Saal, Herbret. "Two Free Spirits," *Newsweek*, Aug. 8, 1977: 52-53.

Santoro, Gene. "Anthony Braxton," *The Nation*, May 8, 1989: 642-44.

Shoemaker, Bill. "Anthony Braxton: The Dynamics of Creativity," *Down Beat*, Mar. 1989: 20-22.

_____ "Eddying Figures," *Down Beat* (review), Nov., 1990: 47.

Smith, Bill. "Anthony Braxton: Saxophone Improvisations Series F," *Coda* (review), Apr. 1974: 15-16.

_____ "The Anthony Braxton Interview," *Coda*, Apr. 1974: 2-8.

Stern, Chip. "Kelvin *7666* = Blip-Bleep," *Village Voice* (review), June 11, 1979: 61.

Tepperman, Barry. "Anthony Braxton: St. Clair Music Library, Toronto, June 16th, 1973," *Coda* (review), Oct., 1973: 43-44.

Tesser, Neil. "Montreux/Berlin Concerts." *Down Beat*, August 20, 1977: 22–23.

Townley, Ray. "Anthony Braxton," *Down Beat*, Feb., 1974: 12-13.

Ventura, Michael. "Hear That Long Snake Moan," *Whole Earth Review* No. 54, Spring 1987: 28.

Musical Recordings

I've listed only the recordings I've discussed. For an up-to-date discography (with compositions and recordings cross-referenced) that also includes some bibliographic material of general interest, order *Anthony Braxton: A Discography, A Complete Listing of the Recordings where Anthony Braxton Appears as Performer or Composer, Indexed by Composition* (1993+, online) from Francesco Martinelli, Lungarno Mediceo 10, 56127, Pisa, Italy.

By Braxton

Traditional Covers

In the Tradition, Vols. 1 & 2 (Inner City IC 2015 & 2045, 1974), with Tete Montoliu, piano; Niels-Henning Orsted Pedersen, bass; and Albert "Tootie" Heath, drums.

Seven Standards 1985, Vols. 1 & 2 (Magenta MA 0203 & 0205, 1985), with Hank Jones, piano; Rufus Reid, bass; and Victor Lewis, drums.

Six Monk's Compositions (1987) (Black Saint BS 120 116-1, 1989), with Mal Waldron, piano; Buell Neidlinger, bass; and Bill Osborne, drums.

Eight (+3) Tristano Compositions 1989 (Hat Art CD 6052, 1990), with John Raskin, bari saxophone; Dred Scott, piano; Cecil McBee, bass; Andrew Cyrille, drums.

Solo Alto

For Alto (Delmark DS 420/1, 1968): *8A, 8F, 8H, 8A/B, 8D, 8C, 8G, 8B.*
Saxophone Improvisations/Series F (Inner City IC 1008, 1972): *8I, 26A, 26J, 26B, 26D, 8J, 26C, 26I, 26F.*
Solo Live at Moers (Ring 01002, 1974): *26B, 26H, 77B, 26E, 26F, 26G.*
Alto Saxophone Improvisations 1979/Language Music (1967) (Arista A2L 8602, 1978/1979): *77A, 77C, 77D, 77E, 26F, 77F, 26B, 77G, 26E, 77H.*
Composition 113 (Sound Aspects SAS 003, 1983).
Solo (London) 1988 (Impetus Records IMP LP 18818, 1988): *106C, 118F(+99G), 138C, 99C, 138E, 99I.*

Duos

Duo (Emanem 3313/4(RI), 1974): open improvisations; with guitarist Derek Bailey.
Live at Wigmore (Inner City 1041, 1974): open improvisations; with guitarist Derek Bailey.
Trio and Duet (Sackville 3007, 1974): *The Song is You, Embraceable You, You Go To My Head*; with bassist David Holland.
Duets 1976 (Arista AL-4101, 1976): *60, 40P, 62*; and an open improvisation post-titled *Nickie*; with pianist Muhal Richard Abrams.
Elements of Surprise (Moers Music MOMU 01036, 1976): *64, 65*; with trombonist George Lewis.
Duets With Anthony Braxton (Sackville 3016, 1977): *40Q, 74A&74B*; with reeds player/composer Roscoe Mitchell.
Birth & Rebirth (Black Saint BSR 0024, 1978): open improvisations; with drummer Max Roach.
One in Two, Two in One (Hat Hut 2R06, 1979): open improvisations; with drummer Max Roach.
For Two Pianos (Arista AL 9559, 1980, released 1982): *95*, performed by pianists Frederic Rzewski and Ursula Oppens.
Four Pieces (Dischi Della quercia Q28015, 1981): *101*; with pianist/composer Giorgio Gaslini.
Open Aspects '82 (Hat Art 1995/96, 1982): open improvisation; with synthesist Richard Teitelbaum.
Six Duets (1982) (Cecma 1005, 1982): *6A & N; 23J; 69A, 69B, & 69P*; with bassist John Lindberg.
Duets 1987 (Ratascan 002, 1987): *86, 134(+96), 40D(96, 108B)*; with percussionist Gino Robair.

Kol Nidre (Sound Aspects 031, 1988): *85 & 87*; with reeds player/composer Andrew Voigt.

Duets, Vancouver 1989 (Music & Arts CD 611): *136, 140(+112+30), 62, 116;* with pianist Marilyn Crispell.

Eight Duets Hamburg 1991 (Music & Arts CD 710): *152–7, 40A*; with bassist Peter Niklas Wilson.

Nine Duets with Mario Pavone (1993) (CD-786 Music & Arts): *6(O), 29, 65, 87, 135*; with bassist Pavone.

Trios

Three Compositions of New Jazz (Delmark DS-415, 1968): *6E, 6D*, and (Leo Smith's) *The Bell*; with multiinstrumentalists Smith and Leroy Jenkins.

B-X°-NO/47A (Affinity 15, 1969): same personnel as above, *6G*.

Silence (Freedom FLP 40123, 1969); same personnel as above, no Braxton compositions.

Company 3 recordings: open improvisations with guitarist Derek Bailey and saxist Evan Parker (Incus 23 & 28; and 29 & 30 [also CD 07]).

This Time (Affinity 25, 1970); same personnel as above, *6H, 6F, 8K*, poem written and recited by Braxton.

Familie (Birth NJ 008, 1972): open improvs with vocalist Jeanne Lee and reeds/vibist Gunter Hampel.

Town Hall 1972 (CD: Art Union TKCB-30108): *6N, 6(O), 6P*; with bassist David Holland, percussionist Phillip Wilson (except on *6P*); and multiinstrumentalist John Stubblefield, percussionist Barry Altschul, and vocalist Jeanne Lee (on *6P*).

Four Compositions (1973) (Denon YX 7506): *23N, 23P, 23M, 23(O)*; with pianist Masahiko Sato, bassist Keiki Midorikawa, and percussionist Hozumi Tanaka (on *23(O)* only). *The Song is You, Embraceable You, You Go To My Head*; with bassist David Holland.

For Trio (Arista AL 4181, 1977): *76*; with multiinstrumentalists Roscoe Mitchell, Douglas Ewart, and Henry Threadgill.

Seven Compositions 1978 (Moers 01066, 1979): *69G, 40F, 69M, 40D, 40I, 69H, 69K; with* trombonist Ray Anderson, bassist John Lindberg, and percussionist Thurman Barker.

Compositions 99, 101, 107 & 139 (Hat Art CD 6019, 1988), with pianist Marianne Schroeder and trombonist Garret List.

7 Compositions (Trio) 1989 (Hat Art CD 6025, 1989): *40D, 40G (+63), 6A, 40J, 110A(+108B+96)*; with bassist Adelhard Roidinger and drummer Tony Oxley.

Quartets

The Complete Braxton (Freedom 400112/3[RI], Arista-Freedom 1902, 1971): *6K, 6J, 6A, 22, 6I, 4, 6L, 6M; with* pianist Chick Corea, bassist/cellist Dave Holland, and percussionist Barry Altschul.

Dona Lee (America 30 AM 6122, 1972): *23L, 23K*; playing alto & soprano sax, flute, and contrabass clarinet, with Michael Smith, piano; Peter Warren, bass; Oliver Johnson, drums.

Town Hall 1972 (CD: Art Union TKCB-30108): *6N, 6(O), 6P*; with bassist David Holland, percussionist Phillip Wilson (except on *6P*); and multiinstrumentalist John Stubblefield, percussionist Barry Altschul, and vocalist Jeanne Lee (on *6P*).

Four Compositions (1973) (Denon YX 7506): *23N, 23P, 23M, 23(O)*; with pianist Masahiko Sato, bassist Keiki Midorikawa, and percussionist Hozumi Tanaka (on *23(O)* only).

New York, Fall 1974 (Arista 4023): *23B, 23C, 23D, 38A, 37, 23A*; with trumpeter Kenny Wheeler, bassist Dave Holland, and percussionist Jerome Cooper (except on *38A & 37*); saxophonists Oliver Lake, Julius Hemphill, and Hamiett Bluiett (on *37*); synthesist Richard Teitelbaum (on *38A*); and violinist Leroy Jenkins (on *23A*).

Quartet Live at Moers Festival (Ring 01010/11, 1974): *23B, 23E, 40(O), 40M, 23F, 23D*; with trumpeter Kenny Wheeler, bassist Dave Holland, and percussionist Barry Altschul.

Five Pieces 1975 (Arista 4064): *23H, 23G, 23E, 40M;* with trumpeter Kenny Wheeler, bassist Dave Holland, and percussionist Barry Altschul.

Montreux/Berlin Concerts (Arista 5002, 1975): *40N, 23J, 40(O), 6C, 6F, 40K, 63* (same personnel as above).

Dortmund (Quartet) 1976 (hat Art 6075): *40F, 23J, 40(O), 6C, 40B;* with trombonist George Lewis, bassist Dave Holland, and percussionist Barry Altschul.

Composition 98 (hat Art CD 6062, 1981): with trumpeter Hugh Ragin, trombonist Ray Anderson, and pianist Marilyn Crispell.

Performance 9/1/79 (hat Hut 2R19): *69C, 69E, 69G, 40F, 69F, 23G, 40J*; with trombonist Ray Anderson, bassist John Lindberg, and percussionist Thurman Barker.

Six Compositions, Quartet (Antilles AN 1005, 1981): *40B, 69N, 40A, 34, 40G, 52*; with pianist Anthony Davis, bassist Mark Helias, and percussionist Ed Blackwell.

Four Compositions (Quartet) 1983 (Black Saint 0066): *105A, 69M, 69(O), 69Q*; with trombonist George Lewis, bassist John Lindberg, and percussionist Gerry Hemingway.

Prag 1984 "Quartet Performance" (sound aspects 038): *105A, 11A, 114, 69H*; with pianist Marilyn Crispell, bassist John Lindberg, and percussionist Gerry Hemingway.

Quartet (Birmingham) 1985 (Leo 202/203): *110A(+96+108B), 69M(+10+33+96), 60(+96+108C), 85(+30+108D), 105B(+5+32+96), 87(108C), 23J, 69H(+31+96), 40(O)*; with pianist Marilyn Crispell, bassist Mark Dresser, and percussionist Gerry Hemingway.

Quartet (Coventry) 1985 (Leo 204/205): *124(+30+96), 88(+108C+30+96), 30, 23G(+30+96), 40N, 69C(+32+96), 96* (drums), *69F, 69B, 96* (bass), *6A* (same personnel as above).

Quartet (London) 1985 (Leo 200/201): *122(+108A), 40(O), collage, 52, 86(+32+96), 30, 115, 105A, 96(percussion), 40F, 121, 116* (same personnel as above).

Five Compositions (Quartet) 1986 (Black Saint 0106): *131, 88(+108C), 124(+96), 122(+108A+96), 101(+31+96+30)*; with pianist David Rosenboom, bassist Mark Dresser, and percussionist Gerry Hemingway.

Willisau (Quartet) 1991 (hat ART CD 61001/4): *160(+5)+40J, 23M(+10), 158(+96)+40L, 40A, 40B, 161, 159, 23C+32+105B(+30), 23M(+10), 40M, 67(+147+96), 140(+147+139+135), 34A, 20+86, 23G(+147+30), 69(O)(+135), 69B, 107(96), 101, 23N(+112+108A+33)*; with pianist Marilyn Crispell, bassist Mark Dresser, and percussionist Gerry Hemingway.

Quartet (Victoriaville) 1992 (Victo CD 021): *159(+131+30+147), 148(+108A+139+147), 161, 158(+108C+147)* (same personnel as above).

Large Ensembles

Creative Music Orchestra (Ring 01024/5/6, 1972): *25*; with 14 players.

Creative Orchestra Music 1976 (Arista 4080): *51, 56, 58, 57, 55, 59*; with 22 players.

For Four Orchestras (Arista A3L 8900, 1978): *82*; with four symphony orchestras.

Composition 96 (Leo 169, 1981): with The Composers and Improvisors Orchestra (37 players)

Ensemble (Victoriaville) 1988 (Victo 07): *141(+20+96+120D), 42*; with saxist Evan Parker, trombonist George Lewis, trumpeter Paul Smoker, vibist Bobby Naughton, bassist Joelle Léandre, and percussionist Gerry Hemingway.

Eugene 1989 (Black Saint BS 120137-2, 1991): *112, 91, 134, 100, 93, 45, 71, 59*; with the Northwest Creative Orchestra (16 players).

Two Compositions (Ensemble) 1989/1991 (hat Art CD 6086): *147, 151*; with the Ensemble Modern Frankfurt (*147*) and the Creative Music Ensemble (*151*).

Composition No. 165 (for 18 instruments) (New Albion NA 050, 1992).

Four (Ensemble) Compositions 1992 (Black Saint 120 124-2): *100, 96, 164, 163*; with 13 players.

By Others

Ellington, Edward Kennedy. *Sacred Concerts*. (Miami Beach, FL: Hansen House, 1979).

Konitz, Lee. *The Lee Konitz Duets*. (Milestone OJCCD-466-2. MSP-9013), 1967.

Lomax, Alan, ed. *Afro-American Spirituals, Work Songs, and Ballads* and *Anglo-American Shanties, Lyric Songs, Dance Tunes, and Spirituals*. Washington, DC: Library of Congress, Division of Music, Recording Laboratory, 1942 and 1956); *Roots of the Blues* and *Sounds of the South*. Atlantic SD 1348 and 1346); and see *Folk Songs of North America*. New York: Dolphin/Doubleday, 1975.

The Carl Stalling Project: Music from Warner Brothers Cartoons, 1936–58. United States: Warner Bros. Records, 1990.

White, B. F. *White Spirituals from the Sacred Harp.* (NW 205 New World Records.)

Miscellaneous

The Music of John Coltrane. Milwaukee, WI: Hal Leonard Publishing, 1991.

Bernstein, Leonard. *The Unanswered Question.* The Norton Lectures (Columbia M4X 33032: 1973).

Braxton, Anthony. Telephone and personal interviews. February 2, 1989; February 25, 1993; October 18, 1993.

Hinton, Robert. "The Black Tradition in American Modern Dance," *American Dance Festival curatorial guide*, project directors Meyers, Gerald E. and Reinhart, Stephanie, 1990: 4.

Images of Another World. BBC/Arts & Entertainment, videotape, 1990.

Ives, Charles. *Symphony No. Four.* New York: Associated Music Publishers, 1965.

Manoff, Tom. Lecture at the University of Oregon, August 16, 1993.

Menuhin, Yehudi (host/narrator). *The Music of Man.* Chicago: Public Media, videotape, 1987.

Mingus, Sue, ed. *Mingus: Not a Fakebook.* Milwaukee, WI: Hal Leonard Publishing, 1991.

Nathan, Hans, ed. *The Complete Works of William Billings.* The American Musicological Society and the Colonial Society of Massachusetts, Boston: University Press of Virginia, 1977.

Radano, M. R. *Anthony Braxton and his Two Musical Traditions: The Meeting of Concert Music and Jazz.* Ann Arbor: University of Michigan, 1985.

Schuller, Günther, ed. *A Collection of the Compositions of Ornette Coleman.* New York: MJQ Music, 1961.

Various authors. *The Grove Dictionary of Music and Musicians.* London: Macmillan; Washington, DC: Groves Dictionaries of Music, 1980.

Various authors. *The New Grove Dictionary of American Music.* London: Macmillan; New York, Groves Dictionaries of Music, 1986.

Various authors. *The New Grove Dictionary of Jazz.* London: Macmillan; New York NY, Groves Dictionaries of Music, 1988.

Walker, Barbara. *The Woman's Encyclopedia of Myths and Secrets.* San Francisco: Harper & Row, 1983.

Sources of display quotes (see above for publishing data):

P. 10 Charles Williams, 8.
P. 27 Anthony Braxton, private conversation (February 2, 1989).
P. 28 Braxton, telephone interview (February 25, 1993).
P. 36 Braxton, telephone interview (February 25, 1993).
P. 39 Braxton, private conversation (February 2, 1989).
P. 44 Dudley Young, xxxv.
P. 52 Francis Bacon, 42–43.
P. 52-53 Robert Grudin, 95.
P. 107 Charles Mingus in Brian Priestley, 192.

P. 118 Theodor Adorno, 62.
P. 146 Albert Murray (*Stomping*), 189.
P. 146 Grudin, 141.
P. 147 Braxton in Henschen, 19.
P. 154 Murray (*Hero*), 81.
P. 154-55 Braxton in Lock, 238; in Carey, 7.
P. 183 Roger Sanjek, 1.
P. 183 Murray (*Stomping*), 251.
P. 184 Murray (*Hero*), 67.
P. 184 Braxton in Townley, 13.
P. 212 Stockhausen, 102.
P. 216-17 Murray (*Hero*), 98.
P. 228 Murray (*Hero*), 98.
P. 263 Grudin, 143.
P. 299 Graham Lock, 21.
P. 304 Lao–Tze, 42.
P. 417 Robert Graves, 177–78.
P. 445 Williams, 8.
P. 446-47 Murray (*Hero*), 107.
P. 463 Grudin, 135.
P. 463 Murray (*Hero*), 98.
P. 463 Braxton (*Composition Notes D*), 521–52.

Index

Recordings:

2 Compositions, 422
5 Pieces, 370
7 Compositions (Trio) 1989, 323, 329
165 (for 18 instruments), 420
Alto Saxophone Improvisations 1979, 241
Alto Saxophone Improvisations 1979/Language Music (1967), 161
B-X^O, 367
Birmingham, 377, 401
Birth & Rebirth, 263
Circle, 378
Circling In, 364
Composition 98 (1984), 168
Composition 113, 163
Compositions 99, 101, 107 & 139, 323
Coventry, 376, 383, 387
Creative Music Orchestra, 419
Creative Orchestra Music 1976, 169, 318, 419, 429, 434
Dona Lee, 157, 360, 370
Dortmund (Quartet) 1976, 360, 377
Duets 1976, 163, 263
Duets 1987, 264
Duets, Vancouver 1989, 264
Eight (+3) Tristano Compositions 1989, 105, 161, 217
Elements of Surprise, 263, 294
Ensemble (Victoriaville) 1988, 420
Eugene (1989), 293, 420, 422, 425, 437
Five Compositions (Quartet) 1986, 168, 408, 401
Five Pieces 1975, 360, 375, 376
For Alto, 86, 161, 236, 244, 253, 366
For Four Orchestras, 420
For Trio, 166, 315, 318
For Two Pianos, 263
Four (Ensemble) Compositions 1992, 420
Four Compositions (1973), 306, 307, 313, 360, 370
Four Compositions (1983), 405, 410
Four Pieces, 263
In the Tradition Vols. 1 & 2, 1974, 160, 217, 220, 371, 374
Kol Nidre, 264
Live at Moers, 373, 374

Live at Wigmore, 263
Montreux/Berlin Concerts, 360, 370, 377
New York, Fall 1974, 360, 370, 373, 374
One in Two, Two in One, 263
Open Aspects '82, 264, 292
Paris Concert, 364
Performance 9/1/79, 166, 361, 376, 405
Prague, 391, 406
Quartet Live at Moers, 360, 370
Quartets London/Birmingham/Coventry 1985, 408
Saxophone Improvisations/Series F, 161
Seven Compositions, 381
Seven Standards 1985, Vols. 1 & 2, 160, 217, 222
Silence, 307, 310
Six Compositions, Quartet (1981), 167, 361, 380
Six Duets (1982), 264
Six Monk's Compositions (1987), 217
Six Pieces, 125
Solo (London) 1988, 250, 253, 381, 401
The Complete Braxton, 360, 367
This Time, 311, 363, 364, 367
Three Compositions of New Jazz, 115, 306, 307, 368
Town Hall, 307, 312, 360, 366, 367
Trio and Duet, 263, 266, 292, 314, 315
Two Compositions (Ensemble) 1989/1991, 420
Willisau, 374, 376, 380, 382, 401

Compositions:

1, 368
2, 368
3, 368
4, 360, 368
5, 368
6(O), 307, 312, 360
6A, 264, 271, 273, 323, 329, 330, 360, 362, 365, 366, 410
6B, 365
6C, 364, 365
6D, 90, 307, 308, 309, 322, 329
6E, 307, 309, 310, 313, 320, 321, 322, 329, 362
6F, 362, 363, 364, 365, 375
6G, 362
6H, 311
6I, 360
6J, 67, 360, 365
6K, 360, 365
6L, 360, 366
6M, 360, 366
6N, 264, 307, 312, 360
6P, 307, 312, 320, 360
7, 368
8A, 236
8A-K, 369
8B, 240, 241
8C, 120, 240
8D, 239, 366
8F, 173, 236
8H, 237
9, 83, 369
10, 368, 369, 371

index

11, 126, 369
12, 369
13, 369
14, 369
15, 369
17, 369
18, 369
19, 369
20, 369, 420
21, 369
22, 360, 369
23(O), 307, 360
23A, 360, 373
23B, 99, 360, 373, 375
23C, 360, 374
23D, 360, 374
23E, 114, 360
23F, 375
23G, 55, 375, 376
23H, 377
23I, 377
23J, 264, 267, 360, 377, 409
23K, 360, 371
23L, 360, 371
23M, 112, 307, 360, 371
23N, 307, 360, 371
23O, 371, 373
23P, 307, 360, 372, 373
24, 378
25, 378, 418, 419, 438
26A–J, 378
26B, 246
26E, 248
26F, 245
27, 378
28, 379
29A–E, 379
30, 264, 376
30–33, 379
32, 387
34, 361, 379
35, 379
36, 314
36, 306, 315, 320, 322, 329, 379
37, 67, 360, 379, 435
38A, 360
38A–B, 379

39, 379
40(O), 360, 384, 409, 383
40A, 271, 361, 380
40B, 361, 380
40D, 264, 323, 329, 381
40F, 361, 381, 410
40G, 323, 329, 381
40H, 382
40I, 382
40J, 323, 329, 382
40K, 360
40L, 382
40M, 360, 382, 383
40N, 61, 62, 360, 383
40P, 263, 275
40Q, 263
41, 434
42, 393, 432, 434
43, 384
44, 384
45, 420, 427
47, 385
48, 385
49, 385, 393
50, 385, 386
51, 384, 419, 435
52, 386
55, 94, 419, 436
56, 419, 435
57, 419, 436
58, 81, 419, 436
59, 419, 420, 429, 437
60, 263, 276, 277, 409
62, 264
62, 263, 276, 277
63, 323, 329, 360, 384
64, 263, 294
65, 263, 297
66, 386
67, 386
68, 386
69A, 264, 273
69B, 264, 273, 387
69C, 361, 387, 389
69E, 361, 390
69F, 361
69G, 361, 390
69H, 407, 409

69J, 329, 332
69K, 391
69M, 391, 409
69N, 361
69O, 391
69P, 264, 273, 366
70, 393
71, 393, 420, 428
73, 317, 318, 319, 393
74A, 263, 298
74B, 263
76, 72, 306, 317, 319, 320, 321, 322, 323, 329
77A, 241, 242
77C, 242
77D, 243
77E, 244
77F, 246
77G, 247
77H, 249
78, 393, 432
82, 169, 420, 431
84, 393, 394
85, 264, 266, 268, 409
86, 264, 267, 268
87, 264, 267, 268, 409
88, 376
89, 393
90, 393, 394
91, 420, 425, 426
93, 420, 425
94, 322, 323, 324, 393
95, 83, 90, 278, 283, 286, 318, 322, 326, 333, 356, 396
96, 89, 264, 323, 382, 392, 395, 396, 397, 398, 400, 401, 404, 409, 420, 425, 426, 429
98, 361, 367, 374, 391, 396, 402, 427
99, 280
99C, 253, 254
99G, 251, 254
99I, 253, 254
100, 404, 420, 425, 427, 428

101, 263, 278, 280, 299, 396
102, 396, 404, 418, 429
103, 402
105A, 64, 396, 403, 404, 405, 406, 409
105B, 278, 333, 409
106C, 250, 252, 254
107, 322, 326, 327, 328, 329, 402
108B, 264, 323, 329, 332
108C, 376
110A, 323, 329, 332, 333, 406, 409
112, 264, 420, 425, 426
113, 163, 164, 170
114, 406, 407
116, 410
116, with pianist Marilyn Crispell, 264
118F, 253, 254
120D, 31, 420
121, 409, 410
122, 409
124, 376, 410
131, 408
134, 264, 420, 427
136, 72, 264
138C, 253, 254
138E, 253, 255
140, 264
141, 31, 420
147, 75, 78, 420, 422, 424
151, 75, 83, 420, 422
161, 413
163, 420
164, 420
165, 420
171, 420, 422

Subjects:

23 series, 370
69 series, 387
AACM, 24, 25, 43, 88, 108, 115, 116, 129, 133, 134, 160, 174,

index

175, 188, 189, 190, 191, 214, 267, 274, 275, 277, 280, 281, 291, 294, 298, 307, 308, 309, 310, 311, 312, 313, 316, 317, 318, 322, 330, 357, 358, 361, 362, 367, 368, 370, 374, 375, 390, 391, 393, 402, 427, 436, 438
Abrams, Muhal Richard, 87, 90, 163, 164, 189, 190, 263, 265, 266, 274, 275, 282, 288, 292, 298, 308, 310, 313, 345, 372, 386, 393, 401, 408
Adams, John, 11, 75
Aebi, Irene, 312
Africa in the West, 43
African American classical music, 130
African Methodist Episcopal Church, 131
Allen, Richard, 58
alphanumerics, 30, 32, 35
Altschul, Barry, 307, 360, 366, 380
Anderson, Fred, 402
Anderson, Laurie, 419
Anderson, Marian, 131
Anderson, Ray, 294, 297, 323, 327, 361, 381, 387
Anderson, T. J., 132
Aquinas, Thomas, 47
Aristotle, 39, 47
Armstrong, Louis, 25, 29, 92, 95, 98, 101, 107, 128, 157, 158, 167, 183, 185, 186, 190, 193, 194, 230, 231, 260, 294, 309, 310, 321, 330, 370, 401
Aryans, 32
Asbury, Francis, 58

Augustine of Hippo, 41, 43, 45
Ayahuasqueros tribe, 29, 84
Ayler, Albert, 59, 84, 105, 112, 113, 114, 115, 157, 158, 175, 189, 194, 241, 253, 254, 275, 278, 280, 290, 294, 308, 312, 330, 340, 375, 389, 391, 424, 428, 439

Bach, Johann Sebastian, 25, 107, 117, 152, 231, 310, 311
Bailey, Derek, 263, 265, 290, 298, 307, 312, 313
Balakrishnan, David, 134
Barker, Thurman, 361, 387
Bartók, Béla, 310
Barton, Todd, 316
Basie, Count, 59, 93, 94, 104, 108, 267, 393, 426, 437
battle-axe cultures, 32
Beat culture, 98, 108
Bechet, Sidney, 87, 91, 92
Beecher, Lyman, 58
Beecher-Stowe, Harriet, 59
Beethoven, Ludwig von, 46, 117, 128
Ben-Jochannon, Yosef A. A., 113
Benson, George, 116
Berkeley, Bishop, 48
Bethune, Blind Thomas, 131
Bigard, Barney, 107
Billings, William, 63, 66, 79, 106, 158
Birth of the Cool, 101
Black Artists Group, 94
Blackwell, Ed, 380
Blakey, Art, 107
blues, 85, 86
Bluiett, Hamiett, 360

Boatner, Edward, 132
bop, 97
Boulez, Pierre, 110
Bowie, Lester, 190
Braxton, Anthony:
"Golden Peak", 396-405; and myth, mysticism, ancient history and occult lore, 16, 24; as composer, 447-467; as conductor, 351-353; as innovator, 17; as traditionalist, 17; as writer, 17, 143, 155-204, 211; Duos, 259-261; occult significance, 262, 299-300; open improv; percussion, 288; with guitar, 290; with percussion, 290; with synthesizer, 292-293; with another horn, 294; with bass, 265; with keyboard, 274-288; co-ordinant system, 166; early musical and personal history, 212-216; feminism, 36; influences, 16, 23-24, 53-134; Large Ensembles, 418-420; early, 438-441; middle, 431-438; occult significance, 417; recent, 420-430; literature on, 10-12; mainstream jazz covers, 227; myth, mysticism, ancient history and occult lore, 27-49; press coverage of, 154; Quartets, 339-341, 356-361; early, 361-378; middle, 380-392; occult significance, 337-339; recent, 405-414; solo alto music, 228-256; Solo music; occult significance, 207-209; symbology and, 13-15, 17-18; Trios, 333; early, 307-314; middle, 314-322; occult significance, 304-307, 314, 322-323, 336; recent, 323-333; works, 368-369, 378-380, 384-387, 392-395
Braxton, Nickie, 263, 400
Brecker Brothers' Dreams, 116
Bridgetower, George, 131
Brubeck, Dave, 101, 192, 213
Burleigh, Harry T., 132
Burton, Gary, 152

C(onnector)-class prototypes, 65
Cage, John, 11, 25, 43, 48, 58, 66, 75, 81, 82, (*4'33"*, 83), 103, 106, 110, 122, 127, 128, 130, 144, 155, 163, 175, 195, 214, 240, 268, 270, 290, 310, 311, 321, 333, 339, 350, 362, 366, 367, 390, 398, 411, 424, 448, 455
Calloway, Cab, 98
Capella, Martianus, 42
Carter, Elliott, 80, 110
chaos, 31
civil rights movement, 98, 108
cobalt series, 31
Coke, Dr. Thomas, 58
Coleman, Ornette, 12, 36, 40, 56, 59, 65, 84, 87, 88, 91, 96, 100, 107, 109, 110, 111,

112, 116, 127, 133, 144, 162, 169, 175, 187, 188, 189, 190, 194, 197, 210, 214, 226, 231, 264, 267, 276, 280, 281, 290, 294, 307, 308, 311, 312, 315, 317, 329, 330, 333, 340, 362, 365, 368, 371, 373, 374, 375, 377, 380, 390, 391, 392, 401, 424, 437, 438, 440, 448
Coleridge-Taylor, Samuel, 132
collage improvisation, 167, 307
Colored American Opera Company, 134
Coltrane, John, 11, 24, 40, 56, 57, 59, 66, 84, 91, 92, 96, 103, 105, 107, 112, 113, 114, 115, 118, 122, 123, 147, 162, 174, 187, 188, 189, 190, 194, 218, 226, 231, 241, 243, 254, 255, 267, 288, 294, 312, 317, 330, 333, 368, 383, 391, 403, 424, 448
Company, 293, 298, 306, 307, 312, 313, 410
Composition Notes, 26, 162, 167, 171, 231, 274, 318, 369, 389, 402
Comte, August, 48
conceptual grafting, 307
Connor, Aaron J. R., 131
Cook, Will Marion, 132
cool, 96, 97, 101, 108
Cooper, Jerome, 360, 370
Copland, Aaron, 11, 75
Corea, Chick, 116, 298, 333, 342, 360, 361, 365, 366

Cowell, Henry, 75
Creative Construction Company, 307, 311, 312, 361, 364, 367, 370, 391
Crispell, Marilyn, 265, 266, 275, 281, 282, 288, 298, 344, 345, 348, 349, 361, 374, 376, 377, 379, 380, 387, 402, 406, 409, 410, 411, 412, 413
Cyrille, Andrew, 217

Da Costa, Noel, 132
Darwin, Charles, 108
Davis, Anthony, 11, 116, 132, 380, 419
Davis, Miles, 36, 56, 57, 66, 92, 96, 101, 102, 104, 107, 116, 167, 187, 190, 194, 213, 218, 231, 268, 317, 333, 401, 402, 448
Davis, Richard, 266
Dawson, William, 132
De nuptiis Philologiae et Mercurii, 42
Debussy, Claude, 101
Descartes, René, 47
Desmond, Paul, 96, 101, 102, 103, 104, 105, 106, 192, 213, 222, 225, 239, 246, 268, 294, 312, 366
Dett, R. Nathaniel, 132
Dickerson, Roger, 132
Dionysius, 38, 45
Dixon, Bill, 327
Dolphy, Eric, 190, 266, 274, 290, 309, 380
Donna Lee, 98, 158
Dorseys, 93
Dresser, Mark, 361, 408, 409, 410, 411, 412
Dudziak, Ursula, 312
Dufay, Guillaume, 66
duos, 263, 266, 291
Dvořák, Antonin, 132

Edwards, Jonathan, 57
Egypt, 35, 36, 37, 40, 42, 43, 66, 86, 87, 110, 113, 117, 122, 130, 132, 134, 187, 188, 190, 195, 196, 199, 200, 202, 203, 208, 227, 228, 293, 299, 303, 304, 306, 307, 314, 323, 336, 338, 372, 395, 414, 418, 445, 446, 450, 452
Ellington, Duke, 57, 85, 92, 93, 94, 107, 108, 118, 128, 147, 167, 169, 176, 183, 190, 194, 299, 317, 435, 436, 466
Emery, James, 323
entoptic images, 34, 452
European improvisers, 116
Evans, Gil, 101, 317
Ewart, Douglas, 315, 319
existentialists, 48

Familie, 307, 311, 312
Favors, Malachi, 190
Feather, Leonard, 177
Feuerbach, Paul, 48
Finney, Charles Grandison, 58
First and Second Great Awakenings of American religion, 57
Fisk Jubilee Singers, 89
Fitzgerald, Ella, 95
FMP, 116
Foster, Stephen, 88
Freeman, Harry Lawrence, 132
Freemasons, 87
Freud, 48, 108
Frisell, Bill, 152

Galileo, Galilei, 47
Gardner, Newport, 84, 131
Gaslini, Giorgio, 263, 266, 275, 278, 281, 282, 288, 290, 299, 347, 408
Gell, Jack, 213
German expressionists, 120
Getz, Stan, 96, 107
Giddins, Gary, 177
Gillespie, Dizzy, 29, 92, 98, 107, 294
Glass, Philip, 11, 75, 419
glossolalia, 57, 59
God-is-Dead theologians, 48
goddess, 35, 36
Gödel, Kurt, 48
Golson, Benny, 297
Goodman, Benny, 11, 93
Gordon, Dexter, 116, 218
Grainger, Percy, 452
gravillic, 104
Gray, Wardell, 104
Great Depression, 93
Greek modes, 44, 66, 187
Greenfield, Elizabeth, 131
Griffin, Johnny, 116

Hakim, Talib Rasul, 84
Hall, Frederick, 132
Hampel, Gunter, 307, 311, 313
Hampton, Lionel, 107
Hancock, Herbie, 116
Hardin, Lil, 95
Hawkins, Coleman, 91, 95, 96, 104, 294
Heath, Albert "Tootie", 217
Hegel, Georg Wilhelm Friedrich, 48, 177
Hemingway, Gerry, 361, 403, 409, 410, 411, 420
Hemmenway, James, 131
Hemphill, Julius, 360
Henderson, Fletcher, 85, 92, 93, 169, 190, 255, 317
Herman, Woody, 11, 101

index

Hermes (Thoth, Mercury, Gabriel), 25
hexachord system of solmization, 71
hieroglyphy, 35
Hildegard of Bingen, 40, 43, 61, 71, 111, 419
Hines, Earl, 107
Holiday, Billie, 95, 96, 190, 194, 226, 282
Holland, David, 154, 263, 265, 266, 267, 268, 270, 274, 298, 307, 312, 315, 333, 346, 360, 361, 366, 370, 374, 377, 380, 393, 408
Holland, Justin, 131

Incus, 116
Ives, Charles, 11, 25, 40, 43, 48, 62, 64, 65, 66, 69, 73, 75, 79, 80, 83, 106, 155, 170, 364, 401, 456

Jacobi, F. H., 48
Jamal, Ahmad, 213
James, George, 86
James, Harry, 93
Jarman, Joseph, 190, 291, 315
Jarrett, Keith, 11
Jazz Age, 93
Jefferson, Blind Lemon, 95
Jenkins, Leroy, 11, 116, 134, 292, 307, 310, 318, 360, 370
Jenoure, Terry, 312
Jesus, 40
Johnson, Frank, 131
Johnson, Hall, 132
Johnson, Oliver, 360
Johnson, Samuel, 48
Jones, Hank, 217
Jones, Quincy, 116
Joplin, Scott, 90, 132
jubilus, 45

Judeo-Christian tradition of flesh-renunciation, 29
Jungians, 45

Kandinsky, Wassily, 120
Kant, Immanuel, 48
Kay, Ulysses, 132
kelvin series, 31
Kenton, Stan, 101
King, Jr., Martin Luther, 59
Kirk, Rashaan Roland, 57, 59
Konitz, 93, 96, 101, 105, 106, 107, 266, 294, 401
Kontra-Punkte, 126

L-C-J series, 378
Lacy, Steve, 11, 109, 225, 294, 298, 376
Lake, Oliver, 360
Lange, Art, 8, 105, 106, 156, 161, 266, 274, 292, 316, 326, 431, 453
Lateef, Yusef, 108
Latin rhythms, 54
Laveau, Marie, 94, 195
Leadbelly, 95
Léandre, Joelle, 420
Lee, Jeanne, 307, 311, 360, 367, 475
Leibniz, Gottfried Wilhelm, 48
Lewis, George, 116, 263, 265, 266, 294, 298, 327, 345, 358, 360, 361, 364, 377, 380, 397, 403, 420
Lewis, John, 109
Lewis, Victor, 217
Lincoln Center, 152
Lindberg, John, 264, 265, 266, 267, 270, 271, 342, 343, 345, 346, 361, 387, 403

List, Garret, 323, 326, 327
Liszt, Franz, 46
Lock, Graham, 8, 11, 12, 18, 56, 57, 86, 93, 102, 103, 104, 113, 115, 117, 122, 130, 145, 147, 148, 149, 154, 156, 165, 175, 180, 190, 212, 218, 255, 270, 281, 299, 329, 331, 401, 408, 429, 464
Logan, Wendell, 132
Lovejoy, Arthur, 47
Lunceford, Jimmie, 92, 93

Machaut, Guilaume de, 62
Mahler, Gustav, 107, 118
Malcolm X, 59, 113
Marable, Fate, 92
Marsalis, Wynton, 116
Marsh, Tina, 312
Marsh, Warne, 93, 96, 101, 102, 103, 104, 105, 106, 161, 218, 294, 308, 401, 435
Marx, Karl, 48
master progression sequence, 167
mathematics, 30
McBee, Cecil, 217
McCall, Steve, 310, 311
McGhee, Howard, 107
medieval Europe, 44
medieval music, 85
Metheney, Pat, 116
Methodism, 57, 58
Midorikawa, Keiki, 307, 360
Millennial, 25, 35, 44, 448, 456
Millennialist, 59
Millennium, 36, 48, 455
Miller, Glenn, 93
mind-altering substances, 29
Mingus, Charles, 40, 57, 59, 87, 88, 92, 93, 107, 108, 109, 111, 112, 120, 122, 169, 187, 218, 254, 267, 299, 309, 317, 371, 373, 380, 401, 426, 431, 436, 448
minimalist, 75
Minstrelsy, 88
Mitchell, Roscoe, 105, 190, 214, 263, 265, 266, 291, 294, 298, 310, 313, 315, 317, 319, 320, 345, 346, 393, 436, 437
modalism, 187
Modern Jazz Quartet, 11
Monk, Thelonious, 11, 56, 57, 90, 92, 99, 103, 104, 109, 161, 167, 186, 187, 188, 190, 218, 219, 226, 268, 376, 380, 422
Montoliu, Tété, 217
Moore, Carman, 132
Moore, Dorothy Rudd, 132
Morgan, Frank, 116
Morton, Jelly Roll, 92
Moten, Bennie, 92
Mozart, Wolfgang Amadeus, 117, 152
Mulligan, Gerry, 101
Muse, 13, 15, 16, 19, 23, 25, 26, 36, 37, 40, 65, 118, 124, 199, 203, 209, 260, 305, 314, 315, 327, 329, 340, 341, 342, 350, 355, 356, 357, 366, 367, 370, 373, 379, 382, 392, 411, 418, 425, 438, 441, 445, 446, 447, 448, 449, 456, 457, 458, 459
Musica Elettronica Vita, 316
Mwanga, Kunlé, 438
mystical pictographs, 30

index **491**

Naughton, Bobby, 420
Negative Confessions, 113
Neidlinger, Buell, 217
Neoplatonism, 43
neumes, 71
New England hymnodists, 62
New Orleans, 44, 91
Nichols, Red, 92
Norman, Jessye, 131
Northwest Creative Orchestra, 420

Oliver, King, 92
Oppens, Ursula, 263, 265, 275, 288, 299, 333
Orpheus, 37, 38
Orphic cult, 37, 38
Ory, Kid, 92, 107
Osborne, Bill, 217
Oxley, Tony, 323, 329

Parham, Charles, 59
Parker, Charlie, 11, 40, 56, 59, 65, 84, 85, 91, 92, 93, 96, 98, 99, 100, 104, 105, 107, 110, 116, 118, 132, 147, 159, 160, 161, 183, 186, 188, 190, 194, 196, 199, 210, 214, 218, 219, 226, 231, 241, 243, 255, 264, 267, 276, 290, 294, 297, 312, 317, 330, 339, 365, 374, 380, 397, 398, 448
Parker, Evan, 294, 298, 307, 312, 420
Partch, Harry, 66, 75, 81, 83, 106, 109, 118
Pascal, Blaise, 48
patriarchy, 36
Pavone, Mario, 274
Pedersen, Niels-Henning Orsted, 217
Pentecostalism, 59
Pepper, Art, 116

Perry, Julia, 132
pictography, 35
Plato, 39, 48, 452
Plotinus, 40
Poincarré, Henri, 48
Pollack, Ben, 92
Popper, Karl, 48
Postelwaite, Joseph, 131
Powell, Bud, 107
Previn, André, 11
Price, Florence, 132
Primate Music, 27
Prime Time, 116
Prohibition, 93
psilocybin, 29
psychotropes, 30
Ptolemy, 40
pulse tracks, 54
Purim, Flora, 312
Pythagoras, 37, 38, 42, 44

Radano, Ronald, 11, 12, 13, 18, 145, 148, 149, 155, 164, 175, 180, 190, 212, 218, 367, 371, 392, 396, 464
Raeburn, Boyd, 101
Ragin, Hugh, 361, 402
Ragtime, 88
Rainey, Ma, 95
Raskin, John, 217
Reich, Steve, 11, 75, 419
Reid, Rufus, 217
restructuralists, 85
Return to Forever, 116
Riegger, Wallingford, 80
Ring Shout, 58
Roach, Max, 263, 265, 288, 298, 398
Robair, Gino, 264, 265, 266, 290
Robert Schumann String Quartet, 167, 281
Robeson, Paul, 131
Roidinger, Adelhard, 323
Rollins, Sonny, 91
Roosevelt College, 24

Rosamond, Johnson, J., 132
Rosicrucians, 87
Rousseau, Jeans-Jacques, 48
Ruggles, Carl, 75
Russell, George, 187
Rzewski, Federic, 263, 265, 266, 281, 288, 299, 333, 379

Saint Georges, Chevalier de, 131
San tribe, 30
Sanders, Pharoah, 59, 105
Santoro, Gene, 148
Sato, Masahiko, 307, 360
Schelling, F. W. J., 48
Schleiermacher, Friedrich, 48
Schönberg, Arnold, 25, 40, 43, 62, 75, 79, 80, 82, 90, 113, 117, 118, 119, 120, 121, 122, 126, 128, 129, 134, 162, 175, 226, 275, 276, 278, 280, 290, 309, 310, 315, 333, 339, 350, 364, 371, 398, 401, 442, 447, 448, 455
Schroeder, Marianne, 280, 323, 326, 328
Schuller, Günther, 11, 109, 111
Scott, Dred, 217
Seeger, Ruth Crawford, 80, 106
Sessions, Roger, 80
Seymour, William J., 60
shape-note music, 62
Shaw, Artie, 93
Shepp, Archie, 186, 220
Shoemaker, Bill, 218, 281, 423
Sidran, Ben, 85
signature logic, 64, 79
Silver, Horace, 107
Skinner, B. F., 48

Smith, Bessie, 95, 183, 194, 290
Smith, Hale, 132
Smith, Leo, 30, 133, 153, 190, 307, 314, 315
Smith, Mamie, 95
Smith, Michael, 360
Smoker, Paul, 420
social Darwinism, 48
Society of Black Composers, 132
Sousa, John Philip, 80, 365, 436
Sowandé, Fela, 113
Still, William Grant, 132
Stitt, Sonny, 116
Stockhausen, Karlheinz, 11, 25, 43, 79, 85, 90, 110, 113, 117, 121, 122, 123, 124, 125, 126, 127, 128, 129, 130, 170, 195, 212, 214, 242, 249, 264, 267, 270, 275, 280, 316, 321, 326, 333, 339, 363, 364, 390, 394, 395, 397, 398, 403, 424, 438, 448, 454, 455
Strauss, Richard, 48
Stravinsky, Igor, 11, 62, 75, 79, 101, 223, 364, 374, 383, 401, 454, 455
Strayhorn, Billy, 218
Stubblefield, John, 307, 360
Sun Ra, 84, 86, 93, 94, 144, 170, 177, 187, 190, 292, 316, 317, 370
Swan, Timothy, 67
Swanson, Howard, 132
Symphony No. Four, 75

Tanaka, Hozumi, 307, 360
Tatum, Art, 90
Taylor, Billy, 107
Taylor, Cecil, 120, 187,

Taylor, Cecil, 11, 36, 84, 89, 90, 109, 120, 162, 187, 188, 189, 190, 192, 194, 229, 231, 281, 374, 391, 401, 424, 428
Teagarden, Jack, 101
Teish, Luisah, 94
Teitelbaum, Richard, 264, 265, 314, 315, 316, 323, 360
Thomson, Virgil, 75
Thornhill, Claude, 101
Threadgill, Henry, 315, 319
Tillis, Frederick, 132
Tri-Axium Writings, 24, 25, 43, 56, 158, 95, 115, 171, 172, 175, 232, 288, 397
Tristano, Lennie, 96, 99, 101, 102, 105, 106, 108, 219, 223, 380, 401
tryptamine hallucinogens, 29
Turtle Island String Quartet, 134

Varése, Edgard, 132
Vaughan, Sarah, 95
vodou, 25, 45, 47, 58, 94, 195, 448, 456
Voigt, Andrew, 264, 265, 266, 294, 298
Voltaire, François Marie Arouet de, 48

Wagner, Richard, 117
Waldron, Mal, 217, 226, 401
Walker, George, 132
Waller, Fats, 90, 98, 159, 442
Warren, Peter, 360
Washington, Dinah, 95, 159
Waters, Ethel, 95

Weather Report, 116
Webb, Chick, 93
Webern, Anton von, 80, 109, 117, 212, 122, 125, 126, 197, 239, 242, 249, 267, 280, 290, 291, 311, 316, 333, 339, 350, 364, 368, 398, 402, 408, 427, 428, 436
Webster, Ben, 243
Wesley brothers, 58
Wesley, John, 58
Western medieval and Renaissance music, 39
Wheeler, Kenny, 294, 332, 360, 361, 370, 374, 375, 377
White, Clarence Cameron, 132
Whiteman, Paul, 92
Whitfield, George, 58
Williams, Henry F., 131
Williams, Tony, 333
Wilson, Olly, 84, 132
Wilson, Peter Niklas 266, 270, 274, 422
Wilson, Phillip, 298, 307, 312, 360
Woods, Phil, 231
Work, John Wesley, 132

Xappo, William, 131
Xenakis, Iannes, 117, 170

Yoruba, 46
Young, La Mont, 175
Young, Lester, 29, 36, 59, 91, 92, 93, 95, 96, 98, 99, 104, 161, 183, 194, 200, 264, 282, 294, 330, 401, 448

Those interested in ordering Anthony Braxton's self-published *Tri-Axium Writings* and *Composition Notes* can write to Frog Peak Music, Box A36, Hanover, NH 03755. Those interested in score availability, recent recordings, recent performances and other activities can write to, fax, phone, e-mail, or (preferably, first) visit The Tri-Centric Foundation, Inc.'s World Wide Web site at the following locations:

The Tri-Centric Foundation
2124 Broadway, Suite 712
New York, NY 10023

Engagements: 212/877-1392
Other: 212/604-4227
Fax: 203/685-2651
E-mail: abraxton@wesleyan.edu
World Wide Web: http://www.wesleyan.edu/music/braxton

Public availability of all music, writings, and scores for educational and performance projects is not yet universal, but is an eventual goal of the Foundation. Some scores are available for perusal at the American Music Center in New York City (212/366-5260), then for rent through the Tri-Centric Foundation. Inquiries by interested presenters, performers, educators, writers, and bandleaders will help build a mailing list for the time when these services and resources are complete.

About the author

Mike Heffley has worked for twenty years as a trombonist/composer and journalist specializing in the post-jazz synthesis of improvisation and composition as pioneered by Anthony Braxton and others. He won a *Down Beat* scholarship in composing/arranging and performance to the Berklee College of Music in Boston in 1965. He returned to his home in the San Francisco Bay Area to begin his career in the circle of players revolving around Rafael (a.k.a. Donald) Garrett, Oliver Johnson, and others. Throughout the 1970s and 1980s he lived in the Pacific Northwest, where he led his own groups and played with many of the region's jazz and new-music artists and began writing reviews, essays, and interviews about the music for major regional and national publications.

His association with Anthony Braxton stems from their 1989 collaborative tour of the Pacific Northwest with Heffley's Northwest Creative Orchestra, which culminated in the internationally critically acclaimed CD *Eugene (1989)*, produced by Braxton and Heffley. That project opened the door to similar collaborations with artists including the late John Carter, Andrew Hill, Vinny Golia, Oliver Lake, the late Julius Hemphill, Marty Ehrlich, Tim Berne, Jay Hoggard, Pheeroan ak-Laff, Mark Helias, and Ursula Oppens.

Heffley has an undergraduate degree in journalism (University of Oregon, 1977), a Master of Arts in Music/Arts Administration (Antioch University, 1993), and is currently on a graduate teaching fellowship as Braxton's assistant in the Ph.D. program in ethnomusicology at Wesleyan University. He serves as co-incorporator and President of the Board of Directors heading Braxton's newly formed Tri-Centric Foundation Inc., a performance and educational organization based in New York City with a mission to present and promote the composer's music.

The Music of Anthony Braxton is his first book. He is currently working on his second, about the Free Music Production (FMP) organization in Berlin, Germany.